# ENGLISH TIBETAN COLLOQUIAL DICTIONARY

# ENGLISH TIBETAN COLLOQUIAL DICTIONARY

C.A. Bell

SECOND EDITION

GYAN

*Published by*

GYAN

Gyan Publishing House
5, Ansari Road
Daryaganj, New Delhi-110002
Phone: 011-47034999, 9811692060
E-mail: books@gyanbooks.com

*Distribution Network*
gyanbooks.com
India, USA, Canada, UK, Australia, France



ISBN : 978-81-212-4365-0 (PB)
First Published, 1920

2nd Impression 2020

*Printed at:* Gyan Press, Delhi.

# English-Tibetan Colloquial Dictionary.

BY

C. A. BELL, C.M.G., C.I.E.

INDIAN CIVIL SERVICE, RETIRED; POLITICAL OFFICER IN SIKKIM; AUTHOR OF "GRAMMAR OF COLLOQUIAL TIBETAN."

SECOND EDITION.

"It is only from its roots in the living generation of men that language can be reinforced with fresh vigour for its seed. What may be called a literate dialect grows ever more and more pedantic and foreign till it becomes at last as unfitting a vehicle for living thought as Monkish Latin."

JAMES RUSSELL LOWELL.

Calcutta:

THE BENGAL SECRETARIAT BOOK DEPOT, WRITERS' BUILDINGS.

1920.

## PREFACE TO SECOND EDITION.

1. In the first edition this dictionary was published as the second part of a "Manual of Colloquial Tibetan," the first part consisting of a Grammar of Colloquial Tibetan. In this second edition both parts have not only been revised, but have also been considerably enlarged. The map accompanying this edition—the latest from the Indian Survey Department—is bulkier than the Royal Geographical Society's map of 1904, with which the first edition was furnished. It has therefore been found best to bring out the Grammar and Dictionary as separate books. The map accompanies the Grammar.

2. The Tibetan words are romanized, as in the first edition, for the convenience of those, who lack either the time or the inclination to master the Tibetan character. But the first Chapter of the Grammar, that on "The alphabet and its pronunciation," is reprinted at the commencement of this dictionary, in order that the student, who learns the Tibetan letters, may understand the structure and the pronunciation of the words more clearly than can be expressed by any system of romanization.

3. Some two thousand fresh words have been added in this edition, which now contains between eleven and twelve thousand words. As Political Officer in Sikkim,—a post to which I have recently been recalled, though I retired from the service of Government ten months ago,—I am in charge of the diplomatic relations of the British Government not only with Sikkim, but with Tibet and Bhutan also. Many therefore of these new words, as well as the revision of a few in the earlier edition, have been gained in conversation with my Tibetan friends of all classes, High Priests, Cabinet Ministers, civil and military officers, shopkeepers, mule-drivers, shepherds, peasants, etc., etc., during my fifteen years' service in Tibet and on the borderland. Among all

these my thanks are especially due to Rai Sahib Kusho Pahlese of the noble family of Pahla in Lhasa. And Mr. David Macdonald, British Trade Agent at Yatung, Tibet, has again rendered valuable assistance.

4. My acknowledgments are also due to the Government of Bengal, who have defrayed the cost of this edition also, in return for its copyright.

5. This book has been adopted as one of the text-books in the High Proficiency examination in the Tibetan language, held under the auspices of the Government of India.

6. In conclusion I must express my pleasure at finding that a second edition was called for owing to the first edition being sold out,—a rare occurrence among books on Tibet,—for it may be hoped that some have found it useful.

GANGTOK, SIKKIM:
*January, 1920.*

C. A. BELL.

## ABBREVIATIONS.

Adj. = adjective.
Adv. = adverb.
Art. = article.
Ch. = Chinese.
Conj. = conjunction.
C.T. = Central Tibet, *i.e.* the provinces of U and Tsang.
Def. = definite.
Do. = ditto.
E.G. = for instance.
F. = female, feminine.
Hin. = Hindi.
Hon. = honorific.
H. hon. = high honorific.
Imp. = imperative.
Inf. = inferior.
Interj. = interjection.
Interr. = interrogative.
Lit. = literally.
M. = male, masculine.
Mon. = Mongolian.
Neg. = negative.
Opp. = opposed.
Post. = postposition.
Pron. = pronoun.
Rel. = relative.
S. = substantive.
Sik. = Sikkimese.
Sup. = superior.
Ts. = Tsang province.
V.I. = verb intransitive.
V.T. = verb transitive.
W. = with.

## ERRATA.

| | | | | |
|---|---|---|---|---|
| Page 8, | column 2, | line 13, | *for* འཛགོ་པ་ | *read* འཛོག་པ་ |
| ,, 11 | ,, 3 | ,, 4 | ,, *ḱa-le* | ,, *ka-le.* |
| ,, 26 | ,, 3 | ,, 23 | ,, *t́sha* | ,, *tsha.* |
| ,, 37 | ,, 2 | ,, 5 | ,, ཚང་བ་ | ,, འཚང་བ་ |
| ,, 50 | ,, 2 | ,, 14 | ,, མཉ་ནདཔོན | ,, མཉན་དཔོན |
| ,, 56 | ,, 2 | ,, 20 | ,, བག་གག་ | ,, བག་ |
| ,, 62 | ,, 3 | ,, 10 | ,, *le-ḱa* | ,, *le-ka.* |
| ,, 71 | ,, 2 | ,, 11 | ,, ཚ་ག་ | ,, ཚོ་ག་ |
| ,, 76 | ,, 2 | ,, 1 | ,, ཨ་བོ་ | ,, ཨ་ལྦ་ |
| ,, 83 | ,, 1 | ,, 4 | ,, Do. | ,, Comforter. |
| ,, 92 | ,, 2 | ,, 2 | ,, ཕེབཔ་ | ,, ཕེབ་པ་ |
| ,, 93 | ,, 2 | ,, 14 | ,, ཆེན་པོ་ | ,, ཆེན་པོ་ |
| ,, 97 | ,, 2 | ,, 2 | ,, ནམ་ ན་ | ,, ནམ་གྱུན་ |
| ,, 97 | ,, 3 | ,, 2 | ,, *nam-gyü* | ,, *nam-gyün.* |
| ,, 115 | ,, 2 | ,, 14 | ,, པེབ་པ་ | ,, ཕེབ་པ་ |
| ,, 122 | ,, 2 | ,, 14 | ,, ད་པེ་ | ,, དཔེ་ |
| ,, 123 | ,, 2 | ,, 4 | ,, སྤྱོད་ | ,, སྤྱོང་ |
| ,, 125 | ,, 2 | ,, 5 | ,, པ.ཤལ་ | " བ.ཤལ་ |
| ,, 129 | ,, 2 | ,, 6 | ,, མཟིགས་ | " གཟིགས་ |

Page 130, column 2, line 8, *for* འཕྲོག་ *read* འཕོག་

,, 142 ,, 2 ,, 14 ,, ཐགུས་ ,, ཐུགས་

,, 151 ,, 2 ,, 4 ,, ཕྲོ་ཉ་ ,, ཕོ་ཉ་

,, 151 ,, 2 ,, 18 ,, སྡིག་ཕ་ ,, སྡིག་པ་

,, 164 ,, 2 ,, 19 ,, སྐུང་ ,, སྐྱུང་

,, 169 ,, 2 ,, 3 ,, འཁྲིར་ ,, འཁྱིར་

,, 182 ,, 1 ,, 7 ,, Forget ,, Forge, *s.*

,, 182 ,, 1 ,, 8 ,, Do, to ,, Forget, to.

,, 182 ,, 3 ,, 16 ,, *wa* ,, *pa*

,, 185 ,, 2 ,, 16 ,, བསྡུ་ ,, དསྡུ་

,, 197 ,, 2 ,, 5 ,, ཚོ་ ,, ཚོ་

,, 209 ,, 1 ,, 6 *after* steel *insert* comma.

,, 211 ,, 3 ,, 17 ,, *lam-lam-gyü* read *lam-gyü.*

,, 219 ,, 2 ,, 14 ,, ལམསང་ ,, ལམ་སང་

,, 228 ,, 2 ,, 17 ,, ཕ་ ,, པ་

,, 238 ,, 2 ,, 13 ,, སྐུར་ ,, སྐྱུར་

,, 238 ,, 2 ,, 14 ,, སྐྱུརནས་ ,, སྐྱུར་ནས་

,, 239 ,, 2 ,, 10 ,, ལམཀྱང་ ,, ལམ་ཀྱང་

,, 244 ,, 2 ,, 5 ,, སྐྱེགྲུབ་ ,, སྐྱེ་གྲུབ་

,, 248 ,, 2 ,, 8 ,, གྲུར་ ,, གྲུབ་

## PREFACE TO FIRST EDITION OF "MANUAL OF COLLOQUIAL TIBETAN."

1. The object of this little work is to provide a practical handbook for those who wish to acquire a speedy knowledge of Colloquial Tibetan. It, therefore, does not deal with the written language, which differs widely from the colloquial, and is useless for conversational purposes.

2. Notwithstanding the political and commercial importance of Tibet it is remarkable that so few Europeans are able to converse with the people in their own tongue. The language is undoubtedly a hard one to acquire on account of the complexity of the grammar, the intricacy of the spelling, the fine shades of pronunciation, the different terminology, known as the honorific, employed in addressing the higher classes, the variety of dialects, and the distinction, already noted, between the literary and spoken language. To minimise these difficulties and to make the approach to the colloquial as easy as possible, is the aim of this handbook. It seeks to do so by giving a minimum of grammatical notes, fully explained by examples, a clear statement of the rules of pronunciation, a simple system of phonetic spelling in the Roman character, a set of conversational exercises and a sufficiently full vocabulary of both common and honorific words to meet the ordinary requirements of conversation with all classes.

3. Tibet is essentially a country of dialects. A well-known proverb says—

།ལུང་པ་རེ་རེ་སྐད་ལུགས་རེ།

།བླ་མ་རེ་རེ་ཆོས་ལུགས་རེ།།

"Every district its own dialect;
Every lama his own doctrine."

Under these circumstances it was necessary to select the dialect most widely spoken, and that of Lhasa has been chosen accordingly. It is not only the dialect of the Central Province, but may be said to be also the *lingua franca* of the whole of Tibet. It is more generally spoken than any other, and is recognized as the most correct form of speech by all.

4. The Vocabulary contains somewhat less than ten thousand Tibetan words, the number of separate English words being some seven thousand or about twice as many as those contained in any colloquial Tibetan vocabulary up to date. The remaining three thousand words are made up of about two thousand honorific words and one thousand extra Tibetan words. Where two or more Tibetan words are given for one English equivalent, all are in common colloquial use and the one placed first is the commonest. It is hoped that the honorific words given may be found useful. Existing vocabularies give but few. A knowledge of honorific words is essential for talking to or of Tibetans of good position. It is hoped also that the exercises in Tibetan handwriting given in Part I, Chapter XVII, may assist any student, who so desires, to learn how to write Tibetan letters and other documents in a clear and correct style.

5. It is recommended that the grammar be used as follows: The rules of each Chapter should be perused and their accompanying examples learnt by heart. The *Words* at the end of the Chapter should then be committed to memory as far as possible, and the exercise (for reading and copying) should be read aloud to the teacher to ensure correct pronunciation, and every word should be understood. After this the other Exercise (for translation) should be translated *vivâ voce* and then written down, care being taken, when writing, to verify the spelling, as very few Tibetan teachers can spell correctly. On the following day the Tibetan half of the reading exercise should be covered up, and the English half re-translated into Tibetan, first *vivâ voce* and then in writing. If the above plan is followed the student will gain the soundest possible knowledge of the language. But if the student has not time for the above thorough system, he should omit the writing of both exercises and limit himself to the *vivâ voce*.

6. As regards teachers it is best to obtain at first one who speaks English. If the teacher can speak the Lhasa language also, so much the better, but very few of the English-speaking Tibetans in the Darjeeling district or in Sikkim are really proficient in the latter. As soon as he can converse a little, the student should change to a Lhasa man that speaks Tibetan only, so as to be certain of always speaking in Tibetan. When the teacher knows English or Hindustani there is always a tendency for the conversation to drop into the latter languages. The Lhasa teacher should of course be as well educated a man as is procurable. The student should also, when he is able to understand and converse a little, call in Tibetans of the Lhasa province to talk to him, one at a time, changing them every two or three weeks. Tibetans are generally ready to talk; they have not the formal constraint of manner which characterizes so many of the Indian races. The more he calls in thus, the better will he be able to understand and reply to any chance Tibetan he meets.

7. A word as to the system of romanization. In this, which is believed to be as phonetic as possible, I had reluctantly to differ from the various systems of my predecessors, as none of them seemed to me to reproduce the sounds in the dialect of Lhasa, though some reproduced those in the Sikkimese and other dialects. The system followed in this book is nearly the same as that recommended to Government for official reports, etc., by Captain O'Connor, C.I.E., Trade Agent at Gyangtse, and the author, but distinguishes the different sounds with greater accuracy than was considered necessary in the Government system.

8. The Tibetan words and syllables in brackets are those used in the simple form of book-language. Where the pronunciation of the literary and spoken form of a word is the same, the literary form alone is given, since the sole object of entering the spoken form is to show the exact pronunciation of the word.

9. In conclusion, I must acknowledge my obligations to the Government of Bengal for their patronage, to the Grammars of the Rev. Graham Sandberg, the Rev. H. A. Jäschke and the Rev.

Father A. Desgodins, and especially to Mr. Henderson's Tibetan Manual, which marks a great advance in the Tibetan colloquial over any of its predecessors. And most of all are my thanks due to Mr. David Macdonald, who has revised this book throughout, and to whose unrivalled knowledge of both colloquial and literary Tibetan are largely due whatever merits the work may possess.

CHUMBI, TIBET:<br>*March*, 1905.

C. A. BELL.

Page 253, column 2, line 8, *for* ལས་ *read* ལཛ་

„ 254 „ 2 „ 5 „ དགངས་ „ དགོངས་

„ 256 „ 1 „ 18 „ *kon* „ *hon.*

„ 259 „ 2 „ 16 „ དགྲོངས་ „ དགོངས་

„ 263 „ 2 „ 7 „ སྤྲེལ་ „ སྦྲེལ་

„ 281 „ 2 „ 2 „ པཞུགས་ „ བཞུགས་

„ 287 „ 2 „ 19 „ ཞལ་ „ ཉལ་

„ 316 „ 2 „ 16 „ སྙིང་སྙིང་ „ སྙི་སྙིང་

„ 321 „ 3 „ 19 „ *nye-ngen* „ *nya-ngen.*

„ 327 „ 2 „ 12 „ ཁ་བ་ „ ཁབ་

„ 340 „ 2 „ 9 „ ཀྲུ་སྨུ་ „ ཀ་སྨུ་

„ 350 „ 2 „ 12 „ ཕྲུཔ་ཤོག་ „ ཕྲུག་ཤོག་

„ 352 „ 2 „ 15 „ འཁོད་བ་ „ འཁོར་བ་

„ 359 „ 2 „ 3 „ ཁྲེད་པ་ „ བྲེད་པ་

„ 360 „ 2 „ 13 „ གདོག་ག་ „ གདོག་པ་

„ 412 „ 2 „ 16 „ ཞུང་ „ གཞུང་

„ 434 „ 2 „ 17 „ བས་མ་པ་ „ བསམ་པ་

„ 439 „ 2 „ 7 „ ཤ་ཛུབདབ་པ་ „ ཤ་ཛུ་བདབ་པ་

„ 447 „ 2 „ 15 „ དང་པོ་ „ དྲང་པོ་

Page 451, column 2, line 1, *for* ཀ་ལི་ *read* ཀ་པཱ་ལི་

,, 468 ,, 2 ,, 10 ,, གན་བ་ ,, གནང་བ་

,, 478 ,, 2 ,, 8 ,, བསླབ་གྭ་ ,, བསླབ་གྲྭ་

,, 491 ,, 2 ,, 15 ,, འབྲུར་ ,, འབྲེུར་

,, 560 ,, 2 ,, 9 ,, གན་ང་བ་ ,, གནང་བ་

,, 562 ,, 3 ,, 5 after *thu-rü* add *chhem-po.*

NOTE.—Where the colloquial and the literary forms differ appreciably, the latter are given in brackets in the Tibetan character. In the romanized Tibetan he colloquial forms alone are given.

## THE ALPHABET AND ITS PRONUNCIATION.

1. The Tibetan Alphabet was originally taken from the Sanskrit Devanagari in the 7th century A.D., but many of the letters, especially in Central Tibet, now represent sounds different from their prototypes. Both the Sanskrit and the Tibetan pronunciations have changed considerably during this period.

2. The Tibetan letters are as follow :—

*Consonants and their romanized equivalents.*

| | Surds. | Aspirates. | Sonants. | Nasals. |
|---|---|---|---|---|
| Gutturals | ཀ་ *ka* | ཁ་ *kha* | ག་ *ḱa* | ང་ *nga* |
| Palatals | ཅ་ *cha* | ཆ་ *chha* | ཇ་ *cȟa* | ཉ་ *nya* |
| Dentals | ཏ་ *ta* | ཐ་ *tha* | ད་ *t́a* | ན་ *na* |
| Labials | པ་ *pa* | ཕ་ *pha* | བ་ *ṕa* | མ་ *ma* |
| Sibilants | ཙ་ *tsa* | ཚ་ *tsha* | ཛ་ *tśa* | |
| Semi-vowels | ཝ་ *wa* | ཞ་ *sȟa* | ཟ་ *śa* | འ་ (not romanized) |
| | ཡ་ *ya* | ར་ *ra* | ལ་ *la* | |
| | ཤ་ *sha* | ས་ *sa* | ཧ་ *ha* | ཨ་ *a* |

3. In this Chapter I endeavour to give as nearly as possible the sound represented by each Tibetan letter. The romanization throughout is intended only as a rough guide to the pronunciation for those who are unable to give the time for studying the exact pronunciation. The consonants when used as initials, *i.e.*, when immediately preceding the vowel of a syllable, are pronounced as below.

ཀ་ The *k* in the Hindustani word *kam*. To be pronounced with the tongue between the teeth and without breathing.

ཁ་ an aspirated *k*, e.g., *block-head*, pronounced in one breath. The same as the aspirated *k* in Hindustani words, *e.g.*, *khana*.

ག་ also a *k* but pronounced through the throat and in a lower tone than ཀ་

ང་ like the *ng* in *coming*. Say *coming in*, eliminating the first four letters *comi*.

ཅ་ *ch* in *chin*. To be pronounced with the tongue between the teeth and without breathing.

ཆ་ *ch* aspirated, e.g., *touch-hands* pronounced in one breath, *i.e.*, like the aspirated *ch* in Hindustani.

ཇ་ is also a *ch* pronounced through the throat and in a lower tone than ཅ་

ཉ་ as the initial sound in *nuisance*.

ཏ་ a Dental *t* to be pronounced with the tongue between the teeth and without breathing. This ཏ་ and ན་ differ from the English *t* and *n*, in that the English letters require the tongue to be placed against the roof of the mouth and so have a heavier sound.

ཐ་ aspirated *t*, e.g., *thora* in Hindustani; or—subject to the difference noted under ཏ་—*pat hard* pronounced in one breath. Not to be confused with the English *th* sound, in words like *the*.

ད་ is like ཏ་ but pronounced through the throat and in a lower tone than ཏ་

ན་ is like English *n*, e.g., in *nest* subject to the difference noted under ཏ་

པ་ like English *p* as in *pear*, to be pronounced with the tongue between the teeth and without breathing.

ཕ་ aspirated *p*, e.g., *stop here* pronounced as one word. Not to be confused with *ph* sound occurring in English words like *phantasy*, etc.

བ་ is also a *p* but pronounced through the throat and in a lower tone than པ་ If it forms the second syllable of a word whose first syllable ends with a vowel or with ང་འ་ར་ or ལ་ it is pronounced as *w*.

མ་ as English *m*, e.g., in *man*.

ཙ་ *ts* is pronounced like *weights* eliminating the letters *weigh*.

To be pronounced with the tongue between the teeth and without breathing.

ཚ་ as *ts* aspirated, *e g.*, in *pats hard* pronounced as one word.

ཛ་ is also a *ts*, but pronounced through the throat and in a lower tone than ཙ་

ཝ་ like *w* in English, *e.g.*, in *wing*.

ཞ་ Something like *sh* in English, but pronounced in a lower tone and more through the throat.

ཟ་ Something like *s* in English, but pronounced in a lower tone and more through the throat.

འ་ has no pronunciation of its own. When it precedes ག་ཇ་ད་བ་ or ཛ་; these letters are pronounced respectively like *g* in *gun*, *j* in *jam*, *d* in *den*, *b* in *bend*, and *ds* in *pads*. See also para. 23

ཡ་ like *y* in English, *e.g.*, in *yacht*.

ར་ is short like *r* in English, *e.g.*, in *rat*. It is never rolled.

ལ་ like *l* in English, *e.g.*, in *linger*.

ཤ་ like *sh* in English, but pronounced sharply and through the teeth.

ས་ like *s* in English, but pronounced sharply and through the teeth.

ཧ་ like *h* aspirated in English, *e.g.*, in *hand*.

ཨ་ When a vowel is initial, either ཨ་ or འ་ is used as its base. The difference in pronunciation of these two is that the throat is opened for ཨ་ and kept closed for འ་ The result is that ཨ་ carries the ordinary vowel sound, whatever the vowel may be; while འ་ in the case of ུ or ོ gives a slight, but very slight sound of *w*; e.g., འུར་ *noise*=something between *ur* and *wur* though more like *ur*.

4. The five vowels are called དབྱངས་ལྔ་ *Yang-nga*: ཨ་ (a) ཨི་ (i) ཨུ་ (u) ཨེ་ (e) ཨོ། (o)

The four vowel-signs are ི *i* ུ *u* ེ *e* ོ *o*.

Every consonant implies a following *a*, unless another vowel is attached. This *a* is sounded like the English *u* in *rub*.

ི named གི་གུ་ *Ki-ku*, like *i* in *in* or *tin*, e.g., མི་ man=*mi*.

ུ named ཞབས་ཀྱུ་ *sKap-kyu*, like *oo* in *root* when initial or final. Like *u* in *pull*, when medial, *e.g.*, གྲུ་ boat=*tru*; ནུབ་ west=*nup*.

ེ named འགྲེང་བུ་ *Deng-bu*, like *e* in *men*. But when final also often like *i* in *tin*, e.g., ལེན་པ་ to take=*lem-pa*; ལྡེ་མིག་ *key*=*di-mi*.

ོ named ན་རོ་ *na-ro*, like *o* in hole; e.g., ལོག་པ་ to come back=*loḱ-pa*.

5. The Tibetan letters with the four vowel-signs are as follow:—

| | | | |
|---|---|---|---|
| ཀི་ *ki.* | ཁུ་ *khu.* | གེ་ *ḱe.* | ངོམས། *ngom.* |
| ཅི་ *chi.* | ཆུ་ *chhu.* | ཇེ་ *cḱe.* | ཉོན། *nyön.* |
| ཏི་ *ti.* | ཐུ་ *thu.* | དེ་ *t́e.* | ནོར། *nor.* |
| པི་ *pi.* | ཕུ་ *phu.* | བེ་ *ṕe.* | མོས། *mö.* |
| ཙི་ *tsi.* | ཚུ་ *tshu.* | ཛེ་ *tśe.* | ཝོལ། *wöl.* |
| ཞི་ *sḱi.* | ཟུ་ *śu.* | འེ་ *e.* | ཡོད། *yö.* |
| རི་ *ri.* | ལུ་ *lu.* | ཤེ་ *she.* | སོང་། *song.* |
| | ཧེ་ *he.* | ཨོཾ། *Om.* | |

(The *o* is named "*le-kor*," and represents the letter མ་).

The above set of examples is that ordinarily used in Tibetan schools and monasteries.

6. **Final Consonants.**—The preceding paragraph shows the ordinary pronunciation of the vowels which is, however, further affected by some of the final consonants. Of final con-

sonants there are only ten; that is to say, though any consonant may begin a syllable only one of these ten consonants may end it. These ten final consonants are as follow:—

ག་ང་ད་ན་བ་མ་འ་ར་ལ་ས་ Let us briefly consider the pronunciation of each as a final, and its effect upon the pronunciation of the preceding vowel.

ག་ is pronounced so slightly as hardly to be heard and shortens the preceding vowel. When followed, however, by another consonant in a second syllable of the same word it is clearly pronounced, and does not affect the pronunciation of the preceding vowel, thus མིག་ eye =*mi*, but འཕོག་པ་ to hit=*phok-pa*.

ང་ is pronounced more sharply than when an initial. It does not affect the pronunciation of the preceding vowel, *e.g.*, མིང་ name=*ming*, but sounded sharply. The sound of final ག་ and ང་ can be obtained from the teacher with but little practice.

ད་ ལ་ ས་ } These all modify the sounds of the preceding vowels *a*, *u* and *o*; i.e., *a* into *e* (in French *les*); *u* into *ü* (in French *sur*); *o* into *ö* (*e.g.*, *hören* in German or *eu* in French *peu*). These modified sounds will, therefore, be romanized into *e*, *ö*, *ü*, respectively.

The final consonant itself is not pronounced; *e.g.*, ལུད་ manure=*lü*, བལ་ wool=*pē*, བྲོས་པ་ to flee=*trö-pa*.

ད་ makes the preceding vowel short; ལ་ and ས་

make it long, thus ལུད་ manure=*lü* (short *u*); but ལུས་ body=*lü* (long *u*).

ན་ modifies vowels as ད་ལ་ and ས་ modify them, but is itself pronounced, *e.g.*, ལན་ answer=*len*. When followed by པ་ཕ་བ་ or མ་ in the same word it is pronounced as *m*, e.g., རིན་པོ་ཆེ་ precious=*rim-po-chhe.*

བ་ མ་ ར་ } Do not affect the pronunciation of the vowel, and are themselves pronounced the same as when initial, *e.g.*, ཚབ་ delegate=*tshaṕ*, ཟམ་པ་ bridge=*śam-pa*, ཟུར་ corner=*śur*. But ར་ like ག་ is sometimes pronounced so lightly as hardly to be heard.

འ་ is not itself pronounced but lengthens the sound of the vowel preceding it. No vowel except the indirect *a* precedes it, *e.g.*, ནམ་མཁའ་ sky=*nam-khā*.

7. **Affix.**—The letter ས་ also occurs as a second final consonant or affix after either of the four letters ག་ང་བ་མ་ It is not pronounced, but in the case of ག་ preceded by *a*, it has the effect of lengthening the *a*, e.g., ལགས་སོ་ yes=*lā-si*. It is sometimes written in an incomplete form below the final consonant thus ལགྶ་སོ་

8. **Sanskrit Letters.**—The following six letters taken from the Sanskrit are occasionally used in the Colloquial language, namely :—

| ཊ་ | ཋ་ | ཌ་ | ཎ་ | ཥ་ | ཀྵ་ |
|---|---|---|---|---|---|
| *tra* | *thra* | *dra* | *na* | *kha* | *khya.* |

ཊ་ is known as *ta-lo-tra,* which means "*ta* reversed is *tra*";

ཎ་ as *na-lo-na,* "*na* reversed is *na*"; and so on.

9. **Examples.**

[The student is recommended to cover the romanized Tibetan letters with a piece of paper and thus to test his knowledge of the alphabet and its pronunciation.]

ཀོ་བ་ leather = *ko-wa.*

སྒར་ encampment = *gar.*

ཤིང་ tree = *shing.*

ཆུ་ water = *chhu.*

ཨ་མ་ mother = *a-ma.*

འོད་ light, *s.* = *ö.*

ཕན་ profit = *phen.*

ཞོན་པ་ to ride = *sḱöm-pa.*

ས་ earth = *sa.*

ཟ་བ་ to eat = *śa-wa.*

དད་པ་ faith = *t́e-pa.*

དང་ and = *t́ang.*

ལས་ཀ་ work = *le-ka.*

ལུག་ sheep = *lŭ.*

ལག་པ་ hand = *laḱ-pa.*

ཇོ་བོ་ lord = *cḱo-wo.*

10. **Diphthongs.**—There are no real diphthongs, but under this head may be classed the combination *ai, oi, ui,* occurring when the one syllable of a word ends in *a, o,* or *u,*

and the next begins with *i*; e.g., རོ་ and འི་ of the corpse = *ro-i*, pronounced almost like *rö*, but with a slight sound of *i*; similarly ཁ and འི་ of the mouth = *kha-i* and almost = *khē*; བུ་ and འི་ of the son = *ṕu-ï* and almost = *ṕü*. In fact the འི་ modifies the preceding vowels in practically the same way as ས་ would do.

The other combinations of vowels are *ao, io, uo, eo, oo, au, iu, eu*; e.g., ཟའོ། ཤིའོ། དུའོ། ཚེའོ། ཇོའོ། གའུ། བྱིའུ། ལེའུ། They are not often used in the colloquial and are not really diphthongs, as each vowel is clearly though rapidly pronounced.

Note that འ་ and not ཨ་ is always used as the base of the second vowel; that is, the letter over which the second vowel must be written; *e.g.*, ཁ and འི་ and not ཁ་ and ཨི་

11. **Compound Consonants.**—These are of two kinds, namely Subjoined and Superadded. These subjoined consonants are:—

ཝ་ཡ་ར་ལ་ and ཧ་ They are known respectively as ཝ་ཟུར་ *wa-śur*, "*wa* on the edge"; ཡ་བཏགས་ *ya-ta*, "*ya* subjoined"; ར་བཏགས་ *ra-ta*, "*ra* subjoined"; ལ་བཏགས་ *la-ta*, "*la* subjoined"; and ཧ་བཏགས་ *ha-ta*, "*ha* subjoined."

**12. Wasurs.**—*Wasur* may be joined to sixteen consonants, *viz.* —

ཀྭ་ ཁྭ་ གྭ་ ཅྭ་ ཉྭ་ ཏྭ་ དྭ་ ཙྭ་ ཚྭ་ ཞྭ་ ཟྭ་ རྭ་ ལྭ་ ཤྭ་ སྭ་ ཧྭ་

The effect on the pronunciation is to lengthen the sound of the vowel in the same way as final འ་ but not quite so much, *e.g.*, ཚྭ་ salt = *tshā.*

13. Of *yatas* there are seven, which are joined to the following letters, thus—

ཀྱ་ *kya*, ཁྱ་ *khya*, གྱ་ *ḱya*, པྱ་ *cha*, ཕྱ་ *chha*, བྱ་ *cḱa*, མྱ་ *nya.*

Note the pronunciation of the last four.

Thus གྱོང་པོ་ hard = *ḱyong-po.*

ཕྱིན་པ་ to go = *chhim-pa.*

བྱ་ bird = *cḱa.*

14. *Rata* is joined to thirteen consonants, namely :—

ཀྲ་ *tra*, ཁྲ་ *thra*, གྲ་ *t́ra.*

ཏྲ་ *tra*, དྲ་ *t́ra.*

པྲ་ pronounced *tra.* or *pa*, ཕྲ་ *thra*, བྲ་ pronounced *t́ra*, *ṕa* or *ra.*

Note that gutturals and labials take the sound of dentals. *Rata* is also joined to ནྲ་ *na*, མྲ་ *ma*, ཤྲ་ *sha*, སྲ་ *sa* or

---

NOTE.—Several English grammars also give ཐྲ་ *thra*, but this is neither given in Tibetan primers nor used in the colloquial language.

*tra* or *hra*, ཧྲ་ *hra*, e.g., ཁྲག་ blood = *thra*, གྲུ་ boat = *t́ru*, དྲིལ་བུ་ bell = *t́ri-ṕu*, བྲིས་པ་ (འབྲི་བ་) to write = *t́ri-pa*, སྲས་ son = *se*, སྲབ་ bridle = *traṕ*.

Note that where any of the first nine *ratas* are followed by the vowels ི or ེ the *r* is pronounced less strongly than when followed by the other vowels. And in no case is the *r* pronounced as strongly as in English.

15. *Hata* in the colloquial language is not used except with ལ་, *e.g.*, ལྷ་ a god = *hla*, the *h* being pronounced before the *l*. It is also joined to ག་ད་བ་ཛ་ and ཌ་ and is then written གྷ་དྷ་བྷ་ཛྷ་ and ཌྷ་ respectively, but these last five cases only occur in transcribing Sanskrit words, and are of little use for colloquial purposes.

16. *La-ta* is joined to six consonants, thus—

ཀླ་གླ་བླ་ཟླ་རླ་སླ་ These are all sounded as *la* in a high tone, except ཟླ་ which is pronounced *da*, e.g., གླུ་ song = *lu* ; ཟླ་བ་ month = *da-wa*.

17. **Examples.**

བྲག་ rock = *t́ra*.

སྨྱུ་གུ་ reed-pen = *nyu-gu*.

སླེ་ཀོག་ basket = *le-ko*.

ངའི་སྲབ་ my bridle = *nge-traṕ*.

ཁྱོད་ཀྱི་སྲོག་ your life = *khyö-kyi so.*

ཁོའི་གླུ་ his song = *khö lu.*

ཞབས་བྲོ་ dance = *sȟaṕ-ro.*

བྲང་ཁོག་ chest (of body) = *ṕang-kho.*

སྲང་འགག་ lane = *hrang-ga.*

18. **Superscribed Consonants.**—There are three of these, namely, ར་ལ་ and ས་ They are placed on the tops of other letters.

ར་ is placed on the top of twelve consonants, thus:

| རྐ་ | རྒ་ | རྔ་ | རྗ་ | རྙ་ | རྟ་ | རྡ་ | རྣ་ | རྦ་ | རྨ་ | རྩ་ | རྫ་ |
|---|---|---|---|---|---|---|---|---|---|---|---|
| *ka* | *ga* | *nga* | *ja* | *nya* | *ta* | *da* | *na* | *ba* | *ma* | *tsa* | *dza.* |

Note that the ར་ is written as ˉ ; except with ཉ་ when the full ར་ is written. Note also that རྒ་ is pronounced as *ga,* རྗ་ as *ja,* རྡ་ as *da,* རྦ་ as *ba* and རྫ་ as *dza.* The others differ from the ordinary ཀ་ང་ etc., in that they are pronounced in higher tone.

19. **Examples.**

རྐང་པ་ foot = *kang-pa,* རྒན་པོ་ old man = *ge-po,* རྒྱན་ ornament = *gyen,* རྡོ་ stone = *do,* རྣོ་པོ་ sharp = *no-po,* རྩ་བ་ root = *tsa-wa,* ལུག་རྫི་ shepherd = *luk-dzi.* The ར་ itself is not pronounced except sometimes when occurring in the second syllables of words; *e.g.*, རྡོ་རྗེ་ sacred thunder-bolt= *dor-je*. When ར་ surmounts a consonant as above, it is named ར་མགོ་ *rang-go*, i.e., ra-head, and the consonant is said to be "tied on" or "subjoined" as the *ya-tas*, *ratas*, etc., above. Thus རྐ་ is named *ra-ka-ta*, i.e., *ra* with *ka* subjoined, རྒ་ is named *ra-ga-ta*, and so on.

20. ལ་ similarly named ལ་མགོ་ *lang-go*, i.e., la-head, is superadded to ten consonants as follow:—

ལྐ་ ལྒ་ ལྔ་ ལྕ་ ལྗ་ ལྟ་ ལྡ་ ལྤ་ ལྦ་ ལྷ་

ལྷ་ is pronounced *hla*. The rest are pronounced in the same way as the corresponding consonants with superadded ར། ལྕ་ and ལྤ་ are pronounced in a high tone as *cha* and *pa* respectively.

21. ས་ similarly named ས་མགོ་ *sang-go*, i.e., sa-head, is superadded to eleven consonants as follow:—

སྐ་ སྒ་ སྔ་ སྙ་ སྟ་ སྡ་ སྣ་ སྤ་ སྦ་ སྨ་ སྩ་

These are pronounced in the same way as the corresponding consonants with superadded ར་ or ལ་ The consonants surmounted by ལ་ or ས་ are similarly said to be "tied on," e.g., ལྔ་ is named *la-nga-ta*, and སྡ་ is named *sa-da-ta*.

22. **Examples.**

ལྔ་ five = *nga.*

སྔ་དྲོ་ morning = *nga-ṫro.*

ལྕགས་ iron = *cha.*

ལྡིང་བ་ to soar (in the air) = *ding-wa.*

སྡིག་པ་ sin = *dik-pa.*

སྨན་ medicine = *men.*

23. **Prefixed Letters.**—The five letters ག་ད་བ་མ་འ་ are found in many words before the initial consonant. These prefixes are not themselves pronounced, but affect the pronunciation in the same way as superadded ར་ལ་ or ས་

ག་ occurs before ཅ་ཉ་ཏ་ད་ན་ཙ་ཞ་ཟ་ཡ་ཤ་ས་

ད་ before ཀ་ག་ང་པ་བ་མ་

བ་ before ཀ་ག་ཙ་ཛ་ཏྟ་ཏ་ད་ན་ཙ་ཛ་ཞ་ཟ་ཟླ་ཤ་ས་

མ་ before ཁ་ག་ང་ཆ་ཇ་ཉ་ཐ་ད་ན་ཚ་ཛ་

འ་ before ཁ་ག་ཆ་ཇ་ཐ་ད་ཕ་བ་ཚ་ཛ་

**Examples.**

| | |
|---|---|
| གཅིག་ one = *chi.* | གདན་ bolster = *den.* |
| གསར་པ་ new = *sa-pa.* | དངུལ་ silver = *ngü.* |

| | |
|---|---|
| བཏང་བ་ to send = *tang-wa.* | བདུན་ seven = *dün.* |
| མཁས་པོ་ skilful = *khe-po.* | འཛོམ་པ་ to assemble = *dzom-pa.* |

24. Confusion might arise in the case of one of the prefixed letters making a word with one of the final consonants, the vowel being the inherent *a*, e.g., དག་ as to whether it represents *tă* or *gā*. The confusion is obviated as follows. If it is the initial ད་, the word is written དག་ *tă*. If it is the prefix, འ་ is added thus, དགའ་ = *gā*.

25. When བ་ as initial consonant follows ད་ as prefix, the combination is either sounded as *w* or not sounded at all. If accompanied by a *yata* or a vowel sign, it is not sounded at all; *e.g.*, དབུགས་ breath = *u*, དབྱངས་ tune, melody = *yang*; དབྱུག་པ་ to throw = *yuk-pa*. If accompanied by *rata*, it follows the ordinary rule of *ratas* (para. 14) and prefixed ད་ (para. 23) and is pronounced *dr*. In other cases it is pronounced as *w*, e.g., དབང་ power, authority = *wang*.

26. **Sentences for Pronunciation.**

Bring some hot water. ཆུ་ཚ་པོ་འཁྱེར་ཤོག་ *chhu tsha-po khe sho.*

This water is not hot. ཆུ་འདི་ཚ་པོ་མི་འདུག་ *chhu di tsha-po min-du.*

It is cold. གྲང་མོ་རེད་ *trang-mo re.*

You can go now. ད་འགྲོ་ཆོག་གི་རེད་ *ta dro chhok-ki-re.*

27. **Irregular Sounds.**—In the following cases the pronunciation is modified for the sake of euphony.

(*a*) *m* and *n* sounds.—When one syllable is followed by another beginning with a prefixed letter the sound of *m* or *n* is often introduced. This occurs especially when the first syllable ends in ག་ *e.g.*

ཕྱག་ལྡེ་ · key, *hon.* = *chhan di.*

ཕྱག་འབྲུ་ grain, *hon.* = *chhan-dru.*

མི་འདུག་ is not = *min-du.*

ན་བཟའ་ clothes, *hon.* = *nam-śa.*

(*b*) *Reduplicated Sounds.*—When the following final consonants, or affixes, namely, ག་གས་ང་ངས་ར་ and ལ་, are followed by པ་ or བ་, the sound of the final consonant is reduplicated, *e.g.*, བཀག་ (འགོགས་) པ་གནང་བ་ to hinder, *hon.* = *kak-ka nang-wa*; གསུངས་པ་རེད་ he said, *hon.* = *sung-nga-re.* ཉར་བ་ གནང་བ་ to take care of, *hon.* = *ngar-ra nang-wa*; ཚིལ་བུ་ fat = *tshil-lu*; དཔོན་པོས་གནང་བ་རེད། the official has given, *pöm-pö nang-nga-re.*

(c) བ་ following a vowel or ལ་. When བ་ follows a vowel its sound is sometimes omitted altogether, *e.g.*, ལྦ་བ་ goitre = *ba-a.*

ཀ་བ་ pillar = *ka-a.*

བ་ after ལ་ is often pronounced as *r*, e.g.,—

རྒྱལ་བ་གནང་བ་ to conquer, hon. = *gye-ra nang-wa.*

(*d*) Other changed sounds

བཞེས་ཐུར་ spoon = *sKip-thu.*

རྒྱ་ར་ (རྒྱ་བྲ་) sweet buck-wheat = *gyap-ra.*

(*e*) There are also other irregular sounds, but it seems unnecessary to enumerate them all here. They will be picked up more easily in the course of conversation.

28. **The Tones.**—In Tibetan the tone, that is to say the pitch of the voice, varies, each word in this language having a tone in which it should be pronounced. It is very important for the student to render these tones with substantial accuracy; otherwise the pronunciation becomes uncertain and many of his words will assume meanings which he does not intend for them.

29. For practical purposes we must discriminate between three tones, *viz.* the high, the medium, and the low. The initial letter and the prefix govern the tone.

*High Tone.*—Use this in a word beginning with a prefix except when the initial letter is ཁ་ག་ཆ་ཇ་ཐ་ད་ཕ་བ་ཚ་ or ཛ་

Use it also with any of the following initials, *viz.* ཀ་ཅ་ཏ་པ་ ཙ་ཤ་ས་ཧ་

*Medium Tone.*—Use this in a word beginning with ཁ་ཆ་ཐ་ཕ་ཚ་ as initals whether with or without prefixes.

*Low Tone.*—Use this in a word beginning with any of the following letters as initials ག་ང་ཇ་ཉ་ད་ན་བ་མ་ཛ་ཝ་ཞ་ཟ་ཡ་ ར་ལ་འ་ also in words in which a prefix precedes the initials ག་ཇ་ད་བ་ or ཛ་ Such initials are in this case, as previously noted in paragraph 23, pronounced as *g*, *j*, *d*, *b* and *dz*, respectively. For effect of ག་ང་ད་བ་ལ་ས་ in lengthening or shortening the preceding vowel see above paras. 6 and 7.

**Examples.**

ཀོ་བ་ leather = *ko-wa*, high tone.

སྤོས་ incense = *pö*, high tone and lengthened.

ཕག་ brick = *pă*, high tone and shortened.

ཆམ་པ་ cold (in the head) = *chham-pa*, medium tone.

ཐབས་ opportunity = *thap̆*, medium tone.

ཐག་པ་ rope = *thak̆-pa*, medium tone and shortened.

ལ་ to (postposition) *la*, low tone.

ལགས་ yes (a polite affirmative) = *lā*, low tone and lengthened.

བོད་ Tibet = *p̆ö*, low tone and shortened.

Note the difference in above examples between སྤོས་ and བོད་ and between ལ་ and ལགས་

30. **Punctuation.**—It will have been noticed from the examples that at the end of each syllable a dot is placed at the top right-hand corner. This dot is named ཚེག *tshe.* A comma, semi-colon or colon is indicated by a vertical line (།) called *she,* a full-stop by a double line (༎) called *nyi-she,* and the end of a chapter by four lines (༎ ༎) called *k̄i-she.* In hand-writing a mark ( ‘ ) is usually placed between each syllable instead of the *tshe,* but is sometimes incorporated with the last letter of the syllable.

31. **Spelling.**—The Tibetan method of spelling words should be acquired, as the teacher, in common with all Tibetans, will use it.

32. Pronounce the first consonant or compound consonant, add the vowel and pronounce the two together.

Thus, ཀོ་ ; *ka-na-ro, ko.* སྐི་ ; *sa-ka-ta, ka, ka k̄i-k̄u, ki.*

It is as if to say *sa* with *ka-ta* makes *ka, ka* with *k̄i-k̄u* makes *ki.*

33. If there is a final consonant, pronounce the whole word with it, then the consonant itself, and then the whole word again. Thus, ཀོང་ ; *ka-na-ro, ko, kong-nga-kong.* Again ཀྱོང་ ; *ka ya-ta, kya, kya-na-ro, kyo, kyong-nga, kyong.*

34. If the vowel is the inherent *a,* pronounce the first consonant, then the whole word, then the final consonant, and then the whole word again, *e.g.* ཁང་ ; *k̄a, k̄ang-nga, k̄ang.* སྒང་ ; *sa-ga-ta, ga, gang-nga, gang.* ལྟོགས་ ; *la-ta-ta, ta, ta-na-ro, to, tok̄-k̄a-sa, tok̄.*

35. When a prefixed letter begins the syllable, *e.g.* གད་ etc., it is pronounced as *ḱa-wo, t́a-wo*; *e.g.* གཉེན; *ḱa-wo-nya-deng-bu, nye, nyen-na, nyen.* དགབ; *t́a-wo-ga, gaṕ-ṕa gaṕ.* This *wo* is pronounced very shortly.

36. A syllable containing only a consonant and the inherent *a*, e.g., མ་, is called *ma-kyang, i e.* "only *ma*," to distinguish it from the consonant accompanied by one of the other vowels. Thus, to enquire whether a syllable is སོ་ or ས་, you may say, "Is it *sa-na-ro* or *sa-kyang*?"

36. **Examples.**

ལུང་ handle. *la sḱaṕ-kyu, lu, lung-nga, lung.*

རས་ cotton. *ra, re-sa, re.*

བཏང་བ་ to send. *ṕa-wo-ta-tang-nga, tang; wa: tang-wa.*

འཁྱུད་པ་ to embrace. *a-wo-kha-ya-ta khya, khya shaṕ-kyu, khyu, khyü-t́a, khyü; pa: khyü-pa.*

དགྲ་ enemy. *tá-wo-ga-ra-ta, dra.*

ལྷ་ spirit. *la-ha-ta, hla.*

བསོད་ནམས་ good fortune. *ṕa-wo-sa-na-ro, so, sö-t́a, sö; na, nam-ma-sa, nam: sö-nam.*

ཞྭ་མོ་ hat. *sḱa-wa-sur, sḱa; ma na-ro, mo: sḱa-mo.*

དཔེ་ཆ་ book. *Tá-wo-pa-deng-bu, pe; chha: pe-chha.*

གློག་ lightning. *ḱa-la-ta, la, la-na-ro, lo, lo-ḱa, lo.*

རྒྱུག་པ་ to run. *ra-ga-ta, ga, ga ya-ta gya, gya sḱap-kyu, gyu, gyuk-ḱa, gyuḱ; pa: gyuk-pa.*

རིགས་བརྒྱུད་ lineage. *ra-ḱi-ḱu, ri, ri-ḱa-sa, riḱ; ṕa-wo-ra-ga-ta, ga, ga ya-ta, gya, gya-sḱap-kyu, gyu, gyü-ťa, gyü: riḱ-gyü.*

37. **Sentences.**

Where are you going to? ཁྱོད་ག་པ་འགྲོ་གི་ཡིན་པ་ *khyö ḱa-pa dro-ḱi yim-pa?*

I am going to Darjiling, Sir. ལགས་ང་རྡོ་རྗེ་གླིང་ལ་འགྲོ་གི་ཡིན་ *lā nga Dor-je-ling lă dro-ḱi yin.*

What have you got in the bundle? རྡོག་ཐྲེད་ནང་ལ་ག་རེ་ཡོད་པ་ *doḱ-thre nang-la ḱa-re yö-pa?*

Different kinds of things, Sir. ལགས་ཆ་ལག་སྣ་ཚོགས་ཡོད་ *lā cha-lă na-tsho yö.*

Have you a tea-pot among them? དེའི་ནང་ལ་ཁོ་ཏིང་ཡོད་པས་ *ťe-ï nang-la kho ting yö-pē?*

Yes, Sir, I have. ལགས་ཡོད་ *lā-yö.*

What is its price? གོང་ག་ཚོད་ཡིན་པ་ *kong ḱa-tshö yim-pa?*

Twenty rupees. ལགས་སྒོར་མོ་ཉི་ཤུ་ཐམ་པ་ཡིན་ *lā gor-mo nyi-shu tham-pa yin.*

Will you let me have it for fifteen rupees? སྒོར་མོ་བཅོ་ལྔ་ལ་གཏོང་གི་ཡིན་པས་ *gor-mo che-nga la tong-ḱi yim-pē?*

No, Sir. ལགས་མིན་ *la-men.*

Well, good-day! འོ་ན་ག་ལེ་རྒྱུག་ *o-na ḱa-le gyu.*

Good-day, Sir! ད་འོ་ན་ག་ལེ་འཆིབ་རྒྱུ་གནང་ *ťa o-na ḱa-le chhiṕ-gyu-nang.*

# ENGLISH-TIBETAN COLLOQUIAL DICTIONARY.

## NOTE.

1. To understand fully the pronunciation of the Tibetan words, and the transliteration into the Roman character, reference should be made to the preliminary chapter on the "The Alphabet and its Pronunciation." It is not possible to represent all the Tibetan sounds by Roman letters with exactitude; hence the importance of mastering that chapter before using this dictionary.

2. Where the colloquial and the literary forms differ appreciably, the latter are given in brackets in the Tibetan character. In the romanized Tibetan the colloquial forms alone are given.

3. Where two or more Tibetan words are entered against the same English word, the first is the one most commonly used.

## A

| | | |
|---|---|---|
| A, An, *art.* | ཅིག་ | *chi.* |
| Do. (in the sense of full or complete) | གང་ | *ḱang.* |
| Aback | རྒྱབ་ལོགས་ལ་ | *gyaṕ-lo-la.* |
| Abaft | གཞུག་ལ་ | *sḱu-la.* |
| Abandon, to | བཞག་པ་ (འཇོག་པ།) སྤང་བ་ | *sḱak-pa ; pang-wa.* |
| Do. *hon.* | གཞོག་ག་ (འཇོག་པ་) གནང་བ་ | *sḱok-ḱa nang-wa.* |
| | སྤོང་ང་ (བ་) གནང་བ་ | *pong-nga nang-wa.* |

| | | |
|---|---|---|
| Abate, to (in price) | བཅག་པ་ (གཅོག་པ་) | *chaḱ-pa.* |
| Do. *hon.* | གཅོག་ག་ (པ་) གནང་བ་ | *chok-ḱa nang-wa.* |
| Abbess | ཨ་ནི་དབུ་མཛད་ | *a-ni um-dze.* |
| Abbot | མཁན་པོ་ | *ḱhem-po.* |
| Abbreviate, to | སྡུད་པ། རྡུམ་རྡུམ་བྱེད་པ་ | *dü-pa; dum dum cḱe-pa.* |
| Abdomen | གྲོ་ཁོག་ (གྲོད་ཁོག་) | *t́ro-kho.* |
| Do. *hon.* | གསོལ་གྲོད་ | *sö-t́rö.* |
| Abide, to | བསྡད་པ་ (སྡོད་པ་) | *de-pa.* |
| Do. *hon.* | བཞུགས་པ་ | *sḱu-pa* |
| Ability | དབང་ | *wang.* |
| Abject | སྡུག་པོ་ | *duḱ-po.* |
| Able, *adj.* | མཁས་པོ་ | *ḱhe-po.* |
| Able, to be | ཐུབ་པ་ | *thuṕ-pa.* |
| Do. *hon.* | ཐུབ་པ་གནང་བ་ | *thuṕ-pa nang-wa.* |
| Able, to be (in the sense of knowing how) | ཤེས་པ་ | *she-pa.* |
| Do. *hon.* | མཁྱེན་པ་ | *khyem-pa.* |
| Able-bodied | སྟོབས་ཆེན་པོ་ | *toṕ chhem-po.* |
| Ablution | ཁྲུས་ | *thrü.* |
| Do. *hon.* | སྐུ་ཁྲུས་ | *ku-thrü.* |

| | | |
|---|---|---|
| Abode | ཁང་པ། ནང་ | *khang-pa; nang.* |
| Do. *hon.* | གཟིམ་ཁང་ | *śim-khang.* |
| Do. *h. hon.* | གཟིམ་ཤག | *śim-sha.* |
| Abolish, to | མེད་པར་བཟོ་བ་ | *me-pa śo-wa.* |
| Do. *hon.* | མེད་པར་བཟོ་བ་གནང་བ་ | *me-pa śo-wa nang-wa.* |
| Abominable | སྐྱུག་བྲོ་བོ་ | *kyuk-ťro-po.* |
| Abortion | བུ་གུ་ཤོར་བ་ | *pu-gu shor-wa.* |
| About (approximately) | ཙ་ (ཙམ་) | *tsa.* |
| About (concerning) | དོན་ལ། སྐོར་ལ་ | *ťön-la; kor-la.* |
| Above (on top of) | སྟེང་ལ། སྒང་ལ་ | *teng-la; gang-la.* |
| Above (higher up a hill) | ཡར་ལ་ | *ya-la.* |
| Abridge, to | སྡུད་པ་ | *dü-pa.* |
| Do. *hon.* | སྡུད་པ་གནང་བ་ | *dü-pa nang-wa.* |
| Abruptly | ལམ་སང་ | *lam-sang.* |
| Abscess | ཤུ་བ་ | *shu-wa.* |
| Do. *hon.* | སྐུ་ཤུ་ | *ku-shu.* |
| Abscond, to | བྲོས་པ་ (འབྲོས་པ་) | *ťrö-pa.* |
| Do. *hon.* | བྲོས་ (འབྲོས་) ཕེབ་པ་ | *ťrö-phe-pa.* |
| Absence | མེད་དུས་ | *me-ťü.* |
| Absent, to be | མེད་པ་ | *me-pa.* |

| | | |
|---|---|---|
| Absolutely (used negatively) | བད་དེ། ཁྱོན་ནས་ | be te ; khyön-n[illegible] |
| Absolve, to | སེལ་བ་ | sel-wa. |
| Do. *hon.* | སེལ་ལ་ (བ་) གནང་བ་ | sel-la nang-wa. |
| Abstain from, to (certain kinds of food, &c.) | སྤང་བ་ | p̣ang·wa. |
| | བཅད་པ་ (གཅོད་པ་) | che-pa. |
| Do. *hon.* | སྤོང་ང་ (བ་) གནང་བ་ | pong-nga nang-wa. |
| | བཅད་ (གཅོད་) པ་གནང་བ་ | che-p̣a nang-wa |
| Absurd, to be | དོན་དག་མེད་པ་ | ťön-ťa me-pa. |
| Abundant | འབེལ་པོ། རྫག་དོ་ | be-po ; dzak-to |
| Abuse, *s.* | སྨད་ར་ | me-ra. |
| Abuse, to. | སྨད་ར་བཏང་ (གཏོང་) བ་ | me-ra tang-wa. |
| Do. *hon.* | སྨད་ར་གཏོང་ང་ (བ་) གནང་བ་ | me-ra tong-ng nang-wa. |
| Do. *inf.* to *sup.* | སྨད་ར་ཞུ་བ་ | me-ra sḳu-wa. |
| Abyss | གཡང་གཟར་པོ་ | yang-ṡar-po. |
| Accede, to | ཁས་ལེན་པ་ | khe-lem-pa. |
| Do. *hon.* | ཞལ་བཞེས་གནང་བ། | sḳe-sḳe nang-wa |
| | ཞལ་གྱིས་བཞེས་པ་ | sḳe-ḳyi sḳe-pa. |
| Accept, to | ལེན་པ་ | lem-pa. |
| Do. *hon.* | བཞེས་པ་ | sḳe-pa. |
| Access, to have | འགྲོ་ཆོག་པ། ཕྱིན་ཆོག་པ་ | dro-chhok-pa ; chhin-chhok-pa. |

| | | |
|---|---|---|
| Access, *hon.* | ཕེབ་ཆོག་པ་ | *phe-chhok-pa.* |
| Accident | བར་ཆད་ | *par-chhe.* |
| Accommodation | ཤོང་ས་ | *shong-sa.* |
| Accompany, to | མཉམ་དུ་ཡོང་བ་ | *nyam-tu yong-wa.* |
| Do. *hon.* | མཉམ་དུ་ཕེབ་པ་ | *nyam-tu phe-pa.* |
| Do. *h. hon.* | ལྷན་རྒྱས་འཆིབ་རྒྱུ་གནང་བ་ | *hlen-gye chhip-gyu nang-wa.* |
| Accomplice | རོགས་ | *ro.* |
| Accomplished, to be (completed) | འཚར་བ་ | *tshar-wa.* |
| Do. *hon.* | གྲུབ་པ་ | *trup-pa.* |
| According to | ནང་བཞིན་ | *nang-skin.* |
| Account | རྩིས་ | *tsi.* |
| Account Book | རྩིས་ཐོ་ | *tsi-tho.* |
| Do. *hon.* | ཕྱག་ཐོ་ | *chha-tho.* |
| Account of, on | རྐྱེན་གྱིས་ | *kyen-kyi.* |
| Accounts, to do | རྩིས་རྒྱབ་པ་ | *tsi-gyap-pa.* |
| Do. *hon.* | ཕྱགས་རྩིས་གནང་བ་ | *ja-tsi nang-wa.* |
| | ཕྱགས་རྩིས་སྐྱོན་པ་ | *ja-tsi kyöm-pa.* |
| Accountant | རྩིས་པ་ | *tsi-pa.* |
| Do. Chief | རྩིས་དཔོན་ | *tsi-pön.* |

| | | |
|---|---|---|
| Accountant, Office of an | རྩིས་ཁང་ | *tsi-khang.* |
| Accumulate, to (money) | བསག་པ་ (གསོག་པ་) | *sak-pa.* |
| Do. *hon.* | བསག་ག་ (གསོག་པ་) གནང་བ་ | *sak-ka nang-wa.* |
| Accurate | ཁྲིག་ཁྲིག། ཏེན་ཏེན་ | *thrik-thrik ; ten-ten.* |
| Accusation | སྙད་ | *nye.* |
| Accuse, to | སྙད་བཙུགས་ (འཛུགས་) པ་ | *nye-tsuk-pa.* |
| Do. *hon.* | སྙད་བཙུགས་ག་ (འཛུགས་པ་) གནང་བ་ | *nye-tsuk-ka nang-wa.* |
| | སྙད་སྐོ་བ་གནང་བ་ | *nye-ko-wa nang-wa.* |
| Accustomed, to be | གོམས་པ་ | *kom-pa.* |
| Do. to become | གོམས་སོང་བ་ | *kom-song-wa.* |
| Ache, *s.* | གཟུག་ | *suk.* |
| Do. *hon.* | སྙུང་གཞི་ | *nyung-ski.* |
| Ache, to | ན་བ་ | *na-wa.* |
| Do. *hon.* | སྙུང་བ་ | *nyung-wa.* |
| Achieve, to | བྱེད་པ་ | *cke-pa.* |
| Do. *hon.* | གནང་བ་ | *nang-wa.* |
| Acid | སྐྱུར་པོ་ | *kyur-po.* |
| Aconite | བཙན་དུག་ | *tsen-ťu.* |
| Acquaintance (friend) | ངོ་ཤེས་པའི་མི་ | *ngo-shem-pe-mi.* |

| | | |
|---|---|---|
| Acquainted, to be | ངོ་ཤེས་པ་ | *ngo-shem-pa.* |
| Do. *hon.* | ཐུགས་ངོ་མཁྱེན་པ་ | *thu-ngo-khyem-pa.* |
| Do. *inf.* to *sup.* | ཞལ་ཚོ་ (ཚོར་) བ་ | *sKe-tsho-wa.* |
| Acquainted, to get | ངོ་ཤེས་བཏང་ (གཏོང་) བ་ | *ngo she tang-wa.* |
| Do. *hon.* | ངོ་ཤེས་གཏོང་ང་ (བ་) གནང་བ་ | *ngo-she tong-nga nang-wa.* |
| Acquire, to | འབྱོར་བ། ཐོབ་པ་ | *jor-wa ; thop-pa.* |
| Do. *hon.* | ཕྱག་འབྱོར་བྱུང་བ་ | *chhan-jor cKung-wa.* |
| Acquirement (skill) | ཡོན་ཏན་ | *yön-ten.* |
| Acquit, to | གློས་པ། བཏང་བ་ | *lö-pa ; tang-wa.* |
| Acquitted, to be (in a case) | བཏང་བཞག་པ་ | *tang-sKak-pa.* |
| Do. *hon.* | བཏང་བཞག་ག་ (པ་) གནང་བ་ | *tang-sKak-ka nang-wa.* |
| Across | ཕར་ | *pha.* |
| Act, to | བྱེད་པ་ | *cKe-pa.* |
| Do. *hon.* | གནང་བ་ | *nang-wa.* |
| Action (law suit) | ཁ་མཆུ་ | *kham-chhu.* |
| Do. (deed) | ལས་ཀ་ | *le-ka.* |
| Do. *hon.* | ཕྱག་ལས་ | *chha-le.* |
| Active | ཧུར་པོ་ | *hur-po.* |
| Actor | ཨ་ཆེ་ལྷ་མོ་ | *a-chhe-hla-mo.* |
| Actress | ཨ་ཆེ་ལྷ་མོ་ | *a-chhe-hla-mo.* |

| | | |
|---|---|---|
| Actual | ངོ་ཐོག་ | *ngo-tho.* |
| Acute (knife) | རྣོ་པོ་ | *no-po.* |
| Adage | གཏམ་དཔེ་ | *tam-pe.* |
| Adams-apple | ཨོག་ལྡོམ་ | *ok-dom.* |
| Add, to | སྣོན་འབེལ་སྤྲད་པ་ | *nöm-be tre-pa.* |
| Do. *hon.* | སྣོན་འབེལ་གནང་བ་ | *nöm-be nang-wa.* |
| Do. (figures) | སྡོམ་པ་ | *dom-pa.* |
| Additional | སྣོན་གས་ | *nön-ke.* |
| Adequate, to be | འགྲིག་པ་ | *drik-pa.* |
| Adhere, to, *v.i.* | འབྱར་བ་ | *jar-wa.* |
| Adieu (to a person departing) | ག་ལེ་ཕེབས་ | *ka-le phe.* |
| Do. (to a person remaining) | ག་ལེ་བཞུགས་ | *ka-le shu.* |
| Adjourn, to | བཞག་པ་ (འཇོག་པ་) | *shak-pa.* |
| Adjourn, to, *hon.* | གཞོག་ག་ (འཇོག་པ་) གནང་བ་ | *shok-ka nang-wa.* |
| Adjust, to | སྒྲིག་པ་ | *drik-pa.* |
| Do. *hon.* | སྒྲིག་ག་ (པ་) གནང་བ་ | *drik-ka nang-wa.* |
| Admiration | མོས་པ་ | *mö-pa.* |
| Admire, to | མོས་པ་བྱེད་པ་ | *mö-pa che-pa.* |

| | | |
|---|---|---|
| Admire, to (things) | སེམས་ཤོར་བ་ | *sem-shor-wa.* |
| Do. *hon.* | ཐུགས་སེམས་ཤོར་བ་ | *thu-sem shor-wa.* |
| Admittance, to grant | མཇལ་ཁ་གནང་བ་ | *je-kha nang-wa.* |
| Admonish, to | བསླབ་བྱ་བྱེད་པ་ | *laṕ-cḱa cḱe-pa.* |
| Do. *hon.* | བསླབ་བྱ་གནང་བ་ | *laṕ-cḱa nang-wa.* |
| Admonition | བསླབ་བྱ་ | *laṕ-cḱa.* |
| Adopted child | གསོས་ཕྲུག་ | *sö-thruḱ.* |
| Adore, to | མོས་གུས་བྱེད་པ་ | *mö-ḱü cḱe-pa.* |
| Adorn, to | རྒྱན་ཆ་བཏགས་ (འདོགས་) པ་ | *gyen-chha taḱ-pa.* |
| Adornment | རྒྱན་ཆ་ | *gyen-chha.* |
| Do. *hon.* | སྐུ་རྒྱན་ | *ku-gyen.* |
| Adrift, to be | ཆུའི་སྒང་ལ་ལྡིང་བ་ | *chhü-gang-la ding-wa.* |
| Adroit | རྩལ་ཆེན་པོ་ | *tse-chhem-po.* |
| Adult | ལོ་དར་མ། གཞོན་པ་ | *lo-t́ar-ma; shöm-pa.* |
| Adulterate, to | འདྲེས་བཏང་ (གཏོང་) བ་ | *dre-tang-wa.* |
| Do. *hon.* | འདྲེས་གཏོང་ང་ (བ་) གནང་བ་ | *dre-tong-nga nang-wa.* |
| Adulterer | ཆལ་པོ་ | *chhe-po.* |
| Adulteress | ཆལ་མོ་ | *chhe-mo.* |
| Advance (of money) | སྔ་ཁྲི་ | *ngam-chhi.* |
| Advantage | ཕན། ཕན་ཐོགས་ | *phen; phen-tho.* |

| | | |
|---|---|---|
| Advantage, *hon.* | ཐུགས་ཕན་ | *thu-phen.* |
| Do. to be of | ཕན་ཐོགས་པ་ | *phen-thoḱ-pa.* |
| Do. *hon.* | ཐུགས་ཕན་གསོ་བ་ | *thu-phen so-wa.* |
| Adversary | དགྲ་ | *dra.* |
| Advice | གྲོས་ | *t́rö.* |
| Advice, to ask | གྲོས་དྲི་ (འདྲི་) བ་ | *t́rö-t́ri-wa.* |
| Do. *hon.* | བཀའ་འདྲི་ཞུ་བ་ | *kan-dri sḱu-wa.* |
| Do. *h. hon.* | བཀའ་སྨོན་ (མོལ) ཞུ་བ་ | *ka-mön sḱu-wa.* |
| Advice, to give | གྲོས་བྱེད་པ་ | *t́rö-cḱe-pa.* |
| Do. *hon.* | བཀའ་གྲོས་གནང་བ་ | *ka-t́rö nang-wa.* |
| Aeroplane | གནམ་གྲུ་ | *nam-t́ru.* |
| Afar, *adv.* | ཐག་རིང་པོ་ | *tha-ring-po.* |
| Affair (business) | ལས་ཀ། དོན་དག་ | *le-ka ; t́ön-t́a.* |
| Do. *hon.* | ཕྱག་ལས། སྐུ་དོན་ | *chha-le ; ku-tön.* |
| Affection | བྱམས་པོ་ | *cḱam-po.* |
| Affectionate, to be | བྱམས་པོ་བྱེད་པ་ | *cḱam-po cḱe-pa.* |
| Do. *hon.* | བྱམས་པོ་གནང་བ་ | *cḱam po nang-wa.* |
| Affirm, to | ལབ་པ་ | *laṕ-pa.* |
| Do. *hon.* | གསུང་བ་ | *sung wa.* |
| Affix, *s.* (grammatical) | རྗེས་འཇུག་ | *jen-ju.* |

| | | |
|---|---|---|
| Affix, to | སྦྲེལ་བ་ | *drel-wa.* |
| Do. *hon.* | སྦྲེལ་ལ་ (བ་) གནང་བ་ | *drel-la nang-wa.* |
| Afflicted, to be | དཀའ་ལས་བྱུང་བ་ | *ꝁa-le cꝁung-wa.* |
| Affliction | དཀའ་ལས་ | *ꝁa-le.* |
| Afford, to | སྟེར་བ་ | *ter-wa.* |
| Do. *hon.* | གནང་བ་ | *nang-wa.* |
| Afloat, to be | ཆུའི་སྒང་ལ་གཡང་ (གཡིང་)བ་ | *chhü-gang-la yang-wa.* |
| Afoot (on foot) | རྐང་ཐང་ལ་ | *kang-thang-la.* |
| Do. *hon.* | ཞབས་ཐང་ལ་ | *sꝁaṕ-thang-la.* |
| Afraid, to be | ཞེད་པ་ | *sꝁe-pa.* |
| Do. *hon.* | ཞེད་པ་གནང་བ་ | *sꝁe-pa nang-wa.* |
| Affray, to commit an | ལག་འཛིང་བྱས་པ་ | *laꝁ-dzing cꝁe-pa.* |
| After | གཞུག་ལ། རྗེས་ལ་ | *sꝁu-la ; je-la.* |
| Afternoon | དགོངས་དག་ | *gong-t́a.* |
| Afterwards | གཞུག་ལ། རྗེས་ལ་ | *sꝁu-la ; je-la.* |
| Again | ཡང་སྐྱར་ | *yang-kyar.* |
| Against, over | ཁ་ཐུག་ལ་ | *kha-thu-la.* |
| Age (of a human being) | ལོ་ | *lo.* |
| Do. *hon.* | དགོང་ལོ་ (དགུང་ལོ་) | *gong-lo.* |
| Age (of an animal) | ན་ | *na.* |

| | | |
|---|---|---|
| Aged, *m.* | རྒ་སྤུ་ (རྒད་པོ་) | *ga-ṕu.* |
| Do. *f.* | རྒ་སྨུ་ (རྒད་མོ་) | *ga-mu.* |
| Do. *hon.* | སྐུ་ནས་བགྲེས་པོ་ | *ku-ne dre-po.* |
| Agent | ལས་ཚབ་ | *le-tshaṕ.* |
| Do. *hon.* | སྐུ་ཚབ་ | *ku-tshaṕ.* |
| Aggravated, to be (angry) | ཚིག་པ་ཟ་བ་ | *tshiḱ-pa śa-wa.* |
| Do. *hon.* | དགོངས་པ་ཚུང་པ་ | *gong-pa tshung-pa.* |
| Agile | ཧུར་པོ་ | *hur po.* |
| Agitate, to (shake) | དཀྲུག་པ་ | *truḱ-pa.* |
| Do. *hon.* | དཀྲུག་ག་ (པ་) གནང་བ་ | *truḱ-ka nang-wa.* |
| Agitated, to be | སེམས་འཚབས་པ་ | *sem tshaṕ-pa.* |
| Do. *hon.* | ཐུགས་སེམས་འཚབས་པ་ གནང་བ་ | *thu-sem tshaṕ-pa nang-wa.* |
| Agony | སྡུག་བསྔལ་ | *du-nge.* |
| Do. *hon.* | ཐུགས་འཁྲལ་ | *thu-thre.* |
| Agree, to | འགྲིག་པ། འཆམ་པ་ | *driḱ-pa ; chham-pa.* |
| Agreeable | མཐུན་པོ་ | *thün-po.* |
| Agreeable (in taste) | ཞིམ་པོ་ | *sḱim-po.* |
| Do. *hon.* | སྤྲོ་པོ་ | *tro-po.* |
| Agreement (bond) | གམ་རྒྱ་ (གན་རྒྱ་) | *ḱam-gya.* |

| | | |
|---|---|---|
| Agriculture | སོ་ནམས་ | *so-nam.* |
| Agriculturist | སོ་ནམས་བྱེད་མཁན་ | *so-nam che-khen.* |
| Ague | ཚད་ནད་ | *tshe-ne.* |
| Ague, to have | འདར་རྒྱབ་པ་ | *dar-gyap-pa* |
| Ahead (in front) | སྔེན་ལ་ ( སྔོན་ལ་ ) | *ngen-la.* |
| Aid | རོགས་ | *ro.* |
| Do. *hon.* | མགོ་འདྲེན་ | *gön-dren.* |
| Aid, to | རོགས་བྱེད་པ་ | *ro-che-pa.* |
| Do. *hon.* | མགོ་འདྲེན་གནང་བ་ | *gön-dren nang-wa.* |
| Ail, to | ན་བ་ | *na-wa.* |
| Do. *hon.* | སྙུང་བ་ | *nyung-wa.* |
| Ailment | ན་ཚ་ | *na-tsha.* |
| Do. *hon.* | སྙུང་བ་ | *nyung-wa.* |
| Air (atmospheric wind) | ལྷགས་པ། རླུང་ | *hlak-pa; lung.* |
| Air (mien) | མདངས། གདོང་ | *dang; dong.* |
| Alarm, to | ཞེད་སྐྲག་སླང་བ་ | *ske-tra lang-wa.* |
| Do. *hon.* | ཞེད་སྐྲག་སློང་ང་ (བ་) གནང་བ་ | *ske-tra long-nga nang-wa.* |
| Alas | ཨ་ཁ་ཁ་ (ཀྱི་མ་) | *a-kha-kha.* |
| Alert | གཅང་པོ་ | *chang-po.* |
| Do. *hon.* | ཐུགས་གཅང་པོ་ | *thu-chang-po.* |

| | | |
|---|---|---|
| Alien | ཕྱོགས་མི་ | *chho-mi.* |
| Alight, to (*e.g.*, from horse) | བབ་པ་ (འབབ་པ་) | *ṕaṕ-pa.* |
| Alight, to be (of fire) | འབར་བ་ | *bar-wa.* |
| Alike | གཅིག་པ་ | *chiḱ-pa.* |
| Alive, to be | གསོན་པོ་ཡོད་པ་ | *söm-po yö-pa.* |
| All | ཚང་མ། ཐམས་ཅད། སྒང་ཁ། རུ་ | *tshang-ma ; tham che ; gang-ḱha ; ru.* |
| All day | ཉིན་གང་ | *nyin-ḱang.* |
| All right (very well) | ལགས་སོ། ལགས་ལགས་སི་ | *la-so ; la-la-si.* |
| Allot, to | བགོད་པ་ | *gö-pa.* |
| Do. *hon.* | བགོད་པ་གནང་བ་ | *gö-pa nang-wa.* |
| Alliance (relation) | བརྒྱུད་ཚ་ | *gyü-tsa.* |
| Do. *hon.* | སྐུ་བརྒྱུད་ | *ku-gyü.* |
| Allied, to be | ཁ་མཐུན་པ་ | *kha-thüm-pa.* |
| Do. *hon.* | ཞལ་མཐུན་གནང་བ་ | *sḱe-thün-nang-wa.* |
| Allotment (share allotted) | སྐེ་ལ་ (སྐལ་བ་) | *ke-la.* |
| Do. *hon.* | སྐུ་སྐལ་ | *ku-ke.* |
| Allow, to | བཅུག་པ་ (འཇུག་པ་) | *chuḱ-pa.* |
| Do. *hon.* | བཅུག་ག་ (འཇུག་པ་) གནང་བ་ | *chuḱ-ḱa nang-wa.* |
| Allowed, to be | ཆོག་པ་ | *chhoḱ-pa.* |

| | | |
|---|---|---|
| Alloy | ལྷད་ | *hle.* |
| Allure, to | སླུ་བ་ | *lu-wa.* |
| All-wise | ཐམས་ཅད་མཁྱེན་པ་ | *tham-che khyem-pa.* |
| Almanack | ཟླ་ཐོ། ལེ་ཐོ་ (ལོ་ཐོ་) | *da-tho ; le-tho.* |
| Do. *hon.* | གཟིགས་ཐོ་ | *śik-tho.* |
| Almighty | སྐུ་དབང་ཆེན་པོ་ | *ku-wang chhem-po.* |
| Almond | རྒྱ་དཀར་སྟར་ཀ་ | *gya-kar tar-ka.* |
| Almost | ཧ་ལམ་ | *ha-lam.* |
| Alms | སྦྱིན་པ་ | *jim-pa.* |
| Alms, to ask | སློང་བ་ | *long-wa.* |
| Alms, to give | སྦྱིན་པ་བཏང་ (གཏོང་) བ་ | *jim-pa tang-wa.* |
| Alone | གཅིག་པོ་ | *chik-po.* |
| Do. *hon.* | སྐུ་རྐྱང་ | *ku kyang.* |
| Along with | དང་མཉམ་དུ་ | *ťang-nyam-ťu.* |
| Aloud | སྐད་ཆེན་པོ་བརྒྱབ་ནས་ | *ke-chhem-po gyap-ne.* |
| Do. *hon.* | གསུང་སྐད་ཆེན་པོ་སྐྱོན་ནས་ | *sung-ke chhem-po kyön-ne.* |
| Alphabet | ཀ་ཁ་ | *ka-kha.* |
| Already | ད་གི་ནས་ | *ťa-ki-ne.* |
| Also | ཡང་ | *yang.* |
| Altar | མཆོད་བཤམས་ | *chhö-sham.* |

| | | |
|---|---|---|
| Alter, to, *v.t.* | རྗེ་བ། སྒྱུར་བ་ | *je-wa ; gyur-wa.* |
| Do. *hon.* | རྗེ་བ་གནང་བ། སྒྱུར་ར་ (བ་) གནང་བ་ | *je-wa nang-wa; gyur-ra nang-wa.* |
| Alter, to (fit of clothes, etc.) | བཟོ་བཅོས་རྒྱབ་པ་ | *śop-chö gyap-pa.* |
| Do. *hon.* | བཟོ་བཅོས་སྐྱོན་པ་ | *śop-chö kyöm-pa.* |
| Alternately | རེ་མེད་ (མོས་) བྱས་ནས་ | *re-me cKe-ne.* |
| Although |཯ང་། རུང་། ན། ཡང་། | *kyang ; rung ; na ; yang.* |
| Altogether (in total) | ཐམས་ཅད་བསྡོམས་ནས་ | *tham-che dom-ne.* |
| Do. (quite) | བད་ | *be.* |
| Alum | སྐྱུར་མོ་ཚ་ | *kyu-mu-tsha.* |
| Always | ནམ་རྒྱུན། དུས་རྒྱུན་ | *nam-gyün ; tü gyün.* |
| Am | ཡོད་ | *yö.* |
| Amass, to | སྡུད་པ་ | *dü-pa.* |
| Do. *hon.* | སྡུད་པ་གནང་བ་ | *dü-pa nang-wa.* |
| Amaze, to | ཡ་མཚན་བྱེད་པ་ | *yam-tshen cKe-pa.* |
| Do. *hon.* | ཡ་མཚན་གནང་བ་ | *yam-tshen nang-wa.* |
| Amazement | ཡ་མཚན་ | *yam-tshen.* |
| Amazing | ཡ་མཚན་པོ་ | *yam-tshem-po.* |
| Ambassador | སྐུ་ཚབ་ | *ku-tshap.* |

| | | |
|---|---|---|
| Amber | སྤོས་ཤེལ་ | *pö-she.* |
| Ambition | མཐོ་འདོད་ | *thon-dö.* |
| Ambitious | མཐོ་འདོད་ཆེན་པོ་ | *thon-dö chhem-po.* |
| Amble (of a horse) | འགྲོས་ | *drö.* |
| Amble, to (horse) | འགྲོས་རྒྱབ་པ་ | *drö-gyap-pa.* |
| Do. *hon.* | ཆིབས་འགྲོས་རྒྱབ་པ་ | *chhim-drö gyap-pa.* |
| Ambling pony | འགྲོས་མ་ | *drö-ma.* |
| Amend, to | བཟོ་སྐྱོར་བྱེད་པ་ | *śo-kyor che-pa.* |
| Do. *hon.* | བཟོ་སྐྱོར་གནང་བ་ | *śo-kyor nang-wa.* |
| Amendment (correction) | ཞུ་དག་ | *shu-ťa.* |
| Amicable | མཐུན་པོ་ | *thüm-po.* |
| Amicable relationship (state of) | མཐུན་ལམ་ | *thün-lam.* |
| Amidst | དཀྱིལ་ལ་ | *kyi-la.* |
| Ammunition | རྫས་རྡེ་ | *dzen-de.* |
| Among | དཀྱིལ་ལ་ | *kyi-la.* |
| Among ourselves (yourselves, themselves) | ནང་ཚག་ | *nang-tsa.* |
| Amount, total | ཁྱོན་བསྡོམས་ | *khyön-dom.* |
| Ample | མང་པོ་ | *mang-po.* |

| | | |
|---|---|---|
| Amusement | རྩེད་མོ་ | *tse-mo.* |
| Do. *hon.* | སྐུ་རྩེད་ | *ku-tse.* |
| Amusement, to have | ཐུགས་སྤྲོ་བཏང་ (གཏོང་) བ་ | *thu-tro tang-wa.* |
| Do. *hon.* | ཐུགས་སྤྲོ་གཏོང་ང་(བ་)གནང་བ་ | *thu-tro tong-nga nang-wa.* |
| Analogy | དཔེ་ | *pe.* |
| Ancestry | རིགས་བརྒྱུད། མི་བརྒྱུད་ | *ri-gyü ; mi-gyü.* |
| Do. *hon.* | སྐུ་བརྒྱུད་ | *ku-gyü.* |
| Ancestry of Lama | གདུང་བརྒྱུད་ | *dung-gyü.* |
| Anchor | གཏིང་རྡོ་ | *ting-do.* |
| Ancient (of former time) | སྔོན་གྱི་ | *ngön-ḱyi.* |
| Do. (old) | སྙིང་པ་ | *nying-pa.* |
| Anciently | སྔོན་ལ། སྔོན་དུས་ | *ngön-la ; ngön-ťü.* |
| And | ཡང་། དང་ | *yang ; ťang.* |
| Anecdote | སྒྲུམ་ (སྒྲུངས་) | *drum.* |
| Anecdote, to relate | སྒྲུམ་ (སྒྲུངས་) བཤད་པ་ | *drum she-pa.* |
| Do. *hon.* | སྒྲུམ་ (སྒྲུངས་) གསུང་བ་ | *drum sung-wa.* |
| Angel | ཕོ་ཉ་ | *pho-nya.* |
| Anger | ཚིག་པ། ཁོང་ཁྲོ་ | *tshik-pa ; khong-thro.* |
| Angle (corner) | ཟུར་ | *śur.* |
| Angry, to be | ཚིག་པ་ཟ་བ། ཁོང་ཁྲོ་ཟ་བ་ | *tshik-pa śa-wa ; khong-thro śa-wa.* |

| | | |
|---|---|---|
| Angry, to be *hon* | དགོངས་པ་ཚུང་པ་ ནམ་མཁྱེན་འགལ་བ་ | *gong-pa tshung-pa ; nam-khyen gel-wa.* |
| Angry and suspicious, to be | བལྟ་ཕྱོགས་བྱེད་པ་ | *ta-chhok cKe-pa.* |
| Do. *hon.* | གཟིགས་ཕྱོགས་གནང་བ་ | *śi-chhok nang-wa.* |
| Angular | ཟུར་མང་པོ་ཡོད་པ་ | *śur-mang-po yö-pa.* |
| Animal | སེམས་ཅན་ | *sem-chen.* |
| Animal (wild) | རི་དྭགས་ | *ri-ťa.* |
| Animal (beast of prey) | གཅན་གཟན་ | *chen-śen.* |
| Ankle | རྐང་པའི་ཚིགས་ཏོག་ | *kang-pe tshik-do* |
| Do. *hon.* | ཞབས་ཀྱི་ཚིགས་ཏོག་ | *sKap-kyi tshik-do.* |
| Annals | ལོ་རྒྱུས་ | *lo-gyü.* |
| Annals (of kings) | རྒྱལ་རབས་ | *gye-rap.* |
| Annihilate, to | ཐམས་ཅད་མེད་པར་བཟོ་བ་ | *tham che me-pa śo-wa.* |
| Announce, to | ལན་ (ལོན་) སྤྲོད་པ། ལན་ (ལོན་) སྐྱེལ་བ་ | *len tre-pa ; len-kyel-wa.* |
| Do. *inf.* to *sup.* | ལྗགས་ལན་ཕུལ་ (འབུལ་) བ་ | *ja-len phü-wa.* |
| Annoy, to | ཁོང་ཁྲོ་སློང་བ | *khong-thro lang-wa.* |
| Do. *hon.* | དགོངས་པ་དཀྲུག་པ་ | *gong-pa truk-pa.* |
| Annoyed, to be | འཚེར་བ་ | *tsher-wa.* |
| Do. *hon.* | ཐུགས་འཚེར་གནང་བ་ | *thu-tsher nang-wa.* |

| | | |
|---|---|---|
| Annually | ལོ་རེ་རེ་ | *lo-re-re.* |
| Anoint, to | བྱུགས་པ་ (འབྱུག་པ།) སྐུ་བ་ | *cḱuk-pa ; ku-wa.* |
| Do. *hon.* | བྱུགས་ཀ་ (འབྱུག་པ་) གནང་བ། བསྐུས་པ་ (སྐུ་བ་) གནང་བ་ | *cḱuk-ka nang-wa ; kü-pa nang-wa.* |
| Another | གཞན་པ། ཡན་པ་ | *sḱem-pa ; yem-pa.* |
| Answer, *s.* | ལན་ | *len.* |
| Do. *hon.* | བཀའ་ལན་ | *ka-len.* |
| Answer, to | ལན་རྒྱབ་པ་ | *len-gyaṕ-pa.* |
| Do. *hon.* | ཞླགས་ལན་སྐྱོན་པ་ | *ja-len kyöm-pa.* |
| Answer, to (in anger) | ཁ་ལན་ལོག་པ་ | *kha-len loḱ-pa.* |
| Answer letter, to | ཡིག་ལན་ལོག་པ། ཡིག་ལན་བཏང་ (གཏོང་) བ་ | *yiḱ-len loḱ-pa; yiḱ-len tang-wa.* |
| Do. *hon.* | ཕྱག་བྲིས་བཀའ་ལན་གནང་བ་ | *chha-ri ka-len nang-wa.* |
| Ant | གྲོག་མ་ | *ťro-ma.* |
| Antagonist | དགྲ་ | *dra.* |
| Antelope | གཙོད་ | *tsö.* |
| Antique | རྙིང་པ་ | *nying-pa.* |
| Anus | ཀུབ་ | *kuṕ.* |
| Do. *hon.* | ཞབས་ཕོངས་ | *sḱam-phong.* |
| Anvil | འོག་ཙ་ | *ok-tsa.* |

| | | |
|---|---|---|
| Anxiety | སེམས་འཁྲལ་ | *sem-thre.* |
| Do. *hon.* | ཐུགས་འཁྲལ་ | *thu-thre.* |
| Anxious, to be | སེམས་འཁྲལ་བྱེད་པ་ | *sem-thre cḱe-pa.* |
| Do. *hon.* | ཐུགས་འཁྲལ་གནང་བ་ | *thuk-thre nang-wa.* |
| Any | གང་ཡང་ | *ḱang-yang.* |
| Anybody (with negative) | སུ་གང་། སུ་ཡང་ | *su-ḱang; su-yang.* |
| Anyhow (in any case) | ག་རེ་ཡིན་ན་ཡང་ | *ḱa-re yin-ne yang.* |
| Apartment | ཁང་མིག | *ḱhang-mik.* |
| Do. *hon.* | གཟིམས་ཆུང་ | *śim-chung.* |
| Ape | སྤྲེའུ་ (སྤྲེའུ་) | *pe-u.* |
| Aperture | སྒི་ཁུང་ | *gi-khung.* |
| Apologize, to | ཐུགས་དགོངས་དག་ཞུ་བ་ | *thu-gong-ṫa sḱu-wa.* |
| Apology | ཐུགས་དགོངས་དག | *thu-gong-ṫa.* |
| Apoplexy | གཟའ་རྒྱབ་པ་ | *śa gyaṗ-pa.* |
| Apothecary's shop | སྨན་ཁང་ | *men-khang.* |
| Apparatus | ལག་ཆ་ | *laḱ-chha.* |
| Apparel | ཆུ་པ་ | *chhu-pa.* |
| Apparel, *hon.* | ན་བཟའ་ | *nam-śa.* |
| Appeal, to | ཞུ་བ་ | *sḱu-wa.* |
| Appear to be, to | ཡིན་འགྲོ་ | *yin-dro.* |

| | | |
|---|---|---|
| Appear, to (to be seen) | མཐོང་བ་ | *thong-wa.* |
| Appear, to cause to (ghost, etc.) | སྤྱན་འདྲེན་ཞུ་བ་ | *chen-dren sḱu wa.* |
| Appearance | དབྱིབས། བཟོ་ལྟ་ | *yiṕ ; sóp-ta.* |
| Appetite | དང་ག་ | *ťang-ka.* |
| Do. *hon.* | གསོལ་དང་ | *sö-ťang.* |
| Applaud, to | སྟོད་ར་བཏང་ (གཏོང་) བ་ | *tö-ra tang-wa.* |
| Do. *hon.* | སྟོད་ར་གཏོང་ང་ (བ་) གནང་བ་ | *tö-ra tong-nga nang-wa.* |
| Do. *inf.* to *sup.* | སྟོད་ར་ཞུ་བ་ | *tö-ra sḱu-wa.* |
| Applause | སྟོད་ར་ | *tö-ra.* |
| Apple | ཀུ་ཤུ་ | *ku-shu.* |
| Application (inferior to superior) | སྙན་ཞུ་ | *nye-sḱu.* |
| Application, written (by inferior to superior) | ཞུ་ཡིག་ | *sḱu-yi.* |
| Apply, to (by inferior to superior) | སྙན་ཞུ་ཕུལ་ (འབུལ་) བ་ | *nye-sḱu-phü-wa.* |
| Apply in writing, to (by inferior to superior) | ཞུ་ཡིག་ཕུལ་བ་ | *sḱu-yi phü-wa.* |
| Appoint, to (an officer) | སྐོ་བ་ | *ko-wa.* |
| Do. *hon.* | བསྐོས་བཞག་གནང་བ་ | *kö-sḱa nang-wa.* |
| Appoint, to (a menial servant) | བཞག་པ་ (འཇོག་པ་) | *sḱak-pa.* |

| | | |
|---|---|---|
| Appoint, to (a menial servant) *hon.* | གཞོག་ག་ (འཛོག་པ་) གནང་བ་ | *sḱok-ka nang-wa.* |
| Approach, to (an object) | འགྲམ་ལ་འགྲོ་བ། འགྲམ་ལ་ཡོང་བ་ | *dram-la dro-wa ; drum-la yong-wa.* |
| Do. *hon.* | འགྲམ་ལ་ཕེབ་པ་ | *dram-la phe-pa.* |
| Approve, to (sanction) | བཀའ་གནང་བ་ | *ka-nang-wa.* |
| Appurtenance | ཙ་ལག་ (ཚ་ལག་) | *cha-la.* |
| Do. *hon.* | སྐུ་ཙས་ (སྐུ་ཚས་) | *ku-che.* |
| Apricot | ཁམ་བུ་ | *kham-ṕu.* |
| Do. (a quick-growing, with good fruit) | ལོ་གསུམ་ཁམ་བུ་ | *lo-sum kham-ṕu.* |
| Do. (dried, from Balti) | མངའ་རིས་ཁམ་བུ་ | *nga-ri kham-ṕu.* |
| Apron | པང་གདན་ | *pang-den.* |
| Do. *hon.* | སྐུ་པང་ | *ku-pang.* |
| Aqueduct | ཡོ་པོ་ (ཡུར་པོ་) | *yo-po.* |
| Arbitrate, to | བར་མི་བྱེད་པ་ | *ṕar-mi cḱe-pa.* |
| Do. *hon.* | བར་མི་གནང་བ་ | *ṕar-mi nang-wa.* |
| Archer | མདའ་པ་ | *da-pa.* |
| Do. *hon.* | ཕྱག་མདའ་གནང་མཁན་ | *chhan-da nang-khen.* |
| Arduous | དཀའ་ལས་ཁག་པོ་ | *ka-le khaḱ-po.* |
| Do. *hon.* | སྐུ་མཉེལ་པོ་ | *ku-nye-po.* |

| | | |
|---|---|---|
| Are | ཡོད། འདུག། རེད་ | *yö ; du ; re.* |
| Area | རྒྱ་ | *gya.* |
| Argue, to | རྩེ་རྒྱབ་པ་ | *tse-gyap̓-pa.* |
| Do. *hon.* | ཞལ་རྩེ་སྐྱོན་པ་ | *sk̄e-tse kyöm-pa.* |
| Argument | རྩོད་པ་ | *tsö-pa.* |
| Arid | སྐམ་པོ་ | *kam po.* |
| Arise, to | ལང་བ་ | *lang-wa.* |
| Do. *hon.* | བཞང་བ་ (བཞེང་བ་) | *sk̄ang-wa.* |
| Do. *h. hon.* | སྐུ་བཞང་ (བཞེང་) གནང་བ་ | *ku-sk̄ang nang-wa.* |
| Arithmetic | རྩིས་ | *tsi.* |
| Do. *hon.* | ལྗགས་རྩིས་ | *ja-tsi.* |
| Arm | ལག་པ་ | *lak̄-pa.* |
| Do. *hon.* | ཕྱག་ | *chha.* |
| Arm, upper | ལག་པའི་ཉ་ | *lak̄-pe-nya.* |
| Do. *hon.* | ཕྱག་གི་ཉ་ | *chha-k̄i-nya.* |
| Armful | པང་ག་ (པ་) གང་ | *pang-k̄a-k̄ang.* |
| Armlet | སྒྲོག་གདུང་ | *dro-dung.* |
| Do. *hon.* | ཕྱག་གདུང་ | *chha-dung.* |
| Armour | ཁྲབ་ | *thrap̓.* |
| Arm-pit | མཆན་ཁུང་ | *chhen-khung.* |

| | | |
|---|---|---|
| Arms (weapon) | མཚོན་ཆ་ | *tshön-chha.* |
| Army | དམག་དཔུང་ | *mak̇-pung.* |
| Do. (first militia, consisting of Tibetan laymen) | འདོན་དམག་ | *dön-ma.* |
| Do. (second militia consisting of Tibetan monks) | སེར་དམག་ | *ser-ma.* |
| Do. (last militia, consisting of all males between 18 and 60) | བཅོ་བརྒྱད་དྲུག་ཅུ་ | *choṗ-gye truk̇-chu.* |
| Around | འཁོར་ལ་ | *khor-la.* |
| Arouse, to (from sleep) | གཉིད་སད་པ་ | *nyi-se-pa.* |
| Do. *hon.* | གཉིད་སད་པ་གནང་བ་ | *nyi-se-pa nang-wa.* |
| Arrange, to | སྒྲིག་པ་ | *drik̇-pa.* |
| Do. *hon.* | སྒྲིག་ག་ (པ་) གནང་བ་ | *drik̇-ka nang-wa.* |
| Arrest, to | ཟིན་པ་ | *ṡim-pa.* |
| Do. *hon.* | ཟིན་པ་གནང་བ་ | *ṡim-pa nang-wa.* |
| Arrive, to | སླེབ་པ་ | *leṗ-pa.* |
| Do. *hon.* | ཕེབ་པ་ | *phe-pa.* |
| Do. *h. hon.* | འཆིབ་རྒྱུ་གནང་བ་ | *chhiṗ-gyu nang-wa.* |
| Arrogant | ཉམས་ཆེན་པོ། ཛ་ཁོག་ཆེན་པོ་ | *nyam-chhem-po; dza-kho chhem-po.* |

| | | |
|---|---|---|
| Arrow | མདའ་ | *da.* |
| Do. *hon.* | ཕྱག་མདའ་ | *chhan-da.* |
| Art, *s.* | ཡོན་ཏན་ | *yön-ten.* |
| Artery | རྩ་ | *tsa.* |
| Artful | གཙང་པོ་ | *chang-po.* |
| Do. *hon.* | ཐུགས་གཙང་པོ་ | *thu-chang-po.* |
| Article | སྤྱད་ལག ། དངོས་རིགས་ | *cha-la ; ngö ri.* |
| Artist (painter) | ལྷ་རི་ (འབྲི་) པ་ | *hla-ri-pa.* |
| As (like) | ནང་བཞིན། འདྲ་པོ་ | *nang-sḱin ; dra-po.* |
| As far as | བར་དུ ། ཐུག་ | *ṕar-ťu ; thu.* |
| Ascend, to | འཛེག་པ་ (འཛེགས་པ་) | *dzaḱ-pa.* |
| Do. *hon.* | འཛེག་ག་ (འཛེགས་པ་) གནང་བ་ | *dzaḱ-ka nang-wa.* |
| Ascent (uphill) | གྱེན་ | *ḱyen.* |
| Ascertain, to | ཧ་གོ་བ་བྱེད་པ་ | *ha-ḱo-wa cḱe-pa.* |
| Do. *hon.* | མཁྱེན་པ་གནང་བ་ | *khyem-pa nang-wa.* |
| Ascetic | སྒོམ་ཆེན་ | *gom-chhen.* |
| Ashamed | ངོ་ཚ་པོ་ | *ngo-tsha-po.* |
| Ashamed, to feel | ངོ་ཚ་བ་ | *ngo-tsha-wa.* |
| Do. *hon.* | ཐུགས་ངོ་ཚ་བ་ | *thu-ngo-ťsha-wa.* |
| Ashes | གོག་ཐལ་ | *ḱo-the.* |

| | | |
|---|---|---|
| Aside | ཟུར་དུ་ | *śur-ťu.* |
| Ask, to | དྲི་བ་ (འདྲི་བ་) | *ťri-wa.* |
| Ask, to (inferior asking superior) | ཞུ་བ་ | *sḱu-wa.* |
| Asleep, to fall | གཉིད་ཁུག་པ་ | *nyi-ḱhuḱ-pa.* |
| Do. *hon.* | མཉན་ (མནལ་) གཟིམ་པ་ | *nye-śim-pa.* |
| Ass | བུང་གུ་ (བོང་བུ་) | *ṕung-ḱu.* |
| Do. (wild) | རྐྱང་ | *kyang.* |
| Assail, to | རུབ་རྒྱབ་པ་ | *ruṕ-gyaṕ-pa.* |
| Assassin | མི་གསོད་མཁན་ | *mi-sö-khen.* |
| Assassinate, to | བསད་པ་ (གསོད་པ་) | *se-pa.* |
| Assault, to | རྡུང་བ་ | *dung-wa.* |
| Do. *hon.* | ཕྱག་འཇུག་ (འཇུས་) གནང་བ་ | *chhan-juḱ nang-wa.* |
| Assemble, to | འཚོགས་པ་ | *tshoḱ-pa.* |
| Do. *hon.* | ཚོགས་འདུ་འཚོགས་ག་ (པ་) གནང་བ་ | *tshon-du-tshoḱ-ḱa nang-wa.* |
| Assembly-hall | ཚོམས་ཆེན་ | *tshom-chhen.* |
| Do. for monks | འདུ་ཁང་ | *du-khang.* |
| Assiduous | བརྩོན་འགྲུས་ཆེན་པོ་ | *tsön-drü chhem-po.* |
| Do. to be | སྙིང་རུས་བྱེད་པ་ | *nying-rü cḱe-pa.* |

| | | |
|---|---|---|
| Assiduous, to be *hon.* | ཐུགས་རུས་གནང་བ་ | *thu-rü nang-wa.* |
| Assist, to | རོགས་བྱེད་པ་ | *ro-cke-pa.* |
| Do. *hon.* | མགོན་འདྲེན་གནང་བ་ | *gön-dren nang-wa.* |
| Assistance | རོགས་ | *ro.* |
| Do. *hon.* | མགོན་འདྲེན་ | *gön-dren.* |
| Assistant | རོགས་བྱེད་མཁན་ | *ro-cke-khen.* |
| Do. *hon.* | མགོན་འདྲེན་གནང་མཁན་ | *gön-dren nang-khen.* |
| Associate | དགའ་པོ་ཉེ་པོ་ | *ga-po nye-po.* |
| Do. *hon.* | ཐུགས་ཉེ་ཆག་པོ་ | *thuk-nye chhak-po.* |
| Associate with, to | དགའ་པོ་ཉེ་པོ་ཡོད་པ་ | *ga-po nye-po yö-pa.* |
| Aster | ཁ་སྐལ་བཟང་མེ་ཏོག | *ke-śang me-to.* |
| Astonish, to | ཡ་མཚན་བྱེད་པ་ | *yam-tshen cke-pa.* |
| Do. *hon.* | ཡ་མཚན་གནང་བ་ | *yam-tshen nang-wa.* |
| Astonished | ཡ་མཚན་པ་ | *yam-tshem-pa.* |
| Astonishing | ཡ་མཚན་པོ་ | *yam-tshem po.* |
| Astonishment | ཡ་མཚན་ | *yam-tshen.* |
| Astride, to put | སྐྱོར་པ་ | *kyöm-pa.* |
| Astrologer | རྩིས་པ་ | *tsi-pa.* |
| Astrology | སྐར་རྩིས་ | *kar-tsi.* |
| Astronomer | རྩིས་པ་ | *tsi-pa.* |

| | | |
|---|---|---|
| Astronomy | སྐར་རྩིས་ | *kar-tsi.* |
| Asunder | སོ་སོ་ | *so-so.* |
| At | ལ་ | *la.* |
| At all (negatively) | རྩ་ནས་ | *tsa-ne.* |
| Athletic | རྩལ་ཆེན་པོ་ | *tse-chhem-po.* |
| Atlas | ས་ཁྲ་ | *sap̓-thra.* |
| At once | ལམ་སང་ | *lam-sang.* |
| Attach, to | རྒྱབ་པ་ | *gyap̓-pa.* |
| Do. *hon.* | སྐྱོན་པ་ | *k̓yöm-pa.* |
| Attach, to (by sticking together) | སྦྱར་བ་ | *jar-wa.* |
| Do. *hon.* | སྦྱར་ར་ (བ་) གནང་བ་ | *j̣ar-ra nang-wa.* |
| Attached, to be (long for) | དྲན་པ་ | *t́rem-pa.* |
| Do. *hon.* | དྲན་པ་གནང་བ་ | *t́rem-pa nang-wa.* |
| Attached, to be (love) | སེམས་ཆགས་པ་ | *sem chhak̓-pa.* |
| Do. *hon.* | ཐུགས་སེམས་ཆགས་པ་ | *thu-sem chhak̓-pa.* |
| Attack, to | རུབ་རྒྱབ་པ་ | *rup̓-gyap̓-pa.* |
| Attain, to | འབྱོར་བ། ཐོབ་པ་ | *jor-wa ; thop̓-pa.* |
| Do. *hon.* | འབྱོར་ར་ (བ་) གནང་བ། ཕྱག་སོན་བྱུང་བ་ | *jor-ra nang-wa ; chhak̓-sön chk̓ung-wa.* |

| | | |
|---|---|---|
| Attempt | བརྩོན་འགྲུས་ | *tsön-drü.* |
| Attempt, to | བརྩོན་འགྲུས་བྱེད་པ་ | *tsön-drü cKe pa.* |
| Do. *hon.* | བརྩོན་འགྲུས་གནང་བ་ | *tsön-drü nang-wa.* |
| Attend, to (servant on master) | ཞབས་ཕྱི་ཞུ་བ་ | *sKap-chhi sKu-wa.* |
| Attend, to (before a superior) | སྐུ་མདུན་ལ་བཙར་བ་ | *kun-dün-la char-wa.* |
| | སྐུ་བཙར་ཞུ་བ་ | *ku-char sKu-wa.* |
| Attend, to (before Lama) | སྐུ་མདུན་ལ་མཇལ་བ་ | *kun-dün-la je-wa.* |
| Attend, to (heed) | ཉན་པ། ཨམ་ཅོག་ཉན་པ་ | *nyem-pa ; am-cho nyem-pa.* |
| Do. *hon.* | གསན་པ། སྙན་ལ་གསན་པ་ | *sem pa ; nyen-la-sem-pa.* |
| Attendant | གཡོག་པོ་ | *yok-po.* |
| Do. *hon.* | ཞབས་ཕྱི་ | *sKap-chhi.* |
| Attendant, female | གཡོག་མོ་ | *yo mo.* |
| Do. *hon.* | ཞལ་ཏ་མ་ | *sKe-ta-ma.* |
| Attentive, to be | ཧུར་ཐག་བྱེད་པ་ | *hur-tha cKe-pa.* |
| Do. *hon.* | ཧུར་ཐག་གནང་བ་ | *hur-tha nang-wa.* |
| Aunt (paternal) | ཨ་ནི་ (ཨ་ནེ་) | *a ni.* |
| Do. (maternal) | སྲུ་མོ་ | *su-mo.* |
| Auspices (omens) | རྟེན་འབྲེལ་ | *tem-dre.* |
| Authentic | དངོས་ནས། ངོ་ཐོག་ | *ngö-ne ; ngo-tho* |
| Author | རྩོམ་མཁན་ | *tsom-khen.* |

| | | |
|---|---|---|
| Author, *hon.* | རྩོམ་པ་གནང་མཁན་ | *tsom-pa nang-khen.* |
| Authority | དབང་ | *wang.* |
| Authorize | དབང་སྤྲད་པ་ | *wang-tre-pa.* |
| Do. *hon.* | དབང་གནང་བ་ | *wang-nang-wa.* |
| Autumn | སྟོན་ཀ་ | *tön-ka.* |
| Auxiliary troops | རྒྱབ་སྣོན་ | *gyam-nön.* |
| Avalanche | གངས་རུད་ | *kang-rü.* |
| Avarice | ཧམ་པ་ | *ham-pa.* |
| Avaricious | ཧམ་པ་ཆེན་པོ་ | *ham-pa chhem-po.* |
| Avenge, to | དགྲ་ལན་ལོག་པ་ | *dra-len lok-pa.* |
| Do. *hon.* | དགྲ་ལན་ལོག་ག་(པ་) གནང་བ་ | *dra-len lok-ka nang-wa.* |
| Avoid, to (a person) | དགྱོལ་བ། ཟུར་ནས་འགྲོ་བ་ | *yö-wa ; śur-ne dro-wa.* |
| Do. *hon.* | གཟུར་ནས་ཕེབ་པ་ | *śur-ne phe-pa.* |
| Awake, to | གཉིད་སད་པ་ | *nyi-se-pa.* |
| Do. *hon.* | མཉན་ (མནལ་) སད་པ་ | *nyen-se-pa.* |
| Await, to | སྒུག་པ་ | *guk-pa.* |
| Do. *hon.* | སྒུག་པ་གནང་བ་ | *guk-pa nang-wa.* |
| Away | ཕར་ | *pha.* |
| Awkward | སྡུག་རུས་ | *duk-rü.* |
| Axe | སྟ་རི་ (སྟ་རེ་) | *ta-ri.* |

| | | |
|---|---|---|
| Ay (yes) | ལགས་སོ། ལགས་ལགས་སི། ལ་ཨོང་ | *la-so ; la-la-si ; la-ong.* |
| Azure | སྔོན་པོ་ | *ngöm-po.* |

# B

| | | |
|---|---|---|
| Baby (of few months) | མ་འབྱར་ | *man-ja.* |
| Baby (older) | ཕྲུ་གུ་ཆུང་ཆུང་ | *pu-gu chhung-chhung.* |
| Do. *hon.* | ཨ་བྲུ་ | *a-wa.* |
| Bachelor | ཕོ་ཧྲང་ང་ | *pho-hrang-nga.* |
| Back (of body) | རྒྱབ་ | *gyap̒.* |
| Do. *hon.* | སྐུ་རྒྱབ་ | *ku-gyap̒.* |
| Back (behind in place) | རྒྱབ་ལ་ | *gyap̒-la.* |
| Backbite | ཁ་བཏང་ (གཏོང་) བ་ | *kha-tang-wa.* |
| Do. *hon.* | ཞལ་གཏོང་ང་ (བ) གནང་བ་ | *sk̒e-tong-nga nang-wa.* |
| Backbone | སྒལ་ཚིགས་ | *ge-tshi.* |
| Do. *hon.* | སྐུ་སྟོད་ཚིགས་ | *ku-tö tshi.* |
| Backside | རྐུབ་ | *kup̒.* |
| Do. *hon.* | ཞབས་ཕོངས་ | *sk̒am-phong.* |
| Backwards | རྒྱབ་ལོགས་ལ་ | *gyap̒-lo-la.* |
| Bad (wicked) | ངན་པ། སྐྱུག་བྲོ་པོ་ | *ngem-pa ; kyuk̒ t̒ro-po.* |
| Do. (decomposed, *e.g.*, of meat) | རུལ་པ་ | *rü-pa.* |
| Do. (of things offensive in smell, &c.) | སྐྱུག་བྲོ་པོ། སྡུག་རུལ་ | *kyuk̒-t̒ro-po ; duk̒-rü.* |

| | | |
|---|---|---|
| Bad, to be (of things generally) | ཡག་པོ་མེད་པ་ | *yak-po me-pa.* |
| Bag (large) | སྒྲེ་མོ་ | *gye-mo.* |
| Do. (small) | ཕད་ཀོག་ | *phe-ḱo.* |
| Do. (made of leather) | ཀྱལ་པ་ | *kye-pa.* |
| Badge | རྟགས་ | *ta.* |
| Baggage | རྡོས་པོ་ | *ťö-po.* |
| Bail | ཁས་ཁྱགས་ | *khe-khya.* |
| Do. *hon.* | ཞལ་ཁྱགས་ | *sḱe-khya* |
| Bail, to | ཁས་ཁྱགས་བྱེད་པ་ | *khe-khya cḱe-pa.* |
| Do. *hon.* | ཞལ་ཁྱགས་གནང་བ་ | *sḱe-khya nang-wa.* |
| Bake, to | བག་ལེབ་སྲེག་པ་ | *ṕa-le traḱ-pa.* |
| Bakshish | གསོལ་རས་ | *sö-re.* |
| Balance (what is wanting) | ལྷག་མ་ | *hla-ma.* |
| Do. (for small weights) | རྒྱ་འཐུར་ | *gya-thu.* |
| Do. (for larger weights) | ཉ་ག་ | *nya-ḱa.* |
| Do. (for very large weights) | རྒྱ་མ་ | *gya-ma.* |
| Balanced evenly, to be | ཡང་ལྗི་མེད་པ་ | *yang ji me-pa.* |
| Bald | ཟངས་ཁོགས་ | *śang-kho.* |
| Do. *hon.* | དབུ་རིལ་ | *u-ri.* |

| | | |
|---|---|---|
| Bale | དོས་པོ་ | *tö-po.* |
| Do. (of wool) | བལ་དོས་ | *ṕe-ťö.* |
| Ball | རྡིའུ་ (རྡེའུ་) | *di-u.* |
| Ball-cartridge | མདེ་རིལ་ | *diḱ-ri.* |
| Ball (of gun) | རྡིག་རིལ་ | *diḱ-ri.* |
| Balloon | རླུང་གྲུ་ | *lung-ťru.* |
| Bamboo | སྨྱུག་མ་ | *nyung-ma.* |
| Banana | སྐྱེ་སྡོང་ *Sik.* | *kye-dong.* |
| Band (gang of men) | ཚོགས་ | *tsho.* |
| Band (hoop) | ཤེན་ | *shen.* |
| Do. (of iron) | ལྕགས་ཤེན་ | *cha-shen.* |
| Do. (of silver) | དངུལ་ཤེན་ | *ngü-shen.* |
| Do. (of brass) | རག་ཤེན་ | *ra-shen.* |
| Do. (of gold) | གསེར་ཤེན་ | *se-shen.* |
| Bandit | ཇག་པ་ | *cḱak-pa.* |
| Bandy-legged | ཀང་ཀྱོག་ | *kang-kyo.* |
| Do. *hon.* | ཞབས་ཀྱོག་ | *sḱaṕ-kyo.* |
| Banish, to | རྒྱང་ཕུད་ (འཕུད་) བཏང་ (གཏོང་) བ་ | *gyam-phü tang-wa.* |

| | | |
|---|---|---|
| Banish, to, *hon.* | རྒྱང་ཕུད་ (འབུད་) གཏོང་ང་ (བ་) གནང་བ་ | *gyam-phü tong-nga nang-wa.* |
| Bank (of river, &c.) | འགྲམ་ | *dram.* |
| Banker | བུན་བདག་ | *ṕün-da.* |
| Banner | དར་འཕྱར་ | *ťar-chhar.* |
| Do. (of victory) | རྒྱལ་མཚན་ | *gyen-tshen.* |
| Banquet | མགྲོན་པོ་ (མགྲོན་) | *dröm-po.* |
| Do. *hon.* | ཐུགས་སྐྲོ་ | *thuḱ-tro.* |
| Do. to give a | མགྲོན་པོ་ (མགྲོན་) བཏང་ (གཏོང་) བ་ | *dröm-po tang-wa.* |
| Do. *hon.* | ཐུགས་སྐྲོ་གཏོང་ང་(བ་)གནང་བ་ | *thuḱ-tro tong-nga nang-wa.* |
| Baptism | ཁྲུས་གསོལ་ | *thrü-sö.* |
| Baptize, to | ཁྲུས་གསོལ་གནང་བ་ | *thrü-sö nang-wa.* |
| Bar | དུམ་བུ་ | *ťum-ṕu.* |
| Barbarian | མཐའ་འཁོབ་པ་ | *tha-khoṕ-pa.* |
| Barber | སྐྲ་བཞར་ར་ (བ་) | *tra-sḱar-ra.* |
| Do. *hon.* | དབུ་སྐྲ་བཞར་མཁན་ | *u-tra sḱar-ḱhen.* |
| Bare (naked) | དམར་ཧྲང་ང་ | *ma-hrang-nga.* |
| Barefooted | ཀང་རྗེན་མ་ | *kang-je-ma.* |
| Do. *hon.* | ཞབས་རྗེན་མ་ | *shaṕ-je-ma.* |

| | | |
|---|---|---|
| Bargain, *s.* | ཚོང་ | *tshong.* |
| Do. to | ཚོང་རྒྱབ་པ་ | *tshong gyaṕ-pa* |
| Do. *hon.* | རྒྱ་ཚོང་གནང་བ་ | *gya-tshong nang-wa.* |
| Bark | པགས་པ་ | *paḱ-pa.* |
| Bark, to (of dogs) | ཆང་བ་ | *chhang-wa.* |
| Barley | ནས་ | *ne.* |
| Do. *hon.* | ཕྱག་འབྲུ་ | *chhan-dru.* |
| Barley-flour | རྩམ་པ་ | *tsam-pa.* |
| Do. *hon.* | གསོལ་ཞིབ་ | *sö-sḱiṕ.* |
| Barn | འབྲུ་ཁང་ | *dru-khang.* |
| Barrel (of gun) | ལྕགས་ཧྲང་ | *cha-hrang.* |
| Barren (of women) | རབས་ཆད་ | *raṕ-chhe.* |
| Do. (of cow) | བཞོས་སྐམ་ | *sḱö-kam.* |
| Barrier (fence) | ར་བ་ | *ra-wa.* |
| Barter | རྗེ་བ་ | *je-wa.* |
| Bashful, to be | ངོ་ཚ་བ་ | *ngo-tsha-wa.* |
| Do. *hon.* | ཞལ་རས་ཚ་བ་ | *sḱe-re tsha-wa.* |
| Basin (for washing hands) | ཏུང་བན་ | *t́ung-ṕen.* |
| Do. (wooden) | གཞོང་པ་ | *sḱong-pa.* |
| Do. (round copper basin) | ཀ་ཏོ་ར་ | *ka-to-ra.* |

| | | |
|---|---|---|
| Basket | སླེ་ཀོག། སླེ་པོ་ | *le-ko; le-po.* |
| Bat | སྒམ་པོ་ (སྒ་ཕོང་) | *gam-po.* |
| Bath | ཆུ་གཞོང་ | *chhu-sKong.* |
| Do. *hon.* | ཆབ་གཞོང་ | *chhaṕ-sKong.* |
| Bathe, to | འཁྲུད་པ་ | *thrü-pa.* |
| Do. *hon.* | འཁྲུད་པ་གནང་བ་ | *thrü-pa nang-wa.* |
| Battle | དམག་ | *ma.* |
| Bay-coloured (horse) | སྐྱང་པོ་ | *kyang-po.* |
| Do. (light) | སྐྱང་དཀར་ | *kyang-ka.* |
| Do. (dark) | སྐྱང་ནག་ | *kyang-na.* |
| Bazaar | ཁྲོམ་ | *throm.* |
| Be, to | རེད་པ། ཡིན་པ། ཡོད་པ། འདུག་པ་ | *re-pa; yim-pa; yö-pa; duk-pa.* |
| Bead | འཕྲང་ང་ (འཕྲེང་བ་) | *thrang-nga.* |
| Do. *hon.* | ཕྱག་འཕྲེང་ | *chhan-threng.* |
| Beak | མཆོ་ལྟོ་ (མཆུ་ལྟོ་) | *chho-to.* |
| Beam, large | གདུང་མ་ | *dung-ma.* |
| Do. small | ལྕམ་ཤིང་ | *cham-shing.* |
| Bean | སྲན་མ་ | *tre-ma.* |
| Bear, to (bring forth) | སྐྱེད་པ་ | *kye-pa.* |

| | | |
|---|---|---|
| Bear, to (bring forth) *hon.* | འཁྲུང་བ་ | *thrung wa.* |
| Bear, to (carry) | འཁྱེར་བ་ | *khyer-wa.* |
| Bear, *s.* | དོམ་ | *tom.* |
| Beard | ཨོག་ཞོལ་ | *ok-sḱö.* |
| Do. (with whiskers) | རྒྱ་ | *gya.* |
| Beard, a person having a | རྒྱའུ་ (རྒྱ་བོ་) | *gya-u.* |
| Beast | དུད་འགྲོ། སེམས་ཅན་ | *t́ün-dro; sem-chen.* |
| Beast (of prey) | གཅན་ཟན་ | *chen-śen.* |
| Beat, to | རྡུང་བ་ | *dung-wa.* |
| Do. *hon.* | ཕྱག་འཇུག་གནང་བ་ | *chhan-ju nang-wa.* |
| Beaten, to be (in a contest) | འཕམ་པ་ | *pham-pa.* |
| Beautiful | མཛེས་པོ་ | *dze-po.* |
| Do. *hon.* | ཐུགས་ཚར་པོ་ | *thu tshar-po.* |
| Beaver | ཆུ་སྲམ་ | *chhu-tram.* |
| Because | རྐྱེན་གྱིས། དོན་ལ་ | *kyen-ḱyi; t́ön-la.* |
| Beckon, to | གཡས་དབྱུག་རྒྱབ་པ་ | *ye-yu gyap̄-pa.* |
| Do. *hon.* | གཡས་དབྱུག་སྐྱོན་པ་ | *ye-yu kyöm-pa.* |
| Become, to | བྱུང་བ་ (འབྱུང་བ་) | *cḱung-wa.* |
| Becoming | འོས་པོ་ | *ö-po.* |

| | | |
|---|---|---|
| Bed | ཉལ་ཁྲི་ | *nye-thri.* |
| Do. *hon.* | གཟིམ་ཁྲི་ | *sim-thri.* |
| Bedaub, to | བྱུགས་པ་ (འབྱུག་པ།) སྐུ་བ་ | *cḱuk-pa ; ku-wa.* |
| Do. *hon.* | བྱུགས་ག་ (འབྱུག་པ་) གནང་བ། སྐུ་བ་གནང་བ་ | *cḱuk-ḱa nang-wa ; ku-wa nang-wa.* |
| Bedding | ཉལ་གཟན་ | *nye-śen.* |
| Do. *hon.* | གཟིམ་གཟན་ | *śim-śen.* |
| Bedroom | ཉལ་ས་ | *nye-sa.* |
| Do. *hon.* | གཟིམ་ཁང་ | *śim-khang.* |
| Bee | སྦྲང་མ་ | *drang-ma.* |
| Bee-hive | སྦྲང་ཚང་ | *drang-tshang.* |
| Beef | གླང་ཤ་ | *lang-sha.* |
| Beer | ཆང་ | *chhang.* |
| Do. *hon.* | མཆོད་ཆང་ | *chhö-chhang.* |
| Do. (spirit) | ཨ་རག་ | *a-ra.* |
| Do. *hon.* | བཞེས་རག་ | *sḱe-ra.* |
| Beer-shop | ཆང་ཁང་ | *chhang-ḱhang.* |
| Beer-seller | ཆང་མ། འཐྲུང་མ་ | *chhang-ma ; thrung-ma.* |
| Bees-wax | སྦྲ་ཚིལ་ | *traḱ ťshi.* |
| Beetle | སྦྲང་བུ་ | *drang-ṕu.* |

| | | |
|---|---|---|
| Befitting, *adj.* | འོས་པོ་ | *ö-po.* |
| Befool, to | མགོ་སྐོར་བ་ | *go-kor-wa.* |
| Do. *hon.* | དབུ་སྐོར་ར་ (བ་) གནང་བ་ | *u-kor-ra nang-wa.* |
| Before (*adv.* & *prep.* of place) | མདུན་ལ་ | *dün-la.* |
| Do. *hon.* | སྐུ་མདུན་ལ་ | *kun-dün-la.* |
| Before (*adv.* & *prep.* of time) | སྔན་ལ་ (སྔོན་ལ) | *ngen-la.* |
| Do. (with verb) | མ་...གོང་ལ་ | *ma...kong-la.* |
| Beg, to (request) | ཞུ་བ་ | *sḱu-wa.* |
| Do. *hon.* | ཞུ་བ་གནང་བ་ | *sḱu-wa nang-wa.* |
| Do. to (alms) | སློང་བ་ | *long-wa.* |
| Do. *hon.* | བསོད་སྙོམས་ཞུ་བ་གནང་བ་ | *sö-nyom sḱu-wa nang-wa.* |
| Beget, to | སྐྱེད་པ་ | *kye-pa.* |
| Do. *hon.* | འཁྲུང་བ་ | *thrung-wa.* |
| Beggar | སྤྲང་གོ་ (སྤྲང་པོ་) | *pang-ḱo.* |
| Begin, to | མགོ་བཙུགས་ (འཛུགས་) པ་ | *go-tsuḱ-pa.* |
| Do. *hon.* | དབུ་བཙུགས་ག་ (འཛུགས་པ་) གནང་བ་ | *u-tsuḱ-ḱa nang-wa.* |
| Beginning | མགོ་ | *go.* |
| Do. in the | སྔོན་དང་པོ་ | *ngön-ťang-po.* |
| Beguile, to | མགོ་སྐོར་བ་ | *go-kor-wa.* |

| | | |
|---|---|---|
| Beguile, to, *hon.* | དབུ་སྐོར་ར་ (བ་) གནང་བ་ | *u-kor-ra nang-wa.* |
| Behalf of, on | དོན་ལ་ | *t́ön-la.* |
| Behaviour | བྱེད་སྟངས་ (སྤྱོད་པ་) | *cḱe-tang.* |
| Behead, to (common person) | སྐེ་བཅད་ (གཅོད་) པ་ | *ke-che-pa.* |
| Do. (superior person) | མགུལ་བཅད་ (གཅོད་) པ་ | *gül-che-pa.* |
| Behind (*adv.* & *prep.*) | རྒྱབ་ལ། གཞུག་ལ་ | *gyaṕ-la ; sḱu-la.* |
| Behind hand, to be | ཕྱི་པོ་བྱེད་པ་ | *chhi-po cḱe-pa.* |
| Do. *hon.* | ཕྱི་པོ་གནང་བ་ | *chhi-po nang-wa.* |
| Behold, to | མཐོང་བ་ | *thong-wa.* |
| Do. *hon.* | གཟིགས་པ་ | *śi-pa.* |
| Belch, to | འགག་དྲི་རྒྱབ་པ་ | *gak-t́ri gyaṕ-pa.* |
| Do. *hon.* | འགག་དྲི་སྐྱོན་པ་ | *gak-t́ri kyöm-pa.* |
| Belief (religion) | དད་པ་ | *t́e-pa.* |
| Believe, to | ཡིད་ཆེས་པ་ | *yi-chhe-pa.* |
| Do. *hon.* | ཐུགས་ཡིད་ཆེས་པ་ | *thu-yi chhe-pa.* |
| Do. (in religious sense) | དད་པ་བྱེད་པ་ | *t́e-pa cḱe-pa.* |
| Do. *hon.* | དད་པ་གནང་བ་ | *t́e-pa nang-wa.* |
| Bell | དྲིལ་བུ་ | *t́ri-ṕu.* |
| Do. *hon.* | ཕྱག་དྲིལ་ | *chha-t́ri.* |
| Bell-metal | ལི་ | *li.* |

| | | |
|---|---|---|
| Bellows | སྦུད་པ་ | *bü-pa.* |
| Do. iron tube of | ཤན་མཆུ་ (སྦུད་མཆུ་) | *shen-chhu.* |
| Belly | གྲོ་ཁོག་ (གྲོད་ཁོག།) ཁོག་པ་ | *t́ro-kho; khok-pa.* |
| Do. *hon.* | གསོལ་གྲོད་ | *sö-t́rö.* |
| Belong, to (to me) | ཡིན་པ་ | *yim-pa.* |
| Do. (to you or to third person) | རེད་པ་ | *re-pa.* |
| Beloved | གཅེས་པོ་ | *che-po.* |
| Below (lower down) | མ་ | *ma.* |
| Do. *prep.* | འོག་ལ། གཤམ་ལ་ | *o-la; sham-la.* |
| Belt | སྐ་རགས་ | *ke-ra.* |
| Do. *hon.* | སྐུ་རགས་ | *ku-ra.* |
| Bench | ཀུབ་ཀྱག། ཁྲིའུ་ཤིང་ | *kuṕ-kya; thri-u-shing.* |
| Do. *hon.* | ཞབས་ཀྱག་ | *shaṕ-kya.* |
| Bend, to, *v.t.* | བཀུག་པ་ (འགུག་པ་) | *kuḱ-pa.* |
| Do. *hon.* | བཀུག་ག་ (འགུག་པ་) གནང་བ་ | *kuḱ-ḱa nang-wa.* |
| Bend, to (stoop) | གུག་གུག་བྱེད་པ་ | *ḱu-ḱu cḱe-pa.* |
| Do. *hon.* | གུག་གུག་གནང་བ་ | *ḱu-ḱu nang-wa.* |
| Beneath | འོག་ལ་ | *o-la.* |
| Benediction | བྱིན་རླབས | *cḱin-laṕ.* |
| Benefaction | མགོ་འདྲེན | *gön-dren.* |

| | | |
|---|---|---|
| Benefactor | མགོ་འདྲེན་གནང་མཁན་ | *gön-dren nang-khen.* |
| Do. *hon.* | དབུ་འདྲེན་གནང་མཁན་ | *u-dren nang-khen.* |
| Benefit, to | ཕན་ཐོགས་པ་ | *phen-thoǩ-pa.* |
| Benefit of, for the | ཕན་པའི་དོན་ལ་ | *phen-pe-tön-la.* |
| Benevolence | དྲིན་ | *ťrin.* |
| Do. *hon.* | བཀའ་དྲིན་ | *ka-ťrin.* |
| Benevolent | དྲིན་ཆེན་པོ་ | *ťrin-chhem-po.* |
| Do. *hon.* | བཀའ་དྲིན་ཆེན་པོ་ | *ka-ťrin chhem-po.* |
| Benevolent, to be | དྲིན་བྱེད་པ་ | *ťrin-cǩe-pa.* |
| Do. *hon.* | བཀའ་དྲིན་གནང་བ་ | *ka-ťrin nang-wa.* |
| Bent, to be | གུག་གུག་བྱས་ནས་བསྡད་ (སྡོད་) པ་ | *ǩu-ǩu cǩe-ne de-pa.* |
| Beseech, to | ཞུ་བ་ཕུལ་ (འབུལ་) བ་ | *sǩu-wa phü-wa.* |
| Beside | ཙ་ལ་ | *tsa-la.* |
| Besides, *prep.* | མ་གཏོགས། མིན་པ་ | *ma-to; mem-pa.* |
| Besmear, to | བྱུགས་པ་ (འབྱུག་པ་) | *cǩuk-pa.* |
| Do. *hon.* | བྱུགས་ཀ་ (འབྱུག་པ་) གནང་བ་ | *cǩuk-ǩa nang-wa.* |
| Besprinkle with water, to | ཆུ་ཆག་རྒྱབ་པ་ | *chhu-chha gyap̌-pa.* |
| Best | ཡག་ཤོས། ཡག་ཐག་ཆོད་ | *yak-shö; yak-thaǩ-chhö.* |
| Bestow, to | སྟེར་བ་ | *ter-wa.* |

| | | |
|---|---|---|
| Bestow, to, *hon.* | གནང་བ་ | *nang-wa.* |
| Bet | རྒྱན་ | *gyen.* |
| Do. *hon.* | སྐུ་རྒྱན་ | *ku-gyen.* |
| Bet, to | རྒྱན་བཞག་ (འཛོག་) པ་ | *gyen-sḱaḱ-pa.* |
| Do. *hon.* | སྐུ་རྒྱན་གཞོག་ག་ (འཛོག་པ་) གནང་བ་ | *ku-gyen sḱoḱ-ka nang-wa.* |
| Betel-nut | གོ་ཡུ་ | *ḱo-yu.* |
| Betray, to | དགྲའི་དབང་ལ་བཏང་ (གཏོང་) བ་ | *dra-i wang-la tang-wa.* |
| Better | ཡག་ག་ | *yaḱ-ḱa.* |
| Better, to get the (in a fight, &c.) | རྒྱལ་བ་ | *gye-wa.* |
| Between | བར་ལ་ | *ṕa-la.* |
| Beware, to | དོགས་ཟོན་བྱེད་པ་ | *ťoḱ-śön cḱe-pa.* |
| Do. *hon.* | ཐུགས་ཟོན་གནང་བ་ | *thuḱ-śön nang-wa.* |
| Bewildered, to be | མགོ་འཁོར་བ་ | *go-khor-wa.* |
| Do. *hon.* | དབུ་འཁོར་ར་ (བ་) གནང་བ་ | *u-khor-ra nang-wa.* |
| Beyond | ཕར་ཕྱོགས་ལ་ | *pha-chho-la.* |
| Bhutan | འབྲུག་ཡུལ་ | *druḱ-yü.* |
| Bhutanese | འབྲུག་པ་ | *druḱ-pa.* |
| Bible | གསུང་རབ་ | *sung-raṕ.* |

| | | |
|---|---|---|
| Bicycle | ཁང་སྒ་རི་ | *ḱang-ga-ri.* |
| Bid, to | བཀའ་གནང་བ་ | *ḱa-nang-wa.* |
| Bier | ཤིང་ཁྲི་ | *shing-thri.* |
| Big | ཆེན་པོ་ | *chhem-po.* |
| Bile | མཁྲིས་པ་ | *thri-pa.* |
| Bill (amount) | རྩིས་ཐོ་ | *tsi-tho.* |
| Do. *hon.* | ཕྱག་ཐོ་ | *chha-tho.* |
| Bill (of bird) | མཆོ་ལྟོ་ (མཆུ་ལྟོ་) | *chho-to.* |
| Billow | བ་རླབས་ | *ba-laṕ.* |
| Bind, to | བསྡམས་པ་ (སྡོམ་པ་) | *dam-pa.* |
| Biography | རྣམ་ཐར་ | *nam-tha.* |
| Do. *hon.* | གསུང་ཐར་ | *sung-tha.* |
| Birch tree | སྟག་པ་ཤིང་ | *taḱ-pa-shing.* |
| Bird | བྱ་ | *cḱa.* |
| Bird-cage | རླུང་ཙེ་ | *lung-tse.* |
| Bird's-nest | བྱ་ཚང་ | *cḱa-tshang.* |
| Birthday | སྐྱེ་ཚེས་ | *ḱye-tshe.* |
| Do. *hon.* | འཁྲུང་ཚེས་ | *thrung-tshe.* |
| Birth, high | སྐྱེ་ས་མཐོ་པོ་ | *ḱye-sa tho-po.* |
| Birth, low | སྐྱེ་ས་དམའ་པོ་ | *ḱye-sa ma-po.* |

| | | |
|---|---|---|
| Birth-place | སྐྱེ་ས། སྐྱེ་སའི་ལུང་པ་ | *kye-sa; kye-se lung-pa.* |
| Do. *hon.* | འཁྲུང་ས་ | *thrung-sa.* |
| Bishop | མཁན་པོ་ | *khem-po.* |
| Bit (of a bridle) | སྲབ་ལྕགས་ | *traṕ-cha.* |
| Bit (piece) | དུམ་བུ་ | *t́um-ṕu.* |
| Bitch | ཁྱི་མོ་ | *khyi-mo.* |
| Bite, to | རྨུག་པ། སོ་རྒྱབ་པ་ | *muk-pa; so-gyaṕ-pa.* |
| Bitter | ཁག་ཁྲིག་ | *khak-thi.* |
| Black | ནག་པོ་ | *nak-po.* |
| Blacksmith | མགར་ར་ (བ་) | *gar-ra.* |
| Bladder | ལྒང་ཕུག་ | *gang-phu.* |
| Blade (of grass) | ལྗང་པ་ | *jang-pa.* |
| Blade (of sword) | དངོ་ | *ngo.* |
| Blame, to | སྐྱོན་བརྡོན་པ་ | *kyön töm-pa.* |
| Do. *hon.* | སྐྱོན་བརྡོན་པ་གནང་བ་ | *kyön töm-pa nang-wa.* |
| Blank | སྟོང་པ་ | *tong-pa.* |
| Blanket | ཉལ་གཟན་ | *nye-śen.* |
| Do. *hon.* | གཟིམ་གཟན་ | *śim-śen.* |
| Blaspheme, to | སྨད་ར་བཏང་ (གཏོང་) བ་ | *me-ra tang-wa.* |
| Do. *hon.* | སྨད་ར་གཏོང་ང་ (བ་) གནང་བ་ | *me-ra tong-nga nang-wa.* |

| | | |
|---|---|---|
| Blaze, *s.* | མེ་ | *me.* |
| Blaze, to (of fire) | འབར་བ་ | *bar-wa.* |
| Bleat, to | ལུག་སྐད་རྒྱབ་པ་ | *luḱ-ke gyaṕ-pa.* |
| Bleed, to, *v.i.* | ཁྲག་འཐོན་པ་ | *thra-thöm-pa.* |
| Do. (of doctor), *v.t.* | ཁྲག་རྒྱབ་པ་ | *thra-gyaṕ-pa.* |
| Blemish, *s.* | སྐྱོན་ | *kyön.* |
| Blend, to | འདྲེ་བ་ | *dre-wa.* |
| Do. *hon.* | འདྲེ་བ་གནང་བ་ | *dre-wa nang-wa* |
| Bless, to | བྱིན་རླབས་གནང་བ་ | *cḱin-laṕ nang-wa.* |
| Do. to (dead person) | བསྔོ་བ་རྒྱབ་པ་ | *ngo-wa gyaṕ-pa.* |
| Blessing (by placing book on head) | བྱིན་རླབས་ | *cḱin-laṕ.* |
| Do. (by laying hand on head) | ཕྱག་དབང་ | *chha-wang.* |
| Blind | ལོང་ང་ (ལོང་བ་) | *long-nga.* |
| Do. *hon.* | སྤྱན་ལོང་ང་ (བ་) | *chen-long-nga.* |
| Blind of one eye | མིག་ཞར་ར་ (བ་) | *mik-sḱar-ra.* |
| Do. *hon.* | སྤྱན་ཞར་ར་ (བ་) | *chen-sḱar-ra.* |
| Blink, to | མིག་བཙུམ་རྒྱབ་པ་ | *mik-tsum gyaṕ-pa.* |
| Do. *hon.* | སྤྱན་བཙུམ་སྐྱོན་པ་ | *chen-tsum kyöm-pa.* |
| Blister, *s.* | ཆུ་གང་ | *chhu-ḱang.* |

| | | |
|---|---|---|
| Blistered, to be | ཆུ་གང་འཐོན་པ་ | *chhu-kang thöm-pa.* |
| Blithe | སྐྱིད་པོ་ | *kyi-po.* |
| Block, to | བཀག་པ་ (འགེགས་པ་) | *kak-pa.* |
| Blockhead | ཀླུགས་པ། གླེན་པ་ | *kuk-pa ; lem-pa.* |
| Blood | ཁྲག་ | *thra.* |
| Do. *hon.* | སྐུ་ཁྲག་ | *ku-thra.* |
| Blossom | མེ་ཏོག་ | *me-to.* |
| Blot, *s.* | ནག་ཐིག་ | *nak-thi.* |
| Blow (with fist) | ཛོག་རམ་ (ཛོག་རིལ་) | *dzo-ram.* |
| Do. (with open palm) | ཐལ་ལྕག་ | *the-cha.* |
| Blow, to, *v.t.* | ཕུ་རྒྱབ་པ་ | *phu-gyaṕ-pa.* |
| Do. *hon.* | ལྗགས་ཕུ་གནང་བ་ | *ja-phu nang-wa.* |
| Do. (of wind), *v.i.* | རྒྱབ་པ་ | *gyaṕ-pa.* |
| Blue | སྔོན་པོ་ | *ngöm-po.* |
| Blue, dark | སྔོ་ནག་ | *ngo-nak.* |
| Blue Book | དེབ་སྔོན་པོ་ | *ťeṕ ngöm-po.* |
| Blue, light | སྔོ་སྐྱ་ | *ngo-kya.* |
| Blunder, to | ཁ་ནོར་བ་ | *kha-nor-wa.* |
| Do. *hon.* | ཞལ་ནོར་ར་ (བ་) གནང་བ་ | *ske-nor-ra nang-wa.* |
| Blunt, to be | རྣོ་པོ་མེད་པ་ | *no-po me-pa.* |

| | | |
|---|---|---|
| Blush, to | ངོ་ཚ་བ་ | *ngo-tsha-wa.* |
| Do. *hon.* | ཞལ་རས་ཚ་བ་གནང་བ། ཐུགས་ངོ་ཚ་བ་གནང་བ་ | *sḱe-re tsha-wa nang-wa ; thu-ngo tsha-wa nang-wa.* |
| Boar | ཕག་པ་ | *phaḱ-pa.* |
| Do. (wild) | རི་ཕག་ | *ri-pha.* |
| Board | སྤང་ལེབ་ | *pang-le.* |
| Boast, to | རང་སྟོད་བྱེད་པ་ | *rang-tö cḱe-pa.* |
| Boat (of wood) | གྲུ་ | *t́ru.* |
| Boatman (of wooden boat) | གྲུ་པ་ | *t́ru-pa.* |
| Do. *hon.* | གྲུ་དཔོན་ | *t́ru-pön.* |
| Boat (of hide) | ཀོ་བ་ | *ko-wa.* |
| Do. *hon.* | ཕེབ་ཀོ་ | *phe-ko.* |
| Boatman (of hide boat) | མཉན་པ་ | *nyem-pa.* |
| Do. *hon.* | མཉ་ནདཔོན་ | *nyem-pön.* |
| Body | གཟུགས་པོ། ལུས་ | *śuḱ-po ; lü.* |
| Do. *hon.* | སྐུ་གཟུགས། སྐུ་ལུས་ | *ku-śuḱ ; ku-lü* |
| Body (corpse of human being) | རོ་ | *ro.* |
| Do. *hon.* | སྐུ་ཕུང་ | *ku-phung.* |
| Body (dead body of animal) | ཤི་རོ་ | *shi-ro.* |
| Boil | གཉན་བུར་ | *nyen-ṕur.* |

| | | |
|---|---|---|
| Boil (watery) | ཆུ་བུར་ | *chhu-ṕur.* |
| Do. to, *v.i.* | འཁོལ་བ་ | *khöl-wa.* |
| Do. *v.t.* | བསྐོལ་བ་ (སྐོལ་བ་) | *kö-wa.* |
| Boiler (cauldron) | དཀྱིལ་ཁྲོ་ | *kyi-thro.* |
| Boiling, *adj.* | ཁོལ་མ་ | *khöl-ma.* |
| Bold | བློ་ཁོག་ཆེན་པོ་ | *lo-kho chhem-po.* |
| Do. *hon.* | ཐུགས་ཁོག་ཆེན་པོ་ | *thu-kho chhem-po.* |
| Bolt | སྒོ་ལྕགས་ | *gön-cha.* |
| Do. *hon.* | གཟིམ་ལྕགས། ཕྱག་ལྕགས་ | *śim-cha; chha-cha.* |
| Bolt, to (of horse), *v.i.* | ངར་ནས་ཕྱིན་པ་ | *ngar-ne chhim-pa.* |
| Bolt, to (door, &c.) | སྒོ་ལྕགས་རྒྱབ་པ་ | *gön-cha gyaṕ-pa.* |
| Do. *hon.* | གཟིམ་ལྕགས་སྐྱོན་པ་ | *śim-cha kyöm-pa.* |
| Bolting, *adj.* (of horse) | འདྲོག་པ་ | *drok-pa.* |
| Bond (for large amount) | གམ་རྒྱ་ (གན་རྒྱ་) | *ḱam-gya.* |
| Do. *hon.* | ཕྱག་གན་ | *chha-gen.* |
| Do. (for small amount) | འཛིན་ | *dzin.* |
| Do. *hon.* | ཕྱག་འཛིན་ | *chhan-dzin.* |
| | བཀའ་འཛིན་ | *kan-dzin.* |
| Bone | རུས་ཁོག་ | *rü-ḱho.* |
| Do. *hon.* | སྐུ་རུས་ | *ku-rü.* |

| | | |
|---|---|---|
| Book | དཔེ་ཆ་ | *pe-chha.* |
| Do. *hon.* | ཕྱག་དཔེ་ | *chha-pe.* |
| Book-language | ཆོས་ཚིག་ | *chhö-tshi.* |
| Book, printed | པར་མ་ | *par-ma.* |
| Do. written | བྲིས་མ་ | *ťri-ma.* |
| Boon | དྲིན་ | *ťrin.* |
| Do. *hon.* | བཀའ་དྲིན་ | *ka-ťrin.* |
| Boot | ལྷམ། ལྷམ་ཁོག་ | *hlam ; hlam-kho.* |
| Do. *hon.* | ཞབས་ཆགས་ | *sǩaṕ-chha.* |
| Boot (of European style) | འཇུ་ཏ་ | *ju-ta.* |
| Bootmaker | དངོ་བཟོ་ | *ngoṕ-śo.* |
| Do. *hon.* | དབུ་མཛད་ | *um-dze.* |
| Borax | ཚ་ལི་ | *tsha-li.* |
| Border | ཟུར་ | *śur.* |
| Do. (of land) | ས་མཚམས་ | *san-tsham.* |
| Bore a hole, to | ཨི་ཁུང་ཕིད་ (འབིག་) པ་ | *i-khung pi-pa.* |
| Born, to be | སྐྱེ་བ་ | *kye-wa.* |
| Do. *hon.* | འཁྲུངས་བ་ | *thrung-wa.* |
| Borrow, to | གཡར་བ་ | *yar-wa.* |
| Do. to (ask a loan) | སྐྱི་བ་ | *kyi-wa.* |

| | | |
|---|---|---|
| Borrow, to, *hon.* | གཡར་པོ་ཞུ་བ་གནང་བ་ | *yar-po sḱu-wa nang-wa.* |
| Bosom | བང་ཁོག་ (བྲང་ཁོག་) | *ṕang-kho.* |
| Do. *hon.* | སྐུ་བང་ (སྐུ་བྲང་) | *ku-ṕang.* |
| Both, *pron.* | གཉིས་ཀ་ | *nyi-ka.* |
| Bothersome | ཅ་སྙུན་པོ་ | *cha-sim-po.* |
| Do. *hon.* | ཐུགས་ཅ་སྙུན་པོ་ | *thu-cha sim-po.* |
| Bottle | ཤེལ་དམ་ | *she-t́am.* |
| Bottom | གཏིང་ | *ting.* |
| Do. (anus) | རྐུབ་ | *kuṕ.* |
| Do. *hon.* | ཞབས་ཕོངས་ | *sḱam-phong* |
| Bough | ཡལ་ག་ | *ye-ḱa.* |
| Bound, to (jump) | མཆོངས་པ། མཆོངས་རྒྱག་རྒྱབ་པ་ | *chhong-pa ; chhong-gya gyaṕ-pa.* |
| Do. *hon.* | མཆོངས་རྒྱག་སྐྱོན་པ་ | *chhong-gya kyöm-pa.* |
| Boundary | ས་མཚམས་ | *san-tsham.* |
| Bountiful | ལག་པ་ཤོག་པོ་ | *laḱ-pa shoḱ-po.* |
| Do. *hon.* | ཕྱག་ཤོག་པོ་ | *chha-shoḱ-po.* |
| Bow (for shooting) | གཞུ་ | *sḱu.* |
| Do. *hon* | ཕྱག་གཞུ་ | *chha-sḱu.* |
| Bow, to (taking hat) | ཕྱག་འབུལ་ཞུ་བ་ | *chham-bü sḱu-wa.* |

| | | |
|---|---|---|
| Bow-legged | ཀང་ཀྱོག་ | *kang-kyo.* |
| Bowel | རྒྱུ་མ་ | *gyu-ma.* |
| Bowl (for drinking tea, &c.) | ཕོར་པ་ | *phor-pa.* |
| Do. *hon.* | མཆོད་ཞལ་ | *chhö-sḱe.* |
| Bowl (of tobacco pipe) | གང་མགོ་ | *ḱang-go.* |
| Box (chest) | སྒམ་ | *gam.* |
| Do. *hon.* | ཕྱག་སྒམ་ | *chha-gam.* |
| Boy | བུ་གུ་ | *pu-gu.* |
| Do. *hon.* | ཨ་ལྭ་ | *a-wa.* |
| Bracelet | སྒྲོག་གདུང་ | *dro-dung.* |
| Do. *hon.* | ཕྱག་གདུང་ | *chha-dung.* |
| Brahma | ཚངས་པ་ | *tshang-pa.* |
| Brahman (caste) | བྲམ་ཟེ་ | *ťram-śe.* |
| Brain | ཀླད་པ་ | *le-pa.* |
| Bramble | ཚེར་མ་ | *tsher-ma.* |
| Bran | ཕུང་མ་ | *phung-ma.* |
| Branch | ཡལ་ག་ | *ye-ḱa.* |
| Brandish, to | དབྱུག་དབྱུག་བྱེད་པ་ | *yu-yu ḱe-pa.* |
| Do. *hon.* | དབྱུག་དབྱུག་གནང་བ་ | *yu-yu nang-wa.* |
| Brandy | ཨ་རག་ | *a-ra.* |

| | | |
|---|---|---|
| Brandy, *hon.* | བཞེས་རག་ | *sḱe-ra.* |
| Brass | རག་ | *ra.* |
| Brave, *adj.* | སྙིང་ཆེན་པོ་ | *nying-chhem-po.* |
| Do. *hon.* | ཐུགས་སྙིང་ཆེན་པོ་ | *thu-nying. chhem-po.* |
| Brawl | རྒྱབ་འདྲེ། འཁྲུག་པ་ | *gyam-dre ; thruḱ-pa.* |
| Bray | བོང་སྐད་རྒྱབ་པ་ | *ṕong-ke-gyaṕ-pa.* |
| Bread | བག་ལེབ་ | *ṕa-le.* |
| Do. *hon.* | བཞེས་བག་ | *sḱe-ṕa.* |
| Breadth | ཞང་ (ཞེང་) | *sḱang.* |
| Break, to, *v.t.* | བཅག་པ་ (གཅོག་པ་) | *chaḱ-pa.* |
| Do. *hon.* | གཅོག་ག་ (གཅོག་པ་) གནང་བ་ | *choḱ-ḱa nang-wa.* |
| Break, to, *v.i.* | འཆག་པ་ | *chhaḱ-pa.* |
| Breakfast (at 10 or 11 A.M.) | ཚ་གདིང་མའི་ཁ་ལག་ | *tsha-ting-me kha-la.* |
| Do. *hon.* | ཚ་གདིང་མའི་ཞལ་ལག་ | *tsha-ting-me sḱe-la.* |
| Breakfast (at 7 to 9 A.M.) | ཞོགས་གེའི་ཁ་ལག་ | *sḱo-ke kha-la.* |
| Do. *hon.* | ཞོགས་གེའི་ཞལ་ལག་ | *sḱo-ke sḱe-la.* |
| Breast | བང་ཁོག་ (བྲང་ཁོག་) | *ṕang-kho.* |
| Do. *hon.* | སྐུ་བང་ (སྐུ་བྲང་) | *ku-ṕang.* |
| Breath | དབུགས་ | *u.* |

| | | |
|---|---|---|
| Breath, *hon.* | ལྗགས་དབུགས་ | *ja-u.* |
| Breathe, to | དབུགས་བཏང་ (གཏོང་) བ་ | *u-tang-wa.* |
| Do. *hon.* | ལྗགས་དབུགས་གཏོང་ང་ (བ་) གནང་བ་ | *ja-u tong-nga nang-wa.* |
| Breathless, to be | དབུགས་བསག་ (གསོག་) པ་ | *u sak-pa.* |
| Do. *hon.* | ལྗགས་དབུགས་བསག་ག་ (གསོག་པ་) གནང་བ་ | *ja-u sak-ka nang-wa.* |
| Breed (of men) | བརྒྱུད་ | *gyü.* |
| Do. *hon.* | སྐུ་བརྒྱུད་ | *ku-gyü.* |
| Do. (of animals) | བརྒྱུད་དག་ | *gyü-ťa.* |
| Breeze | ལྷགས་པ། རླུང་ | *hlak-pa ; lung.* |
| Bribe | ཙིག་ཐོ་ | *tsik-tho.* |
| Do. *hon.* | སྐྱབས་འཇུག་ | *kyam-ju.* |
| Bribe, to give | ཙིག་ཐོ་རྒྱབ་པ་ | *tsik-tho gyap-pa.* |
| Do. (*inf.* to *sup.*) | སྐྱབས་འཇུག་ཞུ་བ་ | *kyam-ju sKu-wa.* |
| Bribe, to take | རྒྱུ་ཟ་བ་ | *gyu-śa-wa.* |
| Do. *hon.* | རྒྱུ་བཞེས་པ་ | *gyu-sKe-pa.* |
| Brick | ས་ཕག་ | *sa-pa.* |
| Brick of tea | ཇ་བག་ | *cKa-pa.* |
| Do. *hon.* | གསོལ་ཇ་བག་ཀག་ | *so-cKa pak-ka.* |

| | | |
|---|---|---|
| Bride | མནའ་མ་ | *na-ma.* |
| Bridegroom | མག་པ་ | *mak-pa.* |
| Bridesmaid | བག་རོགས་ | *ṕa·ro.* |
| Bridge | ཟམ་པ་ | *śam-pa.* |
| Do. *hon.* | ཕེབས་ཟམ་ | *phe-śam.* |
| Bridge, iron | ལྕགས་ཟམ་ | *cha-śam.* |
| Do. *hon.* | ལྕགས་ཀྱི་ཕེབ་ཟམ་ | *cha-kyi phe-śam.* |
| Bridle | སྲབ་ | *traṕ.* |
| Do. *hon.* | ཆིབས་སྲབ་ | *chhiṕ-traṕ.* |
| Brief | ཐུང་ཐུང་ | *thung-thung.* |
| Brier | ཚེར་མ་ | *tsher-ma.* |
| Brigand | ཇག་པ་ | *cḱak-pa.* |
| Bright (clear) | གསལ་པོ་ | *se-po.* |
| Do. (dazzling) | འོད་ཆེན་པོ་ | *ö-chhem-po.* |
| Brightness | འོད་ | *ö.* |
| Brilliant | འོད་ཆེན་པོ་ | *ö-chhem-po.* |
| Brim, to fill to the | དག་དག་ལྡུག་པ་ | *ṫak-ṫak luk-pa.* |
| Do. *hon.* | དག་དག་ལྡུག་ག་ (པ་) གནང་བ་ | *ṫak-ṫak luk-ka nang-wa.* |
| Brimstone | མུ་ཟི་ | *mu-śi.* |
| Bring, to (by carrying) | འཁྱེར་ཡོང་བ་ | *khyer-yong-wa.* |

| | | |
|---|---|---|
| Bring, to, *hon.* | བསྣམས་ (སྣོམ་) ཕེབ་པ་ | *nam-phe-pa.* |
| Bring, to (by leading along, *e.g.*, horse) | འཁྲིད་ཡོང་བ་ | *thri-yong-wa.* |
| Do. *hon.* | འཁྲིད་ཕེབ་པ་ | *thri-phe-pa.* |
| Brink | འགྲམ་ | *dram.* |
| Brisk | ཧུར་པོ་ | *hur-po.* |
| Bristle | ཕག་ཟེ་ | *phak-se.* |
| British | དབྱིན་ཇི་ | *in-ji.* |
| Do. Government | དབྱིན་གཞུང་ | *in-skung.* |
| Broadcloth | འགོ་སྣམ་ | *go-nam.* |
| Broad | ཞང་ (ཞེང་) ཆེན་པོ་ | *skang-chhem-po.* |
| Broad (of land) | རྒྱ་ཆེན་པོ་ | *gya-chhem-po.* |
| Broil | རྒྱབ་འདྲེ་ | *gyam-dre* |
| Broken, to be | ཆག་པ་ | *chhak-pa.* |
| Bronchitis | གློ་ཡུའི་ནད་ | *lo-yü-ne.* |
| Bronze | ཁྲོ་ | *thro.* |
| Brooch | སྐེ་འཕྲུག་ | *ke thru.* |
| Do. *hon.* | མགུལ་འཕྲུག་ | *gü-thru.* |
| Brood, to (of fowls) | སྒོ་ང་བསྙལ་བ་ | *go-nga nyal-wa.* |
| Brook, *s.* | རྒྱུག་ཆུ་ | *gyuk-chhu.* |

| | | |
|---|---|---|
| Broom | ཕྱག་མ་ | *chha-ma.* |
| Broth | ཁུ་བ་ | *khu-a.* |
| Do. *hon.* | སྐྲུང་ཁུ་ (སྐྲུམ་ཁུ་) | *trung-khu.* |
| Broth (made from meat) | ཤ་ཁུ་ | *sha-khu.* |
| Do. *hon.* | སྐྲུང་ཁུ་ (སྐྲུམ་ཁུ་) | *trung-khu.* |
| Brother | སྤུན་ཀྱག་ | *pün-kya.* |
| Do. *hon.* | སྐུ་མཆེད་ | *kum-chhe.* |
| Brother, mother's | ཨ་ཞང་ | *a-sKang.* |
| Do. *hon.* | ཞང་ཞང་ལགས་ | *sKang-sKang-la.* |
| Brother, elder | ཇོ་ཇོ་ | *cKo-cKo.* |
| Do. *hon.* | ཇོ་ལགས་ | *cKo-la.* |
| Brother, younger | སྤུན་ཆུང་ང་ (བ་) | *pün-chhung-nga.* |
| Do. *hon.* | སྐུ་མཆེད་ཆུང་ང་ (བ་) | *kum-chhe chhung-nga* |
| Brother-in-law (wife's brother) | སྐྱེ་དམན་གྱི་སྤུན་ཀྱག་ | *kyi-men kyi pün-kya.* |
| Do. *hon* | སྐུ་ཟླའི་སྐུ་མཆེད་ | *kum-de kum-chhe.* |
| Do. (sister's husband) | སྤུན་ཀྱག་གི་ཁྱོ་ག་ | *pün-kya ki khyo-ga.* |
| Do. *hon.* | སྐུ་མཆེད་ཀྱི་སྐུ་ཟླ་ | *kum-chhe kyi kum-da.* |
| Brown | སྨུག་པོ་ | *muk-po.* |
| Bruised, to be | སྤྲག་པ་ | *trak-pa.* |

| | | |
|---|---|---|
| Bruised, *hon.* | སྤྲག་ག་ (པ་) གནང་བ་ | *trak̔-k̔a nang-wa.* |
| Bruised, to be | ཀི་ཤུས་ལོག་པ་ | *ki-shü lok̔-pa.* |
| Brush | ཕག་ཟེ་ | *pha-śe.* |
| Brute | བྱོལ་སོང་ | *cK̔ö-song.* |
| Bubble | ལྦུ་བ་ | *bu-wa.* |
| Buck | ཤྭ་ (ཤྭ་བ་) | *sha-a.* |
| Bucket | ཆུ་བཟོམ་ | *chhu-śom.* |
| Do. *hon.* | ཆབ་བཟོམ་ | *chhap̔-śom.* |
| Buck wheat, bitter | བྲའུ་ (བྲ་བོ་) | *t̔ra-u.* |
| Do. sweet | གྱ་ཟྲ་ | *gyap̔-ra.* |
| Bud, *s.* | ཐེའུ་ | *theu.* |
| Bud, to | སྐྱེ་བ་ | *kye-wa.* |
| Buddha | སངས་རྒྱས་ | *sang-gye.* |
| Buddhist | ནང་པ་ | *nang-pa.* |
| Buffalo | མ་ཧེ་ | *ma-he.* |
| Buffoonery | སྤྲེ་ཙེད་ | *tre-tse.* |
| Bug | འདྲེ་ཤིག་ | *dre-shi.* |
| Bugle | དམག་དུང་ | *mak̔ t̔ung.* |
| Build, to | བཟོ་བ་ | *śo-wa.* |
| Do. *hon.* | བཟོ་བ་གནང་བ་ | *śo-wa nang-wa.* |

| | | |
|---|---|---|
| Building | ཁང་པ་ | *khang-pa.* |
| Do. *hon.* | གཟིམ་ཁང་ | *śim-khang.* |
| Do. *h. hon.* | གཟིམ་ཤག་ | *śim-sha.* |
| Bulk | ཆེ་ཆུང་ | *chhe-chhung.* |
| Bulky | སྦོམ་པོ་ | *bom-po.* |
| Bull | གླང་། གླང་གོག་ | *lang ; lang-ḱo.* |
| Bullet | རྡིག་རིལ་ (མདེའུ་) | *diḱ-ri.* |
| Bullock | གླང་། གླང་གོག་ | *lang ; lang-ḱo.* |
| Bunch | ཆག་པ་ | *chhaḱ-pa.* |
| Bundle of clothes | གོས་སྒྲིལ་ | *ḱö-dril.* |
| Do. of papers | ཤུག་གུའི་ (ཤོག་བུའི་) ཆག་པ་ | *shuḱ-ḱu-i chhaḱ-pa.* |
| Do. of sticks | ཤིང་འཁུར་ | *shing-khur.* |
| Burden (of animal) | ཁལ། དོས་པོ་ | *khe ; t́ö-po.* |
| Do. (of human being) | རྡོག་ཁྲེད། རྒྱབ་འཁུར་ | *doḱ-thre ; gyaṕ-khur.* |
| Buriat | སྤོ་རས་ཐུ་ | *po-re-thu.* |
| Burn, to, *v.i.* | འཚིག་པ་ | *tshiḱ-pa.* |
| Do. *v.t.* | སྲེག་པ་ | *traḱ-pa.* |
| Burnt-offering | སྦྱིན་སྲེག་ | *jin-se.* |
| Burrhel (sheep) | གནའ་བ་ | *na-wa.* |
| Burst, to, *v.i.* | གས་པ་ (འགས་པ་) | *ḱe-pa.* |

| | | |
|---|---|---|
| Burst, to, *v.t.* | བཅག་པ་ (གཅོག་པ་) | *chak-pa.* |
| Do. *hon.* | གཅོག་ག་ (གཅོག་པ་) གནང་བ་ | *chok-ka nang-wa.* |
| Bury, to | ས་ལ་སྦེད་པ་ | *sa-la be-pa.* |
| Do. *hon.* | ས་སྦེད་གནང་བ་ | *sa-be nang-wa.* |
| Burying-place | དུར་ཁྲོད་ | *ťu-thrö.* |
| Bush | ཤིང་སྡོང་ཆུང་ཆུང་ | *shing-dong chhung-chhung.* |
| Business | ལས་ཀ། དོན་དག་ | *le-ka ; tön-ťa.* |
| Do. *hon.* | ཕྱག་ལས། སྐུ་དོན་ | *chha-le ; ku-tön.* |
| Busy, I am | ང་ཅོག་གི་མི་འདུག ང་དལ་ཀྱི་མི་འདུག | *nga cho-ki min-duk ; nga ťe-kyi min-du.* |
| Busy, he is, *hon.* | ཁོང་ཐུགས་ཅོག་ག་ གནང་གི་མི་འདུག་ | *khong thu-chok-ka nang-gi min-du.* |
| Do. *h. hon.* | སྐུ་གཞོགས་ཐུགས་ཅོག་ག་ (པ་) གནང་གི་མི་འདུག་ | *ku-sko thu-cho-ka nang-yi min-du.* |
| But | ཡིན་ཀྱང་། ཡིན་ན་ཡང་ | *yin-kyang ; yin-na-yang.* |
| Butcher | ཤན་པ། ཡར་པོ་ | *shem-pa ; ya-po.* |
| Butler | གཟིམ་དཔོན་ | *śim-pön.* |
| Butt (of gun) | སྒུམ་ཤིང་། ཉ་གཞུག་ | *gum-shing ; nya-sku.* |
| Butter | མར་ | *mar.* |
| Do. *hon.* | གསོལ་མར་ | *sö-ma.* |

| | | |
|---|---|---|
| Butterfly | ཕྱེ་འདྲེན་མ་ | *chhem-drem-ma.* |
| Butter-milk | དར་ར་ (བ་) | *ťar-ra.* |
| Do. *hon.* | བཞེས་དར་ | *sKe-ťar.* |
| Buttock | ཀུབ་ | *kuṕ.* |
| Do. *hon.* | ཞབས་ཕོངས་ | *sKam-phong.* |
| Button | ཐུབ་ཆི་ | *thuṕ-chhi.* |
| Do. *hon.* | མཀུལ་ཐུབ་ | *gü-thuṕ.* |
| Button-hole | ཐོབ་ལུང་ | *thoṕ-lung.* |
| Do. *hon.* | མཀུལ་ལུང་ | *gü-lung.* |
| Button (of rank) | ཏོག་ | *to.* |
| Do. *hon.* | དབུ་ཏོག་ | *u-to.* |
| Buy, to | ཉོ་བ་ | *nyo-wa.* |
| Do. *hon.* | གཟིགས་པ་ | *śi-pa.* |
| Do. *h. hon.* | ལྗགས་གཟིགས་གནང་བ་ | *ja-śi nang-wa.* |
| Buzz, to | སྦྲང་སྐད་རྒྱབ་པ་ | *drang-ke gyaṕ-pa.* |
| By (*post*) | གིས། ཀྱིས། གྱིས། | *ki ; kyi ; Kyi.* |
| By reason of | རྐྱེན་གྱིས་ | *kyen-Kyi.* |

# C

| | | |
|---|---|---|
| Cabbage | པེ་ཚས་ *ch.* | *pe-tshe.* |
| Cage | ཕྱགས་ཁྲ་ | *cha-thra.* |
| Cairn | རྡོ་སྤུང་ | *do-pung.* |
| Cake | དེན་ཤིན་ *ch.* | *ten-shin.* |
| Do. (of tea) | པག་གག་ | *ṕa-ḱa.* |
| Calamity | བཀྲ་མི་ཤིས་ | *t́ra-mi·shi.* |
| Calculate, to | རྩིས་རྒྱབ་པ་ | *tsi gyaṕ-pa.* |
| Do. *hon.* | ཕྱགས་རྩིས་སྐྱོན་པ་ | *ja-tsi kyöm-pa.* |
| Calculation | རྩིས་ | *tsi.* |
| Do. *hon.* | ཕྱགས་རྩིས | *ja-tsi.* |
| Caldron | དཀྱིལ་ཁྲོ་ | *kyi-thro.* |
| Calendar | ཟླ་ཐོ་ | *da-tho.* |
| Do. *hon.* | གཟིགས་ཐོ་ | *śi tho.* |
| Calf (of the cow) | བེ་བེ་ (བེའུ་) | *ṕe-ṕe.* |
| Do. (of the leg) | རྐང་པའི་ཉ་ | *ḱang-pe nya.* |
| Do. *hon.* | ཞབས་ཀྱི་ཉ་ | *sḱaṕ ḱyi-nya.* |
| Call, to | སྐད་བཏང་ (གཏོང་) བ་ | *ke-tang-wa.* |
| Do. *hon.* | གསུང་གནང་བ། སྐད་གཏོང་ང་ (བ་) གནང་བ་ | *sung-nang-wa; ke-tong-nga nang-wa.* |

| | | |
|---|---|---|
| Call! (a person) | སྐད་གཏོང་ཤོག | *ḱe-tong-sho.* |
| Do. *hon.* | ཕེབས་ཞུས་ཤོག | *pḱe-sḱü-sho.* |
| Do. *h. hon.* | འཆིབ་རྒྱུ་གནང་ཞུས་ཤོག | *chhiṕ-gyu-nang sḱü-sho.* |
| Call, to (on a person) | བཅར་བ | *char-wa.* |
| Call, to (on superior) | སྐུ་མདུན་ལ་བཅར་བ | *ḱun-dün-la char-wa.* |
| Call up, to (a ghost, etc.) | སྤྱན་འདྲེན་ཞུ་བ | *chen-dren sḱu-wa.* |
| Calm (condition of country) | ཀླིངས་ཆགས་པོ། འཇམ་ཐིང་ཐིང | *hling-chaḱ-po; jam-thing-thing.* |
| Cambric | དར་རས | *t́ar-re.* |
| Camel (male or female) | ཨ་མོང་ (རྔ་མོང་) | *a-mong.* |
| Camel hair | ཨ་མོང་སྤུ་ (རྔ་མོང་སྤུ) | *a-mong-pu.* |
| Camp | སྒར | *gar.* |
| Camping ground | སྒར་ས | *ga-sa.* |
| Camphor | ག་བུར | *ḱa-ṕur.* |
| Canal | ཡོ་པོ་ (ཡུར་པོ་) | *yo-po.* |
| Cancel, to (blot out) | སུབ་པ | *suṕ-pa.* |
| Do. *hon.* | སུབ་པ་གནང་བ | *suṕ-pa nang-wa* |
| Cancel, to (set aside) | མེད་པར་བཟོ་བ | *me-pa śo-wa.* |
| Do. *hon.* | མེད་པར་བཟོ་བ་གནང་བ | *me-pa śo-wa nang-wa.* |
| Cancel, to (writing) | བྲིས་སུབ་བཏང་ (གཏོང་) བ | *t́ri-suṕ tang-wa.* |
| Do. *hon.* | བྲིས་སུབ་གནང་བ | *t́ri-suṕ nang-wa.* |

| | | |
|---|---|---|
| Candid | དྲང་པོ་ | *ťrang-po.* |
| Do. *hon.* | ཐུགས་རྒྱུ་དྲང་པོ་ | *thu-gyu ťrang-po.* |
| Candle (of Chinese make) | ལའ་ | *la.* |
| Candle (of English make) | རྒྱ་གར་ལའ་ | *gya-ḱar-la.* |
| Cane | སྤ་ | *pa.* |
| Cannibal | མིའི་ཤ་ཟ་མཁན་ | *mi-i sha-śa-khen.* |
| Cannon | མེ་སྒྱོགས་ | *me-gyo.* |
| Cannon-ball | མེ་སྒྱོགས་ཀྱི་མདེའུ་ | *me-gyoḱ-ḱi di-u.* |
| Canter, to | འཛོག་རྒྱབ་པ་ | *dzo-gyaṕ-pa.* |
| Cap | ཞྭ་མོ་ | *sḱa-mo.* |
| Do. *hon.* | དབུ་ཞྭ་ | *u-sḱa.* |
| Capable | ནུས་པོ་ | *nü-po.* |
| Capable, to be | ཐུབ་པ་ | *thuṕ-pa.* |
| Do. *hon.* | ཐུབ་པ་གནང་བ་ | *thuṕ-pa nang-wa.* |
| Capital, *s.* (as opposed to interest) | ངོ་པོ་ (དངོས་པོ་) | *ngo-po.* |
| Capital (letters) | དབུ་ཅན་ | *u-chen.* |
| Capital, *s.* (chief city) | རྒྱལ་ཁབ། རྒྱལ་ས་ | *gye-khaṕ, gye-sa.* |
| Capital, *adj.* (excellent) | ཡག་ཐག་ཆོད། ཨང་གི་དང་པོ་ | *yaḱ-thaḱ-chhö; ang-gi ťang-po.* |

| | | |
|---|---|---|
| Capitulate, to | མགོ་དགུར་བ་ | *go-gur-wa.* |
| Do. *hon.* | དབུ་དགུར་ར་ (བ་) གནང་བ་ | *u-gur-ra nang-wa.* |
| Capsize, to | མགོ་གཞུག་ལོག་པ་ | *go-sKu lok-pa.* |
| Captain (officer in command of 100 men) | བརྒྱ་དཔོན་ | *gya-pön.* |
| Captive | བཙོན་པ་ | *tsöm-pa.* |
| Capture, to | ཟིན་པ་ (འཛིན་པ་) | *śim-pa.* |
| Do. *hon.* | ཟིན་པ་ (འཛིན་པ་) གནང་བ་ | *śim-pa nang-wa.* |
| Carcass | རོ་ | *ro.* |
| Do. (of animal killed for meat) | ཤི་རོ་ | *shi-ro.* |
| Card | ཡི་གེ་ | *yi-ge.* |
| Cards, playing | ཤོན་ | *shön.* |
| Do. *hon.* | ཕྱག་ཤོན་ | *chha-shön.* |
| Cardamums | སུག་སྨེལ་ | *su-me.* |
| Care (anxiety) | སེམས་འཁྲལ་ | *sem-thre.* |
| Do. *hon.* | ཐུགས་འཁྲལ་ | *thu-thre.* |
| Care, to take (be careful) | བརྟན་བརྟན་བྱེད་པ་ | *ten-ten cKe-pa.* |
| Care of, to take (keep carefully) | ཉར་བ། ཆག་ག་བྱེད་པ་ | *nyar-wa; chak ka cKe-pa.* |

| | | |
|---|---|---|
| Care of, to take *hon.* | ཉར་ར་ (བ་) གནང་བ་ | *nyar-ra nang-wa.* |
| Do. *h. hon.* | ཐུགས་ཅག་གནང་བ་ | *thu-cha nang-wa.* |
| Career (manner of life) | བྱེད་སྟངས་ | *cḱe-tang.* |
| Do. *hon.* | གནང་སྟངས་ | *nang-tang.* |
| Carefully | ཅག་ག་བྱས་ནས་ | *cha-ḱa cḱe-ne.* |
| Do. *hon.* | ཐུགས་ཅག་གནང་ནས་ | *thu-cha nang-ne.* |
| Caress, to | བྱམས་པོ་བྱེད་པ་ | *cḱam-po cḱe-pa.* |
| Do. *hon.* | བྱམས་པོ་གནང་བ་ | *cḱam-po nang-wa.* |
| Carpenter | ཤིང་བཟོ་བ་ | *shing-śo wa.* |
| Do. *hon.* | དབུ་མཛད་ལགས་ | *um-dze-la.* |
| Carpet | ས་གདན་ | *sa-den.* |
| Carriage | ཤིང་རྟ་འཁོར་ལོ་ | *shing-ta ḱhor-lo.* |
| Carrier | དོས་པོ་འཁྱེར་མཁན་ | *tö-po ḱhyer-khen.* |
| Carrot | གུང་ལ་ཕུག་ | *ḱung-la-phuḱ.* |
| Carry, to | འཁྱེར་བ། འཁུར་བ་ | *ḱhyer-wa ; khur-wa.* |
| Do. *hon.* | སྣོམ་པ་ | *nom-pa.* |
| Cart, bullock | གླང་སྒ་རི་ | *lang-ga-ri.* |
| Cartridge | རྡིག་རིལ་ | *diḱ-ri.* |
| Carve to (on wood, iron, etc.) | སྤྲོས་རྒྱབ་པ་ | *trö-gyap̄-pa.* |
| Do. *hon.* | སྤྲོས་སྐྱོན་པ་ | *trö-ḱyöm-pa.* |

| | | |
|---|---|---|
| Cascade | བབ་ཆུ་ (འབབ་ཆུ་) | *ṕaṕ-chhu.* |
| Do. (over rocks) | བྲག་ཆུ་ | *traḱ-chhu.* |
| Case (law suit) | ཁ་མཆུ་ | *ḱham-chhu.* |
| Do. (box) | སྒམ་ | *gam.* |
| Do. *hon.* | ཕྱག་སྒམ་ | *chha-gam.* |
| Do. (covering) | ཤུབས་ | *shuṕ.* |
| Cash | དངུལ་ | *ngü.* |
| Do. *hon.* | ཕྱག་དངུལ་ | *chha-ngü.* |
| Cashier | ཕྱག་མཛོད་ | *chhan-dzö.* |
| Cashmere | ཁ་ཆེའི་ལུང་པ་ | *ḱha-chhe lung-pa.* |
| Cask | ཆུ་རུམ་མ། ཆུ་བཟོམ་ | *chhu-rum-ma ; chhu-śom.* |
| Cast away, to | དབྱུག་པ་ | *yuḱ-pa.* |
| Do. *hon.* | དབྱུག་ག་ (པ་) གནང་བ་ | *yuḱ ḱa nang-wa.* |
| Caste | རུས་ | *rü.* |
| Do. *hon.* | སྐུ་རུས་ | *ḱu-rü.* |
| Castle | རྫོང་ | *dzong.* |
| Castrate, to | ཤ་བཅད་ (གཅོད་) པ་ | *sha-che-pa.* |
| Cat | ཞི་མི་ | *sḱi-mi.* |
| Cataract | ཧ་རི་ལོང་ང་ | *ha-ri-long-nga.* |
| Catarrh | ཆམ་པ་ | *chham-pa.* |

| | | |
|---|---|---|
| Catarrh, *hon.* | མགུལ་ཆམ་ | *gün-chham.* |
| Catch, to | ཟིན་པ་ (འཛིན་པ་) | *śim-pa.* |
| Do. *hon.* | ཟིན་པ་ (འཛིན་པ་) གནང་བ་ | *śim-pa nang-wa.* |
| Catechu | དོས་ཛ་ | *tö-ja.* |
| Caterpillar | ས་འབུ་ | *sa-bu.* |
| Cattle | བ་གླང་ | *ṕa-lang.* |
| Cattle-disease | ཕྱུགས་ནད་ | *chhu ne.* |
| Cauliflower | ཀོ་པི་མེ་ཏོག་ | *ko-pi me-toḱ.* |
| Cause (reason) | རྐྱེན། རྒྱུ་རྐྱེན་ | *kyen ; gyu-kyen.* |
| Cautious, to be | རྟེན་ལྡན་བྱེད་པ་ | *ten-den cḱe-pa.* |
| Do. *hon.* | རྟེན་ལྡན་གནང་བ་ | *ten-den nang-wa.* |
| Cavalry | རྟ་དམག་ | *ta-ma.* |
| Cave of earth | ས་ཕུག་ | *sa-phu.* |
| Cave of rock | བྲག་ཕུག་ | *ťraḱ-phu.* |
| Cavity | ཨི་ཁུང་ | *i-khung.* |
| Cease, to | འཆད་པ་ | *chhe-pa.* |
| Ceaseless | རྒྱུན་མི་ཆད་པ་ | *gyün-mi-chhe-pa.* |
| Ceiling | ཐོག་ཁ་ | *tho-kha.* |
| Celebrated | སྙན་གྲགས་ཆེན་པོ་ | *nyen-ťra chhem-po.* |
| Do. *hon.* | མཚན་སྙན་གྲགས་ཆེན་པོ་ | *tshen nyen-ťra chhem-po.* |

| | | |
|---|---|---|
| Cell (of hermit) | རི་ཁྲོད་ | *ri-thrö.* |
| Do. (of monks) | གྲྭ་ཤག་ | *t́ra-sha.* |
| Cemetery | དུར་ཁྲོད་ | *t́u-thrö.* |
| Censer | སྤོས་ཕོར་ | *pö-phor.* |
| Censure, to | གཤེ་གཤེ་བཏང་ (གཏོང་) བ་ | *she-she tang-wa.* |
| Do. *hon.* | བཀའ་བཀྱོན་གནང་བ་ | *kaṕ-kyön nang-wa.* |
| Centipede | རྐང་བརྒྱ་ལག་བརྒྱ་ | *kang-gya laḱ-gya.* |
| Centre | དཀྱིལ་ | *kyi.* |
| Centurion | བརྒྱ་དཔོན་ | *gya-pön.* |
| Ceremony | ལུགས་སྲོལ་ | *luḱ-sö.* |
| Ceremony (religious) | ཆོ་ག། སྐུ་རིམ་ | *chho-ga; ku-rim.* |
| Certain | ངེས་པ་ | *nge-pa.* |
| Do. *hon.* | ཐུགས་ངེས་པ་ | *thu-nge-pa.* |
| Certainly | ཏེན་ལྡན། ངོ་ཐོག་ | *ten-den; ngo-tho.* |
| Certainty | བརྟན་པོ། ངེས་པ། ཏེན་ལྡན་ | *tem-po; nge-pa; ten-den.* |
| Certificate | བཀའ་ཤོག་ | *ka-sho.* |
| Chaff (of grain) | ཕུང་མ་ | *phung-ma.* |
| Chain, iron | ལྕགས་ཐག་ | *chaḱ-tha.* |
| Do. brass | རག་ཐག་ | *raḱ-tha.* |
| Chair | རྐུབ་ཀྱག། ཁྲིའུ་ཤིང་ | *kuṕ-kya; thri-u-shing.* |

| | | |
|---|---|---|
| Chair, *hon.* | ཞབས་ཀྱག་ | *sKaṕ-kya.* |
| Do. (high chair used as throne) | བཞུགས་ཁྲི་ | *sKuk-thri.* |
| Chairman | འཁྲིད་པ་ | *thri-pa.* |
| Chalk | ས་དཀར། དཀར་རྩི་ | *sa-kar ; kar-tsi.* |
| Chamber | ཁང་མིག་ | *khang-mi.* |
| Do. *hon.* | གཟིམ་ཆུང་ | *śim-chhung.* |
| Chamber, sleeping | ཉལ་ས་ | *nye-sa.* |
| Do. *hon.* | གཟིམ་ཁང་ | *śim-khang.* |
| Chamberlain | གཟིམ་དཔོན་ཆེན་པོ་ | *śim-pön chhem-po.* |
| Chance (accident) | བར་ཆད་ | *ṕar-chhe.* |
| Do. (luck) | བསོ་བདེ་ (བསོད་བདེ་) | *so-de.* |
| Do. *hon.* | སྐུ་བསོད་ | *ku-sö.* |
| Change, to, *v.t.* | སྒྱུར་བ་ | *gyur-wa.* |
| Do. *hon.* | སྒྱུར་ར་ (བ་) གནང་བ་ | *gyur-ra nang-wa.* |
| Change, to, *v.i.* | འགྱུར་བ་ | *gyur-wa.* |
| Change, to, (exchange) | རྗེ་པོ་རྒྱབ་པ་ | *je-po gyaṕ-pa.* |
| Do. *hon.* | རྗེ་པོ་སྐྱོན་པ་ | *je-po kyöm-pa.* |
| Channel (for irrigation) | ཡོ་པོ་ (ཡུར་པོ་) | *yo-po.* |
| Chap, to (of skin) | གས་པ་ | *ke-pa.* |

| | | |
|---|---|---|
| Chapel | ཆོས་ཁང་ | *chhö-khang.* |
| Chapter | ལེའུ་ | *li-u.* |
| Character | བྱེད་སྟངས་ | *cḱe-tang.* |
| Do. *hon.* | གནང་སྟངས་ | *nang-tang.* |
| Charcoal | སོལ་ལ་ (སོལ་བ་) | *sö-la.* |
| Charge, to (price) | གོང་ལབ་པ་ | *ḱong laṕ-pa.* |
| Charge of, to give into | རྩིས་སྤྲོད་པ་ | *tsi tre-pa.* |
| Charge of, to take | རྩིས་ལེན་པ་ | *tsi lem-pa.* |
| Charitable | དགེ་སེམས་ཆེན་པོ་ | *ge sem chhem-po.* |
| Charity (alms) | སྦྱིན་པ། བསོད་སྙོམས་ | *jim-pa; sö-nyom.* |
| Charity of mind | སྙིང་རྗེ། དགེ་སེམས་ | *nying-je; ge-sem.* |
| Charm (amulet) | རྟེན་ | *ten.* |
| Do. (worn on person) | སྲུང་ང་ (སྲུང་བ་) | *trung-nga.* |
| Do. *hon.* | མགུལ་སྲུང་ | *gü-sung.* |
| Charm-box | གའུ་ | *ḱa-u.* |
| Do. *hon.* | མགུལ་གའུ་ | *gü-ḱa-u.* |
| Chase, to | གཞུག་དེད་ཕྱིན་པ་ | *sḱuk-t́e chhim-pa.* |
| Do. *hon.* | གཞུག་དེད་ཞེབ་པ་ | *sḱuk-t́e phe-pa.* |
| Chasm | སེར་ཀ་ | *ser-ka.* |
| Chat, to | ཁ་ལས་བཤད་ (ཤོད་) པ་ | *khaṕ-le she-pa.* |

| | | |
|---|---|---|
| Chat, to *hon.* | ཞལ་ལས་གསུང་བ་ | *sKe-le sung-wa.* |
| Cheap | ཁེ་པོ་ | *khe-po.* |
| Cheat, to | མགོ་སྐོར་བཏང་ (གཏོང་) བ། | *go-kor tang-wa.* |
| | མགོ་སྐོར་བ་ | *go kor-wa.* |
| Do. *hon.* | མགོ་སྐོར་གཏོང་ང་ (བ་) གནང་བ་ | *go-kor tong-nga nang-wa.* |
| Do. *inf.* to *sup.* | དབུ་སྐོར་ཞུ་བ་ | *u-kor sKu-wa.* |
| Check, to (stop) | བཀག་པ་ (འགོགས་པ་) | *kaK-pa.* |
| Do. *hon.* | བཀག་ག་ (བཀག་པ་) གནང་བ་ | *kaK-Ka nang-wa.* |
| Cheek | འདན་ཁོག། འགྲམ་པ་ | *den-kho ; dram-pa.* |
| Do. *hon.* | ཞལ་འགྲམ་ | *sKen-dram.* |
| Cheeky | གྱོང་པོ་ | *Kyong-po.* |
| Cheerful, to be | སེམས་དགའ་བ་ | *sem-ga-wa.* |
| Do. *hon.* | ཐུགས་མཉེས་པ་ | *thu-nye-pa.* |
| Cheese | ཆུར་ར་ | *chhu-ra.* |
| Do. *hon.* | བཞེས་ཆུར་ | *sKip-chhur.* |
| Do. (mixed with butter) | ཐུད་ | *thü.* |
| Do. *hon.* | བཞེས་ཐུད་ | *sKip-thü.* |
| Do. (another kind) | ཆུར་ཞིབ་ | *chhur-sKip.* |

| | | |
|---|---|---|
| Chemist | སྨན་ཚོང་པ་ | *men tshong-pa.* |
| Chess | མིག་དམག་ (མིག་མངས་) | *mi-ma.* |
| Do. *hon.* | སྤྱན་དམག་ (སྤྱན་མངས་) | *chen-ma.* |
| Chest | སྒམ་ | *gam.* |
| Do. *hon.* | ཕྱག་སྒམ་ | *chha-gam.* |
| Do. (of body) | བྲང་ཁོག་ | *ṕang-k̇ho.* |
| Do. *hon.* | སྐུ་བྲང་ | *k̇u-ṕang.* |
| Chestnut (horse), *m.* | སྐྱང་པོ་ | *kyang-po.* |
| Do. *f.* | སྐྱང་མོ་ | *kyang-mo.* |
| Chicken | བྱ་ཕྲུག་ | *cḱaṕ-thru.* |
| Chide, to | གཤེ་གཤེ་བཏང་ (གཏོང་) བ་ | *she-she tang-wa.* |
| Do. *hon.* | བཀའ་བཀྱོན་གནང་བ་ | *kaṕ-kyön nang-wa.* |
| Chief (among officials, etc.) | གཙོ་བོ་ | *tso-o.* |
| Chief Minister | བློན་ཆེན་ | *lön-chhen.* |
| Chiefly | ཕལ་ཆེར་ | *phe-chher.* |
| Chilblains, to suffer from | འཁྱགས་འབོས་འཐེབ་པ་ | *khyaḱ-bö theṕ-pa.* |
| Child | བུ་གུ་ | *pu-gu.* |
| Do. *m. hon.* | སྲས་ | *se.* |
| Do. *f. hon.* | སྲས་མོ་ | *tre-mo* or *se-mo.* |
| Children | བུ་བུ་མོ་ | *ṕu ṕu-mo.* |

| | | |
|---|---|---|
| Children, *hon.* | ཨ་བོ་སྲས་སྲོས་ | *a-wa se-sö.* |
| Chilli | སིལ་པན་ | *si-pen.* |
| Do. *hon.* | སྲུམ་སྨན་ | *trum-men.* |
| Chilly | གྲང་མོ། བསིལ་པོ་ | *ṫrang-mo; si-po.* |
| Do. *hon.* | སྐུ་བསིལ་པོ་ | *ku-si-po.* |
| Chimney | དུ་ཁུང་ (དུད་ཁུང་) | *ṫu-khung.* |
| Chin | མས་ལེ་ | *me-le.* |
| Do. *hon.* | ཞལ་མལ་ (ཞལ་མས་) | *sḱe-mel.* |
| China (country) | རྒྱ་ནག་ | *gya-na.* |
| China, *adj.* (porcelain) | དཀར་ཡོལ་ | *ka-yö.* |
| Do. *hon.* | ཞལ་དཀར་ | *sḱe-ka.* |
| Chinaman | རྒྱ་མི་ | *gya-mi.* |
| Chinese, *adj.* and *s.* | རྒྱ་མི་ | *gya-mi.* |
| Chinese Emperor | རྒྱ་ནག་གོང་མ། གོང་མ་ཆེན་པོ་ | *gya-na kong-ma; kong-ma chhem-po.* |
| Chinese language | རྒྱ་སྐད་ | *gya-ke.* |
| Chink (in wall, etc.) | སེར་ཀ་ | *se-ka.* |
| Chisel | ཟོང་ | *śong.* |
| Choke, to | གློ་སུབ་རྒྱབ་པ་ | *lo-suṕ gyaṕ-pa.* |
| Do. *hon.* | གློ་སུབ་སྐྱོན་པ་ | *lo-suṕ kyöm-pa.* |

| | | |
|---|---|---|
| Choked, to be | འགགས་པ་ | *gak-pa.* |
| Cholera | སྐྱུག་བཤལ་ | *kyuk-she.* |
| Choose, to (appoint) | སྐོ་བ་ | *ko-wa.* |
| Do. *hon.* | སྐོ་བ་གནང་བ་ | *ko-wa nang-wa.* |
| Choose, to (select) | འདམས་པ་ | *dam-pa.* |
| Do. *hon.* | འདམས་པ་གནང་བ་ | *dam-pa nang-wa.* |
| Chop (mutton chop) | ལུག་ཤའི་རྩིབ་མ་ | *luk-she tsi-ma.* |
| Do. *hon.* | གསོལ་སྐྱུམ་ལུག་ཤའི་རྩིབ་མ་ | *sö-trum luk-she tsi-ma.* |
| Do. to (meat) | བཙབ་པ་ | *tsaṕ-pa.* |
| Do. *hon.* | བཙབ་པ་གནང་བ་ | *tsaṕ-pa nang-wa.* |
| Do. to (wood, metal, etc.) | བཅད་པ་ (གཅོད་པ་) | *che-pa.* |
| Do. *hon.* | བཅད་ (གཅོད་) པ་གནང་བ་ | *che-pa nang-wa.* |
| Chopper | ཚེས་དོ་ | *tshe-t́o.* |
| Chopsticks | ཁོ་ཙེ་ *ch.* | *khö-t́se.* |
| Do. *hon.* | བཞེས་ཙེ་ | *sḱe-tse.* |
| Christ | མ་ཤི་ཀ་ | *ma-shi-ka.* |
| Chronicle | ལོ་རྒྱུས་ | *lo-gyü.* |
| Chum (in a monastery) | ཆོས་གྲོགས་ | *chhö-t́ro.* |
| Church | ཆོས་ཁང་ | *chhö-khang.* |
| Churn, *s.* | མདོང་མོ་ | *dong-mo.* |

| | | |
|---|---|---|
| Churn for milk | ཞོ་ལྡོང་ | *sȟo-dong.* |
| Do. for tea | ཇ་ལྡོང་ | *cȟan-dong.* |
| Do. *hon.* | གསོལ་ལྡོང་ | *sön-dong.* |
| Do. to (tea) | སྲུས་པ་ (སྲུབ་པ་) | *sü-pa.* |
| Do. *hon.* | སྲུས་ (སྲུབ་) པ་གནང་བ་ | *sü-pa nang-wa.* |
| Churn, to (milk) | ཞོ་དཀྲོག་པ་ | *sȟo-troǩ-pa.* |
| Cicatrice | རྨ་ཤུལ་ | *ma-shü.* |
| Cinder (hot) | མེ་མདག་ | *men-da.* |
| Cipher (zero) | ཀླད་ཀོར་ | *le-kor.* |
| Circle | སྒོ་སྐོར་ (སྒོར་སྒོར་) | *go-kor.* |
| Circular | ཀོར་ཀོར་ | *kor-kor.* |
| Circumference | སྒོར་ཐིག་ | *gor thiǩ.* |
| Circumstance | རྐྱེན་ | *kyen.* |
| Citadel | རྫོང་ | *dzong.* |
| City | གྲོང་ཁྱེར་ | *ťrong-khyer.* |
| Civil, (honorific, of conversation) | ཞེ་ས་ | *sȟe-sa.* |
| Claim | ཐོབ་སྐལ་ | *thoṕ-ke.* |
| Clairvoyance | མངོན་ཤེས་ | *ngön she.* |
| Do. *hon.* | མངོན་མཁྱེན་ | *ngön-khyen.* |
| Clamour | ཨུར་སྒྲ་ | *u-dra.* |

| | | |
|---|---|---|
| Clap, the hands, to | ལག་པ་རྡབ་པ་ | *laḱ-pa daṕ-pa.* |
| Do. *hon.* | ཕྱག་རྡབ་པ་ | *chha-daṕ-pa.* |
| Clarified butter | མར་ཁུ་ | *mar-khu.* |
| Clarify, to (butter) | མར་བསྐུ་བ་ | *mar sḱu-wa.* |
| Clarionet | རྒྱ་གླིང་ | *gya-ling.* |
| Clasp, to | འཁྱུད་པ་ | *khyü-pa.* |
| Do. *hon.* | འཁྱུད་པ་གནང་བ་ | *khyü-pa nang-wa.* |
| Class (kind) | རིམ་པ་ | *rim-pa.* |
| Do. (in school) | གྲལ་ | *ťre.* |
| Do. *hon.* | བསྐུགས་གྲལ་ | *sḱu-ťre.* |
| Claw | སྡེར་མོ་ | *der-mo.* |
| Clay | འདག་པ་ | *daḱ-pa.* |
| Clean | གཙང་མ་ | *tsang-ma.* |
| Do. to | འཁྲུ་བ་ | *thru-wa.* |
| Do. *hon.* | འཁྲུད་པ་གནང་བ་ | *thrü-pa nang-wa.* |
| Clean, to (by wiping) | འཕྱིད་པ་ | *chhi-pa.* |
| Do. *hon.* | འཇག་ཕྱིད་གནང་བ་ | *ja-chhi nang-wa.* |
| Clean, to (by rubbing and wiping) | འཕྱིད་དར་གཏོང་བ་ | *chhi-ťar tong-wa.* |
| Do. *hon.* | འཇག་འཕྱིད་གནང་བ་ | *ja-chhi nang-wa.* |
| Clean, to (by sweeping) | གེ་རྒྱབ་པ་ | *ḱe-gyaṕ-pa.* |

| | | |
|---|---|---|
| Clean, to (by sweeping) *hon.* | གེ་སྐྱོན་པ་ | *ke-kyöm-pa.* |
| Cleansed (purified) | དག་པོ་ | *ťak-po.* |
| Clear (of glass) | གསལ་པོ་ | *se-po.* |
| Do. (of air) | དྭངས་པོ་ | *tang-po.* |
| Cleave, to (wood etc.) | གཤགས་པ་ (གཤོག་པ་) | *shak-pa.* |
| Do. *hon.* | གཤགས་ག་ (གཤོག་པ་) གནང་བ་ | *shak-ka nang-wa.* |
| Cleft | སེར་ཀ་ | *se-ka.* |
| Clergy | གྲྭ་པ་ | *ťra-pa.* |
| Do. *hon.* | དགེ་འདུན་ | *gen-dün.* |
| Clerk | དྲུང་ཡིག་ | *ťrung-yi.* |
| Do. *hon.* | དྲུང་ཡིག་ལགས་ | *ťrung-yi-la.* |
| Clever | རིག་པ་ཆེན་པོ་ | *rik-pa chhem-po.* |
| Do. *hon.* | ཐུགས་རིག་ཆེན་པོ་ | *thu-rik chhem-po.* |
| Climate | བསིལ་དྲོས་ | *si-ťrö.* |
| Climb, to | འཛག་པ་ (འཛེག་པ་) | *dzak-pa.* |
| Do. *hon.* | འཛག་ག་ (འཛེག་པ་) གནང་བ་ | *dzak-ka nang-wa.* |
| Cling, to | འཇུས་པ་ | *jü-pa.* |
| Do. *hon.* | འཇུས་པ་གནང་བ་ | *jü-pa nang-wa.* |
| Cloak | ཆུ་པ་ | *chhu-pa.* |

| | | |
|---|---|---|
| Cloak. *hon.* | ན་བཟའ་ | *nam-śa.* |
| Clock | ཆུ་ཚོད་འཁོར་ལོ་ | *chhu-ťshö khor-lo.* |
| Cloisonné | ཀུ་ཀུ་ཤ་ | *ḱu-ḱu-sha.* |
| Close to, *adv.* and *post.* | ཙ་ (ཙར།) ཐག་ཉེ་པོ་ | *tsa ; tha-nye-po.* |
| Do. to | བཀག་པ་ (འགེགས་པ་) | *kaḱ-pa.* |
| Do. *hon.* | བཀག་ག་ (འགེགས་པ་) གནང་བ་ | *kaḱ ḱa nang-wa.* |
| Close up, *v.i.* (of flowers, etc.) | ཁ་ཟུམ་པ་ | *kha-śum-pa.* |
| Close fisted | ལག་པ་དམ་པོ་ | *laḱ-pa ťam-po.* |
| Do. *hon.* | ཕྱག་དམ་པོ་ | *chha-ťam po.* |
| Cloth, cotton | རས་ | *re.* |
| Do. *hon.* | སྐུ་རས་ | *ku-re.* |
| Cloth, woollen (of European or Indian make) | འགོ་སྣམ་ | *go-nam.* |
| Do (of Tibetan make) | སྣམ་བུ་ | *nam-ṕu.* |
| Do. *hon.* | ཕྱག་སྣམ་ | *chha-nam.* |
| Clothe, to | གོན་པ་ | *ḱöm-pa.* |
| Do. *hon.* | བཞེས་པ་ | *sḱe-pa.* |
| Clothes | དུག་ལོག་ | *ťu-lo.* |
| Do. *hon.* | ན་བཟའ་ | *nam-śa.* |

| | | |
|---|---|---|
| Clothes, to put on | དུག་ལོག་གོན་པ་ | *ṫu-lo köm-pa.* |
| Do. *hon.* | ན་བཟའ་བཞེས་པ་ | *nam-śa sḱe-pa.* |
| Do. to take off | དུག་ལོག་ཕིས་ (འབུད་) པ་ | *ṫu-lo pi-pa.* |
| Do. *hon.* | ན་བཟའ་བསིལ་བ་ | *nam-śa si-wa.* |
| Cloud (in sky) | སྤྲིན་པ་ | *trim-pa.* |
| Do. (fog) | རྨུགས་པ་ | *muḱ-pa.* |
| Cloudy, to become | འཐིབ་པ་ | *thiṕ-pa.* |
| Clove | ལི་ཤི་ | *li-shi.* |
| Clown | དབུ་འཁོར་ཤུ་མཁན་ | *wu-khor sḱu-khen.* |
| Clumsy | སྡུག་རུལ་ | *duḱ-ru.* |
| Coagulate, to (of blood, etc.) | འཁྱག་པ་ | *khyaḱ-pa.* |
| Coal | རྡོ་སོལ་ | *do-sö.* |
| Coarse | རྩུབ་པོ་ | *tsuṕ-po.* |
| Coast | ཆུ་འགྲམ་ | *chhu-dram.* |
| Coat | ཆུ་པ་ | *chhu-pa.* |
| Do. *hon.* | ན་བཟའ་ | *nam-śa.* |
| Do. of mail | ཁྲབ་ | *thraṕ.* |
| Coax, to (for good object) | བསླབ་བྱ་རྒྱབ་པ་ | *laṕ-cḰa gyaṕ-pa.* |
| Do. *hon.* | བཀའ་སློབ་གནང་བ་ | *ka-loṕ nang-wa.* |
| Coax, to (for bad object) | སླུ་བ་ | *lu-wa.* |

| | | |
|---|---|---|
| Coax, to (for bad object) *hon.* | སླུ་བ་གནང་བ་ | *lu-wa nang-wa.* |
| Cobbler | ཉོ་བཟོ་ | *nyop-so.* |
| Do. *hon.* | སེམས་གསོ་གཏོང་ང་ (བ) གནང་མཁན་ | *sem-so tong-nga nang-khen.* |
| Do. *hon.* (*inf.* to *sup.*) | ཐུགས་གསོ་ཕྱུལ་མཁན་ | *thuk-so phü-khen.* |
| Confidential | གསང་བ་ | *sang-wa.* |
| Cobweb | སྡོམ་ཐག་ | *dom-tha.* |
| Cock | བྱ་ཕོ་ | *cKa-pho.* |
| Code of law | ཁྲིམས་ཡིག་ | *thrim-yi.* |
| Coffer | སྒམ་ | *gam.* |
| Do. *hon.* | ཕྱག་སྒམ་ | *chha-gam.* |
| Coffin | རོ་སྒམ་ | *ro-gam.* |
| Do. *hon.* | སྤུར་སྒམ་ | *pur-gam.* |
| Cohere, to, *v.i.* (stick together) | འབྱར་བ་ | *jar-wa.* |
| Coil, to (of snake) | སྒོ་འཁོར་བྱེད་པ་ | *go-khor cKe-pa.* |
| Coin (silver, value four annas) | ཊཾ་ཀ་ | *tang-ka.* |
| Do. (silver, value two and half annas) | ཞོ་གང་ | *sKo-kang.* |
| Do. (silver, value two annas) | ཕྱེད་གས་ | *chhi-ke.* |

| | | |
|---|---|---|
| Coin (silver, value one anna and one pice) | སྐར་མ་ལྔ་ | ka-ma-nga. |
| Do. (silver, value three pice) | ཁ་གང་ | kha-kang. |
| Do. (silver, value four pies) | ཁ་ཕྱེད་ | khaṕ-chhe. |
| Do. (Chinese pice) | ཏོང་ཙེ་ | ťong-tse. |
| Cold, *adj.* (of body, meat, etc.) | གྲང་མོ། བསིལ་པོ་ | ťrang-mo ; si-po. |
| Do. *hon.* | སྐུ་བསིལ་པོ་ | ku si-po. |
| Do. (to feel) | འཁྱགས་པ་ | khyak-pa. |
| Do. *hon.* | སྐུ་བསིལ་བ་ | ku-si-wa. |
| Cold, *s.* | འཁྱགས་པ་ | khyak-pa. |
| Do. (catarrh) | ཆམ་པ་ | chham-pa. |
| Do. *hon.* | མགུལ་ཆམ་ | gü-chham. |
| Do. to have (in the head) | ཆམ་པ་ན་བ་ | chham-pa na-wa. |
| Do. *hon.* | མགུལ་ཆམ་སྙུང་བ་ | gü-chham nyung-wa. |
| Colic | རྒྱུ་གཟེར་ | gyu-śer. |
| Collar | གོང་ང་ (གོང་བ་) | kong-nga. |
| Do. (after Chinese fashion) | ལིང་ཙེ་ | ling-tse. |

| | | |
|---|---|---|
| Collar (after Chinese fashion) *hon.* | མགུལ་གླིང་ | *gü-ling.* |
| Colleague | རོགས་བྱེད་མཁན་ | *ro-ḱe-khen.* |
| Collect, to | སྡུད་པ་ | *dü-pa.* |
| Do. *hon.* | སྡུད་པ་གནང་བ་ | *dü-pa nang-wa.* |
| Collect, to (wood, etc.) | སྒྲུག་པ་ | *druḱ-pa.* |
| Do. *hon.* | སྒྲུག་ག་ (པ་) གནང་བ་ | *druḱ-ḱa nang-wa.* |
| College (of monks) | གྲྭ་ཚང་ | *ťra-tshang.* |
| Colloquial (language) | ཕལ་སྐད་ | *phe-ke.* |
| Colonel (officer in command of 500 men to 1,000 men) | མདའ་དཔོན་ | *de-pön.* |
| Colour (dye) | ཚོས་ | *tshö.* |
| Do. natural | མདོག་ | *do.* |
| Do. to lose | ཚོས་ཡལ་བ་ | *tshö-ye-wa.* |
| Colt | ཏི་གི་ (ཏིའུ་) | *ti-ḱi.* |
| Do. of an ass | ཨུ་ཏྲི་ | *u-ti.* |
| Column | ཀ་ (ཀ་བ་) | *ka.* |
| Comb | སྐྲ་གཤད་ | *tra-she.* |
| Do. *hon.* | དབུ་ར་ཤད་ | *u-she.* |
| Do. to | སྐྲ་གཤད་པ་ | *tra-she-pa.* |
| Do. *hon.* | དབུ་གཤད་སྐྱོན་པ་ | *u-she kyöm-pa.* |

| | | |
|---|---|---|
| Combat | རྒྱབ་འདྲེ་ | *gyam-dre.* |
| Come, *imp.* | ཤོག་ | *sho.* |
| Do. to | ཡོང་བ་ | *yong-wa.* |
| Do. *hon.* | ཕེབ་པ་ | *phe-pa.* |
| Do. *h. hon.* | འཆིབ་རྒྱུ་གནང་བ་ | *chhiṕ gyu nang-wa.* |
| Come back, to | ལོག་ཡོང་བ་ | *lo yong-wa.* |
| Do. *hon.* | ལོག་ཕེབ་པ་ | *lo-phe-pa.* |
| Do. *h. hon.* | འཆིབ་རྒྱུ་གནང་བ་ | *chhiṕ gyu nang-wa.* |
| Come, to (before *sup.*) | མཇལ་བ་ | *je wa.* |
| Do. *hon.* | མཇལ་ར་ (བ་) གནང་བ་ | *je-ra nang-wa.* |
| Come out, to | འཐོན་པ་ | *thöm-pa.* |
| Do. *hon.* | ཕྱི་ལོགས་ལ་ཕེབ་པ་ | *chhi-lo la pheṕ-pa.* |
| Come together (of persons) | འཛོམ་པ། འཚོགས་པ་ | *dzom-pa ; tshok-pa.* |
| Do. *hon.* | ལྷན་རྒྱས་ཚོགས་པ་གནང་བ་ | *lhen-gye tshok-pa nang-wa.* |
| Comet | དུ་བ་མཇུག་རིང་ | *t́u-wa juk-ring.* |
| Comfortable | སྐྱིད་པོ་ | *kyi-po.* |
| Do. *hon.* | སྤྲོ་པོ་ | *tro-po.* |
| Comic | བགད་མོ་བྲོ་པོ་ | *ge-mo t́ro po.* |
| Do. *hon.* | ཞལ་མོ་བྲོ་པོ་ | *sḱe-mo t́ro-po.* |
| Command, commandment | བཀའ་ | *ka.* |

| | | |
|---|---|---|
| Command, to (give order) | བཀའ་གནང་བ་ | *ka-nang-wa.* |
| Do. to (be in command of) | འགོ་ཁྲིད་བྱེད་པ་ | *go-cKe cKe-pa.* |
| Do. *hon.* | འགོ་ཁྲིད་གནང་བ་ | *go-cKe nang-wa.* |
| Commander | དམག་དཔོན་ | *maǩ-pön.* |
| Commander-in-Chief | སྤྱི་མདའ་ | *chin-da.* |
| Commence, to | མགོ་བཙུགས་ (འཛུགས་) པ་ | *go-tsuǩ-pa.* |
| Do. *hon.* | དབུ་བཙུགས་ (འཛུགས་) པ་ | *u-tsuǩ-pa.* |
| Commencement | ཐོག་མ་ | *tho-ma.* |
| Commend, to | སྟོད་ར་བཏང་ (གཏོང་) བ་ | *ťö-ra tang-wa.* |
| Do. *hon.* | སྟོད་ར་གཏོང་ང་ (བ་) གནང་བ་ | *tö-ra tong-nga nang-wa.* |
| Commendation | སྟོད་ར་ | *tö-ra.* |
| Commerce | ཚོང་ | *tshong.* |
| Do. *hon.* | རྒྱ་ཚོང་ | *gya-tshong.* |
| Commissary (delegate) | ཚབ་ | *tshaṕ.* |
| Do. *hon.* | སྐུ་ཚབ་ | *ku-tshaṕ.* |
| Commit, to | བྱེད་པ་ | *cKe-pa.* |
| Do. *hon.* | གནང་བ་ | *nang-wa.* |
| Do. to (to one's care) | བཅོལ་བ་ (འཆོལ་བ་) | *chöl-wa.* |
| Do. *hon.* | བཅོལ་ར་ (བ་) གནང་བ་ | *chö-ra nang-wa.* |

| | | |
|---|---|---|
| Common, *adj.* (vulgar) | དཀྱུས་མ་ | *kyü-ma.* |
| Do. (plentiful) | འབེལ་པོ་ | *be-po.* |
| Do. (of language *opp.* to *hon.*) | ཞེ་ས་མེད་པ་ | *sKe-sa me-pa.* |
| Do. in (jointly) | མཉམ་འབྲེལ་ | *nyam-dre.* |
| Do. *hon.* | ཕྱག་འབྲེལ་ | *chha-dre.* |
| Companion | རོགས་ | *ro.* |
| Do. (in work) | ལས་རོགས་ | *le-ro.* |
| Do. *hon.* | ཕྱག་འབྲེལ་ | *chha-dre.* |
| Company (of persons) | མི་ཚོགས་ | *mi-tsho.* |
| Compare, to | སྡུར་བ་ | *dur-wa.* |
| Do. *hon.* | སྡུར་ར་ (བ་) གནང་བ་ | *dur ra nang-wa.* |
| Comparison | དཔེ་ | *pe.* |
| Compasses (a pair of) | སྐོར་ཐིག་ | *kor-thi.* |
| Compassion | སྙིང་རྗེ་ | *nying-je.* |
| Do. *hon.* | ཐུགས་རྗེ་ | *thu-je.* |
| Compel, to | ཨུ་ཚུགས་བྱེད་པ་ | *u-tshu cKe-pa.* |
| Do. *hon.* | ཨུ་ཚུགས་གནང་བ་ | *u-tshu nang-wa.* |
| Compelled, to be | དགོས་པ་ | *gö-pa.* |
| Compensate, to | འགྲོ་སོང་སྟེར་བ་ | *dro-song ter-wa.* |
| Compensation | འགྲོ་སོང་ | *dro-song.* |

| | | |
|---|---|---|
| Compete, to | སྡུར་བ་ | *dur-wa.* |
| Do. *hon.* | སྡུར་ར་ (བ་) གནང་བ་ | *dur-ra nang-wa.* |
| Competent | འོས་པོ་ | *ö-po.* |
| Competitor | སྡུར་མཁན་ | *dur-khen.* |
| Do. *hon.* | སྡུར་ར་ (བ་) གནང་མཁན་ | *dur-ra nang-khen.* |
| Compile, to | སྒྲིག་པ་ | *driḱ-pa.* |
| Complain, to (in writing) | སྙན་ཞུ་ཕུལ་ (འབུལ་) བ་ | *nye-sḱu phü ua.* |
| Do. to (verbally) | ཞུ་ཐུག་བྱེད་པ་ | *sḱu-thu cḱe-pa.* |
| Do. *hon.* | ཞུ་ཐུག་གནང་བ་ | *sḱu-thu nang-wa.* |
| Complaint (petition) | སྙན་ཞུ་ | *nye-sḱu.* |
| Complete, to | ཚར་བ་ | *tshar-wa.* |
| Do. *hon.* | འགྲུབ་པ་ | *druṕ-pa.* |
| Completely | བད་དེ་ | *be-ṫe.* |
| Complicated | མགོ་རྙོག་ཚ་པོ་ | *go-nyo tsha-po.* |
| Compliment | ཕྱག་འབུལ་ | *chham-bü.* |
| Compliment, to (a superior) | ཕྱག་འབུལ་ཞུ་བ་ | *chham-bü sḱu-wa.* |
| Do. to (equals) | འདྲིས་མི་བཏང་ (གཏོང་) བ་ | *dri-me tang-wa.* |
| Compose, to (writing, &c.) | རྩོམ་པ་ | *tsom-pa.* |
| Do. *hon.* | རྩོམ་པ་གནང་བ་ | *tsom-pa nang-wa.* |
| Do. *h. hon.* | བཀའ་རྩོམ་གནང་བ་ | *ka tsom nang-wa.* |

| | | |
|---|---|---|
| Comprehend, to (understand) | ཧ་གོ་བ་ | *ha-ko-wa.* |
| Do. *hon.* | མཁྱེན་པ་ | *khyem-pa.* |
| Compress, to | བཙིར་བ་ | *tsir·wa.* |
| Do. *hon.* | བཙིར་ར་ (བ་) གནང་བ་ | *tsir-ra nang-wa.* |
| Comprise, to | སྡུད་པ་ | *dü-pa.* |
| Compromise, to (by mutual concession) | ནང་འགྲིག་བྱེད་པ། བར་འདུམ་བྱེད་པ་ | *nang drik cḱe-pa, par-dum cḱe pa.* |
| Do. *hon.* | བཀའ་བསྡུམ་གནང་བ་ | *nan-dum nang-wa.* |
| Computation | རྩིས་ | *tsi.* |
| Do. *hon.* | ཕྱགས་རྩིས་ | *ja-tsi.* |
| Compute, to | རྩིས་རྒྱབ་པ་ | *tsi-gyaṕ-pa.* |
| Do. *hon.* | ཕྱགས་རྩིས་གནང་བ་ | *ja-tsi nang-wa.* |
| Comrade | རོགས་ | *ro.* |
| Do. *hon.* | ཕྱག་འབྲེལ་ | *chha-dre.* |
| Concave | ཀོང་ཀོང་ | *kong-kong.* |
| Conceal, to | སྦེད་པ་ | *be-pa.* |
| Do. *hon.* | སྦེད་པ་གནང་བ་ | *be-pa nang-wa.* |
| Concede, to | སྟེར་བ་ | *ter-wa.* |
| Do. *hon.* | གནང་བ་ | *nang-wa.* |
| Conceited | ལྟ་བ་མཐོ་པོ་ | *ta-wa tho-po.* |

| | | |
|---|---|---|
| Conceive, to (a child) | བུ་གུ་འཁོར་བ། བུ་ཚ་འཆགས་པ་ | *pu gu khor-wa; pu-tsha chhak-pa.* |
| Do. *hon.* | ཨ་ལྷ་འཁོར་བ་ | *a-wa khor-wa.* |
| Concerning | དོན་ལ། སྐོར་ལ་ | *t́ön-la; kor-la.* |
| Conch-shell | དུང་ | *t́ung.* |
| Do. bracelet | དུང་སྐོར་ | *t́ung-ko.* |
| Do. *hon.* | ཕྱག་དུང་ | *chha-t́ung.* |
| Conclude, to | འཚར་བ་ | *tshar-wa.* |
| Do. *hon.* | འགྲུབ་པ་ | *drup-pa.* |
| Concur, to | མཐུན་པ་ | *thüm-pa.* |
| Do. *hon.* | མཐུན་པ་གནང་བ་ | *thüm-pa nang-wa.* |
| Condemn, to (as judge) | ཁྲིམས་བཏང་ (གཏོང་) བ་ | *thrim-tang-wa.* |
| Condemn, to, *hon.* | ཁྲིམས་གཏོང་ང་ (བ་) གནང་བ་ | *thrim tong-nga nang-wa.* |
| Do. *h. hon.* | བཀའ་ཁྲིམས་གནང་བ་ | *ka-thrim nang-wa.* |
| Condiment | ཤ་སྨན་ | *sha-men.* |
| Condition (state) | གནས་ཚུལ་ | *ne-tshü.* |
| Condole, to | སེམས་གསོ་བཏང་ (གཏོང་) བ་ | *sem-so tang-wa.* |
| Conduct, *s.* | བྱེད་སྟངས | *che-tang.* |
| Do. *hon.* | གནང་སྟངས་ | *nang-tang.* |
| Do. to (towards) | འཁྲིད་ཡོང་བ་ | *thri-yong-wa.* |
| Do. *hon.* | འཁྲིད་ཕེབ་པ་ | *thri-phe-pa.* |

| | | |
|---|---|---|
| Conduct to (away) | འཁྲིད་འགྲོ་བ་ | *thri-dro-wa.* |
| Do. *hon.* | འཁྲིད་ཕེབས་པ་ | *thri-phe-pa.* |
| Conduit (drain) | ཡོ་བོ་ (ཡུར་བོ་) | *yo-po.* |
| Cone of clay (with figures of gods) | ཚ་ཚ་ | *tsha-tsha.* |
| Confer, to (converse) | གྲོས་བྱེད་པ་ | *t́rö-cḱe-pa.* |
| Do. *hon.* | བཀའ་གྲོས་གནང་བ་ | *ka-t́rö nang-wa.* |
| Confer, to (give) | སྟེར་བ་ | *ter-wa.* |
| Do. *hon.* | གནང་བ་ | *nang-wa.* |
| Conference | གྲོས་ | *t́rö.* |
| Do. *hon.* | བཀའ་གྲོས་ | *ka-t́rö.* |
| Confess, to | བཤགས་པ་ | *shaḱ-pa.* |
| Do. *hon.* | མཐོལ་བཤགས་ཕུལ་ (འབུལ་) བ་ | *thö-sha phü-wa.* |
| Do. *h. hon.* | མཐོལ་བཤགས་འབུལ་ལ་ (བ་) གནང་བ་ | *thö-sha bül-la nang-wa.* |
| Confide, to | བློ་གཏད་བྱེད་པ་ | *lo-te cḱe-pa.* |
| Do. *hon.* | བློ་གཏད་གནང་བ་ | *lo-te nang-wa.* |
| Confidence | བློ་གཏད་ | *lo-te.* |
| Confine, to | བཙུག་པ་ (འཛུག་པ་) | *chuḱ-pa.* |
| Do. *hon.* | བཙུག་ག་ (འཛུག་པ་) གནང་བ་ | *chuḱ-ḱa nang-wa.* |

| | | |
|---|---|---|
| Confirm, to (statement etc.) | གཏན་ལྡན་བྱེད་པ་ | *ten·den cḱe-pa.* |
| Do. *hon.* | གཏན་ལྡན་གནང་བ་ | *ten-den nang-wa.* |
| Confiscate, to | གཞུང་བཞེས་བཏང་ (གཏོང་) བ་ | *sḱung-sḱe tang-wa.* |
| Do. *hon.* | གཞུང་བཞེས་གནང་བ་ | *sḱung-sḱe nang-wa.* |
| Confiscation | གཞུང་བཞེས་ | *sḱung-sḱe.* |
| Conflict | རྒྱབ་འདྲེ་ | *gyam-dre.* |
| Confounded, to be | མགོ་འཁོར་བ། མགོ་འཐོམས་པ་ | *go-ḱhor-wa ; go-thom-pa.* |
| Do. *hon.* | དབུ་འཁོར་བ། དབུ་འཐོམས་པ་ | *u-ḱhor-wa ; u-thom-pa.* |
| Confront, to | ར་འཕྲོད་བཏང་ (གཏོང་) བ་ | *raṕ thrö tang-wa.* |
| Do. *hon.* | ར་འཕྲོད་གཏོང་ང་(བ་)གནང་བ་ | *raṕ-thrö tong-nga nang-wa.* |
| Confused, to be | མགོ་འཁོར་བ་ | *go-ḱhor-wa.* |
| Do. *hon.* | དབུ་འཁོར་བ་ | *u-khor-wa.* |
| Confusing (intricate) | མགོ་རྙོག་ཚ་པོ། མགོ་རྙོག་ཆེན་པོ་ | *go-nyo tsha·po ; go-nyo chem·po.* |
| Do. *hon.* | དབུ་རྙོག་ཚ་པོ་ | *u-nyo tsha-po.* |
| Confusion (of speech) | ཁ་རྗོད་ | *khan-jö.* |
| Confusion | མགོ་དཀྲོག་ | *go·tro.* |
| Congeal, to | འཁྱགས་པ་ | *khyaḱ-pa.* |
| Congregate, to | འཛོམས་པ་ | *dzom-pa.* |
| Do. *hon.* | ལྷན་རྒྱས་ཚོགས་པ་ | *hlen-gye tshoḱ-pa.* |

| | | |
|---|---|---|
| Congregation | ཚོགས་ | *tsho.* |
| Conjure, to (do conjuring tricks) | མིག་འཕྲུལ་རྩེད་པ་ | *mik-thrü tse-pa.* |
| Do. *hon.* | མིག་འཕྲུལ་རྩེད་པ་གནང་བ་ | *mik-thrü tse-pa nang-wa.* |
| Conjure, to (implore) | ནན་ཏན་ཞུ་བ་ | *nen-ten sKu-wa.* |
| Do. *hon.* | ནན་ཏན་ཞུ་བ་གནང་བ་ | *nen-ten sKu-wa nang-wa.* |
| Conjure up, to (ghost, etc.) | སྤྱན་འདྲེན་ཞུ་བ་ | *chen-dren sKu-wa.* |
| Do. *hon.* | སྤྱན་འདྲེན་ཞུ་བ་གནང་བ་ | *chen-dren sKu-wa nang-wa.* |
| Conjuring tricks | མིག་འཕྲུལ་ | *mik-thrü.* |
| Do. *hon.* | སྤྱན་འཕྲུལ་ | *chen-thrü.* |
| Conjurer | མིག་འཕྲུལ་རྩེད་མཁན་ | *mik-thrü tse-Khen.* |
| Do. *hon.* | མིག་འཕྲུལ་གནང་མཁན་ | *mik thrü nang-khen.* |
| Connect, to (join together) | འཐུད་པ་ | *thü-pa.* |
| Do. *hon.* | འཐུད་པ་གནང་བ་ | *thü-pa nang-wa.* |
| Conquer, to | རྒྱལ་བ་ | *gye-wa.* |
| Do. *hon.* | རྒྱལ་ར་ (བ་) གནང་བ་ | *gye-ra nang-wa.* |
| Conquered, to be | འཕམ་པ་ | *pham-pa.* |
| Do. *hon.* | ཐུགས་འཕམ་པ་གནང་བ་ | *thu pham-pa nang-wa.* |
| Conscience, to have a | བཟང་ངན་ཤེས་པ་ | *śang-ngen she-pa.* |
| Do. *hon.* | བཟང་ངན་མཁྱེན་པ་ | *śang-ngen khyem-pa.* |
| Conscious, to be | དྲན་པ་ | *t́rem-pa.* |

| | | |
|---|---|---|
| Conscious, to be *hon* | ཐུགས་དྲན་གསོ་བ་ | *thu-tren so-wa.* |
| Consecrate, to | རབ་གནས་བྱེད་པ་ | *rap-ne che-pa.* |
| Do. *hon.* | རབ་གནས་གནང་བ་ | *rap ne nang wa.* |
| Consecration | རབ་གནས་ | *rap-ne.* |
| Consent, to | ཉན་པ་ | *nyem-pa.* |
| Do. *hon.* | གསན་པ་ | *sem pa.* |
| Consequence of, in | རྐྱེན་གྱིས་ | *kyen-kyi.* |
| Consequently | དེའི་རྐྱེན་བྱས་ནས་ | *tei-kyen che-ne.* |
| Consider, to | བསམ་བློ་བཏང་ (གཏོང་) བ་ | *sam lo tang-wa.* |
| Do. *hon.* | ཐུགས་བསམ་བཞེས་པ་ | *thu-sam she-pa.* |
| Considerable number of, a | མང་ཉུང་སྙོམ་པོ་གཅིག་ | *mang-nyung nyom po-chi.* |
| Console, to | སེམས་གསོ་བཏང་ (གཏོང་) བ་ | *sem-so tang-wa.* |
| Do. *inf.* to *sup.* | སེམས་གསོ་ཞུ་བ་ | *sem so shu-wa.* |
| Consonant, *s.* | གསལ་བྱེད་ | *se che.* |
| Conspicuous | མངོན་གསལ་ཆེན་པོ་ | *ngön se chhem-po.* |
| Constable | སྐོར་ཆག་པ་ | *ko-chak-pa.* |
| Constant | བརྟན་པོ་ | *tem-po.* |
| Constantly | རྟག་པ་རེ་བཞིན་ | *tak-pa re-shi.* |
| Constellation | གཟའ་སྐར་ | *za-ka.* |
| Constipation | རྩ་འགག་པ་ | *tsa-gak pa.* |

| | | |
|---|---|---|
| Construct, to | བཟོ་བ་ | *śo-wa.* |
| Do. *hon.* | བཟོ་བ་གནང་བ་ | *śo-wa nang-wa.* |
| Consult, to | གྲོས་དྲི་ (འདྲི་) བ་ | *ťrö-ťri-wa.* |
| Do. *hon.* | བཀའ་གྲོས་གནང་བ་ | *ka ťrö nang-wa.* |
| Consumed, to be | རྫོགས་པ་ | *dzoḱ-pa.* |
| Do. *hon.* | རྫོགས་ག་ (པ་) གནང་བ་ | *dzoḱ-ḱa nang-wa.* |
| Consumption (pulmonary) | གཅོང་ནད་ | *chong-ne.* |
| Contamination | གྲིབ་ | *ťriṕ.* |
| Do. *hon.* | སྐུ་གྲིབ་ | *ku-ťriṕ.* |
| Contemplate, to (consider) | བསམ་བློ་བཏང་ (གཏོང་) བ་ | *sam-lo tang-wa.* |
| Do. *hon.* | ཐུགས་བསམ་བཞེས་པ་ | *thu-sam sḱe-pa.* |
| Do. to (meditate on religious things) | སྒོམ་རྒྱབ་པ་ | *gom-gyaṕ-pa.* |
| Do. *hon.* | སྒོམ་སྐྱོན་པ་ | *gom-kyöm-pa.* |
| Contemporary | ལོ་ཟླ་ | *lon da.* |
| Do. *hon.* | དགོང་ཟླ་ (དགུང་ཟླ་) | *gong-da.* |
| Contend, to (in war) | དམག་རྒྱབ་པ་ | *ma-gyaṕ-pa.* |
| Do. *hon.* | དམག་སྐྱོན་པ་ | *ma-kyöm pa.* |
| Contented, to be | འདོད་པ་གང་བ་ | *dö-pa ḱang-wa.* |
| Do. *hon.* | ཐུགས་འདོད་གང་བ་ | *thung-dö ḱang-wa.* |

| | | |
|---|---|---|
| Continent, *s.* | གླིང་ | *ling.* |
| Continually | ནམ་ ན། དུས་རྒྱུན་ | *nam-gyü ; t́ü-gyün.* |
| Contract, a large written | གན་རྒྱ་ | *ḱam-gya.* |
| Do. a small written | འཛིན་ | *dzin.* |
| Do. *hon.* | བཀའ་འཛིན། ཕྱག་འཛིན་ | *kan-dzin ; chha-dzin.* |
| Do. to let out on | བོགས་མ་ལ་བཏང་ ( གཏོང་ ) བ་ | *ṕok-ma-la tang-wa.* |
| Do. *hon.* | བོགས་གཏོང་གནང་བ་ | *ṕok-tong nang-wa.* |
| Contractor | བོགས་འཛིན་པ་ | *ṕok-dzin-pa.* |
| Contradict, to | རྒྱབ་འགལ་བྱེད་པ་ | *gyam-ge cḱe-pa.* |
| Do. *hon.* | ཐུགས་འགལ་གནང་བ་ | *thuk-ge nang-wa.* |
| Contradictory | རྒྱབ་འགལ་ | *gyam-ge.* |
| Contrite, to be | འགྱོད་པ་སྐྱེད་པ་ | *gyö-pa kye-pa.* |
| Do. *hon.* | ཐུགས་འགྱོད་གནང་བ་ | *thung-gyö nang-wa.* |
| Contrition | འགྱོད་པ་ | *gyö-pa.* |
| Do. *kon.* | ཐུགས་འགྱོད་ | *thung-gyö.* |
| Control | དབང་ | *wang.* |
| Do. *hon.* | སྐུ་དབང་ | *ku-wang.* |
| Control, to | དབང་བྱེད་པ་ | *wang-cḱe-pa.* |
| Do. *hon.* | སྐུ་དབང་གནང་བ་ | *ku-wang nang-wa.* |
| Controversy | རྩོད་པ་ | *tsö-pa.* |

| | | |
|---|---|---|
| Convent | ཨ་ནིའི་དགོན་པ་ | *a-ni-i göm-pa.* |
| Conversation | སྐད་ཆ་ | *ke-chha.* |
| Do. *hon.* | གསུང་གྲོས་ | *sung-ťrö.* |
| Converse, to | སྐད་ཆ་བྱེད་པ་ | *ke-chha cĥe-pa.* |
| Do. *hon.* | གསུང་གྲོས་གནང་བ་ | *sung-ťrö nang-wa.* |
| Do. *inf.* to *sup.* | གསུང་གྲོས་ཞུ་བ་ | *sung-ťrö sĥu-wa.* |
| Convex | འབུར་འབུར་ | *bur-bur.* |
| Convey, to | སྐྱེལ་བ་ | *kye-wa.* |
| Do. *hon.* | སྐྱེལ་ར་ (བ་) གནང་བ་ | *kye-ra nang-wa.* |
| Convulsions (of baby, etc.) | རྒྱལ་གཟེར་རྒྱབ་པ་ | *ge-śer gyaṕ-pa.* |
| Cook | མ་ཆེན་ | *ma-chhen.* |
| Do. to | བཙོས་པ་ (འཚོད་པ་) | *tsö-pa.* |
| Cookroom | ཐབ་ཚང་ | *thaṕ-tshang.* |
| Do. *hon.* | གསོལ་ཐབ་ | *sö-thaṕ.* |
| Cool | གྲང་མོ། བསིལ་པོ་ | *ťrang-mo ; si-po.* |
| Do. *hon.* | སྐུ་བསིལ་པོ་ | *ku-si-po.* |
| Cooly (labourer) | ཨར་པོ་བ་ | *ar-po.* |
| Cooly (carrier of load) | དོས་པོ་འཁྱེར་མཁན། མི་ཧྲང་ | *tö-pokhyer-khen ; mi-hrang.* |
| Copious | མང་པོ། འབེལ་པོ་ | *mang-po ; bé-po.* |
| Copper | ཟངས་ | *śang.* |

| | | |
|---|---|---|
| Coppersmith | ཟངས་བཟོ་བ་ | *śang-śo-wa.* |
| Do. *hon.* | དབུ་མཛོད་ | *um-dze.* |
| Copulate, to | ཀྱོ་བ་ | *gyo-wa.* |
| Copy | དཔེ་ | *pe.* |
| Do. to | དཔེ་ཤུ་བ་ | *pe-shu-wa.* |
| Do. *hon.* | དཔེ་ཤུ་བ་གནང་བ་ | *pe-shu-wa nang-wa.* |
| Copy, true | ངོ་ཤུས་ | *ngo-shü.* |
| Coral | བྱི་རུ་ | *cḱi-ru.* |
| Do. *hon.* | མགུལ་བྱི་ | *gü-cḱi.* |
| Cord | ཐག་པ་ | *thaḱ-pa.* |
| Cork (lid) | ཁ་གཅོད་ | *khaṕ-chö.* |
| Do. *hon.* | ཞལ་གཅོད་ | *śhe-chö.* |
| Corn (grain) | འབྲུ་ | *dru.* |
| Do. *hon.* | ཕྱག་འབྲུ་ | *chhan-dru.* |
| Do. parched | ཡོས་ | *yö.* |
| Do. *hon.* | བཞེས་ཡོས་ | *sḱe-yö.* |
| Corner | ཟུར་ | *śur.* |
| Corporal (in command of 10 men) | བཅུ་དཔོན་ | *chu-pön.* |
| Corpse | རོ་ | *ro.* |
| Do. *hon.* | སྐུ་ཕུང་ (སྐུ་སྤུར་) | *ku-phung.* |

| | | |
|---|---|---|
| Corpulent | རྒྱགས་པ་ | *gyaḱ-pa.* |
| Do. *hon.* | སྐུ་ཤ་འབྱོར་པོ་ | *ku-sha jo-po.* |
| Correct (of words spoken) | སྒྲ་དག་པོ་ | *dra-ṫaḱ-po.* |
| Do. (of a thing done) | དེན་ལྡན་ | *ten-den.* |
| Do. to (any writing) | ཞུ་དག་བྱེད་པ་ | *sḱu-ṫa cḱe-pa.* |
| Do. *hon.* | ཞུ་དག་གནང་བ་ | *sḱu-ṫa nang-wa.* |
| Correction | ཞུ་དག་ | *sḱu-ṫa.* |
| Correctly (of words spoken) | སྒྲ་དག་པོ་བྱས་ནས་ | *dra-ṫaḱ-po cḱe-ne.* |
| Do. (of a thing done) | དེན་ལྡན་བྱས་ནས་ | *ten-den cḱe-ne.* |
| Corrupt, to | མེད་པར་བཟོ་བ་ | *me-pa śo-wa.* |
| Do. *hon.* | མེད་པར་བཟོ་བ་གནང་བ་ | *me-pa śo-wa nang-wa.* |
| Cost | གོང་ | *ḱong.* |
| Do. *hon.* | ལྗགས་གོང་ | *ja-ḱong.* |
| Costly | གོང་ཆེན་པོ་ | *ḱong-chhem-po.* |
| Do. *hon.* | ལྗགས་གོང་ཆེན་པོ་ | *ja-ḱong chhem-po.* |
| Costume | ཆས་ | *chhe.* |
| Cotton | རས་ | *re.* |
| Cotton-cloth | རས་གོས། རས་ཆ་ | *re-ḱö ; re-chha.* |
| Cotton-thread | རས་སྐུད་ | *re-ḱü.* |
| Do. *hon.* | ཕྱག་སྐུད་ | *chha-ḱü.* |

| | | |
|---|---|---|
| Cotton-yarn | སྲིང་ | *sing.* |
| Cotton-wool | སྲིང་བལ་ | *trim-ṕe.* |
| Couch | ཁུབ་ཀྱག། ཁྲིའུ་ཤིང་ | *kuṕ-kya ; thri-u-shing.* |
| Do. *hon.* | ཞབས་ཀྱག་ | *sḱaṕ-kya.* |
| Cough, to | གློ་རྒྱབ་པ་ | *lo-gyaṕ-pa.* |
| Do. *hon.* | མགུལ་གློ་སྐྱོན་པ་ | *gü-lo ḱyöm-pa.* |
| Counsel | གྲོས་ | *t́rö.* |
| Do. *hon.* | བཀའ་གྲོས་ | *ka-t́rö.* |
| Do. to ask | གྲོས་དྲི་ (འདྲི་) བ་ | *t́rö-t́ri-wa.* |
| Do. *hon.* | བཀའ་གྲོས་གནང་བ་ | *ka-t́rö nang-wa.* |
| Council, Head | བཀའ་གཤགས་ལྷན་རྒྱས་ | *ka-sha hlen-gye.* |
| Count, to | གྲངས་ཀ་རྒྱབ་པ་ | *t́rang-ka gyaṕ-pa.* |
| Do. *hon.* | ལྗགས་གྲངས་སྐྱོན་པ་ | *ja-t́rang kyöm-pa.* |
| Countenance | གདོང་ | *dong.* |
| Do. *hon* | ཞལ་རས་ | *sḱe-re.* |
| Counterfeit, *adj.* (of coin) | མ་ཕིན་ | *ma-pin.* |
| Do. (of other things) | རྫུས་མ་ | *dzü-ma.* |
| Do. to (of coin) | མ་ཕིན་བཏང་ (གཏོང་) བ་ | *ma-pin tang-wa.* |
| Do. (of other things) | རྫུས་མ་བཏང་ (གཏོང་) བ་ | *dzü-ma tang-wa.* |
| Counting | གྲངས་ཀ་ | *t́rang-ka.* |

| | | |
|---|---|---|
| Counting, *hon.* | ཕྱགས་གྲངས་ | *ja-ťrang.* |
| Country | ལུང་པ་ | *lung-pa.* |
| Do. (native land) | སྐྱེ་ས་ | *kye-sa.* |
| Do. *hon.* | འཁྲུངས་ས་ | *thrung-sa.* |
| Country (as opposed to town) | གྲོང་སེབ་ | *ťrong-se.* |
| Country-house | གཞི་ཀ་ | *sǩi-ka.* |
| Couple, *s.* (a pair) | ཆ་ | *chha.* |
| Do. (two) | གཉིས། དོ་ | *nyi ; ťo.* |
| Do. a married | ནང་ཚང་གཉིས་ | *nang-tshang-nyi.* |
| Courageous | སྙིང་ཆེན་པོ། བློ་ཁོག་ཆེན་པོ་ | *nying-chhem-po ; lo-kho chhem-po.* |
| Do. *hon.* | ཐུགས་སྙིང་ཆེན་པོ། ཐུགས་ཁོག་ཆེན་པོ་ | *thu-nying chhem-po ; thu-kho chhem-po.* |
| Courier | བང་ཆེན་ | *ṕang-chhen.* |
| Do mounted | ཨ་དྲུང་རྟ་བཞོན་ | *a-trung taṕ-sǩön* |
| Court (of justice) | ཁྲིམས་ཁང་ | *thrim-khang.* |
| Court-yard | སྒོ་ར་ | *go-ra.* |
| Cousin | སྤུན་ཀྱག་ | *pün-kya.* |
| Covenant | ཁ་དེན། ཁ་ཆད་ | *kha-ten ; kha-chhe.* |
| Do. *hon.* | ཞལ་དེན། ཞལ་ཆད་ | *sǩe-ten ; sǩe-chhe.* |
| Cover, *s.* (lid) | ཁ་གཅོད་ | *khaṕ-chö.* |

| | | |
|---|---|---|
| Cover, to | བཀབ་པ་ (འགེབས་པ་) | *kap̔-pa.* |
| Covering | ཁེབས་ | *khep̔.* |
| Covet, to | ཧམ་པ་བྱེད་པ་ | *ham-pa cḱe-pa.* |
| Do. *hon.* | ཧམ་པ་གནང་བ་ | *ham-pa nang-wa.* |
| Covetous | ཧམ་པ་ཆེན་པོ་ | *ham-pa chhem-po.* |
| Covetousness | ཧམ་པ་ | *ham-pa.* |
| Cow | བ་ | *p̔a.* |
| Do. (of yak) | འབྲི་ | *dri.* |
| Coward | སེམས་ཆུང་ཆུང་ | *sem-chhung-chhung.* |
| Do. *hon.* | ཐུགས་སེམས་ཆུང་ཆུང་ | *thu-sem chhung-chhung.* |
| Cowherd | འབྲོག་པ་ | *drok-pa.* |
| Cowshed | བ་ར་ | *p̔a-ra.* |
| Cowry | འགྲོན་བུ་ | *dröm-p̔u.* |
| Crab | སྡིག་སྲིན་ | *dik-sing.* |
| Crack, to, *v.i.* | གས་པ་ (འགས་པ་) | *ḱe-pa.* |
| Do. *hon.* | གས་ (འགས་) པ་གནང་བ་ | *ḱe-pa nang-wa.* |
| Do. a | སེར་ཀ་ | *se-ka.* |
| Crafty | གཡོ་ཆེན་པོ་ | *yo-chhem-po.* |
| Cramp | རྩ་ཁུམས་པ་ | *tsa-khum-pa.* |

| | | |
|---|---|---|
| Crane (bird) | བྱ་ཁྲུང་ཁྲུང་ | cḱa-thrung-thrung. |
| Crawl, to | ཁ་སྦུབ་གོག་པ་ | kha-ṕu ḱok-pa. |
| Crazy | སྨྱོན་པ་ | nyöm pa. |
| Cream | སྤྲི་མ་ | tri-ma. |
| Do. *hon.* | བཞེས་སྤྲི་ | sḱe-tri. |
| Create, to | བཀོད་པ་ | kö-pa. |
| Do. *hon.* | བཀོད་པ་གནང་བ་ | kö-pa nang-wa. |
| Credible | འོས་པ་ | ö-pa. |
| Credit, to | ཡིད་ཆེས་པ་ | yi-chhe-pa. |
| Do. *hon.* | ཐུགས་ཡིད་ཆེས་པ་གནང་བ་ | thu-yi chhe pa nang-wa. |
| Creditor | བུན་བདག་ | ṕün-da. |
| Creed | དད་པ་ | t́e-pa. |
| Creek (in a lake) | མཚོ་ལག་ | tsho-la. |
| Do. (in a river) | ཆུ་ལག་ | chhu-la. |
| Creep, to | ཁ་སྦུབ་གོག་པ་ | ḱa-ṕu ḱok-pa. |
| Crevice | སེར་ཀ་ | se-ka. |
| Crime, to commit | ཁྲིམས་འགལ་བ་ | thrim gel wa. |
| Do. *hon.* | བཀའ་ཁྲིམས་འགལ་ར་ (བ་) གནང་བ་ | ka-thrim ge-ra nang-wa. |
| Criminal, *adj.* | འཛབ་ཆེན་ | dzaṕ-chhen. |

| | | |
|---|---|---|
| Crimson | དམར་པོ་ | *mar-po.* |
| Crippled | ཀང་ཀྱོག་ | *kang-kyo.* |
| Do. *hon.* | ཞབས་ཀྱོག་ | *sKap-kyo.* |
| Crocodile | ཆུ་སྲིན་ | *chhu-sin.* |
| Crooked (with one bend) | གུག་གུག་ | *ku-ku.* |
| Do. (with several bends) | ཀྱོག་ཀྱོག་ | *kyo-kyo.* |
| Crop (of corn, etc.) | སྟོན་ཐོག་ | *tön-tho.* |
| Cross, to | རྒལ་བ་ | *gel-wa.* |
| Do. *hon.* | བརྒལ་ནས་ཕེབ་པ་ | *ge-ne phe-pa.* |
| Do. *h. hon.* | བརྒལ་ནས་འཆིབ་རྒྱུ་གནང་བ་ | *ge-ne chhip-gyu nang-wa.* |
| Cross, to be | ཚིག་པ་ཟ་བ་ | *tshik-pa śa-wa.* |
| Do. *hon.* | དགོངས་པ་ཚུང་བ་ | *gong-pa tshung-wa.* |
| Cross of wood (on which criminals are bound) | རྒྱངས་ཤིང་ | *gyang shing.* |
| Cross-legged | སྐྱིལ་ཀྲུམ་ (སྐྱིལ་ཀྲུང་) | *kyi-trum.* |
| Crow, *s.* | ཁྭ་ཏ་ | *kha-ta.* |
| Do. to (of cock) | ཁྲ་སྐད་རྒྱབ་པ་ | *cKa-ke gyap pa.* |
| Crowd, *s.* | ཚོགས་ | *tshok.* |
| Crown of the head | སྤྱི་གཙུག་ | *chi-tsu.* |
| Do. *hon.* | དབུ་གཙུག་ | *u-tsu.* |

| | | |
|---|---|---|
| Crucify, to | རྒྱངས་ཤིང་ལ་བརྒྱང་ (རྐྱང་) བ་ | *gyang-shing-la. kyang-wa.* |
| Do. *hon.* | རྒྱངས་ཤིང་ལ་རྐྱོང་ང་ (བ་) གནང་བ་ | *gyang-shing la kyong-nga nang-wa.* |
| Cruel, to be | སྙིང་རྗེ་མེད་པ་ | *nying-je me-pa.* |
| Crupper | སྨེད་ | *me.* |
| Crush, to | རྫི་བ་ | *dzi-wa.* |
| Do. *hon.* | རྫི་བ་གནང་བ་ | *dzi-wa nang-wa.* |
| Cry, to (weep) | ངུ་བ་ | *ngu-wa.* |
| Do. *hon.* | ཤུམ་པ་ | *shum-pa.* |
| Crystal | ཤེལ་ | *she.* |
| Cubit | ཁྲུ་ | *thru.* |
| Do. *hon.* | ཕྱག་ཁྲུ་ | *chha-thru.* |
| Cub of fox | ཝ་ཕྲུག་ | *wa-thru.* |
| Do. of bear | དོམ་ཕྲུག་ | *t́om-thru.* |
| Do. of leopard | གཟིག་ཕྲུག་ | *śiḱ-thru.* |
| Do. of tiger | སྟག་ཕྲུག་ | *ta-thru.* |
| Cuckoo | ཁུ་ཡུག་ | *khu-yu.* |
| Culprit | འཛབ་ཆེན་ | *dzaṕ-chhen.* |
| Cultivate, to | ཞིང་ལས་བྱེད་པ་ | *sḱing-le cḱe-pa.* |
| Cultivation | སོ་ནམས་ | *so-nam.* |

| | | |
|---|---|---|
| Cultivator | སོ་ནམས་བྱེད་མཁན་ | *so-nam cħe-khen.* |
| Cunning | གཙང་པོ་ | *chang-po.* |
| Do. *hon.* | ཐུགས་གཙང་པོ་ | *thu-chang-po.* |
| Cup (earthen-ware) | དཀར་ཡོལ་ | *ka-yö.* |
| Do. *hon.* | ཞལ་དཀར་ | *sħe-ka.* |
| Do. (wooden) | ཕོར་པ་ | *phor-pa.* |
| Do. *hon.* | མཆོད་ཞལ་ | *chhö-sħe.* |
| Curds | ཞོ་ | *sħo.* |
| Do. *hon.* | གསོལ་ཞོ་ | *sö-sħo.* |
| Cure, to | དྲག་པ་བཟོ་བ་ | *ťraḱ-pa śo-wa.* |
| Do. *hon.* | དྲག་པ་བཟོ་བ་གནང་བ་ | *ťraḱ-pa śo-wa nang-wa.* |
| Do. (patient, of good position) | སྐུ་དྭངས་ང་ (བ་) བཟོ་བ་ གནང་བ་ | *ku-ťang-nga śo-wa nang wa.* |
| Cured, to be | དྲག་པ་ | *ťraḱ-pa.* |
| Do. *hon.* | སྐུ་དྭངས་པ་ | *ku-ťang-pa.* |
| Curious | ཁྱད་མཚར་པོ་ | *khye-tshar-po.* |
| Curly (of hair) | སུ་ལུ་ | *su-lu.* |
| Current | ཆུ་རྒྱུན་ | *chhu-gyün.* |
| Curse, to | དམོད་མོ་རྒྱབ་པ་ | *mö-mo gyaṕ-pa.* |
| Do. *hon.* | དམོད་མོ་སྐྱོན་པ་ | *mö-mo kyöm-pa.* |

| | | |
|---|---|---|
| Curtail, to | ཉུང་རུ་(དུ་)བཏང་(གཏོང་)བ་ | *nyung-ru tang-wa.* |
| Do. *hon.* | ཉུང་རུ་(དུ་) གཏོང་ང་ (བ་) གནང་བ་ | *nyung-ru tong-nga nang-wa.* |
| Curtain | ཡོལ་ལ་ (ཡོལ་བ་) | *yö-la.* |
| Do. *hon.* | གཟིམ་ཡོལ་ | *śim-yö.* |
| Curve, to | གུག་གུག་བྱེད་པ་ | *kuk-ku che-pa.* |
| Do. *hon.* | གུག་གུག་གནང་བ་ | *kuk-ku nang-wa.* |
| Curved | གུག་གུག་ | *kuk-ku.* |
| Cushion | གདན་ | *den.* |
| Do. *hon.* | བཞུགས་གདན་ | *sku-den.* |
| Cushion (small, placed on chair) | ཁ་གདན་ | *kha-den.* |
| Do. (large, placed on ground) | འབོལ་གདན་ | *bö-den.* |
| Custody (care) | རྩིས་ | *tsi.* |
| Custom (manner) | ལུགས་སྲོལ་ | *luk-sö.* |
| Customs (duty) | ཤོ་ཁྲལ་ | *sho-thre.* |
| Cut, *s.* (blow with whip, etc.) | ལྕག་ | *cha.* |
| Do. (wound) | རྨ་ | *ma.* |
| Cut, to | བཅད་པ་ (གཅོད་པ་) | *che-pa.* |
| Do. *hon.* | བཅད་ (གཅོད་) པ་གནང་བ་ | *che-pa nang-wa.* |
| Cut, to (by chopping) | བཙབ་པ་ | *tsap-pa.* |

| | | |
|---|---|---|
| Cut, to *hon.* (by chopping) | བཙབ་པ་གནང་བ་ | *tsaṕ-pa nang-wa.* |
| Cutch | སྟོད་ཛ་ | *tö-cKa.* |
| Cycle (of 12 years) | ལོ་འཁོར་ | *lo-khor.* |
| Do. (of 60 years) | རབ་བྱུང་ | *rab-cKung.* |
| Cyclone | རླུང་ཚུབ་ | *lung-tshuṕ.* |
| Cylinder | འཁོར་ལོ་ | *khor-lo.* |
| Do. (praying) | མ་ཎི་ | *ma-ni.* |
| Cymbal | རོལ་མོ་ | *rö-mo.* |
| Cypress | ཤུག་པ་ | *shuḱ-pa.* |

# D

| | | |
|---|---|---|
| Dacoit | ཇག་པ་ | *cḱaḱ-pa.* |
| Dagger | ཨམ་གྲི། མགར་ཟོར་ | *am-ṫri ; ga-śo.* |
| Do. *hon.* | ཕྱག་ཞན་ | *chha-shen.* |
| Daily | ཉི་མ་རྟག་པ་རེ་བཞིན་ | *nyi-ma taḱ-pa ri-sḱi.* |
| Dainty | ཡག་པོ་ | *yak-po.* |
| Dairy-farm | འབྲོག་ས་ | *droḱ sa.* |
| Dalai Lama | སྐྱབས་མགོན་རིན་པོ་ཆེ། རྒྱལ་བ་རིན་པོ་ཆེ་ | *kyam-gön rim-po-chhe ; gya-wa rim-po chhe.* |
| Dale | ཀླུངས་ | *lung.* |
| Dam, *s.* (for water) | ཆུ་རགས་ | *chhu-ra.* |
| Damage | སྐྱོན་ | *kyön.* |
| Do. to | སྐྱོན་བྱེད་པ་ | *kyön-cḱe-pa.* |
| Damp | རློན་པ་ | *löm-pa.* |
| Damsel | བུ་མོ་ | *ṕu-mo.* |
| Do. *hon.* | སྲས་མོ་ | *se-mo* or *tre-mo.* |
| Dance, ordinary | ཞབས་བྲོ་ | *sḱaṕ-ro.* |
| Do. with dramatic entertainment | འཁྲབ་པ་ | *thraṕ-pa.* |
| Do. religious, performed by monks | འཆམ་ | *chham.* |

| | | |
|---|---|---|
| Dance, to | ཞབས་བྲོ་རྒྱབ་པ་ | *sḱaṕ-ro gyaṕ-pa.* |
| Do. *hon.* | ཞབས་བཞེས་གནང་བ་ | *sḱaṕ-sḱe nang-wa.* |
| Dandy (sedan-chair) | འཁྱོགས་དཔྱང་ | *gyo-chang.* |
| Do. *hon.* | ཕེབ་དཔྱང་ | *phe-chang.* |
| Danger | ཉེན་ | *nyen.* |
| Dangerous | ཉེན་ཀ་ཆེན་པོ་ | *nyen-ka chhem-po.* |
| Dare, to | ནུས་པ་ | *nü-pa.* |
| Do. *hon.* | ནུས་པ་གནང་བ་ | *nü-pa nang-wa.* |
| Daring | སྙིང་ཆེན་པོ་ | *nying-chhem-po.* |
| Do. *hon.* | ཐུགས་སྙིང་ཆེན་པོ་ | *thu-nying chhem-po.* |
| Dark | ནག་པོ་ | *naḱ-po.* |
| Do. to become (from clouds) | འཐིབས་པ་ | *thiṕ-pa.* |
| Darkness (of night) | མུན་ནག་ | *min-na.* |
| Darling (favourite) | སྙིང་སྡུག་ | *nying-du.* |
| Darn, to | གྲོག་ (སྒྲོག་) དུག་རྒྱབ་པ་ | *t́ro-t́uḱ gyaṕ-pa.* |
| Do. *hon.* | གྲོག་ (སྒྲོག་) དུག་སྐྱོན་པ་ | *t́ro-t́uḱ kyöm-pa.* |
| Dart | མདའ་ | *da.* |
| Do. *hon.* | ཕྱག་མདའ་ | *chhan-da.* |
| Date | ཚེས་པ་ | *tshe-pa.* |
| Daub, to | སྐུ་བ་ | *ku-wa.* |

| | | |
|---|---|---|
| Daub, to *hon.* | སྐུ་བ་གནང་བ་ | *ku-wa nang-wa.* |
| Daughter | བུ་མོ་ | *ṕu-mo.* |
| Do. *hon.* | སྲས་མོ་ | *se-mo.* |
| Daughter-in-law | མནའ་མ་ | *na-ma.* |
| Dawn, *s.* | ནམ་ལངས་ | *nam-lang.* |
| Do. to | ཤར་མདའ་བཏང་ (གཏོང་) བ་ | *shan-da tang-wa.* |
| Day (as opposed to night) | ཉི་མ་ | *nyi-ma.* |
| Do. (of twenty-four hours) | ཞག་པོ་ | *sḱak-po.* |
| Do. *hon.* | བཞུགས་ཞག་ | *sḱu-sḱa.* |
| Do. (all the day long) | ཉིན་གང་ | *nyin-ḱang.* |
| Day, each | ཉི་མ་རེ་རེ་ | *nyi-ma re-re.* |
| Do. every | ཉི་མ་རྟག་པ་རེ་བཞིན་ | *nyi-ma tak-pa ri-sḱi.* |
| Day-break | ནམ་ལངས་ | *nam-lang.* |
| Day after to-morrow | ནངས་ | *nang.* |
| Day before yesterday | ཁའི་ཉི་མ་ | *khe-nyi-ma.* |
| Do. last of a month | གནམ་གང་ | *nam-ḱang.* |
| Dazzling | འོད་ཆེམ་ཆེམ་ | *ö-chhem-chhem.* |
| Dead man (corpse) | རོ་ | *ro.* |
| Do. *hon.* | སྐུ་ཕུང་ | *ku-phung.* |
| Dead, *adj.* (deceased) | ཤི་མཁན་ | *shi-khen.* |

| | | |
|---|---|---|
| Dead, *adj*. (deceased) *hon*. | གྲོངས་མཁན་ | *ťrong-khen.* |
| Do. *h. hon.* | དམ་པ་ | *ťam-pa.* |
| Dead, is | ཤི་སོང་ | *shi-song.* |
| Do. *hon.* | གྲོངས་སོང་ | *ťrong-song.* |
| Do. *h. hon.* | ག་ཤགས་སོང་ (ག་ཤེགས་སོང་) | *sha-song.* |
| Deaf | འོན་པ་ | *öm-pa.* |
| Deal, a great (large quantity) | ཛག་དོ་ | *dzaǩ-ťo.* |
| Dealer | ཚོང་པ་ | *tshong-pa.* |
| Do. *hon.* | ཚོང་དཔོན་ལགས་ | *tshong-pön-la.* |
| Dear (expensive) | གོང་ཆེན་པོ། གུས་པོ་ | *ǩong-chhem-po ; ǩü-po.* |
| Do. *hon.* | ལྗགས་གོང་ཆེན་པོ་ | *ja-ǩong chhem-po.* |
| Dear (beloved) | གཅེས་པོ་ | *che-po.* |
| Debar, to | བཀག་པ་ (འགེགས་པ་) | *kaǩ-pa.* |
| Do. *hon.* | བཀག་ག་ (འགེགས་པ་) གནང་བ་ | *kaǩ-ǩa nang-wa.* |
| Debate, to | རྩོད་པ་རྒྱབ་པ་ | *tsö-pa gyap̌-pa.* |
| Do. *hon.* | ཐུགས་རྩོད་སྐྱོན་པ་ | *thuǩ-tsö kyöm-pa.* |
| Debt | བུ་ལོན་ | *p̌u-lön.* |
| Do. *hon.* | ཕྱག་བུན་ | *chha-p̌ün.* |
| Debtor | བུ་ལོན་ལེན་མཁན་ | *p̌u-lön len-khen.* |

| | | |
|---|---|---|
| Debtor, *hon.* | ཕྱག་བུན་བཞེས་མཁན་ | *chha ṕun she-khen.* |
| Decapitate, to | སྐ་བཅད་ (གཅོད་) པ་ | *ke-che-pa.* |
| Do. (person of high position) | མགུལ་བཅད་ (གཅོད་) པ་ | *gü-che-pa.* |
| Decay, to | རུལ་བ་ | *rül-wa.* |
| Deceased, the | ཤི་མཁན་ | *shi-khen.* |
| Do. *hon.* | གྲོངས་མཁན་ | *ťrong-khen.* |
| Do. *h. hon.* | དམ་པ་ | *ťam-pa.* |
| Deceit | མགོ་སྐོར་ | *go-kor.* |
| Do. *hon.* | དབུ་སྐོར་ | *u-kor.* |
| Deceitful | གཡོ་ཅན། བློ་ཀྱོགས་ཀྱོགས་ | *yo-chen; lo kyok-kyok.* |
| Do. *hon.* | ཐུགས་གཡོ་ཅན། ཐུགས་ཀྱོགས་ཀྱོགས་ | *thu yo-chen; thu kyok-kyok.* |
| Deceive, to | མགོ་སྐོར་བཏང་ (གཏོང་) བ་ | *go-kor tang-wa.* |
| Do. *hon.* | མགོ་སྐོར་གཏོང་ང་ (བ་) གནང་བ་ | *go-kor tong-nga nang-wa.* |
| Do. *inf.* to *sup.* | དབུ་སྐོར་ཞུ་བ་ | *u-kor shu-wa.* |
| Deceiver | མགོ་སྐོར་གཏོང་མཁན་ | *go-kor tong-khen.* |
| Decent (becoming) | འོས་པོ་ | *ö-po.* |
| Deception | གཡོ་སྒྱུ་ | *yo-gyu.* |
| Decide, to (judge) | ཐག་བཅད་ (གཅོད་) པ་ | *tha-che-pa.* |

| | | |
|---|---|---|
| Decide, to (judge) *hon.* | ཐག་གཅོད་པ་གནང་བ་ | *tha-chö-pa nang-wa.* |
| Do. *h. hon.* | ཐུགས་ཐག་གཅོད་པ་གནང་བ་ | *thu-tha chö-pa nang-wa.* |
| Decidedly | ཐག་ཆོད་ | *thak-chhö.* |
| Declare, to | བཤད་པ་ (འཆད་པ་) | *she-pa.* |
| Do. *hon.* | གསུང་བ་ | *sung-wa.* |
| Declivity | ཐུར་ | *thur.* |
| Decorate, to | རྒྱན་ཆ་བཏགས་ (འདོགས་) པ་ | *gyen-chha tak-pa.* |
| Do. *hon.* | སྐུ་རྒྱན་བཏགས་ག་ (འདོགས་པ་) གནང་བ་ | *ku-gyen tak-ka nang-wa.* |
| Decoration | རྒྱན་ཆ་ | *gyen-chha.* |
| Do. *hon.* | སྐུ་རྒྱན་ | *ku-gyen.* |
| Decrease, to (in numbers) | ཉུང་རུ་ (དུ་) ཕྱིན་པ་ | *nyung-ru chhim-pa.* |
| Do. to (in size) | ཆུང་རུ་ (དུ་) ཕྱིན་པ་ | *chhung-ru chhim-pa.* |
| Do. *hon.* | ཆུང་རུ་ (དུ་) ཕེབ་པ་ | *chhung-ru-phe-pa.* |
| Decree (of court of justice) | བཀའ་ཁྲིམས་ | *ka-thrim.* |
| Do. (of secular authority) | བཀའ་ཤོག་ | *ka-sho.* |
| Do. (religious) | ཆོས་ཁྲིམས་ | *chhö-thrim.* |
| Decrepit | འཁོགས་པ་ | *khok-pa.* |
| Dedicate, to | རབ་གནས་བྱེད་པ་ | *ram-ne che-pa.* |
| Do. *hon.* | རབ་གནས་གནང་བ་ | *ram-ne nang-wa.* |

| | | |
|---|---|---|
| Dedication | རབ་གནས་ | *ram-ne.* |
| Deduct, to | འཐེན་པ་ | *them-pa.* |
| Do. *hon.* | འཐེན་པ་གནང་བ་ | *them-pa nang-wa.* |
| Deed | ལས་ཀ་ | *le-ka.* |
| Do. *hon.* | ཕྱག་ལས་ | *chha-le.* |
| Deep | གཏིང་རིང་པོ་ | *ting-ring-po.* |
| Deer | ཤ་ (ཤ་བ་) | *sha.* |
| Do. male | ཤ་ཕོ་ | *sha-pho.* |
| Do. female | ཤ་མོ་ | *sha-mo.* |
| Do. young | ཤ་ཕྲུག་ | *sha-thru.* |
| Deface, to | སུབ་པ་ | *suṕ-pa.* |
| Do. *hon.* | སུབ་པ་གནང་བ་ | *suṕ-pa nang-wa.* |
| Defamation | སྨད་ར་ | *me-ra.* |
| Defame, to | སྨད་ར་བཏང་ (གཏོང་) བ་ | *me-ra tang-wa.* |
| Do. *hon.* | སྨད་ར་གཏོང་ང་(བ་)གནང་བ་ | *me-ra tong-nga nang-wa.* |
| Defeat, to | རྒྱལ་བ་ | *gye-wa.* |
| Do. *hon.* | རྒྱལ་ར་ (བ་) གནང་བ་ | *gye-ra nang-wa.* |
| Defeated, to be | འཕམ་པ་ | *pham-pa.* |
| Do. *hon.* | འཕམ་པ་གནང་བ་ | *pham-pa nang-wa.* |
| Defect | སྐྱོན་ | *kyön.* |

| | | |
|---|---|---|
| Defective | སྐྱོན་ཆེན་པོ་ | *kyön-chhem-po.* |
| Defend, to | བསྐྱབས་པ་ (སྐྱོབ་པ།) སྐྱོང་བ་ | *kyap-pa; kyong-wa.* |
| Do. *hon.* | སྐྱབས་འཇུག་གནང་བ་ | *kyam-juk nang-wa.* |
| Defendant | ཞུ་གདུག་བྱེད་པའི་ཁ་ཐེག་ | *sKu-tuk cKe-pe khap-the.* |
| Defer, to | པ་རུ་བཞག་ (འཇོག་) པ་ | *pa-ru sKak-pa.* |
| Do. *hon.* | པ་རུ་གཞོག་ག་གནང་བ་ | *pa-ru sKok-Ka nang-wa.* |
| Deficient | ཆད་པ་ | *chhe-pa.* |
| Defile, to | བཙོག་པ་བཟོ་བ་ | *tsok-pa śo-wa.* |
| Do. *hon.* | བཙོག་པ་བཟོ་བ་གནང་བ་ | *tsok-pa śo-wa nang-wa.* |
| Defilement | གྲིབ་ | *t́rip.* |
| Define, to | དོན་དག་བཤད་ (འཆད་) པ་ | *t́ön-t́a she-pa.* |
| Do. *hon.* | སྐུ་དོན་གསུང་བ་ | *ku-t́ön sung-wa.* |
| Definite (certain) | ངེས་པ། ཏེན་ཏེན་ | *nge-pa; ten-ten.* |
| Do. *hon.* | ཐུགས་ངེས་པ་ | *thu-nge-pa.* |
| Definitely | ཏེན་ཏེན་བྱས་ནས་ | *ten-ten cKe-ne.* |
| Deformed, to be | དབང་པོ་མ་ཚང་བ་ | *wang-po ma-tshang-wa.* |
| Defraud, to | མགོ་སྐོར་བཏང་ (གཏོང་) བ་ | *go-kor tang-wa.* |
| Do. *hon.* | མགོ་སྐོར་གཏོང་ང་ (བ་) གནང་བ་ | *go-kor tong-nga nang-wa.* |
| Degenerate, to | ཉམས་པ་ | *nyam-pa.* |

| | | |
|---|---|---|
| Degenerate, to *hon.* | ཐུགས་ཉམས་པ་ | *thu-nyam-pa.* |
| Degrade, to | གོ་གནས་ཕབ་པ་ | *ko-ne p̓ap̓-pa.* |
| Degree (series) | རིམ་པ་ | *rim-pa.* |
| Do. (rank) | གོ་གནས་། གོ་ས་ | *ko-ne ; ko-sa.* |
| Degrees, by | རིམ་བཞིན་ | *rim-s̈hin.* |
| Dejected, to be | མི་...དགའ་བ་ | *mi...ga-wa.* |
| Do. *hon.* | མཉེས་པོ་མི་...གནང་བ་ | *nye-po mi... nang-wa.* |
| Do. *h. hon.* | ཐུགས་དགྱེས་པོ་མི་...གནང་བ་ | *thu-gye-po mi ...nang-wa.* |
| Deity | ལྷ་ | *hla.* |
| Delay | འགོར་པོ་ | *gor-po.* |
| Delay, without | འགོར་པོ་མ་བྱེད་པར་ | *gor-po ma-c̈he-par.* |
| Do. *hon.* | ཐུགས་འགོར་མེད་པ་ | *thung-gor me-pa.* |
| Delay, to | འགོར་པོ་བྱེད་པ་ | *gor-po c̈he-pa.* |
| Do. *hon.* | ཐུགས་འགོར་གནང་བ་ | *thung-gor nang-wa.* |
| Delegate | ཚབ་ | *tshap̓.* |
| Do. *hon.* | སྐུ་ཚབ་ | *ku-tshap̓.* |
| Delegate, to | ངོ་ཚབ་བཏང་ (གཏོང་) བ་ | *ngo-tshap̓ tang-wa.* |
| Do. *hon.* | སྐུ་ཚབ་གཏོང་ང་ (བ་) གནང་བ་ | *ku-tshap̓ tong-nga nang-wa.* |
| Deliberate, to | གྲོས་བྱེད་པ་ | *t̓rö-c̈he-pa.* |
| Do. *hon.* | བཀའ་གྲོས་གནང་བ་ | *ka-t̓rö nang-wa.* |

| | | |
|---|---|---|
| Delicate (weak), to be | ཐང་པོ་མེད་པ་ | thang-po me-pa. |
| Delicious | ཞིམ་ཐག་ཆོད་ | sḱim-thaḱ-chhö. |
| Do. *hon.* | སྤྲོ་ཐག་ཆོད་ | trö-thaḱ-chhö. |
| Delight | དགའ་ཚོར་ | ga-tshor. |
| Do. *hon.* | མཉེས་ཚོར་ | nye-tshor. |
| Delight in, to take | དགའ་བ་ | ga-wa. |
| Do. *hon.* | མཉེས་པོ་གནང་བ་ | nye-po nang-wa. |
| Do. *h. hon.* | ཐུགས་དགྱེས་པོ་གནང་བ་ | thu-gye-ṗo nang-wa. |
| Deliver, to (rescue) | བསྐྱབས་པ་ (སྐྱོབ་པ།) སྐྱོང་བ་ | kyaṗ-pa; kyong-wa. |
| Do. *hon.* | སྐྱབས་འཇུག་གནང་བ་ | kyam-juḱ nang wa. |
| Deliver, to (give) | སྤྲད་པ་ | tre-pa. |
| Do. *hon.* | གནང་བ་ | nang-wa. |
| Deliverance | ཐར་པ་ | thar pa. |
| Delude, to | མགོ་སྐོར་བཏང་ (གཏོང་) བ་ | go-kor tang-wa. |
| Do. *hon.* | མགོ་སྐོར་གཏོང་ང་(བ་)གནང་བ་ | go-kor tong-nga nang-wa. |
| Do. *inf.* to *sup.* | དབུ་སྐོར་ཞུ་བ་ | u-kor sḱu-wa. |
| Deluge (flood) | ཆུ་རུད་ | chhu-rü. |
| Demand, to | དགོ་ (དགོས་) ཟེར་བ་ | go-ṡer-wa. |
| Do. *hon.* | དགོ་ (དགོས) གསུང་བ་ | go-sung-wa. |

| | | |
|---|---|---|
| Demeanour | བྱེད་སྟངས་ | *cKe-tang.* |
| Do. *hon.* | གནང་སྟངས་ | *nang-tang.* |
| Demented | སྨྱོན་པ་ | *nyöm-pa.* |
| Demi-god | ལྷ་མ་ཡིན་ | *lha-ma-yin.* |
| Demolish, to | བཤིག་པ་ (འཇིག་པ་) | *shik-pa.* |
| Do. *hon.* | བཤིག་ག་ (འཇིག་པ་) གནང་བ་ | *shik-ka nang-wa.* |
| Demon | གདོང་འདྲེ། བདུད་ | *dong-dre; dü.* |
| Den | ཚང་ | *tshang.* |
| Denomination | ཆོས་ལུགས་ | *chhö-lu.* |
| Dense | འཐུག་པོ་ | *thuk-po.* |
| Deny, to | རྒྱབ་འགལ་བྱེད་པ་ | *gyam-ge cKe-pa.* |
| Do. *hon.* | རྒྱབ་འགལ་གནང་བ་ | *gyam-ge nang-wa.* |
| Depart, to | འཐོན་པ། ཕྱིན་པ་ | *thöm-pa; chhim-pa.* |
| Do. *hon.* | ཕེབ་པ་ | *phe-pa.* |
| Do. *h. hon.* | འཆིབ་རྒྱུ་གནང་བ་ | *chhip-gyu nang-wa.* |
| Departed (deceased) | ཤི་མཁན་ | *shi-khen.* |
| Do. *hon.* | གྲོངས་མཁན་ | *trong-khen.* |
| Do. *h. hon.* | དམ་པ་ | *tam-pa.* |
| Depend upon, to | བློས་ (བློ་) བཀལ་བ་ | *lö-kel-wa.* |

| | | |
|---|---|---|
| Depend upon, to *hon.* | ཐུགས་བློ་བཀལ་ར་ (བ་) གནང་བ་ | *thu-lo ke-ra nang-wa.* |
| Deportment | བྱེད་སྟངས་ | *cḱe-tang.* |
| Do. *hon.* | གནང་སྟངས་ | *nang-tang.* |
| Deposit, to | བཞག་པ་ (འཇོག་པ་) | *sḱaḱ-pa.* |
| Do. *hon.* | གཞོག་ག་ (འཇོག་པ་) གནང་བ་ | *sḱoḱ-ḱa nang-wa.* |
| Depositary | མཛོད་ | *dzö.* |
| Depraved, *adj.* | སྡུག་རུལ་ | *duḱ-rü.* |
| Deprive, to | འཕྲོག་པ་ | *throḱ-pa.* |
| Do. *hon.* | འཕྲོག་ག་ (པ་) གནང་བ་ | *throḱ-ḱa nang wa.* |
| Depth | གཏིང་རིང་ཐུང་ | *ting-ring-thung.* |
| Depute, to (send) | ཚབ་བཏང་ (གཏོང་) བ་ | *tshaṕ-tang-wa.* |
| Do. *hon.* | སྐུ་ཚབ་གཏོང་ང་ (བ་) གནང་བ་ | *ku-tshaṕ tong-nga nang-wa.* |
| Deputy | ཚབ་ | *tshaṕ.* |
| Do. *hon.* | སྐུ་ཚབ་ | *ku-tshaṕ.* |
| Derangement | སྐྱོན་ | *kyön.* |
| Descend, to | བབ་ (འབབ་) ཡོང་བ་ (or འགྲོ་བ་) | *ṕaṕ-yong-wa* (or *dro-wa*). |
| Do. *hon.* | བབ་ (འབབ་) ཕེབ་པ་ | *ṕaṕ-phe-pa.* |

| | | |
|---|---|---|
| Descend, to *h. hon.* | བབ་ (འབབ་) འཆིབ་ཀྱུ་ གནང་བ་ | *ṕaṕ-chhiṕ-gyu nang-wa.* |
| Descendants | རིགས་བརྒྱུད། མི་བརྒྱུད་ | *ri-gyü ; mi-gyü.* |
| Do. *hon.* (of laymen) | སྐུ་བརྒྱུད་ | *ku-gyü.* |
| Do. *hon.* (of lamas) | གདུང་བརྒྱུད་ | *dung-gyü.* |
| Descent | ཐུར་ | *thur.* |
| Describe, to | བཤད་པ་ (འཆད་པ་) | *she-pa.* |
| Do. *hon.* | གསུང་བ་ | *sung-wa.* |
| Desert, *s.* | བྱེ་ཐང་ | *cḰe-thang.* |
| Do. to | སྤང་བ་ | *pang-wa.* |
| Do. *hon.* | སྤོང་ང་ (བ) གནང་བ་ | *pong-nga nang-wa.* |
| Deserve, to | འོས་པ་ | *ö-pa.* |
| Design (sketch) | རི་མོ་ | *ri-mo.* |
| Do. (pattern) | དཔེ་ | *pe.* |
| Do. to (sketch, &c.) | རི་མོ་བྲིས་པ་ (འབྲི་བ་) | *ri-mo t́ri-pa.* |
| Do. *hon.* | རི་མོ་བྲིས་པ་ (འབྲི་བ་) གནང་བ་ | *ri-mo t́ri-pa nang-wa.* |
| Design, to (copy) | དཔེ་བྲིས་པ་ (འབྲི་བ་) | *pe t́ri-pa.* |
| Do. *hon.* | དཔེ་བྲིས་པ་ (འབྲི་བ་) གནང་བ་ | *pe t́ri-pa nang-wa.* |
| Desire, *s.* | འདོད་པ་ | *dö-pa.* |
| Do. *hon.* | ཐུགས་འདོད་ | *thung-dö.* |

| | | |
|---|---|---|
| Desire, to | འདོད་པ་བྱེད་པ་ | *dö-pa cKe-pa.* |
| Do. *hon.* | ཐུགས་འདོད་གནང་བ་ | *thung-dö nang-wa.* |
| Desist, to | སྤང་བ་ | *pang-wa.* |
| Do. *hon.* | སྤོང་ང་ (བ) གནང་བ་ | *pong-nga nang-wa.* |
| Despair, to | ཡིད་སྨུག་པོ་བྱེད་པ་ | *yi muk-po cKe-pa.* |
| Despatch, to | བཏང་བ་ (གཏོང་བ་) | *tang-wa.* |
| Do. *hon.* | གཏོང་ང་ (བ་) གནང་བ་ | *tong-nga nang-wa.* |
| Desperate, to be (hopeless) | བློ་ (ཁོ་) ཐག་བཅད་ (གཅོད་) པ་ | *lo-tha che-pa.* |
| Despise, to | དམའ་འབེབས་བྱེད་པ་ | *ma-beṕ cKe-pa.* |
| Do. *hon.* | དམར་འབེབས་གནང་བ་ | *ma-beṕ nang-wa* |
| Do. *inf.* to *sup.* | དམའ་འབེབས་ཞུ་བ་ | *ma-beṕ sKu-wa.* |
| Despondent, to be | སེམས་སྐྱོ་བ་ | *sem-kyo-wa.* |
| Do. *hon.* | ཐུགས་སེམས་སྐྱོ་བ་གནང་བ་ | *thu-sem kyo-wa nang-wa.* |
| Destiny (fate) | བསོ་བདེ་ (བསོད་བདེ་) | *so-de.* |
| Do. *hon.* | སྐུ་བསོད་ | *ku-sö.* |
| Destitute | གང་ཡང་མེད་པ་ | *Kang-yang me-pa.* |
| Destroy, to | མེད་པ་ (པར་) བཟོ་བ་ | *me-pa śo-wa.* |
| Do. *hon.* | མེད་པ་ (པར་) བཟོ་བ་གནང་བ་ | *me-pa śo-wa nang-wa.* |
| Detail, in | ཞིབ་པ་ | *sKiṕ-pa.* |

| | | |
|---|---|---|
| Detailed account | ཐོ་ | *tho.* |
| Do. *hon.* | ཕྱག་ཐོ་ | *chha-tho.* |
| Detain, to | བཀག་པ་ (འགོགས་པ་) | *kak-pa.* |
| Do. *hon.* | བཀག་ག་ (པ་) གནང་བ་ | *kak-ka nang-wa.* |
| Determine, to | ཐག་བཅད་ (གཅོད་) པ་ | *tha-che-pa.* |
| Do. *hon.* | ཐག་གཅོད་པ་གནང་བ་ | *tha-chö-pa nang-wa.* |
| Do. *h. hon.* | ཐུགས་ཐག་གཅོད་པ་གནང་བ་ | *thu-tha chö-pa nang-wa.* |
| Detest, to | དགྲ་བྱེད་པ་ | *dra-cḱe-pa.* |
| Do. *hon.* | དགྲ་གནང་བ་ | *dra nang-wa.* |
| Device | ཇུས་ | *chü.* |
| Do. *hon.* | སྐུ་ཇུས་ | *ku-cḱü.* |
| Devil | གདོང་འདྲེ། བདུད་ | *dong-dre ; dü.* |
| Devotee (hermit) | མཚམས་པ། སྒོམ་ཆེན་ | *tsham-pa ; gom-chhen.* |
| Devotion (faith) | དད་པ་ | *t́e-pa.* |
| Devour, to | ཧ་ཕེ་ཧོ་ཕེ་ (ཧབ་ཧོབ་) ཟ་བ་ | *ha-phe ho-phe śa-wa.* |
| Do. *hon.* | ཧ་ཕེ་ཧོ་ཕེ་ (ཧབ་ཧོབ་) བཞེས་པ་ | *ha-phe ho-phe sḱe-pa.* |
| Devout | ཆོས་སེམས་ཆེན་པོ་ | *chhö-sem chhem-po.* |
| Dew | ཟིལ་པ་ | *śi-pa.* |
| Dexterous | གཅང་པོ་ | *chang-po.* |
| Do. *hon.* | ཐུགས་གཅང་པོ་ | *thu-chang-po.* |

| | | |
|---|---|---|
| Diadem | ཅོད་པན་ | *chö-pen.* |
| Dialect | སྐད་ལུགས་ | *ke-lu.* |
| Diamond | རྡོ་རྗེ་ཕ་ལམ་ | *do-je pha-lam.* |
| Diarrhœa | བཤལ་ནད་ | *she-ne.* |
| Do. to have | འགྲིམ་པ། བཤལ་བ་ | *drim-pa ; she-wa.* |
| Do. *hon.* | འགྲིམ་པ་གནང་བ། བཤལ་ར་ (བ་) གནང་བ་ | *drim-pa nang-wa ; she-ra nang wa.* |
| Dice, to play at | ཤོ་རྒྱབ་པ་ | *sho-gyap̍-pa.* |
| Do. *hon.* | ཕྱག་ཤོ་སྐྱོན་པ་ | *chha-sho kyöm-pa.* |
| Dictionary | ཚིག་མཛོད་ | *tshik̍-dzö.* |
| Die, Dice, *s.* | ཤོ་ | *sho.* |
| Do. *hon.* | ཕྱག་ཤོ་ | *chha-sho.* |
| Die, to | ཤི་བ་ | *shi-wa.* |
| Do. *hon.* | གྲོངས་པ་ (འགྲོང་བ་) | *ťrong-pa.* |
| Do. *h. hon.* | གཤགས་པ་ (གཤེགས་པ་) | *shak-pa.* |
| Die, to (of great Lama) | སྐུ་ཞིང་ལ་ཕེབ་པ་ | *ku-sKing-la phe-pa.* |
| Diet | ཁ་ལག། ལྟོ་ཆས་ | *kha-la ; top̍-chhe.* |
| Do. *hon.* | ཞལ་ལག་ | *sKe-la.* |
| Differ, to | ཁྱད་ཡོད་པ་ | *khye yö-pa.* |
| Do. *hon.* | ཐུགས་ཁྱད་ཡོད་པ་ | *thu-khye yö-pa.* |

| | | |
|---|---|---|
| Difference | ཁྱད། ཧེ་བག | *khye ; he-pa.* |
| Do. *hon.* | ཐུགས་ཁྱད་ | *thu-khye.* |
| Different | མི་གཅིག་པ་ | *mi-chik-pa.* |
| Difficult | དཀའ་ལས་ཁག་པོ་ | *ka-le khak-po.* |
| Do. *hon.* | སྐུ་མཉེལ་པོ་ | *ku-nye-po.* |
| Dig, to | རྐོ་བ་ | *ko-wa.* |
| Do. *hon.* | རྐོ་བ་གནང་བ་ | *ko-wa nang-wa.* |
| Digest, to | འཇུ་བ་ | *ju-wa.* |
| Do. *hon.* | འཇུ་བ་གནང་བ་ | *ju-wa nang-wa.* |
| Dignity | གོ་ས། གོ་གནས་ | *ko-sa ; ko-ne.* |
| Dilate, to | ཁ་ཕྱེ་བ་ | *kha-chhe wa.* |
| Dilatory | སྙ་སི་དགུ་སི་ | *nya-si gu-si.* |
| Diligence | སྙིང་རུས་ | *nying-rü.* |
| Do. *hon.* | ཐུགས་རུས་ | *thuk-rü.* |
| Diligence, to use | སྙིང་རུས་བྱེད་པ་ | *nying-rü che-pa.* |
| Do. *hon.* | ཐུགས་རུས་གནང་བ་ | *thuk rü nang-wa.* |
| Diligent | སྙིང་རུས་ཆེན་པོ་ | *nying-rü chhem-po.* |
| Do. *hon.* | ཐུགས་རུས་ཆེན་པོ་ | *thuk-rü chhem-po.* |
| Diligently | སྙིང་རུས་བྱས་ནས་ | *nying-rü che-ne* |
| Do. *hon.* | ཐུགས་རུས་གནང་ནས་ | *thuk-rü nang-ne* |

| | | |
|---|---|---|
| Dim | ཧྲབ་ཧྲིབ་ | *hraṕ-hriṕ.* |
| Dimension | ཆེ་ཆུང་ | *chhe-chhung.* |
| Diminish, to (in number) | ཉུང་རུ་ (དུ་) འགྲོ་བ་ | *nyung-ru dro-wa.* |
| Do. to (in size) | ཆུང་རུ་ (དུ་) འགྲོ་བ་ | *chhung-ru dro-wa.* |
| Do. *hon.* | ཆུང་རུ་ (དུ་) ཕེབ་པ་ | *chhung-ru phe-pa.* |
| Dinner (in evening) | དགོང་མོའི་ཁ་ལག་ | *gong-mö kha-la.* |
| Do. *hon.* | དགོང་མོའི་ཞལ་ལག་ | *gong-mö sḱe-la.* |
| Dip, to (into water, &c.) | བཙུག་པ་ (འཛུག་པ་) | *chuḱ-pa.* |
| Do. *hon.* | བཙུག་ག་ (པ་) གནང་བ་ | *chuḱ-Ḱa nang-wa.* |
| Diploma | བཀར་ཤོག་ | *ka-sho.* |
| Direction | ཕྱོགས་ | *chho.* |
| Directly | ལམ་སང་ | *lam sang.* |
| Dirt | བཙོག་པ་ | *tsoḱ-pa.* |
| Do. *hon.* | སྐུ་བཙོག་ | *ku-tso.* |
| Dirt (mud) | རྫབ་ | *dzaṕ.* |
| Dirty | བཙོག་པ་ | *tsoḱ-pa.* |
| Do. to make | བཙོག་པ་བྱེད་པ་ | *tsoḱ-pa cḱe-pa.* |
| Do. *hon.* | སྐུ་བཙོག་གནང་བ་ | *ku-tso nang-wa.* |
| Dirty, to become | བཙོག་པ་ཤོར་བ་ | *tsoḱ-pa shor-wa.* |
| Do. *hon.* | སྐུ་བཙོག་ཤོར་བ་ | *ku-tso shor-wa.* |

| | | |
|---|---|---|
| Disadvantageous, to be | ཕན་ཐོགས་མེད་པ་ | *phen-tho me-pa.* |
| Do. *hon.* | ཐུགས་ཕན་མི་གསོ་བ་ | *thu-phen mi so-wa.* |
| Disagree, to | མི་མཐུན་པ་ | *mi thüm-pa.* |
| Do. *hon.* | མཐུན་པ་མི་གནང་བ་ | *thüm-pa mi nang-wa.* |
| Disappear, to | ཡལ་བ་ | *ye-wa.* |
| Disbelieve, to | ཡིད་མི་ཆེས་པ་ | *yi mi chhe-pa.* |
| Do. *hon.* | ཐུགས་ཡིད་མི་ཆེས་པ་གནང་བ་ | *thu-yi mi chhe-pa nang-wa.* |
| Disc | འཁོར་ལོ་ | *khor-lo.* |
| Discharge, to (dismiss) | དགོངས་པ་སྟེར་བ་ | *gong-pa ter-wa.* |
| Do. *hon.* | དགོངས་པ་གནང་བ་ | *gong-pa nang-wa.* |
| Discharge, to (fire off) | རྒྱབ་པ་ | *gyap-pa.* |
| Do. *hon.* | སྐྱོན་པ་ | *kyöm-pa.* |
| Discharge to (free) | བཏང་བ་ (གཏོང་བ་) | *tang-wa.* |
| Do. *hon.* | གཏོང་ང་ (བ་) གནང་བ་ | *tong-nga nang-wa.* |
| Disciple | ཉེ་གནས་ | *nye-ne.* |
| Discipline | ཁྲིག་ལམ་ | *drik-lam.* |
| Discontented, to be | འདོད་པ་མི་ཁང་བ་ (འཁེངས་པ་) | *dö-pa mi khang-wa.* |
| Do. *hon.* | ཐུགས་འདོད་མི་ཁང་བ་ (འཁེངས་པ་) | *thung-dö mi khang-wa.* |

| | | |
|---|---|---|
| Discourse | སྐད་ཆ་ | *ke-chha.* |
| Do. *hon.* | གསུང་གྲོས་ | *sung-ťrö.* |
| Discourse, to | སྐད་ཆ་བྱེད་པ་ | *ke-chha cKe-pa.* |
| Do. *hon.* | གསུང་གྲོས་གནང་བ་ | *sung-ťrö nang-wa.* |
| Discover, to (see) | མཐོང་བ་ | *thong-wa.* |
| Do. *hon.* | མཟིགས་པ་ | *śi-pa.* |
| Discreet (in speech) | ཁ་བཙན་པོ་ | *kha tsem-po.* |
| Do. *hon.* | ཞལ་བཙན་པོ་ | *sKe tsem-po.* |
| Discuss, to | རྩོད་པ་རྒྱབ་པ་ | *tsö-pa gyaṕ-pa.* |
| Do. *hon.* | རྩོད་པ་སྐྱོན་པ་ | *tsö-pa kyöm-pa.* |
| Disease | ན་ཚ་ | *na-tsha.* |
| Do. *hon.* | སྙུང་གཞི་ | *nyung-sKi.* |
| Disgrace | ཞབས་འདྲེན་ | *sKam-dren.* |
| Disgraced, to be | ཞབས་འདྲེན་ཞུ་བ་ | *sKam-dren sKu-wa.* |
| Do. *hon.* | ཞབས་འདྲེན་ཞུ་བ་གནང་བ་ | *sKam-dren sKu-wa nang-wa.* |
| Disguised, to be | ཆ་ལུགས་མི་གཅིག་པ་སྤྲད་པ་ | *chha-lu mi-chik-pa tre-pa.* |
| Do. *hon.* | ཆ་ལུགས་མི་གཅིག་པ་བཞེས་པ་ | *chha-lu mi-chik-pa sKe-pa.* |
| Disgusting | སྐྱུག་བྲོ་པོ་ | *kyuk-ťro-po.* |
| Dish | སྡེར་མ་ | *der-ma.* |
| Do. *hon.* | གསོལ་སྡེར་ | *sö-der.* |

| | | |
|---|---|---|
| Disheartened | སེམས་སྐྱོ་པོ་ | *sem-kyo-po.* |
| Disk | འཁོར་ལོ་ | *khor-lo.* |
| Dislike, to | མི་དགའ་བ་ | *mi-ga-wa.* |
| Do. *hon.* | མི་མཉེས་པ་ | *mi-nye-pa.* |
| Dislocate, to (joint) | ཚིགས་སྒྲོག་པ་ | *tshik-throk-pa.* |
| Dismantle, to | བཤིག་པ་ (འཇིག་པ་) | *shik-pa.* |
| Do. *hon.* | བཤིག་ག་ (པ་) གནང་བ་ | *shik-k̓a nang-wa.* |
| Dismiss, to (*e.g.*, servant) | དགོངས་འཕྲོག་བཏང་ (གཏོང་) བ། | *gong-pho tang-wa;* |
| | གནས་དབྱུང་བཏང་ (གཏོང་) བ་ | *ne-yung tang-wa.* |
| Do. *hon.* | གནས་དབྱུང་གཏོང་ང་ (བ་) གནང་བ། | *ne-yung tong-nga nang-wa;* |
| | དགོངས་འཕོག་གནང་བ་ | *gong-pho nang-wa.* |
| Dismount, to | བབ་པ་ (འབབ་པ་) | *p̓ap̓-pa.* |
| Do. *hon.* | ཆིབས་གཞོལ་གནང་བ་ | *chhip̓-sk̓ö nang-wa.* |
| Disobey, to | ཁ་ལ་མི་ཉན་པ་ | *kha-la mi-nyem pa.* |
| Do. *hon.* | ཞལ་ལ་མི་གསན་པ་ | *sk̓e-la mi-sem-pa.* |
| Disorder | མགོ་དཀྲོག་ | *go tro.* |
| Dispatch, to | བཏང་བ་ (གཏོང་བ་) | *tang-wa.* |
| Do. *hon.* | གཏོང་ང་ (བ་) གནང་བ་ | *tong-nya nang-wa.* |

| | | |
|---|---|---|
| Dispensary | སྨན་ཁང་ | *men-khang.* |
| Disperse, to, *v.i.* | གྲོལ་བ། གྲེས་པ་ | *t́röl-wa ; ḱye-pa.* |
| Do. *hon.* | ལྷན་རྒྱས་གྲོལ་ར་(བ་) གནང་བ་ | *l̈hen-gye t́rö-ra nang-wa.* |
| Disposition (temper) | སེམས་ | *sem.* |
| Do. *hon.* | ཐུགས་སེམས་ | *thu-sem.* |
| Disputation | རྩོད་པ་ | *tsö-pa.* |
| Dispute | ལབ་གཞི། རྩོད་པ་ | *laṕ-shi ; tsö-pa.* |
| Do. to | རྩོད་པ་རྒྱབ་བ་ | *tsö-pa gyaṕ-pa.* |
| Do. *hon.* | རྩོད་པ་སྐྱོན་པ་ | *tso-pa kyöm-pa.* |
| Disrobe, to | ཕྱིས་པ་ (འཕུད་པ་) | *pi-pa.* |
| Do. *hon.* | ཕྱིས་ (འཕུད་) པ་གནང་བ་ | *pi-pa nang-wa.* |
| Dissatisfied, to be | འདོད་པ་མི་ཁང་བ་(འཁེངས་པ) | *dö-pa mi-khang-wa.* |
| Do. *hon.* | ཐུགས་འདོད་མི་ཁང་བ་ (འཁེངས་པ་) | *thung-dö mi-khang-wa.* |
| Dissension | སྡེ་དཀྲུག་ | *de-tru.* |
| Dissimilar | མི་གཅིག་པ་ | *mi-chiḱ-pa.* |
| Dissimilarity | ཁྱད་པར་ | *khye-par.* |
| Do. *hon.* | ཐུགས་ཁྱད་ | *thu-khye.* |
| Dissolve, to | བཞུ་བ་ | *sḱu-wa.* |
| Do. *hon.* | བཞུ་བ་གནང་བ་ | *sḱu-wa nang-wa.* |

| | | |
|---|---|---|
| Dissuade, to | སེམས་སྒྱུར་བ་ | *sem-gyur-wa.* |
| Do. *hon.* | ཐུགས་སེམས་སྒྱུར་ར་ (བ་) གནང་བ་ | *thu-sem gyur-ra nang-wa.* |
| Distance | ཐག་རིང་ཐུང་ | *tha-ring-thung.* |
| Do. *hon.* | ཕེབ་ཐག་རིང་ཐུང་ | *phep̌-tha-ring-thung.* |
| Distant | ཐག་རིང་པོ་ | *tha-ring-po.* |
| Do. *hon.* | ཕེབ་ཐག་རིང་པོ་ | *phep̌-tha-ring-po.* |
| Distinct (clear) | གསལ་པོ་ | *se-po.* |
| Distinction, to make a | དབྱེན་ (དབྱེ་བ་) ཕྱེ་བ་ | *yen chhe-wa.* |
| Distinction (difference) | ཁྱད་ | *khye.* |
| Do. *hon.* | ཐུགས་ཁྱད་ | *thu-khye.* |
| Distinctly (intelligibly) | སྒྲ་དག་པོ་ | *dra-ťaǩ-po.* |
| Distinguish, to | དབྱེན་ (དབྱེ་བ་) ཕྱེ་བ་ | *yen-chhe-wa.* |
| Do. *hon.* | དབྱེན་ (དབྱེ་བ) ཕྱེ་བ་གནང་བ་ | *yen-chhe-wa nang-wa.* |
| Distinguished (well-known) | སྐད་གྲགས་ཆེན་པོ་ | *ke-ťra chhem-po.* |
| Do. *hon.* | མཚན་སྙན་གྲགས་ཆེན་པོ་ | *tshen-nyen-ťra chhem-po.* |
| Distress | སྡུག་བསྔལ་ | *du-nge.* |
| Distressed, to be | སེམས་སྡུག་པ་ | *sem-duǩ-pa.* |
| Do. *hon.* | ཐུགས་སེམས་སྡུག་ག་ (པ་) གནང་བ་ | *thu-sem duǩ-ka nang-wa.* |

| | | |
|---|---|---|
| Distribute, to | བགོད་པ། བགོ་བཤའ་རྒྱབ་པ་ | *gö-pa ; goṗ-sha gyaṗ-pa.* |
| Do. *hon.* | བགོད་པ་གནང་བ། བགོ་བཤའ་སྐྱོན་པ་ | *gö-pa nang-wa ; goṗ-sha kyöm-pa.* |
| District (tract of country) | ལུང་པ། ཡུལ་ | *lung-pa ; yü.* |
| Do, (jurisdiction of a dzong pön) | རྫོང་ཁག་ | *dzong-kha.* |
| Distrust, to | བློས་མི་ཁེད་པ་ | *lö mi khe-pa.* |
| Do. *hon.* | ཐུགས་བློས་མི་ཁེད་པ་ | *thuk-lö mi khe-pa.* |
| Disturbance | རྒྱབ་འདྲེ་ | *gyam-dre.* |
| Do. *hon.* | གསུང་འཁྲུག་ | *sung-thru.* |
| Ditch | ཆུ་དོང་ | *chhu-ťong.* |
| Dive, to | ཆུའི་གདིང་ལ་འཛུལ་འགྲོ་བ་ | *chhu-i-ting-la dzü-dro-wa.* |
| Divers (various) | སོ་སོ་ | *so-so.* |
| Divest, to (of clothes) | ཕྱིས་པ་ (འཕྱིད་པ་) | *pi-pa.* |
| Do. *hon.* | ཕྱིས་ (འཕྱིད་) པ་གནང་བ་ | *pi-pa nang-wa.* |
| Divide, to | བགོད་པ། བགོ་བཤའ་རྒྱབ་པ་ | *gö-pa ; goṗ-sha gyaṗ-pa.* |
| Do. *hon.* | བགོད་པ་གནང་བ་ | *gö-pa nang-wa.* |
| Divorce, to | ཁ་བྲལ་ (འབྲལ་) བ་ | *kha-ťrel-wa.* |
| Do. *hon.* | ཁ་བྲལ་ར་ (འབྲལ་བ་) གནང་བ་ | *kha-ťre-ra nang-wa.* |
| Divorce money (paid to divorce) | དབྱུག་འཇལ་ | *yuk-je.* |
| Dizzy, to be | མགོ་ཡུ་འཁོར་བ་ | *go-yu khor-wa.* |

| | | |
|---|---|---|
| Dizzy, to be *hon.* | དབུ་ཡུ་འཁོར་བ་ | *u-yu khor-wa.* |
| Do, to | བྱེད་པ་ | *cḱe-pa.* |
| Do. *hon.* | གནང་བ་ | *nang-wa.* |
| Do, that will (that is enough) | ད་འགྲིག་ག་ | *t́a-drik-ḱa.* |
| Doctor | ཨམ་ཆི་ (ཨེམ་ཆི་) | *am-chhi.* |
| Do. *hon.* | ཨམ་ (ཨེམ་) ཆི་ལགས་ | *am-chhi-la.* |
| Doctrine | ཆོས་ལུགས་ | *chhö-lu.* |
| Document | འཛིན་ | *dzin.* |
| Do. *hon.* | ཕྱག་འཛིན་ | *chha-dzin.* |
| Dog | ཁྱི་ | *khyi.* |
| Do. *hon.* | གཟིམ་ཁྱི་ | *śim-khyi.* |
| Dog (for hunting) | ཤ་ཁྱི་ | *sha-khyi.* |
| Dominion | རྒྱལ་ཁག་ | *gye-kha.* |
| Dominoes, to play at | སྦག་རྒྱབ་པ་ | *ba gyaṕ-pa.* |
| Do. *hon.* | ཕྱག་སྦག་སྐྱོན་པ་ | *chha-ba kyöm-pa.* |
| Donkey | བུང་གུ་ (བོང་བུ་) | *ṕung-gu.* |
| Door | སྒོ་ | *go.* |
| Do. *hon.* | གཟིམ་སྒོ་ | *śim-go.* |
| Door (large outside) | རྒྱལ་སྒོ་ | *gye-go.* |
| Door-frame | སྒོའི་རེ་བཞི་ | *gö-riṕ-sḱi.* |

| | | |
|---|---|---|
| Door-keeper | སྒོ་རག་པ་ (སྒོ་སྲུང་པ་) | *go-ra-pa.* |
| Dose (of medicine) | སྨན་ཐུན་ | *men-thün.* |
| Dot | ཚག་ (ཚེག) | *tsha.* |
| Double | གཉིས་ལྡབ་ | *nyi-daṕ.* |
| Doubt | ཐེ་ཚོམ་ | *the-tshom.* |
| Do. to | ཐེ་ཚོམ་ཟ་བ་ | *the-tshom śa-wa.* |
| Do. *hon.* | ཐེ་ཚོམ་གནང་བ་ | *the-tshom nang-wa.* |
| Doubtful | གཉིས་བཟོ་ | *nye-śo.* |
| Dough | སྤགས་ | *pa.* |
| Dove | ཏུད་ཏུད་ཀུ་ཀུ་ | *t́u-t́u ku-ku.* |
| Down | མར་ | *ma.* |
| Down hill | ཐུར་ | *thur.* |
| Down there | མ་གི་ | *ma-gi.* |
| Downwards | མར་ | *ma.* |
| Doze, to | གཉིད་ཙོག་རྒྱབ་པ་ | *nyi-tso gyaṕ-pa.* |
| Do. *hon.* | མཉན་ (མནལ་) ཙོག་སྐྱོན་པ་ | *nye-tso kyöm-pa.* |
| Drag, to | འཐེན་པ་ | *them-pa.* |
| Do. *hon.* | འཐེན་པ་གནང་བ་ | *them-pa nang-wa.* |
| Dragon | འབྲུག་ | *druḱ.* |
| Drain (on ground) | ཡོ་པོ་ (ཡུར་པོ་) | *yo-po.* |

| | | |
|---|---|---|
| Drain (on roof of house) | ཨོག་ཆུ་ | *o-chhu.* |
| Draw, to (pull) | འཐེན་པ་ | *them-pa.* |
| Do. *hon.* | འཐེན་པ་གནང་བ་ | *them-pa nang-wa.* |
| Draw lots, to | མོ་རྒྱབ་པ་ | *mo-gyap̂-pa.* |
| Do. *hon.* | ཕྱག་མོ་སྐྱོན་པ་ | *chha-mo kyöm-pa.* |
| Draw up, to (documents &c.) | རྩོམ་པ་ | *tsom-pa.* |
| Do. *hon.* | རྩོམ་པ་གནང་བ་ | *tsom-pa nang-wa.* |
| Do. *h. hon.* | བཀའ་རྩོམ་གནང་བ | *ḱa-tsom nang-wa.* |
| Draw out, to (in length) | རིང་དུ་བཏང་ (གཏོང་) བ་ | *ring-ťu tang-wa.* |
| Do. *hon.* | རིང་དུ་གཏོང་ང་ (བ་) གནང་བ་ | *ring-ťu tong-nga nang-wa.* |
| Draw pictures, to | རི་མོ་བྲིས་པ་ (འབྲི་བ་) | *ri-mo ťri-pa.* |
| Do. *hon.* | རི་མོ་བྲིས་པ་ (འབྲི་བ་) གནང་བ་ | *ri-mo ťri-pa nang-wa.* |
| Drawers (in table, &c.) | ཤུར་སྒམ་ (ཤུབས་སྒམ་) | *shur-gam.* |
| Drawers, chest of | སྒམ་ | *gam.* |
| Do. *hon.* | ཕྱག་སྒམ་ | *chha-gam.* |
| Drawers (garment) | གོ་ཐུང་ (གོས་ཐུང་།) དོར་མ་ | *ḱo-thung ; ťo-ma.* |
| Do. *hon.* | ཞབས་ཁྱེན། ཞབས་དོར་ | *sḱap-khyen ; sḱap-ťo.* |
| Dread, to | ཞེད་པ་ | *sḱe-pa.* |
| Do. *hon.* | ཞེད་པ་གནང་བ་ | *sḱe-pa nang-wa* |

| | | |
|---|---|---|
| Dreadful | ཞེད་སྐྲག་ཚ་པོ་ | *sḱe-tra tsha-po.* |
| Dream | གཉིད་ལམ་ | *nyi-lam.* |
| Do. *hon.* | མཉན་ལམ་ (མནལ་ལམ་) | *nye-lam.* |
| Dream, to | གཉིད་ལམ་བཏང་ (གཏོང་) བ་ | *nyi-lam tang-wa.* |
| Do. *hon.* | མཉན་ (མནལ་) ལམ་གཏོང་ང་ (བ་) གནང་བ་ | *nye-lam tong-nga nang-wa.* |
| Dress | དགུ་ལོག་ | *ṫu-lo.* |
| Do. *hon.* | ན་བཟའ་ | *nam-śa.* |
| Dress, to (clothe) | གྱོན་པ་ | *ḱyöm-pa.* |
| Do. *hon.* | བཞེས་པ་ | *sḱe-pa.* |
| Dress ostentatiously, to | དང་འདོད་བྱེད་པ་ | *ṫang-dö cḱe-pa.* |
| Do. *hon.* | ཐུགས་དང་འདོད་གནང་བ་ | *thu ṫang-dö nang-wa.* |
| Dried | སྐམ་པོ་ | *kam-po.* |
| Drill, to (soldiers) | དམག་སྦྱོང་བྱེད་པ་ | *ma-jong cḱe-pa.* |
| Do. *hon.* | དམག་སྦྱོང་གནང་བ་ | *ma-jong nang-wa.* |
| Drink, to | འཐུང་བ་ | *thung-wa.* |
| Do. *hon.* | བཞེས་པ་ | *sḱe-pa.* |
| Drinking-water | འཐུང་ཡ་གི་ཆུ་ | *thung-ya-ḱi chhu.* |
| Do. *hon.* | བཞེས་ཡ་གི་ཆབ་ | *sḱe-ya-ḱi chhaṕ.* |
| Drip, to (of water) | ཐིགས་པ་རྒྱབ་པ་ | *thiḱ-pa gyaṕ-pa.* |

| | | |
|---|---|---|
| Drive, to (pursue) | དེད་པ་ | *ťe-pa.* |
| Do. *hon.* | དེད་པ་གནང་བ་ | *ťe-pa nang-wa.* |
| Drop | ཐིགས་པ་ | *thiǩ-pa.* |
| Drop, to, *v.t.* | བཏང་བ་ (གཏོང་བ་) | *tang-wa.* |
| Do. *hon.* | གཏོང་ང་ (བ་) གནང་བ་ | *tong-nga nang-wa.* |
| Drop, to *v.i.* | གཟག་པ་ | *śaǩ-pa.* |
| Dropsy, to have | གཟུགས་པོ་ལ་ཆུ་བསགས་ (གསོག་) པ་ | *śuǩ-po-la chhu-saǩ-pa.* |
| Do. *hon.* | སྐུ་གཟུགས་ལ་ཆབ་བསགས་ (གསོག་) པ་ | *ku-śuǩ-la chhap̍ saǩ-pa.* |
| Dross (alloy) | ལྷེད་ | *hle.* |
| Drowned, to be | ཆུ་ལ་ཤོར་བ་ | *chhu-la shor-wa.* |
| Do. *hon.* | ཆབ་ལ་ཤོར་ར་ (བ་) གནང་བ་ | *chhap̍-la shor-ra nang-wa.* |
| Drug | སྨན་ | *men.* |
| Do. *hon.* | གསོལ་སྨན་ | *sö-men.* |
| Drum | རྔ་ | *nga.* |
| Do. *hon.* | ཕྱག་རྔ་ | *chha-nga.* |
| Drum-skin | རྔ་ལྤགས་ | *nga-pa.* |
| Drum-stick | རྔ་ཡོག་ (རྔ་དབྱུགས་) | *nga-yo.* |
| Drunk | ར་བཟི་ | *rap̍-śi.* |

| | | |
|---|---|---|
| Drunk, to be | ར་བཟི་བ་ | *ra-śi-wa.* |
| Do. *hon.* | སྐུ་ར་གྲད་པ་ | *ku-ra be-pa.* |
| Drunken fit, to quarrel in a | ར་བཟི་བྱེད་པ། ཀྱོང་ཁོང་བྱེད་པ་ | *rap-śi cKe-pa ; kyong-khong cKe-pa.* |
| Do. *hon.* | ར་བཟི་གནང་བ། ཀྱོང་ཁོང་གནང་བ་ | *rap-śi nang-wa ; kyong-khong nang-wa.* |
| Dry | སྐམ་པོ་ | *kam-po.* |
| Dry to | བསྐམ་པ་ (སྐེམ་པ་) | *kam-pa.* |
| Duck | ཡ་ཚེ་ ch. | *ya-tse.* |
| Dull (stupid) | ལྐུགས་པ། གླེན་པ་ | *kuk-pa ; lem pa.* |
| Dumb | ཁ་ལྐུགས་པ་ | *kha-kuk-pa.* |
| Do. *hon.* | ཞལ་ལྐུགས་པ་ | *sKe-kuk-pa.* |
| Dung (of sheep, goats, mice, etc.) | རིལ་མ་ | *ri-ma.* |
| Do. of horse | རྟའི་སྦངས་ | *te-bang.* |
| Do. of cattle | ལྕུ་བ་ (ལྕི་བ་) | *chu-a.* |
| Do. of human beings. | སྐྱག་པ་ | *kyak-pa.* |
| Dupe, to | མགོ་སྐོར་བཏང་ (གཏོང་) བ་ | *go-kor tang-wa.* |
| Do. *hon.* | མགོ་སྐོར་གཏོང་ང་ (བ་) གནང་བ་ | *go-kor tong-nga nang-wa.* |
| Durable | ཀྲོག་ཆེན་པོ་ | *tro-chhem-po.* |

| | | |
|---|---|---|
| During | དུས་ལ་ | *tü-la.* |
| Dusk | ས་རིབ་ (སྲོད་ཇུབ་) | *sa-rip.* |
| Dust | ཐལ་ལ (ཐལ་བ་) | *thel-la.* |
| Dust-storm | ཐལ་རླུང་ | *the-lung.* |
| Duty (tax) | ཤོ་ཁྲལ་ | *sho-thre.* |
| Dwarf | མི་ཆུང་དེ་ལེབ་ | *mi-chhung te-le.* |
| Do. *hon.* | སྐུ་གཟུགས་ཆུང་ཆུང་ | *ku-śuḱ chhung-chhung.* |
| Dwell, to | བསྡད་པ་ (སྡོད་པ་) | *de-pa.* |
| Do. *hon.* | བཞུགས་པ་ | *sḱu-pa.* |
| Do. *h. hon.* | བཞུགས་གདན་འཇགས་པ་ | *sḱu-den jaḱ-pa.* |
| Dweller | སྡོད་མཁན་ | *dö-khen.* |
| Do. *hon.* | བཞུགས་མཁན་ | *sḱu-khen.* |
| Do. *h. hon.* | བཞུགས་གདན་འཇགས་མཁན་ | *sḱu-den ja-khen.* |
| Dwelling, *s.* | ཁང་པ། ནང་། སྡོད་ས་ | *khang-pa ; nang ; dö-sa.* |
| Do. *hon.* | གཟིམ་ཁང་། བཞུགས་ས་ | *śim-khang ; sḱuḱ-sa.* |
| Do. *h. hon.* | གཟིམ་ཤག། བཞུགས་གདན་འཇགས་ས་ | *śim-sha ; sḱu-den ju-sa.* |
| Dwindle, to (in size) | ཆུང་རུ་ (ཏུ་) འགྲོ་བ་ | *chhung-ru dro-wa.* |
| Do. *hon.* | ཆུང་རུ་ (དུ་) ཕེབ་པ་ | *chhung-ru phe-pa.* |
| Dwindle, to (in numbers) | ཉུང་རུ་ (དུ་) འགྲོ་བ་ | *nyung-ru dro-wa.* |

| | | |
|---|---|---|
| Dye | ཚོས་ | *tshö.* |
| Do. red lac | རྒྱ་ཚོས་ | *gya-tshö.* |
| Dye, to | ཚོས་རྒྱབ་པ་ | *tshö-gyap̍-pa.* |
| Do. *hon.* | ཚོས་སྐྱོན་པ་ | *tshö-kyöm-pa.* |
| Dynasty | རྒྱལ་བརྒྱུད་ | *gye-gyü.* |
| Dysentery | འཁྲུ་ནད་ | *thru-ne.* |
| Dyspepsia | ལྟོ་མ་འཇུ་བའི་ནད་ | *to ma-ju-we ne.* |

# E

| | | |
|---|---|---|
| Each | རེ་རེ་ | *re-re.* |
| Eager | སྙིང་འདོད་པོ། སྙིང་བྲོ་པོ་ | *nying-dö-po ; nying-ťro-po.* |
| Eager to do | བྱེད་སྙིང་འདོད་པོ་ | *cKe-nying dö-po.* |
| Eager to go | འགྲོ་སྙིང་འདོད་པོ་ | *dro-nying dö-po.* |
| Eagle | གོ་བོ་ | *ko-wo.* |
| Ear | ཨམ་མཆོག་ (རྣ་མཆོག་) | *am-chho.* |
| Do. *hon.* | སྙན་མཆོག་ | *nyen-chho.* |
| Ear-hole | ཨམ་མཆོག་ (རྣ་མཆོག་) གི་ཨི་ཁུང་ | *am-chho-ki i-khung.* |
| Do. *hon.* | སྙན་མཆོག་གི་ཨི་ཁུང་ | *nyen-chho-ki i-khung.* |
| Ear of corn | སྙེ་མ་ | *nye-ma.* |
| Early (in morning) | སྔ་པོ་ | *nga-po.* |
| Earnest, *adj.* | སྙིང་རུས་ཆེན་པོ་ | *nying-rü chhem-po.* |
| Do. *hon.* | ཐུགས་རུས་ཆེན་པོ་ | *thu-rü chhem-po.* |
| Earnestly | སྙིང་རུས་བྱས་ནས་ | *nying-rü cKe-ne.* |
| Earring (man's) | སོ་བྱིས་ (སོ་གོང་) | *so-cKi.* |
| Do. *hon.* | སྙན་བྱིས་ | *nyen-cKi.* |
| Earring (woman's) | ཨས་སྐོར་ | *e-kor.* |
| Do. *hon.* | སྙན་སྐོར་ | *nyen-kor.* |

| | | |
|---|---|---|
| Earring (of turquoises) | གཟི་གཡུ་ | *sí-yu.* |
| Do. *hon.* | སྙན་གཡུ་ | *nye-yu.* |
| Earth | ས་ | *sa.* |
| Earthen vessel | ཁོག་མ་ | *kho-ma.* |
| Do. *hon.* | བཞེས་ཁོག་ | *sḱe-kho.* |
| Earthenware | རྫ་སྣོད་ | *dza-nö.* |
| Earthquake | ས་གཡོམ་ (ས་གཡོས།) ས་འགྱུལ་ | *sa-yom ; sa-gü.* |
| Earth-work | ས་ལས་ | *sap-le.* |
| Easily | ལས་སླ་པོ་ | *le-la-po.* |
| East | ཤར་ | *shar.* |
| Easy | ལས་སླ་པོ་ | *le-la-po.* |
| Eat, to | ཟ་བ་ | *śa-wa.* |
| Do. *hon.* | བཞེས་པ་ | *sḱe-pa.* |
| Eating-house | ཟ་ཁང་ | *śa-khang.* |
| Echo | བ་ཆ་ (བྲག་ཆ་) | *ṕa-chha.* |
| Do. to | བ་ཆ་ (བྲག་ཆ་) འཁོར་བ་ | *ṕa-chha khor-wa.* |
| Eclipse of the moon | ཟླ་འཛིན་ | *dan-dzin.* |
| Do. of the sun | ཉིན་འཛིན་ | *nyin-dzin.* |
| Edict | བཀའ་རྒྱ་ | *ka-gya.* |

| | | |
|---|---|---|
| Edge (of knife, etc.) | ངོ་ | *ngo.* |
| Do. (of land, water, etc.) | ཚར། འགྲམ་ | *tsa ; dram.* |
| Do. (of table, etc.) | ཟུར་ | *śur.* |
| Edged | རྣོ་པོ་ | *no-po.* |
| Edible, to be | ཟ་ཉན་པ་ | *śa-nyem-pa.* |
| Do. *hon.* | མཆོད་ཉན་པ་ | *chhö-nyem-pa.* |
| Editor | རྩོམ་པ་རྒྱབ་མཁན་ | *tsom-pa gyaṕ-khen.* |
| Educate, to | ཡི་གེ་བསླབས་ (སློབ་) པ། སྦྱོང་དར་སྤྲོད་པ་ | *yi-ge laṕ-pa ; jong-ťar tre-pa.* |
| Do. *hon.* | ཕྱག་བྲིས་བསླབས་ (སློབ་) པ་གནང་བ་ | *chha-ri laṕ-pa nang-wa.* |
| Efface, to | སུབ་པ་ | *suṕ-pa.* |
| Do. *hon.* | སུབ་པ་གནང་བ་ | *suṕ-pa nang-wa.* |
| Effect, to (perform) | བྱེད་པ་ | *cḱe-pa.* |
| Do. *hon.* | གནང་བ་ | *nang-wa.* |
| Effects (goods) | ཅ་ལག་ (ཆ་ལག་) | *cha-la.* |
| Do. *hon.* | སྐུ་ཅས་ (སྐུ་ཆས་) | *ku-che.* |
| Effort | བརྩོན་འགྲུས་ | *tsön-drü.* |
| Effort, to make an | བརྩོན་འགྲུས་བྱེད་པ་ | *tsön-drü cḱe-pa.* |
| Do. *hon.* | ཐུགས་བརྩོན་གནང་བ་ | *thuḱ-tsön nang-wa.* |

| | | |
|---|---|---|
| Egg | སྒོ་ང་ | *go-nga.* |
| Do. *hon.* | བཞེས་སྒོང་ | *ske-gong.* |
| Egg, white of an | དཀར་སྤྲིན་ | *kar-trin.* |
| Eggs, to lay | སྒོ་ང་བཏང་ (གཏོང་) བ་ | *go-nga tang-wa.* |
| Eight | བརྒྱད་ | *gye.* |
| Eighteen | བཅོ་བརྒྱད་ | *chop-gye.* |
| Eighteenth | བཅོ་བརྒྱད་པ་ | *chop-gye-pa.* |
| Eighth | བརྒྱད་པ་ | *gye-pa.* |
| Eightieth | བརྒྱད་བཅུ་པ་ | *gye-chu-pa.* |
| Eighty | བརྒྱད་བཅུ་ | *gye-chu.* |
| Either, *conj.* | ཡང་མེན་ན། ཡང་ན་ | *yang-men-na ; yang-na.* |
| Eject to | བཏོན་པ་ (འདོན་པ་) | *töm-pa.* |
| Do. *hon.* | བཏོན་ (འདོན་) པ་གནང་བ་ | *töm-pa nang-wa.* |
| Elbow | གྲུ་མོ་ | *t're-mo.* |
| Elder, *adj.* | རྒན་པ་ | *gem-pa.* |
| Elder brother | ཇོ་ཇོ་ | *cKo-cKo.* |
| Do. *hon.* | ཇོ་ལགས་ | *cKo-la.* |
| Eldest | རྒན་ཤོས་ | *gen-shö.* |
| Do. *hon.* | བགྲེས་ཤོས་ | *dre-shö.* |
| Elect, to (appoint) | སྒོ་བ་ | *ko-wa.* |

| | | |
|---|---|---|
| Elect, to (appoint) *hon.* | སྐོ་བ་གནང་བ་ | *ko-wa-nang-wa.* |
| Electric light | གློག་ཞུ་ | *lok-sku.* |
| Elegant | འདྲ་ཆགས་པོ་ | *dra-chhak-po.* |
| Element (fire, earth, etc.) | འབྱུང་བ་ | *jung-wa.* |
| Elephant | གླང་པོ་ཆེ། གླང་ཆེན་ | *lang-po-chhe; lang-chhen.* |
| Elevation | མཐོ་དམན་ | *tho-men.* |
| Eleven | བཅུ་གཅིག་ | *chuk-chi.* |
| Eleventh | བཅུ་གཅིག་པ་ | *chuk-chi-pa.* |
| Else | དེ་མིན་ན་ | *te-min-na.* |
| Elsewhere | གཞན་པ་ | *skem-pa.* |
| Embarrassed, to be | མགོ་འཐོམས་པ་ | *go-thom-pa.* |
| Do. *hon.* | དབུ་འཐོམས་པ་ | *u-thom-pa.* |
| Ember | མེ་མདག་ | *men da.* |
| Emblem | རྟགས་ | *ta.* |
| Embrace, to | འཁྱུད་པ་ | *khyü-pa.* |
| Do. *hon.* | འཁྱུད་པ་གནང་བ་ | *khyü-pa nang-wa.* |
| Embroidery | ཀྱིང་ཁབ་ (ཀྱིང་ཁེབས་) | *kying-khap.* |
| Do. gold | ཟར་བབས་ | *śar-pap.* |
| Do. best quality | རྒྱ་གསེར་ | *gya-ser.* |
| Emerald | མ་རྒད་ | *ma-ge.* |

| | | |
|---|---|---|
| Emetic | སྐྱུག་སྨན་ | *kyuk-men.* |
| Eminence, *s.* | སྒང་། རྩེ་ | *gang ; tse.* |
| Eminent, *adj.* | སྐད་གྲགས་ཆེན་པོ་ | *ke-t́ra chhem-po.* |
| Do. *hon.* | སྙན་གྲགས་ཆེན་པོ་ | *nyen-t́ra Chhem-po.* |
| Emperor | རྒྱལ་པོ་ | *gye-po.* |
| Do. of China | རྒྱ་ནག་གོང་མ་ | *gya-na ḱong-ma.* |
| Emperor's administration | རྒྱལ་སྲིད་ | *gye-si.* |
| Empire | རྒྱལ་ཁམས་ | *gyeng-kham.* |
| Employ, to | སྐོ་བ་ | *ko-wa.* |
| Do. *hon.* | སྐོ་བ་གནང་བ་ | *ko-wa nang-wa.* |
| Employ, to (servant) | བཞག་པ་ (འཛོག་པ་) | *sḰak-pa.* |
| Do. *hon.* | གཞོག་ག་ (པ་) གནང་བ་ | *sḰok-ḱa nang-wa.* |
| Employment | ལས་ཀ་ | *le-ka.* |
| Do. *hon.* | ཕྱག་ལས་ | *chha-le.* |
| Empty, *adj.* | སྟོང་པ་ | *tong-pa.* |
| Do. to | སྟོང་པ་བཟོ་བ་ | *tong-pa śo-wa.* |
| Do. *hon.* | སྟོང་པ་བཟོ་བ་གནང་བ་ | *tong-pa śo-wa nang-wa.* |
| Enabled, to be | ཐུབ་པ་ | *thuṕ-pa.* |
| Do. *hon.* | ཐུབ་པ་གནང་བ་ | *thuṕ-pa nang-wa.* |
| Enamelware | ཀུ་ཀུ་ཤ་ | *ḱu-ḱu-sha.* |

| | | |
|---|---|---|
| Encamp, to | སྒར་རྒྱབ་པ་ | *gar-gyap-pa.* |
| Do. *hon.* | སྒར་སྐྱོན་པ་ | *gar-kyöm-pa.* |
| Encampment | སྒར་ | *gar.* |
| Encircle, to | སྐོར་བ་ | *kor-wa.* |
| Do. *hon.* | སྐོར་ར་ (བ་) གནང་བ་ | *kor-ra nang-wa.* |
| Enclosure (fence) | ར་བ་ | *ra-wa.* |
| Encounter, to (meet) | ཐུག་པ་ | *thuk-pa.* |
| Do. *inf.* meeting *sup.* | མཇལ་བ་ | *jel-wa.* |
| Encourage, to | བློ་ཁོག་ཆེ་རུ་བཏང་ (གཏོང་) བ་ | *lo-kho chhe-ru tang-wa.* |
| Do. *hon.* | བློ་ཁོག་ཆེ་རུ་གཏོང་ང་ (བ་) གནང་བ་ | *lo-kho chhe-ru tong-nga nang-wa.* |
| End | མཐའ་ | *tha.* |
| Do. to be at an (consumed) | རྫོགས་པ་ | *dzok-pa.* |
| Do. to be at an (accomplished) | འཚར་བ་ | *tshar-wa.* |
| Endeavour, to | བརྩོན་འགྲུས་བྱེད་པ་ | *tsön-drü che-pa.* |
| Do. *hon.* | ཐུགས་བརྩོན་གནང་བ་ | *thu-tsön nang-wa.* |
| Endless | རྫོགས་རྒྱུ་མེད་པ་ | *dzo-gyu me-pa.* |
| Endure, to, *v.t.* | བཟོད་པ་སྒོམ་པ་ | *śö-pa gom-pa.* |
| Do. *hon.* | བཟོད་པ་སྒོམ་པ་གནང་བ་ | *śö-pa gom-pa nang-wa.* |
| Enemy. | དགྲ་ | *dra.* |

| | | |
|---|---|---|
| Energetic | བརྩོན་པོ། སྙིང་རུས་ཆེན་པོ་ | *tsöm-po ; nying-rü chhem-po.* |
| Do. *hon.* | ཐུགས་རུས་ཆེན་པོ་ | *thuk-rü chhem-po.* |
| Engage on hire, to | གླ་པ་ | *la-pa.* |
| Do. *hon.* | གླ་གནང་བ་ | *la nang-wa.* |
| Enhance, to | འཕར་བ་ | *phar-wa.* |
| Enjoin, to | བཀའ་གནང་བ་ | *ka-nang-wa.* |
| Enough, to be | འགྲིག་པ་ | *drik-pa.* |
| Enjoy, to | སྐྱིད་པོ་བྱེད་པ་ | *kyi-po cke-pa.* |
| Do. *hon.* | སྤྲོ་པོ་གནང་བ་ | *tro-po nang-wa.* |
| Enlarge, to | ཆེ་རུ་བཏང་ (གཏོང་) བ་ | *chhe-ru tang-wa.* |
| Do. *hon.* | ཆེ་རུ་གཏོང་ང་ (བ་) གནང་བ་ | *chhe-ru tong-nya-nang-wa.* |
| Enmity | གཏིང་ནད་ | *ting-ne.* |
| Enormous | ཆེ་ཐག་ཆོད་ | *chhe-thak-chhö.* |
| Enquire, to (ask) | དྲི་བ་ (འདྲི་བ་) | *tri-wa.* |
| Do. *hon.* | བཀའ་འདྲི་གནང་བ་ | *kan-dri nang-wa.* |
| Enquire, to (investigate) | ཞིབ་དཔྱོད་བྱེད་པ་ | *skip-chö cke-pa.* |
| Do. *hon.* | ཞིབ་དཔྱོད་གནང་བ་ | *skip-chö nang-wa.* |
| Do. *h. hon.* | བཀའ་ཞིབ་གནང་བ་ | *ka-skip nang-wa.* |
| Ensnare, to | རྙི་བཙུགས་ (འཛུགས་) པ་ | *nyi-tsuk-pa.* |

| | | |
|---|---|---|
| Ensnare, to *hon.* | ཉི་བཙུགས་ག་ (འཛུགས་པ་) གནང་བ་ | *nyi-tsuk-ka nang-wa.* |
| Enter, to | འཛུལ་བ་ | *dzü-wa.* |
| Do. *hon.* | ཕེབ་པ་ | *phe-pa.* |
| Do. *h. hon.* | འཆིབ་གྱུ་གནང་བ་ | *chhip-gyu nang-wa.* |
| Entertainment (feast) | མགྲོན་པོ་ | *dröm-po.* |
| Do. *hon.* | ཐུགས་སྤྲོ་ | *thu-tro.* |
| Entice, to | སླུ་བ་ | *lu-wa.* |
| Do. *hon.* | སླུ་བ་གནང་བ་ | *lu-wa nang-wa.* |
| Entire | ཚང་མ། ཐམས་ཅད། སྒང་ཁ་ | *tshang-ma; tham-che; gang-kha.* |
| Entirely | བད་དེ་ | *be-ťe.* |
| Entomb, to | ས་སྦེད་བཏང་ (གཏོང་) བ་ | *sa-be tang-wa.* |
| Do. *hon.* | ས་སྦེད་གཏོང་ང་ (བ་) གནང་བ་ | *sa-be tong-nga nang-wa.* |
| Entrails | གྱུ་མ་ | *gyu-ma.* |
| Do. *hon.* | སྐུ་གྱུ་ | *ku gyu.* |
| Entreat, to | ཞུ་བ་ | *sǩu-wa.* |
| Entrust, to | བཅོལ་ (འཚོལ་) གཞོག་ (འཇོག་) པ་ | *chö-sǩok-pa.* |
| Do. *hon.* | བཅོལ་ (འཆོལ་) གཞོག་ག་ (འཇོག་པ་) གནང་བ་ | *chö-sǩok-ka nang-wa.* |

| | | |
|---|---|---|
| Envelope (Tibetan) | རྒྱ་མ་ | *gya-ma.* |
| Do. (English) | ཡིག་ཤུབས་ | *yiḱ-shuṕ.* |
| Envious | ཕྲ་དོག་ཚ་པོ་ | *thra-ťo tsha-po.* |
| Envoy | ཕྲོ་ཉ་ | *pho-nya.* |
| Envy, *s.* | ཕྲ་དོག་ | *thra-ťo.* |
| Envy, to | ཕྲ་དོག་བྱེད་པ་ | *thra-ťo cḱe-pa.* |
| Do. *hon.* | ཕྲ་དོག་གནང་བ་ | *thra-ťo nang-wa.* |
| Epilepsy | གཟའ་ནད་ | *śa-ne.* |
| Epistle | ཡི་གེ་ | *yi-ge.* |
| Do. *hon.* | ཕྱག་བྲིས་ | *chha ri.* |
| Equal | གཅིག་པ། འདྲ་འདྲ་ | *chiḱ-pa ; dran-dra.* |
| Equitable | འདྲ་དྲང་ | *dra-ťrang.* |
| Erase, to | སྤུབ་པ་ | *suṕ-pa.* |
| Do. *hon.* | སྤུབ་པ་གནང་བ་ | *suṕ-pa nang-wa.* |
| Erect | ཀྱེ་རེ་ | *kye-re.* |
| Do. to stand | ཀྱེ་རེ་ལང་བསྡད་ (སྡོད་) པ་ | *kye-re lang-de-pa.* |
| Do. *hon.* | ཀྱེ་རེ་བཞེང་(བཞེང་)བཞུགས་པ་ | *kye-re sḱang-sḱu-pa.* |
| Erect, to (build) | རྩིག་པ་ | *tsiḱ-pa.* |
| Do. *hon.* | རྩིག་ག་ (པ་) གནང་བ་ | *tsiḱ-ḱa nang-wa.* |
| Err, to | ནོར་བ་ | *nor-wa.* |

| | | |
|---|---|---|
| Err, to *hon.* | ནོར་ར་ (བ་) གནང་བ་ | *nor-ra nang-wa.* |
| Error | ནོར་ | *nor.* |
| Eruption (on skin) | ལྦ་ཚ་ (ལྦ་བ་) | *ba-tsha.* |
| Escape, to | ཤོར་བ་ | *shor-wa.* |
| Escort, *s.* | སྐུ་སྲུང་། | *ku-sung.* |
| | དཔུང་རོགས་ | *pung-ro.* |
| Do. to | དཔུང་རོགས་འཁྲིད་པ་ | *pung-ro thri-pa.* |
| Do. *hon.* | དཔུང་རོགས་འཁྲིད་པ་གནང་བ་ | *pung-ro thri-pa nang-wa.* |
| Do. to (of person in superior position) | སྐུ་སྲུང་འཁྲིད་པ་གནང་བ་ | *ku-sung thri-pa nang-wa.* |
| Especially | ཁྱད་པར་དུ་ | *khye par-ťu.* |
| Eternal | རྫོགས་རྒྱུ་མེད་པ། མཐའ་མེད་པ་ | *dzo-gyu-me-pa; tha-me-pa.* |
| Europe | ཕྱི་གླིང་ | *chhi-ling.* |
| European, *adj.* | ཕྱི་གླིང་གི་ | *chhi-ling-ki.* |
| Do. (a man) | ཕྱི་གླིང་གི་མི་ | *chhi-ling-ki-mi.* |
| Evaporate, to | ཡལ་བ་ | *ye-wa.* |
| Even, *adj.* (level) | སྙོམས་པོ་ | *nyom-po.* |
| Even, *adv.* | ཡང་ | *yang.* |
| Evening | དགོང་མོ་ | *gong-mo.* |
| Do. this | དོ་དགོང་ | *ťo-gong.* |

| | | |
|---|---|---|
| Evenly balanced, to be | ཡང་ སྙི་མེད་པ་ | *yang-ji me-pa.* |
| Events, at all | གང་ཡིན་ཀྱང་། ག་རེ་ཡིན་རུང་ | *kang-yin-kyang ; ka-re yin-rung.* |
| Ever (always) | ནམ་རྒྱུན། དུས་རྒྱུན། རྟག་པ་རེ་བཞིན་ | *nam-gyün ; tü-gyün ; tak-pa re-shi.* |
| Everlasting | རྫོགས་རྒྱུ་མེད་པ། མཐའ་མེད་པ་ | *dzo-gyu me-pa ; tha me-pa.* |
| Every | རེ་རེ་ | *re-re.* |
| Everybody | མི་སྐང་ཁ་ | *mi gang-kha.* |
| Every day | ཞག་མ་རེ་རེ་ | *sha-ma re-re.* |
| Every kind | སྣ་ཚོགས་ | *na-tsho.* |
| Everywhere | ག་ས་ག་ལ་ | *ka sa ka-la.* |
| Evidence | རྒྱུ་མཚན་ | *gyum-tshen.* |
| Evident | ངེས་པ། དངོས་ནས་ | *nge-par ; ngön-ne.* |
| Evil | ངན་པ་ | *ngen-pa.* |
| Evil spirit | འདྲེ་ | *dre.* |
| Exact | ཁྲིག་ཁྲིག་ | *thrik-thri.* |
| Exactly | རང་ | *rang.* |
| Exactly so | ད་ག་རེད་ | *ta-ka-re.* |
| Do. *hon.* | ད་ག་རང་རེད་ | *ta-ka rang-re.* |
| Do. *h. hon.* | བཀའ་གནང་རང་རེད་ | *ka-nang rang-re.* |

|  |  |  |
|---|---|---|
| Exaggerate, to | སྐད་ཆ་སྒྲོ་འདོགས་པ་ | *ke-chha dro-dok-pa.* |
| Exalt, to | མཐོ་ས་སྐྱེལ་བ་ | *tho-sa kyel-wa.* |
| Do *hon.* | མཐོ་ས་སྐྱེལ་ར་ (བ་) གནང་བ་ | *tho-sa kye-ra nang-wa.* |
| Examination (of student) | རྒྱུགས་ | *gyuk.* |
| Do. (investigation) | ཞིབ་དཔྱོད་ | *sKiṕ-chö.* |
| Do. *hon.* | བཀའ་ཞིབ་ | *ka-sKiṕ.* |
| Examine, to (student) | རྒྱུགས་ལེན་པ་ | *gyuk-lem-pa.* |
| Do. *hon.* | རྒྱུགས་བཞེས་པ་ | *gyuk-sKe-pa.* |
| Examine, to (investigate) | ཞིབ་དཔྱོད་བྱེད་པ་ | *sKiṕ-chö cKe-pa.* |
| Do. *hon.* | ཞིབ་དཔྱོད་གནང་བ་ | *sKiṕ-chö nang-wa.* |
| Do. *h. hon.* | བཀའ་ཞིབ་གནང་བ་ | *ka-sKiṕ nang-wa.* |
| Examined, to be (student) | རྒྱུགས་ཕུལ་ (འབུལ་) བ་ | *gyuk-phül-wa.* |
| Example | དཔེ་ | *pe.* |
| Example, for | དཔེ་ན་ཡིན་ན། དཔེ་ན་ (དཔེར་ན་) | *pe-na yin-na; pe-na.* |
| Excavation | དོང་ | *t́ong.* |
| Excavate, to | རྐོ་བ་ | *ko-wa.* |
| Do. *hon.* | རྐོ་བ་གནང་བ་ | *ko-wa nang-wa.* |
| Exceed, to | ལྷག་པ་ | *hlak-pa.* |
| Exceedingly | ཐག་ཆོད་ | *thak-chhö.* |

| | | |
|---|---|---|
| Exceedingly many | མང་ཐག་ཆོད་ | *mang-thaḱ-chhö.* |
| Excellency, His | རིན་པོ་ཆེ་ | *rim-po-chhe.* |
| Excellent | ཡག་ཐག་ཆོད་ | *yaḱ-thaḱ-chhö.* |
| Except | མ་གཏོགས། མིན་པ་ (མིན་པ་) | *ma-to ; mem-pa.* |
| Exchange | རྗེ་པོ་རྒྱབ་པ་ | *je-po gyaṕ-pa.* |
| Do. *hon.* | རྗེ་པོ་སྐྱོན་པ་ | *je-po ḱyöm-pa.* |
| Excessive | མང་ཐག་ཆོད། ཛག་ཏོ་ | *mang-thaḱ-chhö ; dzaḱ-ťo.* |
| Excessive appetite | གྲོད་ཁོག་ཆེན་པོ་ | *ťrö-kho chhem-po.* |
| Exclaim, to | སྐད་བཏང་ (གཏོང་) བ་ | *ke-tang-wa.* |
| Do. *hon.* | སྐད་གཏོང་ང་ (བ་) གནང་བ་ | *ke tong-nga nang wa.* |
| Excluding (except) | མ་གཏོགས། མིན་པ་ (མིན་པ་) | *ma-to ; mem-pa.* |
| Excrement (human) | སྐྱག་པ་ | *kyaḱ-pa.* |
| Excuse, *s.* | ཁ་འདྲི་ | *khan-dri.* |
| Do. *hon.* | ཞལ་འདྲི་ | *sḱen-dri.* |
| Excuses, to make | ཁ་འདྲི་བཤད་པ་ | *khan-dri she-pa.* |
| Do. *hon.* | ཞལ་འདྲི་གནང་བ་ | *sḱen-dri nang-wa.* |
| Do. *inf.* to *sup.* | ཁ་འདྲི་ཞུ་བ་ | *khan dri sḱu-wa.* |
| Exercise, literary | ཡིག་རྒྱུགས་ | *yiḱ-gyu.* |
| Exert one's self, to | སྙིང་རུས་བྱེད་པ་ | *nying-rü cḱe-pa.* |
| Do. *hon.* | ཐུགས་རུས་གནང་བ་ | *thuḱ-rü nang-wa.* |

| | | |
|---|---|---|
| Exhausted, to be (tired) | ཐང་ཆད་པ་ | *thang-chhe-pa.* |
| Do. *hon.* | སྐུ་ཐང་ཆད་པ་གནང་བ་ | *ku thang chhe-pa nang-wa.* |
| Exhaustion | ངལ་ | *ngel.* |
| Do. *hon.* | སྐུ་ངལ་ | *ku-ngel.* |
| Exhibit, to | བསྟན་པ་ (སྟོན་པ་) | *tem-pa.* |
| Exist, to | ཡོད་པ་ | *yö-pa.* |
| Exhort, to | བསླབ་བྱ་བྱེད་པ་ | *lap̓-cḱa cḱe-pa.* |
| Do. *hon.* | བསླབ་བྱ་གནང་བ་ | *lap̓-cḱa nang-wa.* |
| Do. *h. hon.* | བཀའ་སློབ་གནང་བ་ | *ka-lop̓ nang-wa.* |
| Exhortation | བསླབ་བྱ་ | *lap̓-cḱa.* |
| Do. *hon.* | བཀའ་སློབ་ | *ka lop̓.* |
| Exorcise, to | དམ་ལ་བཏགས་ (འདོགས་) པ་ | *ťam-la tak-pa.* |
| Do. *hon.* | དམ་འདོགས་གནང་བ་ | *ťam-dok nang-wa.* |
| Expanse | ཁ་ཞེང་ | *kha-sḱeng.* |
| Expect, to (wait for) | སྒུག་བསྡད་ (སྡོད་) པ་ | *gu-de pa.* |
| Do. *hon.* | སྒུག་བཞུགས་པ་ | *gu sḱu-pa.* |
| Expect, to (hope for) | རེ་བ་བྱེད་པ་ | *re-wa cḱe pa.* |
| Do. *hon.* | ཐུགས་རེ་གནང་བ་ | *thu-re nang-wa.* |
| Expectation | རེ་བ་ | *re-wa.* |
| Do. *hon.* | ཐུགས་རེ་ | *thu-re.* |

| | | |
|---|---|---|
| Expedite, to | བྲེལ་བ་བྱེད་པ་ | *ťre-wa cḱe-pa.* |
| Do. *hon.* | ཐུགས་བྲེལ་གནང་བ་ | *thuk-ťre nang-wa.* |
| Expel, to | བཏོན་པ་ (འདོན་པ་) | *töm-pa.* |
| Do. *hon.* | འདོན་པ་གནང་བ་ | *döm-pa nang-wa.* |
| Expense | འགྲོ་སོང་ | *dro-song.* |
| Do. *hon.* | ཐུགས་འགྲོན་ (ཐུགས་འགྲོ་) | *thung-drön.* |
| Expensive | གོང་ཆེན་པོ། གུས་པོ་ | *kong-chhem-po ; ḱü-po.* |
| Do. *hon.* | ལྗགས་གོང་ཆེན་པོ་ | *ja-kong chhem-po.* |
| Experienced (skilled) | མཁས་པོ་ | *khe-po.* |
| Explain, to | ངོ་སྤྲོད་སྤྲད་པ། དོན་དག་བཤད་པ་ | *ngo-trö tre-pa ; ťon-ťa she-pa.* |
| Do. *hon.* | ངོ་སྤྲོད་གནང་བ། སྐུ་དོན་གསུང་བ་ | *ngo-trö nang-wa ; ku-ťön sung-wa.* |
| Explain, to (by sign) | ལག་བརྡ་བྱེད་པ་ | *lak-da cḱe-pa.* |
| Do. *hon.* | ཕྱག་བརྡ་གནང་བ་ | *chha-da nang-wa.* |
| Explanation (apology) | སེབ་བཀྲོལ་ | *seṕ-trö.* |
| Exports | འཐོན་ཁུངས་ | *thön-khung.* |
| Extensive | རྒྱ་ཆེན་པོ་ | *gya-chhem-po.* |
| External | ཕྱིའི་ | *chhi-i.* |
| Extinct, to become | ཆད་པ་ | *chhe-pa.* |

| | | |
|---|---|---|
| Extinguish, to | བསད་པ་ (གསོད་པ་) | *se-pa.* |
| Do. *hon.* | གསོད་པ་གནང་བ་ | *sö-pa nang-wa.* |
| Extort, to | དབང་ཡོད་བྱས་ནས་ལེན་པ་ | *wang-yö cḱe-ne lem-pa.* |
| Extra | འཕེབ་པ་ | *theṕ-pa.* |
| Extract, to | བཏོན་པ་ (འདོན་པ་) | *töm-pa.* |
| Do. *hon.* | འདོན་པ་གནང་བ་ | *döm-pa nang-wa.* |
| Extraction (descent) | རྒྱུད་ | *gyü.* |
| Extraordinary | ཡ་མཚན་པོ། ཁྱད་མཚར་པོ། | *yam-tshen po ; khye-tsha-po.* |
| Extremity | མཐའ་ | *tha.* |
| Exult, to (rejoice) | དགའ་བ་ | *ga-wa.* |
| Do. *hon.* | མཉེས་པོ་གནང་བ་ | *nye-po nang-wa.* |
| Do. *h. hon.* | ཐུགས་དགྱེས་པོ་གནང་བ་ | *thu-gye-po nang-wa.* |
| Exultation | དགའ་ཚོར་ | *ga-tshor.* |
| Eye | མིག་ | *miḱ.* |
| Do. *hon.* | སྤྱན་ | *chen.* |
| Eye-ball | མིག་རིལ་ | *miḱ-ri.* |
| Do. *hon.* | སྤྱན་རིལ་ | *chen-ri.* |
| Eye-brow | མིག་ཟི་ (མིག་ཟྀ་) | *miḱ-śi.* |
| Do. *hon.* | སྤྱན་ཟི་ (སྤྱན་ཟྀ་) | *chen-śi.* |
| Eye-glass | མིག་ཤེར་ (མིག་ཤེལ་) | *miḱ-sher.* |

| | | |
|---|---|---|
| Eye-glass, *hon.* | སྤྱན་ཤེར་ (སྤྱན་ཤེལ་) | *chen-sher.* |
| Eye-lash | མིག་སྤུ་ | *mik-pu.* |
| Do. *hon.* | སྤྱན་སྤུ་ | *chem-pu.* |
| Eye-lid | མིག་ལྤགས་ | *mik-pa.* |
| Do. *hon.* | སྤྱན་ལྤགས་ | *chem-pa.* |
| Eye-lid, lower | མིག་ལྤགས་སྨད་ | *mik-pa me.* |
| Do. *hon.* | སྤྱན་ལྤགས་སྨད་ | *chem-pa me.* |
| Eye-lid, upper | མིག་ལྤགས་ཡས་ | *mik pa-ye.* |
| Do. *hon.* | སྤྱན་ལྤགས་ཡས་ | *chem-pa ye.* |
| Eye-shade (of hair) | མིག་ར་ | *mik-ra.* |
| Do. *hon.* | སྤྱན་ར་ | *chen-ra.* |

# F

| | | |
|---|---|---|
| Fable | སྒྲུམ་ (སྒྲུང་) | *drum.* |
| Do. *hon.* | ཞལ་སྒྲུམ་ (ཞལ་སྒྲུང་) | *sḱe-drum.* |
| Fabrication (lie) | ཧམ་པ། སྐྱག་རྫུན་ | *ham-pa ; kyak-dzün.* |
| Do. *hon.* | ཞལ་རྫུན་ | *sḱe-dzün.* |
| Face | གདོང་ | *dong.* |
| Do. *hon.* | ཞལ་རས་ | *sḱe-re.* |
| Facsimile | འདྲ་ཤུས་ | *dra-shü.* |
| Fact | དོན་སྙིང་ | *ťön-nying.* |
| Factory | བཟོ་ཁང་ | *śo-khang.* |
| Fade, to (wither) | སྙིད་པ་ | *nyi-pa.* |
| Do. to (of colour) | གཤུད་པ་ | *sḱü pa.* |
| Fail, to (miss) | མི་…ཐུབ་པ་ | *mi…thuṕ-pa.* |
| Do. *hon.* | མི་…ཐུབ་པ་གནང་བ་ | *mi…thuṕ-pa nang-wa.* |
| Fail, without (in any event) | ཡིན་གཅིག་མིན་གཅིག། ངེས་ལྡན་ | *yin-chi min-chi ; ten-den.* |
| Faint-hearted | སེམས་ཆུང་ཆུང་། སྙིང་ཆུང་ཆུང་ | *sem chhung-chhung ; nying-chhung-chhung.* |
| Do. *hon.* | ཐུགས་སེམས་ཆུང་ཆུང་ | *thu-sem chhung-chhung.* |

| | | |
|---|---|---|
| Faint, to | དྲན་མེད་བརྒྱལ་བ་ | *t́ren me gye-wa.* |
| Do. *hon.* | དྲན་མེད་བརྒྱལ་ར་ (བ་) གནང་བ་ | *t́ren me gye-ra nang-wa.* |
| Fair | མཛེས་པོ་ | *dze-po.* |
| Do. *hon.* | ཐུགས་ཚར་པོ་ | *thu tshar-po.* |
| Fair (just) | ཁྲིམས་དྲང་པོ་ | *thrim-t́rang-po.* |
| Do. *hon.* | བཀའ་ཁྲིམས་དྲང་པོ་ | *ka-thrim t́rang-po* |
| Fairy | ལྷ་མོ་ | *hla-mo.* |
| Faith | དད་པ་ | *t́e-pa.* |
| Faithful | དམ་ཚིག་ཡག་པོ་ | *t́am-tshi yaḱ-po.* |
| Fakir | གྲུབ་ཐོབ་ | *t́ruṕ-tho.* |
| Falcon | ཁྲ་ | *thra.* |
| Fall, to (on ground which one is already touching) | འགྱེལ་བ་ | *gye-wa.* |
| Do. *hon.* | འགྱེལ་ར་ (བ་) གནང་བ་ | *gye-ra nang-wa.* |
| Fall, to (from a height) | གཟགས་པ་ (འཛོག་པ་) | *śaḱ-pa.* |
| Do. *hon.* | གཟགས་ག་ (འཛོག་པ་) གནང་བ་ | *śaḱ-ka nang-wa.* |
| Fall, to (descend) | བབ་ (འབབ་) ཡོང་བ་ (or འགྲོ་བ་) | *ṕaṕ-yong-wa* (or *dro-wa*). |

| | | |
|---|---|---|
| Fall, to (descend) *hon.* | བབ་ (འབབ་) ཕེབ་པ་ | *ṕaṕ-phe-pa.* |
| Do. *h. hon.* | བབ་ (འབབ་) འཆིབ་རྒྱུ་གནང་བ་ | *ṕaṕ-chhiṕ-gyu nang-wa.* |
| Fall head-over-heels, to | མགོ་གཞུག་ལོག་པ་ | *go-sḱu loḱ-pa.* |
| Do. to (in drops) | འཐིག་པ་རྒྱབ་པ་ | *thiḱ-pa gyaṕ-pa.* |
| Do. to (of flood, etc.) | ཆག་པ་ | *chhaḱ-pa.* |
| Fallow | ས་སྟོང་ | *sa-tong.* |
| False | ཧམ་ཟ། སྐྱག་རྫུན། | *ham-pa ; kyaḱ-dzün.* |
| Falsehood | ཧམ་པ། སྐྱག་རྫུན་ | *ham-pa ; ḱyaḱ-dzün.* |
| Do. *hon.* | ཞལ་རྫུན་ | *sḱe-dzün.* |
| Falter, to (waver) | ཐེ་ཚོམ་ཟ་བ་ | *the-tshom śa-wa* |
| *Do. hon.* | ཐེ་ཚོམ་གནང་བ་ | *the-tshom nang-wa.* |
| Fame | སྐད་གྲགས་ | *ke-ṫra.* |
| Do. *hon.* | སྙན་གྲགས་ | *nyen-ṫra.* |
| Familiar | ཀློ་དཀར། ཉེ་པོ་ | *lo-ka ; nye-po.* |
| Family | མི་ཚང་ | *mi-tshang.* |
| Family (lineage) | རིགས་བརྒྱུད་ | *ri-gyü.* |
| Do. *hon.* | སྐུ་བརྒྱུད་ | *ku-gyü.* |
| Family, member of | ནང་མི་ | *nang-mi.* |
| Family priest | མཆོད་གནས་ | *chhö-ne.* |

| | | |
|---|---|---|
| Famine | མུ་གེ་ | *mu-ke.* |
| Famous (celebrated) | སྐད་གྲགས་ཆེན་པོ་ | *ke-tra chhem-po.* |
| Do. *hon.* | སྙན་གྲགས་ཆེན་པོ་ | *nyen-tra chhem-po.* |
| Fan | རླུང་ཡབ་ | *lung-yap.* |
| Fancy (opinion) | བསམ་པ་ | *sam-pa.* |
| Do. *hon.* | ཐུགས་སེམས་ | *thu-sem.* |
| Fancy (wish) | འདོད་པ་ | *dö-pa.* |
| Do. *hon.* | ཐུགས་འདོད་ | *thung-dö.* |
| Fancy, to (like) | དགའ་བ་ | *ga-wa.* |
| Do. *hon.* | ཐུགས་མཉེས་པ་ | *thu-nye-pa.* |
| Do *h. hon.* | ཐུགས་དགྱེས་པ་ | *thu-gye-pa.* |
| Fancy to, (suppose) | བསམ་པ་ | *sam-pa.* |
| Do. *hon.* | དགོངས་པ་ | *gong-pa.* |
| Fang (of tiger, etc.) | མཆེ་བ་ | *chhe-wa.* |
| Far | ཐག་རིང་པོ་ | *tha-ring-po.* |
| Do. how | ཐག་རིང་ཐུང་ག་ཚོད་ | *tha-ring-thung ka-tshö.* |
| Fare (food) | ཁ་ལག། ལྟོ་ | *kha-la ; to.* |
| Do *hon.* | ཞལ་ལག་ | *she-la.* |
| Farewell! (to person going away) | འོ་ན་གྱུག་ཨ་ | *o-na gyu-a.* |
| Do. *hon* | ག་ལེ་ཕེབས་ | *ka-le phe* |

| | | |
|---|---|---|
| Farewell! (to person going away) *h. hon.* | ག་ལེ་འཆིབ་རྒྱུ་གནང་ | *ka-le chhip-gyu-nang.* |
| Farewell! (to person remaining) | འོ་ན་སྡོད་ཨ་ | *o-na dö-a.* |
| Do. *hon.* | ག་ལེ་བཞུགས་ | *ka-le sKu.* |
| Do. *h. hon.* | ག་ལེ་བཞུགས་གདན་འཇག་ | *ka-le sKu-den-ja.* |
| Farm | ཕ་གཞིས་ | *pha-sKi.* |
| Farmer | སོ་ནམས་བྱེད་མཁན་ | *so-nam cKe-khen.* |
| Farming, *s.* (agriculture) | སོ་ནམས་ | *so-nam.* |
| Farrier | རྨིག་ལྕགས་རྒྱབ་མཁན་ | *mik-cha gyang-khen.* |
| Farther | ཕ་ཙ་ (ཕར་ཙམ་) | *pha-tsa.* |
| Fascinate, to | བློ་ལ་ཕྱིན་པ་ | *lo-la chhim-pa.* |
| Do. *hon.* | ཐུགས་ལ་ཕེབ་པ་ | *thu-la phe-pa.* |
| Fashion (custom) | ལུགས་སྲོལ་ | *luk-sö.* |
| Do. (form) | བཟོ་ལྟ་ | *śop-ta.* |
| Do. *hon.* | སྐུ་བཟོ་ | *ku-śo.* |
| Fast (faithful) | དམ་ཚིག་ཡག་པོ་ | *tam-tshi yak-po.* |
| Do. (firm) | བརྟན་པོ་ | *tem-po.* |
| Do. (quick) | མགྱོགས་པོ་ | *gyok-po.* |
| Do. *hon.* | རྩོལ་པོ་ | *tsö-po.* |
| Fast, to | སྨྱུང་གནས་སྲུང་བ་ | *nyung-ne sung-wa.* |

| | | |
|---|---|---|
| Fast, to, *hon.* | སྨྱུང་གནས་སྲུང་ང་ (བ་) གནང་བ་ | *nyung-ne sung-nga nang-wa.* |
| Fasten, to (with rope, etc.) | བསྡམས་པ་ (སྡོམ་པ་) | *dam-pa.* |
| Do. *hon.* | བསྡམས་ (སྡོམ་) པ་གནང་བ་ | *dam-pa nang-wa.* |
| Fasten, to (with glue, etc.) | སྦྱར་བ་ | *jar-wa.* |
| Do. *hon.* | སྦྱར་ར་ (བ་) གནང་བ་ | *jar-ra nang-wa.* |
| Fasten on, to (affix) | སྦྲེལ་བ་ | *drel-wa.* |
| Do. *hon.* | སྦྲེལ་ལ་ (བ་) གནང་བ་ | *drel-la nang-wa.* |
| Fasting, *s.* | སྨྱུང་གནས་ | *nyung-ne.* |
| Fat, *adj.* | ཤ་རྒྱགས་པ་ | *sha-gyak-pa.* |
| Do. *hon.* | སྐུ་ཤ་འབྱོར་པོ་ | *ku-sha jor-po.* |
| Fat, *s.* (suet, lard) | ཚིལ་ལུ་ (ཚིལ་བུ་) | *tshi-lu.* |
| Do. *hon.* | བཞེས་ཚིལ་ | *ske-tshi.* |
| Fate | བསོ་བདེ་ (བསོད་བདེ་) | *so-de.* |
| Do. *hon.* | སྐུ་བསོད་ | *ku-sö.* |
| Father | ཨ་ཕ་ | *a-pha.* |
| Do. *hon.* | ཡབ་ | *yaṕ.* |
| Fatherland | ལུང་པ་ | *lung-pa.* |
| Do. *hon.* | འཁྲུངས་ས་ | *thrung-sa.* |
| Father-in-law | པ་ལགས། གྱོས་པོ་ | *pa-la ; kyö-po.* |

| | | |
|---|---|---|
| Fatigue | ངལ་ | *ngel.* |
| Do. *hon.* | སྐུ་ངལ་ | *ku-ngel.* |
| Fatigued, to be | ཐང་ཆད་པ་ | *thang-chhe-pa.* |
| Do. *hon.* | སྐུ་ཐང་མཉེལ་བ་ | *ku-thang nye-wa.* |
| Fatiguing | དཀའ་ལས་ཁག་པོ་ | *ka-le khak-po.* |
| Do. *hon.* | སྐུ་མཉེལ་པོ་ | *ku-nye-po.* |
| Fault | སྐྱོན་ | *kyön.* |
| Favour | དྲིན་ | *trin.* |
| Do. *hon.* | བཀའ་དྲིན་ | *ka-trin.* |
| Favourite (official, etc.) | མིག་གསལ་ | *mik-se.* |
| Do. *hon.* | སྤྱན་གསལ་ | *chen-se.* |
| Fawn | ཤ་ཕྲུག་ | *sha-thru.* |
| Fear | ཞེད་སྐྲག་ | *ske-tra.* |
| Fear, to | ཞེད་པ་ | *ske-pa.* |
| Do. to *hon.* | ཞེད་པ་གནང་བ་ | *ske-pa nang-wa.* |
| Fearful | ཞེད་སྐྲག་ཚ་པོ་ | *ske-tra tsha-po.* |
| Fearless, to be | ཞེད་རྒྱུ་ཙ་ནས་མེད་པ་ | *ske-gyu tsa-ne me-pa.* |
| Feast | མགྲོན་པོ་ | *dröm-po.* |
| Do. *hon.* | ཐུགས་སྤྲོ་ | *thuk-tro.* |
| Feather (small) | སྤུ་ | *pu.* |

| | | |
|---|---|---|
| Feather (large) | སྒྲོ་ | *dro.* |
| Features | བཟོ་བལྟ་ | *sop-ta.* |
| Fee | ངན་པ། གླ་ | *ngem-pa ; la.* |
| Feeble (infirm) | ཀྱ་རེ་ཀྱོ་རེ། ཉ་རེ་(ར)ཉོ་རེ་ | *kya-re kyo-re ; nya-re nyo-re.* |
| Do. *hon.* | སྐུ་ཀྱོར་ཀྱོར་ | *ku-kyor-kyor.* |
| Feed, to, *v.t.* | ལྟོ་སྟེར་བ་ | *to ter-wa.* |
| Do. *hon.* | ལྟོ་གསོལ་རས་གནང་བ་ | *to sö-re nang-wa.* |
| Do. *inf.* to *sup.* | ཞལ་ལག་ཕུལ་ (འབུལ་) བ་ | *ske la phü-wa.* |
| Feed, to, *v.i.* | ཁ་ལག་ཟ་བ། ལྟོ་ཟ་བ་ | *kha-la śa-wa ; to śa-wa* |
| Do. *hon.* | ཞལ་ལག་བཞེས་པ་ | *ske-la ske-pa.* |
| Feel, to, (touch) | ཐུག་པ་ | *thuk-pa.* |
| Do. *hon.* | ཐུག་ག་ (པ་) གནང་བ་ | *thuk-ka nang-wa.* |
| Feel cold, to | འཁྱགས་པ་ | *khyak-pa.* |
| Do. *hon.* | སྐུ་བསིལ་ར་ (བ་) གནང་བ་ | *ku-si-ra nang-wa* |
| Feign, to | གྱོད་བཤད་པ་ | *kyö-she-pa* |
| Do. *hon.* | གྱོད་གསུང་བ་ | *kyö-sung-wa.* |
| Feign illness, to | ན་ཚུ་ (རྫུ) བཏབ་ (འདེབས་) པ་ | *na-tshu tap-pa.* |
| Do. *hon.* | སྙུང་ཚུ་ (རྫུ) བཏབ་ (འདེབས་) པ་ | *nyung-tshu tap-pa.* |
| Feign stupidity, to. | ལྐུགས་ཚུལ་བཏབ་(འདེབས་)པ་ | *kuk-tshü tap-pa.* |

| | | |
|---|---|---|
| Feign stupidity, to, *hon.* | ལྐུགས་ཚུལ་གསུང་བ་ | *kuḱ-tshü sung-wa.* |
| Fellow-labourer | ལས་རོགས་ | *le-ro.* |
| Do. *hon.* | ཕྱག་སྦྲེལ་ | *chha-drel.* |
| Fellow-traveller | ལམ་རོགས་ | *lam-ro.* |
| Do. *hon.* | ཕེབ་རོགས་ | *pheṕ-ro.* |
| Felon | བཙོན་པ་ | *tsöm-pa.* |
| Felt | ཕྱིང་པ་ | *chhing-pa.* |
| Female | མོ་ | *mo.* |
| Fence | ར་བ་ | *ra-wa.* |
| Ferment, to (wine) | བསྙིལ་བ་ (སྙིལ་བ་) | *nyel-wa.* |
| Fern | སྐྱེ་མ་ | *kye-ma.* |
| Ferocious (of human beings) | ངན་པ་ | *ngem-pa.* |
| Do. (of animals) | ཚུབ་པོ་ | *tshuṕ-po.* |
| Ferry | གྲུ་ཁ་ | *t́ru-kha.* |
| Ferry-boat | གྲུ་ | *t́ru.* |
| Do. *hon.* | ཕེབ་གྲུ་ | *pheṕ t́ru.* |
| Ferry-man | གྲུ་པ་ | *t́ru-pa.* |
| Do. *hon.* | གྲུ་དཔོན་ | *t́ru-pön.* |
| Fertile | ལུད་ཆུ་འཛོམ་པོ་ | *lü-chhu dzom-po.* |
| Fervent | སྙིང་རུས་ཆེན་པོ་ | *nying-rü chhem-po.* |

| | | |
|---|---|---|
| Fervent, *hon.* | ཐུགས་རྩུས་ཆེན་པོ་ | *thu-rü chhem-po* |
| Festival | དུས་ཆེན་ | *tü-chhen.* |
| Fetch, to (by carrying) | འཁྱེར་བ་ | *khyer-wa.* |
| Do. *hon.* | སྣོམ་པ་ | *nom-pa.* |
| Fetch, to (by leading) | འཁྲིད་པ་ | *thri-pa.* |
| Do. *hon.* | འཁྲིད་པ་གནང་བ་ | *thri-pa nang-wa.* |
| Fetlock, fore (of horse) | ལག་གུག་ | *lak-ku.* |
| Do. hind | རྐང་གུག་ | *kang-ku.* |
| Fetters (for hands) | ལག་ལྕགས་ | *lak-cha.* |
| Do. (for feet) | རྐང་ལྕགས་ | *kang-cha.* |
| Fever | ཚད་པ་ | *tshe-pa.* |
| Do. *hon.* | སྐུ་ཚད་ | *ku-tshe.* |
| Fever, to have | ཚད་པ་ན་བ་ | *tshe-pa na-wa.* |
| Do. *hon.* | སྐུ་ཚད་སྙུང་བ་ | *ku-tshe nyung-wa.* |
| Few | ཏོག་ཙ་ (ཏོག་ཚོད་) | *tok-tsa.* |
| Do., only a | ཁ་ཤས་ཅིག་ | *kha-she-chi.* |
| Fibre | རྒྱུས་པ་ | *gyü-pa.* |
| Fickle, to be | བརྟན་པོ་…མེད་པ་ | *tem-po ...... me-pa.* |
| Fiddle | པི་ཝང་ | *pi-wang.* |
| Field | ཞིང་ཁ་ | *sking-kha.* |

| | | |
|---|---|---|
| Fiend | བདུད་ | *dü.* |
| Fierce (of human beings) | ངན་པ་ | *ngem-pa.* |
| Do. (of animals) | ཚུབ་པོ་ | *tshup-po.* |
| Fifteen | བཅོ་ལྔ་ | *chö-nga.* |
| Fifteenth | བཅོ་ལྔ་པ་ | *chö-nga-pa.* |
| Fifth | ལྔ་པ་ | *nga-pa.* |
| Fiftieth | ལྔ་བཅུ་པ་ | *ngap-chu-pa.* |
| Fifty | ལྔ་བཅུ་ | *ngap-chu.* |
| Fight | རྒྱབ་འདྲེ་ | *gyam-dre.* |
| Do. to (with words or blows) | རྒྱབ་འདྲེ་རྒྱབ་པ་ | *gyam-dre gyap-pa.* |
| Do. *hon.* | གསུང་འཁྲུག་སྐྱོན་པ་ | *sung-thru kyöm-pa.* |
| Fight, to (make war) | དམག་རྒྱབ་པ་ | *ma-gyap-pa.* |
| Do. *hon.* | དམག་སྐྱོན་པ་ | *ma-kyöm-pa.* |
| Fight, to (with blows) | འཛིང་བ་ | *dzing-wa.* |
| Do. *hon.* | འཛིང་རེས་གནང་བ་ | *dzing-re nang-wa.* |
| Figurative | སྙན་ངག་ | *nye-nga.* |
| Figure (painting) | རི་མོ་ | *ri-mo.* |
| Do. (number) | ཨང་གི་ | *ang-ki.* |
| Do. (shape) | བཟོ་བལྟ་ | *śop-ta.* |
| Do. *hon.* | སྐུ་བཟོ་ | *ku-śo.* |

| | | |
|---|---|---|
| File | ལྕགས་སག་ | *chak-sa.* |
| Fill, to | གང་བླུག་པ་ | *kang-luk-pa.* |
| Do. *hon.* | གང་བླུག་ག་ (པ་) གནང་བ་ | *kang-luk-ka nang-wa.* |
| Do. *inf.* to *sup.* | གང་སྐུ་བ་ | *kang-sku-wa.* |
| Filter (for tea) | ཇ་ཚགས་ | *cka-tsha.* |
| Filthy | བཙོག་པ་ | *tsok-pa.* |
| Do. *hon.* | སྐུ་བཙོག་ | *ku-tso.* |
| Filthy, to be | བཙོག་པ་ཡོད་པ་ | *tsok-pa yö-pa.* |
| Do. to become | བཙོག་པ་ཤོར་བ་ | *tsok-pa shor-wa.* |
| Do. *hon* | སྐུ་བཙོག་ཤོར་བ་ | *ku-tso shor-wa.* |
| Fin | ཤོག་པ་ | *shok-pa.* |
| Final | གཞུག་ཤོས་ | *skuk-shö.* |
| Find, to | རྙེད་པ་ | *nye-pa.* |
| Do. *hon.* | རྙེད་པ་གནང་བ་ | *nye-pa nang-wa.* |
| Fine (beautiful) | མཛེས་པོ་ | *dze-po.* |
| Do. (minute) | ཞིབ་པོ་ | *skip-po.* |
| Do. (thin, of round objects) | ཕྲ་པོ་ | *thra-po.* |
| Do. (thin, of flat objects) | སྲབ་པོ་ | *trap-po.* |
| Fine, *s.* | དངོས་པོའི་ཉེས་པ་ | *ngö pö nye-pa.* |

| | | |
|---|---|---|
| Fine, *hon.* | དངོས་པོའི་བཀའ་ཉེས་ | *ngö-pö ka-nye.* |
| Fine, to | དངོས་པོའི་ཉེས་པ་བཏང་ (གཏོང་) བ་ | *ngö-pö nye-pa tang-wa.* |
| Do. *hon.* | དངོས་པོའི་བཀའ་ཉེས་གནང་བ་ | *ngö-pö ka-nye nang wa.* |
| Fine (for murder, paid as compensation to the relatives of the deceased) | སྟོང་ | *tong.* |
| Do. (for theft) | བརྐུས་འཇལ་ (རྐུ་འཇལ་) | *kün-jel.* |
| Finger | མཛུག་གུ་ | *dzu-ku.* |
| Do. *hon.* | ཕྱག་མཛུག་ | *chhan-dzu.* |
| Finger (fore-finger) | མཛུག་གུ་ | *dzu-ku* |
| Do. (middle finger) | དཀྱིལ་མཛུག་ | *kyi-dzu.* |
| Do. (third finger) | སྲིན་མཛུག་ | *trin-dzu.* |
| Do. (little finger) | མཛུག་ཆུང་། ཨི་ཆུང་ང་ | *dzuk-chhung; i-chhung-nga.* |
| Finger-nail | སེན་མོ་ | *sen-mo.* |
| Do. *hon.* | ཕྱག་སེན་ | *chha-sen.* |
| Finish, to (complete) | འཚར་བ་ | *tshar wa.* |
| Do. *hon.* | འགྲུབ་པ་ | *drup-pa.* |
| Fir-tree (Abies Webbiana) | གདུང་ཤིང་ | *dung-shing.* |

| | | |
|---|---|---|
| Fire | མེ་ | *me.* |
| Do. *hon.* | ཞུགས་མེ་ | *sḱu-me.* |
| Fire, to catch | མེ་ཤོར་བ་ | *me-shor-wa.* |
| Fire, to, *v.t.* | མེ་སྦར་བ་ | *me-bar-wa.* |
| Fire a gun, to | མེ་མདའ་རྒྱབ་པ་ | *men-da gyaṕ-pa.* |
| Do. to *hon.* | ཕྱག་མདའ་སྐྱོན་པ་ | *chhan-da-kyöm-pa.* |
| Fire-place | ཐབ་ | *thaṕ.* |
| Fire-works | ཤོག་པག་ | *sho-pa.* |
| Firm (not shaky) | བརྟན་པོ་ | *tem-po.* |
| Do. (tight) | དམ་པོ་ | *t́am-po.* |
| Firmament | གནམ། ནམ་མཁའ་ | *nam ; nam-kha.* |
| First | དང་པོ་ | *t́ang-po.* |
| Firstborn | རྒན་པ་ | *gem-pa.* |
| First class (excellent) | ཨང་གི་དང་པོ་ | *ang-ki t́ang-po.* |
| First-rate | ཨང་གི་དང་པོ་ | *ang-ḱi t́ang-po.* |
| Firstly | དང་པོ་ (དང་པོར་) | *t́ang-po.* |
| Fish | ཉ་ | *nya.* |
| Do. to | ཉ་ཟིན་པ་ | *nya śim-pa.* |
| Do. *hon.* | ཉ་ཟིན་པ་གནང་བ་ | *nya śim-pa nang-wa.* |
| Fish-bone | ཉ་རུས་ | *nya-rü.* |

| | | |
|---|---|---|
| Fisherman | ཉ་རྡུང་ང། ཉ་ཟིན་མཁན་ | *nyap dung-nga ; nya-śim-khen.* |
| Fish-hook | ལྕགས་ཀྱུ། ཉ་ཀྱུག་ | *cha-kyu ; nya-ku.* |
| Fishing-net | ཉ་དོལ་ | *nya-ťöl.* |
| Fish's fin | ཉའི་ཤོག་པ་ | *nya-i shok-pa.* |
| Fissure | སེར་ཀ་ | *ser-ka.* |
| Fist | ཛོག་མགོ་ | *dzong-go.* |
| Fisted, close- | ལག་པ་དམ་པོ་ | *lak-pa ťam-po.* |
| Do. *hon.* | ཕྱག་དམ་པོ་ | *chha-ťam-po.* |
| Fit, to (of clothes, &c.) | འགྲིག་པ་ | *drik-pa.* |
| Do. *hon.* | འགྲིག་ག་ (པ་) གནང་བ་ | *drik-ka nang-wa.* |
| Fitful, to be | བརྟན་པོ་མེད་པ་ | *tem-po....me-pa.* |
| Fitting (proper) | འོས་པོ་ | *ö-po.* |
| Do. to be | འགྲིག་པ་ | *drik-pa.* |
| Five | ལྔ་ | *nga.* |
| Fix, to (place) | བཞག་པ་ (འཛོག་པ་) | *sȟak-pa.* |
| Do. *hon.* | གཞོག་ག་ (པ་) གནང་བ་ | *sȟok-ka nang-wa.* |
| Fix a time, to | དུས་ཚོད་བྱེད་པ་ | *tü-tshö cȟe-pa.* |
| Do. *hon.* | དུས་ཚོད་གནང་བ་ | *ťü tshö nang-wa.* |
| Flag, large | དར་ཆེན་ | *ťar-chhen.* |
| Do. small | དར་ལྕོག་ | *ťar-cho.* |

| | | |
|---|---|---|
| Flagstaff | དར་ཤིང་ | *t́ar-shing.* |
| Flame | མེ་ལྕེ་ | *me-che.* |
| Flannel, thin | ཐེར་མ་ | *ther-ma.* |
| Do. thick | སྤྲུ་རུག་ | *pu-ru.* |
| Flat | ལེབ་ལེབ་ | *leṕ-leṕ.* |
| Flatten, to | ལེབ་ལེབ་བཟོ་བ་ | *leṕ-leṕ śo-wa.* |
| Do. *hon.* | ལེབ་ལེབ་བཟོ་བ་གནང་བ་ | *leṕ-leṕ śo-wa nang-wa.* |
| Flatter, to | དཔལ་ལས་བཤད་པ་ | *pe-le she-pa.* |
| Do. *inf.* to *sup* | དཔལ་ལས་ཞུ་བ་ | *pe-le sḱu-wa.* |
| Flaunt, to (boast) | རང་སྟོད་བྱེད་པ་ | *rang-tö cḱe-pa.* |
| Flavour | བྲོ་བ་ | *t́ro-wa.* |
| Do. *hon.* | ལྗགས་བྲོ་ | *ja-t́ro.* |
| Flaw | སྐྱོན་ | *kyön.* |
| Flay, to | ཤུ་བ་ | *shu-wa.* |
| Do. *hon.* | ཤུ་བ་གནང་བ་ | *shu-wa nang-wa.* |
| Flea | འཇོ་འོ་ (འཇུ་བ་) | *jo.* |
| Flee, to | བྲོས་ཕྱིན་པ་ | *ṕö chhim-pa.* |
| Do. *hon.* | བྲོས་ཕེབ་པ་ | *ṕö-pheṕ-pa.* |
| Do. *h. hon.* | བྲོས་འཆིབ་ རྒྱུ་གནང་བ་ | *ṕö chhiṕ-gyu nang-wa.* |

| | | |
|---|---|---|
| Fleet (quick) | མགྱོགས་པོ་ | *gyok-po.* |
| Do. *hon.* | རྩོལ་པོ་ | *tsö-po.* |
| Flesh | ཤ་ | *sha.* |
| Do. *hon.* | སྐུ་ཤ་ | *ku-sha.* |
| Flesh, for eating, *hon.* | གསོལ་སྐྲུང་ (གསོལ་སྐྲུམ་) | *sö-trung.* |
| Fleshy (fat) | ཤ་རྒྱགས་པ་ | *sha-gyak-pa.* |
| Do. *hon.* | སྐུ་ཤ་འབྱོར་པོ་ | *ku-sha jor-po.* |
| Flexible | མཉེན་པོ་ | *nyem-po.* |
| Fling, to | དབྱུག་པ་ | *yuk-pa.* |
| Do. *hon.* | དབྱུག་ག་ (པ་) གནང་བ་ | *yuk-ka nang-wa.* |
| Flint | མེ་རྡོ་ | *me-do.* |
| Flip, to | ཨེ་ཀོག་གཞུ་བ་ | *e-ko sku-wa.* |
| Float, to | ལྡིང་བ་ | *ding-wa.* |
| Flock, *s.* | ཁྱུ་ | *khyu.* |
| Flog, to | གཞུ་བ་ | *sku-wa.* |
| Flood | ཆུ་རུད་ | *chhu rü.* |
| Do. to | ཆུ་ཡིས་གནན་པ་ | *chhu-yi nem-pa.* |
| Floor, boarded | སྤང་ལེབ་ | *pang-lep.* |
| Do. of earth | ས་ | *sa.* |
| Do. plastered | ཞལ་ (ཞལ་ལ་ | *ska-la.* |

| | | |
|---|---|---|
| Flour, barley | ཙམ་པ་ | *tsam-pa.* |
| Do. *hon.* | གསོལ་ཞིབ་ | *sö-sKiṕ.* |
| Flour, wheat | གྲོ་ཞིབ་ | *t́ro-sKiṕ.* |
| Do. rice | འབྲས་ཙམ་ | *dre-tsam.* |
| Flourishing | གཡང་ཆེན་པ་ | *yang-chhem-po.* |
| Flout, to (scoff) | ཀྱག་ཀྱག་བྱས་ནས་ལབ་པ་ | *kya-kya cKe-ne laṕ-pa.* |
| Do. *hon.* | ཀྱག་ཀྱག་གནང་ནས་གསུང་བ་ | *kya-kya nang-ne sung-wa.* |
| Flout, to (insult) | སྨད་ར་བཏང་ (གཏོང་) བ་ | *me-ra tang-wa.* |
| Do. *hon.* | སྨད་ར་གཏོང་ང་ (བ་) གནང་བ་ | *me-ra tong-nga nang-wa.* |
| Flow, to | རྒྱུག་པ་ | *gyuḱ-pa.* |
| Flow out, to | འཐོན་པ་ | *thöm-pa.* |
| Flower | མེ་ཏོག་ | *me-to.* |
| Do. garden. | མེ་ཏོག་ལྡུམ་ར་ | *me-to dum-ra.* |
| Fluently | ཆུ་རྒྱུག་རྒྱུག་ | *chhu-gyuḱ-gyu.* |
| Fluid (food) | ཁུ་བ་ | *khu-wa.* |
| Flute (small) | གླིང་བུ་ | *ling-ṕu.* |
| Flute (large, held across the body) | ཕྲེད་གླིང་ | *thre-ling.* |
| Do. *hon.* | ཞལ་གླིང་ | *sKe-ling.* |
| Fly, *s.* | སྦྲང་མ་ | *drang-ma.* |
| Do. to (of bird) | འཕིར་བ་ (འཕུར་བ་) | *phir-wa.* |

| | | |
|---|---|---|
| Foal, *s.* | རྟེ་གི་ (རྟེའུ་) | *ti-ki.* |
| Do. of an ass | ཨུ་རྟེའི་ (ཨུ་རྟེ་) | *u-ti-i.* |
| Foam | ལྦུ་བ་ | *bu-wa.* |
| Fodder (grass and grain) | རྩ་ཆག་ | *tsa-chha.* |
| Foe | དགྲ་ | *dra.* |
| Fog | སྨུགས་པ་ | *muk-pa.* |
| Fold, to | ལྟབ་རྩིས་ (རྩིགས་) རྒྱབ་པ་ | *taṕ-tsi gyaṕ-pa.* |
| Do. *hon.* | ལྟབ་རྩིས་ (རྩིགས་) སྐྱོན་པ་ | *taṕ-tsi kyöm-pa.* |
| Foliage | ལོ་མ་ | *lo-ma.* |
| Folk | མི་ | *mi.* |
| Follow, to | གཞུག་ལ་ཕྱིན་པ་ | *sḱu-la chhim-pa.* |
| Do. *hon.* | གཞུག་ལ་ཕེབ་པ་ | *sḱu-la phe-pa.* |
| Do. *h. hon.* | གཞུག་ལ་འཆིབ་རྒྱུ་གནང་བ་ | *sḱu-la chhiṕ-gyu nang-wa.* |
| Fond of, to be (of persons and things) | ཞེན་ཆགས་བྱེད་པ་ | *sḱen-chha cḱe-pa.* |
| Do. *hon.* | ཞེན་ཆགས་གནང་བ་ | *sḱen-chha nang-wa.* |
| Fondle, to | བྱམས་པོ་བྱེད་པ་ | *cḱam po cḱe-pa.* |
| Do. *hon.* | བྱམས་པོ་གནང་བ་ | *cḱam-po nang-wa.* |
| Fondness | བྱམས་པོ་ | *cḱam-po.* |
| Food | ཁ་ལག། ལྟོ་ | *kha-la; to.* |
| Do. *hon.* | ཞལ་ལག་ | *sḱe-la.* |

| | | |
|---|---|---|
| Fool | གླེན་པ། ལྐུགས་པ་ | *lem-pa ; kuḱ-pa.* |
| Foolhardy (rash) | ཁ་མེད་མིག་མེད་ | *kha-me miḱ-me.* |
| Foolish (weak in intellect) | ལྐུགས་པ། གླེན་པ་ | *kuḱ-pa ; lem-pa.* |
| Do. (senseless, of things) | དོན་མེད་ | *tön-me.* |
| Foot | རྐང་པ་ | *kang-pa.* |
| Do. *hon.* | ཞབས་ | *sḱaṕ.* |
| Foot, to go on | རྐང་ཐང་ལ་འགྲོ་བ་ | *kang-thang-la dro-wa.* |
| Do. *hon.* | ཞབས་ཐང་ལ་ཕེབ་པ་ | *sḱaṕ-thang-la pheṕ-pa.* |
| Do. *h. hon.* | ཞབས་ཐང་ལ་འཆིབ་རྒྱུ་གནང་བ་ | *sḱaṕ-thang-la chhiṕ-gyu nang-wa.* |
| Foot and mouth disease | ཁ་ཚ་ | *kha-tsha.* |
| Foot-bridge | ཟམ་པ་ཆུང་ཆུང་ | *śam-pa chhung-chhung.* |
| Do. *hon.* | ཕེབ་ཟམ་ཆུང་ཆུང་ | *pheṕ-śam. chhung-chhung.* |
| Foot-path | རྐང་ཐང་ལ་འགྲོ་ས་ | *kang-thang-la dro-sa.* |
| Do. *hon.* | ཞབས་ཐང་ལ་ཕེབ་ས་ | *sḱaṕ-thang-la pheṕ-sa.* |
| Foot-path (alongside of cliff) | འཕྲང་ | *thrang.* |
| Foot-print | རྐང་རྗེས་ | *kang-je.* |
| Do. *hon.* | ཞབས་རྗེས་ | *sḱaṕ-je.* |
| Foot-race | མི་རྒྱུག་ | *mi-gyu.* |
| Foot-soldier | དམག་མི་ | *ma-mi.* |

| | | |
|---|---|---|
| Footstool | རྐང་སྟེགས་ | *kang-teḱ.* |
| Do. *hon.* | ཞབས་སྟེགས་ | *sḱap-teḱ.* |
| For (because) | ག་རེ་རེད་ཟེར་ན་ | *ka-re re śe-na.* |
| For instance | དཔེ་ན་ (དཔེར་ན་) | *pe-na.* |
| For the sake of | དོན་ལ་ | *ťön-la.* |
| Forage (grass) | རྩྭ་ | *tsa.* |
| Forbear, to | ཁོག་པ་བྱེད་པ་ | *khoḱ-pa cḱe-pa.* |
| Do. *hon.* | ཐུགས་ཁོག་གནང་བ་ | *thu-kho nang-wa.* |
| Forbear, to (of monks) | བཟོད་པ་སྒོམ་པ་ | *śö-pa gom-pa.* |
| Do. *hon.* | བཟོད་པ་བཞེས་པ་ | *śö-pa sḱe-pa.* |
| Forbid, to | བཀག་པ་ (འགེགས་པ་) | *kaḱ-pa.* |
| Do. *hon.* | བཀག་ག་ (འགེགས་པ་) གནང་བ་ | *kaḱ-ḱa nang-wa.* |
| Forbidding (repulsive) | སྐྱུག་བྲོ་པོ་ | *kyuḱ-ťro-po.* |
| Force (strength) | ཤེད་ | *she.* |
| Do. *hon.* | སྐུ་ཤེད་ | *ku-she.* |
| Force (authority) | དབང་ | *wang.* |
| Do. *hon.* | སྐུ་དབང་ | *ku-wang.* |
| Force, to (compel) | ཨུ་ཚུགས་བྱེད་པ་ | *u-tshu cḱe-pa.* |
| Do. *hon.* | ཨུ་ཚུགས་གནང་བ་ | *u-tshu nang-wa.* |

| | | |
|---|---|---|
| Forcible | ཤུགས་ཆེན་པོ་ | *shuk-chhem-po.* |
| Ford, *s.* | རབ་ | *rap.* |
| Forearm | ལག་ངར་ | *la-ngar.* |
| Do. *hon.* | ཕྱག་ངར་ | *chha-ngar.* |
| Forecast | ལུང་བསྟན་ | *lung-ten.* |
| Do. *hon.* | བཀའ་ལུང་ | *ka-lung.* |
| Forego, to (renounce) | སྤང་བ་ | *pang-wa.* |
| Do. *hon.* | སྤོང་ང་ (བ་) གནང་བ་ | *pong-nga nang-wa.* |
| Foregoing | སྔོན་གྱི་ | *ngön-kyi.* |
| Forehead | དཔལ་ཁོག་ (ཐོད་པ་) | *pe-kho.* |
| Do. *hon.* | དབུ་དཔལ་ | *u-pe.* |
| Foreign | ཕྱི་གླིང་ | *chhi-ling.* |
| Foreigner | ཕྱི་གླིང་ང་ (བ་) | *chhi-ling-nga.* |
| Foreign country | ཕི་ (ཕྱི་) གླིང་ལུང་པ་ | *phi-ling lung-pa.* |
| Foreign Secretary | ཕྱི་རྒྱའི་བློན་ཆེན་ | *chhi-gye lön-chhen.* |
| Foreknowledge | མངོན་ཤེས་ | *ngön-she.* |
| Do. *hon.* | མངོན་མཁྱེན་ | *ngön-khyen.* |
| Forenoon (8 a.m. to 10 a.m.) | ཚ་དིང་ | *tsha-ting.* |
| Forerunner | སྔན་ (སྔོན་) བགྲོད་པ་ | *ngen-drö-pa.* |
| Foretell, to | མངོན་ཤེས་ཤེས་པ་ | *ngön-she she-pa.* |

| | | |
|---|---|---|
| Foretell, to, *hon.* | མངོན་མཁྱེན་མཁྱེན་པ་ | *ngön-khyen khyem-pa.* |
| Foretell, to (in a trance) | ལུང་བསྟན་ (སྟོན་) པ་ | *lung-tem-pa.* |
| Do. *hon.* | ལུང་བསྟན་ (སྟོན་) པ་གནང་བ་ | *lung-tem pa nang-wa.* |
| Forest | ཤིང་ནགས། ནགས་གསེབ་ | *shing-na ; nak-seṕ.* |
| Forever | ནམ་རྒྱུན། དུས་རྒྱུན་ | *nam-gyün ; ťü-gyün.* |
| Forget | བཟོ་ཐབ་ | *śo-thaṕ.* |
| Do. to | རྗེད་པ། བརྗེད་ནས་མེད་པ་ | *je-pa ; je-ne-me-pa.* |
| Do. *hon.* | བསྙེལ་བ། ཐུགས་བསྙེལ་ཤོར་བ་ | *nyel-wa ; thu-nye shor-wa.* |
| Forgive, to | དགོངས་པ་བཏང་ (གཏོང་) བ། སྙིང་རྗེ་ལྟ་བ་ | *gong-pa tang-wa ; nying-je ta-wa.* |
| Do. *hon.* | དགོངས་པ་གཏོང་ང་ (བ་) གནང་བ། སྙིང་རྗེ་གཟིགས་པ་ | *gong-pa tong-nga nang-wa ; nying-je śik-pa.* |
| Fork | ཤ་འཛིན་ | *shan-dzin.* |
| Form, *s.* (shape) | བཟོ་བལྟ་ | *śoṕ-ta.* |
| Do. *hon.* | སྐུ་བཟོ་ | *ku-śo.* |
| Form, to (make) | བཟོ་བ་ | *śo-wa.* |
| Do. *hon.* | བཟོ་བ་གནང་བ་ | *śo-wa nang wa.* |
| Formally | ལུགས་སྲོལ་ནང་བཞིན་ | *luḱ-sö nang-sḱin.* |
| Former | སྔོན་གྱི། དང་པོ་ | *ngön-kyi ; ťang-po.* |

| | | |
|---|---|---|
| Formerly (a short time ago) | སྔན་ལ་ (སྔོན་ལ་) | *ngen-la.* |
| Do. (a long time ago) | སྔར་ | *ngar.* |
| Formidable | ཞེད་སྐྲག་ཚ་པོ་ | *sKe-tra tsha-po.* |
| Forsake, to | དབྱུག་བཞག་ (འཇོག་) པ་ | *yuk-sKak-pa.* |
| Do. *hon.* | དབྱུག་ག་ (པ་) གནང་བ་ | *yuk-Ka nang-wa.* |
| Fort | རྫོང་ | *dzong.* |
| Forthwith | ལམ་སང་། ལམ་ཀྱང་ | *lam-sang ; lam-kyang.* |
| Fortieth | བཞི་བཅུ་པ་ | *sKip-chu-pa.* |
| Fortification | འཛིང་ར་ | *dzing-ra.* |
| Fortnight | བདུན་ཕྲག་གཉིས། བདུན་གཉིས་ | *dün-thra nyi ; dün-nyi.* |
| Fortress | རྫོང་ | *dzong.* |
| Fortunate | བསོ་ (བསོད་) བདེ་ཆེན་པོ། བསོད་ནམས་ཆེན་པོ་ | *so-de chhem-po ; sö-nam chhem-po.* |
| Do. *hon.* | སྐུ་བསོད་ཆེན་པོ་ | *ku-sö chhem-po.* |
| Fortune, good | བསོ་བདེ་ (བསོད་བདེ་།) བསོད་ནམས་ | *so-de ; sö-nam.* |
| Do. *hon.* | སྐུ་བསོད་ | *ku-sö.* |
| Fortune, bad | བསོ་ (བསོད་) བདེ་སྐམ་པོ། བསོད་ནམས་ཆུང་ཆུང་ | *so-de kam-po ; sö-nam chhung-chhung.* |

| | | |
|---|---|---|
| Fortune, bad, *hon.* | སྐུ་བསོད་ཆུང་ཆུང་ | *ku-sö chhung-chhung.* |
| Forty | བཞི་བཅུ་ | *śhiṕ-chu.* |
| Foster, to | གསོ་བ་ | *so-wa.* |
| Do. *hon.* | གསོ་བ་གནང་བ་ | *so-wa nang-wa.* |
| Foul | བཙོག་པ་ | *tsoḱ-pa.* |
| Do. *hon.* | སྐུ་བཙོག་ | *ḱu-tsho.* |
| Foul, to be | བཙོག་པ་ཡོད་པ་ | *tsoḱ-pa yö-pa.* |
| Do. to become | བཙོག་པ་ཤོར་བ་ | *tsoḱ-pa shor-wa.* |
| Do. *hon.* | སྐུ་བཙོག་ཤོར་བ་ | *ḱu-tso shor-wa.* |
| Found, to (institute) | བཙུགས་པ་ (འཛུགས་པ་) | *tsuḱ-pa.* |
| Do. *hon.* | བཙུགས་ག་ (འཛུགས་པ་) གནང་བ་ | *tsuḱ-ḱa nang-wa.* |
| Foundation of wall | རྩིག་རྟེན་ | *tsiḱ-ten.* |
| Fountain | ཆུ་མིག་ | *chhu-mi.* |
| Four | བཞི་ | *sḱi.* |
| Fourth | བཞི་པ་ | *sḱi-pa.* |
| Fourteen | བཅུ་བཞི་ | *chuṕ-sḱi.* |
| Fourteenth | བཅུ་བཞི་པ་ | *chuṕ-sḱi-pa.* |
| Fowl | བྱ་ | *cḱa.* |
| Do. domestic | བྱ་དེ་ | *cḱa-te.* |

| | | |
|---|---|---|
| Fox | ཝ་མོ་ | *wa-mo.* |
| Fractured, to be (of bones) | རུས་ཁོག་ཆག་པ་ | *rü-kho chhak-pa.* |
| Fragment | ཆག་དུམ་ | *chhak-tum.* |
| Fragrance | དྲི་མ་ | *t́ri-ma.* |
| Frail (infirm) | ཀྱ་རེ་ཀྱོ་རེ། ཉ་རེ་ (ར་) ཉོ་རེ་ | *kya-re kyo-re ; nya-re nyo-re.* |
| Do. *hon.* | སྐུ་ཀྱོར་ཀྱོར་ | *ku-kyor-kyor.* |
| Frame, *s.* | ཁྲི་ | *thri.* |
| Do. to (construct) | བཟོ་བ་ | *śo-wa.* |
| Do. *hon.* | བཟོ་བ་གནང་བ་ | *śo-wa nang-wa.* |
| Frank | དྲང་པོ་ | *t́rang-po.* |
| Do. *hon.* | ཐུགས་རྒྱུ་དྲང་པོ་ | *thu-gyu t́rang-po.* |
| Frankincense | སྤོས་ | *pö.* |
| Frankly | མ་་་གསང་བ་ | *ma...sang-wa.* |
| Fraud, to commit | མགོ་སྐོར་བ་ | *go-kor-wa.* |
| Do. *hon.* | མགོ་སྐོར་ར་ (བ་) གནང་བ་ | *go-kor-ra nang-wa.* |
| Do. *inf.* on *sup.* | བཀུ་སྐོར་ཞུ་བ་ | *u-kor sḱu-wa.* |
| Free, to, *v.t.* | ཐར་ར་ (བར་) བྱེད་པ། བཏང་ (གཏོང་) བ་ | *thar-ra cḱe-pa ; tang-wa.* |
| Do. *hon.* | ཐར་ར་ (བར་) གནང་བ། གཏོང་ང་ (བ་) གནང་བ་ | *thar-ra nang-wa ; tong-nga nang-wa.* |

| | | |
|---|---|---|
| Free, to become | ཐར་བ་ | *thar-wa.* |
| Free, to (by ransom) | བླུ་བ་ | *lu-wa.* |
| Do. *hon.* | བླུ་བ་གནང་བ་ | *lu-wa nang-wa.* |
| Freedom | ཐར་པ་ | *thar-pa.* |
| Freeze, to | ཁྱགས་པ་ཆགས་པ་ | *khyak-pa chhak-pa.* |
| Frequently | ཚར་མང་པོ་ | *tshar mang-po.* |
| Fresco | རི་མོ་ | *ri-mo.* |
| Fresh | གསར་པ་ | *sa-pa.* |
| Fret, to | སེམས་འཁྲུལ་བྱེད་པ། སེམས་འཚབས་པ་ | *sem thre cḱe-pa ; sem-tshaṕ-pa.* |
| Do. *hon.* | ཐུགས་འཁྲུལ་གནང་བ། ཐུགས་སེམས་འཚབས་པ་གནང་བ་ | *thuḱ-thre nang-wa ; thu-sem tshaṕ-pa nang-wa.* |
| Friction (disagreement) | འཁྲུག་གཞི་ | *thruḱ-sḱi.* |
| Friday | གཟའ་པ་སངས་ | *śa-pa-sang.* |
| Friend, *m.* | གྲོགས་པོ་ | *ťrok-po.* |
| Friend, *f.* | གྲོགས་མོ་ | *ťro-mo.* |
| Friendly relationship (between governments, etc.) | མཐུན་ལམ་ | *thün-lam.* |
| Friends, to make | གྲོགས་པོ་རྒྱབ་པ་ | *ťrok-po gyaṕ-pa.* |

| | | |
|---|---|---|
| Friends, to make, *hon.* | གྲོགས་པོ་སྐྱོན་པ་ | *ťrok̄-po kyöm-pa.* |
| Fright (fear) | ཞེད་སྐྲག་ | *sk̄e-tra.* |
| Frighten | ཞེད་སྐྲག་སླང་བ་ | *sk̄e-tra lang-wa.* |
| Do. *hon.* | ཞེད་སྐྲག་སློང་ང་ (བ་) གནང་བ་ | *sk̄e-tra long-nga nang-wa.* |
| Frightened, to be | ཞེད་པ་ | *sk̄e-pa.* |
| Do. *hon.* | ཞེད་པ་གནང་བ་ | *sk̄e-pa nang-wa.* |
| Frightful | ཞེད་སྐྲག་ཚ་པོ་ | *sk̄e-tra tsha-po.* |
| Frigid | གྲང་མོ། བསིལ་པོ་ | *ťrang-mo ; si-po.* |
| Do. *hon.* | སྐུ་བསིལ་པོ་ | *ku-si-po.* |
| Fringe (of thread, etc.) | ཁ་ཚར། སྣེ་ཚར་ | *kha-tshar ; ne-tshar.* |
| Frivolous | དོན་གནད་ཆུང་ཆུང་ | *ťön-ne chhung-chhung.* |
| Do. *hon.* | ཐུགས་དོན་ཆུང་ཆུང་ | *thuk̄-ťön chhung-chhung.* |
| Frog | སྦལ་པ་ | *be-pa.* |
| From | ནས་ | *ne.* |
| From within | ནང་ནས་ | *nang-ne.* |
| Front of, in (ahead) | སྔན་ལ་ (སྔོན་ལ་) | *ngen-la.* |
| Do. (in presence of) | མདུན་ལ་ | *dün-la.* |
| Do. *hon.* | སྐུ་མདུན་ལ་ | *kun-dün-la.* |
| Front tooth | མདུན་སོ་ | *dün-so.* |
| Do. *hon.* | མདུན་གྱི་ཚེམས་ | *dün-kyi-tshem.* |

| | | |
|---|---|---|
| Frontier | ས་མཚམས་ | *san-tsham.* |
| Frost | ཁྱགས་པ་ | *khyak-pa.* |
| Frost-bitten, to be | གངས་ཀྱིས་འཚིག་པ་ | *ḱang-ki tshik-pa.* |
| Froth | ལྦུ་བ་ | *bu-wa.* |
| Frown, to | ངོ་ནག་སྡུ་བ་ | *ngo-na du-wa.* |
| Frozen, to be | ཁྱགས་པ་ཆགས་པ་ | *khyak-pa chhak-pa.* |
| Fruit (of crops) | འབྲས་བུ་ | *dre-ṕu.* |
| Fruit of tree (as orange, etc.) | ཤིང་འབྲས་ | *shing-dre.* |
| Fruitful (fertile) | ལུད་ཆུ་འཛོམ་པོ་ | *lü--chhu dzom-po.* |
| Fruitless, to be (useless) | ཕན་མི་ཐོགས་པ་ | *phen mi thok-pa.* |
| Do. *hon.* | ཐུགས་ཕན་མི་གསོ་བ་ | *thu-phen mi so-wa.* |
| Fry, to | རྔོད་པ་ | *ngö-pa.* |
| Do. *hon.* | རྔོད་པ་གནང་བ་ | *ngö-pa nang-wa.* |
| Frying-pan | ཚལ་སླང་ | *tshe-lang* |
| Fuel | མེ་ཤིང་ | *me-shing.* |
| Fulfil, to | སྒྲུབ་པ་ | *drup-pa.* |
| Do. *hon.* | སྒྲུབ་པ་གནང་བ་ | *drup-ṕa nang-wa.* |
| Fulfilled, to be | ཚར་བ་ | *tshar-wa.* |
| Do. *hon.* | གྲུབ་པ་ | *t́rup-pa.* |
| Full | གང་ | *ḱang.* |

| | | |
|---|---|---|
| Fun | བལྟས་མོ་ | *te-mo.* |
| Function (work) | ལས་ཀ་ | *le-ka.* |
| Do. *hon.* | ཕྱག་ལས་ | *chha-le.* |
| Functionary | དཔོན་པོ་ | *pöm-po.* |
| Fundament | ཀུབ་ | *kuṕ.* |
| Do. *hon.* | ཞབས་ཕོངས་ | *sḱam-phong.* |
| Fungus | ཤ་མོ་ | *sha-mo.* |
| Funny | བགད་མོ་བྲོ་པོ་ | *ge-mo t́ro-po.* |
| Do. *hon.* | ཞལ་མོ་བྲོ་པོ་ | *sḱe-mo t́ro-po.* |
| Fur-coat | པགས་ཚ་ | *paḱ-tsha.* |
| Do. *hon.* | སྐུ་ཚ་ | *ku-tsha.* |
| Furnace | ཐབ་ | *thaṕ.* |
| Furnish, to (supply) | སྒྲུབ་པ་ | *druṕ-pa.* |
| Do. *hon.* | སྒྲུབ་པ་གནང་བ་ | *druṕ-pa nang-wa.* |
| Furniture | ཅ་ལག་ (ཆ་ལག་) | *cha-la.* |
| Do. *hon.* | སྐུ་ཅས་ (སྐུ་ཆས་) | *ku-che.* |
| Furrow | རོལ་ | *rö.* |
| Further (in distance) | ཕ་ཙ་ (ཕར་ཙམ་) | *pha-tsa.* |
| Do. (again) | ད་རུང་ཡང་། ཡང་སྐྱར་ | *t́a-rung-yang; yang-kyar.* |
| Fuse (for gun) | སྦིད་ཏི་ (སྦིད་ཏེ) | *bi-di.* |

| | | |
|---|---|---|
| Futile, to be (useless) | ཕན་མི་ཐོགས་པ་ | *phen mi thok-pa.* |
| Do. *hon.* | ཐུགས་ཕན་མི་གསོ་བ་ | *thu-phen mi so-wa.* |
| Future | གཤུག་ལ་ | *sKu-la.* |

# G

| | | |
|---|---|---|
| Gaiety | དགའ་ཚོར་ | *ga-tshor.* |
| Gain (profit) | ཁེ་བཟང་ | *kheṕ-śang.* |
| Do. *hon.* | སྐུ་ཁེ་ | *ku-khe.* |
| Gain a profit, to | ཁེ་བཟང་ཟ་བ་ | *kheṕ-śang śa-wa.* |
| Do. *hon.* | སྐུ་ཁེ་བཞེས་པ་ | *ku-khe ske-pa.* |
| Gain victory, to | རྒྱལ་བ་ | *gye-wa.* |
| Do. *hon.* | རྒྱལ་ར་ (བ་) གནང་བ་ | *gye-ra nang-wa.* |
| Gain, to (obtain) | འབྱོར་བ། ཐོབ་པ་ | *jor-wa ; thoṕ-pa.* |
| Do. *hon.* | ཕྱག་འབྱོར་ཡོང་བ་ | *chhan-jor yong-wa.* |
| Gainsay, to (deny) | རྒྱབ་འགལ་ལབ་པ་ | *gyam-ge ƚaṕ-pa.* |
| Do. *hon.* | རྒྱབ་འགལ་གསུང་བ་ | *gyam-ge sung-wa.* |
| Gainsay, to (dispute) | རྩོད་པ་རྒྱབ་པ་ | *tsö-pa gyaṕ-pa.* |
| Do. *hon.* | རྩོད་པ་སྐྱོན་པ་ | *tsö-pa kyöm-pa.* |
| Gait | འགྲོ་སྟངས་ | *dro-tang.* |
| Do. *hon.* | ཕེབ་སྟངས་ | *pheṕ-tang.* |
| Gale | ལྷགས་པ་ཚ་པོ་ | *hlaḱ-pa tsha-po.* |
| Gall (malignant feeling) | གནོད་སེམས་ | *nö-sem.* |
| Gall-bladder | མཁྲིས་པ་ | *thri-pa.* |
| Gallant, *adj.* | སྙིང་ཆེན་པོ་ | *nying-chhem-po.* |

| | | |
|---|---|---|
| Gallant *hon.* | ཐུགས་སྙིང་ཆེན་པོ་ | *thu-nying chhem-po.* |
| Gallop, to | ཞམ་བེས་བཏང་ (གཏོང་) བ་ | *sḰam-ṗe tang-wa.* |
| Do. *hon.* | ཆིབས་ཞམ་གནང་བ་ | *chhiṗ-sḰam nang-wa* |
| Gamble, to | ཤོ་རྒྱབ་པ་ | *sho-gyaṗ-pa.* |
| Do. *hon.* | ཕྱག་ཤོ་སྐྱོན་པ་གནང་བ་ | *chhu-sho kyöm-pa nang-wa.* |
| Gambler | ཤོ་པ་ | *sho-pa.* |
| Game (play) | རྩེད་མོ་ | *tse-mo.* |
| Do. *hon.* | སྐུ་རྩེད་ | *ku-tse.* |
| Game (wild animals) | རི་དགས་ | *ri-ṫa.* |
| Gander | འང་པ་ (ངང་པ་) | *ang-pa.* |
| Gang | ཚོགས་ | *tsho.* |
| Gaol | བཙོན་ཁང་ | *tsön-khang.* |
| Gaoler | བཙོན་སྲུང་ང་ (པ་) | *tsön-sung-nga.* |
| Gap | སེར་ཀ་ | *se-ka.* |
| Gape, to (of wounds) | ཁ་བཞག་བཤད་ (ཤོད་) པ་ | *kha-sḰa de-pa.* |
| Do. (yawn) | ཨ་སྦྱོང་རྒྱབ་པ་ | *a-tong gyaṗ-pa.* |
| Do. *hon.* | ཨ་སྦྱོང་སྐྱོན་པ་ | *a-tong kyöm-pa.* |
| Garb | དུག་ལོག་ | *ṫu-lo.* |
| Do. *hon.* | ན་བཟའ་ | *nam-śa.* |
| Garden | ལྡུམ་ར་ | *dum-ra.* |

| | | |
|---|---|---|
| Garden, flower | མེ་ཏོག་གི་ལྡུམ་ར་ | me-tok-ki dum-ra. |
| Do. vegetable | ཚས་གཡང་ཙེ་ ch. | tshe-yang-tse. |
| Do. public | གླིང་ཀ་ | ling-ka. |
| Gardener | གླིང་སྲུང་ང་ (པ་) | ling-sung-nga. |
| Gargle, to | ཁ་བ་ཤལ་བ་ཤལ་བཏང་ (གཏོང་) བ་ | kha-she-she tang wa. |
| Do. *hon.* | ཞལ་བ་ཤལ་བ་ཤལ་གནང་བ་ | ske she-she nang-wa. |
| Garland | མེ་ཏོག་འཕྲང་ང་ (འཕྲེང་བ་) | me-to thrang-nga. |
| Garlic | སྒོག་པ་ | gok-pa. |
| Do. *hon.* | བཞེས་སྒོག་ | ske-go. |
| Garment | དུག་ལོག་ | t́u-lo. |
| Do. *hon.* | ན་བཟའ་ | nam-śa. |
| Garnish, to (adorn) | རྒྱན་ཆ་བཏགས་ (འདོགས་) པ་ | gyen-cha tak-pa. |
| Garrison | དམག་སྒར་ | ma-ga. |
| Garter (for Tibetan boots) | ལྷམ་སྒྲོག་ | hlam-dro. |
| Do. *hon.* | ཞབས་སྒྲོག་ | skap-dro. |
| Gas | དུ་བའི་རླངས་པ་ | t́u-we lang-pa. |
| Gas, poisonous | དུག་རླངས་ | t́uk-lang |
| Gate (small) | ཕྱི་སྒོ་ | chhi-go. |

| | | |
|---|---|---|
| Gate (small), *hon.* | གཟིམ་སྒོ་ཕྱི་སྒོ་ | *śim-go chhi-go.* |
| Gate (large) | རྒྱལ་སྒོ་ | *gye-go.* |
| Do. *hon.* | གཟིམ་སྒོ་རྒྱལ་སྒོ་ | *śim-yo gye-go.* |
| Gather, to (pick up) | སྒྲུག་པ་ | *druk-pa.* |
| Do. *hon.* | སྒྲུག་ག་ (པ་) གནང་བ་ | *druk-ka nang-wa.* |
| Gather, to (pluck off tree) | གཏོག་པ་ | *tok-pa.* |
| Do. *hon.* | གཏོག་ག་ (པ་) གནང་བ་ | *tok-ka nang-wa.* |
| Gather, to (collect) *v.t.* | སྡུད་པ་ | *dü-pa.* |
| Do. *hon.* | སྡུད་པ་གནང་བ་ | *dü-pa nang-wa.* |
| Gather, to (assemble) *v.i.* | འཚོགས་པ། འཛོམས་པ་ | *tsoḳ-pa ; dzom-pa.* |
| Do. *hon.* | ལྷན་རྒྱས་གནང་བ་ | *hlen-gye nang-wa.* |
| Gaunt | ཤ་སྐམ་པོ་ | *sha kam-po.* |
| Do. *hon.* | སྐུ་ཤ་སྐམ་པོ་ | *ku-sha kam-po.* |
| Gay, to be | དགའ་བ། སྐྱིད་པོ་བྱས་ནས་སྡོད་པ་ | *ga-wa ; kyi-po cḱe-ne dö-pa.* |
| Do. *hon.* | མཉེས་པོ་གནང་བ། སྤྲོ་པོ་གནང་ནས་བཞུགས་པ་ | *nye-po nang-wa ; tro-po nang-ne sḱuk-pa.* |
| Do. *h. hon.* | ཐུགས་དགྱེས་པོ་གནང་བ་ | *thu-gye-po nang-wa.* |
| Gaze, to | ལྟ་བ་ | *ta-wa.* |
| Do. *hon.* | གཟིགས་པ་ | *śi-pa.* |

| | | |
|---|---|---|
| Gelding | ཕོ་རྟ་ | *pho-ta.* |
| Gem | ནོར་བུ་ | *nor-ṕu.* |
| Gender | ཕོ་མོ་ | *pho-mo.* |
| Genealogy (of laymen) | རིགས་བརྒྱུད། མི་བརྒྱུད་ | *ri-gyü ; mi-gyü.* |
| Do. *hon.* | སྐུ་བརྒྱུད་ | *ku-gyü.* |
| Do. *hon.* (of lamas) | གདུང་བརྒྱུད་ | *dung-gyü.* |
| Generally | ཕལ་ཆེར་ | *phe-chher.* |
| Generate, to | སྐྱེད་པ་ | *kye-pa.* |
| Generation | མི་བརྒྱུད་ | *mi-gyü.* |
| Generosity | དྲིན་ | *t́rin.* |
| Do. *hon* | བཀའ་དྲིན་ | *ka-t́rin.* |
| Generous | ལག་པ་ཤོག་པོ་ | *laḱ-pa shoḱ-po.* |
| Do. *hon.* | ཕྱག་ཤོག་པོ་ | *chha-shoḱ-po.* |
| Genius | རིག་པ་ | *riḱ-pa.* |
| Do. *hon.* | ཐུགས་རིག་ | *thu-ri.* |
| Gentian | ཏིག་ཏ་ | *tiḱ-ta.* |
| Gentile | ཕྱི་པ་ | *chhi-pa.* |
| Gentle | འཇམ་པོ་ | *jam-po.* |
| Do. in speech | ཁ་འཇམ་པོ་ | *kha jam-po.* |
| Do. *hon.* | ཞལ་འཇམ་པོ་ | *sḱe jam-po.* |

| | | |
|---|---|---|
| Gentle (tame, of animals) | མཉེན་པོ་ | *nyem-po.* |
| Gentleman | སྐུ་དྲག་ | *ku-ťra.* |
| Gently (slowly) | ག་ལེ་ | *ḱa-le.* |
| Do. (not roughly) | འཇམ་པོ་བྱས་ནས་ | *jam-po cḱe-ne.* |
| Do. *hon.* | འཇམ་པོ་གནང་ནས་ | *jam po nang-ne.* |
| Genuine | ངོ་ཐོག། དངོས་ནས་ | *ngo-tho ; ngö-ne.* |
| Geography | འཛམ་གླིང་རྒྱས་བཤད་ | *dzam-ling gye-she.* |
| Germinate, to | སྐྱེ་བ་ | *kye-wa.* |
| Do. to cause to | སྐྱེད་པ་ | *kye-pa.* |
| Gesture | བརྡབ་ (བརྡ་) | *daṕ.* |
| Gesture of hand | ལག་བརྡབ་ (ལག་བརྡ་) | *laḱ-daṕ.* |
| Do. *hon.* | ཕྱག་བརྡབ་ (ཕྱག་བརྡ་) | *chha-daṕ.* |
| Gesture of foot | རྐང་བརྡབ་ (རྐང་བརྡ་) | *kang·daṕ.* |
| Do. *hon.* | ཞབས་བརྡབ་ (ཞབས་བརྡ་) | *sḱaṕ-daṕ.* |
| Get, to | འབྱོར་བ། ཐོབ་པ་ | *jor-wa ; thoṕ-pa.* |
| Do. *hon.* | ཕྱག་འབྱོར་ཡོང་བ་ | *chhan-jor yong-wa.* |
| Get by heart, to | བློ་ལ་ཟིན་པ་ | *lo-la śim-pa.* |
| Do. *hon.* | ཐུགས་བློ་ལ་ཟིན་པ་གནང་བ་ | *thu-lo-la śim-pa nang-wa.* |
| Get well, to | དྲག་པ་ | *ťraḱ-pa.* |
| Do. *hon.* | སྐུ་དྭང་བ་ | *ku-ťang-wa.* |

| | | |
|---|---|---|
| Get through, to | ཐར་བ་ | *thar-wa.* |
| Get up, to, *v.i.* | ལང་བ་ | *lang-wa.* |
| Do. *hon.* | བཞང་བ་ (བཞེངས་པ་) | *sKang-wa.* |
| Do. *h. hon.* | སྐུ་བཞང་ (བཞེངས་) གནང་བ་ | *ku-sKang nang-wa.* |
| Ghastly (horrible) | ཞེད་སྐྲག་ཚོ་པོ་ | *sKe-tra tsha-po.* |
| Ghost | གདོང་འདྲེ། འདྲེ་ | *dong-dre ; dre.* |
| Giant | མི་ཆེན་པོ་ | *mi-chhem-po.* |
| Do. (mythological) | མི་རྒོད་ | *mi-gö.* |
| Gibberish | དོན་དག་མེད་པའི་སྐད་ཆ་ | *ťon-ťa me-pe ke-chha.* |
| Gibe, to | ཀྱག་ཀྱག་བྱས་ནས་ལབ་པ་ | *kya-kya cKe-ne lap̄-pa.* |
| Do. *hon.* | ཀྱག་ཀྱག་གནང་ནས་གསུང་བ་ | *kya-kya nang-ne sung-wa.* |
| Giddy, to be | མགོ་ཡུ་འཁོར་བ། བཟི་ཡོམ་ཡོམ་བྱེད་པ་ | *go-yu khor-wa ; si-yom-yom cKe-pa.* |
| Do. *hon.* | དབུ་ཡུ་འཁོར་བ་ | *u-yu khor-wa.* |
| Gift (alms to poor) | སྦྱིན་པ་ | *jim-pa.* |
| Do. (to Lama) | འབུལ་བ་ | *bül-wa.* |
| Do. (tip) | ཆང་རིན་ | *chhang-rin.* |
| Do. *hon.* | གསོལ་རས། ཁྲུང་རིན་ | *sö-re ; thrung-rin.* |
| Gigantic | ཆེ་ཐག་ཆོད་ | *chhe-thak-chhö.* |
| Giggle, to | ཁ་ཚེ་ཚེ་བྱེད་པ་ | *kha tshe-tshe cKe-pa.* |

| | | |
|---|---|---|
| Giggle, to, *hon.* | ཞལ་ཚེ་ཚེ་གནང་བ་ | *she tshe-tshe nang wa.* |
| Gild, to (images, etc.) | མཚར་གསེར་བཏང་ (གཏོང་) བ་ | *tsha-ser tang-wa.* |
| Do. *hon.* | མཚར་གསེར་གཏོང་ང་ (བ་) གནང་བ་ | *tsha-ser tong-nga nang wa.* |
| Gilding | མཚར་གསེར་ | *tsha-ser.* |
| Gilt, *s.* | མཚར་གསེར་ | *tsha-ser.* |
| Gilt, to | མཚར་གསེར་བཏང་ (གཏོང་) བ་ | *tsha-ser tang-wa.* |
| Gimlet | སོར་ | *sor.* |
| Ginger | སྒ་སྨུག་ | *ga-mu.* |
| Girdle | སྐེ་རགས་ | *ke-ra.* |
| Do. *hon.* | སྐུ་སྐེ། སྐུ་རགས་ | *ku-ke ; ku-ra.* |
| Girl | བུ་མོ་ | *ṕu-mo.* |
| Do. *hon.* | སྲས་མོ་ | *se-mo* or *tre-mo.* |
| Girth (of saddle) | གློ་ | *lo.* |
| Do. *hon.* | ཆིབས་གློ་ | *chhiṕ-lo.* |
| Gist (of letter, etc.) | དོན་སྙིང་ | *t́ön-nying.* |
| Give, to | སྟེར་བ་ | *ter-wa.* |
| Do. *hon.* | གནང་བ་ | *nang-wa.* |
| Give, to (to superior) | ཕུལ་བ་ (འབུལ་བ་) | *phü-wa.* |
| Do. *hon.* | འབུལ་ར་ (བ་) གནང་བ་ | *bü-ra nang-wa.* |

| | | |
|---|---|---|
| Give over, to (deliver) | སྤྲད་པ་ | *tre-pa.* |
| Do. *hon.* | གནང་བ་ | *nang-wa.* |
| Give up, to (sins, certain kinds of foods, etc.) | སྤང་བ་ | *pang-wa.* |
| Do. *hon.* | སྤོང་ང་ (བ་) གནང་བ་ | *pong-nga nang-wa.* |
| Glacier | འཁྱགས་རུམ་ | *khya-rum.* |
| Glad, to be | དགའ་བ་ | *ga-wa.* |
| Do. *hon.* | མཉེས་པོ་གནང་བ་ | *nye-po nang-wa.* |
| Do. *h. hon.* | ཐུགས་དགྱེས་པོ་གནང་བ་ | *thu-gye-po nang-wa.* |
| Gladness | དགའ་ཚོར་ | *ga-tshor.* |
| Do. *hon.* | མཉེས་ཚོར་ | *nye-tshor.* |
| Glaring | འོད་ཆེམ་ཆེམ་ | *ö-chhem-chhem.* |
| Glass | ཤེལ་ | *she.* |
| Do. (looking glass) | ཤེལ་སྒོ་ | *she-go.* |
| Do. *hon.* | སྤྱན་ཤེལ་ | *chen-she.* |
| Gleam, to | འོད་རྒྱབ་པ་ | *ö gyap-pa.* |
| Do. (of the sun) | ཤར་བ་ | *shar-wa.* |
| Do. (of the moon) | ཟླ་དཀར་ཤར་བ་ | *da-ka shar-wa.* |
| Glee | དགའ་ཚོར་ | *ga-tshor.* |
| Gleeful, to be | དགའ་བ་ | *ga-wa.* |

| | | |
|---|---|---|
| Gleeful, to be *hon.* | མཉེས་པོ་གནང་བ་ | *nye-po nang-wa.* |
| Do. *h. hon.* | ཐུགས་དགྱེས་པོ་གནང་བ་ | *thu-gye-po nang-wa.* |
| Glimmer, to | འོད་རྒྱབ་པ་ | *ö gyaṕ-pa.* |
| Do. (of the moon) | ཟླ་དཀར་ཤར་བ་ | *da-ka shar-wa.* |
| Glisten, to | འོད་རྒྱབ་པ་ | *ö gyaṕ-pa.* |
| Glistening, *adj.* | འོད་ཆེན་པོ་ | *ö chhem-po.* |
| Glitter, to | འོད་རྒྱབ་པ་ | *ö gyaṕ-pa.* |
| Globe | རིལ་རིལ་ | *ri-ri.* |
| Globular | རིལ་རིལ་ | *ri-ri.* |
| Gloom | མུན་ནག་ | *mi-na.* |
| Glomy, to be (low-spirited) | སེམས་སྐྱོ་སྣང་བྱེད་པ་ | *sem kyo-nang cḱe-pa.* |
| Do. *hon.* | ཐུགས་སེམས་སྐྱོ་སྣང་གནང་བ་ | *thu-sem kyo-nang nang-wa.* |
| Glorious (in appearance) | གཟི་བརྗིད་ཆེན་པོ་ | *śi-ji chhem-po.* |
| Do. (celebrated) | སྐད་གྲགས་ཆེན་པོ་ | *ke-ťra chhem-po.* |
| Do. *hon.* | སྙན་གྲགས་ཆེན་པོ་ | *nyen-ťra chhem-po.* |
| Glory (splendour) | གཟི་བརྗིད་ | *śi-ji.* |
| Glossary | མིང་མཛོད་ | *ming-dzö.* |
| Glossy (of silk) | ཀོན་ཡག་པོ་ | *kön-yaḱ-po.* |
| Do. (of wool or cotton) | རྩིག་ག་ (པ་) ཡག་པོ་ | *tsiḱ-ka yaḱ-po.* |
| Glove | ལག་ཤུབས་ | *laḱ-shuṕ.* |

| | | |
|---|---|---|
| Glove, *hon.* | ཕྱག་ཤུབས་ | *chha-shup.* |
| Glue | སྤྱིང་ (སྤྱིན་) | *ping.* |
| Gluttonous | གྲོད་ཆེན་པོ་ | *trö-chhem-po.* |
| Gnash teeth, to | སོ་བདར་བ་ | *so-dar-wa.* |
| Do. *hon.* | ཚེམས་བདར་ར་ (བ་) གནང་བ་ | *tshem dar-ra nang-wa.* |
| Gnat | སྲིན་སྦྲང་ | *sin-drang.* |
| Gnaw, to | མུར་བ་ | *mur-wa.* |
| Do. *hon.* | མུར་ར་ (བ་) གནང་བ་ | *mur-ra nang-wa.* |
| Go, to | འགྲོ་བ་ | *dro-wa.* |
| Do. *hon.* | ཕེབ་པ། ཐྲས་པ་ | *phe-pa ; the-pa.* |
| Do. *h. hon.* | འཆིབ་སྒྱུ་གནང་བ་ | *chhip-gyu nang-wa* |
| Go after, to | གཞུག་ལ་ཕྱིན་པ་ | *sKu-la chhim-pa.* |
| Do. *hon.* | གཞུག་ལ་ཕེབ་པ་ | *sKu-la phe-pa.* |
| Do. *h. hon.* | གཞུག་ལ་འཆིབ་སྒྱུ་གནང་བ་ | *sKu-la chhip-gyu nang-wa.* |
| Go-between | བར་མི་ | *par-mi.* |
| Godown | དོས་ཁང་ | *tö-khang.* |
| Go down, to (hill, etc.) | ཐུར་ལ་བབ་ (འབབ་) པ་ | *thur-la pap-pa.* |
| Do. *hon.* | ཐུར་ལ་ཕེབ་པ་ | *thur-la phe-pa.* |
| Go down, to (diminish, of flood, etc.) | འཆག་པ་ | *chhak-pa.* |
| Go out, to | འཐོན་པ་ | *thöm-pa.* |

| | | |
|---|---|---|
| Go out, to, *hon.* | འཐོན་པ་གནང་བ་ | *thöm-pa nang-wa.* |
| Go round, to | འཁོར་བ་ | *khor-wa.* |
| Do. *hon.* | འཁོར་ར་ (བ་) གནང་བ་ | *khor-ra nang-wa.* |
| Go up, to | འཛག་པ་ (འཛེག་པ་). | *dzak-pa.* |
| Do. *hon.* | འཛག་ག་ (འཛེག་པ་) གནང་བ་ | *dzak-ka nang-wa.* |
| Gaol | བཙོན་ཁང་ | *tsön-khang.* |
| Gaoler | བཙོན་སྲུང་ང་ (པ་) | *tsön-sung-nga.* |
| Goat | ར་ | *ra.* |
| Goat, he- | ར་ཕོ་ | *ra-pho.* |
| Goat, she- | ར་མོ་ | *ra-mo.* |
| Goblin | གདོང་འདྲེ། འདྲེ་ | *dong-dre ; dre.* |
| God | ཀུན་མཆོག་ (དཀོན་མཆོག་) | *kün-chho.* |
| God, a | ལྷ་ | *hla.* |
| Goddess, a | ལྷ་མོ་ | *hla-mo.* |
| Godless | ཆོས་སེམས་མེད་པ་ | *chho sem me-pa.* |
| Goggles | མིག་ཤེལ་ | *mik-she.* |
| Do. *hon.* | སྤྱན་ཤེལ་ | *chen-she.* |
| Goitre | ལྦ་བ་ | *ba-a.* |
| Do. *hon.* | མགུལ་ལྦ་ | *gü-ba.* |
| Gold | གསེར་ | *se.* |

| | | |
|---|---|---|
| Gold, *hon.* | ཕྱག་གསེར་ | *chha-se.* |
| Golden (made of gold) | གསེར་གྱི་ | *se ki.* |
| Do. (colour) | སེར་པོ་ | *se-po.* |
| Goldsmith | གསེར་བཟོ་བ་ | *ser-śo-wa.* |
| Gong | འཁར་རྔ་ | *kha-nga.* |
| Gonorrhoea | གྲང་གཞི་ | *ṫrang-ski.* |
| Good, *adj.* | ཡག་པོ་ | *yak-po.* |
| Do. (virtuous) | བཟང་པོ་ | *śang-po.* |
| Good, *s.* (advantage) | ཕན་ | *phen.* |
| Good for, to be | ཕན་ཐོགས་པ་ | *phen thok-pa.* |
| Do. *hon.* | ཐུགས་ཕན་གསོ་བ་ | *thu-phen so-wa.* |
| Good-bye! (to person going) | འོ་ན་རྒྱུག་ཨ་ | *o-na gyu-a.* |
| Do. *hon.* | ཀ་ལེ་ཕེབས་ | *ka-le-phe.* |
| Do. *h. hon.* | ཀ་ལེ་འཆིབ་རྒྱུ་གནང་ | *ka-le chhip-gyu-nang.* |
| Good-bye! (to person remaining) | འོ་ན་སྡོད་ཨ་ | *o-na dö-a.* |
| Do. *hon.* | ཀ་ལེ་བཞུགས་ | *ka-le sku.* |
| Do. *h. hon.* | ཀ་ལེ་བཞུགས་གདན་འཇག་ | *ka-le sku-den ja.* |
| Goods | ཅ་ལག་ (ཆ་ལག་) | *cha-la.* |
| Do. *hon.* | སྐུ་ཅས་ (སྐུ་ཆས་) | *ku-che.* |
| Good-tempered | རྒྱུ་མ་རིང་པོ་ | *gyu-ma ring-po.* |

| | | |
|---|---|---|
| Good-tempered *hon.* | ཐུགས་རྒྱུ་རིང་པོ་ | *thuk-gyu ring-po.* |
| Goose | ངང་པ་ | *ngang-pa.* |
| Gorge | རོང་ | *rong.* |
| Gorgeous (of persons) | རྔམ་ཟྲིག་ (བརྗིད་) ཆེན་པོ་ | *ngam-śi chhem-po.* |
| Gossamer | སྡོམ་ཐག་ | *dom-tha.* |
| Gossip, to | ལབ་ལབ་ཇུང་བ། ཁ་ལས་ཟ་ཤད་པ་ | *laṗ-laṗ dung-wa; khaṗ-le she-pa.* |
| Do. *hon.* | ཞལ་ཞོག་གནང་བ། ཞལ་ལས་གསུང་བ་ | *sKe-sKo nang-wa; sKel-le sung-wa.* |
| Gout | འབམ་ | *bam.* |
| Do. *hon.* | སྐུ་འབམ་ | *kun-bam.* |
| Govern, to | དབང་བྱེད་པ་ | *wang-che-pa.* |
| Do. *hon.* | སྐུ་དབང་གནང་བ་ | *ku-wang nang-wa.* |
| Govern a country, to (secular government) | རྒྱལ་སྲིད་གནང་བ་ | *gye-si nang-wa.* |
| Do. (spiritual government) | ཆོས་སྲིད་གནང་བ་ | *chhö-si, nang-wa.* |
| Government | གཞུང་། གཞུང་ཐོག་ | *sKung; sKung tho.* |
| Do. Tibetan | སྡེ་པ་གཞུང་ | *de-pa sKung.* |
| Government revenue | ཞུང་གི་འབབ་ | *sKung gi baṗ.* |
| Governor | བཀའ་བློན་ | *ka-lön.* |
| Gown | ཆུ་པ་ | *chhu-pa.* |

| | | |
|---|---|---|
| Gown, *hon.* | ན་བཟའ་ | *nam-śa.* |
| Grace (favour) | བཀའ་དྲིན། ཐུགས་རྗེ་ | *ka-ṫrin ; thuk-je.* |
| Graceful | མཛེས་པོ་ | *dze-po.* |
| Gracious | དྲིན་ཆེན་པོ་ | *ṫrin-chhem-po.* |
| Do. *hon.* | བཀའ་དྲིན་ཆེན་པོ་ | *ka-ṫrin-chhem-po.* |
| Grade (rank) | གོ་ས། གོ་གནས། རིམ་པ་ | *k̄o-sa ; k̄o-ne ; rim-pa.* |
| Gradually | ག་ལེ་ག་ལེ་ | *k̄a-le k̄a-le.* |
| Grain (for human beings) | འབྲུ་ | *dru.* |
| Do. *hon.* | ཕྱག་འབྲུ་ | *chhan-dru.* |
| Grain (for animals) | ཆག་ | *chha.* |
| Grain, parched | ཡོས་ | *yö.* |
| Do. *hon.* | བཞེས་ཡོས་ | *sk̄e-yö.* |
| Grammar (orthography) | དག་ཡིག་ | *ṫak-yi.* |
| Granary | འབྲུ་བཀང་འཇུག་ འབྲུ་ཁང་ | *dru-kang-juk ; dru-khang.* |
| Grand | ཆེན་པོ་ | *chhem-po.* |
| Grand-daughter | བུའི་བུ་མོ། བུ་མོའི་བུ་མོ་ | *ṕu-i ṕu-mo ; ṕu-mö ṕu-mo.* |
| Grandfather | པོ་འོ་ | *po-o.* |
| Do. *hon.* | པོ་འོ་ལགས་ | *po-o-la.* |
| Grandmother | རྨོ་འོ་ | *mo-o.* |

| | | |
|---|---|---|
| Grandmother, *hon.* | རྨོ་འོ་ལགས་ | *mo-o-la.* |
| Grandson (son's son) | བུའི་བུ་ | *ṕu-ï-ṕu.* |
| Do. (daughter's son) | བུ་མོའི་བུ་ | *ṕu-mö-ṕu.* |
| Grant, to | སྟེར་བ་ | *ter-wa.* |
| Do. *hon.* | གནང་བ་ | *nang-wa.* |
| Grape (fruit) | རྒུན་འབྲུམ་ | *gün-drum.* |
| Grasp, to | ཟིན་པ་ (འཛིན་པ་) | *śim-pa.* |
| Do. *hon.* | ཟིན་ (འཛིན་) པ་གནང་བ་ | *śim-pa nang-wa.* |
| Grasp, to (understand) | ཧ་གོ་བ་ | *ha-ko-wa.* |
| Do. *hon.* | མཁྱེན་པ་ | *khyem-pa.* |
| Do. *h. hon.* | དགོངས་པ་རྟོགས་པ་ | *gong pa tok-pa.* |
| Grasping (avaricious) | ཧམ་པ་ཆེན་པོ་ | *ham-pa chhem-po.* |
| Grass | རྩ་ | *tsa.* |
| Grateful | བཀའ་དྲིན་ཆེན་པོ་ | *ka-t́rin chhem-po.* |
| Grateful, to be | དྲིན་དྲན་པ་ | *t́rin t́rem-pa.* |
| Do. *hon.* | དྲིན་དྲན་པ་གནང་བ་ | *t́rin t́rem-pa nang-wa.* |
| Do. *inf.* to *sup.* | བཀའ་དྲིན་དྲན་པ་ | *ka-t́rin t́rem-pa.* |
| Gratification (pleasure) | དགའ་ཚོར་ | *ga-tshor.* |
| Do. *hon.* | མཉེས་ཚོར་ | *nye-tshor.* |
| Gratified, to be | དགའ་བ་ | *ga-wa.* |

| | | |
|---|---|---|
| Gratified, to be, *hon.* | ཐུགས་མཉེས་པ་ | *thu-nye-pa.* |
| Do. *h. hon.* | ཐུགས་དགྱེས་པ་ | *thu-gye-pa.* |
| Grating (for windows) | ཁྲ་མ་ (དྲ་མ་) | *thra-ma.* |
| Do. iron | ལྕགས་ཁྲ་ (ལྕགས་དྲ་) | *chhak-thra.* |
| Gratitude | བཀའ་དྲིན་སྙིང་བཅང་ | *ka-ťrin nying-chang.* |
| Gratuity (tip) | ཆང་རིན་ | *chhang-rin.* |
| Do. *hon.* | གསོལ་རས། ཁྲུང་རིན་ | *sö-re ; trung-rin.* |
| Grave, *s.* | དུར་ཁུང་ | *ťur-khung.* |
| Grave, *adj.* (important) | གནད་ཁག་ཆེན་པོ། གལ་ཆེན་པོ་ | *nen-kha chhem-po ; ke chhem-po.* |
| Gravity (importance) | གནད་ཁག་ | *nen-kha.* |
| Gravy | ཤ་ཁུ་ | *sha-khu.* |
| Do. *hon.* | སྐྲུང་ཁུ་ (སྐྲུམ་ཁུ་) | *trung-khu.* |
| Gray | སྔོ་སྐྱ་ | *ngoṕ-kya.* |
| Graze, to (eat grass) | རྩ་ཟ་བ་ | *tsa śa-wa.* |
| Grease | ཚིལ་ལུ་ (ཚིལ་བུ་) | *tshi-lu.* |
| Do. liquid | སྣུམ་རྩི་ | *num-tsi.* |
| Greasy | ཞག་རྩི་ཆེན་པོ་ | *sḱak-tsi chhem-po.* |
| Great | ཆེན་པོ་ | *chhem-po.* |
| Greed | ཧམ་པ་ | *ham-pa.* |

| | | |
|---|---|---|
| Greedy (avaricious) | འདོད་པ་ཆེན་པོ་ | *dö-pa chhem-po.* |
| Do. (gluttonous) | གྲོད་ཆེན་པོ་ | *ṫrö-chhem-po.* |
| Green | ལྗང་ཁུ་ | *jang-khu.* |
| Green (of grass) | སྔོན་པོ་ | *ngöm po.* |
| Greet, to (by raising the hands) | ཐབ་མཇལ་བྱེད་པ་ | *dam-jel cḱe pa.* |
| Do. *hon.* | ཐབ་མཇལ་གནང་བ་ | *dam-jel nang-wa.* |
| Greet, to, *inf.* to *sup.* (by removing the hat) | ཕྱག་འབུལ་ཞུ་བ་ | *chham-bü sḱu-wa.* |
| Do. (by kneeling) | ཕྱག་འཚལ་བ་ | *chha tshe-wa.* |
| Do. *hon.* | སྐུ་ཕྱག་འཚལ་ར་ (བ་) གནང་བ་ | *ku-chha tshe-ra nang-wa.* |
| Greet, to (by (postration) | བརྐྱང་ཕྱག་འཚལ་བ་ | *kyang-chha tshe-wa.* |
| Do. *hon.* | བརྐྱང་ཕྱག་འཚལ་ར་ (བ་) གནང་བ་ | *kyang-chha tshe-ra nang-wa.* |
| Grey | སྔོ་སྐྱ་ | *ngoṕ-kya.* |
| Grief (in serious matters) | སྡུག་བསྔལ། སེམས་འཁྲལ་ | *du-nge ; sem-thre.* |
| Do. *hon.* | ཐུགས་འཁྲལ་ | *thuḱ-thre.* |
| Grieve, to, *v. i.* (in serious matters) | སྡུག་བསྔལ་བྱེད་པ། མྱ་ངན་བྱེད་པ་ | *du-nye cḱe-pa ; nya-ngen cḱe-pa.* |
| Do. *hon.* | ཐུགས་ངན་གནང་བ་ | *thu-ngen nang-wa.* |

| | | |
|---|---|---|
| Grieve, to, *v.i.* (in lesser matters) | སེམས་སྐྱོ་བ། སེམས་སྡུག་པ་ | *sem-kyo-wa*; *sem-duk-pa.* |
| Do. *hon.* | ཐུགས་སེམས་སྡུག་ག (པ་) གནང་བ་ | *thu-sem duk-ka nang-wa.* |
| Grim | ཞེད་སྐྲག་ཚ་པོ་ | *sKe-tra tsha-po.* |
| Grind, to (steel the teeth) | བདར་བ་ | *dar-wa.* |
| Do. *hon.* | བདར་ར་ (བ་) གནང་བ་ | *dar-ra nang-wa.* |
| Grind, to (corn) | བཏགས་པ་ (འཐག་པ་) | *taK-pa.* |
| Grindstone (for knives, &c.) | རྡར་རྡོ་ | *dar-do.* |
| Do. (for corn) | རང་འཐག་ | *rang-tha.* |
| Grip, to | ཟིན་པ་ (འཛིན་པ་) | *śim-pa.* |
| Do. *hon.* | ཟིན་ (འཛིན་) པ་གནང་བ་ | *śim-pa nang-wa.* |
| Groan, to | སྐད་ཤོར་བ་ | *ke-shor-wa.* |
| Do. *hon.* | གསུང་སྐད་ཤོར་ར་ (བ་) གནང་བ་ | *sung-ke shor-ra nang-wa.* |
| Grog-shop | ཆང་ཁང་ | *chhang-khang.* |
| Grog-seller | ཆང་མ་ | *chhang-ma.* |
| Groom | ཆིབས་དཔོན་ | *chhip-pön.* |
| Do. *hon.* | ཆིབས་དཔོན་ལགས་ | *chhip-pön-la.* |
| Grotto | བྲག་ཕུག་ | *traK-phu.* |
| Ground | ས་ | *sa.* |

| | | |
|---|---|---|
| Ground-rent | ས་གླ་ | *saṕ-la.* |
| Group | ཚོགས་ | *tsho.* |
| Grouse, sand | གངས་ཀ་ལིང་ | *ḱang-ka-ling.* |
| Grove, pleasure | གླིང་ཀ་ | *ling-ka.* |
| Grow, to | ཆེ་རུ་ཆེ་རུ་འགྲོ་བ་ | *chhe-ru chhe-ru dro-wa.* |
| Do. *hon.* | ཆེ་རུ་ཆེ་རུ་ཕེབ་པ་ | *chhe-ru chhe-ru phe-pa.* |
| Grow dark, to | ས་རིབ་ (འགྲིབས་) པ་ | *sa-riṕ-pa.* |
| Grow old, to | རྒད་རུ་རྒད་རུ་འགྲོ་བ་ | *ge-ru ge-ru dro-wa.* |
| Do. *hon.* | བགྲེས་རུ་བགྲེས་རུ་ཕེབ་པ་ | *dre-ru dre-ru phe-pa.* |
| Gruel | བག་ཐུག་ | *ṕa thu.* |
| Do. *hon.* | བཞེས་ཐུག་བག་ཐུག་ | *shé-thu ṕa-thu.* |
| Gruff (surly) | གྱོང་པོ་ | *ḱyong-po.* |
| Grunt, to | སྐད་རྒྱབ་པ་ | *ḱe-gyaṕ-pa.* |
| Guarantee | ཁས་ཁྱགས་ | *khe-khya.* |
| Do. *hon.* | ཞལ་ཁྱགས་ | *sKe-khya.* |
| Guarantee, to | ཁས་ཁྱགས་བྱེད་པ་ | *khe-khya cKe-pa.* |
| Do. *hon.* | ཞལ་ཁྱགས་གནང་བ་ | *sKe-khya nang-wa.* |
| Guarantor | ཁས་ཁྱགས་བྱེད་མཁན་ | *khe-khya cKe-khen.* |
| Do. *hon.* | ཞལ་ཁྱགས་གནང་མཁན་ | *sKe-khya nang-khen.* |
| Guard, *s.* | སྲུང་མཁན་ | *sung-khen.* |

| | | |
|---|---|---|
| Guard, to (a place, &c.) | སྲུང་བ་ | *sung-wa.* |
| Do. *hon.* | སྲུང་ང་ (བ་) གནང་བ་ | *sung-nga nang-wa.* |
| Guard, to (take care of goods, &c.) | ཉར་བ་ | *nyar-wa.* |
| Do. *hon.* | ཉར་ར་ (བ་) གནང་བ་ | *nyar-ra nang-wa.* |
| Do. *h. hon.* | ཐུགས་ཅག་གནང་བ་ | *thu-cha nang-wa.* |
| Guardian | མགོ་འདོན་བྱེད་མཁན་ | *gon-dön cKe-khen.* |
| Guess, *s.* | ཚོད་ | *tshö.* |
| Guest | མགྲོན་པོ་ | *dröm-po.* |
| Do. *hon.* | སྐུ་མགྲོན་ | *kun-drön.* |
| Guide, *s.* | ལམ་རྒྱུད་བྱེད་མཁན། ལམ་ཁ་བསྟན་ (སྟོན་) མཁན་ | *lam-gyü cKe-khen; lam-kha ten-khen.* |
| Do. *hon.* | ལམ་རྒྱུད་གནང་མཁན་ | *lam-lam-gyü nang-khen.* |
| Guide, to | ལམ་རྒྱུད་བྱེད་པ། ལམ་ཁ་བསྟན་ (སྟོན་) པ་ | *lam-gyü cKe-pa; lam-kha tem-pa.* |
| Do. *hon.* | ཕེབས་ལམ་རྒྱུད་གནང་བ་ | *phep-lam-gyü nang-wa.* |
| Guile | གཡོ་སྒྱུ་ | *yo-gyu.* |
| Guileful | གཡོ་སྒྱུ་ཚ་པོ་ | *yo-gyu tsha-po.* |
| Guilt | སྐྱོན། ཉེས་པ་ | *kyön; nye-pa.* |
| Guiltless | ཉེས་པ་མེད་པ་ | *nye-pa me-pa.* |

| | | |
|---|---|---|
| Guilty | སྐྱོན་ཆེན་པོ། ཉེས་པ་ཆེན་པོ་ | *kyön-chhem-po; nye-pa chhem po* |
| Guinea-pig | ཨབ་ར་ | *ab-ra.* |
| Guitar | སྒྲ་སྙན་ | *dram-nyen.* |
| Do. *hon.* | ཕྱག་སྙན་ | *chha-nyen.* |
| Gull, to | མགོ་སྐོར་བཏང་ (གཏོང་) བ་ | *go-kor tang-wa.* |
| Do. *hon.* | མགོ་སྐོར་གཏོང་ང་ (བ་) གནང་བ་ | *go-kor tong-nga nang-wa.* |
| Do. *inf.* to *sup.* | དབུ་སྐོར་ཞུ་བ་ | *u-kor sku-wa.* |
| Gullet | མིག་པ་ (མིད་པ་) | *mik-pa.* |
| Do. *hon.* | མགུལ་མིག་ | *gü-mi.* |
| Gully | སང་འགག་ | *hrang-ga.* |
| Gum | སྤྱིང་ (སྤྱིན་) | *ping.* |
| Do. for closing envelopes, etc. | ཁ་སྤྱིང་ (ཁ་སྤྱིན་) | *kha-ping.* |
| Do. *hon.* | ཞལ་སྤྱིང་ (ཞལ་སྤྱིན་) | *ske-ping.* |
| Gum (of teeth) | སོ་ཉིང་ | *so-nying.* |
| Do. *hon.* | ཚེམས་ཉིང་ | *tshem-nying.* |
| Gun | མེ་མདའ་ | *men-da.* |
| Do. *hon.* | ཕྱག་མདའ་ | *chhan-da.* |
| Gun-barrel | ལྕགས་ཧྲང་ | *cha-hrang.* |

| | | |
|---|---|---|
| Gun-fuse | སྦིད་རྫི་ (སྦིད་རྡི་) | *bi-di.* |
| Gun, hammer of | སྐམ་པ་ | *kam-pa.* |
| Gun-powder | རྫས་ | *dze.* |
| Gun, ramrod of | སིན་འབིད་ | *sim-bi.* |
| Gun-rest (of Tibetan fashion) | མེ་མདའི་རུ་ | *men-de ru.* |
| Do. *hon.* | ཕྱག་མདའི་རུ་ | *chhan-de ru.* |
| Gun, stock of | སྒྲུམ་ཤིང་ | *gum-shing.* |
| Do. trigger of | སྐམ་པ་ | *kam-pa.* |
| Guts | རྒྱུ་མ་ | *gyu-ma.* |
| Do. *hon.* | སྐུ་རྒྱུ་ | *ku-gyu.* |
| Gutter (on ground) | ཡོ་པོ་ (ཡུར་པོ་) | *yo-po.* |
| Do. (on roof of house) | འོག་ཆུ་ | *o-chhu.* |

# H

| | | |
|---|---|---|
| Habit (custom) | ལུགས་སྲོལ་ | *luk-sö.* |
| Habitation | ཁང་པ། ནང་། སྡོད་ས་ | *khang-pa; nang; dö-sa.* |
| Do. *hon.* | གཟིམ་ཁང་། བཞུགས་ས་ | *śim-khang; sku-sa.* |
| Do. *h. hon* | གཟིམ་ཤག། བཞུགས་གདན་འཛེགས་ས་ | *śim-sha; sku-den ja-sa.* |
| Habitually | རྟག་པར། ནམ་རྒྱུན་ | *tak-pa; nam-gyün.* |
| Haemorrhoids (piles) | གཞང་ཐྲོར་ | *ťrang-thor.* |
| Haft | ཡུ་བ་ | *yu-wa.* |
| Hag | མ་རྒན་ | *ma-gen.* |
| Hail, *s.* | སེར་ར་ (སེར་བ་) | *se-ra.* |
| Hail, to (hail-storm) | སེར་ར་ བཏང་ (གཏོང་) བ་ | *se-ra tang-wa.* |
| Do. to (call) | སྐད་བཏང་ (གཏོང་) བ་ | *ke-tang-wa.* |
| Do. *hon.* | གསུངས་སྐད་གནང་བ། སྐད་གཏོང་ང་ (བ་) གནང་བ་ | *sung-ke nang-wa; ke tong-nya nang-wa.* |
| Hair (on human head) | སྐྲ་ | *tra.* |
| Do. *hon.* | དབུ་སྐྲ་ | *u-tra.* |
| Hair, to wash the | སྐྲ་འཁྲུད་པ་ | *tra thrü-pa.* |
| Do. *hon.* | དབུ་བསིལ་གནང་བ་ | *u-si nang-wa.* |
| Hair, a single | སྐྲ་ཁང་གཅིག་ | *tra-kang chi.* |

| | | |
|---|---|---|
| Hairs, two | སྐྲ་རྐང་གཉིས་ | *tra-kang-nyi.* |
| Hair (of animals, and human hair other than that on head) | སྤུ་ | *pu.* |
| Do. a single | སྤུ་རྐང་གཅིག་ | *pu-kang-chi.* |
| Do. two | སྤུ་རྐང་གཉིས་ | *pu-kang nyi.* |
| Hair-brush | ཕག་ཟེ་ | *phak-śe.* |
| Half | ཕྱེད་ཀ་ | *chhe-ka.* |
| Hall of assembly | ཚོམས་ཆེན་ | *tshom-chhen.* |
| Do. for monks | འདུ་ཁང་ | *du-khang.* |
| Halo | འོད་སྐོར་ | *ö-kor.* |
| Halt, to | ཞག་ས་སྡོད་པ་ | *sKak-sa dö-pa.* |
| Do. *hon.* | བཞུགས་ཞག་གནང་བ་ | *sKuk-sKa nang-wa.* |
| Halter | ཐོ་མགོ་ (ཐུར་མགོ | *thong-go.* |
| Halting-place (for the day) | ཞག་ས་ | *sKak-sa.* |
| Do. *hon.* | བཞུགས་ཞག་ | *sKu-sKa.* |
| Hammer | ཐོ་བ་ | *tho-wa.* |
| Do. of gun | སྐམ་པ་ | *kam-pa.* |
| Hamper, *s.* | སླེ་ཀོག་ (སླེ་པོ་) | *le ko.* |
| Do. *hon.* | ཕྱག་སླེ་ | *chha-le.* |
| Hamper, to (hinder). | བཀག་པ་ (འགེགས་པ་) | *kak-pa.* |

| | | |
|---|---|---|
| Hamper, to (hinder) *hon.* | བཀག་ག་ (འགེགས་པ་) གནང་བ་ | *kaḱ-ḱa nang-wa.* |
| Hand | ལག་པ་ | *laḱ-pa.* |
| Do. *hon.* | ཕྱག་ | *chha.* |
| Handcuff, to | ལག་ལྕགས་རྒྱབ་པ་ | *laḱ-cha gyaṕ-pa.* |
| Handcuffs | ལག་ལྕགས་ | *laḱ-cha.* |
| Handful a | སྤར་ར་ (བ་) གང་ | *bar-ra ḱang.* |
| Do. *hon.* | ཕྱག་གང་ | *chha-ḱang.* |
| Handicraft | ལས་ཀ་ | *le-ḱa.* |
| Do. *hon.* | ཕྱག་ལས་ | *chha-le.* |
| Handkerchief | སྣ་འཕྱིད་ | *naṕ-chhi.* |
| Do. *hon.* | ཤངས་འཕྱིད་ | *shang-chhi.* |
| Handkerchief (compliment-ary) | ཁ་བཏགས་ | *kha-ta.* |
| Do. *hon.* | མཇལ་དར་ | *je-t́ar.* |
| Handle, straight (of knife, &c.) | ཡུ་བ་ | *yu-wa.* |
| Do. *hon.* | ཕྱག་ཡུ་ | *chha-yu.* |
| Handle, curved (of kettle, &c.) | ལུང་ | *lung.* |
| Do. *hon.* | ཕྱག་ལུང་ | *chha-lung.* |
| Handle, to | འཆང་བ་ | *chhang-wa.* |
| Do. *hon.* | འཆང་ང་ (བ་) གནང་བ་ | *chhang-nga nang-wa.* |

| | | |
|---|---|---|
| Handmaid | གཡོག་མོ་ | *yo-mo.* |
| Do. *hon.* | ཞལ་ལྟ་མ་ | *ske-ta-ma.* |
| Handsome | ཚར་པོ། མཛེས་པོ་ | *tshar-po; dze-po.* |
| Do. *hon.* | ཐུགས་ཚར་པོ་ | *thu tshar·po.* |
| Handwriting | ཡི་གེ་ | *yi-ge.* |
| Do. *hon.* | ཕྱག་བྲིས་ | *chha-ri.* |
| Hang, to, *v. t.* | བཀལ་བ་ (འགེལ་བ་) | *kel-wa.* |
| Do. *hon.* | བཀལ་ར་ (འགེལ་བ་) གནང་བ་ | *ke-ra nang-wa.* |
| Hang, to (a man) | སྐེ་ལ་ཐག་པ་བསྡམས་ནས་ བསད་ (གསོད་) པ་ | *ke-la thak-pa dam-ne se-pa.* |
| Hanker after, to | དྲན་པ་ | *trem-pa* |
| Do. *hon.* | ཐུགས་དྲན་པ་གནང་བ་ | *thu-trem-pa nang wa.* |
| Happen, to | བྱུང་བ་ (འབྱུང་བ་) | *chung-wa.* |
| Happiness | དགའ་ཚོར་ | *ga·tshor.* |
| Do. *hon.* | མཉེས་ཚོར་ | *nye-tshor.* |
| Happy (comfortable) | སྐྱིད་པོ་ | *kyi-po.* |
| Do. *hon.* | སྤྲོ་པོ་ | *tro-po.* |
| Happy, to be | དགའ་བ་ | *ga-wa.* |
| Do. *hon.* | མཉེས་པོ་གནང་བ་ | *nye-po nang-wa.* |
| Do. *h. hon.* | ཐུགས་དགྱེས་པོ་གནང་བ་ | *thu-gye-po nang-wa.* |

| | | |
|---|---|---|
| Harass, to | སྡུག་པོ་བཏང་ (གཏོང་) བ་ | *duk-po tang-wa.* |
| Do. *hon.* | སྡུག་པོ་གཏོང་ང་ (བ་) གནང་བ་ | *duk-po tong-nga nang-wa.* |
| Hard (arduous) | དཀའ་ལས་ཁག་པོ་ | *ka-le khak-po.* |
| Do. *hon.* | སྐུ་མཉེལ་པོ། སྐུ་ལས་ཁག་པོ་ | *ku-nye-po ; ku-le khak-po.* |
| Hard (of substance) | མཁྲགས་པོ་ (མཁྲེགས་པོ་) | *thrak-po.* |
| Hard-hearted, to be | སྙིང་རྗེ་མེད་པ་ | *nying-je me-pa.* |
| Do. *hon.* | ཐུགས་རྗེ་མེད་པ་ | *thuk-je me-pa.* |
| Hardship | དཀའ་ལས་ | *ka-le.* |
| Hardware (of iron things) | ལྕགས་ཅས་ (ལྕགས་ཆས་) | *cha-che.* |
| Do. (of copper things) | ཟངས་ཅས་ (ཟངས་ཆས་) | *śang-che.* |
| Hardy | གཟུགས་པོ་ཐང་པོ་ | *śuk-po thang-po.* |
| Do. *hon.* | སྐུ་གཟུགས་ཐང་པོ་ | *ku-śu thang-po.* |
| Hare | རི་གོང་ (རི་བོང་) | *re-kong.* |
| Hare-lip | ཞོ་རལ་ | *sho-re.* |
| Hare-year | ཡོས་ལོ་ | *yö-lo.* |
| Harlot | ཆལ་མོ། གཞང་ཚོང་མ། སྨད་ཚོང་མ་ | *chhe-mo ; skang-tshong-ma ; me-tshong-ma.* |
| Harm, *s.* | སྐྱོན་ | *kyön.* |
| Harm, to | སྐྱོན་བྱེད་པ་ | *kyön-che-pa.* |
| Do. *hon.* | སྐྱོན་གནང་བ་ | *kyön-nang-wa.* |

| | | |
|---|---|---|
| Harm, to (by witchcraft, &c.) | གནོད་པ་ | *nö-pa.* |
| Do. *hon.* | གནོད་པ་གནང་བ་ | *nö-pa nang-wa.* |
| Harmony, to be in | མཐུན་པ་ | *thüm-pa.* |
| Harp | སྒྲ་སྙན་ | *dram-nyen.* |
| Do. *hon.* | ཕྱག་སྙན་ | *chha-nyen.* |
| Harsh | གྱོང་པོ་ | *kyong-po.* |
| Hart | ཤ་བ་ | *sha a.* |
| Harvest | སྟོན་ཐོག་ | *tön-tho.* |
| Haste | བྲེལ་བ་ | *tre-wa.* |
| Do. *hon.* | ཐུགས་བྲེལ་ | *thu-tre.* |
| Hasten, to | མགྱོགས་པོ་བྱེད་པ་ | *gyok-po cke-pa.* |
| Do. *hon.* | རྩོལ་པོ་གནང་བ་ | *tsö-po nang-wa.* |
| Do. *h. hon.* | ཐུགས་རྩོལ་པོ་གནང་བ་ | *thu tsö-po nang-wa.* |
| Hastily | ལམ་སང་ | *lam-sang.* |
| Hasty (quick) | མགྱོགས་པོ་ | *gyok-po* |
| Do. *hon.* | རྩོལ་པོ་ | *tsö-po.* |
| Hasty (rash) | ཁ་མེད་མིག་མེད་ | *kha-me mik-me.* |
| Hate, to | སྡང་པོ་བྱེད་པ་ | *dang-po cke-pa.* |
| Do. *hon.* | སྡང་པོ་གནང་བ་ | *dang-po nang-wa.* |
| Hat | ཞྭ་མོ་ | *ska-mo.* |

| | | |
|---|---|---|
| Hat, *hon.* | དབུ་ཞྭ་ | *u-sKa.* |
| Hatchet | སྟ་རི། སྟ་གྲི་ | *ta-ri ; ta-ťri.* |
| Hateful | སྐྱུག་བྲོ་པོ་ | *kyuḱ-ťro-po.* |
| Haughtiness | ཉམས། ཛ་ཁོག་ | *nyam ; dza-kho.* |
| Haughty | ཉམས་ཆེན་པོ། ཛ་ཁོག་ཆེན་པོ་ | *nyam-chhem-po; dza-kho chhem-po.* |
| Haul, to | འཐེན་པ་ | *them-pa* |
| Do. *hon.* | འཐེན་པ་གནང་བ་ | *them-pa nang-wa.* |
| Haunt, *s.* | ཚང་ | *tshang.* |
| Have, to | ཡོད་པ་ | *yö-pa.* |
| Have, I | ང་ལ་ཡོད་ | *nga-la yö.* |
| Haversack | ལྟོ་ཕད་ | *to-phe.* |
| Hawk | ཁྲ་ | *thra.* |
| Hay | གཟན་པ། རྩྭ་སྐམ་པོ་ | *śem-pa ; tsa-kam-po.* |
| Do. *hon.* | ཆིབས་རྩྭ་ | *chhiṕ-tsa.* |
| Hay-fork | ཁེ་རག་ (ཁ་དྲག་) | *kheṕ-ra.* |
| Hay-sickle | ཟོར་ར་ (ཟོར་བ་) | *śor-ra.* |
| Hazard | ཉེན་ཁ | *nyen-kha.* |
| Hazardous | ཉེན་ཁ་ཆེན་པོ་ | *nyen-kha chhem-po.* |
| Haze | སྨུགས་པ་ | *muk-pa.* |
| He | ཁོ། ཁོ་རང་ | *kho ; kho-rang.* |

| | | |
|---|---|---|
| He, *hon.* | ཁོང་ | *khong.* |
| Head | མགོ་ | *go.* |
| Do. *hon.* | དབུ་ | *u.* |
| Head (leader) | མགོ་པ་ | *go-pa.* |
| Head, having a shaved (as a monk) | མགོ་རིལ་ | *go-ri.* |
| Do. *hon.* | དབུ་རིལ་ | *u-ri.* |
| Headache, to have | མགོ་ན་བ་ | *go-na-wa.* |
| Do. *hon.* | དབུ་སྙུང་བ་ | *u-nyung-wa.* |
| Headman | འགོ་བྱེད་ | *go-ch́e.* |
| Headstrong | གྱོང་པོ་ | *ḱyong-po.* |
| Heal, to | དྲག་ག་ (པ་) བཟོ་བ་ | *t́rak-ḱa śo-wa.* |
| Do. *hon.* | དྲག་ག་ (པ་) བཟོ་བ་གནང་བ་ | *t́rak-ḱa śo-wa nang-wa.* |
| Heal, to (patient of good position) | སྐུ་དང་ང་ (པ་) བཟོ་བ་གནང་བ་ | *ku-t́ang-nga śo-wa nang-wa.* |
| Healed, to be | དྲག་པ་ | *t́rak-pa.* |
| Do. *hon.* | སྐུ་དང་བ་ | *ku-t́ang-wa.* |
| Health | གཟུགས་པོ། ཁམས་ | *śuk-po ; kham.* |
| Do. *hon.* | སྐུ་གཟུགས། སྐུ་ཁམས་ | *ku-śuk ; kung-kham.* |
| Healthy | གཟུགས་པོ་བདེ་པོ་ | *śuk-po de-po.* |
| Do. *hon.* | སྐུ་གཟུགས་བཟང་པོ་ | *ku-śuk śang-po.* |

| | | |
|---|---|---|
| Heap, *s.* | སྤུང་ | *pung.* |
| Heap, to | སྤུང་བ་ | *pung-wa.* |
| Do. *hon.* | སྤུང་ང་ (བ་) གནང་བ་ | *pung-nga nang-wa.* |
| Hear, to | གོ་བ། ཨམ་མཆོག་གོ་བ་ | *Ḱo-wa ; am-chho ḱo-wa.* |
| Do. *hon.* | གསན་པ། སྙན་ལ་གསན་པ་ | *sem-pa ; nyen-la sem-pa.* |
| Hearken, to | ཉན་པ་ | *nyem-pa.* |
| Do. *hon.* | གསན་པ་ | *sem-pa.* |
| Hearsay (report) | སྐད་ཆ། གཏམ་ | *ḱe-chha ; tam.* |
| Heart | སྙིང་ | *nying.* |
| Do. *hon.* | ཐུགས་སྙིང་། སྐུ་སྙིང་ | *thu-nying ; ḱu-nying.* |
| Heart, to learn by | བློ་ལ་ཟིན་པ་ | *lo-la śim-pa.* |
| Do. *hon.* | ཐུགས་ལ་ཟིན་པ་གནང་བ་ | *thu-la śim-pa nang-wa.* |
| Hearth | ཐབ་ | *thaṕ.* |
| Do. *hon.* | གསོལ་ཐབ་ | *sö-thaṕ.* |
| Heartily | སྙིང་རུས་བྱས་ནས་ | *nying-rü cḱe-ne.* |
| Do. *hon.* | ཐུགས་རུས་གནང་ནས་ | *thuḱ-rü nang-ne.* |
| Heat | ཚད་པ་ | *tshe-pa.* |
| Do. *hon.* | སྐུ་ཚད་ | *ḱu-tshe.* |
| Heathen | ཕྱི་པ་ | *chhi pa.* |
| Heaven (sky) | གནམ། ནམ་མཁའ་ | *nam ; nam-ḱha.* |

| | | |
|---|---|---|
| Heavy | ལྗི་པོ་ | *ji-po.* |
| Hedge | ར་བ་ | *ra-a.* |
| Hedgehog | གཟིག་སྨོ་ | *śiḱ-mo.* |
| Heed, to | ཉན་པ་ | *nyem-pa.* |
| Do. *hon.* | གསན་པ་ | *sem-pa.* |
| Heel | རྟིང་པ་ | *ting-pa.* |
| Do. *hon.* | ཞབས་མཐིལ་ (ཞབས་རྟིང་) | *sḱaṕ-thil.* |
| Heifer | པེ་བེ་ | *pe-ṕe.* |
| Height (of human being) | རིང་ཐུང་ | *ring-thung.* |
| Do. (of inanimate objects) | མཐོ་དམན་ | *tho-men.* |
| Heir | ནོར་གྱི་བདག་པོ་ | *nor-kyi dak-po.* |
| Heiress | ནོར་གྱི་བདག་པོ་ | *nor-ḱyi daḱ-po.* |
| Hell | དམྱལ་ལ་ (བ་) | *nyel-la.* |
| Helmet | རྨོག་ | *mo.* |
| Do. *hon.* | དབུ་རྨོག་ | *u-mo.* |
| Help | རོགས་ | *ro.* |
| Do. *hon.* | མགོ་འདྲེན་ | *gön-dren.* |
| Help, to | རོགས་བྱེད་པ་ | *ro cḱe-pa.* |
| Do. *hon.* | མགོ་འདྲེན་གནང་བ་ | *gön-dren nang-wa.* |
| Helper | རོགས་བྱེད་མཁན་ | *ro-cḱe-khen.* |

| | | |
|---|---|---|
| Helper, *hon.* | མགོ་འདྲེན་གནང་མཁན་ | *gön-dren nang-khen.* |
| Helpful, to be (useful) | ཕན་ཐོགས་པ་ | *phen-thok-pa.* |
| Do. *hon.* | ཐུགས་ཕན་གསོ་བ་ | *thu-phen so-wa.* |
| Helpless | རོགས་ ‥ མེད་པ་ | *ro.....me pa.* |
| Hem, *s.* | སྙེ། སྙེ་མོ་ | *ne ; ne-mo.* |
| Hem, to | སྙེ་ནས་འཚེམ་པ་ | *ne-ne tshem-pa.* |
| Do. *hon.* | སྙེ་ནས་འཚེམ་པ་གནང་བ་ | *ne-ne tshem-pa nang-wa.* |
| Hemp | སོ་མ་ར་ཙ་ | *so-ma ra-tsa.* |
| Hen | བྱ་མོ་ | *cḱa-mo.* |
| Hence (from this place) | འདི་ནས་ | *di-ne.* |
| Do. (therefore) | དེའི་རྐྱེན་བྱས་ནས། དེའི་རྐྱེན་གྱིས་ | *t́e-i-kyen cḱe-ne ; t́e-i kyen-kyi.* |
| Henceforth | ད་ནས་ཕྱིན་ཆད་ | *t́a-ne chhin-chhe.* |
| Her | མོའི་ | *mö.* |
| Herd | ཁྱུ་ | *khyu.* |
| Herdsman | རྫི་བོ་ | *dzi-o.* |
| Do. of cattle | བ་རྫི་ | *ṕa-dzi.* |
| Do. of goats | ར་རྫི་ | *ra-dzi.* |
| Do. of horses | རྟ་རྫི་ | *ta-dzi.* |
| Do. of hogs | ཕག་རྫི་ | *phak-dzi.* |

| | | |
|---|---|---|
| Herdsman of sheep | ལུག་རྫི་ | *luk-dzi.* |
| Do. of yaks | གཡག་རྫི་ | *ya-dzi.* |
| Do. of donkeys | བོང་རྫི་ | *ṕong-dzi.* |
| Do. of fowls | བྱ་རྫི་ | *cḱa-dzi.* |
| Here | འདིར་ | *de.* |
| Hereafter | ད་ནས་ཕྱིན་ཆད་ | *t́a-ne chhin-chhe.* |
| Heresy | ཆོས་ལོག་ | *chhö lo.* |
| Heresy, to commit. | ཆོས་ལོག་བྱེད་པ་ | *chhö-lo cḱe-pa.* |
| Herewith | འདི་དང་མཉམ་དུ་ | *di-t́ang nyam-t́u.* |
| Heritage | ནོར་སྐལ་ | *nor-ke.* |
| Hermit | སྒོམ་ཆེན་ | *gom-chhen.* |
| Hermitage | དབེན་གནས་ | *en-ne.* |
| Hero | དཔའ་བོ་ | *pa-o.* |
| Heroine | དཔའ་མོ་ | *pa-mo.* |
| Hers | མོའི་ | *mö.* |
| Herself | མོ་རང་ | *mo-rang.* |
| Hesitate, to | ཐེ་ཚོམ་ཟ་བ་ | *the-tshom śa-wa.* |
| Do. *hon.* | ཐེ་ཚོམ་གནང་བ་ | *the-tshom nang-wa.* |
| Hesitation | ཐེ་ཚོམ་ | *the-tshom.* |
| Hew, to (length ways) | གཤག་པ་ | *shak-pa.* |

| | | |
|---|---|---|
| Hew, to (breadthways) | བཙབ་པ་ | *tsaṕ-pa.* |
| Hiccough, to | ཨི་ཀ་རྒྱབ་པ་ | *i-ka gyaṕ-pa.* |
| Hidden (concealed) | སྦས་པ་ | *be-pa.* |
| Do. (secret) | གསང་བ་ | *sang-wa.* |
| Hide, *s.* (*e.g.* of yak, bullock, &c.) | ཀོ་བ་ | *ko-wa.* |
| Do. (*i.e.* skin of sheep, goat, &c.) | པགས་པ་ | *paḱ-pa.* |
| Hide, to, *v.t.* | སྦེད་པ་ | *be-pa.* |
| Do. *hon.* | སྦེད་པ་གནང་བ་ | *be-pa nang-wa.* |
| Hide, to, *v.i.* | ཡིབ་པ་ | *yiṕ-pa.* |
| Do. *hon.* | ཡིབ་པ་གནང་བ་ | *yiṕ-pa nang-wa.* |
| Hideous | ཞེད་སྣག་ཚ་པོ་ | *sḱe-tra tsha-po.* |
| Hierarchy | ཆོས་སྲིད་ | *chhö-si.* |
| High (of things, rank of persons | མཐོ་པོ་ | *tho-po.* |
| Highway | རྒྱ་ལམ་ | *gya-lam.* |
| Hill | རི་ | *ri.* |
| Do. up | གྱེན་ | *kyen.* |
| Do. down | ཐུར་ | *thur.* |
| Hilt | ཡུ་བ་ | *yu-wa.* |
| Him | ཁོ་ལ་ | *kho-la.* |

| | | |
|---|---|---|
| Himself | ཁོ་རང་ | *kho-rang.* |
| Hinder, to | བཀག་པ་ (འགེགས་པ) | *kak-pa.* |
| Do. *hon.* | བཀག་ཀ་ (འགེགས་པ་) གནང་བ་ | *kak-ka nang-wa.* |
| Hind-foot | རྐང་པ་ | *kang-pa.* |
| Hindrance | བཀག་ཆ་ | *kak-chha.* |
| Hinge (of Tibetan make) | ཏིང་པ་ | *ting-pa.* |
| Hip (of body) | དཔྱི་མགོ་ | *ching-go.* |
| Hire (wages) | གླ། ཕོགས་ | *la ; pho.* |
| Hire, to | གླས་པ་ | *le-pa.* |
| Hired workman | མི་གླ། གླ་པ་ | *mi-la ; la-pa.* |
| His | ཁོའི་ | *khö.* |
| History | ལོ་རྒྱུས། རྣམ་ཐར་ | *lo-gyü ; nam-tha.* |
| Do. *hon.* | གསུང་ཐར་ | *sung-tha.* |
| Hit, to | ཁེས་པ། འཕོག་པ་ | *khe-pa ; phok-pa.* |
| Hit at, to (with a stick, fists, &c.) | གཞུ་བ་ | *sku-wa.* |
| Hit, a | ལྕག་ | *cha.* |
| Hither | ཚུར། འདི་རུ་ | *tshur ; di-ru.* |
| Hitherto | ད་ཐུག་བར་དུ་ | *ta-thu par-tu.* |
| Hive (of bees) | སྦྲང་ཚང་ | *drang-tshang.* |

| | | |
|---|---|---|
| Hoard | བཀང་འཇུག་ | *kang-juk.* |
| Hoar-frost | བ་མོ་ | *ṕa-mo.* |
| Hoarse, to be | སྐད་འཛེར་བ་ | *ke dzer-wa.* |
| Hobbling (lame) | རྐང་ཀྱོག་ | *kang-kyo.* |
| Do. *hon.* | ཞབས་ཀྱོག་ | *s̕kaṕ-kyo.* |
| Hobgoblin | གདོང་འདྲེ། འདྲེ་ | *dong-dre ; dre.* |
| Hoe | འཇོར་ (ཏོག་ཙེ་) | *jo.* |
| Hoe, to | རྐོ་བ་ | *ko-wa.* |
| Hog | ཕག་པ་ | *phak-pa.* |
| Hoist, to | ཡར་འཕྱར་བ་ | *yar-chhar-wa.* |
| Hold, to (catch hold of) | ཟིན་པ་ (འཛིན་པ་) | *śim-pa.* |
| Do. *hon.* | ཟིན་ (འཛིན་) པ་གནང་བ་ | *śim-pa nang-wa.* |
| Hold up, to | སྟེན་པ་ | *tem-pa.* |
| Hole (made by human being or animal) | ཁུང་ | *khung.* |
| Do. (formed by nature) | ཨི་ཁུང་ | *i-khung.* |
| Hole, peep- | སོ་ཁུང་ | *so-khung.* |
| Holiday | དགོངས་པ་ | *gong-pa.* |
| Hollo! *interj.* | ཝེ | *we.* |
| Hollow, *s.* (in the ground) | ཀོང་སྟོང་ | *kong-tong.* |

| | | |
|---|---|---|
| Hollow, *adj.* (of metals, manufactured articles, &c.) | ཁོག་སྟོང་ | *khoḱ-tong.* |
| Hollyhock | ཧ་ལོ་མེ་ཏོག་ | *ha-lo me-to.* |
| Holy | དམ་པ། ཆོས་ལྡན་ | *ťam-pa chhön-den.* |
| Homage, to do | ཕྱག་འཚལ་བ་ | *chha-tshe-wa.* |
| Home | ནང་། ཁང་པ་ | *nang ; khang-pa.* |
| Do. *hon.* | གཟིམ་ཁང་ | *śim-khang.* |
| Do. *h. hon.* | གཟིམ་ཤག་ | *śim-sha.* |
| Home, at | ནང་ལ་ | *nang-la.* |
| Home-sick, to be | ལུང་པ་དྲན་པ་ | *lung-pa ťrem-pa.* |
| Honest | དྲང་པོ་ | *ťrang-po.* |
| Do. *hon.* | ཐུགས་དྲང་པོ་ | *thu-ťrang-po.* |
| Honey | སྦྲང་རྩི་ | *drang-tsi.* |
| Honour (respect) | བསྙེན་བཀུར་ | *nyen-kur.* |
| Honour, to | བསྙེན་བཀུར་བྱེད་པ་ | *nyen-kur cḱe-pa.* |
| Do. *inf.* to *sup.* | བསྙེན་བཀུར་ཞུ་བ་ | *nyen-kur sḱu-wa.* |
| Hood (as scarf wound round the face to protect from cold, &c.) | ཁ་དཀྲིས་ | *kha-tri.* |
| Do. *hon.* | ཞལ་དཀྲིས་ | *sḱe-tri.* |
| Hoof | རྨིག་པ་ | *mik-pa.* |

| | | |
|---|---|---|
| Hook | ཀྱུག་ | *kuk.* |
| Hook, fish- | ཉ་ཀྱུག་ | *nya-kuk.* |
| Hook, iron- | ལྕགས་ཀྱུ་ | *cha-kyu.* |
| Hookah | ཧོར་ཁ་ *Hind.* | *hor-kha.* |
| Do. *hon.* | བཞེས་ཧོར་ | *ske-hor.* |
| Hookah, bowl of | ཅི་ལིམ་ *Hind.* | *chi-lim.* |
| Hoop | ཤན་ | *shen.* |
| Do. iron | ལྕགས་ཤན་ | *cha-shen.* |
| Hoopoe | པུ་པུ་ཁུ་ཤུད་ (པུ་ཤུད་) | *pu-pu khu-shü.* |
| Hope | རེ་བ་ | *re-wa.* |
| Do. *hon.* | ཐུགས་རེ་ | *thu-re.* |
| Hope, to | རེ་བ་བྱེད་པ་ | *re-wa che-pa.* |
| Do. *hon.* | ཐུགས་རེ་གནང་བ་ | *thu-re nang-wa.* |
| Hopeless, to be | རེ་བ་མེད་པ་ | *re-wa me-pa.* |
| Do. *hon.* | ཐུགས་རེ་མེད་པ་ | *thu re me pa.* |
| Horizon | མཐོང་བའི་འཁོར་ | *thong-we khor.* |
| Horn | ར་ཅོ་ | *ra-cho.* |
| Hornet | སྦྲང་མ་ | *drang-ma.* |
| Hornless | ཨ་ཡུ་ | *a-yu.* |
| Horoscope | སྐྱེ་སྐར་རྟགས་པ་ | *kye-ka tak-pa.* |

| | | |
|---|---|---|
| Horoscope, *hon.* | འཁྲུངས་སྐར་རྟགས་པ་ | *thrung-ka tak-pa.* |
| Horrible | ཞེད་སྐྲག་ཚ་པོ་ | *sḱe-tra tsha-po.* |
| Horrid | ཞེད་སྐྲག་ཚ་པོ་ | *sḱe-tra tsha-po.* |
| Horrifying | ཞེད་སྐྲག་ཚ་པོ་ | *sḱe-tra tsha-po.* |
| Horror | ཞེད་སྐྲག་ | *sḱe-tra.* |
| Horse | རྟ་ | *ta* |
| Do. *hon.* | ཆིག་པ་ (ཆིབས་པ་) | *chhiḱ-pa.* |
| Horse, Chinese | སིང་རྟ་ | *sing-ta.* |
| Horse, Indian country-bred | རྟི་པི་ཅག་ | *ti pi-cha.* |
| Horse, saddle | ཞོན་རྟ་ | *sḱön-ta.* |
| Do. *hon.* | ཆིབས་པ་ | *chhiḱ-pa.* |
| Horse, pack | ཁལ་རྟ་ | *khe-ta.* |
| Horse, saddle (of very high official or lama) | ཆིབས་ཆེན་ | *chhiṕ-chhen.* |
| Horse-dung | རྟའི་སྦངས་ | *te-bang.* |
| Horse-hair (of the tail) | རྟ་རྔ་ | *ta-nga.* |
| Horse-whip | རྟ་ལྕག་ | *te-cha.* |
| Do. *hon.* | ཆིབས་ལྕག་ | *chhiṕ-cha.* |
| Horseman | རྟ་པ་ | *ta-pa.* |
| Horsemen, body of | རྟ་རག་ | *taṕ-ra.* |
| Do. *hon.* | ཆིབས་རག་ | *chhiṕ-ra.* |

| | | |
|---|---|---|
| Horse-shoe | རྨིག་ལྕགས་ | *mik-cha.* |
| Hospitable | ལག་པ་ཤོག་པོ་ | *lak-pa shok-po.* |
| Do. *hon.* | ཕྱག་ཤོག་པོ་ | *chha-shok-po.* |
| Hospital | སྨན་ཁང་ | *men-khang.* |
| Host (army) | དམག་ | *ma.* |
| Do. (crowd of persons) | མི་དཔུང་ | *mi-pung.* |
| Do. (owner of house, inn, &c.) | གནས་པོ་ | *ne-po.* |
| Hostess | གནས་མོ་ | *ne-mo.* |
| Hot | ཚ་པོ་ | *tsha-po.* |
| Hot-tempered | རླུང་ལང་པོ་ | *lung lang-po.* |
| Do. *hon.* | སྐུ་རླུང་བཞང་པོ་ | *ku-lung sKang-po.* |
| Hot (of weather) | ཚད་པ་ཚ་པོ་ | *tshe-pa tsha-po.* |
| Hot, to be (of body) | ཚད་པ་འཚིག་པ་ | *tshe-pa tshik-pa.* |
| Do. *hon.* | སྐུ་ཚད་ཚ་པོ་བྱུང་བ་ | *ku-tshe tsha-po cKung-wa.* |
| Hotel | གནས་ཚང་ | *ne-tshang.* |
| Hotel charges | གནས་གླ་ | *ne-la.* |
| Hotel-keeper | གནས་པོ་ | *ne-po.* |
| Do. *f.* | གནས་མོ་ | *ne-mo.* |
| Hound | ཁྱི་ | *khyi.* |
| Do. *hon.* | གཟིམ་ཁྱི་ | *śim-khyi.* |

| | | |
|---|---|---|
| Hour | ཆུ་ཚོད་ | *chhu-tshö.* |
| House | ནང་། ཁང་པ་ | *nang ; khang-pa.* |
| Do. *hon.* | གཟིམ་ཁང་ | *śim-k̇hang.* |
| Do. *h. hon.* | གཟིམ་ཤག་ | *śim-sha.* |
| House-owner | ཁང་བདག་ | *khang-dak̇.* |
| House agent | ཁང་གཉེར་ | *khang-nyer.* |
| House, care-taker of | ཁང་སྲུང་ང་ (བ་) | *khang-sung-nga.* |
| House-rent | ཁང་གླ་ | *khang-la.* |
| Household | ནང་མི་ | *nang-mi.* |
| Housewife | གནས་མོ་ | *ne-mo.* |
| Do. *hon.* | སྙི་སྙིང་ལགས་ | *nyi-nying-la.* |
| Hovel | ནང་ཆུང་། ཁང་ཆུང་ | *nang-chhung ; k̇hang-chhung.* |
| How | ག་འདྲས་ | *k̇an-dre.* |
| How much | ག་ཚོད་ | *k̇a-tshö.* |
| Howbeit | ག་རེ་ཡིན་ནས་ | *ka-re yin-ne.* |
| However | ཡིན་ནས། ཡིན་ཀྱང་། ཡིན་ན་ཡང་ | *yin-ne ; yin-k̇yang ; yin-na-yang.* |
| Howl, to (of dogs) | སྡུག་སྐད་རྒྱབ་པ་ | *duk-k̇e gyaṗ-pa.* |
| Do. (of children crying) | ངུ་བ་ | *ngu-wa.* |
| Hug, to | འཁྱུད་པ་ | *khyü-pa.* |

| | | |
|---|---|---|
| Huge | ཆེ་ཐག་ཆོད་ | *chhe-thaḱ-chhö.* |
| Hullo! (expression of surprise) | ཨ་ཙི | *a-tsi.* |
| Human | མིའི་ | *mi-i.* |
| Humble | སེམས་ཆུང་ཆུང་ | *sem-chhung-chhung.* |
| Do. *hon.* | ཐུགས་སེམས་ཆུང་ཆུང་ | *thuḱ sem chhung-chhung.* |
| Humid | རློན་པ་ | *löm-pa.* |
| Humorous | བགད་མོ་བྲོ་པོ་ | *ge-mo t́ro-po.* |
| Do. *hon.* | ཞལ་མོ་བྲོ་པོ་ | *sḱe-mo t́ro-po.* |
| Hunch-back | སྒོད་དགུར་ | *tö-gur.* |
| Hundred | བརྒྱ་ཐམ་པ་ | *gya-tham-pa.* |
| Hundredth | བརྒྱ་ཐམ་པ་ | *gya-tham-pa.* |
| Hunger | ལྟོགས་པ་ | *toḱ-pa.* |
| Do. *hon.* | བཀྲེས་པ་ | *tre pa.* |
| Hungry, to be | གྲོ་ (གྲོད་) ཁོག་ལྟོགས་པ་ | *t́ro ḱho toḱ-pa.* |
| Do. *hon.* | གསོལ་གྲོད་དཀྲེས་པ་ | *sö-t́rö tre-pa.* |
| Hunt, to | ཁྱི་ར་རྒྱབ་པ་ | *khyi-ra gyaṕ-pa.* |
| Hunter | ཁྱི་ར་བ་ | *khyi-ra-wa.* |
| Hurricane | ལྷགས་པ་ཚ་པོ་ | *hlak-pa tsha-po.* |
| Do. (with rain) | ཆར་རླུང་ | *chhar-lung.* |
| Hurry, to | མགྱོགས་པོ་བྱེད་པ་ | *gyoḱ-po cḱe-pa.* |

| | | |
|---|---|---|
| Hurry, to, *hon.* | རྩོལ་པོ་གནང་བ་ | *tsö-po nang-wa.* |
| Do. *h. hon.* | ཐུགས་རྩོལ་པོ་གནང་བ་ | *thu tsö-po nang-wa.* |
| Hurry, in a great | བྲེལ་བ་ཚ་པོ་བྱས་ནས་ | *ťre-wa tsha-po cḱe-ne.* |
| Do. *hon.* | མཛད་བྲེལ་ཆེན་པོ་གནང་ནས་ | *dze-ťre chhem-po nang-ne.* |
| Hurt (physical) | རྨ་ | *ma.* |
| Do. (by witchcraft, etc.) | གནོད་པ་ | *nö-pa.* |
| Hurt, to (physically) | རྨ་བཟོ་བ་ | *ma-śo-wa.* |
| Do. (by witchcraft, etc.) | གནོད་པ་བྱེད་པ་ | *nö-pa cḱe-pa.* |
| Hurt, to (impair) | སྐྱོན་བྱེད་པ་ | *kyön-cḱe-pa.* |
| Do. *hon.* | སྐྱོན་གནང་བ་ | *kyön-nang-wa.* |
| Hurt, to be | སྐྱོན་བྱེད་པ་ | *kyön-cḱe-pa.* |
| Husband | ཁྱོ་ག་ | *khyo-ḱa.* |
| Husbandman | སོ་ནམས་བྱེད་མཁན་ | *sö-nam cḱe-khen.* |
| Husband and wife | བཟའ་ཚང་ | *śa-tshang.* |
| Husbandry (agriculture) | སོ་ནམས་ | *sö-nam.* |
| Husk (of grain) | པགས་པ་ | *paḱ-pa.* |
| Hut | ནང་ཆུང་། ཁང་ཆུང་ | *nang-chhung; khang-chhung.* |
| Hydrophobia | ཁྱི་སྨྱོན་ | *khyim-nyön.* |
| Hymn | མགུར་མ་ | *gur-ma.* |

# I

| | | |
|---|---|---|
| I | ང་ | *nga.* |
| Do. myself | ང་རང་ | *nga-rang.* |
| Ice | ཁྱག་པ་ | *khyaḱ-pa.* |
| Icicle | ཁྱག་པ་ | *khyaḱ pa.* |
| Icy, to be | ཁྱག་པ་ཡོད་པ་ | *khyaḱ-pa yö-pa.* |
| Idea (purport) | དོན་ | *t́ön.* |
| Do. *hon.* | སྐུ་དོན་ | *ku-t́ön.* |
| Idea (opinion) | བསམ་པ་ | *sam-pa.* |
| Do. *hon.* | ཐུགས་སེམས་ | *thu-sem.* |
| Identical | གཅིག་པ་ | *chiḱ-pa.* |
| Identify, to | ངོ་འཕྲོད་སྤྲད་པ་ | *ngo-thrö tre-pa.* |
| Do. *hon.* | ངོ་འཕྲོད་གནང་བ་ | *ngo-thrö nang-wa.* |
| Idiom | སྐད་ལུགས་ | *ke-lu.* |
| Idiot | ལྐུགས་པ། གླེན་པ་ | *kuḱ-pa ; lem-pa.* |
| Idiotic (stupid) | ལྐུགས་པ། གླེན་པ་ | *kuḱ-pa ; lem-pa.* |
| Idle | རྒྱུ་མ་རིང་པོ། ལེ་ལོ་ཆེན་པོ་ | *gyu-ma ring po; le-lo chhem-po.* |
| Do. *hon.* | ཐུགས་རྒྱུ་རིང་པོ་ | *thu-gyu ring-po.* |
| Idol | སྐུ་འདྲ་ | *ḱun-dra.* |
| If | གལ་སྲིད་……ན་ | *Ḱe-si...na.* |

| | | |
|---|---|---|
| Ignite, to | འབར་བ་ | *bar-wa.* |
| Ignoble | སྐྱེ་ས་དམའ་པོ་ | *kye-sa ma-po.* |
| Ignominious | ངོ་ཚ་པོ་ | *ngo-tsha-po.* |
| Ignominy | ངོ་ཚ་ | *ngo-tsha.* |
| Ignoramus | ལྐུགས་པ་ | *kuk-pa.* |
| Ignorant | ཡོན་ཏན་མེད་པ་ | *yön-ten me-pa.* |
| Do. *hon.* | སྐུ་ཡོན་མེད་པ་ | *ku-yön me-pa.* |
| Ill, to be | ན་བ་ | *na-wa.* |
| Do. *hon.* | སྙུང་བ་ | *nyung-wa.* |
| Illegal | ཁྲིམས་མེད་ | *thrim-me.* |
| Ill-fated | བསོད་བདེ་མེད་པ། བསོད་བདེ་ཆུང་ཆུང་། | *so-de me-pa; so-de chhung-chhung.* |
| Do. *hon.* | སྐུ་བསོད་མེད་པ། སྐུ་བསོད་ཆུང་ཆུང་ | *ku-sö me-pa; ku-sö chhung-chhung.* |
| Ill-feeling, to cherish | སེམས་ལ་ངན་པ་བྱས་ནས་བཞག་ (འཛོག་) པ་ | *sem-la ngem-pa cKe-ne sKak-pa.* |
| Ill-luck | བསོད་བདེ་མེད་པ་ | *so-de me-pa.* |
| Do. *hon.* | སྐུ་བསོད་མེད་པ་ | *ku-sö me-pa.* |
| Ill-natured | སེམས་ངན་པ་ | *sem-ngem-pa.* |
| Do. *hon.* | ཐུགས་སེམས་ངན་པ་ | *thu-sem ngem-pa.* |

| | | |
|---|---|---|
| Ill-will | སྙིང་ནད་ | *nying-ne.* |
| Illegal | ཁྲིམས་མེད་ | *thrim-me.* |
| Illegitimate | ཁྲིམས་མེད་ | *thrim-me.* |
| Illicit | ཁྲིམས་མེད་ | *thrim-me.* |
| Illimitable | ཚོད་མེད་པ་ | *tshö-me-pa.* |
| Illiterate, to be | ཡོན་ཏན་མེད་པ་ | *yön-ten me-pa.* |
| Do. *hon.* | སྐུ་ཡོན་མེད་པ་ | *ḱu-yön me-pa.* |
| Illness | ན་ཚ་ | *na·tsha.* |
| Do. *hon.* | སྙུང་གཞི་ | *nyung·sḱi.* |
| Illuminate, to | འོད་རྒྱབ་པ་ | *ö-gyaṕ-pa.* |
| Illusion (optical) | མིག་འཁྲུལ་ | *miḱ·thrü.* |
| Illusive | མིག་འཁྲུལ་ཆེན་པོ་ | *miḱ-thrü chhem-po.* |
| Illustrate, to | དཔེ་སྦྱར་ནས་བཤད་པ་ | *pe-jar-ne she-pa.* |
| Do. *hon.* | དཔེ་སྦྱར་ནས་གསུང་བ་ | *pe-jar ne sung-wa.* |
| Illustration | དཔེ་ | *pe.* |
| Illustrious | སྐད་གྲགས་ཆེན་པོ་ | *ḱe-t́ra chhem-po.* |
| Do. *hon.* | མཚན་སྙན་གྲགས་ཆེན་པོ་ | *tshen nyen-t́ra chhem-po.* |
| Image (idol) | སྐུ་འདྲ་ | *ḱun dra.* |
| Imagination | དམིགས་པ་ | *miḱ-pa.* |
| Imagine, to (think) | བསམ་པ་ | *sam·pa.* |

| | | |
|---|---|---|
| Imagine, to (think), *hon.* | ཐུགས་བསམ་བཞེས་པ་ | *thu-sam sKe-pa.* |
| Imbecile | ལྐུགས་པ། གླེན་པ་ | *kuk-pa ; lem-pa.* |
| Imbrue, to (soak) | སྦང་བ་ | *bang-wa.* |
| Do. *hon.* | སྦང་ང་ (བ་) གནང་བ་ | *bang-nga nang-wa.* |
| Imitate, to | མིག་འདྲེན་བྱེད་པ་ | *mik-dren cKe-pa.* |
| Immaculate, to be | སྐྱོན་མེད་པ་ | *kyön me pa.* |
| Immaterial (without substance) | གཟུགས་མེད་ | *śu-me.* |
| Immeasurable (very great) | ཆེ་ཐག་ཆོད་ | *chhe thak-chhö.* |
| Do. to be | ཚོད་མེད་པ་ | *tshö me pa* |
| Immediately | ལམ་སང་། ལམཀྱང་ | *lam-sang ; lam-kyang.* |
| Immense | རྒྱ་ཆེན་པོ། ཆེ་ཐག་ཆོད་ | *gya-chhem-po ; chhe thak-chhö.* |
| Immoderate, to be | ཚོད་མེད་པ་ | *tshö-me-pa.* |
| Do. *hon.* | ཐུགས་ཚོད་མེད་པ་ | *thuk-tshö me-pa.* |
| Immodest, to be | ངོ་ཚ་མེད་པ་ | *ngo-tsha me-pa.* |
| Immoral | བྱེད་སྟངས་ངན་པོ་ | *cKe-tang ngem-po.* |
| Do. *hon.* | གནང་སྟངས་ངན་པོ་ | *nang-tang ngem-po.* |
| Immortal, to be | ཤི་རྒྱུ་...མེད་པ་ | *shi-gyu...me-pa.* |
| Do *hon.* | བཤག་ (གཤེགས་) རྒྱུ་... མེད་པ་ | *sha-gyu...me-pa.* |
| Immovable | གཡོ་རྒྱུ་མེད་པ་ | *yo-gyu me-pa.* |

| | | |
|---|---|---|
| Impair, to | སྐྱོན་བྱེད་པ་ | *kyön-c̓he-pa.* |
| Do. *hon.* | སྐྱོན་གནང་བ་ | *kyön-nang-wa.* |
| Impale, to | ཤིང་ལ་བཀལ་ནས་བསད་ (གསོད་) པ་ | *shing-la ke-ne se-pa.* |
| Impart, to | སྟེར་བ་ | *ter-wa.* |
| Do. *hon.* | གནང་བ་ | *nang-wa.* |
| Impartial | ཉེ་རིང་མེད་པ་ | *nye-ring me-pa.* |
| Impartial (of judges) | ཁྲིམས་དྲང་པོ་ | *thrim ťrang-po.* |
| Do. *hon.* | བཀའ་ཁྲིམས་དྲང་པོ་ | *ka-thrim ťrang-po.* |
| Impassable, to be | མི་...ཐར་བ་ | *mi...thar-wa.* |
| Impassive | དྲན་པ་བརྒྱལ་བ་ | *ťrem-pa gyel-wa.* |
| Impede, to | བཀག་པ་ (འགེགས་པ་) | *kaḱ-pa.* |
| Do. *hon.* | བཀག་ག་ (འགེགས་པ་) གནང་བ་ | *kaḱ ka nang-wa.* |
| Impediment | བཀག་ཆ་ | *kaḱ-chha.* |
| Imperceptible, to be | མཐོང་རྒྱུ་....མེད་པ་ | *thong-gyu me-pa.* |
| Imperfect | མི་དག་པ་ | *mi ťak-pa.* |
| Imperfection (defect) | སྐྱོན་ | *kyön.* |
| Imperial | རྒྱལ་པོའི་ | *gye-pö.* |
| Imperishable, to be | ཆག་རྒྱུ་མེད་པ་ | *chha-gyu me-pa.* |

| | | |
|---|---|---|
| Impertinent | འཛིང་པ་སྦོམ་པོ། གྱོང་པོ་ | jing-pa bom-po ; kyong-po. |
| Impetuous | རུ་ངར་པོ་ | ru-ngar-po. |
| Do. *hon.* | ཐུགས་རུ་ངར་པོ་ | thuk-ru ngar-po. |
| Impious | ཆོས་སེམས་མེད་པ་ | chhö-sem me-pa. |
| Implements | ལག་ཆ་ | lak-chha. |
| Implore, to | ཞུ་བ་ | sku-wa. |
| Do. *hon.* | ཞུ་བ་གནང་བ་ | sku-wa nang-wa. |
| Impolite | གྱོང་པོ་ | kyong-po. |
| Import (meaning) | དོན་དག་ | tön-ta. |
| Do. *hon.* | སྐུ་དོན་ | ku-tön. |
| Importance | གནད་ཁག་ | nen kha. |
| Important | གནད་ཁག་ཆེན་པོ། གལ་ཆེན་པོ་ | nen-kha chhem-po, ke-chhem-po. |
| Impose, to (lay on) | སྐྱུལ་བ་ | kü-wa. |
| Impose on, to (deceive) | མགོ་སྐོར་བ་ | go-kor-wa. |
| Do. *hon.* | དབུ་སྐོར་ར་ (བ་) གནང་བ་ | u-kor-ra nang-wa. |
| Do. *inf.* to *sup.* | དབུ་སྐོར་ཞུ་བ་ | u-kor sku wa. |
| Imposition (deceit) | མགོ་སྐོར་ | go-kor. |
| Do. *hon.* | དབུ་སྐོར་ | u-kor. |
| Impossible | མི་ཐུབ་པ་ | mi-thup-pa. |

| | | |
|---|---|---|
| Impost (general) | ཁྲལ། འབབ་ | *thre ; baṕ.* |
| Do. (customs-duty) | ཤོ་ཁྲལ་ | *sho-thre.* |
| Do. (on land) | ས་ཁྲལ་ | *sa-thre.* |
| Imposture | མགོ་སྐོར་ | *go-kor.* |
| Do. *hon.* | དབུ་སྐོར་ | *u-kor.* |
| Impotent, to be | སྟོབས་འཆག་པ་ | *toṕ-chhak-pa.* |
| Do. *hon.* | སྐུ་སྟོབས་འཆག་པ་ | *ku-toṕ chhak-pa.* |
| Impracticable, to be | བྱེད་...མི་ཐུབ་པ་ | *cḱe...mi thuṕ-pa.* |
| Imprecate, to | དམོད་མོ་རྒྱབ་པ་ | *mö-mo gyaṕ-pa.* |
| Do. *hon.* | དམོད་མོ་སྐྱོན་པ་ | *mö-mo kyöm-pa.* |
| Impression, thumb | མཛུག་ཐེ་ | *dzuḱ-the.* |
| Imprison, to | བཙོན་ལ་བཅུག་ (འཇུག་) པ་ | *tsön-la chuk-pa.* |
| Improper | མི་ཆོག་པ་ | *mi-chhoḱ-pa.* |
| Improve, to | བཟོ་སྐྱོར་བྱེད་པ་ | *śo-kyor cḱe-pa.* |
| Do. *hon.* | བཟོ་སྐྱོར་གནང་བ་ | *śo-kyor nang-wa.* |
| Impudent | འཇིང་པ་སྦོམ་པོ། གྱོང་པོ་ | *jing-pa bom-po ; kyong-po.* |
| Impure | སྐྱུག་བྲོ་པོ་ | *kyuk-ťro-po.* |
| Impurity | གྲིབ་ | *ťriṕ.* |
| Impute wrongly, to | ཡ་ལ་བཞག་ (འཇོག་) པ་ | *ya-la sḱak-pa.* |
| Do. *hon.* | ཡ་ལ་གཞོག་ག་ (པ་) གནང་བ་ | *ya-la-sḱoḱ-ka nang-wa.* |

| | | |
|---|---|---|
| In (inside) | ནང་ལ་ | *nang-la.* |
| Inaccessible | བཙན་པོ་ | *tsem-po.* |
| Inaccurate, to be | མི་ ་ ་དག་པ་ | *mi...ťaḱ-pa.* |
| Inadequate, to be | མི་ ་ ་འགྲིག་པ་ | *mi...driḱ-pa.* |
| Inattentive, to be | སེམས་གཡེང་ནས་བསྡད་ (སྡོད་) པ་ | *sem-yang-ne de-pa.* |
| Do. *hon.* | ཐུགས་སེམས་གཡེང་ནས་བཞུགས་པ་ | *thuḱ-sem yang-ne sḱuḱ-pa.* |
| Inauspicious day | གཡང་གཟའ་ | *yang-śa.* |
| Incalculable | གྲངས་མེད་ | *ťrang-me.* |
| Incantation | སྔགས་ | *nga.* |
| Incapable | མི་ ་ ་ཐུབ་པ་ | *mi...thuṕ-pa.* |
| Incarcerate, to | བཙོན་ལ་བཅུག་ (འཇུག་) པ་ | *tsön-la chuḱ-pa.* |
| Incarnate, to be | སྤྲུལ་བ་ | *trül-wa.* |
| Incarnation (of a deity) | སྤྲུལ་སྐུ་ | *trül-ku.* |
| Incautious | སྣང་དག་མེད་པ་ | *nang-ťa me-pa.* |
| Incense, *s.* | སྤོས་ | *pö.* |
| Incense, to | ཁོང་ཁྲོ་སློང་བ་ | *khong-thro lang-wa.* |
| Do. *hon.* | དགོངས་པ་དཀྲུག་པ་ | *gong-pa truḱ-pa.* |
| Incessant | རྒྱུན་ཆད་རྒྱུ་མེད་པ་ | *gyün-chhe-gyu me-pa.* |

| | | |
|---|---|---|
| Incessantly | ནམ་རྒྱུན། དུས་རྒྱུན་ | *nam-gyün; tü-gyün.* |
| Inch (breadth of a finger) | སོར་ | *sor.* |
| Inclination | འདོད་པ་ | *dö-pa.* |
| Do. *hon.* | ཐུགས་འདོད་ | *thung-dö.* |
| Incline, to (lean against) | སྦོ་སྙེ་རྒྱབ་པ་ | *bo-nye gyaṕ-pa.* |
| Do. *hon.* | སྦོ་སྙེ་སྐྱོན་པ་ | *bo-nye kyöm-pa.* |
| Inclined to be | འདོད་པ་ཡོད་པ་ | *dö-pa yö-pa.* |
| Do. *hon.* | ཐུགས་འདོད་ཡོད་པ་ | *thung-dö yö-pa.* |
| Inclosure | ར་བ་ | *ra-wa.* |
| Include, to | སྡོམ་པ་ | *dom-pa.* |
| Income | ཐོབ་ཐང་ | *thoṕ-thang.* |
| Incompetent, to be | འོས་པོ་མེད་པ་ | *ö-po me-pa.* |
| Do. *hon.* | ཐུགས་འོས་པོ་མེད་པ་ | *thuḱ-ö-po me-pa.* |
| Incomplete, to be | མི་ཚང་བ་ | *mi tshang-wa.* |
| Inconstant, to be | བརྟན་པོ་མེད་པ་ | *tem-po me-pa.* |
| Incorporeal | གཟུགས་པོ་མེད་པ་ | *śuk-po me-pa.* |
| Incorrect | མ་དག་པ་ | *ma-ṫak-pa.* |
| Increase, to (in numbers) | འཕེལ་བ་ | *phe-wa.* |
| Do. (in price) | འཕར་བ་ | *phar-wa.* |
| Do. (in size) | ཆེ་རུ་ཆེ་རུ་འགྲོ་བ་ | *chhe-ru chhe-ru dro-wa.* |

| | | |
|---|---|---|
| Increase, to (in size), *hon.* | ཆེ་རུ་ཆེ་རུ་ཕེབ་པ་ | *chhe-ru chhe-ru phe-pa.* |
| Indeed | དེན་དེན། ངོ་ཐོག་ | *ten-ten ; ngo-tho.* |
| Indefatigable | སྙིང་རུས་ཆེན་པོ་ | *nying-rü chhem-po.* |
| Do. *hon.* | ཐུགས་རུས་ཆེན་པོ་ | *thu-rü chhem-po.* |
| Indefinite | དན་པོ་མེད་པ་ | *tem-po me-pa.* |
| Indented | ཀྱོང་ཀྱོང་ | *kyong-kyong.* |
| Independent | རང་མགོ་འཐོན་པ་ | *rang-go thöm-pa.* |
| Indestructible | ཆག་རྒྱུ་མེད་པ་ | *chha-gyu me-pa.* |
| Index | ཐོ་ | *tho.* |
| India (plains of) | རྒྱ་ཐང་ | *gya-thang.* |
| India | རྒྱ་གར་ | *gya-kar.* |
| Indian | རྒྱ་གར་གྱི་ | *gya-kar-kyi.* |
| Indicate, to | མིག་སྟོན་པ་ | *mi-töm-pa.* |
| Do. *hon.* | མིག་སྟོན་པ་གནང་བ་ | *mi-töm-pa nang-wa.* |
| Do. *inf.* to *sup.* | སྤྱན་ཕེབ་ཞུ་བ་ | *chem-phe sku-wa.* |
| Indifferent, to be | སྣང་དག་མི་བྱེད་པ་ | *nang-ta mi-che-pa.* |
| Indigent | སྐྱོ་པོ་ | *kyo-po.* |
| Indigestion | ལྟོ་མ་འཇུ་བའི་ནད་ | *to ma ju-we ne.* |
| Indignant, to be | ཁོང་ཁྲོ་ཟ་བ། ཚིག་པ་ཟ་བ་ | *khong-thro śa-wa ; tshik-pa śa-wa.* |

| | | |
|---|---|---|
| Indignant, to be, *hon.* | དགོངས་པ་ཚུང་པ། རྣམ་མཁྱེན་འགལ་བ་ | *gong-pa tshung-pa ; nam-khyen gel-wa.* |
| Indignation | ཚིག་པ། ཁོང་ཁྲོ་ | *tshik-pa ; khong-thro.* |
| Do. *hon.* | དགོངས་ཚུང་། རྣམ་མཁྱེན་ | *gong-tshung ; nam-khyen.* |
| Indigo | རམས་ | *ram.* |
| Indisposed, to be (unwell) | བདེ་པོ་མེད་པ། གཟུགས་པོ་ཐང་པོ་མེད་པ་ | *de-po me-pa ; śuk-po thang-po me-pa.* |
| Do. *hon.* | སྐུ་གཟུགས་ཐང་པོ་མེད་པ་ | *ku-śuk thang-po me-pa.* |
| Indisposition (illness) | ན་ཚ་ | *na-tsha.* |
| Do. *hon.* | སྙུང་གཞི་ | *nyung-ski.* |
| Indistinct | གསལ་པོ་མེད་པ་ | *se-po me-pa.* |
| Indolent | རྒྱུ་མ་རིང་པོ། ལེ་ལོ་ཆེན་པོ་ | *gyu-ma ring-po ; le-lo chhem-po.* |
| Do. *hon.* | ཐུགས་རྒྱུ་རིང་པོ་ | *thu-gyu ring-po.* |
| Indra | ལྷའི་དབང་པོ་རྒྱ་བྱིན་ | *hlaï-wang-po gya-jin.* |
| Induce, to | ཨུ་ཚུགས་བྱེད་པ་ | *u-tshu che-pa.* |
| Do. *hon.* | ཨུ་ཚུགས་གནང་བ་ | *u-tshu nang-wa.* |
| Industrious | སྙིང་རུས་ཆེན་པོ་ | *nying-rü chhem-po.* |
| Do. *hon.* | ཐུགས་རུས་ཆེན་པོ་ | *thu-rü chhem-po.* |
| Industry | སྙིང་རུས་ | *nying-rü.* |
| Do. *hon.* | ཐུགས་རུས་ | *thuk-rü.* |

| | | |
|---|---|---|
| Ineffaceable, to be | སུབ་...མི་ཐུབ་པ་ | *sup...mi thup-pa.* |
| Inefficient, to be | འོས་པོ་...མེད་པ་ | *ö-po...me-pa.* |
| Inequitable, to be (unjust) | དྲང་པོ་...མེད་པ་ | *trang-po...me-pa* |
| Inert, to be | ཧུར་པོ་...མེད་པ་ | *hur-po.. me-pa.* |
| Inexhaustible | ཛོགས་རྒྱུ་མེད་པ་ | *dzo-gyu me-pa.* |
| Inexorable | སྨྲ་བ་ལན་གཅིག་ | *ma-wa len-chi.* |
| Inexpensive | ཁེ་པོ། གོང་ཆུང་ཆུང་ | *khe-po ; kong-chhung-chhung.* |
| Infallible, to be | མི་ནོར་བ་ | *mi-nor-wa.* |
| Infamy | མིང་ངན་ | *ming ngen.* |
| Infant | ཕྲུ་གུ་ཆུང་ཆུང་ | *pu-gu chhung-chhung.* |
| Do. *hon.* | ཨ་ལྷྭ་ཆུང་ཆུང་ | *a-wa chhung-chhung.* |
| Infant (of a few weeks only) | མ་འབྱར་ | *man-ja.* |
| Infantry | དམག་དཔུང་ | *mak-pung.* |
| Infelicitous (unfortunate) | བསོད་བདེ་མེད་པ། བསོད་བདེ་ཆུང་ཆུང་ | *so-de me-pa ; so-de chhung-chhung.* |
| Do. *hon.* | སྐུ་བསོད་མེད་པ། སྐུ་བསོད་ཆུང་ཆུང་ | *ku-sö me-pa ; ku-sö chhung-chhung.* |
| Inferior (of things) | སྡུག་པོ་ | *duk-po.* |
| Do. (in rank of persons) | དམའ་པོ་ | *ma-po.* |
| Infertile | རྩ་ཆུ་འཛོམ་པོ་...མེད་པ་ | *tsa-chhu dzom-po...me-pa.* |

| | | |
|---|---|---|
| Infidel | ཕྱི་པ་ | *chhi-pa.* |
| Infinite | ཚོད་མེད་པ་ | *tshö me-pa.* |
| Infirm | ཤེད་མེད་པ་ | *she me-pa.* |
| Do. *hon.* | སྐུ་ཤེད་ཆུང་ཆུང་ | *ku-she chhung-chhung.* |
| Inflame, to (with anger) | ཁོང་ཁྲོ་སློང་བ་ | *khong-thro lang-wa.* |
| Do. *hon.* | དགོངས་པ་དཀྲུག་པ་ | *gong-pa truk-pa.* |
| Inflammation | ཚ་བ་ | *tsha-wa.* |
| Do. of bone | རུ་གཟུག་རྒྱར་པ་ | *ru-śuk gyap-pa.* |
| Do. of joint | ཚིགས་ཚ་བ་ | *tshi tsha-wa.* |
| Do. of muscle | རྩ་གཞི་འབར་བ་ | *tsap-ski bar-wa.* |
| Inflamed, to be (of hands, &c.) | འཚིག་པ་ | *tshik-pa.* |
| Inflate, to | གམ་ཕུ་རྒྱང་བ་ | *kam-phu gyang-wa.* |
| Inflexible (stubborn) | གྱོང་པོ་ | *kyong-po.* |
| Influence | དབང་ | *wang.* |
| Do. *hon.* | སྐུ་དབང་ | *ku-wang.* |
| Influential | དབང་ཆེན་པོ་ | *wang-chhem-po.* |
| Do. *hon.* | སྐུ་དབང་ཆེན་པོ་ | *ku-wang chhem-po.* |
| Inform, to | ལན་སྤྲོད་པ་ | *len-trö-pa.* |
| Do. *inf.* to *sup.* | ཞུགས་ལན་ཕུལ་ (འབུལ་) བ་ | *ja-len phü-wa.* |
| Do. *sup.* to *inf.* | བཀའ་ལན་གནང་བ་ | *ka-len nang-wa.* |

| | | |
|---|---|---|
| Information (news) | གནས་ཚུལ། གསར་འགྱུར་ | *ne-tshül ; sang gyu.* |
| Informer | ལན་སྤྲད་མཁན་ | *len-tre-khen.* |
| Ingenious | ཇུས་མཁས་པོ་ | *cKü-khe-po.* |
| Do. *hon.* | སྐུ་ཇུས་མཁས་པོ་ | *ku-cKü khe-po.* |
| Inhabit, to | བསྡད་པ་ (སྡོད་པ་) | *de-pa.* |
| Do. *hon.* | བཞུགས་པ་ | *sKu-pa.* |
| Inhale, to | དབུགས་འཐེན་པ་ | *u-them-pa.* |
| Do. *hon.* | ལྗགས་དབུགས་འཐེན་པ་ གནང་བ་ | *ja-u them-pa nang-wa.* |
| Inherit, to | སྐལ་ལ་ (བ་) ཐོབ་པ་ | *ke-la thoṗ-pa.* |
| Do. *hon.* | སྐུ་སྐལ་ཐོབ་པ་ | *ku-ke thoṗ-ṗa.* |
| Inheritance | ཐོབ་སྐལ་ | *thoṗ-ke.* |
| Do. *hon.* | སྐུ་སྐལ་ | *ku-ke.* |
| Inhibit, to (forbid) | བཀག་པ་ (འགོགས་པ་) | *kaǩ-pa.* |
| Do. *hon.* | བཀག་ག་ (འགོགས་པ་) གནང་བ་ | *kaǩ-ǩa nang-wa.* |
| Inhuman, to be | སྙིང་རྗེ་མེད་པ་ | *nying-je me-pa.* |
| Do. *hon.* | ཐུགས་རྗེ་མེད་པ་ | *thuǩ-je me-pa.* |
| Inimical, to be | དགྲ་བྱེད་པ་ | *dra-cKe-pa.* |
| Do. *hon.* | དགྲ་གནང་བ་ | *dra-nang-wa.* |

| | | |
|---|---|---|
| Iniquitous | ངན་པོ་ | *ngem-po.* |
| Do. *hon.* | ཐུགས་ངན་པོ་ | *thu ngem-po.* |
| Iniquity | ཉེས་པ། སྡིག་པ་ | *nye-pa ; diḱ-pa.* |
| Do. *hon.* | སྐུ་སྡིག་ | *ku-di.* |
| Inject, to | བཅུག་པ་ (འཇུག་པ་) | *chuḱ-pa.* |
| Do. *hon.* | བཅུག་ག་ (འཇུག་པ་) གནང་བ་ | *chuḱ-ḱa nang-wa.* |
| Injunction | བཀའ་ | *ḱa.* |
| Injure, to (by witchcraft, etc.) | གནོད་པ་བྱེད་པ་ | *nö-pa cḱe-pa.* |
| Do. (physically) | རྨ་བཟོ་བ་ | *ma-śo-wa.* |
| Do. (impair) | སྐྱོན་བྱེད་པ་ | *kyön-cḱe-pa.* |
| Do. *hon.* | སྐྱོན་གནང་བ་ | *kyön-nang-wa.* |
| Injured, to be | སྐྱོན་བྱེད་པ་ | *kyön-cḱe-pa.* |
| Injury | གནོད་པ་ | *nö-pa.* |
| Injustice, to do | ཁྲིམས་མེད་བྱེད་པ་ | *thrim-me cḱe-pa.* |
| Do. *hon.* | ཁྲིམས་མེད་གནང་བ་ | *thrim-me nang-wa.* |
| Ink | སྣག་ཚ་ | *naḱ-tsha.* |
| Do. *hon.* | ཕྱག་སྣག་ | *chha-na.* |
| Ink-pot | སྣག་བུམ་ | *naḱ-ṕum.* |
| Do. *hon.* | ཕྱག་བུམ་ | *chha-ṕum.* |
| Ink, red | མཚལ་ | *tshe.* |

| | | |
|---|---|---|
| Inlet (bay) | ཆུ་ལྷག་ | *chhu-hla.* |
| Inmate (fellow-lodger) | ལྟོ་ཚང་། ཐབ་རོགས་ | *to-tshang ; thaṕ-ro.* |
| Inn | གནས་ཚང་ | *ne-tshang.* |
| Inn-keeper | གནས་པོ་ | *ne-po.* |
| Do. *f.* | གནས་མོ་ | *ne-mo.* |
| Inner | ནང་གི་ | *nang-ki.* |
| Innocent | ཉེས་པ་མེད་པ་ | *nye-pa me-pa.* |
| Innumerable | གྲངས་མེད་ | *ťrang me.* |
| Inoculate, to (for smallpox) | ལྷ་འབྲུམ་བཙུགས་ (འཛུག་) པ་ | *hlan-drum tsuǩ-pa.* |
| Do. *hon.* | ལྷ་འབྲུམ་བཙུགས་ཀ་ (འཛུགས་པ་) གནང་བ་ | *hlan-drum tsuǩ-ǩa nang-wa.* |
| Inordinate, to be. | ཚོད་མེད་པ་ | *tshö me-pa.* |
| Do. *hon.* | ཐུགས་ཚོད་མེད་པ་ | *thuǩ-tshö me-pa.* |
| Inquire, to (ask) | དྲི་བ་ (འདྲི་བ་) | *ťri-wa.* |
| Do. *hon.* | བཀའ་འདྲི་གནང་བ་ | *kan-dri nang-wa.* |
| Do. *inf.* to *sup.* | ཞུ་བ་ | *sǩu-wa.* |
| Inquire, to (into a matter) | རྩད་གཅོད་པ་ | *tse chö-pa.* |
| Do. *hon.* | རྩད་གཅོད་གནང་བ་ | *tse-chö nang-wa.* |
| Inquire, to (investigate) | ཞིབ་དཔྱོད་བྱེད་པ་ | *sǩiṕ-chö cǩe-pa.* |
| Do. *hon.* | ཞིབ་དཔྱོད་གནང་བ་ | *sǩiṕ-chö nang-wa.* |

| | | |
|---|---|---|
| Inquire, to (investigate) *h. hon.* | བཀའ་ཞིབ་གནང་བ་ | *ka-skip nang-wa.* |
| Inquiry (investigation) | ཞིབ་དཔྱོད་ | *skip-chö.* |
| Do. *hon.* | བཀའ་ཞིབ་ | *ka-skip.* |
| Insane | སྨྱོན་པ་ | *nyöm-pa.* |
| Insane, to be | སྨྱོ་བ་ | *nyo-wa.* |
| Inscription | རྡོ་བཀོད་ | *do-kö.* |
| Insect | འབུ་ | *bu.* |
| Insensible, to become | དྲན་པ་འཐོར་བ་ | *ťrem-pa thor-wa.* |
| Inseparable, to be | བྲལ་ (འབྲལ་) མི་ཐུབ་པ་ | *ťre...mi-thup-pa.* |
| Insert, to | བཙུགས་པ་ (འཛུགས་པ་) | *tsuk-pa.* |
| Do. *hon.* | བཙུགས་ག་ (འཛུགས་པ་) གནང་བ་ | *tsuk-ka nang-wa.* |
| Inside, *prep.* | ནང་ལ་ | *nang-la.* |
| Insignificant (of matters) | དོན་དག་ཆུང་ཆུང་ | *ťön ťa chhung-chhung.* |
| Do. *hon.* | སྐུ་དོན་ཆུང་ཆུང་ | *ku-ťön chhung-chhung.* |
| Insincere, to be | དྲང་པོ་……མེད་པ། དངོས་ནས་……མི་བྱེད་པ་ | *ťrang-po . me-pa ; ngön-ne ...mi che-pa.* |
| Insist, to | ཨུ་ཚུགས་བྱེད་པ་ | *u-tshu che-pa.* |
| Do. *hon.* | ཨུ་ཚུགས་གནང་བ་ | *u tshu nang-wa.* |
| Insolent | འཛིང་པ་སྦོམ་པོ། ཀྱོང་པོ་ | *jing-pa bom-po; kyong-po.* |

| | | |
|---|---|---|
| Insoluble | ཞུ…མི་ཐུབ་པ་ | *sku…mi thup-pa.* |
| Inspect, to | ལྟ་བ་ | *ta-wa.* |
| Do. *hon.* | གཟིགས་པ་ | *śi pa.* |
| Installation (of a ruler) | ཁྲི་འདོན་ | *thrin-dön.* |
| Instance | དཔེ་ | *pe.* |
| Instance, for | དཔེ་ན་ (དཔེར་ན་) | *pe-na.* |
| Instant, in an (presently) | ཧྲིབ་ཙམ་ཅིག་ལ་ | *hrip-tsa-chi-la.* |
| Instantaneously | ལམ་སང་། ལམ་ཀྱང་ | *lam-sang ; lam-kyang.* |
| Instantly | ལམ་སང་། ལམ་ཀྱང་ | *lam-sang ; lam-kyang.* |
| Instead of | ཚབ་ལ་ | *tshap-la.* |
| Instigate, to | ངན་པ་བསླབས་ (སློབ་) པ་ | *ngen-pa lap-pa.* |
| Institute, to | བཙུགས་པ་ (འཛུགས་པ་) | *tsuk-pa.* |
| Instruct, to | བསླབས་པ་ (སློབ་པ་) | *lap-pa.* |
| Do. *hon.* | བསླབས་ (སློབ་) པ་གནང་བ་ | *lap-pa nang-wa.* |
| Instructor | དགེ་རྒན། སློབ་དཔོན་ | *ge-gen ; lo-pön.* |
| Do. (of Lama) | ཡོངས་འཛིན་ | *yong-dzin.* |
| Instrument | ལག་ཆ་ | *lak-chha.* |
| Insufficient | མི་…ལྡང་བ་ | *mi…dang wa.* |
| Insult, *s.* | སྨད་ར་ | *me-ra.* |
| Insult, to | སྨད་ར་བཏང་ (གཏོང་) བ་ | *me-ra tang-wa.* |

| | | |
|---|---|---|
| Insult, to, *hon.* | སྨད་ར་གཏོང་ང་ (བ་) གནང་བ་ | *me-ra tong-nga nang-wa.* |
| Insurrection | སྡེ་འཁྲུག | *de-thruḱ.* |
| Intellect | བློ་གྲོས་ | *lo-ťro.* |
| Intellectual | བློ་གྲོས་ཆེན་པོ་ | *lo-ťro chhem-po.* |
| Do. *hon.* | དགངས་པ་ཆེན་པོ་ | *gong-pa chhem-po.* |
| Intelligence (news) | གནས་ཚུལ། གསར་འགྱུར་ | *ne-tshül; sang-gyu.* |
| Do. (understanding) | རིག་པ་ | *rik-pa.* |
| Do. *hon.* | ཐུགས་རིག་ | *thu-ri.* |
| Intelligent | རིག་པ་ཡག་པོ་ | *rik-pa yaḱ-po.* |
| Do. *hon.* | ཐུགས་རིག་ཡག་པོ་ | *thu-ri yaḱ-po.* |
| Intemperate, to be | ཚོད་མེད་པ་ | *tshö-me-pa.* |
| Do. *hon.* | ཐུགས་ཚོད་མེད་པ་ | *thuḱ-tshö me-pa.* |
| Intend, to (purpose) | སེམས་ལ་བསམ་པ་ | *sem-la sam-pa.* |
| Do. *hon.* | ཐུགས་ལ་དགོངས་པ་ | *thuḱ-la gong-pa.* |
| Intent, *s.* | དོན་དག་ | *ťön-ťa.* |
| Do. *hon.* | སྐུ་དོན་ | *ku-ťön.* |
| Intention | དོན་དག་ | *ťön-ťa.* |
| Do. *hon.* | སྐུ་དོན་ | *ku-ťön.* |
| Inter, to (bury) | ས་ལ་སྦས་པ་ | *sa-la be-pa.* |
| Intercede, to | བར་མི་བྱེད་པ་ | *ṕar-mi cḱe-pa.* |

| | | |
|---|---|---|
| Intercede, to, *hon.* | བར་མི་གནང་བ་ | *par-mi nang-wa.* |
| Intercourse, to have (conversation) | སྐད་ཆ་བྱེད་པ་ | *ke-chha ch́e-pa.* |
| Do. *hon.* | གསུང་གྲོས་གནང་བ་ | *sung-t́rö nang-wa.* |
| Do. *inf. w. sup.* | གསུང་གྲོས་ཞུ་བ་ | *sung-t́rö sḱu-wa.* |
| Interdict, to (forbid) | བཀག་པ་ (འགེགས་པ) | *kaḱ-pa.* |
| Do. *hon.* | བཀག་ག་ (འགེགས་པ་) གནང་བ་ | *kaḱ-ḱa nang-wa.* |
| Interest (on loan) | སྐྱེད་ | *kye.* |
| Do. *hon.* | ཕྱགས་སྐྱེད་ | *ja-kye.* |
| Interior, *s.* (of a building) | ནང་ | *nang.* |
| Do. (of a country) | གྲོང་གསེབ་ | *t́rong-se.* |
| Internal | ནང་གི་ | *nang-ḱi.* |
| Interpose, to (intercede) | བར་མི་བྱེད་པ་ | *ṕar-mi ch́e-pa.* |
| Do. *hon.* | བར་མི་གནང་བ་ | *ṕar-mi nang-wa.* |
| Interpreter | ལོ་ཙཱ་བ་ | *lo-tsa-wa.* |
| Interrogate, to | དྲི་བ་ (འདྲི་བ་) | *t́ri-wa.* |
| Do. *hon.* | བཀའ་འདྲི་གནང་བ་ | *kan-dri nang-wa.* |
| Interrupt, to | བཀག་པ་ (འགེགས་པ་) | *kaḱ-pa.* |
| Do. *hon.* | བཀག་ག་ (འགེགས་པ་) གནང་བ་ | *kaḱ-ḱa nang-wa.* |

| | | |
|---|---|---|
| Interruption | བཀག་ཆ་ | *kak-chha.* |
| Interstice | སེར་ཀ་ | *ser-ka.* |
| Interview (with lama) | མཇལ་ཁ་ | *je-kha.* |
| Do. (with official) | སྐུ་མཇལ་ | *ku-ja* |
| Interview, to (lama) | མཇལ་ཁ་ཞུ་བ་ | *je-kha sku-wa.* |
| Do. (official) | སྐུ་བཅར་ཞུ་བ་ | *ku-cha sku-wa.* |
| Intestines | རྒྱུ་མ་ | *gyu-ma.* |
| Intimate, *adj.* | དགའ་པོ་ཉེ་པོ་ | *ga-po nye-po.* |
| Do. *hon.* | ཐུགས་ཉེ་ཆགས་པོ་ | *thuk-nye chhak-po.* |
| Intimidate, to | ཞེད་སྐྲག་སླང་བ་ | *ske-tra lang-wa.* |
| Do. *hon.* | ཞེད་སྐྲག་སློང་ང་ (བ་) གནང་བ་ | *ske-tra long-nga nang-wa.* |
| Into | ནང་ལ་ | *nang-la.* |
| Intolerable (pain) | སྒོང་ (སྒོམ་) མི་ཐུབ་པ་ | *gong mi thup-pa.* |
| Do. *kon.* | སྒོང་ང་ (སྒོམ་པ་) གནང་མི་ཐུབ་པ་ | *gong-nga nang mi thup-pa.* |
| Intonation | མདངས་ | *dang.* |
| Intoxicated | ར་བཟི་ | *ra-śi.* |
| Do. to be | ར་བཟི་བ་ | *ra-śi-wa.* |
| Do. *hon.* | སྐུ་ར་བྲེད་པ་ | *ku-ra be-pa.* |

| | | |
|---|---|---|
| Intrepid. | སྙིང་ཆེན་པོ་ | nying-chhem-po. |
| Do. *hon.* | ཐུགས་སྙིང་ཆེན་པོ་ | thu-nying chhem-po. |
| Intricate | མགོ་ཉོག་ཚ་པོ་ | go-nyo tsha-po. |
| Do. *hon.* | དབུ་ཉོག་ཚ་པོ་ | u-nyo tsha-po. |
| Intrigue | གྲོས་ངན་ | t́rö-ngen. |
| Intrinsic (real) | ངོ་ཐོག། དངོས་ནས་ | ngo-tho ; ngö-ne. |
| Inundate, to | ཆུ་ཡིས་གནན་ (གནོན་) པ་ | chhu-yi nem-pa. |
| Inundation | ཆུ་རུད་ | chhu-rü. |
| Invalid, *s.* | ནད་པ་ | ne-pa. |
| Do. *hon.* | སྙུང་མཁན་ | nyung-khen. |
| Invective | སྨད་ར་ | me-ra. |
| Inveigle, to | སླུ་བ་ | lu-wa. |
| Do. *hon.* | སླུ་བ་གནང་བ་ | lu-wa nang-wa. |
| Inventory | བརྗེད་ཐོ་ | je-tho. |
| Do. *hon.* | བསྙེལ་ཐོ་ | nye-tho. |
| Invert, to (up-side down) | མགོ་གཞུག་ལོག་པ། ཨ་ལོག་རྒྱབ་པ་ | go-sḱu loḱ pa ; a-lo gyaṕ-pa. |
| Do. *hon.* | མགོ་གཞུག་ལོག་ག་ (པ་) གནང་བ། ཨ་ལོག་རྒྱབ་པ་གནང་བ་ | go-sḱu-loḱ-ḱa nang-wa ; a-lo gyaṕ-pa nang-wa. |

| | | |
|---|---|---|
| Invert, to (back to front) | ཁ་ཕྱོགས་ལོག་པ་ | *kha-chho lok-pa.* |
| Do. *hon.* | ཞལ་ཕྱོགས་ལོག་ག་ (པ་) གནང་བ་ | *sKe-chho lok-ka nang-wa.* |
| Investigate, to | ཞིབ་དཔྱོད་བྱེད་པ་ | *sKip-chö cKe-pa.* |
| Do. *hon.* | ཞིབ་དཔྱོད་གནང་བ | *sKip-chö nang-wa.* |
| Do. *h. hon.* | བཀའ་ཞིབ་གནང་བ་ | *ka-sKip nang-wa.* |
| Investigation | ཞིབ་དཔྱོད་ | *sKip-chö.* |
| *Do.* *hon.* | བཀའ་ཞིབ་ | *ka-sKip.* |
| Invincible | གླགས་.....མི་ཁ་བ་ | *la...mi kha-wa.* |
| Invisible | མི་.....མཐོང་བ་ | *mi ..thong-wa.* |
| Invite, to (request) | ཞུ་བ་ | *sKu-wa.* |
| Do. *hon.* | ཞུ་བ་གནང་བ་ | *sKu-wa nang-wa.* |
| Invite, to (guest) | སྐད་བཏང་ (གཏོང་) བ་ | *ke-tang-wa.* |
| Do. *hon.* | གདན་འདྲེན་ཞུ་བ་ | *den-dren sKu-wa.* |
| Involved (intricate) | མགོ་རྙོག་ཚ་པོ་ | *go-nyo tsha-po.* |
| Inward | ནང་གི་ | *nang-ki.* |
| Irascible | རུ་ངར་པོ་ | *ru-ngar-po.* |
| Do. *hon.* | ཐུགས་རུ་ངར་པོ་ | *thu-ru ngar-po.* |
| Ire | ཚིག་པ། ཁོང་ཁྲོ་ | *tshik-pa ; khong-thro.* |
| Do. *hon.* | དགོངས་ཚུང་། ནམ་མཁྱེན་ | *gong-tshung ; num-khyen.* |

| | | |
|---|---|---|
| Iris | སི་ལིང་ལྗང་པ་ | *si-ling jang-pa.* |
| Irksome | དཀའ་ལས་ཁག་པོ་ | *ka-le khak-po.* |
| Do. *hon.* | སྐུ་མཉེལ་པོ་ | *ku-nye-po.* |
| Iron, *s.* | ལྕགས་ | *cha.* |
| Iron, *s.* (for clothes) | དབུར་དེ་ | *ur-te.* |
| Iron, *adj.* | ལྕགས་ཀྱི་ | *cha-kyi.* |
| Irrational | དོན་མེད་ | *tön-me.* |
| Irreligious, to be | ཆོས་སེམས་མེད་པ་ | *chhö-sem me-pa.* |
| Do. *hon.* | ཆོས་སེམས་མི་གནང་བ་ | *chhö-sem mi-nang-wa.* |
| Irreparable, to be | ཐབས་མེད་པ་ | *thap-me-pa.* |
| Irresistible, to be | བཀག······མི་ཐུབ་པ་ | *kak...mi thup-pa.* |
| Irresolute, to be | བརྟན་བརྟན······མེད་པ་ | *ten-ten...me-po.* |
| Irritable | རུ་ངར་པོ་ | *ru-ngar-po.* |
| Do. *hon.* | ཐུགས་རུ་ངར་པོ་ | *thu-ru ngar-po.* |
| Irritate, to | ཁོང་ཁྲོ་སློང་བ་ | *khong-thro lang-wa.* |
| Do. *hon.* | དགོངས་པ་དཀྲུག་པ་ | *gong-pa truk-pa.* |
| Is | རེད། འདུག་ | *re ; du.* |
| Island | གླིང་ཕྲན་ | *ling-thren.* |
| Isolated place | དབེན་གནས་ | *en-ne.* |
| Issue (result) | སྙིང་པོ་ | *nying-po.* |

| | | |
|---|---|---|
| Issue, to (come out) | འཐོན་པ་ | *thöm-pa.* |
| Do. *hon.* | ཕེབ་འཐོན་གནང་བ་ | *phep̍-thön nang-wa.* |
| Do. *h. hon.* | ཕྱོགས་ཕེབས་གནང་བ་ | *chho-phe nang-wa.* |
| It | དེ། འདི་ | *t́e; di.* |
| Itch, *s.* | རྔོ་ | *ngo.* |
| Itch, to (of body) | ཟ་བ། གཡའ་བ་ | *śa-wa; ya-wa.* |
| Itching disease, to have | རྔོ་ཤོར་བ། རྔོ་རྒྱབ་པ་ | *ngo-shor-wa; ngo-gyap̍-pa.* |
| Itself | འདི་རང་། དེ་རང་ | *di-rang; t́e-rang.* |
| Ivory | བ་སོ་ | *p̍a-so.* |
| Ivy | ཐག་འཁྱུད་མེ་ཏོག་ | *tha-khyü me-tok̍.* |

# J

| | | |
|---|---|---|
| Jackal | ཁྱི་སྤྱང་ | *khyip-chang.* |
| Jackass | བུང་གུ་ (བོང་བུ་) | *pung-gu.* |
| Jackdaw | སྐྱུང་ཀ་ | *kyung-ka.* |
| Jacket (without sleeves) | ཕྱུ་ཕྱུར་ | *ja-ja.* |
| Do. *hon.* | ན་བཟའ་ཕྱུ་ཕྱུར་ | *nam-śa ja-ja.* |
| Jacket (with sleeves) | འགོག་ཙེ་ | *go-tse.* |
| Do. *hon.* | ན་བཟའ་འགོག་ཙེ་ | *nam-śa go-tse.* |
| Jade (stone) | གཡང་ཏྲི་ | *yang-tri.* |
| Jail | བཙོན་ཁང་ | *tsön-khang.* |
| Jailor | བཙོན་སྲུང་ང་ (བ་) | *tsön-sung-nga.* |
| Jangle, to (wrangle) | རྒྱབ་འདྲེ་རྒྱབ་པ་ | *gyam-dre gyap-pa.* |
| Do. *hon.* | གསུང་འཁྲུག་སྐྱོན་པ་ | *sung-thru kyöm-pa.* |
| Jar | ཛ་བུམ་ | *dza-pum.* |
| Jaundice | སེར་ནད་ | *ser-ne.* |
| Jaunt, to (ramble) | ཆམ་ཆམ་ (འཁྱམས་འཁྱམས་) བྱེད་པ་ | *chham-chham che-pa.* |
| Do. *hon.* | སྐུ་ཆམ་ (འཁྱམས་) གནང་བ་ | *kün-chham nang-wa.* |
| Javelin | མདུང་ | *dung.* |

| | | |
|---|---|---|
| Javelin, *hon.* | ཕྱག་མདུང་ | *chhan-dung.* |
| Jaw | འགྲམ་པ་ | *dram-pa.* |
| Jealous | ཕྲག་དོག་ཚ་པོ་ | *thra-ťo tsha-po.* |
| Jealousy | ཕྲག་དོག་ | *thra-ťo.* |
| Jealousy (between husband and wife) | མིག་སེར་ | *miǩ-ser.* |
| Jeer, to | ཀྱག་ཀྱག་བྱས་ནས་ལབ་པ་ | *kya-kya cȟe-ne lap̌ pa.* |
| Do. *hon.* | ཀྱག་ཀྱག་གནང་ནས་གསུང་བ་ | *kya-kya nang-ne sung-wa.* |
| Jelly (meat) | ཕིག་ཕིག་ | *phiǩ-phi.* |
| Jest, to | ཁབ་ལས་བཤད་པ་ | *khap̌-le she-pa.* |
| Do. *hon.* | ཞལ་ལས་གསུང་བ་ | *sǩe-le sung-wa.* |
| Do. *h. hon.* | ཞལ་ལས་གསུང་ང་ (བ་) གནང་བ་ | *sǩe-le sung-nga nang-wa.* |
| Jester | དབུ་འཁོར་ཞུ་མཁན་ | *u-khor sǩu-khen.* |
| Jesus | ཡེ་ཤུ་ | *ye-shu.* |
| Jew | ཡ་ཧུ་དཱ་པ་ | *ya-hu-da-pa.* |
| Jewel | ནོར་བུ་ | *nor-p̌u.* |
| Job (work) | ལས་ཀ་ | *le-ka.* |
| Jockey (for making horses) | རྟ་སྦྱོང་མཁན་ | *ta-jang-khen.* |
| Do. (for racing) | རྟ་རྒྱུག་བཏང་མཁན་ | *tap̌-gyu tang-khen.* |

| | | |
|---|---|---|
| Join, to | སྦྲེལ་བ། འཐུད་པ་ | *drel-wa ; thü-pa.* |
| Do. *hon.* | སྦྲེལ་ལ་ (བ་) གནང་བ། འཐུད་པ་གནང་བ་ | *drel-la nang-wa ; thü-pa nang-wa.* |
| Join, to (by glueing together, &c.) | སྦྱར་བ་ | *jar-wa.* |
| Do. *hon.* | སྦྱར་ར་ (བ་) གནང་བ་ | *jar-ra nang-wa.* |
| Joint, *s.* (of body) | ཚིགས་ | *tshiḱ.* |
| Jointly | མཉམ་སྦྲེལ་ | *nyam-drel.* |
| Do. *hon.* | ཕྱག་སྦྲེལ་ | *chha-drel.* |
| Joke, to | ཁབ་ལས་བཤད་པ་ | *khaṕ-le she-pa.* |
| Do. *hon.* | ཞལ་ལས་གསུང་བ་ | *sḱe-le sung-wa.* |
| Do. *h. hon.* | ཞལ་ལས་གསུང་ང་ (བ་) གནང་བ་ | *sḱe-le sung-nga nang-wa.* |
| Jollity | དགའ་ཚོར་ | *ga-tshor.* |
| Do. *hon.* | མཉེས་ཚོར་ | *nye-tshor.* |
| Jolly | དགའ་པོ་ | *ga-po.* |
| Joss-stick | སྤོས་ | *pö.* |
| Do. *hon.* | གཟིམ་སྤོས་ | *śim-pö.* |
| Journey | ལམ་ཀ་ | *lang-ka.* |
| Do. *hon.* | ཕེབ་ལམ་ | *pheṕ-lam.* |
| Joviality | དགའ་ཚོར་ | *ga-tshor.* |

| | | |
|---|---|---|
| Joviality, *hon.* | མཉེས་ཚོར་ | *nye-tshor.* |
| Joy | དགའ་ཚོར་ | *ga-tshor.* |
| Do. *hon.* | མཉེས་ཚོར་ | *nye-tshor.* |
| Joyful, to be | དགའ་བ་ | *ga-wa.* |
| Do. *hon.* | མཉེས་པོ་གནང་བ་ | *nye-po nang-wa.* |
| Do. *h. hon.* | ཐུགས་དགྱེས་པོ་གནང་བ་ | *thu-gye-po nang-wa.* |
| Judge, *s.* (if a Chinaman) | ཁྲིམས་དཔོན་ | *thrim-pön.* |
| Do. (if a Tibetan) | མི་དཔོན་ | *mi-pön.* |
| Judge, to | ཁྲིམས་བཅད་ (གཅོད་) པ་ | *thrim-che-pa.* |
| Do. *hon.* | ཁྲིམས་གཅོད་པ་གནང་བ་ | *thrim-chö-pa nang-wa.* |
| Judgment (opinion) | བསམ་པ་ | *sam-pa.* |
| Do. *hon.* | ཐུགས་སེམས་ | *thu-sem.* |
| Judgment (legal) | བཅད་མཚམས། ཁྲ་མ་ | *che-tsham ; thra-ma.* |
| Do. to apply for | ཁྲ་མ་ཞུ་བ་ | *thra-ma sKu-wa.* |
| Do. to pass | ཁྲ་མ་གནང་བ་ | *thra-ma nang-wa.* |
| Judgment-hall | ལས་ཁང་ (ལས་ཁུངས་) | *le-khung.* |
| Jug | ཆུ་སྣོད་ | *chhu-nö.* |
| Do. *hon.* | ཆབ་སྣོད་ | *chhap-nö.* |
| Juggle, to (conjure) | མིག་འཕྲུལ་རྩེད་པ་ | *mik-thrü tse-pa.* |
| Do. *hon.* | མིག་འཕྲུལ་རྩེད་པ་གནང་བ་ | *mik-thrü tse-pa nang-wa.* |

| | | |
|---|---|---|
| Juggler | མིག་འཕྲུལ་རྩེད་མཁན་ | *miḱ-thrü tse-khen.* |
| Do. *hon.* | མིག་འཕྲུལ་རྩེད་པ་གནང་མཁན་ | *miḱ-thrü tse-pa nang-khen.* |
| Jugglery | མིག་འཕྲུལ་ | *miḱ-thrü.* |
| Juice | ཁུ་བ་ | *khu-wa.* |
| Jump, to | མཆོངས་པ། མཆོངས་རྒྱག་རྒྱབ་པ་ | *chhong pa ; chhong-gya gyaṕ-pa.* |
| Do. *hon.* | མཆོངས་རྒྱག་སྐྱོན་པ་ | *chhong-gya kyöm-pa.* |
| Junction of roads | ལམ་འཛོམ་ | *lam-dzom.* |
| Do. of rivers | ཆུ་འཛོམ་ | *chhu-dzom.* |
| Jungle | ཤིང་ནགས་ | *shing-na.* |
| Juniper | ཤུག་པ་ | *shuḱ-pa.* |
| Do. (another kind) | སྤ་མ་ | *pa-ma.* |
| Jurisdiction | ས་གནས་ | *sa-ne.* |
| Just, *adj.* | ཁྲིམས་དྲང་པོ་ | *thrim-t́rang-po.* |
| Do. *hon.* | བཀའ་ཁྲིམས་དྲང་པོ་ | *ḱa-thrim t́rang-po.* |
| Just, *adv.* | རང་ | *rang.* |
| Just by | རྩ་ལ་ (རྩར་) | *tsa-la.* |
| Just now | ད་ལྟ་རང་ | *t́an-da-rang.* |
| Just so! (like that) | ད་ག་རེད་ | *t́a-ḱa re.* |
| Do. *hon.* | ལགས་ད་ག་རང་རེད་ | *la-t́a-ḱa-rang re.* |

| | | |
|---|---|---|
| Just so ! (like that) *h. hon.* | ལགས་བཀའ་གནང་རང་རེད་ | *la ka nang-rang re.* |
| Justice | ཁྲིམས་དྲང་པོ་ | *thrim ťrang-po.* |
| Do. *hon.* | བཀའ་ཁྲིམས་དྲང་པོ་ | *ka-thrim ťrang-po.* |
| Justly | ཁྲིམས་ནང་བཞིན་ | *thrim nang-sƙin.* |
| Do. *hon.* | བཀའ་ཁྲིམས་ནང་བཞིན་ | *ka-thrim nang-sƙin.* |
| Jute | སོ་མ་ར་ཙ་ | *so-ma ra-tsa.* |
| Juvenile | གཞོན་པ། ལོ་གཞོན་གཞོན་ | *sƙöm pa ; lo sƙön-sƙön.* |

# K

| | | |
|---|---|---|
| Keen (not blunt) | རྣོ་པོ་ | *no-po.* |
| Keen (eager) | སྙིང་འདོད་པོ། སྙིང་བྲོ་པོ་ | *nying-dö-po ; nying ťro-po.* |
| Keep, to (have the care of) | ཉར་བ། ཅག་ག་བྱེད་པ་ | *nyar-wa ; cha-ǩa cǩe-pa.* |
| Do. *hon.* | ཉར་ར་ (བ་) གནང་བ། ཐུགས་ཅག་གནང་བ་ | *nyar-ra nang-wa ; thuǩ-cha nang-wa.* |
| Keep, to (retain) | བཞག་པ་ (འཛོག་པ་) | *sǩaǩ-pa.* |
| Do. *hon.* | གཞོག་ག་ (འཛོག་པ་) གནང་བ་ | *sǩok-ǩa nang-wa.* |
| Keeper (guard) | སྲུང་མཁན་ | *sung-khen.* |
| Kennel | ཁྱི་ཚང་ | *khyi-tshang.* |
| Kerosene oil | ས་སྣུམ་ | *sa num.* |
| Kettle (for tea) | ཁོ་ཏི་ | *kho-ti.* |
| Do. *hon.* | གསོལ་ཏི་ | *sö-ti.* |
| Key | ལྡེ་མིག་ | *di-mi.* |
| Do. *hon.* | ཕྱག་ལྡེ་ | *chhan-di.* |
| Kham (province in Eastern Tibet) | ཁམས་ | *kham.* |
| Kham, inhabitant of | ཁམས་པ་ | *kham-pa.* |
| Kick | རྡོག་རྒྱག་ | *dong-gya.* |

| | | |
|---|---|---|
| Kick, to | རྡོག་རྒྱག་གཞུ་བ་ | *dong-gya sḱu-wa.* |
| Do. *hon.* | ཞབས་རྡོག་གཞུ་བ་གནང་བ་ | *shap-do sḱu-wa nang-wa.* |
| Kid, *s.* | རེ་ཀོག་ (ར་ཕྲུག་) | *re-ko.* |
| Kidney | ཨ་རི་མཁལ་རི་ | *a-ri khe-ri.* |
| Kill, to | བསད་པ་ (གསོད་པ་) | *se-pa.* |
| Do. *hon.* | བཀྲོངས་པ་ (འགྲོང་བ་) | *trong-pa.* |
| Do. *h. hon.* | བཀྲོངས་ང་ (འགྲོང་བ་) གནང་བ་ | *trong-nga nang-wa.* |
| Kind, *s.* (sort) | རྒྱུ་ | *gyu.* |
| Kind, *adj.* | དྲིན་ཆེན་པོ་ | *t́rin chhem-po.* |
| Do. *hon.* | བཀའ་དྲིན་ཆེན་པོ་ | *ka-t́rin chhem-po.* |
| Kindle, to (fire) | བཏང་བ་ (གཏོང་བ་) | *tang-wa.* |
| Do. *hon.* | གཏོང་ང་ (བ་) གནང་བ་ | *tong-nga nang-wa.* |
| Kindly | དྲིན་ཆེན་པོ་ | *t́rin-chhem-po.* |
| Do. *hon.* | བཀའ་དྲིན་ཆེན་པོ་ | *ka-t́rin chhem-po.* |
| Kindness | དྲིན་ | *t́rin.* |
| Do. *hon.* | བཀའ་དྲིན་ | *ka-t́rin.* |
| Kindness, to do | དྲིན་བྱེད་པ་ | *t́rin cḰe-pa.* |
| Do. *hon.* | བཀའ་དྲིན་གནང་བ་ | *ka-t́rin nang-wa.* |
| Kindred (relatives) | ཉེ་བ་ | *nye-wa.* |

| | | |
|---|---|---|
| Kindred (relatives) *hon.* | སྐུ་གཉེན་ | *ku-nyen.* |
| Kinds, different | སྣ་ཚོགས་ | *na-tsho.* |
| King | རྒྱལ་པོ་ | *gye-po.* |
| King's business (administration) | རྒྱལ་སྲིད་ | *gye-si.* |
| Kingdom | རྒྱལ་ཁབ་ | *gye-khaṕ.* |
| Kiss, to | ཁ་སྐྱེལ་བ་ | *kha-kyel-wa.* |
| Do. *hon.* | ཞལ་སྐྱེལ་ལ་ (བ་) གནང་བ་ | *sḱe-kyel-la nang-wa.* |
| Kitchen | ཐབ་ཚང་ | *thaṕ-tshang.* |
| Do. *hon.* | གསོལ་ཐབ་ | *sö-thaṕ.* |
| Kitchen-garden | ཚལ་ཡང་ཙེ་ | *tshe-yang-tse.* |
| Kite (bird) | པིང་ཀྱུ་མ་ | *ping-kyu-ma.* |
| Kitten | ཞིམ་ཕྲུག་ | *sḱim-thru.* |
| Knapsack | ལྟོ་ཕད་ | *to-phe.* |
| Knave | བསྟན་བཞིག། འཛབ་ཆེན་ | *ten-sḱi; dzaṕ-chhen.* |
| Knee | པུས་མོ་ | *pi mo.* |
| Do. *hon.* | ཞབས་པུས་ | *sḱaṕ-pi.* |
| Knee-joint | པུས་མོའི་ཚིགས་ | *pi-mö-tshik.* |
| Do. *hon.* | ཞབས་པུའི་ཚིགས་ | *sḱaṕ-pi-i tshik.* |
| Kneel, to | པུས་མོ་བཙུག་ (འཛུགས་) པ་ | *pi-mo tsuk-pa.* |

| | | |
|---|---|---|
| Kneel, to *hon.* | ཞབས་པུས་བཙུག་ག་ (འཛུགས་པ་) གནང་བ་ | *sḱaṕ-pi tsuk-ka nang-wa.* |
| Knife | གྲི་ | *t́ri.* |
| Do. *hon.* | ཕྱག་ཤན་ | *chha-shen.* |
| Knife, clasp | ལྟབ་གྲི་ | *taṕ-t́ri.* |
| Do. *hon.* | ཕྱག་ཤན་ལྟབ་གྲི་ | *chha-shen taṕ-t́ri.* |
| Knit, to | སླེ་བ་ | *le-wa.* |
| Do. *hon.* | སླེ་བ་གནང་བ་ | *le-wa nang wa.* |
| Knitting-needle | ལྕགས་མདའ་ | *chan-da.* |
| Knock, to | དག་དག་བཏང་ (གཏོང་) བ་ | *taḱ-ta tang-wa.* |
| Do. *hon* | དག་དག་གཏོང་ང་ (བ་) གནང་བ་ | *taḱ-ta tong nga nang-wa.* |
| Knocking, *s.* (on door, &c.) | དག་དག་ | *taḱ-ta.* |
| Knot, *s.* | མདུད་པ་ | *dü-pa.* |
| Do. *hon.* | ཕྱག་མདུད་ | *chhan-dü.* |
| Knot, to | མདུད་པ་རྒྱབ་པ་ | *dü-pa gyaṕ-pa.* |
| Do. *hon.* | ཕྱག་མདུད་སྐྱོན་པ་ | *chhan-dü kyöm-pa.* |
| Knot, to untie a | མདུད་པ་བཤིག་པ་ | *dü-pa sḱik-pa.* |
| Do. *hon.* | ཕྱག་མདུད་བཤིག་ག་ (པ་) གནང་བ་ | *chhan-dü sḱik-ka nang-wa.* |

| | | |
|---|---|---|
| Know, to (things) | ཤེས་པ་ | *she-pa.* |
| Do. *hon.* | མཁྱེན་པ་ | *khyem-pa.* |
| Do. *h. hon.* | དགོངས་པ་རྟོགས་པ་ | *yong-pa toḱ-pa.* |
| Know, to (persons) | ངོ་ཤེས་པ་ | *ngo-shem-pa.* |
| Know, to (a person of good position) | ཞལ་ཚོ་ (ཚོར་) བ་ | *sḱe-tsho-wa.* |
| Do. *hon.* | ཐུགས་ངོ་མཁྱེན་པ་ | *thu-ngo khyem-pa.* |
| Knowledge (in general) | ཤེས་བྱ། ཡོན་ཏན་ | *she-cḱa ; yön-ten.* |
| Do. *hon.* | སྐུ་ཡོན་ | *ku-yön.* |
| Knowledge (as to a specific matter) | རྒྱུས་ | *gyü.* |
| Knuckle | ལག་པའི་ཚིགས་ | *lak-pe tshiḱ.* |
| Do. *hon.* | ཕྱག་གི་ཚིགས་ | *chha-ḱi tshiḱ.* |

# L

| | | |
|---|---|---|
| Laborious (difficult) | དཀའ་ལས་ཁག་པོ་ | *ka-le khak-po.* |
| Do. *hon.* | སྐུ་མཉེལ་པོ་ | *ku-nye-po.* |
| Labour (pangs of child-birth) | སྐྱེ་གཟུག་ | *kye-śu.* |
| Do. (work) | ལས་ཀ་ | *le-ka.* |
| Do. *hon.* | ཕྱག་ལས་ | *chha-le.* |
| Labour, forced | འུ་ལག་ | *u-la.* |
| Do. hired | མི་ལག་ | *mi-la.* |
| Labour, to | ལས་ཀ་བྱེད་པ་ | *le-ka cḱe-pa.* |
| Do. *hon.* | ཕྱག་ལས་གནང་བ་ | *chha-le nang-wa.* |
| Labourer | མི་གླ་ | *mi-la.* |
| Labourer's hire, a | གླ་ | *la.* |
| Lac (dye) | རྒྱ་ཚོས་ | *gya-tshö.* |
| Lac (number) | འབུམ་ | *bum.* |
| Lacerate, to | གཤག་པ་ | *shak-pa.* |
| Do. *hon.* | གཤག་ག་ (པ་) གནང་བ་ | *shak-ka nang-wa.* |
| Lack, to | མི་..ཚང་བ་ | *mi..tshang-wa.* |
| Lad | བུ་གུ་ | *pu-gu.* |
| Do. *hon.* | ཨ་ཝ་ | *a-wa.* |
| Ladak (name of province) | ལ་དྭགས་ | *la-dak.* |

| | | |
|---|---|---|
| Ladder | ཀན་ཙ་ (སྐས་འཛེག་) | *ken-tsa.* |
| Do. *hon.* | ཕེབ་སྐས་ | *phep-ke.* |
| Lade, to | ཁལ་བཀལ་ (འགེལ་) བ་ | *khe kel-wa.* |
| Do. *hon.* | ཁལ་བཀལ་ལ་ (བ་) གནང་བ་ | *khe kel-la nang-wa.* |
| Ladle, *s.* | སྐྱོགས་ | *kyo.* |
| Do. *hon.* | གསོལ་སྐྱོགས། ཕྱག་སྐྱོགས་ | *sö-kyo ; chha-kyo.* |
| Ladle, to | སྐྱོགས་ཀྱིས་བླུག་པ་ | *kyo-kyi luk-pa.* |
| Do. *hon.* | གསོལ་སྐྱོགས་ཀྱིས་བླུག་ག་ (པ་) གནང་བ་ | *sö-kyo-kyi luk-ka nang-wa.* |
| Ladle, to, *inf.* to *sup.* | གསོལ་སྐྱོགས་ཀྱིས་ཞུ་བ་ | *sö-kyo-kyi sKu-wa.* |
| Lady (wife of well-to-do villager) | སྙི་སྙིང་ལགས་ | *nyi- nying-la.* |
| Do. (wife of ordinary official) | ལྕམ་སྐུ་གཞོགས་ | *cham-ku-sKo.* |
| Do. (third grade and upwards) | ལྷ་ལྕམ་སྐུ་གཞོགས་ | *hla-cham ku-sKo.* |
| Lady, young | སྲས་མོ་ | *se-mo.* |
| Lag, to | འགོར་བ་ | *gor-wa.* |
| Do. *hon.* | ཕེབ་འགོར་གནང་བ་ | *phe-gor nang-wa.* |
| Lahoul (name of province) | གར་ཞ་ | *Kar-sKa.* |
| Laity | ཨ་འུ། འཇིག་རྟེན་པ་ | *a-u ; jik-tem-pa.* |

| | | |
|---|---|---|
| Lair | ཚང་ | *tshang.* |
| Lake | མཚོ་ | *tsho.* |
| Lakh (number) | འབུམ་ | *bum.* |
| Lama | བླ་མ་ | *la-ma.* |
| Lama, Grand (of Lhasa) | སྐྱབས་མགོན་རིན་པོ་ཆེ་ | *kyam-gön rim-po-chhe.* |
| Lama, Grand (of Tashi Hlüm-po) | པན་ཆེན་རིན་པོ་ཆེ་ | *pen-chhen rim-po-chhe.* |
| Lamb | ལུག་ཕྲུག། ལུ་གུ་ | *luk-thru; lu-ku.* |
| Lame | ཀང་ཀྱོག་ | *kang-kyo.* |
| Do. *hon.* | ཞབས་ཀྱོག་ | *shap-kyo.* |
| Lament, to | སྡུག་བསྔལ་བྱེད་པ། མྱ་ངན་བྱེད་པ་ | *du-nge che pa; nya-ngen che-pa.* |
| Do. *hon.* | ཐུགས་ངན་གནང་བ་ | *thu-ngen nang-wa.* |
| Lamentation | མྱ་ངན་ | *nya-ngen.* |
| Lamp | ཞུ་མར་ | *shu-ma.* |
| Do. *hon.* | གཟིམ་ཞུ་ | *śim shu.* |
| Lamp (as offering to deity) | མཆོད་མེ་ | *chhö-me* |
| Lance, *s.* | མདུང་ | *dung.* |
| Do. *hon.* | ཕྱག་མདུང་ | *chhan-dung.* |
| Lancet | ཙའུ་ | *tsa-u.* |

| | | |
|---|---|---|
| Land (earth) | ས་ | *sa.* |
| Do. (landed property) | ས་ཆ་ | *sa-chha.* |
| Do. (country) | ལུང་པ། ཡུལ་ | *lung-pa ; yü.* |
| Landing-place | གྲུ་ཁ་ | *t́ru-kha.* |
| Landlady (of inn, etc.) | གནས་མོ་ | *ne-mo.* |
| Do. *hon.* | གནས་མོ་ལགས་ | *ne-mo-la.* |
| Landlord (of inn, etc.) | གནས་པོ་ | *ne-po.* |
| Do. *hon.* | གནས་པོ་ལགས་ | *ne-po-la.* |
| Landlord (of land) | སའི་བདག་པོ་ | *sa-i daḱ-po.* |
| Landslip | ས་རུད་ | *sa-rü.* |
| Land-tax | ས་ཁྲལ་ | *sa-thre.* |
| Lane | སྲང་འགག་ | *hrang-ga.* |
| Language | སྐད་ | *ke.* |
| Do. (honorific) | ཞེ་ས་ | *sḱe-sa.* |
| Language (common, *i.e.* non-honorific) | ཞེ་ས་མེད་པའི་སྐད་ཆ་ | *sḱe-sa me-pe ke-chha.* |
| Do. (colloquial) | ཕལ་སྐད། ཕལ་ཚིག་ | *phe-ke ; phe-tshi.* |
| Do. (literary) | ཆོས་སྐད། ཆོས་ཚིག་ | *chhö-ke ; chhö-tshi.* |
| Languid | སྙོབ་པོ་ | *nyoṕ-po.* |
| Lank (of persons and animals) | ཤ་སྐམ་པོ་ | *shá kam-po.* |
| Do. *hon.* (of persons) | སྐུ་ཤ་སྐམ་པོ་ | *ku-sha kam-po.* |

| | | |
|---|---|---|
| Lank (of animals) *hon.* | བཞེས་ཤ་སྐམ་པོ་ | *ske sha kam-po.* |
| Lantern | སྒང་ཞུ་ (སྒོང་ཞུ་) | *gang-sku.* |
| Do. *hon.* | ཕེབ་ཞུ་ | *phep-sku.* |
| Lap, *s.* (of women) | པང་པ་ | *pang-pa.* |
| Do. *hon.* | སྐུ་པང་ | *ku-pang.* |
| Lap up, to (water, &c.) | ལྡག་པ་ | *dak-pa.* |
| Lapsus linguae, to make a | ཁ་ཤོར་བ་ | *kha-shor-wa.* |
| Do. *hon.* | ཞལ་བཞེས་གནང་བ་ | *ske-ske nang-wa.* |
| Larch | ཟྲ་ཤིང་ | *śa-shing.* |
| Lard | ཕག་ཚིལ་ | *phak tshi.* |
| Large | ཆེན་པོ་ | *chhem-po.* |
| Large (of country, etc.) | རྒྱ་ཆེན་པོ་ | *gya-chhem-po.* |
| Larynx | སྐེ་ | *ke.* |
| Do. *hon.* | མགུལ་ | *gü.* |
| Lascivious | འདོད་ཆགས་ཆེན་པོ་ | *dö-chha chhem-po.* |
| Lasciviousness | འདོད་ཆགས་ | *dö-chha.* |
| Lash (of a whip) | རྟ་ལྕག་ | *ta-cha.* |
| Do. *hon.* | ཆིབས་ལྕག་ | *chhip-cha.* |
| Lash, to | རྟ་ལྕག་གཞུ་བ་ | *ta-cha sku-wa.* |
| Do. *hon.* | ཆིབས་ལྕག་སྐྱོན་པ་ | *chhip-cha kyöm-pa.* |

| | | |
|---|---|---|
| Lass | བུ་མོ་ | *ṕu-mo.* |
| Do. *hon.* | སྲས་མོ་ | *se-mo.* |
| Lassitude | ངལ་ | *ngel.* |
| Do. *hon.* | སྐུ་ངལ་ | *ku-ngel.* |
| Last, *adj.* | གཞུག་ཤོས་ | *shuk-shö.* |
| Do. *adv.* (at last) | གཞུག་ལ་ | *shuk-la.* |
| Last night | མདངས་དགོངས་ | *dang-yong.* |
| Last year | ཟླ་སྙིང་ (ན་ཉིང་) | *da-nying.* |
| Last, to | ཐུབ་པ་ | *thuṕ-pa.* |
| Lasting (durable) | ཀྲོག་ཆེན་པོ་ | *tro chhem-po.* |
| Latch | ཨ་ཤིང་ | *a-shing.* |
| Latchet | ལྷམ་སྒྲོགས་ | *hlam-dro.* |
| Do. *hon* | ཞབས་སྒྲོགས་ | *shaṕ-dro.* |
| Late | ཕྱི་པོ་ | *chhi-po.* |
| Late, to be | ཕྱི་པོ་བྱེད་པ་ | *chhi-po che-pa.* |
| Late, the (the deceased) | ཤི་མཁན་ | *shi-khen.* |
| Do. *hon.* | གྲོང་མཁན་ | *t́rong-khen.* |
| Do. *h. hon.* | དམ་པ་ | *t́am-pa.* |
| Lately | ཁ་སང་ | *kha-sang.* |
| Latent | སྦེད་པ་ | *be-pa.* |

| | | |
|---|---|---|
| Later on (afterwards) | གཞུག་ལ་ | *sKu-la.* |
| Latest | གཞུག་ཤོས་ | *sKuk-shö.* |
| Latter | གཞུག་མ་ | *sKuk ma.* |
| Laud, to | སྟོད་ར་བཏང་ (གཏོང་) བ་ | *tö-ra tang-wa.* |
| Do. *hon.* | སྟོད་ར་གཏོང་ང་ (བ་) གནང་བ་ | *tö-ra tong-nga nang-wa.* |
| Do. *inf.* to *sup.* | སྟོད་ར་ཞུ་བ་ | *tö-ra sKu-wa.* |
| Laugh, *s.* | བགད་མོ་ | *ge-mo.* |
| Laugh, to | བགད་མོ་བགད་པ། བགད་མོ་ཤོར་བ་ | *ge-mo ge-pa; ye mo shor-wa.* |
| Do. *hon.* | ཞལ་མོ་བཞེས་པ། ཞལ་མོ་ཤོར་བ་ | *sKe-mo sKe-pa; sKe-mo shor-wa.* |
| Laughable | བགད་མོ་བྲོ་བོ་ | *ge-mo ťro-po.* |
| Do. *hon.* | ཞལ་མོ་བྲོ་བོ་ | *sKe-mo ťro-po.* |
| Laughter | བགད་མོ་ | *ge-mo.* |
| Do. *hon.* | ཞལ་མོ་ | *sKe-mo.* |
| Lavish (profuse) | འབེལ་པོ། ཛག་དོ་ | *be po; dzak-to.* |
| Law | ཁྲིམས་ | *thrim.* |
| Do. *hon.* | བཀའ་ཁྲིམས་ | *ka-thrim.* |
| Law (religious) | ཆོས་ཁྲིམས་ | *chhö-thrim.* |
| Law, to go to | རྒྱུ་རྐྱེན་ཞུ་བ། ཁྲིམས་ལ་ཞུ་བ་ | *gyu-kyen sKu-wa; thrim-la sKu-wa.* |

| | | |
|---|---|---|
| Laws, to obey | ཁྲིམས་འཁྱེར་བ། ཁྲིམས་འཁུར་བ་ | *thrim khyer-wa ; thrim khur-wa.* |
| Law-court | ཁྲིམས་ས་ | *thrim-sa.* |
| Do. *hon.* | བཀའ་ཁྲིམས་ཀྱི་ས་ཆ་ | *ka-thrim-kyi sa-chha.* |
| Lawful | ཁྲིམས་མཐུན་ | *thrim-thün.* |
| Lawfully | ཁྲིམས་ནང་བཞིན་ | *thrim-nang-skin.* |
| Do. *hon.* | བཀའ་ཁྲིམས་ནང་བཞིན་ | *ka-thrim nang-skin.* |
| Lawless | ཁྲིམས་མེད་ | *thrim-me.* |
| Lawn | ཐང་ | *thang.* |
| Law-suit | ཁ་མཆུ་ | *kham-chhu.* |
| Lay, to (place) | བཞག་པ་ (འཇོག་པ་) | *skak-pa.* |
| Do. *hon.* | གཞོག་ག་ (འཇོག་པ་) གནང་བ་ | *skok-ka nang-wa.* |
| Lay, to (spread) | བཏིང་པ་ (འདིང་བ་) | *ting-pa.* |
| Do. *hon.* | བཏིང་ང་ (འདིང་བ་) གནང་བ་ | *ting-nga nang-wa.* |
| Lay, to | བཞག་པ་ (འཇོག་པ་) | *skak-pa.* |
| Do. *hon.* | གཞོག་ག་ (འཇོག་པ་) གནང་བ་ | *skok-ka nang-wa.* |
| Lay, to (down) | བསྙལ་བ་ (སྙོལ་བ་) | *nye-wa.* |
| Do. *hon.* | བསྙལ་ལ་ (སྙོལ་བ་) གནང་བ་ | *nye-la nang-wa.* |
| Lay, to (eggs) | བཏང་བ་ (གཏོང་བ་) | *tang-wa.* |
| Lay the foundation of, to | རྩིག་རྟེན་བཏིང་ (འདིང་) བ་ | *tsik-ten ting-wa.* |

| | | |
|---|---|---|
| Lay the foundation of, to, *hon.* | རྩིག་སྟན་བཏིང་ང་ (བ་) གནང་བ་ | *tsik-ten ting-nga nang-wa.* |
| Layman | ཨཱུ། འཇིག་རྟེན་པ་ | *a-u ; jik-tem-pa.* |
| Lazy | རྒྱུ་མ་རིང་པོ། ལེ་ལོ་ཆེན་པོ་ ཅན་ | *gyu-ma ring-po ; le-lo chhem-po* |
| Do. *hon.* | ཐུགས་རྒྱུ་རིང་པོ་ | *thu-gyu ring-po.* |
| Lead, *s.* (metal) | ཞ་ཉེ་ | *sKa-ni.* |
| Lead (red-lead) | སི་ནྡྷུ་ར་ | *sin-dhu-ra.* |
| Lead, to (towards) | འཁྲིད་ཡོང་བ་ | *thri-yong-wa.* |
| Do. *hon.* | འཁྲིད་ཕེབ་པ་ | *thri-phe-pa.* |
| Lead, to (away) | འཁྲིད་འགྲོ་བ་ | *thri-dro-wa.* |
| Do *hon.* | འཁྲིད་ཕེབ་པ་ | *thri-phe-pa.* |
| Leader | མགོ་པ་ | *go-pa.* |
| Leaf (of a tree) | ལོ་མ། འདབ་མ་ | *lo-ma ; da-ma.* |
| Do. (of a book) | ཤོག་ལེབ་ | *shok-le.* |
| Leak, to (of water) | འཛག་པ་ | *dzak-pa.* |
| Lean, *adj.* (of animals and persons) | ཤ་སྐམ་པོ་ | *sha-kam-po.* |
| Do. *hon.* (of persons) | སྐུ་ཤ་སྐམ་པོ་ | *ku-sha kam-po.* |
| Do. *hon.* (of meat) | བཞེས་ཤ་སྐམ་པོ་ | *sKe-sha kam-po.* |
| Lean, to (against) | སྙེ་བསྡད་ (སྡོད་) པ་ | *nye-de-pa.* |

| | | |
|---|---|---|
| Lean, to (against) *hon.* | སྐུ་སྙེ་གནང་ནས་བཞུགས་པ་ | *ku-nye nang-ne sKu-pa.* |
| Do. *h. hon.* | སྐུ་སྙེ་གནང་ནས་བཞུགས་གདན་འཇག་པ་ | *ku-nye nang-ne sKu-den ja-pa.* |
| Lean, to (back) | རྒྱབ་བསྙེས་བྱས་ནས་བསྡད་ (སྡོད་) པ་ | *gyap-nye cKe-ne de-pa.* |
| Do. *hon.* | སྐུ་བསྙེས་གནང་ནས་བཞུགས་པ་ | *ku-nye nang-ne sKu-pa.* |
| Leap, to | མཆོངས་པ། མཆོངས་རྒྱག་རྒྱབ་པ་ | *chhong-pa ; chhong-gya gyap-pa.* |
| Do. *hon.* | མཆོངས་རྒྱག་སྐྱོན་པ་ | *chhong-gya kyöm-pa.* |
| Learn, to | བསླབས་པ་ (སློབ་པ་) | *lap-pa.* |
| Do. *hon.* | བསླབས་ (སློབ་) པ་གནང་བ་ | *lap-pa nang-wa.* |
| Learn, to (by heart) | བློ་ལ་ཟིམ་པ་ (བཟུང་བ་) | *lo-la śim-pa.* |
| Do. *hon.* | ཐུགས་བློ་ལ་ཟིམ་པ་ (བཟུང་བ་) གནང་བ་ | *thuk-lo la śim-pa nang-wa.* |
| Learned | ཤེས་བྱ་ཆེན་པོ། ཡོན་ཏན་ཆེན་པོ་ | *she-cKa chhem-po ; yön-ten chhem po.* |
| Do. *hon.* | སྐུ་ཡོན་ཆེན་པོ་ | *ku-yön chhem-po.* |
| Learner (novice) | ཨེན་ཆུང་ | *en-chhung.* |
| Learning | ཤེས་བྱ། ཡོན་ཏན་ | *she-cKa ; yön-ten.* |

| | | |
|---|---|---|
| Learning, *hon.* | སྐུ་ཡོན་ | *ku-yön.* |
| Lease, *s.* | བཀའ་བཏན་ | *ka-ten.* |
| Do. to (let out on) | བོགས་མ་ལ་བཏང་ (གཏོང་) བ་ | *po-ma-la tang-wa.* |
| Do. *hon.* | བོགས་མ་ལ་གཏོང་ང་ (བ་) གནང་བ་ | *po-ma-la tong-nga nang-wa.* |
| Least | ཆུང་ཤོས་ | *chhung-shö.* |
| Leather | ཀོ་བ་ | *ko-wa.* |
| Leave of absence | དགོངས་པ་ | *gong-pa.* |
| Leave, to (depart) | འཐོན་པ། ཕྱིན་པ་ | *thöm-pa ; chhim-pa.* |
| Do. *hon.* | ཕེབ་པ་ | *phep pa.* |
| Do. *h. hon.* | འཆིབ་རྒྱུ་གནང་བ་ | *chhip-gyu nang-wa.* |
| Leave off, to (renounce) | སྤང་བ་ | *pang-wa.* |
| Do. *hon.* | སྤོང་ང་ (བ་) གནང་བ་ | *pong-nga nang-wa.* |
| Leave, to (a country, etc.) | བཞག་ནས་ཡོང་བ་ | *sKa-ne yong-wa.* |
| Do. *hon.* | བཞག་ནས་ཕེབ་པ་ | *sKa-ne phe-pa.* |
| Do. *h hon.* | བཞག་ནས་འཆིབས་རྒྱུ་གནང་བ་ | *sKa-ne chhip gyu nang-wa.* |
| Leave, to ask for | དགོངས་པ་ཞུ་བ་ | *gong-pa sKu-wa.* |
| Do. *hon.* | དགོངས་ཞུ་གནང་བ་ | *gong-sKu nang-wa.* |
| Leave, to grant | དགོངས་པ་སྟེར་བ་ | *gong-pa ter-wa.* |
| Do. *hon.* | དགོངས་པ་གནང་བ་ | *gong-pa nang-wa.* |

| | | |
|---|---|---|
| Leaven (for fermenting liquor) | ཆང་རྩི་ | *chhang-tsi.* |
| Do. (for fermenting dough for bread) | ཕྱེ་སྨན་ | *chhi-men.* |
| Leaves (in a book), number of | ཤོག་གྲངས་ | *shok-trang.* |
| Leavings (things left) | ལྷག་མ་ | *hla-ma.* |
| Lecherous | འདོད་ཆགས་ཆེན་པོ་ | *dö-chha chhem-po.* |
| Lechery | འདོད་ཆགས་ | *dö-chha.* |
| Leech | པད་པ་ | *pe-pa.* |
| Left, *adj.* (opp. to right) | གཡོན་ | *yön.* |
| Left, to be (not expended) | ལྷག་མ་ལུས་པ་ | *hla-ma lü-pa.* |
| Left, to be (behind) | ལས་ (ལུས་) ནས་མེད་པ་ | *le-ne me-pa.* |
| Do. *hon.* | ལས་ (ལུས་) པ་གནང་བ་ | *le-pa nang-wa.* |
| Left-handed | གཡོན་ལག་ | *yön-la.* |
| Do. *hon.* | ཕྱག་གཡོན་ལག་ | *chha-yön-la.* |
| Leg | རྐང་པ་ | *kang-pa.* |
| Do. *hon.* | ཞབས་ | *skap.* |
| Leg (of mutton, etc.) | རྐང་ཤ་ | *kang-sha.* |
| Legal | ཁྲིམས་མཐུན་ | *thrim-thün.* |
| Legally | ཁྲིམས་ནང་བཞིན་ | *thrim-nang-skin.* |

| | | |
|---|---|---|
| Legally, *hon.* | བཀའ་ཁྲིམས་ནང་བཞིན་ | *ka-thrim nang-sKin.* |
| Legend | རྣམ་ཐར་ | *nam-tha.* |
| Legged, bandy | རྐང་ཀྱོག་ | *kang-kyo.* |
| Do. *hon.* | ཞབས་ཀྱོག་ | *sKap-kyo.* |
| Legible, to be | ཀློག་ཤེས་པ་ | *lok-she-pa.* |
| Do. *hon.* | ལྗགས་ཀློག་གནང་མཁྱེན་པ་ | *ja-lo nang khyem-pa.* |
| Legitimate (lawful) | ཁྲིམས་མཐུན་ | *thrim-thün.* |
| Legitimately | ཁྲིམས་ནང་བཞིན་ | *thrim nang-sKin.* |
| Do. *hon.* | བཀའ་ཁྲིམས་ནང་བཞིན་ | *ka-thrim nang-sKin.* |
| Leisure | ལོང་ | *long.* |
| Leisure, to sit at | ལྷོད་ལྷོད་བསྡད་ (སྡོད་) པ་ | *hlö-hlö de-pa.* |
| Do. *hon.* | ཐུགས་ལྷོད་ལྷོད་བཞུགས་པ་ | *thu-hlö-hlö sKu-pa.* |
| Lend, to | གཡར་བ་ | *yar-wa.* |
| Do. *hon.* | གཡར་པོ་གནང་བ་ | *yar-po nang wa.* |
| Length | རིང་ཐུང་ | *ring-thung.* |
| Length, at (afterwards) | གཞུག་ལ། རྗེས་ལ་ | *sKu-la ; je-la.* |
| Lengthen, to | རིང་དུ་བཏང་ (གཏོང་) བ་ | *ring-ťu tang-wa.* |
| Do. *hon.* | རིང་དུ་གཏོང་ང་ (བ་) གནང་བ་ | *ring-ťu tong nga nang-wa.* |
| Lengthy | རིང་པོ་ | *ring-po.* |
| Lenient, to be | འཆ་ཡང་གནང་བ་ | *chha-yang nang-wa.* |

| | | |
|---|---|---|
| Leopard | གཟིག་ | *śik.* |
| Leper (male) | མཛེ་པོ་ | *dze-po.* |
| Do. (female) | མཛེ་མོ་ | *dze-mo.* |
| Leprosy | མཛེ་ | *dze.* |
| Leprous, to be | མཛེ་རྒྱབ་པ་ | *dze-gyap̄-pa.* |
| Do. *hon.* | མཛེ་སྐྱོན་པ་ | *dze kyöm-pa.* |
| Less | ཉུང་བ་ | *nyung-wa.* |
| Lessen, to, *v.i.* | ཉུང་རུ་ཕྱིན་པ་ | *nyung-ru chhim pa.* |
| Do. to, *v.t.* | ཉུང་རུ་བཏང་ (གཏོང་) བ་ | *nyung-ru tang-wa.* |
| Do. *hon.* | ཉུང་རུ་གཏོང་ང་ (བ་) གནང་བ་ | *nyung ru tong-nga nang-wa.* |
| Lessen, to (price) | བཅག་པ་ (གཅོག་པ་) | *chak̄-pa.* |
| Do. *hon.* | གཅོག་ག་ (པ་) གནང་བ་ | *chok̄-k̄a nang-wa.* |
| Lesson | ཡིག་རྒྱུགས་ | *yi-gyuk̄.* |
| Let, to (allow) | བཅུག་པ་ (འཇུག་པ་) | *chuk-pa.* |
| Do. *hon.* | བཅུག་ག་ (པ་) གནང་བ་ | *chuk-k̄a nang-wa.* |
| Let, to (down) | ཕབ་པ་ (འབེབས་པ་) | *phap̄-pa.* |
| Let, to (let in, let loose, etc.) | བཏང་བ་ (གཏོང་བ་) | *tang-wa.* |
| Do. *hon.* | གཏོང་ང་ (བ་) གནང་བ་ | *tong-nga nang-wa.* |
| Let off, to | བཏང་བ་ (གཏོང་བ་) | *tang-wa.* |
| Do. *hon.* | གཏོང་ང་ (བ་) གནང་བ་ | *tong-nga nang-wa.* |

| | | |
|---|---|---|
| Letter (epistle) | ཡི་གེ་ | *yi-ge.* |
| Do. *hon.* | ཕྱག་བྲིས་ | *chha ri.* |
| Level, *adj.* | སྙོམས་པོ་ | *nyom-po.* |
| Lewd | འདོད་ཆགས་ཆེན་པོ་ | *dö-chha chhem-po.* |
| Lewdness | འདོད་ཆགས་ | *dö-chha.* |
| Lhasa | ལྷ་ས་ | *hla-sa.* |
| Lhasa man, a | ལྷ་སཱ་ | *hla-sā.* |
| Liar | ཧམ་པ་ཤོད་མཁན་ | *ham-pa shö-khen.* |
| Libation | གསེར་སྐྱེམས་ | *ser-kyem.* |
| Libel, *s.* | སྨད་ར་ | *me-ra.* |
| Libel, to | སྨད་ར་བཏང་ (གཏོང་) བ་ | *me-ra tang-wa.* |
| Do. *hon.* | སྨད་ར་གཏོང་ང་ (བ་) གནང་བ་ | *me-ra tong-nga nang-wa.* |
| Do *inf.* to *sup.* | སྨད་ར་ཞུ་བ་ | *me-ra shu wa.* |
| Liberal | ལག་པ་ཤོག་པོ་ | *lak-pa shok-po.* |
| Do. *hon.* | ཕྱག་ཤོག་པོ་ | *chha-shok-po.* |
| Liberate, to | བཏང་བ་ (གཏོང་བ་) | *tang-wa.* |
| Liberated, to be | ཐར་བ་ | *thar-wa.* |
| Liberty | ཚེ་ཐར་ | *tshe-thar.* |
| Do. to be at (to be allowed) | ཚོག་པ་ | *chhok-pa.* |

| | | |
|---|---|---|
| Liberty, to be set at | ཚེ་ཐར་བཏང་ (གཏོང་) བ་ | *tshe-thar tang-wa.* |
| Do. *hon.* | ཚེ་ཐར་གཏོང་ང་ (བ་) གནང་བ་ | *tshe-thar tong-nga nang-wa.* |
| Libidinous | འདོད་ཆགས་ཆེན་པོ་ | *dö-chha chhem-po.* |
| Library | དཔེ་ཆ་ཁང་ | *pe-chha-khang.* |
| Do. *hon.* | ཕྱག་དཔེ་ཁང་ | *chha-pe-khang.* |
| License | བཀའ་ཤོག་ | *ka-sho.* |
| Licentious | འདོད་ཆགས་ཆེན་པོ་ | *dö-chha chhem-po.* |
| Licentiousness | འདོད་ཆགས་ | *dö-chha.* |
| Lick, to (of animals) | ལྡག་པ་ | *dak-pa.* |
| Do. (of persons) | ལྕེ་ལ་ (ལྡག་) རྒྱབ་པ་ | *che-la gyap-pa.* |
| Do. *hon.* | ལྕེ་ལ་ (ལྡག་) སྐྱོན་པ་ | *che-la kyöm-pa.* |
| Lid | ཁ་གཅོད། ཁ་ | *khap-chö ; kha.* |
| Lid (of the eye) | མིག་པགས་ | *mik-pa.* |
| Lie, *s.* | ཧམ་པ། ཀྱག་རྫུན་ | *ham-pa ; kyak-dzün.* |
| Do. *hon.* | ཞལ་རྫུན་ | *ske-dzün.* |
| Lie, to (tell untruth) | ཧམ་པ་བཤད་ (ཤོད་) པ། ཀྱག་རྫུན་བཤད་ (ཤོད་) པ་ | *ham-pa she-pa ; kyak-dzün she-pa.* |
| Do. *hon.* | ཞལ་རྫུན་གནང་བ་ | *ske-dzün nang-wa.* |
| Lie, to (down) | ཉལ་བསྡད་ (སྡོད་) པ་ | *nye-de-pa.* |
| Do. *hon.* | གཟིམ་བཞུགས་པ་ | *sim-sku-pa.* |

| | | |
|---|---|---|
| Lieu of, in (instead of) | ཚབ་ | *tshaṕ.* |
| Do. *hon.* | སྐུ་ཚབ་ | *ku-tshaṕ.* |
| Life | སྲོག། ཚེ་ | *so* or *hro ; tshe.* |
| Do. *hon.* | སྐུ་སྲོག། སྐུ་ཚེ་ | *ku-so ; ku-tshe.* |
| Life-time | ཚེ་གང་ | *tshe-ḱang.* |
| Do. *hon.* | སྐུ་ཚེ་གང་ | *ku-tshe-ḱang.* |
| Lift, to | ཡར་ཀྱག་ (འཁྱོག་) པ། ཡར་ལེན་པ་ | *yar-kyak-pa ; yar-lem-pa.* |
| Do. *hon.* | ཡར་ཀྱག་ག་ (འཁྱོག་པ་) གནང་བ་ | *yar-kyak-ḱa nang-wa.* |
| Light, *s.* (lamp) | ཞུ་མར་ | *sḱu-ma.* |
| Do. *hon.* | གཟིམ་ཞུ་ | *śim-sḱu.* |
| Light, *s.* (brightness) | འོད་ | *ö.* |
| Light, *adj.* (bright) | འོད་ཆེན་པོ་ | *ö chhem-po.* |
| Light, *adj.* (not heavy) | ཡང་པོ་ | *yang-po.* |
| Light, to (fire) | བཏང་བ་ (གཏོང་བ་) | *tang-wa.* |
| Do. *hon.* | གཏོང་ང་ (བ་) གནང་བ་ | *tong-nga nang-wa.* |
| Light, to (lamp) | སྦར་བ་ | *par-wa.* |
| Do. *hon.* | སྦར་ར་ (བ་) གནང་བ་ | *par-ra nang-wa.* |
| Lightning, *s.* | གློག་ | *lo.* |

| | | |
|---|---|---|
| Lightning (forked) | འཁྱུག་ | *khyu.* |
| Lightning (sheet), to flash | གློག་རྒྱབ་པ་ | *lo gyaṕ-pa.* |
| Do. (forked), to flash | འཁྱུག་རྒྱབ་པ་ | *khyu gyaṕ-pa.* |
| Like (similar) | ནང་བཞིན། འདྲ་པོ་ | *nang-sḱin ; dra-po.* |
| Like, to | དགའ་བ་ | *ga-wa.* |
| Do. *hon.* | ཐུགས་མཉེས་པོ་གནང་བ་ | *thu-nye-po nang-wa.* |
| Do. *h. hon.* | ཐུགས་དགྱེས་པོ་གནང་བ་ | *thu-gye-po nang-wa.* |
| Like this | འདི་འདྲ་ | *din-dra.* |
| Like that | དེ་འདྲ་ | *t́en-dra.* |
| Likely, it is | ཡིན་འགྲོ། ཡིན་པ་འདྲ་ | *yin-dro ; yim-pa-dra.* |
| Likeness (form) | བཟོ་བསྟ་ | *śoṕ-ta.* |
| Do. *hon.* | སྐུ་བཟོ་ | *ku-śo.* |
| Likewise | ཡང་ | *yang.* |
| Limb (of human beings) | འཟུགས་ཀྱི་ཡན་ལག་ | *śuk-kyi yen-la.* |
| Do. *hon.* | སྐུ་གཟུགས་ཀྱི་ཡན་ལག་ | *ku-śuk-kyi yen-la.* |
| Limb (of animals) | སྒུག་ལག་ | *suḱ-la.* |
| Lime | ས་དཀར། དཀར་རྩི་ | *sa-kar ; kar-tsi.* |
| Limit | མཐའ་ | *tha.* |
| Limitation | ཚོད་ | *tshö.* |
| Do. *hon.* | ཐུགས་ཚོད་ | *thu-tshö.* |

| | | |
|---|---|---|
| Limp, to | རྐང་པ་འཁྱོག་འཁྱོག་བྱེད་པ་ | *kang-pa khyo-khyo che-pa.* |
| Do. *hon.* | ཞབས་འཁྱོག་འཁྱོག་གནང་བ་ | *shap khyo-khyo nang-wa.* |
| Limpid (clear) | དྭངས་པོ་ | *ťang-po.* |
| Line | ཐིག་ | *thi.* |
| Line (in a book) | ཡིག་ཕྲེང་ | *yik-threng.* |
| Lineage (of laymen) | རིགས་བརྒྱུད། མི་བརྒྱུད་ | *ri-gyü ; mi-gyü.* |
| Do. *hon.* | སྐུ་བརྒྱུད་ | *ku-gyü.* |
| Do. *hon.* (of lamas) | གདུང་བརྒྱུད་ | *dung-gyü.* |
| Linen | རས་ | *re.* |
| Do. *hon.* | སྐུ་རས་ | *ku-re.* |
| Linger, to | འགོར་བ་ | *gor-wa.* |
| Do. *hon.* | ཕེབ་འགོར་གནང་བ་ | *phe-gor nang-wa.* |
| Lining | ནང་ཤ་ | *nang-sha.* |
| Link, to | འཐུད་རྒྱབ་བ་ | *thü-gyap-pa.* |
| Do. *hon.* | འཐུད་སྐྱོན་པ་ | *thü-kyöm-pa.* |
| Lion | སེང་གེ་ | *seng-ge.* |
| Lioness | སེང་གེ་མོ་ | *seng-ge-mo.* |
| Lip | མཆུ་ཏོ་ | *chho-to.* |
| Do. *hon.* | ཞལ་མཆུ་ | *she-chhu.* |
| Lip, upper | ཡ་མཆུ་ | *yen-chhu.* |

| | | |
|---|---|---|
| Lip, lower | མ་མཆུ་ | *men-chhu.* |
| Liquefy, to | ཞུ་བ་ | *sḱu-wa.* |
| Liquid | ཁུ་བ་ | *khu-wa.* |
| Liquid medicine | འཐུང་སྨན་ | *thung-men.* |
| Liquor, distilled | ཨ་རག་ | *a-ra.* |
| Do. *hon.* | བཞེས་རག་ | *sḱe-ra.* |
| List | ཐོ་ | *tho* |
| Do. *hon.* | ཕྱག་ཐོ་ | *chha-tho.* |
| Listen, to | ཉན་པ། ཨམ་ཆོག་ཉན་པ་ | *nyem-pa ; am-chho nyem-pa.* |
| Do. *hon.* | གསན་པ། སྙན་ལ་གསན་པ་ | *sem-pa ; nyen-la sem-pa.* |
| Literary language | ཆོས་སྐད་ | *chhö-ke.* |
| Literature | ཆོས་ | *chhö.* |
| Little | ཆུང་ཆུང་ | *chhung-chhung.* |
| Little, a (few) | ཏོག་ཙ། ཉུང་ཉུང་ | *tok-tsa ; nyung-nyung.* |
| Little time, a | ཧྲིབ་ཙ་ (ཙམ་) ཅིག་ | *hrip-tsa-chi.* |
| Live, *adj.* | གསོན་པོ་ | *söm-po.* |
| Live, to (dwell) | བསྡད་པ་ (སྡོད་པ་) | *de-pa.* |
| Do. *hon.* | བཞུགས་པ་ | *sḱu-pa.* |
| Do. *h. hon.* | བཞུགས་གདན་འཇག་པ་ | *sḱu-den jak-pa.* |
| Lively | ཧུར་པོ། གཅང་པོ་ | *hur-po ; chang-po.* |

| | | |
|---|---|---|
| Liver | མཆིན་པ་ | *chhim-pa.* |
| Do. *hon.* | སྐུ་མཆིན་ | *ku-chhin.* |
| Living, *adj.* | གསོན་པོ་ | *söm-po.* |
| Lizard, sand (small) | བྱེ་མ་ཉུ་གུ་ | *cḱe-ma nyu-gu.* |
| Lizard, rock (large) | ཙམ་པ་ཁ་རལ་ | *tsam-pa kha-re.* |
| Lo ! | ལྟོས་ཤིག་ | *tö-shi.* |
| Load (of an animal) | ཁལ། དོ་པོ་ | *khe ; t́o-po.* |
| Do. (of human being) | རྡོག་ཐྲེད། རྒྱབ་འཁུར་ | *dok-thre ; gyaṕ-khur.* |
| Load, to (animal) | ཁལ་བཀལ་ (འགེལ་) བ་ | *khe-ke-wa.* |
| Do. to (of human being) | རྡོག་ཐྲེད་སྐུར་བ་ | *dok-thre kur-wa.* |
| Load, to (a gun) | རྫས་རྫོང་རྒྱབ་པ་ | *dze-dzong gyaṕ-pa.* |
| Do. *hon.* | རྫས་རྫོང་སྐྱོན་པ་ | *dze-dzong kyöm-pa.* |
| Loadstone | རྡོ་ཁབ་ལེན་ | *do-khaṕ-len.* |
| Loaf | བག་ལེབ་ | *ṕa-le.* |
| Loafer (tramp) | རྒྱལ་ཁམས་སྐོར་མཁན་ | *gyeng-kham kor khen.* |
| Loan | བུ་ལོན་ | *ṕu-lön.* |
| Loathe, to | སྡང་པོ་བྱེད་པ་ | *dang-po cḱe-pa.* |
| Do. *hon.* | སྡང་པོ་གནང་བ་ | *dang-po nang-wa.* |
| Locality | ས་ཆ་ | *sa-chha.* |
| Lock, *s.* | སྒོ་ལྕགས་ | *gön-cha.* |

| | | |
|---|---|---|
| Lock, *hon.* | གཟིམ་ལྕགས། ཕྱག་ལྕགས་ | *śim-cha ; chha-cha.* |
| Lock, to | སྒོ་ལྕགས་རྒྱབ་པ་ | *gön-cha gyaṕ-pa.* |
| Do. *hon.* | གཟིམ་ལྕགས་སྐྱོན་པ་ | *śim-cha kyöm-pa.* |
| Locust | ཨ་ཚ་ཚག་པ་ | *a-tsha tshaḱ-pa.* |
| Lodging-house | གནས་ཚང་ | *ne-tshang.* |
| Lodging-house, landlady of | གནས་མོ་ | *ne-mo.* |
| Do. *hon.* | གནས་མོ་ལགས་ | *ne-mo-la.* |
| Lodging-house, landlord of | གནས་པོ་ | *ne-po.* |
| Do. *hon.* | གནས་པོ་ལགས་ | *ne-po-la.* |
| Lofty | མཐོ་པོ་ | *tho-po.* |
| Log (piece of wood) | ཤིང་དུམ་ | *shing-t́um.* |
| Loins | རྐེད་པ་ | *ke-pa.* |
| Do. *hon.* | སྐུ་རྐེད་ | *ku-ke.* |
| Loiter, to | འགོར་བ་ | *gor-wa.* |
| Do. *hon.* | ཕེབ་འགོར་གནང་བ་ | *phe-gor nang-wa.* |
| Lonely | གཅིག་པོ་ | *chiḱ-po.* |
| Do. *hon.* | སྐུ་རྐྱང་ | *ku-kyang.* |
| Lonely place | དབེན་གནས་ | *en-ne.* |
| Long | རིང་པོ་ | *ring-po.* |
| Long for, to | དྲན་པ་ | *t́rem-pa.* |

| | | |
|---|---|---|
| Long for, to, *hon.* | ཐུགས་དྲན་པ་གནང་བ་ | *thu-t̃rem-pa nang-wa.* |
| Long life, to have | ཚེ་རིང་བ་ | *tshe-ring-wa.* |
| Do. *hon.* | སྐུ་ཚེ་རིང་བ་ | *ku-tshe ring-wa.* |
| Long-lived | ཚེ་རིང་པོ་ | *tshe-ring-po.* |
| Do. *hon.* | སྐུ་ཚེ་རིང་པོ་ | *ku-tshe ring-po.* |
| Look, to | ལྟ་བ་ | *ta-wa.* |
| Do. *hon.* | གཟིགས་པ་ | *śi-pa.* |
| Look for, to (search) | འཚོལ་བ་ | *tshö-wa.* |
| .Do. *hon.* | འཚོལ་ལ་ (བ་) གནང་བ་ | *tshö-la nang-wa.* |
| Looking-glass | ཤེལ་སྒོ་ | *she-go.* |
| Loom | འཐག་ཁྲི་ | *thak̃-thri* |
| Loop | ལུང་ | *lung.* |
| Loop-button | ཐུབ་ལུང་ | *thup̃-lung.* |
| Do. *hon.* | མགུལ་ལུང་ | *gü-lung.* |
| Loose (not tight) | ལྷུག་ལྷུག་ | *lhu-lhu.* |
| Do. (lascivious) | འདོད་ཆགས་ཆེན་པོ་ | *dö-chha chhem-po.* |
| Loose, to (liberate) | བཏང་བ་ (གཏོང་བ་) | *tang-wa.* |
| Do. *hon.* | གཏོང་ང་ (བ་) གནང་བ་ | *tong-nga nang-wa.* |
| Loose, to (slacken) | ལྷོད་ལྷོད་བཏང་ (གཏོང་) བ་ | *hlö-hlö tang-wa.* |

| | | |
|---|---|---|
| Loose, to (slacken), *hon.* | ལྷོད་ལྷོད་གཏོང་ང་ (བ་) གནང་བ་ | *hlö-hlö tong-nga nang-wa.* |
| Loosen, to | ལྷུག་ལྷུག་བྱེད་པ་ | *lhu-lhu ck̔e-pa.* |
| Do. *hon.* | ལྷུག་ལྷུག་གནང་བ་ | *lhu-lhu nang-wa.* |
| Lord | དཔོན་པོ་ | *pöm-po.* |
| Lose, to | བརླགས་པ་ | *la-pa.* |
| Lose, to (in business transaction) | གྱོང་འཕོག་པ་ | *k̔yong phok̔-pa.* |
| Do. *hon.* | སྐུ་གྱོང་འཕོག་ག་ (པ་) གནང་བ་ | *ku-k̔yong phok̔-ka nang-wa.* |
| Lose, to (battle, law-suit, etc.) | ཤོར་བ | *shor-wa.* |
| Do. *hon.* | ཤོར་ར་ (བ་) གནང་བ་ | *shor-ra nang-wa.* |
| Loss | གྱོང་ | *k̔yong.* |
| Loss of appetite | དང་ཁ་མེད་པ་ | *t̔ang-kha me-pa.* |
| Do. *hon.* | གསོལ་དང་མེད་པ་ | *sö-t̔ang-me-pa.* |
| Lost, it is | བརླགས་ནས་མི་འདུག | *la-ne min-du.* |
| Do. *hon.* | བརླགས་ག་ (པ་) གནང་ནས་མི་འདུག | *lak̔-ka nang-ne min-du.* |
| Lot (many) | མང་པོ་ | *mang-po.* |
| Do. (very many) | གཡོ་མ་སུ་ | *yo-ma-su.* |
| Do. (chance) | མོ་ | *mo.* |
| Do. *hon.* | ཕྱག་མོ་ | *chha-mo* |

| | | |
|---|---|---|
| Lot (fortune) | བསོ་བདེ་ (བསོད་བདེ་) | *so-de.* |
| Do. *hon.* | སྐུ་བསོད་ | *ku-sö.* |
| Lot (share) | སྐལ་ལ་ (སྐལ་བ་) | *ke-la* |
| Do. *hon.* | སྐུ་སྐལ་ | *ku-ke.* |
| Lots, to draw | མོ་རྒྱབ་པ་ | *mo-gyaṕ-pa.* |
| Do. *hon.* | ཕྱག་མོ་སྐྱོན་པ་ | *chha-mo kyöm-pa.* |
| Lotus | པད་པ་ | *pe-ma.* |
| Loud (noisy) | སྐད་ཆེན་པོ་ | *ke chhem-po.* |
| Do. *hon.* | གསུང་སྐད་ཆེན་པོ་ | *sung-ke chhem-po.* |
| Louse | ཤིག་ | *shi.* |
| Do. *hon.* | སྐུ་ཤིག་ | *ku-shi.* |
| Love | བྱམས་པོ་ | *cKam-po.* |
| Love, to | བྱམས་པོ་བྱེད་པ་ | *cKam-po cKe-pa.* |
| Do. *hon.* | བྱམས་པོ་གནང་བ་ | *cKam-po nang-wa.* |
| Lovely | ཚར་པོ། མཛེས་པོ་ | *tshar-po ; dze-po.* |
| Do. *hon.* | ཐུགས་ཚར་པོ་ | *thu-tshar-po.* |
| Lover | སྙིང་སྡུག་ | *nying-du.* |
| Low | དམའ་པོ་ | *ma-po.* |
| Low (cheap) | ཁེ་པོ་ | *khe-po.* |
| Low, to be (shallow) | གཏིང་རིང་པོ་མེད་པ་ | *ting-ring-po me-pa.* |

| | | |
|---|---|---|
| Lower part of a thing | སྨད་ | *me.* |
| Lower tooth | སྨད་སོ་ | *me-so.* |
| Do. *hon.* | སྨད་ཀྱི་ཚེམས་ | *me-kyi tshem.* |
| Lowland | སྨད་ | *me.* |
| Lowly | སེམས་ཆུང་ཆུང་ | *sem-chhung-chhung.* |
| Do. *hon.* | ཐུགས་སེམས་ཆུང་ཆུང་ | *thuk-sem chhung-chhung.* |
| Low-spirited, to be | སེམས་སྐྱོ་སྣང་བྱེད་པ་ | *sem-kyo-nang ch́e-pa* |
| Do. *hon.* | ཐུགས་སེམས་སྐྱོ་སྣང་གནང་བ་ | *thu-sem kyo-nang nang-wa.* |
| Loyal, to be | བཀའ་མཐུན་ཞུ་བ་ | *ka-thün sḱu-wa.* |
| Lucid | སྒྲ་དག་པོ་ | *dra-ťak-po.* |
| Luck (good) | བསོད་བདེ། བསོད་ནམས་ | *so-de ; sö-nam.* |
| Do. *hon.* | སྐུ་བསོད་ | *ku-sö.* |
| Luck (bad) | བསོད་བདེ་སྐམ་པོ། བསོད་ནམས་ཆུང་ཆུང་ | *so-de kam-po ; sö-nam chhung-chhung.* |
| Do. *hon.* | སྐུ་བསོད་ཆུང་ཆུང་ | *ku-sö chhung-chhung.* |
| Lucky | བསོད་བདེ་ཆེན་པོ། བསོད་ནམས་ཆེན་པོ་ | *so-de chhem-po ; sö-nam chhem-po.* |
| Do. *hon.* | སྐུ་བསོད་ཆེན་པོ་ | *ku-sö chhem-po.* |
| Ludicrous | དགད་མོ་བྲོ་པོ་ | *ge-mo ťro-po.* |

| | | |
|---|---|---|
| Ludicrous, *hon.* | ཞལ་མོ་བྲོ་པོ་ | *sḱe-mo tro-po.* |
| Luggage | ཅ་ལག་ (ཆ་ལག་) | *cha-la.* |
| Do. *hon.* | སྐུ་ཅས་ (སྐུ་ཆས་) | *ku-che.* |
| Lugubrious, to be | སེམས་སྐྱོ་བ། སེམས་སྡུག་པ་ | *sem-kyo-wa ; sem-duḱ-pa.* |
| Do. *hon.* | ཐུགས་སེམས་སྐྱོ་བ་གནང་བ། ཐུགས་སེམས་སྡུག་ག་ (པ་) གནང་བ་ | *thu-sem kyo-wa nang-wa. thu-sem duḱ-ḱa nang-wa.* |
| Lukewarm | དྲོན་འཇམ་ | *t́rön-jam.* |
| Lumbago, to have | སྐེད་པ་ན་བ་ | *ke-pa na-wa.* |
| Do. *hon.* | སྐུ་སྐེད་སྙུང་བ་ | *ku-ke nyung-wa.* |
| Luminous | འོད་ཆེན་པོ་ | *ö chhem-po.* |
| Lump | རྡོག་རྡོག་ | *doḱ-do.* |
| Lunatic | སྨྱོན་པ་ | *nyöm-pa.* |
| Lunch | ཉིན་གུང་ཁ་ལག་ | *nyin-ḱung kha-la.* |
| Do. *hon.* | ཉིན་གུང་ཞལ་ལག་ | *nyin-ḱung sḱe-la.* |
| Lungs | གློ་ (གློ་བ་) | *lo.* |
| Do. *hon.* | སྐུ་གློ་ | *ku-lo.* |
| Lurk, to | ཡིབ་ནས་བསྡད་ (སྡོད་) པ་ | *yiṕ-ne de-pa.* |
| Do. *hon.* | ཡིབ་ནས་བཞུགས་པ་ | *yiṕ-ne sḱu-pa.* |
| Lust | འདོད་ཆགས་ | *dö-chha.* |

| | | |
|---|---|---|
| Lustful | འདོད་ཆགས་ཆེན་པོ་ | *dö-chha chhem-po.* |
| Lustre | གཟི་བརྗིད། འོད་ | *śi-ji ; ö.* |
| Lustrous | གཟི་བརྗིད་ཆེན་པོ། འོད་ཆེན་པོ་ | *śi-ji chhem-po ; ö chhem-po.* |
| Lusty | ཤེད་ཆེན་པོ་ | *she chhem-po.* |
| Do. *hon.* | སྐུ་ཤེད་ཆེན་པོ་ | *ku-she chhem-po.* |
| Luxuriant | འབེལ་པོ་ | *be-po.* |
| Lynx | དབྱི་ | *i.* |

# M

| | | |
|---|---|---|
| Machine, sewing | ཚེམ་བུའི་འཁོར་ལོ་ | tshem-bü ḱhor-lo. |
| Mad | སྨྱོན་པ་ | nyöm-pa. |
| Mad, to be | སྨྱོ་བ་ | nyo-wa. |
| Madam | ལྕམ་སྐུ་གཞོགས་ | cham-ku-sḰo. |
| Magazine | མཛོད་ | dzö. |
| Magic | མིག་འཕྲུལ་ | miḱ-thrü. |
| Magician | མིག་འཕྲུལ་སྟོན་མཁན་ | miḱ-thrü tön-khen. |
| Magistrate, city (Chinaman) | ཁྲིམས་དཔོན་ | thrim-pön. |
| Do. (Tibetan) | མི་དཔོན་ | mi-pön. |
| Do. in charge of district | རྫོང་དཔོན་ | dzong-pön. |
| Magnanimity | དྲིན་ | ťrin. |
| Do. *hon.* | བཀའ་དྲིན་ | ka-ťrin. |
| Magnanimous | དྲིན་ཆེན་པོ་ | ťrin chhem-po. |
| Do. *hon.* | བཀའ་དྲིན་ཆེན་པོ་ | ka-ťrin chhem-po. |
| Magnet | རྡོ་ཁབ་ལེན་ | do-khaṕ-len. |
| Magnificent | གཡང་མཛེས་ | yang-dze. |
| Magnitude | ཆེ་ཆུང་ | chhe-chhung. |
| Magnolia | ཙམ་པ་ཀ་ *Hin.* | tsam-pa-ka. |
| Magpie | ཀྲ་ཀ་ (སྐྲ་ཀ་) | tra-ka. |

| | | |
|---|---|---|
| Mahommedan | ཁ་ཆེ་ | *kha-chhe.* |
| Maid, maiden | བུ་མོ་ | *ṕu-mo.* |
| Do. *hon.* | སྲས་མོ་ | *se-mo* or *tre-mo.* |
| Maid-servant | གཡོག་མོ་ | *yo-mo.* |
| Do. of person of high rank | ཞལ་ཏ་མ་ | *sḱe-ta-ma.* |
| Main point | དོན་སྙིང་ | *t́ön-nying.* |
| Mainly | ཕལ་ཆེར་ | *phe-chher.* |
| Maintain, to (affirm) | ལབ་པ་ | *laṕ-pa.* |
| Do. *hon.* | གསུང་བ་ | *sung-wa.* |
| Maintain, to (nourish) | གསོ་བ་ | *so-wa.* |
| Do. *hon.* | གསོ་བ་གནང་བ་ | *so-wa nang-wa.* |
| Maize | ཀྐན་ཛོམ་ | *ken-dzom.* |
| Majestic | གཟི་བརྗིད་ཆེན་པོ་ | *śi-ji chhem-po.* |
| Majesty, His | རིན་པོ་ཆེ་ | *rim-po-chhe.* |
| Major (officer in command of 250 to 500 men) | རུ་དཔོན་ | *ru-pön.* |
| Majority, the | མང་ང་ (མང་བ་) | *mang-nga.* |
| Make, to | བྱེད་པ་ | *cḱe-pa.* |
| Do. *hon.* | གནང་བ་ | *nang-wa.* |
| Make, to (construct) | བཟོ་བ་ | *śo-wa.* |

| | | |
|---|---|---|
| Make, to (construct), *hon.* | བཟོ་བ་གནང་བ་ | *śo-wa nang-wa.* |
| Maker | བཟོ་མཁན་ | *śo-khen.* |
| Do. *hon.* | བཟོ་བ་གནང་མཁན་ | *śo-wa nang-khen.* |
| Malady | ན་ཚ་ | *na-tsha.* |
| Do. *hon.* | སྙུང་གཞི་ | *nyung-sKi.* |
| Male | ཕོ་ | *pho.* |
| Malediction, to pronounce | དམོད་མོ་རྒྱབ་པ་ | *mö-mo gyaṕ-pa.* |
| Do. *hon.* | དམོད་མོ་སྐྱོན་པ་ | *mö-mo kyöm-pa.* |
| Malefactor | འཛབ་ཆེན་ | *dzaṕ-chhen.* |
| Malice | གནོད་སེམས་ | *nö-sem.* |
| Malicious | སེམས་ངན་པོ་ | *sem ngem-po.* |
| Do. *hon.* | ཐུགས་སེམས་ངན་པོ་ | *thu-sem ngem-po.* |
| Malign, to | སྨད་ར་བཏང་ (གཏོང་) བ་ | *me-ra tang-wa.* |
| Do. *hon.* | སྨད་ར་གཏོང་ང་ (བ་) གནང་བ་ | *me-ra tong-nga nang-wa.* |
| Do. *inf.* to *sup.* | སྨད་ར་ཞུ་བ་ | *me-ra sKu-wa.* |
| Malignant | སེམས་ངན་པོ་ | *sem ngem-po.* |
| Do. *hon.* | ཐུགས་སེམས་ངན་པོ་ | *thu-sem ngem-po.* |
| Malignity | གནོད་སེམས་ | *nö-sem.* |
| Mallet | ཤིང་གི་ཐོ་བ་ | *shing-ki tho-a.* |
| Maltreat, to | སྡུག་པོ་བཏང་ (གཏོང་) བ་ | *duk-po tang-wa.* |

| | | |
|---|---|---|
| Maltreat, to, *hon.* | སྡུག་པོ་གཏོང་ང་(བ་)གནང་བ་ | *duk-po tong-nga nang-wa.* |
| Mamma | ཨ་མ་ | *a-ma.* |
| Do. *hon.* | ཡུམ་ | *yum.* |
| Mammon | ནོར་ལྷ་ | *nor-hla.* |
| Man | མི་ | *mi.* |
| Do. a short | ཏེ་པོ་ | *te-po.* |
| Man-servant | གཡོག་པོ་ | *yok-po.* |
| Do. of person in good position | ཞབས་ཕྱི་ | *sȟaṕ-chhi.* |
| Manacles | ལག་ལྕགས་ | *lak-cha.* |
| Manage, to (supervise) | དོ་དམ་བྱེད་པ་ | *ťo-ťam cȟe-pa.* |
| Do. *hon.* | དོ་དམ་གནང་བ་ | *ťo-ťam nang-wa.* |
| Manager | དོ་དམ་པ་ | *ťo-ťam-pa.* |
| Do. *hon.* | དོ་དམ་གནང་མཁན་ | *ťo-ťam nang-khen.* |
| Mandate | བཀའ་ | *ka.* |
| Do. written (of Government) | བཀའ་རྒྱ་ | *ka-gya.* |
| Mane (of horse, etc.) | ཟེ་ | *śe.* |
| Do. (of lion) | རལ་པ་ | *re-pa.* |
| Mange | རྔོ་ | *ngo.* |
| Do. to have | རྔོ་ཤོར་བ་ | *ngo-shor-wa.* |

| | | |
|---|---|---|
| Manger | ཁྲེས་ར་ (ཁྲེས་) | *ťre-ra.* |
| Mangle, to (tear) | བཀོག་པ་ (འགོག་པ་) | *koǩ-pa.* |
| Do. *hon.* | བཀོག་ག་ (འགོག་པ་) གནང་བ་ | *koǩ-ǩa nang-wa.* |
| Maniac | སྨྱོན་པ་ | *nyöm-pa.* |
| Manifest, *adj.* | མངོན་ནས། ངོ་ཐོག་ | *ngön-ne ; ngo-tho.* |
| Manifold | སྣ་ཚོགས་ | *na-tsho.* |
| Mankind | མི་རིགས་ | *mi-ri.* |
| Manly (brave) | སྙིང་ཆེན་པོ། བློ་ཁོག་ཆེན་པོ་ | *nying-chhem-po ; lo-kho chhem-po.* |
| Do. *hon.* | ཐུགས་སྙིང་ཆེན་པོ། ཐུགས་ཁོག་ཆེན་པོ་ | *thu-nying chhem-po ; thu-kho chhem po.* |
| Manner (custom) | ལུགས་སྲོལ་ | *luǩ-sö.* |
| Do. (behaviour) | བྱེད་སྟངས་ | *cǩe-tang.* |
| Do. *hon.* | གནང་སྟངས་ | *nang-tang.* |
| Manœuvre, to (troops) | དམག་སྦྱོང་བྱེད་པ་ | *ma-jong cǩe-pa.* |
| Do. *hon.* | དམག་སྦྱོང་གནང་བ་ | *ma-jong nang-wa.* |
| Mansion | གཟིམ་ཤག། ཕོ་བྲང་ | *śim-sha ; pho-ťrang.* |
| Mantle | ཆུ་པ་ | *chhu-pa.* |
| Do. *hon.* | ན་བཟའ་ | *nam-śa.* |

| | | |
|---|---|---|
| Manufacture, to | བཟོ་བ་ | *śo-wa.* |
| Do. *hon.* | བཟོ་བ་གནང་བ་ | *śo-wa nang-wa.* |
| Manure | ལུད་ | *lü.* |
| Manuscript | བྲིས་མ་ | *ťri-ma.* |
| Many | མང་པོ་ | *mang-po.* |
| Many, very | ཧ་ཅང་མང་པོ། གཡོ་མ་སུ་ | *ha chang mang-po ; yo-ma-su.* |
| Many, too | ལྷག་པོ་ | *hlaḱ-po.* |
| Many, how | ག་ཚོད་ | *ḱa-tshö.* |
| Map | ས་ཁྲ་ | *saṕ-thra.* |
| Mar, to | སྐྱོན་བྱེད་པ་ | *kyön-cḱe-pa.* |
| Do. *hon.* | སྐྱོན་གནང་བ་ | *kyön-nang-wa.* |
| March, to | འགྲོ་བ་ | *dro wa.* |
| Do. *hon.* | ཕེབ་པ་ | *phe-pa.* |
| Do. *h. hon.* | འཆིབ་སྒྱུ་གནང་བ་ | *chhiṕ-gyu nang-wa.* |
| Mare | རྒོད་མ་ | *gö-ma.* |
| Margin | མཐའ་ | *tha.* |
| Marigold | གུར་གུམ་མེ་ཏོག་ | *ḱur-ḱum me-to.* |
| Mark | རྟགས་ | *ta.* |
| Mark, to (observe) | མིག་ལྟ་བ་ | *miḱ-ta-wa.* |
| Do. *hon.* | གཟིགས་པ་ | *śi-pa.* |

| | | |
|---|---|---|
| Marked (famous) | སྐད་གྲགས་ཆེན་པོ་ | *ke-ťra chhem-po.* |
| Do. *hon.* | སྙན་གྲགས་ཆེན་པོ་ | *nyen-ťra chhem-po.* |
| Market-place | ཁྲོམ་ | *throm.* |
| Marriage. | ཆང་ས་ | *chhang-sa.* |
| Do. *hon.* | འཁྲུང་ས་ | *thrung-sa.* |
| Marry, to (take a wife) | མནའ་མ་ལེན་པ་ | *na-ma lem-pa.* |
| Do. *hon.* | མནའ་མ་བཞེས་པ་ | *na-ma sKe-pa.* |
| Marry, to (take a husband) | མག་པ་བསླང་ (སློང་) བ་ | *mak-pa lang-wa.* |
| Do. *hon.* | སྐུ་བག་བཞེས་པ་ | *ku-ṕa sKe-pa.* |
| Marvel, *s.* | ཡ་མཚན་ | *yam tshen.* |
| Marvel, to | ཁྱད་མཚར་པོ་བྱེད་པ་ | *khye-tsha-po cKe-pa.* |
| Marvellous | ཡ་མཚན་པོ། ཁྱད་མཚར་པོ་ | *yam-tshem-po; khye-tsha-po.* |
| Mask | འབག་ | *ba.* |
| Do. *hon.* | ཞལ་འབག་ | *sKem-ba.* |
| Mason | རྡོ་བཟོ་བ་ | *doṕ-śo-wa.* |
| Masquerade | འཆམ་ | *chham.* |
| Do. *hon.* | སྐུ་འཆམ་ | *kun-chham.* |
| Massage, to | འཕུར་འཕུར་བྱེད་པ་ | *phu-phu cKe-pa.* |
| Massive (bulky) | སྦོམ་པོ་ | *bom-po.* |
| Do. (heavy) | ལྗི་པོ་ | *ji-po.* |

| | | |
|---|---|---|
| Mast (flag-staff) | དར་པོ་ཆེ་ | *ťar-po-chhe.* |
| Master | སྦྱིན་བདག ། བདག་པོ་ | *jin-da ; dak-po.* |
| Do. *hon.* | དཔོན་པོ་ | *pöm-po.* |
| Mastery (power) | དབང་ | *wang.* |
| Do. *hon.* | སྐུ་དབང་ | *ku-wang.* |
| Mastiff | འབྲོག་ཁྱི་ | *drok-khyi.* |
| Mart | ཁྲོམ་ | *throm.* |
| Mat | གདན་ | *den.* |
| Match (lucifer) | མུ་ཟི་ | *mu-śi.* |
| Match-box | མུ་ཟིའི་སྒམ་ཆུང་ | *mu-śi gam-chhung.* |
| Mate | རོགས་ | *ro.* |
| Material, *s.* | རྒྱུ་ | *gyu.* |
| Material, *adj.* (important) | གནད་ཁག་ཆེན་པོ། གལ་ཆེན་པོ་ | *nen-kha chhem-po ; ke chhem-po.* |
| Maternal aunt | སྲུ་མོ་ | *su-mo.* |
| Matter (substance) | རྒྱུ་ | *gyu.* |
| Do. (pus) | རྣག་ | *na.* |
| Mattress | འབོལ་གདན་ | *bö-den.* |
| Do. *hon.* | བཞུགས་འབོལ་ | *skum-böl.* |
| Mature, to be | ཚོས་པ་ | *tshö-pa.* |

| | | |
|---|---|---|
| Maxim | གཏམ་དཔེ་ | *tam-pe.* |
| Me | ང་ལ་ | *nga-la.* |
| Meadow | སྤང་ | *pang.* |
| Meagre (lean) | ཤ་སྐམ་པོ་ | *sha-kam-po.* |
| Do. *hon.* | སྐུ་ཤ་སྐམ་པོ་ | *ku-sha kam-po.* |
| Meagre (scanty) | ཉུང་ཉུང་ | *nyung-nyung.* |
| Meal (food taken at one time) | ཁ་ལག། ལྟོ། ལྟོ་ཆས་ | *kha-la ; to ; top-chhe.* |
| Do. *hon.* | ཞལ་ལག་ | *sḱe-la.* |
| Mean (vulgar) | དཀྱུས་མ་ | *kyü-ma.* |
| Mean (stingy) | ལག་པ་དམ་པོ་ | *laḱ-pa t́am-po.* |
| Do. *hon.* | ཕྱག་དམ་པོ་ | *chha t́am-po.* |
| Mean, to (purpose) | སེམས་ལ་བསམ་པ་ | *sem-la sam-pa.* |
| Do. *hon.* | ཐུགས་ལ་དགོངས་པ་ | *thuḱ-la gong-pa.* |
| Meaning | དོན་དག་ | *tön-t́a.* |
| Do. *hon.* | སྐུ་དོན་ | *ku-tön.* |
| Means, *s.* | ཐབས་ | *thaṕ.* |
| Means, by all | ངེས་པར་ | *nge-par.* |
| Means, by what | ག་འདྲས་ | *ḱan-dre.* |
| Meantime, in the | ཁབ་སུ་ | *khaṕ-su.* |

| | | |
|---|---|---|
| Meanwhile, in the | ཁབ་སུ་ | *khaṕ-su.* |
| Measles | གསིལ་པ་ | *si-pa.* |
| Measure, *s.* | ཚད་ | *tshe.* |
| Measure, to | འཇལ་བ་ | *je-wa.* |
| Do. *hon.* | འཇལ་ར་ (བ་) གནང་བ་ | *je-ra nang-wa.* |
| Meat | ཤ་ | *sha.* |
| Do. *hon.* | བཞེས་ཤ་ | *sKe-sha.* |
| Mechanic | བཟོ་མཁན་ | *śo-khen.* |
| Mediate, to | བར་མི་བྱེད་པ་ | *ṕar-mi cKe-pa.* |
| Do. *hon.* | བར་མི་གནང་བ་ | *ṕar-mi nang-wa.* |
| Mediator | བར་མི་བྱེད་མཁན་ | *ṕar-mi cKe-khen.* |
| Medicine | སྨན་ | *men.* |
| Medicine for internal use | ཁོང་སྨན་ | *khong-men.* |
| Medicine, mineral | ས་སྨན་ | *sa-men.* |
| Meditate, to | བསམ་པ་ | *sam-pa.* |
| Do. *hon.* | དགོངས་པ་ | *gong-pa.* |
| Meditate, to (on religious affairs) | སྒོམ་རྒྱབ་པ་ | *gom-gyaṕ-pa.* |
| Do. *hon.* | སྒོམ་སྐྱོན་པ་ | *gom-kyöm-pa.* |
| Meditation, religious | ཏིང་ངེ་འཛིན་ | *ting-nge dzin.* |

| | | |
|---|---|---|
| Medium (of quality) | འབྲིང་ཅིག། ཁྲིག་ཁྲིག་ཅིག་ | *dring-chi ; thriḱ-thri-chi.* |
| Meek | སེམས་ཆུང་ཆུང་ | *sem-chhung-chhung.* |
| Do. *hon.* | ཐུགས་སེམས་ཆུང་ཆུང་ | *thuḱ-sem-chhung-chhung.* |
| Meek in speech | ཁ་འཇམ་པོ་ | *kha jam-po.* |
| Do. *hon.* | ཞལ་འཇམ་པོ་ | *sḱe jam-po.* |
| Meet, to | ཐུག་པ་ | *thuḱ-pa.* |
| Do. (a superior) | མཇལ་བ་ | *je-wa.* |
| Do. (between two of high position) | མཇལ་ར་ (བ་) གནང་བ་ | *je-ra nang-wa.* |
| Meeting | ཐུག་ཕྲད་ | *thuḱ-thre.* |
| Do. *hon.* | མཇལ་ཕྲད་ | *je-thre.* |
| Melancholy, to be | སེམས་སྐྱོ་སྣང་བྱེད་པ་ | *sem-kyo-nang cḱe-pa.* |
| Do. *hon.* | ཐུགས་སེམས་སྐྱོ་སྣང་གནང་བ་ | *thu-sem kyo-nang nang-wa.* |
| Melt, to | ཞུ་བ་ | *sḱu-wa.* |
| Memoir (story) | རྣམ་ཐར་ | *nam-tha.* |
| Memory | དྲན་པ་ | *t́rem-pa.* |
| Do. *hon.* | ཐུགས་དྲན་ | *thu-t́ren.* |
| Menace, to | འཛྀག་འཛྀག་ (འཛིག་འཛིག་) བཏང་ (གཏོང་) བ་ | *dziḱ-dziḱ tang-wa.* |
| Mend, to | སྒྲོག་པ་ | *droḱ-pa.* |

| | | |
|---|---|---|
| Mend, to, *hon.* | སྒྲོག་ག་ (པ་) གནང་བ་ | *drok-ka nang-wa.* |
| Mend, to (by patching) | ལྷན་པ་རྒྱབ་པ་ | *hlem-pa gyap-pa.* |
| Do. *hon.* | ལྷན་པ་སྐྱོན་པ་ | *hlem-pa kyöm-pa.* |
| Mendacious, to be | ཧམ་པ་ཤོད་པ། ཀྱག་རྫུན་ཤོད་པ་ | *ham-pa shö-pa ; kyak-dzün shö-pa.* |
| Do. *hon.* | ཞལ་རྫུན་གསུང་བ་ | *ske-dzün sung-wa.* |
| Mendicant | སྤང་ཀོ་ (སྤྲང་པོ་) | *pang-ko.* |
| Menses | ཟླ་མཚན་ | *da-tshen.* |
| Menstruate, to | ཟླ་ཁྲག་རྒྱབ་པ་ | *da-thra, gyap-pa.* |
| Mention, to | ལབ་པ་ | *lap-pa.* |
| Do. *hon.* | གསུང་བ་ | *sung-wa.* |
| Merchandise | ཚོང་ཟོག་ | *tshong-śo.* |
| Merchant | ཚོང་པ་ | *tshong-pa.* |
| Do. *hon.* | ཚོང་དཔོན་ | *tshong-pön.* |
| Merciful | སྙིང་རྗེ་ཆེན་པོ་ | *nying-je chhem-po.* |
| Do. *hon.* | ཐུགས་རྗེ་ཆེན་པོ་ | *thuk-je chhem-po.* |
| Merciless, to be | སྙིང་རྗེ་མེད་པ་ | *nying-je me-pa.* |
| Do. *hon.* | ཐུགས་རྗེ་མེད་པ་ | *thuk-je me-pa.* |
| Mercury | དངུལ་ཆུ་ | *ngü-chhu.* |
| Mercy | སྙིང་རྗེ་ | *nying-je.* |

| | | |
|---|---|---|
| Mercy, *hon.* | ཐུགས་རྗེ་ | *thuk-je.* |
| Merely | ཤ་སྟག་ | *sha-ta.* |
| Merit | དགེ་བ། ཚོགས་ | *ge-wa ; tsho.* |
| Do. to accumulate | ཚོགས་བསག་ (གསོག་) པ་ | *tsho sak-pa.* |
| Do. *hon.* | ཚོགས་གསོག་ག་ (པ་) གནང་བ་ | *tsho sok-ka nang-wa.* |
| Merit, to | འོས་པ་ | *ö-pa.* |
| Merriment | དགའ་ཚོར་ | *ga-tshor.* |
| Do. *hon.* | མཉེས་ཚོར་ | *nye-tshor.* |
| Merry, to be | དགའ་བ། སྐྱིད་པོ་བྱས་ནས་སྡོད་པ་ | *ga-wa ; kyi-po cKe-ne dö-pa.* |
| Do. *hon.* | མཉེས་པོ་གནང་བ། སྤྲོ་པོ་གནང་ནས་བཞུགས་པ་ | *nye-po nang-wa ; tro-po nang-ne shuk-pa.* |
| Do. *h. hon.* | ཐུགས་དགྱེས་པོ་གནང་བ་ | *thu-gye-po nang-wa.* |
| Message | ལན་ | *len.* |
| Do. *hon.* | བཀའ་ལན་ | *ka-len.* |
| Messenger | བང་ཆེན་ | *ṕang-chhen.* |
| Method (means) | ཐབས་ | *thaṕ.* |
| Do. (custom) | ལུགས་སྲོལ་ | *luk-sö.* |
| Mewing, *s.* (of cat) | སྨྱོའོ་ | *me-o.* |

| | | |
|---|---|---|
| Mid-day | ཉིན་གུང་ | *nyin-kung.* |
| Middle, *s.* | དཀྱིལ་ | *kyi.* |
| Do. (waist) | རྐེད་པ་ | *ke-pa.* |
| Do. *hon.* | སྐུ་རྐེད་ | *ku-ke.* |
| Middle, *adj.* | འབྲིང་ཙམ། ཁྲིག་ཁྲིག་ཙམ་ | *dring-chi ; thrik-thri-chi.* |
| Middle of, in the | དཀྱིལ་ལ་ | *kyi-la.* |
| Midnight | ནམ་ཕྱེད་ | *nam-chhe.* |
| Midst, in the | དཀྱིལ་ལ་ | *kyi-la.* |
| Mien | བཟོ་ལྟ་ | *śop-ta.* |
| Do. *hon.* | སྐུ་བཟོ་ | *ku-śo.* |
| Might (official authority) | དབང་ | *wang.* |
| Do. *hon.* | སྐུ་དབང་ | *ku-wang.* |
| Might (physical) | ཤེད་ | *she.* |
| Do. *hon.* | སྐུ་ཤེད་ | *ku-she.* |
| Mighty (officially) | དབང་ཆེན་པོ་ | *wang chhem-po.* |
| Do. *hon.* | སྐུ་དབང་ཆེན་པོ་ | *ku-wang chhem-po.* |
| Mighty (physically) | ཤེད་ཆེན་པོ་ | *she chhem-po.* |
| Do. *hon.* | སྐུ་ཤེད་ཆེན་པོ་ | *ku-she chhem-po.* |
| Milch cow | བཞོན་མ་ | *skö-ma.* |
| Mild in speech | ཁ་འཇམ་པོ་ | *kha jam-po.* |

| | | |
|---|---|---|
| Mild in speech, *hon.* | ཞལ་འཇམ་པོ་ | *sḱe jam-po.* |
| Mild (of climate) | བསིལ་དྲོས་སྙོམ་པོ་ | *si-ṫrö nyom-po.* |
| Militia (first) see "army" | འདོན་དམག | *döm-ma.* |
| Do. (second) | སེར་དམག་ | *ser-ma.* |
| Do. (final) | བཅོ་བརྒྱད་དྲུག་ཅུ་ | *choṕ-gye truk-chu.* |
| Milk | འོ་མ་ | *o-ma.* |
| Do. *hon.* | བཞེས་འོ་ | *sḱe-o.* |
| Milk, to | བཞོ་བ་ | *sḱo-wa.* |
| Do. *hon.* | བཞོ་བ་གནང་བ་ | *sḱo-wa nang-wa.* |
| Milk-jug | འོ་སྣོད་ | *o-nö.* |
| Million | ས་ཡ་ | *sa-ya.* |
| Mimic, to | ལན་ལྟོས་བྱེད་པ་ | *len-tö cḱe-pa* |
| Do. *hon.* | ལན་ལྟོས་གནང་བ་ | *len-tö nang-wa.* |
| Mimicry | ལན་ལྟོས་ | *len-tö* |
| Mina (bird) | མི་ན་ *Hin.* | *me-na.* |
| Mince, to | བཙབ་པ་ | *tsaṕ-pa.* |
| Do. *hon.* | བཙབ་པ་གནང་བ་ | *tsaṕ-pa nang-wa.* |
| Mind | བློ། སེམས་ | *lo ; sem.* |
| Do. *hon.* | ཐུགས་ | *thu.* |
| Mind, to (take care of) | ཉར་བ་ | *nyar-wa.* |

| | | |
|---|---|---|
| Mind, to (take care of), *hon.* | ཉར་ར་ (བ་) གནང་བ་ | *nyar-ra nang-wa.* |
| Mind! never | ཨའུ་ཙེ་ | *a-u-tse.* |
| Mine, *pron.* | ངའི་ | *nge.* |
| Mingle, to, *v.i.* | འདྲེ་བ་ | *dre-wa.* |
| Mingle, to, *v.t.* | བསྲེ་བ་ | *tre-wa.* |
| Do. *hon.* | བསྲེ་བ་གནང་བ་ | *tre-a nang-wa.* |
| Minister of the Grand Council at Lhasa | ས་དབང་ཆེན་པོ། ཞབས་པད། བཀའ་བློན་ | *sa-wang chhem-po ; shaṗ-pe ; ka-lön.* |
| Minister, Chief | བློན་ཆེན་ | *lön-chhen.* |
| Mint | དངུལ་པར་ཁང་ | *ngü-par-khang.* |
| Minute, *adj.* | ཞིབ་ཞིབ་ | *shiṗ-shiṗ.* |
| Miracle | ཡ་མཚན་ | *yam-tshen.* |
| Miraculous | ཡ་མཚན་པོ། ཁྱད་མཚར་པོ་ | *yam-tshem-po ; khye-tsha-po.* |
| Mire | འདམ། རྫབ་ | *dam ; dzaṗ.* |
| Mirror | ཤེལ་སྒོ་ | *she-go.* |
| Mirth | དགའ་ཚོར་ | *ga-tshor.* |
| Do. *hon.* | མཉེས་ཚོར་ | *nye-tshor.* |
| Mirthful, to be | དགའ་བ་ | *ga-wa.* |
| Do. *hon.* | མཉེས་པོ་གནང་བ་ | *nye-po nang-wa.* |
| Do. *h. hon.* | ཐུགས་དགྱེས་པོ་གནང་བ་ | *thu-gye-po nang-wa.* |

| | | |
|---|---|---|
| Mischief | སྐྱོན་ | *kyön.* |
| Miscreant | འཛབ་ཆེན་ | *dzap-chhen.* |
| Miserable (unhappy) | སྡུག་བསྔལ་ཆེན་པོ་ | *dung-nge chhem-po.* |
| Do. *hon.* | ཐུགས་བསྔལ་ཆེན་པོ་ | *thuk-nge chhem-po.* |
| Miserliness | སེར་སྣ་ | *ser-na.* |
| Miserly | སེར་སྣ་ཆེན་པོ་ | *ser-na chhem-po.* |
| Misery | སྡུག་བསྔལ་ | *dung-nge.* |
| Do. *hon.* | ཐུགས་བསྔལ་ | *thuk-nge.* |
| Misfortune | བསོད་བདེ་སྐམ་པོ་ | *so-de kam-po.* |
| Do. *hon.* | སྐུ་བསོད་ཆུང་ཆུང་ | *ku-sö chhung-chhung.* |
| Mist | སྨུགས་པ་ | *muk-pa.* |
| Mistake, to | ནོར་བ་ | *nor-wa.* |
| Do. *hon.* | ནོར་ར་ (བ་) གནང་བ་ | *nor-ra nang-wa.* |
| Mistake in speech, to make a | ཁ་ནོར་བ་ | *kha-nor-wa.* |
| Do. *hon.* | ཞལ་ནོར་བ་ | *ske nor-wa.* |
| Mistress (wife of well-to-do villager) | སྙིང་སྙིང་ལགས་ | *nyi-nying-la.* |
| Mistress (wife of ordinary official) | ལྕམ་སྐུ་གཞོགས་ | *cham-ku-sko.* |
| Do. (third grade and upwards) | ལྷ་ལྕམ་སྐུ་གཞོགས་ | *hla-cham ku-sko.* |

| | | |
|---|---|---|
| Misunderstood, to be | ཀོ་ལོག་བྱུང་བ་ | *k̇o-lok cK̇ung-wa.* |
| Do. *hon.* | གསན་འཛོལ་བྱུང་བ་ | *sen-dzöl cK̇ung-wa.* |
| Mix, to, *v.t.* | བསྲེ་བ་ | *tre-wa.* |
| Do. *hon.* | བསྲེ་བ་གནང་བ་ | *tre-a nang-wa.* |
| Mix, to, *v.i.* | འདྲེ་བ་ | *dre-wa.* |
| Mock, to | ཀྱག་ཀྱག་བྱས་ནས་ལབ་པ་ | *kya-kya cK̇e-ne lap̍-pa.* |
| Do. *hon.* | ཀྱག་ཀྱག་གནང་ནས་གསུང་བ་ | *kya kya nang-ne sung-wa.* |
| Mode (custom) | ལུགས་སྲོལ་ | *luk-sö.* |
| Do. (method) | ཐབས་ | *thap̍.* |
| Model | དཔེ་ | *pe.* |
| Modelled well- (of metal-work, wood-work, etc.) | བཀོད་པ་དོད་པོ་ | *kö-pa ťö-po.* |
| Moderate, to be | ཚོད་ཟིན་པ་ | *tshö-śim-pa.* |
| Modern | དེ་རིང་སང་གི་ | *ťe-ring sang-k̇i.* |
| Modest, to be | དམའ་ས་ཟིན་པ་ | *ma-sa śim-pa.* |
| Do. *hon.* | དམའ་ས་ཟིན་པ་གནང་བ་ | *ma-sa śim-pa nang-wa.* |
| Mohammadan | ཁ་ཆེ་ | *kha-chhe* |
| Moist | རློན་པ་ | *löm-pa.* |
| Moisten, to | སྦང་བ་ | *bang-wa.* |
| Do. *hon.* | སྦང་ང་ (བ་) གནང་བ་ | *bang-nga nang-wa.* |

| | | |
|---|---|---|
| Moisture (of ground) | བཞའ་ཚེན་ | *sKa-tshen.* |
| Molar tooth | འགྲམ་སོ་ | *dram-so.* |
| Do. *hon.* | ཞལ་འགྲམ་གྱི་ཚེམས་ | *sKe-dram-kyi tshem.* |
| Mole | སྨན་ (སྨེ་བ་) | *men.* |
| Molest, to | སྡུག་པོ་བཏང་ (གཏོང་) བ་ | *duK-po tang-wa.* |
| Do. *hon.* | སྡུག་པོ་གཏོང་ང་ (བ་) གནང་བ་ | *duK-po tong-nga nang-wa.* |
| Moment (importance) | གནད་ཁག་ | *nen-kha.* |
| Moment, in a | ཧྲིབ་ཙ་ (ཙམ་) ཅིག་ | *hriṕ-tsa-chi.* |
| Momentous | གནད་ཁག་ཆེན་པོ། གལ་ཆེན་པོ་ | *nen-kha chhem-po ; Ke chhem-po.* |
| Monarch | རྒྱལ་པོ་ | *gye-po.* |
| Monarch's administration | རྒྱལ་སྲིད་ | *gye-si.* |
| Monastery | དགོན་པ་ | *göm-pa.* |
| Monday | གཟའ་ཟླ་བ་ | *śa-da-wa.* |
| Money | དངུལ་ | *ngü.* |
| Mongol, Mongolian | སོག་པོ་ | *soK-po.* |
| Monk | གྲྭ་པ་ | *t́ra-pa.* |
| Do. *hon.* | དགེ་འདུན་ | *gen-dün.* |
| Monkey | སྤེའུ་ (སྤྲེའུ་) | *pe-u.* |
| Monstrous (huge) | ཆེ་ཐག་ཆོད་ | *chhe-thaK-chhö.* |

| | | |
|---|---|---|
| Monstrous (horrible) | ཞེད་སྣག་ཚ་པོ་ | *sḱe-tra tsha-po.* |
| Month | ཟླ་བ་ | *da-wa.* |
| Month, 1st half of | ཟླ་སྟོད། ཚེས་ཤར་ | *da-tö ; tshe-shar.* |
| Do. middle of | ཟླ་དཀྱིལ། ཚེས་དཀྱིལ་ | *da-kyi ; tshe-kyi.* |
| Do. last half of | ཟླ་སྨད། ཟླ་མཇུག། ཚེས་གཞུག་ | *da-me ; dan-juḱ ; tshe-sḱu.* |
| Do. last day of | ནམ་གང་ | *nam-ḱang.* |
| Moon | ཟླ་བ་ | *da-wa.* |
| Moonlight | ཟླ་དཀར་ | *da-ka.* |
| Moonlight, to be | ཟླ་དཀར་ཤར་བ་ | *da-ka shar-wa.* |
| Moral, *adj.* (of persons) | ཚུལ་ལྡན་ | *tshün-den.* |
| Morality | ཚུལ་ཁྲིམས་ | *tshü-thrim.* |
| More | མང་ང་ (མང་བ།) ལྷག་ག་ (ལྷག་པ་) | *mang-nga ; hlaḱ-ḱa.* |
| Moreover | ད་འདོ་ (ད་གདོས་) | *t́an-do.* |
| Morning | ཞོགས་གས། སྔ་དྲོ་ | *sḱoḱ-ḱe ; nga-t́ro.* |
| Do. (before dawn) | ཐོ་རངས་ | *tho-rang.* |
| Do. forenoon (eight to ten o'clock) | ཚ་དིང་ | *tsha-ting.* |
| Morrow | སང་ཉིན་ | *sang-nyi.* |

| | | |
|---|---|---|
| Morsel, a | དག་ག་ཅིག་ | t́ak-ḱa-chi. |
| Mortal, *s.* | མི་ | *mi.* |
| Mortar (for pounding) | སྒོག་དིང་ | *gok-ting.* |
| Do. (cannon) | མེ་སྒྱོགས་ | *me-gyok.* |
| Mortification (shame) | ངོ་ཚ་ | *ngo-tsha.* |
| Mortified, to feel | ངོ་ཚ་བ་ | *ngo-tsha-wa* |
| Do. *hon.* | ཐུགས་ངོ་ཚ་བ་ | *thu-ngo tsha-wa.* |
| Mosquito | དུག་སྦྲང་ | *t́uk-drang.* |
| Most | མང་ཤོས་ | *mang-shö.* |
| Most part, for the | ཕལ་ཆེར་ | *phe-chher.* |
| Moth | ཕྱེ་འདྲེན་མ་ | *chhem-drem-ma.* |
| Mother | ཨ་མ་ | *a-ma.* |
| Do. *hon.* | ཡུམ་སྐུ་གཞོགས་ | *yum-ku-sḱo.* |
| Do. *h. hon.* | ལྷ་ཡུམ་སྐུ་གཞོགས་ | *hla-yum ku-sḱo* |
| Do. (of Dalai and Tashi Lamas) | རྒྱལ་ཡུམ་སྐུ་གཞོགས་ | *gye-yum ku-sḱo.* |
| Mother of pearl | ཉ་ཕྱིས་ | *nyaṕ-chhi.* |
| Motive | དོན་དག་ | *t́ön-t́a.* |
| Do. *hon.* | སྐུ་དོན་ | *ku-tön.* |
| Mould (for shaping) | པར་ | *par.* |

| | | |
|---|---|---|
| Mouldy, to be | ཧམ་པ་རྒྱབ་པ་ | *ham-pa gyaṗ-pa.* |
| Mound | ས་ཕུང་ | *sa-phung.* |
| Mount for photograph | པར་གྱི་རྒྱབ་ཤ་ཤོག་བུ་ | *par-kyi gyaṗ-sha shok-ku.* |
| Mount, to (a horse, &c.) | ཞོན་པ་ | *sKöm-pa.* |
| Do. *hon.* | འཆིབ་པ་ | *chhiṗ-pa.* |
| Mount, to (rise) | ལང་བ་ | *lang-wa.* |
| Do. *hon.* | བཞང་བ་ (བཞེང་བ་) | *sKang-wa.* |
| Do. *h. hon.* | སྐུ་བཞང་ (བཞེང་) གནང་བ་ | *ku-sKang nang-wa.* |
| Mount, to (climb) | འཛེག་པ་ (འཛེག་པ་) | *dzaK-pa.* |
| Do. *hon.* | འཛེག་ག་ (འཛེག་པ་) གནང་བ་ | *dzaK-Ka nang-wa.* |
| Mountain | རི་ | *ri.* |
| Do. snowy | གངས་རི་ | *Kang-ri.* |
| Mountain-pass | ལ་ | *la.* |
| Mourn, to | སྡུག་བསྔལ་བྱེད་པ། མྱ་ངན་བྱེད་པ་ | *du-nge cKe-pa; nye-ngen cKe-pa.* |
| Do. *hon.* | ཐུགས་ངན་གནང་བ་ | *thu-ngen nang-wa.* |
| Mouse | ཙི་ཙི་ | *tsi-tsi.* |
| Moustache | ཨ་ར་ | *a-ra.* |
| Do. *hon.* | ཞལ་ར་ | *sKe-ra.* |

| | | |
|---|---|---|
| Mouth | ཁ་ | *kha.* |
| Do. *hon.* | ཞལ་ | *she.* |
| Mouthful | ཁམ་རྡོག་ཅིག་ | *kham-do-chi.* |
| Move, to (go) | འགྲོ་བ་ | *dro-wa.* |
| Do. *hon.* | ཕེབ་པ། ཐམས་པ་ | *phe-pa; the-pa.* |
| Do. *h. hon.* | འཆིབ་རྒྱུ་གནང་བ་ | *chhip-gyu nang-wa* |
| Move, to (persuade) | བསླབ་བྱ་བྱེད་པ་ | *lap-cha che-pa.* |
| Do. *hon.* | བཀའ་སློབ་གནང་བ་ | *ka-lop nang-wa.* |
| Mow, to | རྔ་བ་ | *nga-wa.* |
| Do. *hon.* | རྔ་བ་གནང་བ་ | *nga-wa nang-wa.* |
| Much (many) | མང་པོ་ | *mang po.* |
| Do. (very many) | གཡོ་མ་སུ་ | *yo-ma-su.* |
| Much, too | ལྷག་པ། ལྷག་མ་ | *hlak-pa; hla-ma.* |
| Much, very | ཧ་ཅང་མང་པོ་ | *ha-chang mang-po.* |
| Mud | འདམ། རྫབ་ | *dam; dzap.* |
| Muddy (of water) | རྙོག་པོ་ | *nyok-po.* |
| Muhammadan | ཁ་ཆེ་ | *kha-chhe.* |
| Mule | དྲེ་ | *tre.* |
| Mule, baggage | ཁལ་དྲེ་ | *khe-tre.* |
| Mule, riding | ཞོན་དྲེ་ | *shön-tre.* |

| | | |
|---|---|---|
| Mule, riding, *hon.* | ཆིབས་དྲེ་ | *chhip-ťre.* |
| Muleteer | དྲེལ་པ་ | *ťre-pa.* |
| Multitude (of men) | མི་ཚོགས་ | *mi-tsho.* |
| Mumps | འགྲམ་པ་སྐྲང་བ་ | *dram-pa trang-wa.* |
| Murder, to | བསད་པ་ (གསོད་པ་) | *se-pa.* |
| Do. *hon.* (*inf.* to *sup.*) | བཀྲོངས་པ་ | *trong-pa.* |
| Do. *hon.* (between two of high position) | བཀྲོངས་ང་ (པ་) གནང་བ་ | *trong-nga nang-wa.* |
| Murderer | མི་བསད་མཁན་ | *mi-se-khen.* |
| Murky, to become (from clouds) | འཐིབས་པ་ | *thip-pa.* |
| Muscle | རྩ་ | *tsa.* |
| Muse, to (meditate) | བསམ་པ་ | *sam-pa.* |
| Do. *hon.* | དགོངས་པ་ | *gong-pa.* |
| Mushroom (two kinds) | དཀར་ཤ། སེར་ཤ་ | *ka-sha ; se-sha.* |
| Musk | གླ་རྩི་ | *la-tsi.* |
| Musk-deer | གླ་བ་ | *la-wa.* |
| Do. the young one of a | གླ་ཕྲུག་ | *la-thru.* |
| Musket | མེ་མདའ་ | *men-da.* |
| Musket-ball | རྡེའུ་ | *di-u.* |

| | | |
|---|---|---|
| Mussalman | ཁ་ཆེ་ | *kha-chhe.* |
| Must, *v.i.* | དགོ་བ་ (དགོས་པ་) | *go-wa.* |
| Mustard | པེ་གང་ | *pe-kang.* |
| Muster, to, *v.i.* | འཚོགས་པ། འཛོམས་པ་ | *tshok-pa ; dzom-pa.* |
| Do. *hon.* | ལྷན་རྒྱས་གནང་བ་ | *hlen-gye nang-wa.* |
| Musty, to be | ཧམ་པ་རྒྱབ་པ་ | *ham-pa gyap-pa.* |
| Mute, *s.* (dumb person) | ལྐུགས་པ་ | *kuk-pa.* |
| Mute, to be (silent) | ཁ་ཁ་བསྡད་ (སྡོད་) པ་ | *kha-kha de-pa.* |
| Do. *hon.* | ཞལ་རགས་བཞུགས་པ་ | *ske-ra sku-pa.* |
| Mutton | ལུག་ཤ་ | *luk-sha.* |
| My | ངའི་ | *nge.* |
| Myrabolam | ཨ་རུ་ | *a-ru.* |
| Myrrh | ཨ་ག་རུ་ | *a-ka-ru.* |
| Myself | ང་རང་ | *nga-rang.* |
| Mystified, to be | མགོ་འཐོམས་པ་ | *go-thom-pa.* |
| Do. *hon.* | དབུ་འཐོམས་པ་གནང་བ་ | *u-thom-pa nang-wa.* |
| Myth | སྒྲུང་ | *drum.* |

# N

| | | |
|---|---|---|
| Nail | གཟེར་ | *śer.* |
| Do. finger | ལག་པའི་སེན་མོ་ | *laḱ-pe se-mo.* |
| Do. *hon.* | ཕྱག་སེན་ | *chhaḱ-se.* |
| Nail, toe | རྐང་པའི་སེན་མོ་ | *kang-pe se-mo.* |
| Do. *hon.* | ཞབས་སེན་ | *shaṕ-se.* |
| Nail, iron | ལྕགས་གཟེར་ | *chaḱ-śer.* |
| Do. wooden | ཕུར་པ་ | *phur-pa.* |
| Nail, to | ལྕགས་གཟེར་རྒྱབ་པ་ | *chaḱ-śer gyaṕ-pa.* |
| Do. *hon.* | ལྕགས་གཟེར་སྐྱོན་པ་ | *chaḱ-śer kyöm-pa.* |
| Naked | དམར་ཧྲང་ང་ | *mar-hrang-nga.* |
| Name | མིང་ | *ming.* |
| Do. *hon.* | མཚན་ | *tshen.* |
| Name, to | མིང་འདོགས་པ་ | *ming doḱ-pa.* |
| Do. *hon.* | མཚན་འདོགས་པ་ | *tshen doḱ-pa.* |
| Nap (sleep) | གཉིད་ | *nyi.* |
| Do. *hon.* | མཉལ་ (མནལ་) | *nye.* |
| Napkin | པང་ཁེབས་ | *pang-kheṕ.* |
| Do. *hon.* | སྐུ་ཁེབས་ | *ku-kheṕ.* |
| Narrate, to | བཤད་པ་ | *she-pa.* |

| | | |
|---|---|---|
| Narrate, to, *hon.* | གསུང་བ་ | *sung-wa.* |
| Narrative | རྒྱུ་རྐྱེན། ལོ་རྒྱུས་ | *gyu-kyen; lo-gyü.* |
| Narrow | དོག་པོ། སྦུགས་སྦུབ་དོག་པོ་ | *ťok-po; bu-su ťok-po.* |
| Nasty | སྐྱུག་བྲོ་པོ་ | *kyuk-ťro-po.* |
| Nation | མི་བརྒྱུད། རིགས་བརྒྱུད་ | *mi-gyü; ri-gyü.* |
| Native land | སྐྱེ་ས་ | *kye-sa.* |
| Do. *hon.* | འཁྲུངས་ས་ | *thrung-sa.* |
| Nature (species) | བརྒྱུད་ | *gyü.* |
| Do. of different | སྣ་ཚོགས་ | *na-tsho.* |
| Naught (cipher) | ཀླད་སྐོར་ | *le-kor.* |
| Naughty | ངན་པ་ | *ngem-pa.* |
| Nauseating | སྐྱུག་བྲོ་པོ་ | *kyuk-ťro-po.* |
| Navel | ལྟེ་ (ལྟེ་བ་) | *te.* |
| Near, *adj.* | ཉེ་པོ། ཐག་ཉེ་པོ། ཚར། འགྲམ་ལ་ | *nye-po; tha-nye-po; tsa; dram-la.* |
| Nearly (almost) | ཧ་ལམ། ག་ཆེན་ | *ha-lam; ka-chhen.* |
| Neat | འདྲ་ཆགས་པོ་ | *dra-chhak-po.* |
| Necessary | དགོས་པ་ | *gö-pa.* |
| Necessity | དགོས་པ། མཁོ་ཆེ་ | *gö-pa; kho-chhe* |
| Neck | སྐེ་ | *ke.* |

| | | |
|---|---|---|
| Neck, *hon.* | མགུལ་ | *gü.* |
| Neck, back of | མཇིང་པ་ | *jing-pa.* |
| Do. *hon.* | མགུལ་མཇིང་ | *gü-jing.* |
| Necklace | སྐེ་རྒྱན་ | *ke-gyen.* |
| Do. *hon.* | མགུལ་རྒྱན་ | *gü-gyen.* |
| Nectar | བདུད་རྩི་ | *dü-tsi.* |
| Need, to (require) | དགོས་པ་ | *gö-pa.* |
| Do. *hon.* | ཐུགས་དགོས་པ་ | *thu-gö-pa.* |
| Need, *s.* (necessity) | དགོས་པ། མཁོ་ཆེ་ | *gö-pa; kho-chhe.* |
| Needful | དགོས་པ་ | *gö-pa.* |
| Needfulness | དགོས་པ། མཁོ་ཆེ་ | *gö-pa; kho-chhe.* |
| Needle | ཁབ་ | *khaṕ.* |
| Do. *hon.* | མགུལ་ཁབ་ | *gü-khaṕ.* |
| Needle, eye of | ཁབ་མིག་ | *khaṕ-mi.* |
| Do. *hon.* | མགུལ་ཁབ་མིག་ | *gü-khaṕ-mi.* |
| Needle, point of | ཁབ་རྩེ་ | *khaṕ-tse.* |
| Do. *hon.* | མགུལ་ཁབ་རྩེ་ | *gü-khaṕ-tse.* |
| Needy (poor) | སྐྱོ་པོ། སྙེམས་ཆུང་ (ཉམས་ཆུང་) | *kyo-po; nyem-chhung.* |
| Nefarious | ངན་པོ་ | *ngem-po.* |

| | | |
|---|---|---|
| Nefarious, *hon.* | ཐུགས་ངན་པོ་ | *thu ngem-po.* |
| Negotiate, to | འགྲིག་ཆགས་བྱེད་པ་ | *drik-chha che-pa.* |
| Do. *hon.* | འགྲིག་ཆགས་གནང་བ་ | *drik-chha nang-wa.* |
| Negotiation | བཀའ་མོལ། འགྲིག་ཆགས་ | *ka-mön ; drik-chha.* |
| Neigh, to | རྟ་སྐད་རྒྱབ་པ་ | *ta-ke gyaṕ-pa.* |
| Neighbour | ཁྱིམ་མཚེས་ | *khyim-tshe.* |
| Neighbourhood | ཉེ་འཁོར་ | *nye-khor.* |
| Nepal | བལ་ཡུལ་ | *ṕe-yü.* |
| Nepalese | བལ་པོ་ | *ṕe-po.* |
| Nephew | ཚ་བོ་ | *tsha-wo.* |
| Nerve | ཆུ་རྒྱུས་ | *chhu-gyü.* |
| Nest | ཚང་ | *tshang.* |
| Net | རྒྱ། དྲ་བ་ | *gya ; t́ra-a.* |
| Do. fish | ཉ་དོལ། ཉ་རྒྱ་ | *nya-tö ; nya-gya.* |
| Nettle, *s.* | ཟྭ་པོ་ | *śa-po.* |
| Nettle, to (irritate) | ཁོང་ཁྲོ་སློང་བ་ | *khong-thro lang-wa.* |
| Do. *hon.* | དགོངས་པ་དཀྲུག་པ་ | *gong-pa truk-pa.* |
| Neuralgia | ཡ་མ་ | *ya-ma.* |
| Never | རྩ་ནས་...མ། མ་ནས་...མ་ | *tsa-ne...ma ; ma-ne...ma.* |
| Never mind! | ཨའུ་ཚེ་ | *a-u-tse.* |

| | | |
|---|---|---|
| Nevertheless | ཡིན་ནས། ཡིན་ཀྱང་། ཡིན་ན་ཡང་ | *yin-ne ; yin-kyang ; yin-na-yang.* |
| New | གསར་པ་ | *sa-pa.* |
| New year | ལོ་གསར་ | *lo-sa.* |
| News | གནས་ཚུལ། གསར་འགྱུར་ | *ne-tshü ; sang-gyu.* |
| Newspaper | གསར་འགྱུར་ཤོག་གུ་ | *sang-gyu shok-ku.* |
| Next (at the side of) | ཙར། འགྲམ་ལ་ | *tsa ; dram-la.* |
| Next (afterwards) | གཤུག་ལ། རྗེས་ལ་ | *sku-la ; je-la.* |
| Nice (accurate) | ཁྲིག་ཁྲིག། ཏེན་ཏེན་ | *thrik-thrik ; ten-ten.* |
| Nice (in flavour) | ཞིམ་པོ་ | *skim-po.* |
| Do. *hon.* | སྤྲོ་པོ་ | *tro-po.* |
| Nice (pleasant) | དར་པོ། ཡག་པོ་ | *ťar-po ; yak-po.* |
| Nickname | མིང་འདོགས། མིང་ངན་ | *ming-do ; ming-ngen.* |
| Niece | ཚ་མོ་ | *tsha-mo.* |
| Niggardly | ལག་པ་དམ་པོ་ | *lak-pa ťam-po.* |
| Do. *hon.* | ཕྱག་དམ་པོ་ | *chha ťam-po.* |
| Nigh | ཉེ་པོ། ཐག་ཉེ་པོ། ཙར། འགྲམ་ལ་ | *nye-po ; tha-nye-po ; tsa ; dram-la.* |
| Night | མཚན། དགོངས་མོ་ | *tshen ; gong-mo.* |
| Night, last | མདང་དགོངས་ | *dang-gong.* |

| | | |
|---|---|---|
| Night, in the middle of the | ནམ་ནག་གུང་། མཚན་ནག་གུང་ | *nam-na ḱung; tshen-na-ḱung.* |
| Night-attack, to make | མཚན་ཐིག་ (མཚན་དེབ་) རྒྱབ་པ་ | *tshen-thi gyaṕ-pa.* |
| Nimble | ཧུར་པོ། མགྱོགས་པོ་ | *hur-po; gyok-po.* |
| Do. *hon.* | རྩོལ་པོ་ | *tsö-po.* |
| Nine | དགུ་ | *gu.* |
| Nineteen | བཅུ་དགུ་ | *chu-gu.* |
| Nineteenth | བཅུ་དགུ་པ་ | *chu-gu-pa.* |
| Ninetieth | དགུ་བཅུ་པ་ | *guṕ-chu-pa.* |
| Ninety | དགུ་བཅུ་ཐམ་པ་ | *guṕ-chu tham-pa.* |
| Ninny | ལྐུགས་པ། གླེན་པ། | *ḱuk-pa; lem-pa.* |
| Ninth | དགུ་པ་ | *gu-pa.* |
| Nipple (of breast) | འོ་མའི་རྩེ། ནུ་སོར་ | *o-me-tse; nu-sor.* |
| Do. *hon.* | ཆབ་ཞོའི་རྩེ་ | *chhaṕ-sḱö-tse.* |
| Noble, *s.* | སྐུ་དྲག་ | *ku-ťra.* |
| Do. *adj.* (illustrious) | སྐད་གྲགས་ཆེན་པོ་ | *ḱe-ťra chhem-po.* |
| Do. *hon.* | མཚན་སྙན་གྲགས་ཆེན་པོ་ | *tshen-nyen-ťra chhem-po.* |
| Nobleman | སྐུ་དྲག་ | *ku-ťra.* |
| Nobody | སུ་ཡང་ w. neg. | *su-yang* (w. neg.) |
| Nod, to | མགོ་འཇོག་འཇོག་བྱེད་པ་ | *go jok-jok ćhe-pa.* |

| | | |
|---|---|---|
| Nod, to, *hon.* | དབུ་འཇོག་འཇོག་གནང་བ་ | *u jok-jok nang-wa.* |
| Noise | ཅུར་སྒྲ་ | *u-dra.* |
| Noise, to make a | ཅུར་སྒྲ་རྒྱབ་པ་ | *u-dra gyap-pa.* |
| Do. *hon.* | ཅུར་སྒྲ་སྐྱོན་པ་ | *u-dra kyöm-pa.* |
| Noisome | སྐྱུག་བྲོ་པོ་ | *kyuk-tro-po.* |
| Nomad | འབྲོག་པ་ | *drok-pa.* |
| Nominate, to | སྐོ་བ་ | *ko-wa.* |
| Do. *hon.* | སྐོ་བ་གནང་བ་ | *ko-wa nang-wa.* |
| None (nobody) | སུ་ཡང་ w. neg. | *su-yang* (w. neg.) |
| Do. (nothing) | ག་གས་ (གང་ཡང་) w. neg. | *ka-ke* (w. neg.) |
| Nonsensical | དོན་མེད་ | *tön-me.* |
| Nook | ཟུར་ | *sur.* |
| Noon | ཉིན་གུང་ | *nyin-kung.* |
| Noose | ཞགས་པ་ | *skak-pa.* |
| North | བྱང་ | *ckang.* |
| Northward | བྱང་ངོས། བྱང་ཕྱོགས་ | *ckang-ngö ; ckang-chho.* |
| Nose | སྣ་ཁུག་ (སྣ་) | *na-khu.* |
| Do. *hon.* | ཤངས་ | *shang.* |
| Nostril | སྣ་ཁུག་གི་ཨི་ཁང་ (སྣ་ཁུང་) | *na-khu-ki i-khang.* |

| | | |
|---|---|---|
| Nostril, *hon.* | ཤངས་ཀྱི་ཨི་ཁང་ (ཤངས་ཁུང་) | *shang-kyi i-khang.* |
| Not | མ། མི་ | *ma ; mi.* |
| Not at all | རྩ་ནས་ w. neg. | *tsa-ne* (w. neg.) |
| Notable (celebrated) | སྙན་གྲགས་ཆེན་པོ་ | *nyen-ťra chhem-po.* |
| Do. *hon.* | མཚན་སྙན་གྲགས་ཆེན་པོ་ | *tshen nyen-ťra chhem-po.* |
| Note, *s.* (letter) | ཡི་གེ་ | *yi-ge.* |
| Do. *hon.* | ཕྱག་བྲིས་ | *chha-ri.* |
| Note, *s.* (reputation) | སྐད་གྲགས་ | *ke-ťra.* |
| Do. *hon.* | སྙན་གྲགས་ | *nyen-ťra.* |
| Note, to (observe) | མིག་ལྟ་བ་ | *mik-ta-wa.* |
| Do. *hon.* | གཟིགས་པ་ | *śi-pa.* |
| Noted | སྐད་གྲགས་ཆེན་པོ་ | *ke-ťra chhem-po.* |
| Do. *hon.* | མཚན་སྙན་གྲགས་ཆེན་པོ་ | *tshen-nyen-ťra chhem-po.* |
| Nothing | ག་གས་ (གང་ཡང་) w. neg. | *ka-ke* (w. neg.) |
| Notice | ལན་ (ལོན་) | *len.* |
| Notice, to (mention) | ལབ་པ་ | *lap-pa.* |
| Do. *hon.* | གསུང་བ་ | *sung-wa.* |
| Notice, to (see) | མིག་ལྟ་བ་ | *mik-ta-wa.* |
| Do. *hon.* | གཟིགས་པ་ | *śi-pa.* |

| | | |
|---|---|---|
| Notification (of Government) | བཀའ་རྒྱ་ | *ka-gya.* |
| Do. (of official) | བསྐུལ་གདམ་ | *kü-tam.* |
| Notion (opinion) | བསམ་པ་ | *sam-pa.* |
| Do. *hon.* | ཐུགས་སེམས་ | *thu-sem.* |
| Notorious | སྐད་གྲགས་ཆེན་པོ་ | *ke-ťra chhem-po.* |
| Notwithstanding | ཡིན་ནས། ཡིན་ཀྱང་། ཡིན་ན་ཡང་ | *yin-ne ; yin-kyang ; yin-na-yang.* |
| Noun | མིང་སྒྲ་ | *ming-dra.* |
| Nourish, to | གསོ་བ་ | *so-wa.* |
| Do. *hon.* | གསོ་བ་གནང་བ་ | *so-wa nang-wa.* |
| Novel (new) | གསར་པ་ | *sa-pa.* |
| Novice, religious | དགེ་ཚུལ་ | *ge-tshü.* |
| Now (at this time) | ད་ལྟ་ | *ťan-da.* |
| Now (well, yes) | འོ་ན་ | *o-na.* |
| Now-a-days | དེ་རིང་སང་། དེང་སང་ | *ťe-ring-sang ; ťeng-sang.* |
| Now and then | མཚམས་མཚམས་ | *tsham-tsham.* |
| Nowhere | ག་པ་···མ། ག་རེ་···མ་ | *ǩa-pa...ma ; ǩa-re...ma.* |
| Noxious | སྐྱུག་བྲོ་པོ་ | *kyuǩ-ťro-po.* |
| Nude | དམར་ཧྲང་ང་ | *mar-hrang-nga.* |
| Nullify, to | མེད་པར་བཟོ་བ་ | *me-pa ŝo-wa.* |

| | | |
|---|---|---|
| Nullify, to, *hon.* | མེད་པར་བཟོ་བ་གནང་བ་ | *me-pa śo-wa nang-wa.* |
| Number (numeral) | གྲངས་ཀ། ཨང་ཀི་ | *ťrang-ka; ang-ki.* |
| Do. amount | མང་ཉུང་ | *mang-nyung.* |
| Number, to | གྲངས་ཀ་རྒྱབ་པ་ | *ťrang-ka gyaṕ-pa.* |
| Do. *hon.* | ཕྱགས་གྲངས་སྐྱོན་པ་ | *ja-ťrang kyöm-pa.* |
| Numberless | གྲངས་མེད་ | *ťrang-me.* |
| Numerous | མང་པོ་ | *mang-po.* |
| Numerous, very | གཡོ་མ་སུ་ | *yo-ma-su.* |
| Nun | ཨ་ནི | *a-ni.* |
| Do. *hon.* | རྗེ་བཙུན་ | *je-tsün.* |
| Nuptials | ཆང་ས་ | *chhang-sa.* |
| Do. *hon.* | འཁྲུང་ས་ | *thrung-sa.* |
| Nurse (of children) | དབུ་རྫི། བུ་རྫི་ | *u-dzi; ṕu-dzi.* |
| Do. *hon.* | ཞལ་ལྟ་མ་ | *sḱe-ta-ma.* |
| Nurture, to | གསོ་བ་ | *so-wa.* |
| Do. *hon.* | གསོ་བ་གནང་བ་ | *so-wa nang-wa.* |
| Nutmeg | ཛ་ཏི་ | *dza-ti.* |
| Nutrition | ཁ་ལག། ལྟོ་ | *kha-la; to.* |
| Do. *hon.* | ཞལ་ལག་ | *sḱe-la.* |

# O

| | | |
|---|---|---|
| Oar | གྲུ་སྐྱ་ | *ṫru-kya.* |
| Oath | མནའ་ | *na.* |
| Do. *hon.* | དབུ་མནའ་ | *u-na.* |
| Oath, to take an | མནའ་སྐྱེལ་བ་ | *na kyel-wa.* |
| Do. *hon.* | དབུ་མནའ་བཞེས་པ་ | *u-na sḱe-pa.* |
| Obdurate, to be (hard-hearted) | སྙིང་རྗེ་མེད་པ་ | *nying-je me-pa.* |
| Do. *hon.* | ཐུགས་རྗེ་མེད་པ་ | *thuḱ-je me-pa.* |
| Obdurate, to be (obstinate) | གྱོང་པོ་ | *ḱyong-po.* |
| Obedient | ཁ་ལ་ཉན་པོ་ | *kha-la nyem-po.* |
| Do. *hon.* | ཞལ་ལ་གསན་པོ་ | *sḱe-la sem-po.* |
| Obeisance, to make (by kneeling) | ཕྱག་འཚལ་བ་ | *chha-tshe-wa.* |
| Do. *hon.* | སྐུ་ཕྱག་འཚལ་ལ་(བ་)གནང་བ་ | *ku-chha tshe-la nang-wa.* |
| Obeisance, to make (by removing hat) | ཇབ་མཇལ་བྱེད་པ་ | *dam-jel cḱe-pa.* |
| Do. *hon.* | ཇབ་མཇལ་གནང་བ་ | *dam-jel nang-wa.* |
| Obeisance, to make (by raising hand) | ཕྱག་འབུལ་ཞུ་བ་ | *chham-bü sḱu-wa.* |
| Do. *hon.* | ཕྱག་འབུལ་ཞུ་བ་གནང་བ་ | *chham-bü sḱu-a nang-wa.* |
| Obeisance, to make (by prostration) | ཕྱག་འཚལ་བ་ | *chha-tshe-wa.* |

| | | |
|---|---|---|
| Obeisance, to make (by prostration), *hon.* | སྐུ་ཕྱག་འཚལ་བ་ | *ku-chha tshe-wa.* |
| Obese | ཤ་རྒྱགས་པ་ | *sha-gyak-pa.* |
| Do. *hon.* | སྐུ་ཤ་འབྱོར་པོ་ | *ku-sha jor-po.* |
| Obey, to | ཁ་ལ་ཉན་པ་ | *kha-la nyem-pa.* |
| Do. *hon.* | ཞལ་ལ་གསན་པ་ | *sh̓e-la sem-pa.* |
| Obey laws, to | ཁྲིམས་འཁྱེར་བ། ཁྲིམས་འཁུར་བ་ | *thrim khyer-wa; thrim khur-wa.* |
| Object (intention) | དོན་དག་ | *t̓ön-t̓a.* |
| Do. *hon.* | སྐུ་དོན་ | *ku-t̓ön* |
| Object, to | བཀག་པ་ (འགེགས་པ་) | *kak-pa.* |
| Do. *hon.* | བཀག་ཀ་ (འགེགས་པ་) གནང་བ་ | *kak-k̓a nang-wa.* |
| Obliged, to be (thankful) | དྲིན་དྲན་པ་ | *t̓rin t̓rem-pa.* |
| Do. *hon.* | དྲིན་དྲན་པ་གནང་བ་ | *t̓rin t̓rem-pa nang-wa.* |
| Do. *inf.* to *sup.* | བཀའ་དྲིན་དྲན་པ་ | *ka-t̓rin t̓rem-pa* |
| Obliging | དྲིན་ཆེན་པོ་ | *t̓rin chhem-po.* |
| Do. *hon.* | བཀའ་དྲིན་ཆེན་པོ་ | *ka-t̓rin chhem-po.* |
| Oblique | ཀྱོག་ཀྱོག་ | *kyok-kyo.* |
| Obliterate, to | སུབ་པ་ | *sup-pa.* |

| | | |
|---|---|---|
| Obliterate, to, *hon.* | སྦུབ་པ་གནང་བ་ | *sup-pa nang-wa.* |
| Obscure (dark) | ནག་པོ་ | *nak-po.* |
| Do. (undefined) | ཏན་པོ་མེད་པ་ | *tem-po me-pa.* |
| Obscurity (darkness) | མུན་ནག་ | *min-na.* |
| Observe, to | མིག་ལྟ་བ་ | *mik-ta-wa.* |
| Do. *hon.* | གཟིགས་པ་ | *śi-pa.* |
| Obstacle | བཀག་ཆ་ | *kak-chha.* |
| Obstinate | གྱོང་པོ་ | *kyong-po.* |
| Obstruct, to | བཀག་པ་ (འགེགས་པ་) | *kak pa.* |
| Do. *hon.* | བཀག་ག་ (འགེགས་པ་) གནང་བ་ | *kak-ka nang-wa.* |
| Obtain, to | འབྱོར་བ། ཐོབ་པ་ | *jor wa ; thop-pa.* |
| Do. *hon.* | ཕྱག་འབྱོར་ཡོང་བ་ | *chhan-jor yong-wa.* |
| Obtuse (dull) | ལྐུགས་པ། གླེན་པ་ | *kuk-pa ; lem-pa.* |
| Occasion (cause) | ཀྱེན། རྒྱུ་ཀྱེན་ | *kyen ; gyu-kyen.* |
| Do. (opportunity) | ཐབས་ | *thap.* |
| Do. (time) | དུས། དུས་ཚོད་ | *tü ; tü-tshö.* |
| Occasionally | མཚམས་མཚམས་ | *tsham-tsham.* |
| Do. *hon.* | ཐུགས་སངས་ཐུགས་སངས་ལ་ | *thuk-sang thuk-sang la.* |
| Occupation | ལས་ཀ་ | *le-ka.* |

| | | |
|---|---|---|
| Occupation, *hon.* | ཕྱག་ལས་ | *chha-le.* |
| Occupied with work, to be | བྲེལ་བ་ཡོད་པ་ | *t́re-wa yö-pa.* |
| Do. *hon.* | ཐུགས་བྲེལ་ཡོད་པ་ | *thu-t́re yö-pa.* |
| Occur, to | ཡོང་བ་ | *yong-wa.* |
| Ocean | རྒྱ་མཚོ་ | *gyam-tsho.* |
| O'clock | ཆུ་ཚོད་ | *chhu-tshö.* |
| Odd (not a pair) | ཡ་གཅིག་ | *ya-chi.* |
| Odious | སྐྱུག་བྲོ་པོ་ | *kyuk-t́ro-po.* |
| Odour | དྲི་མ་ | *t́ri-ma.* |
| Odour, to have | དྲི་མ་ཁ་བ་ | *t́ri-ma kha-wa.* |
| Of, *post.* | གི། ཀྱི། གྱི་ | *ki ; kyi ; ḱyi.* |
| Off, *adv.* | ནས་ | *ne.* |
| Offal | བཙོག་པ་ | *tsok-pa.* |
| Offence (anger) | ཚིག་པ། ཁོང་ཁྲོ་ | *tshik-pa ; khong-thro.* |
| Do. (insult) | སྨད་ར་ | *me-ra.* |
| Do. (moral fault) | ཉེས་པ་ | *nye-pa.* |
| Offence, to commit | ཉེས་པ་བསག་ (གསོག་) པ་ | *nye-pa sak-pa.* |
| Do. *hon.* | སྐུ་སྡིག་བསག་ག་ (གསོག་པ་) གནང་བ་ | *ku-di sak-ka-nang-wa.* |
| Offence, to give | ཁོང་ཁྲོ་སློང་བ་ | *khong-thro lang-wa.* |

| | | |
|---|---|---|
| Offence, to give, *hon.* | དགོངས་པ་དཀྲུག་པ་ | *gong-pa truk-pa.* |
| Offence, to take | འཚེར་བ་ | *tsher-wa.* |
| Do. *hon.* | ཐུགས་འཚེར་གནང་བ་ | *thu-tsher nang-wa.* |
| Offend, to | དམའ་འབེབས་བྱེད་པ་ | *mam-be cKe-pa.* |
| Do. *hon.* | དམའ་འབེབས་གནང་བ་ | *mam-be nang-wa.* |
| Offensive (disgusting) | སྐྱུག་བྲོ་པོ་ | *kyuk-tro-po.* |
| Do. (insolent) | འཛིང་པ་སྦོམ་པོ། ཀྱོང་པོ་ | *jing-pa bom-po; kyong-po.* |
| Offer, to | སྟེར་བ་ | *ter-wa.* |
| Do. *hon.* | གནང་བ་ | *nang-wa.* |
| Do. *inf.* to *sup.* | ཕུལ་བ་ (འབུལ་བ་) | *phü-wa.* |
| Offering (presents) | འབུལ་བ་ | *bül-wa.* |
| Do. (sacrifice) | མཆོད་པ་ | *chhö-pa.* |
| Office (employment) | ལས་ཀ་ | *le-ka.* |
| Do. *hon.* | ཕྱག་ལས་ | *chha-le.* |
| Office-room | ཡིག་ཚང་ | *yik-tshang.* |
| Officer | དཔོན་པོ་ | *pöm-po.* |
| Official | དཔོན་པོ་ | *pöm-po.* |
| Officiate, to | ལས་ཚབ་བྱེད་པ་ | *le-tshap cKe-pa.* |
| Do. *hon.* | སྐུ་ཚབ་གནང་བ་ | *ku-tshap nang-wa.* |
| Offspring | ཕྲུ་གུ་ | *pu-gu.* |

| | | |
|---|---|---|
| Often | ཚར་མང་པོ་ | *tshar mang-po.* |
| Oh ! | ཨ་ཁ་ཁ་ | *a-kha-kha.* |
| Oil | སྣུམ་ | *num.* |
| Do. (kerosene) | ས་སྣུམ་ | *sa-num.* |
| Ointment | བྱུགས་པ་ | *cḱuk-pa.* |
| Old (of persons and animals) | རྒ་པུ་ (རྒད་པོ་) | *ga-pu.* |
| Old man | རྒ་པུ་ (རྒད་པོ་) | *ga-pu.* |
| Do. *hon.* | བགྲེས་པོ་ | *dre-po.* |
| Old woman | རྒ་མུ་ (རྒད་མོ་) | *ga-mu.* |
| Do. *hon.* | བགྲེས་མོ་ | *dre-mo.* |
| Old (of things) | རྙིང་པ་ | *nying-pa.* |
| Old, to grow | རྒས་པ་ | *ge-pa.* |
| Do. *hon.* | བགྲེས་པ་ | *dre-pa.* |
| Omen | རྟེན་འབྲེལ་ | *tem-dre.* |
| Omit, to | སུབ་པ་ | *suṕ-pa.* |
| Do. *hon.* | སུབ་པ་གནང་བ་ | *suṕ-pa nang-wa.* |
| On | སྒང་ལ། སྟེང་ལ་ | *gang-la ; teng-la.* |
| Once | ཚར་གཅིག། ཐེངས་གཅིག་ | *tshar-chi ; theng-chi.* |
| Once, at (immediately) | ལམ་སང་ | *lam-sang.* |

| | | |
|---|---|---|
| Once more | ད་འདོ་ (ད་འདོས་) ཚར་གཅིག། ད་རུང་ཚར་གཅིག་ | *ťan-ťo tshar-chi ; ťa-rung tshar-chi.* |
| One | གཅིག་ | *chi.* |
| One (in the sense of one full or complete) | གང་ | *ǩang.* |
| One-eyed | ཞར་ར་ (ཞར་བ།) མིག་ཞར་ | *sǩar-ra ; mik-sǩar.* |
| Onion | བཙོང་ | *tsong.* |
| Only, *adj.* (alone) | གཅིག་པོ་ | *chiǩ-po.* |
| Do. *adv.* (entirely) | ཤ་སྟག་ | *sha-ta.* |
| Onward (forward) | སྔེན་ལ་ (སྔོན་ལ་) | *ngen-la.* |
| Open, to | ཁ་ཕྱེས་ (འབྱེད་) པ་ | *ǩha-chhe-pa.* |
| Do. *hon.* | ཁ་ཕྱེས་ (འབྱེད་) པ་གནང་བ་ | *ǩha-chhe-pa nang wa.* |
| Open (frank) | དྲང་པོ་ | *ťrang-po.* |
| Do. *hon.* | ཐུགས་རྒྱུ་དྲང་པོ་ | *thu-gyu ťrang-po.* |
| Opening | ཨི་ཁུང་ | *i-ǩhung.* |
| Openly (frankly) | མ·····གསང་བ་ | *ma...sang-wa.* |
| Operation | གྲིས་བཤག་པ་ | *ťri-shaǩ-pa.* |
| Opinion | བསམ་པ་ | *sam-pa.* |
| Do. *hon.* | ཐུགས་སེམས་ | *thu-sem.* |
| Opium | གཡའ་ཕིན། *Ch.* ཉལ་ཐ་ཁ་ | *ya-phin ; nye-tha-ǩha.* |

| | | |
|---|---|---|
| Opponent | དགྲ་ | *dra.* |
| Opportunity | ཐབས་ | *thaṕ.* |
| Oppose, to (dispute) | རྩོད་པ་རྒྱབ་པ་ | *tsö-pa gyaṕ-pa.* |
| Do. *hon.* | རྩོད་པ་སྐྱོན་པ་ | *tsö-pa kyöm-pa.* |
| Oppose, to (thwart) | བཀག་པ་ (འགེགས་པ་) | *kaḱ-pa.* |
| Do. *hon.* | བཀག་ག་ (འགེགས་ག་) གནང་བ་ | *kaḱ-ka nang-wa.* |
| Opposite (different) | མི་…གཅིག་པ་ | *mi ..chiḱ-pa.* |
| Do. (facing) | ཁ་ཐུག་ལ་ | *kha-thu-la.* |
| Opposite side | ཕར་ཕྱོགས་ | *pha-chho.* |
| Oppress, to (press against) | གནན་པ་ (ནོན་པ་) | *nem-pa.* |
| Do. *hon.* | གནན་ (ནོན་) པ་གནང་བ་ | *nem-pa nang-wa.* |
| Oppress, to (use severely) | སྡུག་པོ་བཏང་ (གཏོང་) བ། བཟོ་བལྟ་བཟོ་བ་ | *duḱ-po tang-wa; śoṕ-ta śo-wa.* |
| Do. *hon.* | སྡུག་པོ་བཏོང་ང་ (བ་) གནང་བ་ | *duḱ-po tong-nga nang wa.* |
| Opthalmia | མིག་ནད་ | *miḱ-ne.* |
| Do. *hon.* | སྤྱན་སྣུང་བ་ | *chen nyung-wa.* |
| Optical deception | མིག་འཁྲུལ་ | *mik-thrü.* |
| Option | ཐང་ | *thang.* |
| Opulent | ཕྱུག་པོ། ཅ་ (ཆ་) ལག་ཆེན་པོ་ | *chhuḱ-po; cha-la chhem-po.* |

| | | |
|---|---|---|
| Opulent, *hon.* | སྐུ་ཅས་ (ཆས་) ཆེན་པོ་ | *ku-che chhem-po.* |
| Or | ཡང་མིན་ན། ཡང་ན་ | *yang-men-na; yang-na.* |
| Oracle (prophecy) | ལུང་བསྟན་ | *lung-ten.* |
| Do. *hon.* | བཀའ་ལུང་ | *ka-lung.* |
| Oracle, to deliver (by beads or dice) | མོ་རྒྱབ་པ་ | *mo-gyap-pa.* |
| Do. *hon.* | ཕྱག་མོ་སྐྱོན་པ་ | *chha-mo kyöm-pa.* |
| Oral | ཁའི་ | *khe.* |
| Orally | ཁ་ནས་ | *kha-ne.* |
| Orange | ཚ་ལུམ་མ་ (པ་) | *tsha-lum-ma.* |
| Orchard | ལྡུམ་ར་ | *dum-ra.* |
| Order, *s.* (command) | བཀའ་ | *ka.* |
| Order (rank) | གོ་ས། གོ་གནས། རིམ་པ་ | *ko-sa; ko-ne; rim-pa.* |
| Order, written (of Government) | བཀའ་རྒྱ་ | *ka-gya.* |
| Do. (of official) | བསྐུལ་གཏམ་ | *kü-tam.* |
| Do. verbal (of official) | བཀའ་ཁྱབ། བཀའ་བཀོད་ | *ka-khyap; ka-kö.* |
| Do. (written judgment in a judicial case). | བཅད་མཚམས། ཁྲ་མ་ | *che-tsham; thra-ma.* |
| Do. (series) | རིམ་པ་ | *rim-pa.* |
| Do. (rank) | གྲལ་ | *tre.* |

| | | |
|---|---|---|
| Order, to | བཀའ་གནང་བ་ | *ka-nang-wa.* |
| Order, to (things from shop, etc.) | མངག་པ་ | *ngaḱ-pa.* |
| Do. *hon.* | བཀའ་མངག་གནང་བ་ | *ka-nga nang-wa.* |
| Order to, in | དོན་ལ་ | *t́ön-la.* |
| Ordinarily | ཕལ་ཆེར་ | *phe-chher.* |
| Ordinary language, *opp.* to *hon.* | ཞེ་ས་མེད་པ་ | *sḱe-sa me-pa.* |
| Ordinary (in quality) | དཀྱུས་མ་ | *kyü-ma.* |
| Orifice | ཨི་ཁུང་ | *i-khung.* |
| Origin | བྱུང་སྟངས་ (འབྱུང་ཁུང་) | *cḱung-tang.* |
| Ornament | རྒྱན་ཆ་ | *gyen-chha.* |
| Do. *hon.* | སྐུ་རྒྱན་ | *ku-gyen.* |
| Orphan | དྭ་ཕྲུག་ | *t́a-thru.* |
| Orthography | དག་ཡིག་ | *t́aḱ-yi.* |
| Ostentatious | ཉམས་དོད་པོ་ | *nyam-t́ö-po.* |
| Do. *hon.* | སྐུ་ཉམས་དོད་པོ་ | *ku-nyam t́ö-po.* |
| Other | གཞན་པ། ཡན་པ་ | *sḱem-pa ; yem-pa.* |
| Otter | སྲམ་ | *hram.* |
| Ought | དགོས་པ་ | *gö-pa* |
| Our | ང་ཚོའི་ | *nga-tshö.* |

| | | |
|---|---|---|
| Out (outside) | ཕྱི་ལོགས་ལ་ | *chhi-lo-la.* |
| Out of | ནས་ | *ne.* |
| Outcry | ཨུར་སྒྲ་ | *u-dra.* |
| Outlet | སྒོ་ | *go.* |
| Outside, *adv.* | ཕྱི་ལོགས་ལ་ | *chhi-lo-la.* |
| Outward | ཕྱིའི་ | *chhi-i.* |
| Oven | ཐབ་ | *thap̓.* |
| Do. *hon.* | གསོལ་ཐབ་ | *sö-thap̓.* |
| Over (above) | ཡ་གེའི་ | *ya-ke.* |
| Do. (more) | ལྷག་ | *hla.* |
| Overbear, to | རྒྱལ་བ། ཀླག་འཁས་པ་ | *gye-wa ; la khe-pa.* |
| Do. *hon.* | རྒྱལ་ར (བ་) གནང་བ། ཀླག་འཁས་ར་ (པ་) གནང་བ་ | *gye-ra nang-wa ; la khe-ra nang-wa.* |
| Overbearing | ཉམས་ཆེན་པོ། ཛ་ཁོག་ཆེན་པོ་ | *nyam-chhem-po ; dza-kho chhem-po.* |
| Overcome, to | རྒྱལ་བ། ཀླག་འཁས་པ་ | *gye-wa ; la khe-pa.* |
| Do. *hon.* | རྒྱལ་ར་ (བ་) གནང་བ། ཀླག་འཁས་ར་ (པ་) གནང་བ་ | *gye-ra nang-wa ; la khe-ra nang-wa* |

| | | |
|---|---|---|
| Overflow, to | ལྷུད་པ་ | *lü-pa.* |
| Overpower, to | རྒྱལ་བ། ལྷག་འཁས་པ་ | *gye-wa ; la khe-pa.* |
| Do *hon.* | རྒྱལ་ར་ (བ་) གནང་བ། ལྷག་འཁས་ར་ (པ་) གནང་བ་ | *gye-ra nang-wa ; la khe-ra nang-wa.* |
| Overtake, to | རྗེས་ཟིན་པ་ | *je-śim-pa.* |
| Do. *hon.* | རྗེས་ཟིན་པ་གནང་བ་ | *je-śim-pa nang-wa.* |
| Do. *inf.* to *sup.* | ཕེབ་རྗེས་ཟིན་པ་ | *phep-je śim-pa.* |
| Overthrow, to | རྒྱལ་བ་ | *gye-wa.* |
| Do. *hon.* | རྒྱལ་ར་ (བ་) གནང་བ་ | *gye-ra nang-wa.* |
| Overturn, to | མགོ་གཞུག་ལོག་པ། ཨ་ལོག་རྒྱབ་པ་ | *go-sku lok-pa ; a-lo gyap-pa.* |
| Do. *hon.* | མགོ་གཞུག་ལོག་ག་ (པ་) གནང་བ། ཨ་ལོག་སྐྱོན་པ་ | *go-sku lok-ka nang-wa ; a-lo kyöm-pa.* |
| Owe, to | བུ་ལོན་གཟུག་པ་ | *pu-lön śuk-pa.* |
| Do. *hon.* | ཕྱག་བུན་གཟུག་པ་ | *chha-pün śuk-pa.* |
| Owl | འུག་པ་ | *uk-pa.* |
| Own, *adj.* | རང་གི་ | *rang-ki.* |
| Owner | བདག་པོ་ | *dak-po.* |
| Ox | གླང་། གླང་གོག་ | *lang ; lang-ko.* |

# P

| | | |
|---|---|---|
| Pace (stride) | གོམ་པ་ | *ḱom-pa.* |
| Do. *hon.* | ཞབས་གོམ་ | *sḱap-ḱom.* |
| Paces (of a horse) | འགྲོས་ | *drö.* |
| Do. *hon.* | ཆིབས་འགྲོས་ | *chhiṕ-drö.* |
| Pack (load) | ཁལ་ | *ḱhe.* |
| Pack on, to (load) | བཀལ་བ་ (འགེལ་བ་) | *kel-wa.* |
| Do. *hon.* | བཀལ་ར་ (འགེལ་བ་) གནང་བ་ | *ke ra nang-wa.* |
| Pack-horse | ཁལ་རྟ་ | *khe-ta.* |
| Pack-mule | ཁལ་དྲེ་ | *khe-t́re.* |
| Pack-pony | ཁལ་རྟ་ | *khe-ta.* |
| Pack-saddle | སྒ་ | *ga.* |
| Packet of paper, large | ཤོག་སྒྲིལ་ | *shoḱ-dri.* |
| Do. small | ཤོག་གུའི་ (ཤོག་བུའི་) ཚག་པ་ | *shoḱ-ḱü chhaḱ-pa.* |
| Padlock | སྒོ་ལྕགས་ | *gö-cha.* |
| Do. *hon.* | གཟིམ་ལྕགས། ཕྱག་ལྕགས་ | *śim-cha; chha-cha.* |
| Pagan | ཕྱི་པ་ | *chhi-pa.* |
| Page of book | ཤོག་ལེབ་ | *shoḱ-le.* |
| Do. number of, in a book | ཤོག་གྲངས་ | *shoḱ-t́rang.* |
| Do. (attendant) | གཡོག་པོ་ | *yoḱ-po.* |

| | | |
|---|---|---|
| Page (attendant), *hon.* | ཞབས་ཕྱི་ | *shaṕ-chhi.* |
| Pail (of wood) | ཟོ་ལག་ | *śo-la.* |
| Do. (of iron) | ལྕགས་ཀྱི་ཟོ་ལག་ | *cha-kyi śo-la.* |
| Pain, bodily | གཟུག་ | *śu.* |
| Do. *hon.* | སྙུང་གཟུག་ | *nyung-śu.* |
| Pain, mental | སྡུག་བསྔལ་ | *dung-nge.* |
| Do. *hon.* | ཐུགས་འཁྲལ་ | *thuk-thre.* |
| Pain (punishment by beating) | ཁྲིམས་ | *thrim.* |
| Do. *hon.* | བཀའ་ཁྲིམས་ | *ka-thrim.* |
| Pain (punishment by fine) | ཉེས་པ། ཆད་པ་ | *nye-pa ; chhe-pa.* |
| Do. *hon.* | བཀའ་ཉེས། བཀའ་ཆད | *ka-nye ; ka-chhe.* |
| Painful | གཟུག་ཆེན་པོ་ | *śuk·chhem-po.* |
| Painstaking | སྙིང་རུས་ཆེན་པོ་ | *nying-rü chhem-po.* |
| Paint, *s.* | ཚོན་ | *tshön.* |
| Paint, to (cover with colour) | ཚོན་བཏང་ (གཏོང་) བ་ | *tshön tang-wa.* |
| Do. *hon.* | ཚོན་གཏོང་ང་ (བ་) གནང་བ་ | *tshön tong-nga nang-wa.* |
| Paint, to (picture) | བྲིས་པ་ (འབྲི་བ་) | *ṫri-pa.* |
| Do. *hon.* | བྲིས་པ་ (འབྲི་བ་) གནང་བ་ | *ṫri-pa nang-wa.* |
| Painter | ལྷ་བྲི་ (འབྲི་) པ་ | *hlaṕ-ri-pa.* |

| | | |
|---|---|---|
| Painting | རི་མོ་ | *ri-mo.* |
| Pair | ཆ་ | *chha.* |
| Palace | ཕོ་བྲང་ | *pho-t́rang.* |
| Palanquin | མགྱོགས་དཔྱང་ (འཁྱོགས་དཔྱང་) | *gyo-chang.* |
| Do. *hon.* | ཕེབ་དཔྱང་ | *pheṕ-chang.* |
| Palate | དཀན་ | *ken.* |
| Pale | དཀར་པོ་དཀར་ཀྱང་ | *kar-po kar-kyang.* |
| Pallid | དཀར་པོ་དཀར་ཀྱང་ | *kar-po kar-kyang.* |
| Palm (of hand) | ལག་མཐིལ་ | *laḱ-thi.* |
| Do. *hon.* | ཕྱག་མཐིལ་ | *chha-thi.* |
| Palsy | གྲུམ་བུ་ཆུ་སེལ་ | *t́rum-ṕu chhu-se.* |
| Paltry | དོན་དག་ཆུང་ཆུང་ | *t́ön-t́a chhung-chhung.* |
| Do. *hon.* | སྐུ་དོན་ཆུང་ཆུང་ | *ku t́ön chhung-chhung.* |
| Pan | སླ་ང་ | *la-nga.* |
| Pang, mental | སྡུག་བསྔལ་ | *du-nge.* |
| Do. *hon.* | ཐུགས་འཁྲལ་ | *thu-thre.* |
| Pang, physical | གཟུག་ | *śu.* |
| Do. *hon.* | སྙུང་གཟུག་ | *nyung-śu.* |
| Pankah | རླུང་ཡབ་ | *lung-yaṕ.* |

| | | |
|---|---|---|
| Pang (of grief) | སྡུག་བསྔལ་ | *dung-nge.* |
| Pant, to (for breath) | དབུགས་བསགས་ (གསོག་) པ་ | *u sak-pa.* |
| Do. *hon.* | ལྗགས་དབུགས་བསགས་ཀ་ (གསོག་པ་) གནང་བ་ | *ja-u sak-ka nang-wa.* |
| Pant, to (when the breath is taken away by cold water) | ཧམ་པ་ | *ngam-pa.* |
| Do. *hon.* | ཧམ་པ་གནང་བ་ | *ngam-pa nang-wa.* |
| Pantaloons | གོས་ཐུང་། དོར་མ་ | *ko-thung ; ťor-ma.* |
| Do. *hon.* | ཞབས་དོར་ | *sǩap-ťo.* |
| Panther | གཟིག་ | *śik.* |
| Pantry | གཉེར་ཚང་ | *nyer-tshang.* |
| Paper | ཤུ་གུ་ (ཤོག་བུ་) | *shu-gu.* |
| Do. *hon.* | ཕྱག་ཤོག་ | *chha-sho.* |
| Parable | དཔེ། འདྲ་དཔེ་ | *pe ; dra-pe.* |
| Paradise | བདེ་བ་ཅན་གྱི་ཞིང་ཁམས་ | *de-wa-chen-kyi sǩing-kham.* |
| Parasol | ཉི་གདུགས་ | *nyi-du.* |
| Do. *hon.* | དབུ་གདུགས་ | *u-du.* |
| Parcel (round) | ཐུམ་དི་ | *thum-ťi.* |
| Parcel out, to | བགོད་པ། བགོ་བ་ཤའ་རྒྱབ་པ་ | *gö-pa ; goṕ-sha gyaṕ-pa.* |

| | | |
|---|---|---|
| Parcel out, to, *hon.* | བགོད་པ་གནང་བ། བགོ་བཤའ་སྐྱོན་པ་ | *gö-pa nang-wa ; gop̍-sha kyöm-pa.* |
| Parched (dry) | སྐམ་པོ་ | *kam-po.* |
| Pardon | དགོངས་པ་ | *gong-pa.* |
| Pardon, to | དགོངས་པ་བཏང་ (གཏོང་) བ་ | *gong-pa tang-wa.* |
| Do. *hon.* | དགོངས་པ་གཏོང་ང་ (བ་) གནང་བ་ | *gong-pa tong nga nang-wa.* |
| Pardon, to ask | ཐུགས་དགོངས་དག་ཞུ་བ་ | *thu-gong-t̍a shu-wa.* |
| Pare, to | པགས་པ་ཤུ་བ་ | *pak̍-pa shu-wa.* |
| Do. *hon.* | པགས་པ་ཤུ་བ་གནང་བ་ | *pak̍-pa shu-wa nang-wa.* |
| Parents | ཕ་མ་ | *pha-ma.* |
| Do. *hon.* | ཡབ་ཡུམ་ | *yap̍-yum.* |
| Park | གླིང་ཀ་ | *ling-ka.* |
| Parrot | ཨའུ་ནེ་ཙོ། ནེ་ཙོ་ | *a-u-nen-tso ; nen-tso.* |
| Parsimonious | ལག་པ་དམ་པོ་ | *lak̍-pa t̍am-po.* |
| Do. *hon.* | ཕྱག་དམ་པོ་ | *chha-t̍am-po.* |
| Part | ཐུམ་བུ་ | *t̍um-p̍u.* |
| Do. (share) | སྐལ་ལ་ (སྐལ་བ་) | *ke-la.* |
| Do. *hon.* | སྐུ་སྐལ་ | *ku-ke.* |
| Part, to | ཁ་གྱེས་པ་ (འགྱེ་བ་) | *kha-kye-pa.* |

| | | |
|---|---|---|
| Part, to, *hon.* | ཞལ་གྲེས་ར་ (འགྲེ་བ་) གནང་བ་ | *sKe-kye-ra nang-wa.* |
| Partial, to be (biassed) | ཉེ་རིང་བྱེད་པ་ | *nye-ring-cKe-pa.* |
| Do. *hon.* | ཉེ་རིང་གནང་བ་ | *nye-ring nang-wa.* |
| Particular (exact) | ཁྲིག་ཁྲིག། ཏེན་ཏེན་ | *thrik-thrik; ten-ten.* |
| Particularly | ཁྱད་པར་དུ་ | *khye-par-tu.* |
| Partly | ཏོག་ཙ་ | *tok-tsa.* |
| Partner (in business) | ཚོང་རོགས་ | *tshong-ro.* |
| Party (faction) | ཕྱོགས་ | *chho.* |
| Do. (in law-suit) | རྒྱོད་ཡ་ | *kyo-ya.* |
| Pass, *s.* (over mountains) | ལ་ | *la.* |
| Pass, to (go), *v.i.* | འགྲོ་བ་ | *dro-wa.* |
| Do. *hon.* | ཕེབ་པ་ | *phe-pa.* |
| Pass, to, *h. hon.* | འཆིབ་རྒྱུ་གནང་བ་ | *chhip-gyu nang-wa.* |
| Pass the time, to | མགོ་འཁོར་བ་ | *go-khor-wa.* |
| Do. *hon.* | དབུ་འཁོར་བ་ | *u-khor-wa.* |
| Passenger (traveller) | འགྲུལ་པ་ | *drü-pa.* |
| Passion (rage) | ཚིག་པ། ཁོང་ཁྲོ་ | *tshik-pa; khong-thro.* |
| Do. *hon.* | དགོངས་པ། རྣམ་མཁྱེན་ | *gong-pa; nam-khyen.* |
| Passion (lust) | འདོད་ཆགས་ | *dö-chha.* |

| | | |
|---|---|---|
| Passionate | རུ་ངར་པོ་ | *ru-ngar-po.* |
| Passport | ལམ་ཡིག་ | *lam-yi.* |
| Pastime (game) | རྩེད་མོ་ | *tse-mo.* |
| Do. *hon.* | སྐུ་རྩེད་ | *ku-tse.* |
| Pastry-puff | མོག་མོག་ | *mo mo.* |
| Do. *hon.* | བཞེས་མོག་ | *sḱe-mo.* |
| Patch, *s.* | ལྷན་པ་ | *hlem-pa* |
| Patch, to | ལྷན་པ་རྒྱབ་པ་ | *hlem-pa gyaṕ pa.* |
| Do. *hon.* | ལྷན་པ་སྐྱོན་པ་ | *hlem-pa kyöm-pa.* |
| Path | ལམ་ཀ་ | *lang-ka.* |
| Do. *hon.* | ཕེབ་ལམ་ | *pheṕ-lam.* |
| Path (by cliff) | ཕྲང་ | *thrang.* |
| Patience (forbearance) | བཟོད་པ་ | *śö-pa.* |
| Patient, to be (to endure) | བཟོད་པ་སྒོམ་པ་ | *śö-pa gom pa.* |
| Do. *hon.* | བཟོད་པ་སྒོམ་པ་གནང་བ་ | *śö-pa gom-pa nang-wa.* |
| Patiently, to wait | བསྒུགས་བསྡད་ (སྡོད་) པ་ | *gu de-pa.* |
| Do. *hon.* | བསྒུགས་བཞུགས་པ་ | *gu sḱuk-pa.* |
| Patron | མགོན་འདྲེན་གནང་མཁན་ | *gön-dren nang-khen.* |
| Patronage | མགོན་འདྲེན་ | *gön-dren.* |
| Patronize, to | མགོན་འདྲེན་གནང་བ་ | *gön-dren nang-wa.* |

| | | |
|---|---|---|
| Pattern | དཔེ་ | *pe.* |
| Do. (sample) | སྤྱུས་ཚད་ | *pü-tshe.* |
| Pauper | ཉམས་ཆུང་། སྐྱོ་པོ་ | *nyem chhung; kyo-po.* |
| Paw | སྡེར་མོ་ | *der-mo.* |
| Pawn, to | གཏའ་མ་བཞག་ (འཇོག) པ་ | *ta-ma shak-pa.* |
| Do. *hon.* | གཏའ་མ་གཞོག་ག་ (འཇོག་པ་) གནང་བ་ | *ta-ma shok-ka nang-wa.* |
| Pay | གླ། ཕོགས་ | *la ; pho.* |
| Do. *hon.* | གསོལ་ཕོགས་ | *sö-pho.* |
| Pay, to | གླ་སྤྲད་པ། ཕོགས་སྤྲད་པ་ | *la-tre-pa ; pho-tre-pa.* |
| Do. *hon.* | གླ་གནང་བ། ཕོགས་གནང་བ་ | *la nang-wa ; pho nang-wa.* |
| Pay back, to | སྐྱིན་ཚབ་སྤྲད་པ་ | *kyin-tshaṕ tre-pa.* |
| Do. *hon.* | སྐྱིན་ཚབ་གནང་བ་ | *kyin-tshaṕ nang-wa.* |
| Do. *inf.* to *sup.* | སྐྱིན་ཚབ་ཕུལ་ (འབུལ་) བ་ | *kyin-tshaṕ phü-wa.* |
| Pay taxes, to | ཁྲལ་འཇལ་བ་ | *thre je-wa.* |
| Paymaster | ཕོགས་དཔོན་ | *pho-pön.* |
| Pea | སྲན་མ་ | *trem-ma.* |
| Peace | སྐྱིད་པོ། དུས་བདེ་པོ་ | *kyi-po ; tü de-po.* |
| Peaceable (condition of country) | གླིངས་ཆག་པོ། འཇམ་ཐིང་ཐིང་ | *hling-chhak-po; jam-thing-thing.* |

| | | |
|---|---|---|
| Peaceful (condition of country) | ལྷིངས་ཆག་པོ། འཇམ་ཐིང་ཐིང་ | *hling-chhak-po; jam-thing-thing.* |
| Peach | ཁམ་བུ་ | *kham-pu.* |
| Peacock | རྨ་བྱ་ | *map-cha.* |
| Peak (of mountain) | རྩེ་ | *tse.* |
| Pear | ལི་ | *li.* |
| Do. *hon.* | བཞེས་སླི་ | *ske-li.* |
| Pearl | མུ་ཏིག་ | *mu-ti.* |
| Do. *hon.* | དབུ་ཏིག་ | *u-ti.* |
| Peasant | སོ་ནམ་བྱེད་མཁན་ | *so-nam che-khen.* |
| Pebble | རྡོ་ཧྲུག་ | *do-hru.* |
| Peculiar | ཁྱད་མཚར་པོ། ཡ་མཚན་པོ་ | *khye-tsha po; yam-tshem-po.* |
| Pedestrian | རྐང་ཐང་ང་ (པ་) | *kang-thang-nga.* |
| Peel, *s.* | པགས་པ་ | *pak-pa.* |
| Peel, to | པགས་པ་ཤུ་བ་ | *pak pa shu-wa.* |
| Do. *hon.* | པགས་པ་ཤུ་བ་གནང་བ་ | *pak-pa shu-wa nang-wa.* |
| Peg, iron | ལྕགས་ཕུར་ | *cha-phu.* |
| Do. wooden | ཕུར་པ་ | *phu pa.* |
| Pelt, to (stone) | གཞུ་བ་ | *sku-wa.* |
| Do. *hon.* | གཞུ་བ་གནང་བ་ | *sku-wa nang-wa.* |

| | | |
|---|---|---|
| Pen | སྙུ་གུ་ | *nyu-ku.* |
| Do. *hon.* | ཕྱག་སྙུ་ | *chha-nyu.* |
| Penalty | ཆད་པ། ཉེས་པ་ | *chhe-pa ; nye-pa.* |
| Do. *hon.* | བཀའ་ཆད། བཀའ་ཉེས་ | *ka chhe ; ka-nye.* |
| Pencil | སྙུ་གུ་ | *nyu-ku.* |
| Do. *hon.* | ཕྱག་སྙུ་ | *chha-nyu.* |
| Pending | མ་ཚར་བ་ | *ma-tshar-wa.* |
| Penetrate, to (enter) | འཛུལ་བ་ | *dzü-wa.* |
| Do. (pierce) | ཕིགས་པ་ (འབིགས་པ་) | *phi-pa.* |
| Do. *hon.* | འབིགས་ག་ (པ་) གནང་བ་ | *bi-ka nang-wa.* |
| Penis | མཇེ། ཕོ་རྟགས་ | *je ; pho-ta.* |
| Do. *hon.* | སོ་མཇེ་ | *so je.* |
| Penurious | སྐྱོ་པོ། སྙེམས་ཆུང་ (ཉམས་ཆུང་) | *kyo-po ; nyem-chhung.* |
| People | མི་ | *mi.* |
| Do. (nation) | མི་བརྒྱུད། རིགས་བརྒྱུད་ | *mi-gyü ; ri-gyü.* |
| Pepper | ཕོ་བ་རིལ་བུ་ | *pho-wa ri-pu.* |
| Peradventure | གཅིག་བྱེད་ན་ | *chik-che-na.* |
| Perceive, to (with the eye) | མཐོང་བ་ | *thong-wa.* |
| Do. *hon.* | གཟིགས་པ་ | *śi-pa.* |

| | | |
|---|---|---|
| Perceive, to (understand) | ཤེས་པ། ཧ་གོ་བ་ | *she-pa ; ha-ḱo-wa.* |
| Do. *hon.* | མཁྱེན་པ་ | *khyem-pa.* |
| Do. *h. hon.* | དགོངས་པ་རྟོགས་པ་ | *gong-pa toḱ-pa.* |
| Perfect (possessed of grace, glory, and wealth) | ཕུན་སུམ་ཚོགས་པ་ | *phün-sum tshoḱ-pa.* |
| Perform, to | བྱེད་པ་ | *cḱe-pa.* |
| Do. *hon.* | གནང་བ་ | *nang-wa.* |
| Perfume | དྲི་མ་ | *t́ri-ma.* |
| Perhaps | གཅིག་བྱེད་ན་ | *chiḱ-cḱe-na.* |
| Peril | ཉེན་ཁ་ | *nyen-kha.* |
| Perilous | ཉེན་ཁ་ཆེན་པོ་ | *nyen-kha chhem-po.* |
| Period | དུས། བསྐལ་པ་ | *tü, kel-pa.* |
| Perish, to | ཞི་བ་ | *shi-wa.* |
| Do. *hon.* | གྲོངས་པ་ (འགྲོང་བ་) | *t́rong-pa.* |
| Do. *h. hon.* | བཞགས་པ་ | *shaḱ-pa.* |
| Permission | དགོངས་པ་ | *gong-pa.* |
| Permit, to | བཅུག་པ་ (འཇུག་པ་) | *chuḱ-pa.* |
| Do. *hon.* | བཅུག་ག་ (འཇུག་པ་) གནང་བ་ | *chuḱ-ka nang-wa.* |
| Permitted, to be | ཆོག་པ་ | *chhoḱ-pa.* |
| Perpetual | རྒྱུན་ཆད་རྒྱུ་མེད་པ་ | *gyün-chhe-gyu me-pa.* |

| | | |
|---|---|---|
| Perpetually | ནམ་རྒྱུན། དུས་རྒྱུན་ | *nam-gyün; tü-gyün.* |
| Perplexed, to be | མགོ་འཐོམས་པ་ | *go-thom-pa.* |
| Do. *hon.* | དབུ་འཐོམས་པ་གནང་བ་ | *u thom-pa nang-wa.* |
| Perplexing | མགོ་ཉོག་ཚ་པོ་ | *go-nyo tsha-po.* |
| Perplexity | མགོ་ཉོག་ | *go-nyo.* |
| Persecute, to | གནོད་པ་བྱེད་པ་ | *nö-pa che-pa.* |
| Do. *hon.* | གནོད་པ་གནང་བ་ | *nö-pa nang-wa.* |
| Persecution | གནོད་པ་ | *nö-pa.* |
| Perseverance | སྙིང་རུས་ | *nying-rü.* |
| Do. *hon.* | ཐུགས་རུས་ | *thu-rü.* |
| Persevere, to | སྙིང་རུས་བྱེད་པ་ | *nying-rü che-pa.* |
| Do. *hon.* | ཐུགས་རུས་གནང་བ་ | *thuk-rü nang-wa.* |
| Persia | ཏ་ཟིག་ | *ta-śi.* |
| Persian | ཏ་ཟིག་པ་ | *ta śik-pa.* |
| Persist, to | ཨུ་ཚུགས་བྱེད་པ་ | *u tshu che-pa.* |
| Do. *hon.* | ཨུ་ཚུགས་གནང་བ་ | *u-tshu nang-wa* |
| Persistence | ཨུ་ཚུགས་ | *u-tshu.* |
| Person | མི་ | *mi.* |
| Personally | རང་ | *rang.* |
| Perspiration | རྔུལ་ནག་ | *ngü-na.* |

| | | |
|---|---|---|
| Perspire, to | རྔུལ་ནག་འཐོན་པ་ | *ngü-na thöm-pa.* |
| Do. *hon.* | རྔུལ་ནག་འཐོན་པ་གནང་བ་ | *ngü-na thöm-pa nang-wa.* |
| Persuade, to | བསླབ་བྱ་བྱེད་པ་ | *lap̍-cḱa cḱe-pa.* |
| Do. *hon.* | བཀའ་སློབ་གནང་བ་ | *ka-lop̍ nang-wa.* |
| Peruse, to | ཀློག་པ་ | *loḱ-ṗa.* |
| Do. *hon.* | ལྗགས་ཀློག་གནང་བ་ | *ja-lo nang-wa.* |
| Perverse | གྱོང་པོ་ | *ḱyong-po.* |
| Pessimistic, to be (hopeless) | རེ་བ་མེད་པ་ | *re-wa me-pa.* |
| Do. *hon.* | ཐུགས་རེ་མེད་པ་ | *thu-re me-pa.* |
| Pestle | ཡ་གྱུག། གཏུན་རིལ་ | *ya-gya ; ting-ri.* |
| Pet, to | གཅེས་པོ་བྱེད་པ་ | *che-po cḱe-pa.* |
| Do. *hon.* | གཅེས་པོ་གནང་བ་ | *che-po nang-wa.* |
| Petition | སྙན་ཞུ་ | *nye-sḱu.* |
| Petition, to | སྙན་ཞུ་ཞུ་བ་ | *nye-sḱu sḱu-wa.* |
| Petroleum | ས་སྣུམ་ | *sa-num.* |
| Petticoat | སྨད་གཡོགས་ | *me-yo.* |
| Do. *hon.* | ཞབས་ཁྱེན་ | *sḱap̍-khyen.* |
| Petty (matter) | དོན་གནད་ཆུང་ཆུང་ | *ṫön-ne chhung-chhung.* |
| Do. *hon.* | ཐུགས་དོན་ཆུང་ཆུང་ | *thuk-ṫön chhung-chhung.* |

| | | |
|---|---|---|
| Pewter | ཏིག་ཚ་ | *tik-tsha.* |
| Phantom | གདོང་འདྲེ། འདྲེ་ | *dong-dre; dre.* |
| Pheasant, Blood | ཟེ་མོ་ | *se-mo.* |
| Do. Monal | བྱ་མདངས་ | *ĉKam-dang.* |
| Phlegm | ལུད་པ་ | *lü-pa.* |
| Do. *hon.* | ལྗགས་ལུད་ | *ja-lü.* |
| Photographic mount | པར་གྱི་རྒྱབ་ཤ་ཤོག་གུ་ (བུ་) | *par-kyi gyap-sha shok-ku.* |
| Phthisis | གཅོང་ནད་ | *chong-ne.* |
| Physic | སྨན་ | *men.* |
| Do. *hon.* | གསོལ་སྨན་ | *sö-men.* |
| Physician | ཨེམ་ཆི་ | *am-chhi.* |
| Do. *hon.* | ཨེམ་ཆི་ལགས་ | *am-chhi-la.* |
| Pick, to (flowers, etc.) | གཏོག་ག་ | *tok-pa.* |
| Do. *hon.* | གཏོག་ག་ (པ་) གནང་བ་ | *tok-ka nang-wa.* |
| Pick, to (a quarrel) | སྙད་སྐོ་བ་ | *nye-ko-wa.* |
| Do. (choose) | འདམ་པ་ | *dam-pa.* |
| Do. *hon.* | འདམ་པ་གནང་བ་ | *dam-pa nang-wa.* |
| Pick up, to | ཡར་སྒྲུག་པ། ཡར་ཁྱག (འཁྱགས་) པ་ | *ya-druk-pa; ya-khyak-pa.* |

| | | |
|---|---|---|
| Pick up, to, *hon.* | ཡར་སྒྲུག་ག་ (པ་) གནང་བ། ཡར་ཁྱག་ག་ (འཁྱོགས་པ་) གནང་བ་ | *ya-druḱ-ḱa nang-wa ; ya-khyak-ḱa nang-wa.* |
| Pictorial representation | རི་མོ་ | *ri-mo.* |
| Picture | ཐང་ཀ་ | *thang-ka.* |
| Do. *hon.* | ཞལ་ཐང་ | *sḱe-thang.* |
| Piebald (horse) | རྟ་ཁྲ་ | *taṕ-thra.* |
| Piece | ཏུམ་བུ་ | *t́um-ṕu.* |
| Do. (round in shape) | རྡོག་རྡོག་ | *doḱ-do.* |
| Do. (roll of cotton cloth) | ཐ་ན་ *Hind.* | *tha-na.* |
| Do. (roll of silk) | ཡུག་ | *yuk.* |
| Do. (roll of woollen cloth) | བུབས་ | *ṕuṕ.* |
| Pierce, to | ཕིགས་པ་ (འབིགས་པ་) | *phi-pa.* |
| Do. *hon.* | འབིགས་ག་ (པ་) གནང་བ་ | *bi-ḱa nang-wa.* |
| Piety | ཆོས་སེམས། དགེ་སེམས་ | *chhö-sem ; ge-sem.* |
| Pig | ཕག་པ་ | *phak-pa.* |
| Pig-sty | ཕག་ཚང་ | *phak-tshang.* |
| Pig-tail | ལྕང་ལོ་ | *chang-lo.* |
| Do. *hon.* | དབུ་ལྕང་ | *u-chang.* |
| Pigeon | འང་ཀུ། (ཕུག་རོན་) | *ang-ku.* |

| | | |
|---|---|---|
| Pike (spear) | མདུང་ | *dung.* |
| Do. *hon.* | ཕྱག་མདུང་ | *chhan-dung.* |
| Pile, *s.* | སྤུང་ | *pung.* |
| Pile, to | སྤུང་ནས་བཞག་ (འཇོག་) པ་ | *pung-ne sKak-pa.* |
| Do. *hon.* | སྤུང་ནས་གཞོག་ག་ (པ་) གནང་བ་ | *pung-ne sKok-ka nang-wa.* |
| Piles | གྲང་ཐོར་ | *trang-thor.* |
| Pilgrim | གནས་སྐོར་ར་ (པ་) | *ne-kor-ra.* |
| Pilgrimage | གནས་སྐོར་ | *ne-kor.* |
| Do. to go on | གནས་སྐོར་ལ་འགྲོ་བ་ | *ne-kor-la dro-wa.* |
| Do. *hon.* | གནས་སྐོར་ལ་ཕེབ་པ་ | *ne-kor-la phe-pa.* |
| Do. *h. hon.* | གནས་སྐོར་ལ་འཆིབ་རྒྱུ་ གནང་བ་ | *ne-kor-la chhip-gyu nang-wa.* |
| Pill | རིལ་བུ་ | *ri-pu.* |
| Pillage, to (rob) | ཇག་པ་རྒྱབ་པ་ | *cKak-pa gyap-pa.* |
| Pillar | ཀ་བ་ | *ka-a.* |
| Pillow | སྔས། སྔས་འབོལ་ | *nge ; ngem böl.* |
| Do. *hon.* | དབུ་སྔས་ | *u-nge.* |
| Pimple | ཐོར་པ་ | *thor-pa.* |
| Do. *hon.* | མགུལ་ཐོར་ | *gü-thor.* |

| | | |
|---|---|---|
| Pin | གཟེར་ | *śer.* |
| Pincers | སྐམ་པ་ | *kam-pa.* |
| Pinch, to | སེན་འཐོག་རྒྱབ་པ་ | *sem-tho gyaṕ-pa.* |
| Do. *hon.* | སེན་འཐོག་སྐྱོན་པ་ | *sem-tho kyöm-pa.* |
| Pinch, to (twisting the skin) | ཤ་བཙུས་ (འཛུས་) རྒྱབ་པ་ | *shaṕ-chü gyaṕ-pa.* |
| Do. *hon.* | ཤ་བཙུས་ (འཛུས་) སྐྱོན་པ་ | *shaṕ-chü kyöm-pa.* |
| Pine-tree (Pinus Excelsa) | ཐང་ཤིང་ | *thang-shing.* |
| Pinnacle | ལྷ་བཙུགས། ལྕོག་ | *hla-tsuḱ ; cho.* |
| Pious | ཆོས་སེམས་ཆེན་པོ་ | *chhö-sem chhem-po.* |
| Pipe (musical) instrument) | གླིང་བུ་ | *ling-ṕu.* |
| Do. *hon.* | ཞལ་གླིང་ | *she-ling.* |
| Pipe (tobacco) | གང་ཟག་ | *Ḱang-śa.* |
| Do. *hon.* | བཞེས་ཟག་ | *sḰe-śa.* |
| Pistol | ཁྲོ་མདའ་ | *trom-da.* |
| Pit | ས་དོང་། དོང་ | *sa-ťong ; ťong.* |
| Pitch (of the voice) | གདངས་ | *dang.* |
| Pitcher . | ཆུ་སྣོད། ཆུ་བན་ | *chhu-nö ; chhu-ṕen.* |
| Pitiless, to be | སྙིང་རྗེ་…མེད་པ་ | *nying-je...me-pa.* |
| | ཁྲམས་སྙིང་རྗེ་…མེད་པ་ | *cḰum-nying-je ...me-pa.* |
| Do. *hon.* | ཐུགས་རྗེ་…མེད་པ་ | *thuḱ-je...me-pa.* |

| | | |
|---|---|---|
| Pity | སྙིང་རྗེ། བྱམས་སྙིང་རྗེ་ | *nying-je; cham-nying-je.* |
| Do. *hon.* | ཐུགས་རྗེ་ | *thuk-je.* |
| Place, *s.* | ས་ཆ་ | *sa-chha.* |
| Place, to | བཞག་པ་ (འཇོག་པ་) | *shak-pa.* |
| Do. *hon.* | གཞོག་ག་ (འཇོག་པ་) གནང་བ་ | *shok-ka nang-wa.* |
| Place in, to | བཅུག་པ་ (འཇུག་པ་) | *chuk-pa.* |
| Do. *hon.* | བཅུག་ག་ (འཇུག་པ་) གནང་བ་ | *chuk-ka nang-wa.* |
| Placenta | ཤ་མ་ | *sha-ma* |
| Plague | གཉན་ནད་ | *nyen-ne.* |
| Plain | ཐང་ | *thang.* |
| Plain, *adj.* (clear) | གསལ་པོ་ | *se-po.* |
| Do. (level) | སྙོམས་པོ་ | *nyom-po.* |
| Plaintiff | ཞུ་གདུག་བྱེད་པོ་ | *sku-tuk che-po.* |
| Do. *hon.* | ཞུ་གདུག་གནང་མཁན་ | *sku-tuk nang-khen.* |
| Plait (of hair) | ལྕང་ལོ་ | *chang-lo.* |
| Do. *hon.* | དབུ་ལྕང་ | *u-chang.* |
| Plan (pattern) | རི་མོ་ | *ri-mo.* |
| Do. (map) | ས་ཁྲ་ | *sap-thra.* |
| Do. (contrivance) | ཐབས་ | *thap.* |
| Plane | སྦུ་ལྷན | *bu-hlen.* |

| | | |
|---|---|---|
| Plane, to | སྦྲུ་སྣན་རྒྱབ་པ་ | *bu-hlen gyap-pa.* |
| Do. *hon.* | སྦྲུ་སྣན་སྐྱོན་པ་ | *bu hlen kyöm-pa.* |
| Planet | གཟའ་ | *śa.* |
| Plank | སྤང་ལེབ་ | *pang-le.* |
| Plant, to | བཙུགས་པ་ (འཛུགས་པ་) | *tsuk-pa.* |
| Do. *hon.* | བཙུགས་ག་ (འཛུགས་པ་) གནང་བ་ | *tsuk-ka nang-wa.* |
| Plantain | སྐྱེ་སྡོང་ *Sik.* | *kye-dong.* |
| Plat, to (weave) | འཐག་འཐག་པ་ | *tha thak-pa.* |
| Do. *hon.* | འཐག་ཐག་ག་གནང་བ་ | *tha thak-ka nang-wa.* |
| Plate | སྡེར་མ། ཐར་དཔག་ | *der-ma ; tha-pa.* |
| Do. *hon.* | གསོལ་སྡེར་ | *sö-der.* |
| Play | རྩེད་མོ་ | *tse-mo.* |
| Do. *hon.* | སྐུ་རྩེད་ | *ku-tse.* |
| Play, to | རྩེད་མོ་རྩེ་བ་ | *tse mo tse-wa.* |
| Do. *hon.* | སྐུ་རྩེད་གནང་བ་ | *ku-tse nang-wa.* |
| Play-fellow | རྩེད་རོགས་ | *tse-ro.* |
| Do. *hon.* | སྐུ་རྩེད་གནང་རོགས་ | *ku-tse nang-ro.* |
| Plea (controversy) | ལབ་གཞི། རྩོད་པ་ | *lap-ski ; tsö-pa.* |
| Plead, to | ཞུ་བ་ | *sku-wa.* |

| | | |
|---|---|---|
| Plead, to, *hon.* | ཞུ་བ་གནང་བ་ | *sKu-wa nang-wa.* |
| Pleader | བར་མི་བྱེད་མཁན་ | *ṕar-mi cKe-khen.* |
| Do. *hon.* | བར་མི་གནང་མཁན་ | *ṕar-mi nang-khen.* |
| Pleasant | སྐྱིད་པོ་ | *kyi-po.* |
| Do. *hon.* | སྤྲོ་པོ་ | *tro-po.* |
| Please, if you | རོགས་གནང་། རོགས་བྱེད་ | *ro nang ; ro-cKe.* |
| Pleased, to be | དགའ་བ་ | *ga-wa.* |
| Do. *hon.* | ཐུགས་མཉེས་པ་ | *thu nye-pa.* |
| Do. *h. hon.* | ཐུགས་དགྱེས་པ་ | *thu-gye-pa.* |
| Pleasure | དགའ་ཚོར་ | *ga-tshor.* |
| Do. *hon.* | མཉེས་ཚོར་ | *nye-tshor.* |
| Pledge | གཏའ་མ་ | *ta-ma.* |
| Plenteous | འབེལ་པོ། རྫག་ཏོ་ | *be-po ; dzak-ťo.* |
| Plentiful | འབེལ་པོ། རྫག་ཏོ་ | *be-po ; dzak-ťo.* |
| Pliable | མཉེན་པོ་ | *nyem-po.* |
| Pliant (flexible) | མཉེན་པོ་ | *nyem-po.* |
| Plough, *s.* | གཤོལ་ | *shö.* |
| Plough, to | རྨོན་པ་རྒྱབ་པ་ | *möm-pa gyaṕ-pa.* |
| Ploughman | རྨོན་པ་རྒྱབ་མཁན། ཐོན་མཁན་ (ཐོང་པ་) | *möm-pa gyang-khen ; thön-khen.* |

| | | |
|---|---|---|
| Pluck, to (*e.g.* from tree) | གཏོག་པ་ | *toḱ-pa.* |
| Do. *hon.* | གཏོག་ག་ (པ་) གནང་བ་ | *toḱ-ḱa nang-wa.* |
| Plump | ཤ་རྒྱགས་པ་ | *sha-gyaḱ-pa.* |
| Do. *hon.* | སྐུ་ཤ་འབྱོར་པོ་ | *ku-sha jor-po.* |
| Plunder, to (by stealth) | རྐུ་བ་ | *ku-wa.* |
| Do. (by highway robbery) | ཇག་པ་རྒྱབ་པ་ | *cḱak-pa gyaṕ pa.* |
| Pneumonia | བད་ཁྲག་ | *ṕe-thra.* |
| Pocket | ཨམ་བག་ | *am-ṕa.* |
| Do. *hon.* | སྐུ་བག་ | *kum-ṕa.* |
| Pock-mark | འབར་ཙག་ | *bar-tsa.* |
| Pod | གང་བུ་ | *ḱam-ṕu.* |
| Do. *hon.* | བཞེས་གང་ | *sḱe-ḱam.* |
| Poem | སྙན་ངག་ | *nye-nga.* |
| Poet | སྙན་ངག་བྲིས་མཁན་ | *nye-nga t́ri-khen.* |
| Point (*e.g.*, of nail) | རྩེ་ | *tse.* |
| Do. (of argument) | དོན་དག་ | *t́ön-t́a.* |
| Do. *hon.* | སྐུ་དོན་ | *ku-t́ön.* |
| Point out, to (indicate) | མིག་སྟོན་པ་ | *mi-töm-pa.* |
| Do. *hon.* | མིག་སྟོན་པ་གནང་བ་ | *mi-töm-pa nang-wa.* |

| | | |
|---|---|---|
| Point out, to (indicate) *inf.* to *sup.* | སྤྱན་ཕེབ་ཞུ་བ། སྤྱན་དར་ཞུ་བ་ | *chem-phe shu-wa ; chen-tar shu-wa.* |
| Poised evenly, to be | ཡང་ལྗི་མེད་པ་ | *yang-ji me-pa.* |
| Poison | དུག་ | *ťu.* |
| Do. *hon.* | གསོལ་དུག་ | *sö-ťu.* |
| Policeman | སྐོར་ལྕག་པ་ | *ko-chak-pa.* |
| Policy | ལུགས་སྲོལ་ | *luk-sö.* |
| Polite language | ཞེ་ས་ | *she-sa.* |
| Pollute, to | བཙོག་པ་བཟོ་བ་ | *tsok-pa ŝo-wa.* |
| Do. *hon.* | བཙོག་པ་བཟོ་བ་གནང་བ་ | *tsok-pa ŝo-wa nang-wa.* |
| Pollution | གྲིབ་ | *ťrip.* |
| Do. *hon.* | སྐུ་གྲིབ་ | *ku-ťrip.* |
| Pond | ཆུ་འཁྱིལ་ | *chhu-khyil.* |
| Ponder, to | བསམ་བློ་བཏང་ (གཏོང་) བ་ | *sam-lo tang-wa.* |
| Do *hon.* | ཐུགས་བསམ་བཞེས་པ་ | *thu-sam she-pa.* |
| Ponderous (heavy) | ལྗི་པོ་ | *ji-po.* |
| Pony | རྟ་ | *ta.* |
| Do. *hon.* | ཆིབས་པ་ | *chhik-pa.* |
| Pony, riding | ཞོན་རྟ་ | *shön-ta.* |
| Do. *hon.* | ཆིབས་པ་ | *chhik-pa.* |

| | | |
|---|---|---|
| Pony, riding (of very high official or lama) | ཆིབས་ཆེན་ | *chhiṕ-chhen.* |
| Pony, pack | ཁལ་རྟ་ | *khe-ta.* |
| Pool (small) | ཆུ་འཁྱིལ་ | *chhu-khyil.* |
| Poor | སྐྱོ་པོ། སྙིམས་ཆུང་ (ཉམས་ཆུང་) | *kyo-po ; nyem-chhung.* |
| Poplar | སྤྱར་པ་ | *ja-pa.* |
| Poppy | སྟོབས་ལྡན་མེ་ཏོག་ | *tom-den me to.* |
| Population | མི་གྲངས་ | *mi-ťrang.* |
| Porch | ཕྱི་སྒོ་ | *chhi-go.* |
| Porcupine | གཟིག་མོ་ | *śiḱ-mo.* |
| Pork | ཕག་ཤ་ | *phaḱ-sha.* |
| Porridge | པག་ཐུག་ | *ṕa-thu.* |
| Do. *hon.* | བཞེས་པག་པག་ཐུག་ | *sḱe-ṕa ṕa-thu.* |
| Portent | རྟེན་འབྲེལ་ | *tem-dre.* |
| Portion | སྐལ་ལ་ (སྐལ་བ་) | *ke-la.* |
| Do. *hon.* | སྐུ་སྐལ་ | *ku-ke.* |
| Position (in society) | རྒྱུད་ | *gyü.* |
| Positive | རྟེན་རྟེན་ | *ten-ten.* |
| Possessor | བདག་པོ་ | *daḱ-po.* |

| | | |
|---|---|---|
| Possible, to be | ཐུབ་པ་ | *thup-pa.* |
| Post (pillar) | ཀ་བ་ | *ka-a.* |
| Post-office | ཡིག་ཁང་ | *yik-khang.* |
| Posterior (anus) | ཀུབ་ | *kup.* |
| Do. *hon.* | ཞབས་ཕོང་ | *sKam-phong.* |
| Postpone, to (adjourn) | བཞག་པ་ (འཇོག་པ་) | *sKak-pa.* |
| Do. *hon.* | གཞོག་ག་ (འཇོག་པ་) གནང་བ་ | *sKok-ka nang-wa.* |
| Posture | བཛབ་ (བཛ་) | *dap.* |
| Pot | ཁོག་མ་ | *kho-ma.* |
| Do. earthen | ཛ་ཁོག་ | *dza-kho.* |
| Do. flower | མེ་ཏོག་ཁོག་མ་ | *me-to kho-ma.* |
| Potato | ཞོ་ཀོག་ | *sKo-ko.* |
| Do. (a sweet variety) | གྲོ་མ་ | *tro-ma.* |
| Do. *hon.* | བཞེས་གྲོ་ | *sKe-tro.* |
| Potency | དབང་ | *wang.* |
| Do. *hon.* | སྐུ་དབང་ | *ku-wang.* |
| Potter | ཛ་མཁན་ | *dza-khen.* |
| Pouch (for tobacco) | ཐ་ཁུག་ | *tha-khu.* |
| Do. *hon.* | བཞེས་ཁུག་ | *sKe-khu.* |

| | | |
|---|---|---|
| Pound, to (crush) | རྫོག་པ་ | *dzok-pa.* |
| Do. *hon.* | རྫོག་ག་ (པ་) གནང་བ་ | *dzok-ka nang-wa.* |
| Pour, to | བླུག་པ་ | *luk-pa.* |
| Do. *hon.* | བླུག་ག་ (པ་) གནང་བ་ | *luk-ka nang-wa.* |
| Powder | ཕྱེ་མ་ | *chhe-ma.* |
| Do. gun | རྫས་ | *dze.* |
| Power (official) | དབང་ | *wang.* |
| Do. *hon.* | སྐུ་དབང་ | *ku-wang.* |
| Power (physical) | ཤེད་ | *she.* |
| Do. *hon.* | སྐུ་ཤེད་ | *ku-she.* |
| Powerful (officially) | དབང་ཆེན་པོ་ | *wang chhem-po.* |
| Do. *hon.* | སྐུ་དབང་ཆེན་པོ་ | *ku-wang chhem-po.* |
| Powerful (physically) | ཤེད་ཆེན་པོ་ | *she chhem-po.* |
| Do. *hon.* | སྐུ་ཤེད་ཆེན་པོ་ | *ku-she chhem-po.* |
| Practicable, to be | ཐུབ་པ་ | *thup-pa.* |
| Practice (custom) | ལུགས་སྲོལ་ | *luk-sö.* |
| Practise, to | སྦྱང་བ་ | *jang-wa.* |
| Do. *hon.* | སྦྱང་ང་ (བ་) གནང་བ་ | *jang-nga nang-wa.* |
| Praise, *s.* | སྟོད་ར་ | *tö-ra.* |
| Praise, to | སྟོད་ར་བཏང་ (གཏོང་) བ་ | *tö-ra tang-wa.* |

| | | |
|---|---|---|
| Praise, to, *hon.* | སྟོད་ར་གཏོང་ང་ (བ་) གནང་བ་ | *tö-ra tong-nga nang-wa.* |
| Do. *inf.* to *sup.* | སྟོད་ར་ཞུ་བ་ | *tö-ra sKu-wa.* |
| Pray, to (request) | ཞུ་བ་ | *sKu-wa.* |
| Do. *hon.* | ཞུ་བ་གནང་བ་ | *sKu-wa nang-wa.* |
| Pray to deity, to (extempore prayer) | སྨོན་ལམ་བཏབ་ (འདེབས་) པ་ | *mö-lam tap-pa.* |
| Do. *hon.* | ཐུགས་སྨོན་གནང་བ་ | *thu-mön nang wa.* |
| Do. (written prayers) | ཁ་འདོན་བྱེད་པ་ | *khan-dön che-pa.* |
| Do. *hon.* | ཞལ་འདོན་གནང་བ་ | *sKen-dön nang-wa.* |
| Prayer (extempore) | སྨོན་ལམ་ | *mö-lam.* |
| Do. *hon.* | ཐུགས་སྨོན་ | *thu-mön.* |
| Prayer (written) | ཁ་འདོན་ | *khan-dön.* |
| Do. *hon.* | ཞལ་འདོན་ | *sKen-dön.* |
| Prayer-wheel | མ་ཎི། ལག་སྐོར་ | *ma-ni ; la-kor.* |
| Do. *hon.* | ཕྱག་སྐོར་ | *chha-kor.* |
| Preach, to | ཆོས་བཤད་པ་ | *chhö she-pa.* |
| Do. *hon.* | བཀའ་ཆོས་གསུང་བ་ | *ka-chhö sung-wa.* |
| Precede, to | སྔན་ (སྔོན་) ལ་འགྲོ་བ་ | *ngen-la dro-wa.* |
| Do. *hon.* | སྔན་ (སྔོན་) ལ་ཕེབས་པ་ | *ngen-la phe-pa.* |

| | | |
|---|---|---|
| Precede, to, *h. hon.* | སྔན་ (སྔོན་) ལ་འཆིབ་རྒྱུ་གནང་བ་ | *ngen-la chhip-gyu nang-wa.* |
| Preceding | སྔོན་གྱི། དང་པོ་ | *ngön-kyi ; ťang-po.* |
| Precept (maxim) | གདམས་དཔེ་ | *tam-pe.* |
| Precious | རྩ་ཆེན་པོ་ | *tsa-chhem-po.* |
| Precipice | གཡང་ | *yang.* |
| Precipitate (rash) | ཁ་མེད་མིག་མེད་ | *kha-me mik-me.* |
| Precise | ཁྲིག་ཁྲིག། ཏེན་ཏེན་ | *thrik-thrik ; ten-ten.* |
| Precisely | རང་ | *rang.* |
| Preclude, to | བཀག་པ་ (འགེགས་པ་) | *kak-pa.* |
| Do. *hon.* | བཀག་ག་ (འགེགས་པ་) གནང་བ་ | *kak-ka nang-wa.* |
| Predict, to | མངོན་ཤེས་བཤད་པ་ | *ngön-she she-pa.* |
| Do. *hon.* | མངོན་མཁྱེན་གསུང་བ་ | *ngön-khyen sung-wa.* |
| Prediction | ལུང་བསྟན་ | *lung-ten.* |
| Do. *hon.* | བཀའ་ལུང་ | *ka-lung.* |
| Prefix, *s.* | སྔོན་འཇུག་ | *ngön-ju.* |
| Pregnant, to be | པུ་གུ་སྐྱེད་རྒྱུ་ཡོད་པ་ | *pu-gu kye-gyu yö-pa.* |
| Do. *hon.* | ཨ་ཝ་འཁྲུང་རྒྱུ་ཡོད་པ་ | *a-wa thrung-gyu yö-pa.* |
| Prejudice | རྣམ་རྟོག་ | *nam-to.* |

| | | |
|---|---|---|
| Prepare, to | གྲལ་སྒྲིག་བྱེད་པ་ | *ťra-dri cKe-pa.* |
| Do. *hon.* | གྲལ་སྒྲིག་གནང་བ་ | *ťra-dri nang-wa.* |
| Prerogative | ཐོབ་ཐང་ | *thop̌-thang.* |
| Presage, *s.* | རྟེན་འབྲེལ་ | *tem dre.* |
| Presence of, in the | མདུན་ལ་ | *dün-la.* |
| Do. *hon.* | སྐུ་མདུན་ལ་ | *kun-dün-la.* |
| Present, *s.* (alms to poor) | སྦྱིན་པ་ | *jim-pa.* |
| Do. (to lama) | འབུལ་བ་ | *bül-wa.* |
| Do. (tip) | ཆང་རིན་ | *chhang-rin.* |
| Do. *hon.* | གསོལ་རས། ཁྲུང་རིན་ | *sö-re; thrung-rin.* |
| Present, to | སྟེར་བ་ | *ter-wa.* |
| Do. *hon.* | གནང་བ་ | *nang-wa.* |
| Do. *inf.* to *sup.* | ཕུལ་བ་ | *phü-wa.* |
| Do. *hon.* | འབུལ་ར་ (བ་) གནང་བ་ | *bü-ra nang wa.* |
| Present, to be | བསྡད་ (སྡོད་) ཡོད་པ་ | *de yö-pa.* |
| Do. *hon.* | བཞུགས་ཡོད་པ་ | *sKu yö-pa.* |
| Do. *h. hon.* | བཞུགས་གདན་འཛག་ཡོད་པ་ | *sKu-den-ja yö-pa.* |
| Present, at | ད་ལྟ་ | *ťan-da.* |
| Presently (in a few minutes) | ཧྲིབ་ཙ་ (ཙམ་) གཅིག། མགྱོགས་པོ་ | *hrip-tsa-chi; gyok-po.* |

| | | |
|---|---|---|
| Preserve, to (keep care of) | ཉར་བ་ | *nyar-wa.* |
| Do. *hon.* | ཉར་ར་ (བ་) གནང་བ་ | *nyar-ra nang-wa.* |
| Do. *h. hon.* | ཐུགས་ཅག་གནང་བ་ | *thuk-cha nang-wa.* |
| Press, to (physically) | གནན་པ་ (གནོན་པ་) | *nem-pa.* |
| Do. *hon.* | གནན་ (གནོན་) པ་གནང་བ་ | *nem-pa nang-wa.* |
| Press, to (insist) | ཨུ་ཚུགས་བྱེད་པ་ | *u-tshu cḱe-pa.* |
| Do. *hon.* | ཨུ་ཚུགས་གནང་བ་ | *u-tshu nang-wa.* |
| Pressing (work) | ཁྲལ་ཁྲལ་བྱེད་དགོས་ཡ་ | *thre-thre cḱe gö-ya.* |
| Pretend, to | གྱོད་བ་ཤད་པ་ | *ḱyö she-pa.* |
| Do. *hon.* | གྱོད་གསུང་བ་ | *ḱyö sung-wa.* |
| Pretty (of woman) | ཚར་པོ། མཛེས་པོ་ | *tshar-po; dze-po.* |
| Do. *hon.* | ཐུགས་ཚར་པོ་ | *thu tshar-po.* |
| Pretty (of things) | སྙིང་རྗེ་པོ་ | *nying-je-po.* |
| Prevail over, to (overcome) | རྒྱལ་བ། ཀླག་འཁས་པ་ | *gye-wa; la khe-pa.* |
| Do. *hon.* | རྒྱལ་ར་ (བ་) གནང་བ། ཀླག་འཁས་ར་ (པ་) གནང་བ་ | *gye-ra nang-wa; la khe-ra nang-wa.* |
| Prevent, to | བཀག་པ་ (འགེགས་པ་) | *kaḱ-pa.* |
| Do. *hon.* | བཀག་ཀ་ (འགེགས་པ་) གནང་བ་ | *kaḱ-ka nang-wa.* |

| | | |
|---|---|---|
| Previous | སྔོན་གྱི། དང་པོ་ | *ngön-kyi; tang-po.* |
| Previously | སྔན་མ། སྔོན་ལ་ | *ngen-ma; ngen-la.* |
| Price | གོང་། རིན་ | *kong; ring.* |
| Do. *hon.* | ཕྱགས་གོང་ | *ja-kong.* |
| Prick, to | བཙུགས་པ་ (འཛུགས་པ་) | *tsuk-pa.* |
| Do. *hon.* | བཙུགས་ག་ (འཛུགས་པ་) གནང་བ་ | *tsuk-ka nang-wa.* |
| Pride | ཉམས། ཛོག་ཁོག་ | *nyam; dza-kho.* |
| Priest | བླ་མ་ | *la-ma.* |
| Prince | རྒྱལ་སྲས་ | *gye-se.* |
| Princess | རྒྱལ་པོའི་སྲས་མོ་ | *gye-pö se-mo.* |
| Principal | ཆེ་ཤོས་ | *chhe-shö.* |
| Do. (of a loan) | མ་རྩ་ | *ma-tsa.* |
| Principally | ཕལ་ཆེར་ | *phe-chher.* |
| Principle (origin) | བྱུང་སྟངས་ (འབྱུང་ཁུང་) | *cKung-tang.* |
| Do. (cause) | རྐྱེན། རྒྱུ་རྐྱེན་ | *kyen; gyu-kyen.* |
| Do. (motive) | དོན་དག་ | *tön-ta.* |
| Do. *hon.* | སྐུ་དོན་ | *ku-tön.* |
| Print, to | པར་རྒྱབ་པ་ | *par-gyap-pa.* |
| Do. *hon.* | སྐུ་པར་སྐྱོན་པ་ | *ku-par kyöm-pa.* |

| | | |
|---|---|---|
| Printed matter | པར་མ་ | *par-ma.* |
| Printer | པར་པ་ | *par-pa.* |
| Printer (cutter of types) | པར་རྐོད་ (རྐོ་) པ་ | *par-kö-pa.* |
| Do. *hon.* | པར་དཔོན་ | *par-pön.* |
| Printing-office | པར་ཁང་ | *par-khang.* |
| Prior, *adj.* | སྔོན་གྱི། དང་པོ་ | *ngön-kyi ; ťang-po.* |
| Prison | བཙོན་ཁང་ | *tsön-khang.* |
| Prisoner | བཙོན་པ་ | *tsöm-pa.* |
| Private | གསང་བ་ | *sang-wa.* |
| Private property, *hon.* | སྐུ་སྒེར་གྱི་སྐུ་ཆས་ | *ku-ger-kyi ku-chhe.* |
| Privately | གསང་བ་བྱས་ནས་ | *sang-wa cǩe-ne.* |
| Do. *hon.* | གསང་བ་གནང་ནས་ | *sang-wa nang-ne.* |
| Privilege (right) | ཐོབ་ཐང་ | *thoṕ-thang.* |
| Prize | གསོལ་རས་ | *sö-re.* |
| Probably | གཅིག་བྱེད་ན་ | *chiǩ-cǩe-na.* |
| Probationer (in monastery) | ཨེན་ཆུང་ | *en-chhung.* |
| Proceed, to | འགྲོ་བ། ཕྱིན་པ་ | *dro-wa ; chhim-pa.* |
| Do. *hon.* | ཕེབ་པ། ཐེགས་པ་ | *phe-pa ; the-pa.* |
| Do. *h. hon.* | འཆིབ་སྒྱུ་གནང་བ་ | *chhiṕ-gyu nang-wa.* |
| Proclaim, to | སྒྲོག་པ་ | *droǩ-pa.* |

| | | |
|---|---|---|
| Proclaim, to, *hon.* | སྒྲོག་ག་ (པ་) གནང་བ་ | *drok-ka nang-wa.* |
| Proclamation (of Government) | བཀའ་རྒྱ་ | *ka-gya.* |
| Do. (of official) | བསྒྲུལ་གཏམ་ | *kü-tam.* |
| Procrastinating | ཉ་སི་དགུ་སི་ | *nya-si-gu-si.* |
| Procreate, to | སྐྱེད་པ་ | *kye-pa.* |
| Procure, to | འབྱོར་བ། ཐོབ་པ་ | *jor-wa ; thop-pa.* |
| Do. *hon.* | ཕྱག་འབྱོར་ཡོང་བ་ | *chhan-jor yong-wa.* |
| Prodigal (profuse) | འབེལ་པོ། ཛག་ཏོ་ | *be-po ; dzak-to.* |
| Prodigious | ཆེ་ཐག་ཆོད་ | *chhe-thak-chhö.* |
| Prodigy | ཡ་མཚན་ | *yam-tshen.* |
| Produce, to (bring) | འཁྱེར་ཡོང་བ་ | *khyer-yong-wa.* |
| Do. *hon.* | བསྣམས་ (སྣོམ་) ཕེབ་པ་ | *nam-phe-pa.* |
| Productive (of soil) | ལུད་ཆུ་འཛོམ་པོ་ | *lü-chhu dzom-po.* |
| Profane | ཆོས་སེམས་མེད་པ་ | *chhö-sem me-pa.* |
| Profession | ལས་ཀ་ | *le-ka.* |
| Do. *hon.* | ཕྱག་ལས་ | *chha-le.* |
| Professor | མཁན་པོ་ | *khem-po.* |
| Profit | ཁེ་བཟང་ | *khep-śang.* |
| Do. *hon.* | སྐུ་ཁེ་ | *ku-khe.* |
| Profit, to make a | ཁེ་བཟང་ཟབ་ | *khep-śang śa wa.* |

| | | |
|---|---|---|
| Profit, to make a, *hon.* | སྐུ་ཁེ་བཞེས་པ་ | *ku-khe sḱe-pa.* |
| Profitable, to be | ཕན་ཐོགས་པ་ | *phen-thoḱ-pa.* |
| Do. *hon.* | ཐུགས་ཕན་གསོལ་བ་ | *thu-phen söl-wa.* |
| Profound (deep) | གཏིང་རིང་པོ་ | *ting-ring-po.* |
| Profuse | འབེལ་པོ། ཛག་ཏོ་ | *be-po ; dzaḱ-ťo.* |
| Progeny | ཕྲུ་གུ་ | *pu-gu.* |
| Prognostication | ལུང་བསྟན་ | *lung ten.* |
| Do. *hon.* | བཀའ་ལུང་ | *ka-lung.* |
| Prohibit, to | བཀག་པ་ (འགེགས་པ་) | *kak·pa.* |
| Do. *hon.* | བཀག་ག་ (འགེགས་པ་) གནང་བ་ | *kaḱ-ka nang-wa.* |
| Prolific (of soil) | ལུད་ཆུ་འཛོམ་པོ་ | *lü-chhu dzom-po.* |
| Prominent (eminent) | སྐད་གྲགས་ཆེན་པོ་ | *ke-ťra chhem-po.* |
| Do. *hon.* | སྙན་གྲགས་ཆེན་པོ་ | *nyen-ťra chhem-po.* |
| Promise, to | ཁས་བླང་བ་ | *khe-lang-wa.* |
| Do. *hon.* | ཞལ་བཞེས་པ་ | *sḱe-sḱe-pa.* |
| Promoted, to be | གོ་གནས་འཕར་བ་ | *ḱo-ne phar-wa.* |
| Do. *hon.* | གོ་གནས་འཕར་ར་ (བ་) གནང་བ་ | *ḱo-ne phar-ra nang-wa.* |
| Promptly | མགྱོགས་པོར་ | *gyoḱ-po.* |

| | | |
|---|---|---|
| Promptly, *hon.* | རྩོལ་པོར་ | *tsö-p̊o.* |
| Promulgate, to | སྒྲོག་པ་ | *drok-pa.* |
| Do. *hon.* | སྒྲོག་ག་ (པ་) གནང་བ་ | *drok-ka nang-wa.* |
| Pronunciation | ལབ་སྟངས། ཤོད་སྟངས་ | *lap̊-tang; shö-tang.* |
| Do. *hon.* | གསུང་སྟངས་ | *sung-tang.* |
| Proof | རྟགས་ | *ta.* |
| Prop, *s.* | ཀ་སྐྱོར་ | *ka-kyor.* |
| Prop, to | སྐྱོར་བ་ | *kyor-wa.* |
| Do. *hon.* | སྐྱོར་ར་ (བ་) གནང་བ་ | *kyor-ra nang-wa.* |
| Proper (befitting) | འོས་པོ་ | *ö-po.* |
| Property (in land) | ས་ཆ་ | *sa-chha.* |
| Do. (in goods) | ཆ་ལག་ | *cha-la.* |
| Do. *hon.* | སྐུ་ཆས་ | *ku-che.* |
| Prophecy | ལུང་བསྟན་ | *lung-ten.* |
| Do. *hon.* | བཀའ་ལུང་ | *ka-lung.* |
| Prophesy, to | མངོན་ཤེས་ཤེས་པ་ | *ngön-she she-pa.* |
| Do. *hon.* | མངོན་མཁྱེན་མཁྱེན་པ་ | *ngön-khyen khyem-pa.* |
| Propitious | རྟེན་འབྲེལ་ཡག་པོ་ | *tem-dre yak-po.* |
| Proportion | ཚོད་ | *tshö.* |
| Proprietor | བདག་པོ་ | *dak-po.* |

| | | |
|---|---|---|
| Prose | ལྷུག་མ་ | *lhuk-ma.* |
| Prosperity (good fortune) | བསོ་བདེ་ (བསོད་བདེ།) བསོད་ནམས་ | *so-de ; sö-nam.* |
| Do. *hon.* | སྐུ་བསོད་ | *ku-sö.* |
| Prosperous | གཡང་ཆེན་པོ་ | *yang-chhem-po.* |
| Prostrate one-self, to | ཕྱག་འཚལ་བ་ | *chha-tshe-wa.* |
| Do. *hon.* | སྐུ་ཕྱག་འཚལ་ར་ (བ་) གནང་བ་ | *ku-chha tshe-ra nang-wa.* |
| Prostitute | ཆལ་མོ། ཞང་ཚོང་མ་ | *chhe-mo ; śhang-tshong-ma.* |
| Protect, to | སྲུང་བ་ | *sung-wa.* |
| Do. *hon.* | སྲུང་ང་ (བ་) གནང་བ་ | *sung-nga nang-wa.* |
| Protector | སྐྱབས་མགོན་ | *kyam-gön.* |
| Protectorate (over a country) | སྐྱབས་ཁོངས་ | *kyap-khong.* |
| Proud | ཉམས་ཆེན་པོ། རྫག་ཁོག་ཆེན་པོ་ | *nyam-chhem-po ; dza-kho chhem-po.* |
| Prove, to (a case) | ར་འཕྲོད་པ་ | *ra-thrö-pa.* |
| Do. *hon.* | ར་འཕྲོད་པ་གནང་བ་ | *ra-thrö-pa nang-wa.* |
| Prove, to (test) | ཚོད་ལྟ་བ་ | *tshö ta-wa.* |
| Do. *hon.* | ཚོད་གཟིགས་པ་ | *tshö śi-pa.* |

| | | |
|---|---|---|
| Proverb | གཏམ་དཔེ་ | *tam-pe.* |
| Provide, to | སྒྲུབ་པ་ | *drup-pa.* |
| Do. *hon.* | སྒྲུབ་པ་གནང་བ་ | *drup-pa nang-wa.* |
| Province | ཞིང་ཆེན། ཁུལ་ | *sKing-chhen; khü.* |
| Provisions | ཁ་ལག། ལྟོ་ | *kha-la; to.* |
| Do. *hon.* | ཞལ་ལག་ | *sKe-la.* |
| Provisions for journey | ལམ་ཆས་ | *lam-chhe.* |
| Provoke, to (annoy) | ཁོང་ཁྲོ་སློང་བ་ | *khong-thro lang-wa.* |
| Do. *hon.* | དགོངས་པ་དཀྲུག་པ་ | *gong-pa truk-pa.* |
| Proximity | ཉེ་འཁོར་ | *nye-khor.* |
| Proxy | ཚབ་ | *tshap.* |
| Do. *hon.* | སྐུ་ཚབ་ | *ku-tshap.* |
| Prudence (wisdom) | བློ་གྲོས་ | *lo-trö.* |
| Prudent | མཁས་པོ་ | *khe-po.* |
| Puddle (small pool) | ཆུ་འཁྱིལ་ | *chhu-khyil.* |
| Puff (pastry) | མོག་མོག་ | *mo-mo.* |
| Do. *hon.* | བཞེས་མོག་ | *sKe-mo.* |
| Pull, to | འཐེན་པ་ | *them-pa.* |
| Do. *hon.* | འཐེན་པ་གནང་བ་ | *them-pa nang-wa.* |
| Pull, to (of horses) | ངར་པོ་བྱེད་པ་ | *ngar-po cKe-pa.* |

| | | |
|---|---|---|
| Pulling, *adj.* (of horses) | ངར་པོ་ | *ngar-po.* |
| Pulse (of the body) | རྩ་ | *tsa.* |
| Do. *hon.* | ཕྱག་རྩ་ | *chha-tsa* |
| Punctually | ཏེན་ཏེན་བྱས་ནས། མ་འཕྱུག་པ་བྱས་ནས་ | *ten-ten che-ne; ma-chhuk-pa che-ne.* |
| Do. *hon.* | ཏེན་ཏེན་གནང་ནས། མ་འཕྱུག་པ་གནང་ནས་ | *ten-ten nang-ne; ma-chhuk-pa nang-ne.* |
| Pungent | ཁ་ཚ་པོ་ | *kha-tsha-po.* |
| Do. *hon.* | ཞལ་ཚ་པོ་ | *she-tsha-po.* |
| Punish, to (by fine) | ཉེས་པ་བཏང་ (གཏོང་) བ་ | *nye-pa tang-wa.* |
| Do. *hon.* | བཀའ་ཉེས་གནང་བ་ | *ka-nye nang-wa.* |
| Punish, to (by beating) | ཁྲིམས་བཏང་ (གཏོང་) བ་ | *thrim tang-wa.* |
| Do. *hon.* | བཀའ་ཁྲིམས་གནང་བ་ | *ka-thrim nang-wa.* |
| Punishment (by fine) | ཉེས་པ། ཆད་པ་ | *nye-pa; chhe-pa.* |
| Do. *hon.* | བཀའ་ཉེས། བཀའ་ཆད་ | *ka-nye; ka-chhe.* |
| Punishment (by beating) | ཁྲིམས་ | *thrim.* |
| Do. *hon.* | བཀའ་ཁྲིམས་ | *ka-thrim.* |
| Pupil | བསླབ་ཕྲུག་ | *lap-thru.* |
| Do. (monk) | དགེ་ཕྲུག་ | *ge-thru.* |
| Puppy | ཨ་ཡོ་ (ཁྱི་ཕྲུག་) | *a-yo.* |

| | | |
|---|---|---|
| Purchase, to | ཉོ་བ་ | *nyo-wa.* |
| Do. *hon.* | གཟིགས་པ་ | *śi-pa.* |
| Pure | གཙང་མ་ | *tsang-ma.* |
| Purgative | འགྲིན་སྨན། བཤལ་སྨན་ | *dri-men; she-men.* |
| Purge, to | འགྲིན་པ། བཤལ་བ་ | *drim-pa; she-wa* |
| Do. *hon.* | འགྲིན་པ་གནང་བ། བཤལ་ར་ (བ་) གནང་བ་ | *drim-pa nang-wa; she-ra nang-wa.* |
| Purified | དག་པོ་ | *ťak-po.* |
| Purple | རྒུན་འབྲུམ་མདོག་ | *gün-drum-do.* |
| Purport | དོན་དག་ | *ťön-ťa.* |
| Do. *hon.* | སྐུ་དོན་ | *ku-ťön.* |
| Purpose, *s.* | དོན་དག་ | *ťön-ťa.* |
| Do. *hon.* | སྐུ་དོན་ | *ku-tön.* |
| Purpose, to | སེམས་ལ་བསམས་པ་ | *sem-la sam-pa.* |
| Do. *hon.* | ཐུགས་ལ་དགོངས་པ་ | *thuk-la gong-pa.* |
| Purr, to | ངུག་པ་རྒྱབ་པ་ | *nguk-pa gyap-pa.* |
| Purse | སྦྲ་ཁུག (སྦྲིད་ཁུག) | *ba-khu.* |
| Do. *hon.* | ཕྱག་ཁུག་ | *chha-khu.* |
| Pursue, to | གཞུག་རྗེད་ཕྱིན་པ་ | *sǩuk-de chhim-pa.* |
| Do. *hon.* | གཞུག་རྗེད་ཕེབ་པ་ | *sǩuk-de phe-pa.* |

| | | |
|---|---|---|
| Pus | རྣག་ | *na.* |
| Do. *hon.* | སྐུ་རྣག་ | *ku-na.* |
| Push, to | འབེད་ཀྱག་བཏང་ (གཏོང་) བ་ | *be-kya tang-wa.* |
| Do. *hon.* | འབེད་ཀྱག་གཏོང་ང་ (བ་) གནང་བ་ | *be-kya tong-nga nang-wa.* |
| Pustule | ཐོར་པ་ | *thor-pa.* |
| Do. *hon.* | མཁྱུལ་ཐོར་ | *gü-thor.* |
| Put, to (place) | བཞག་པ་ (འཇོག་པ་) | *sKak-pa.* |
| Do. *hon.* | བཞོག་ག་ (འཇོག་པ་) གནང་བ་ | *sKok-ka nang-wa.* |
| Put in, to | བཅུག་པ་ (འཇུག་པ་) | *chuk-pa.* |
| Do. *hon.* | འཇུག་ག་ (པ་) གནང་བ་ | *juk-ka nang-wa.* |
| Put in order, to | སྒྲིག་པ་ | *drik-pa.* |
| Do. *hon.* | སྒྲིག་ག་ (པ་) གནང་བ་ | *drik-ka nang-wa.* |
| Put on, to (clothes) | གོན་པ་ | *köm-pa.* |
| Do. *hon.* | བཞེས་པ་ | *sKe-pa.* |
| Put off, to (defer) | པ་རུ་བཞག་ (འཇོག་) པ་ | *pa-ru sKak-pa.* |
| Do. *hon.* | པ་རུ་གཞོག་ག་ (འཇོག་པ་) གནང་བ་ | *pa-ru sKok-ka nang-wa.* |
| Put off, to (divest) | ཕྱིས་པ་ (འཕུད་པ་) | *pi-pa.* |
| Do. *hon.* | ཕྱིས་ (འཕུད་) པ་གནང་བ་ | *pi-pa nang-wa.* |

| | | |
|---|---|---|
| Putrefy, to | རུལ་འགྲོ་བ་ | *rü-dro-wa.* |
| Putrid, to be | རུལ་བ་ | *rü-wa.* |
| Puzzled, to be | མགོ་འཐོམས་པ་ | *go-thom-pa.* |
| Do. *hon.* | དབུ་འཐོམས་པ་གནང་བ་ | *u-thom-pa nang-wa.* |

# Q

| | | |
|---|---|---|
| Quaint | ཡ་མཚན་པོ། ཁྱད་མཚར་པོ་ | *yam-tshen-po ; khye-tsha-po.* |
| Quake, to (shudder) | འདར་བ་ | *dar-wa.* |
| Do. *hon.* | སྐུ་འདར་སྐྱོན་པ་ | *kün-dar kyöm-pa.* |
| Qualified | འོས་པོ་ | *ö-po.* |
| Quality | ཡག་ཉེས། སྤུས་ཁ་ | *ya-nye ; pü-kha.* |
| Quarrel | རྒྱབ་འདྲེ་ | *gyam-dre.* |
| Do. *hon.* | གསུང་འཁྲུག་ | *sung-thru.* |
| Quarrel, to | རྒྱབ་འདྲེ་རྒྱབ་པ་ | *gyam-dre gyap-pa.* |
| Do. *hon.* | གསུང་འཁྲུག་སྐྱོན་པ་ | *sung-thru kyöm-pa.* |
| Quarrel, to pick a | སྙད་སྐོ་བ་ | *nye-ko-wa.* |
| Quarrelsome | རུ་ངར་པོ་ | *ru-ngar-po.* |
| Queen | རྒྱལ་མོ་ | *gye-mo.* |
| Queen-consort | རྒྱལ་པོའི་བཙུན་མོ་ | *gye-pö tsö-mo.* |
| Queer | ཁྱད་མཚར་པོ་ | *khye-tsha-po.* |
| Query, to (question) | དྲི་བ་ (འདྲི་བ་) | *ťri-wa.* |
| Do. *hon.* | བཀའ་འདྲི་གནང་བ་ | *kan-dri nang-wa.* |
| Do. *inf.* to *sup.* | ཞུ་བ་ | *sKu-wa.* |
| Question, to | དྲི་བ་ (འདྲི་བ་) | *ťri-wa.* |
| Do. *hon.* | བཀའ་འདྲི་གནང་བ་ | *kan-dri nang-wa.* |

| | | |
|---|---|---|
| Queue (pig-tail) | ལྕང་ལོ་ | *chang-lo.* |
| Do. *hon.* | དབུ་ལྕང་ | *u-chang.* |
| Quick (rapid) | མགྱོགས་པོ་ | *gyok-po.* |
| Do. *hon.* | རྩོལ་པོ་ | *tsö-po.* |
| Quick (active) | ཧུར་པོ་ | *hur-po.* |
| Do. (clever) | རིག་པ་ཆེན་པོ་ | *rik-pa chhem-po.* |
| Do. *hon.* | ཐུགས་རིག་ཆེན་པོ་ | *thu-rik chhem-po.* |
| Quick (irritable) | རུ་ངར་པོ་ | *ru-ngar-po.* |
| Do. *hon.* | ཐུགས་རུ་ངར་པོ་ | *thu-ru ngar-po.* |
| Quick (living) | གསོན་པོ་ | *söm-po.* |
| Quickly (rapid-ly) | མགྱོགས་པོར་ | *gyok-po.* |
| Do. *hon.* | རྩོལ་པོར་ | *tsö-po.* |
| Quick-silver | དངུལ་ཆུ་ | *ngü-chhu.* |
| Quiet (of persons) | ཁ་ཉུང་ཉུང་ | *kha nyung-nyung.* |
| Do. *hon.* | ཞལ་ཉུང་ཉུང་ | *ske nyung-nyung.* |
| Quiet (of places) | ཁ་གུ་སིམ་པོ་ | *kha-ku sim-po.* |
| Do. (calm condition of country) | ལྷིང་ཆགས་པོ། འཇམ་ཐིང་ཐིང་ | *hling-chhak-po; jam-thing-thing.* |
| Do. (of horses) | ལྷིང་བུ་ | *hling-pu.* |
| Quilt | ཉལ་གཟན་ | *nye-sen.* |

| | | |
|---|---|---|
| Quilt, *hon.* | གཟིམ་གཟན་ | *śim-śen.* |
| Quill-pen | སྒྲོ་སྨྱུག་ | *dro-nyu.* |
| Quit, to (depart) | འཐོན་པ། ཕྱིན་པ་ | *thöm-pa ; chhim-pa.* |
| Do. *hon.* | ཕེབ་པ་ | *phe-pa.* |
| Do. *h. hon.* | འཆིབ་ཀྱུ་གནང་བ་ | *chhiṕ-gyu nang-wa.* |
| Quit, to (a country, etc.) | བཞག་ནས་ཡོང་བ་ | *sḱa-ne yong-wa.* |
| Do. *hon.* | བཞག་ནས་ཕེབ་པ་ | *sḱa-ne phe-pa.* |
| Do. *h. hon.* | བཞག་ནས་འཆིབ་ཀྱུ་གནང་བ་ | *sḱa-ne chhiṕ-gyu nang-wa.* |
| Quite (used negatively) | ཐད་དེ། ཁྱོན་ནས་ | *be-ťe ; khyön-ne.* |
| Quite so ! | ད་ག་རང་རེད་ | *ťa-ḱa-rang-re.* |
| Do. *hon.* | ལགས་ད་ག་རང་རེད་ | *la ťa-ḱa-rang-re.* |
| Do. *h. hon.* | བཀའ་གནང་རང་རེད་ | *ka-na-rang-re.* |
| Quiver, *s.* | མདའ་དོང་ | *da-ťong.* |
| Quiver, to (of animate things) | འདར་བ་ | *dar-wa.* |
| Do. *hon.* | སྐུ་འདར་སྐྱོན་པ་ | *kün-dar kyöm-pa.* |
| Quiver, to (of inanimate things) | འཁྲུག་པ་ | *thruḱ-pa.* |
| Quota | སྐལ་ལ་ (སྐལ་བ་) | *ke-la.* |
| Do. *hon.* | སྐུ་སྐལ་ | *ku-ke.* |

# R

| | | |
|---|---|---|
| Rabbit | རི་གོང་ (རི་བོང་) | *ri-ḱong.* |
| Rabid | སྨྱོན་པ་ | *nyöm-pa.* |
| Rabid, to be | སྨྱོ་བ་ | *nyo-wa.* |
| Race, foot | མི་རྒྱུག་ | *mi-gyu.* |
| Do. horse | རྟ་རྒྱུག་ | *ta-gyu.* |
| Race (tribe) | མི་བརྒྱུད། རིགས་བརྒྱུད་ | *mi-gyü ; ri-gyü.* |
| Radiance | གཟི་བརྗིད། འོད་ | *śi-ji ; ö.* |
| Radiant | གཟི་བརྗིད་ཆེན་པོ། འོད་ཆེན་པོ་ | *śi-ji chhem-po ; ö chhem-po.* |
| Radish | ལ་ཕུག་ | *la-phu.* |
| Do. *hon.* | བཞེས་ལབ་ | *sḱe-laṕ.* |
| Rafter | ལྕམ་ | *cham.* |
| Rag | ཨ་ཚོར་ | *a-chho.* |
| Do. *hon.* | ཞལ་ཚོར་ | *sḱe-chho.* |
| Rage | ཚིག་པ། ཁོང་ཁྲོ་ | *tshiḱ-pa ; khong-thro.* |
| Do. *hon.* | དགོངས་ཚུང་། ནམ་མཁྱེན་ | *gong-tshung ; nam-khyen.* |
| Ragged | བཙབ་རལ་ (ཧྲུལ་པོ་) | *tsaṕ-re.* |
| Railing (fence) | ར་བ་ | *ra-wa.* |
| Do. iron | ལྕགས་ཀྱི་ར་བ་ | *cha-kyi ra-wa.* |
| Raiment | དུག་ལོ་ | *t́u-lo.* |

| | | |
|---|---|---|
| Raiment, *hon.* | ན་བཟའ་ | *nam-śa.* |
| Rain | ཆར་པ་ | *chhar-pa.* |
| Do. *hon.* | སྐུ་ཆར་ | *sku-chhar.* |
| Rain, light shower of | སྤྲིན་ཆར་ | *tring-chhar.* |
| Do. mixed with hail | དྲག་ཆར་ | *ťrak-chhar.* |
| Rain, to | ཆར་པ་བཏང་ (གཏོང་) བ་ | *chhar-pa tang-wa.* |
| Do. *hon.* | སྐུ་ཆར་བཏང་ (གཏོང་) བ་ | *sku-chhar tang-wa.* |
| Rain heavily, to | ཆར་པ་ཞེ་སྤྲག་རྒྱབ་པ་ | *chhar-pa ske-tra gyaṕ-pa.* |
| Rainbow | འཇའ་ | *ja.* |
| Raise up, to | ཡར་ཀྱག་ (འཁྱོག་) པ། ཡར་ལེན་པ་ | *yar-kyak-pa; yar-lem-pa.* |
| Do. *hon.* | ཡར་ཀྱག་ག་ (འཁྱོག་པ་) གནང་བ་ | *yar-kyak-ka nang-wa.* |
| Raisin | རྒུན་འབྲུམ་དཀར་པོ་ | *gün-drum ka-po* |
| Rake | རྒྱ་གཟེབ་ | *gya-śeṕ.* |
| Ram | ལུག་ཕོ་ | *luk-pho.* |
| Ramble, to | ཆམ་ཆམ་ (འཁྱམས་ འཁྱམས་) བྱེད་པ་ | *chham-chham cke-pa.* |
| Do. *hon.* | སྐུ་ཆམ་ (འཁྱམས་) གནང་བ་ | *kün-chham nang-wa.* |
| Ramrod of gun | སིན་འབིད་ | *sim-bi.* |

| | | |
|---|---|---|
| Rancid | ཁ་རྩུབ་པོ་ | *kha-tsup̍-po.* |
| Rancour | གནོད་སེམས་ | *nö-sem.* |
| Range, to (rove over) | ཆམ་ཆམ་ (འཁྱམས་འཁྱམས་) ལ་འགྲོ་བ་ | *chham-chham la dro-wa.* |
| Do. *hon.* | སྐུ་ཆམ་ (འཁྱམས་) ལ་ཕེབ་པ་ | *kün-chham la phe-pa.* |
| Do. *h. hon.* | སྐུ་ཆམ་ (འཁྱམས་) ལ་འཆིབ་ཀྱུ་གནང་བ་ | *kün-chham la chhip̍-gyu nang-wa.* |
| Rank (degree) | གོ་ས། གོ་གནས། རིམ་པ་ | *ko-sa ; ko-ne ; rim-pa.* |
| Do. (row) | གྲལ་ | *t̍re.* |
| Ransack, to | ཧག་པ་རྒྱབ་པ་ | *cHak-pa gyap̍-pa.* |
| Ransom (for killing a man) | སྟོང་ | *tong.* |
| Ransom, to | བླུ་བ་ | *lu-wa.* |
| Do. *hon.* | བླུ་བ་གནང་བ་ | *lu-wa nang-wa.* |
| Rap, *s.* (on door, etc.) | དག་དག་ | *tak-tak.* |
| Rap, to | དག་དག་བཏང་ (གཏོང་) བ་ | *tak-tak tang-wa.* |
| Do. *hon.* | དག་དག་གཏོང་ང་ (བ་) གནང་བ་ | *tak-tak tong-nga nang-wa.* |
| Rapacious | འདོད་པ་ཆེན་པོ། ཧམ་པ་ཚ་པོ་ | *dö-pa chhem-po ; ham-pa tsha-po.* |
| Rapacity | ཧམ་པ་ | *ham-pa.* |
| Rapid | མགྱོགས་པོ་ | *gyok-po.* |

| | | |
|---|---|---|
| Rapid, *hon.* | རྩོལ་པོ་ | *tsö-po.* |
| Rare | དཀོན་པོ་ | *köm-po.* |
| Rascal | བསྟན་བཞིག། འཛབ་ཆེན་ | *ten-sKi ; dzap-chhen.* |
| Rase, to | བཤིག་པ་ (འཇིག་པ་) | *shik-pa.* |
| Do. *hon.* | བཤིག་ག་ (འཇིག་པ་) གནང་བ་ | *shik-ka nang-wa* |
| Rash, *adj.* | ཁ་སྨེད་མིག་མེད་ | *kha-me mik-me.* |
| Rat | ཙི་ཙི་ (ཙིག་གི་) | *tsi-tsi.* |
| Rate (price) | གོང་ | *Kong.* |
| Do. *hon.* | ལྗགས་གོང་ | *ja-Kong.* |
| Rate (tax) | ཁྲལ། འབབ་ | *thre ; bap.* |
| Do. on land | ས་ཁྲལ་ | *sa-thre.* |
| Ratify, to (confirm) | གདན་ལྡན་བྱེད་པ་ | *ten-den cKe-pa.* |
| Do. *hon.* | གདན་ལྡན་གནང་བ་ | *ten-den nang-wa.* |
| Rattle, to, *v.t.* | དཀྲོག་དཀྲོག་བཏང་ (གཏོང་) བ་ | *trok-tro tang-wa.* |
| Do. *hon.* | དཀྲོག་དཀྲོག་གཏོང་ང་ (བ་) གནང་བ་ | *trok-tro tong-nga nang-wa.* |
| Ravage, to (rob) | ཇག་པ་རྒྱབ་པ་ | *cKak-pa gyap-pa.* |
| Raven | ཕོ་རོག་ | *pho-ro.* |

| | | |
|---|---|---|
| Ravine | རོང་ | *rong.* |
| Raw (uncooked) | རྗེན་པ་ | *jem-pa.* |
| Do. (of weather) | གྲང་མོ། བསིལ་པོ་ | *ťrang-mo ; si-po.* |
| Do. *hon.* | སྐུ་བསིལ་པོ་ | *ku-si-po.* |
| Ray | འོད་གཟེར་ | *ö-śer.* |
| Raze, to | བཤིག་པ་ (འཇིག་པ་) | *shiḱ-pa.* |
| Do. *hon.* | བཤིག་ག་ (འཇིག་པ་) གནང་བ་ | *shiḱ-ḱa nang-wa.* |
| Razor | སྐྲ་གྲི་ | *tra-ťri.* |
| Reach, to (by stretching hand, etc.) | སྙོབ་པ་ | *nyoṕ-pa.* |
| Do. *hon.* | སྙོབ་པ་གནང་བ་ | *nyoṕ-pa nang-wa.* |
| Reach, to (arrive at) | སླེབ་པ་ | *leṕ-pa.* |
| Do. *hon.* | ཕེབ་པ་ | *phe-pa.* |
| Do. *h. hon.* | འཆིབ་རྒྱུ་གནང་བ་ | *chhiṕ-gyu nang-wa.* |
| Read, to | ཀློག་པ་ | *loḱ-pa.* |
| Do. *hon.* | ཀློག་ག་ (པ་) གནང་བ་ | *loḱ-ḱa nang-wa.* |
| Do. *h. hon.* | ལྗགས་ཀློག་གནང་བ་ | *ja-lo nang-wa.* |
| Ready | གྲལ་སྒྲིག་ | *ťra-dri.* |
| Ready, to make | གྲལ་སྒྲིག་བྱེད་པ་ | *ťra-dri ḱhe-pa.* |

| | | |
|---|---|---|
| Ready, to make, *hon.* | གྲ་སྒྲིག་གནང་བ་ | *t̕ra-dri nang-wa.* |
| Real | ངོ་ཐོག། དངོས་ནས་ | *ngo-tho ; ngö-ne.* |
| Do. (of price, etc.) | ཡང་ཏིག་ | *yang-tik.* |
| Realise, to (obtain) | འབྱོར་བ། ཐོབ་པ་ | *jor-wa ; thop-pa.* |
| Do. *hon.* | ཕྱག་འབྱོར་ཡོང་བ་ | *chhan-jor yong-wa.* |
| Realise, to (understand) | ཤེས་པ། ཧ་གོ་བ་ | *she-pa ; ha-ko-wa.* |
| Do. *hon.* | མཁྱེན་པ་ | *khyem-pa.* |
| Do. *h. hon.* | དགོངས་པ་རྟོགས་པ་ | *gong-pa tok-pa.* |
| Really | ངེས་པར། དངོས་ནས་དྲང་ནས་ | *nge-par ; ngö-ne t̕rang-ne.* |
| Realm (kingdom) | རྒྱལ་སྲིད་ | *gye-si.* |
| Reap, to | རྔ་བ་ | *nga-wa.* |
| Do. *hon.* | རྔས་པ་གནང་བ་ | *nge-pa nang-wa.* |
| Reaper | རྔ་མཁན་ | *nga-khen.* |
| Do. *hon.* | རྔ་བ་གནང་མཁན་ | *nga-a nang-khen.* |
| Rear, in the | རྒྱབ་ལ་ | *gyap-la.* |
| Reason (mind) | བློ། སེམས་ | *lo ; sem.* |
| Do. *hon.* | ཐུགས་ | *thu.* |
| Reason (purpose) | དོན་དག། རྒྱུ་ | *t̕on-t̕a.* |
| Do. *hon.* | སྐུ་དོན་ | *ku-t̕ön.* |
| Reason, to (argue) | རྩེ་རྒྱབ་པ་ | *tse gyap-pa.* |

| | | |
|---|---|---|
| Reason, to (argue), *hon.* | ཞལ་རྩེ་སྐྱོན་པ་ | *she-tse kyöm-pa.* |
| Reasoning | རྩོད་པ་ | *tsö-pa.* |
| Rebel, to | སྡེ་འཁྲུག་པ་ | *de-thruk-pa.* |
| Rebellion | སྡེ་འཁྲུག་ | *de-thru.* |
| Rebuke, *s.* | གཤེ་གཤེ་ | *she-she.* |
| Do. *hon.* | བཀའ་བཀྱོན་ | *kap-kyön* |
| Rebuke, to | གཤེ་གཤེ་བཏང་ (གཏོང་) བ་ | *she-she tang-wa.* |
| Do. *hon.* | བཀའ་བཀྱོན་གནང་བ་ | *kap-kyön nang-wa.* |
| Recede, to (retreat) | ཕྱིར་ལོག་རྒྱབ་པ་ | *chhi-lo gyap-pa.* |
| Do. *hon.* | ཕྱིར་ལོག་སྐྱོན་པ་ | *chhi-lo kyöm-pa.* |
| Receipt | འཛིན་ | *dzin.* |
| Do. *hon.* | ཕྱག་འཛིན་ | *chhan-dzin.* |
| Receive, to | འབྱོར་བ། ཐོབ་པ་ | *jor-wa; thop-pa.* |
| Do. *hon.* | ཕྱག་འབྱོར་ཡོང་བ་ | *chhan-jor yong-wa.* |
| Recent | གསར་པ་ | *sa-pa.* |
| Recently | ཁ་སང་ནས་ | *kha-sang-ne.* |
| Recite, to | ཆོས་ཀློག་པ་ | *chhö lok-pa.* |
| Do. *hon.* | ཆོས་ཀློག་ག་ (པ་) གནང་བ་ | *chhö lok-ka nang-wa.* |
| Reckless | ཁ་མེད་མིག་མེད་ | *kha-me mik-me.* |
| Reckon, to | རྩིས་རྒྱབ་པ་ | *tsi-gyap-pa.* |

| | | |
|---|---|---|
| Reckon, to, *hon.* | ཕྱག་རྩིས་སྐྱོན་པ་ | *ja-tsi kyöm-pa.* |
| Reckoning | རྩིས་ | *tsi.* |
| Do. *hon.* | ཕྱག་རྩིས་ | *ja-tsi.* |
| Recline, to | ཉལ་ནས་བསྡད་ (སྡོད་) པ་ | *nye-ne de-pa.* |
| Do. *hon.* | གཟིམ་ནས་བཞུགས་པ་ | *śim-ne sḱu-pa.* |
| Recluse | སྒོམ་ཆེན་ | *gom-chhen.* |
| Recognise, to (a person) | ངོ་ཤེས་པ་ | *ngo-shem-pa.* |
| Do. *hon.* | ཐུགས་ངོ་མཁྱེན་པ། ཞལ་ཚོར་བ་ | *thu-ngo khyem-pa; she-tsho-wa.* |
| Recollect, to | དྲན་གསོ་བ་ | *t́ren-so-wa.* |
| Do. *hon.* | ཐུགས་དྲན་གསོ་བ་གནང་བ་ | *thu-t́ren so-wa nang-wa.* |
| Recollection | དྲན་པ་ | *t́rem-pa.* |
| Do. *hon.* | ཐུགས་དྲན་ | *thu-t́ren.* |
| Reconcile, to | ནང་སྒྲིག་བྱེད་པ་ | *nang-dri cḱe-pa.* |
| Do. *hon.* | ནང་སྒྲིག་གནང་བ་ | *nang-dri nang-wa.* |
| Reconciliation | ནང་སྒྲིག་ | *nang-dri.* |
| Record | ཐོ་ | *tho.* |
| Do. *hon.* | ཕྱག་ཐོ་ | *chha-tho.* |
| Recover, to (health) | དྲག་པ་ | *t́rak-pa.* |
| Do. *hon.* | སྐུ་དྭངས་པ་ | *ku-t́ang-pa.* |

| | | |
|---|---|---|
| Recover, to (find) | རྙེད་པ་ | *nye-pa.* |
| Do. *hon.* | རྙེད་པ་གནང་བ་ | *nye-pa nang-wa.* |
| Recreation (game) | རྩེད་མོ་ | *tse-mo.* |
| Do. *hon.* | སྐུ་རྩེད་ | *ku-tse.* |
| Recreation, to have | ཐུགས་སྤྲོ་བཏང་ (གཏོང་) བ་ | *thu-tro tang-wa.* |
| Do. *hon.* | ཐུགས་སྤྲོ་གཏོང་ང་ (བ་) གནང་བ་ | *thu-tro tong-nga nang-wa.* |
| Rectify, to (correct) | ཞུ་དག་བྱེད་པ་ | *sǨu-ťa cǨe-pa.* |
| Do. *hon.* | ཞུ་དག་གནང་བ་ | *sǨu-ťa nang-wa.* |
| Red | དམར་པོ་ | *ma-po.* |
| Redeem, to | བླུ་བ་ | *lu-wa.* |
| Do. *hon.* | བླུ་བ་གནང་བ་ | *lu-wa nang-wa.* |
| Redeemer | སྐྱབས་མགོན་ | *kyam-gön.* |
| Redemption | ཐར་པ་ | *thar-pa.* |
| Reduce in number, to | ཉུང་རུ་ (དུ་) བཟོ་བ་ | *nyung-ru ṡo-wa.* |
| Do. *hon.* | ཉུང་རུ་ (དུ་) བཟོ་བ་གནང་བ་ | *nyung-ru ṡo-wa nang-wa.* |
| Reduce in price, to | གོང་བཅག་ (གཅོག་) པ་ | *ǩong chaǩ-pa.* |
| Do. *hon.* | ལྗགས་གོང་གཅོག་ག་ (པ་) གནང་བ་ | *ja-ǩong chok-ǩa nang-wa.* |
| Reduce, to (conquer) | རྒྱལ་བ། ཀླག་འཁྲས་པ་ | *gye-wa ; la khe-pa.* |

| | | |
|---|---|---|
| Reduce, to (conquer), *hon.* | རྒྱལ་ར་ (བ་) གནང་བ། ཀླག་འཁས་ར་ (པ་) གནང་བ་ | *gye-ra nang-wa ; la khe-ra nang-wa.* |
| Reduce, to (degrade) | གོ་གནས་བབ་པ་ | *ḱo-ne ṕaṕ-pa.* |
| Reed | སྨྱུག་མ་ | *nyung-ma.* |
| Reel, to (stagger) | འཁྱོར་ནས་འགྲོ་བ་ | *khyor-ne dro-wa.* |
| Do. *hon.* | སྐུ་འཁྱོར་ནས་ཕེབ་པ་ | *ku-khyor-ne phe-pa.* |
| Do. *h. hon.* | སྐུ་འཁྱོར་ནས་འཆིབ་རྒྱུ་གནང་བ་ | *ku-khyor-ne chhiṕ-gyu nang-wa.* |
| Reflect, to | བསམ་བློ་བཏང་ (གཏོང་) བ་ | *sam-lo tang-wa.* |
| Do. *hon.* | ཐུགས་བསམ་བཞེས་པ་ | *thu-sam sḱe-pa.* |
| Reform, to (amend) | བཟོ་སྐྱོར་བྱེད་པ་ | *ś o-kyor cḱe-pa.* |
| Do. *hon.* | བཟོ་སྐྱོར་གནང་བ་ | *ś o-kyor nang-wa.* |
| Refrain, to (forbear) | ཁོག་པ་བྱེད་པ་ | *khoḱ-pa cḱe-pa.* |
| Do. *hon.* | ཐུགས་ཁོག་གནང་བ་ | *thu-kho nang-wa* |
| Refuge (shelter) | སྐྱབས་གནས་ | *kyam-ne.* |
| Refuse, to (withhold) | མི···སྟེར་བ་ | *mi...ter-wa.* |
| Do. *hon.* | མི···གནང་བ་ | *mi...nang-wa.* |
| Refuse, to (a request) | མི···ཉན་པ་ | *mi...nyem-pa.* |
| Do. *hon.* | མི···གསན་པ་ | *mi...śem-pa.* |
| Regard, to (look at) | ལྟ་བ་ | *ta-wa.* |

| | | |
|---|---|---|
| Regard, to (look at), *hon.* | གཟིགས་པ་ | *śi-pa.* |
| Regarding (concerning) | དོན་ལ། སྐོར་ལ་ | *tön-la ; kor-la.* |
| Regent | རྒྱལ་ཚབ་ | *gye-tshap.* |
| Regent of Tibet | བོད་རྒྱལ་པོ་ | *pö-gye-po.* |
| Regiment | དམག་དཔུང་ | *ma-pung.* |
| Region | ལུང་པ་ | *lung-pa.* |
| Register, *s.* | ཐོ་ | *tho.* |
| Do. *hon.* | ཕྱག་ཐོ་ | *chha-tho.* |
| Register, to | ཐོ་ཕྲིས་པ་ (འཕྲི་བ་) | *tho-ṫri-pa.* |
| Do. *hon.* | ཕྱག་ཐོ་སྐྱོན་པ་ | *chha-tho kyöm-pa.* |
| Regret, *s.* (heavy sorrow) | སྡུག་བསྔལ། སེམས་འཁྲལ་ | *du-nge ; sem-thre.* |
| Do. *hon.* | ཐུགས་འཁྲལ་ | *thuk-thre.* |
| Regret, *s.* (repentance) | འགྱོད་པ་ | *gyö-pa.* |
| Do. *hon.* | ཐུགས་འགྱོད་ | *thung-gyö.* |
| Regret, to, *v.i.* (heavy sorrow) | སྡུག་བསྔལ་བྱེད་པ། མྱ་ངན་བྱེད་པ་ | *du-nge che-pa ; nya-ngen che-pa.* |
| Do. *hon.* | ཐུགས་ངན་གནང་བ་ | *thu-ngen nang-wa.* |
| Regret, to, *v.i.* (in lesser matters) | སེམས་སྐྱོ་བ། སེམས་སྡུག་པ་ | *sem-kyo-wa ; sem-duk-pa.* |
| Do. *hon.* | ཐུགས་སེམས་སྐྱོ་བ་གནང་བ་ | *thu-sem kyo-wa nang-wa.* |
| Regulate, to (arrange) | སྒྲིག་པ་ | *drik-pa.* |

| | | |
|---|---|---|
| Regulate, to (arrange), *hon.* | སྒྲིག་ག་ (བ་) གནང་བ་ | *drik-ka nang-wa.* |
| Regulation (law) | ཁྲིམས་ | *thrim.* |
| Do. *hon.* | བཀའ་ཁྲིམས་ | *ka-thrim.* |
| Regulation (religious) | ཆོས་ཁྲིམས་ | *chhö-thrim.* |
| Reign, *s.* | རྒྱལ་སྲིད་ | *gye-si.* |
| Reign, to | རྒྱལ་སྲིད་གནང་བ་ | *gye-si nang-wa.* |
| Reinforcement | རྒྱབ་སྣོན་ | *gyam-nön.* |
| Reins | སྲབ་ཐག་ | *traṕ-tha.* |
| Reject, to | སྤང་བ་ | *pang-wa.* |
| Do. *hon.* | སྤོང་ང་ (བ་) གནང་བ་ | *pong-nga nang-wa.* |
| Rejoice, to | དགའ་བ་ | *ga-wa.* |
| Do. *hon.* | མཉེས་པོ་གནང་བ་ | *nye-po nang-wa.* |
| Do. *h. hon.* | ཐུགས་དགྱེས་པོ་གནང་བ་ | *thu-gye-po nang-wa.* |
| Rejoicing, *s.* | དགའ་ཚོར་ | *ga-tshor.* |
| Relate, to | བཤད་པ་ | *she-pa.* |
| Do. *hon.* | གསུང་བ་ | *sung-wa.* |
| Relation | ཉེ་བ་ | *nye-wa.* |
| Do. *hon.* | སྐུ་གཉེན་ | *ku-nyen.* |
| Relative, *s.* | ཉེ་བ་ | *nye-wa.* |
| Do. *hon.* | སྐུ་གཉེན་ | *ku-nyen.* |

| | | |
|---|---|---|
| Relative to (concerning) | དོན་ལ། སྐོར་ལ་ | *tön-la; kor-la.* |
| Release, to | ཐར་ར་ (བར་) བྱེད་པ། བཏང་བ་ (གཏོང་བ་) | *thar-ra cKe-pa; tang-wa.* |
| Do. *hon.* | ཐར་ར་ (བར་) གནང་བ། གཏོང་ང་ (བ་) གནང་བ་ | *thar-ra nang-wa; tong-nga nang-wa.* |
| Release, to (by ransom) | བླུ་བ་ | *lu-wa.* |
| Do. *hon.* | བླུ་བ་གནང་བ་ | *lu-wa nang-wa.* |
| Released, to be | ཐར་བ་ | *thar-wa.* |
| Relentless, to be | སྙིང་རྗེ་མེད་པ་ | *nying-je me-pa.* |
| Do. *hon.* | ཐུགས་རྗེ་མེད་པ་ | *thuk-je me-pa.* |
| Reliable | བློས་ (བློ་) ཁེལ་བ་ | *lö khe-wa.* |
| Do. *hon.* | ཐུགས་བློས་ཁེལ་བ་ | *thu-lö khe-wa.* |
| Reliance | བློ་གདད་ | *lo-te.* |
| Relief (help) | རོགས་ | *ro.* |
| Do. *hon.* | མགོ་འདྲེན་ | *gön-dren.* |
| Relief (in coming troops) | རྗེས་ཚབ་ | *je-tshap.* |
| Relieve, to (help) | རོགས་བྱེད་པ་ | *ro cKe-pa.* |
| Do. *hon.* | མགོ་འདྲེན་གནང་བ་ | *gön-dren nang-wa.* |
| Religion | ཆོས་ | *chhö.* |
| Religion, to practise | ཆོས་བྱེད་པ་ | *chhö cKe-pa.* |

| | | |
|---|---|---|
| Religion, to practise, *hon.* | སྐུ་ཆོས་གནང་བ་ | *ku-chhö nang-wa.* |
| Religious | ཆོས་སེམས་ཆེན་པོ་ | *chhö-sem chhem-po.* |
| Relinquish, to (abandon) | སྤང་བ་ | *pang-wa.* |
| Do. *hon.* | སྤོང་ང་ (བ་) གནང་བ་ | *pong-nga nang-wa.* |
| Relish, *s.* (taste) | བྲོ་བ་ | *t́ro-a.* |
| Do. *hon.* | ལྗགས་བྲོ་ | *ja-t́ro.* |
| Rely on, to | བློས་ (བློ་) བཀལ་བ་ | *lö kel-wa.* |
| Do. *hon.* | ཐུགས་བློ་བཀལ་ར་ (བ་) གནང་བ་ | *thu-lo ke-ra nang-wa.* |
| Remain, to | བསྡད་པ་ (སྡོད་པ་) | *de-pa.* |
| Do. *hon.* | བཞུགས་པ་ | *sḱu-pa.* |
| Do. *h. hon.* | བཞུགས་གདན་འཇག་པ་ | *sḱu-den jak-pa.* |
| Remainder | ལྷག་མ་ | *hla-ma.* |
| Remains (corpse) | རོ་ | *ro.* |
| Do *hon.* | སྐུ་སྤུར། སྐུ་ཕུང་ | *ku-pur ; ku-phung.* |
| Do. *hon.* (of lamas) | སྐུ་གདུང་ | *ku-dung.* |
| Remarkable | ཁྱད་མཚར་པོ་ | *khye-tsha-po.* |
| Remedy, to | བཅོས་ཐབས་བྱེད་པ་ | *chö-thaṕ cḱe-pa.* |
| Do. *hon.* | བཅོས་ཐབས་གནང་བ་ | *chö-thaṕ nang-wa.* |
| Remember, to | དྲན་གསོ་བ་ | *t́ren-so-wa.* |

| | | |
|---|---|---|
| Remember, to, *hon.* | ཐུགས་དྲན་གསོ་བ་གནང་བ་ | *thu-t́ren so-wa nang-wa.* |
| Remembrance | དྲན་པ་ | *t́rem-pa.* |
| Do. *hon.* | ཐུགས་དྲན་ | *thu-t́ren.* |
| Remind, to | དྲན་གསོས་བཏང་ (གཏོང་) བ་ | *t́ren-sö tang-wa.* |
| Do. *hon.* | དྲན་གསོས་གནང་བ་ | *t́ren-sö nang-wa.* |
| Do. *inf.* to *sup.* | བསྙེལ་གསོལ་ཞུ་བ་ | *nye-sö shu-wa.* |
| Reminder | དྲན་གསོ་ | *t́ren-so.* |
| Do. *hon.* | བསྙེལ་གསོ་ | *nye-so.* |
| Remorse (regret) | འགྱོད་པ་ | *gyö-pa.* |
| Do. *hon.* | ཐུགས་འགྱོད་ | *thung-gyö.* |
| Remorseless, to be (merciless) | སྙིང་རྗེ་མེད་པ་ | *nying-je me-pa.* |
| Do. *hon.* | ཐུགས་རྗེ་མེད་པ་ | *thuk-je me-pa.* |
| Remote | ཐག་རིང་པོ་ | *tha-ring-po.* |
| Do. *hon.* | ཕེབ་ཐག་རིང་པོ་ | *phep-tha-ring-po.* |
| Remove, to | ཕར་ཤིད་པ་ | *pha shi-pa.* |
| Do. *hon.* | ཕར་ཤིད་པ་གནང་བ་ | *pha shi-pa nang-wa.* |
| Remove, to (take off) | ཕྱིས་པ་ (འབུད་པ་) | *pi-pa.* |
| Do. *hon.* | བསིལ་ར་ (བ་) གནང་བ་ | *si-ra nang-wa.* |
| Remuneration | རྔན་པ་ | *ngem-pa.* |
| Rend, to | གཤག་པ་ | *shak-pa.* |

| | | |
|---|---|---|
| Rend, to, *hon.* | གཤག་ཀ་ (པ་) གནང་བ་ | *shak-ka nang-wa.* |
| Renounce, to (sins, certain kinds of foods, etc.) | སྤང་བ་ | *pang-wa.* |
| Do. *hon.* | སྤོང་ང་ (བ་) གནང་བ་ | *pong-nga nang-wa.* |
| Renown | སྐད་གྲགས་ | *ke-t́ra.* |
| Do. *hon.* | སྙན་གྲགས་ | *nyen-t́ra.* |
| Renowned | མིང་ཆེན་པོ་ | *ming chhem-po.* |
| Do. *hon.* | མཚན་ཆེན་པོ་ | *tshen chhem-po.* |
| Rent | སེར་ཀ་ | *se-ka.* |
| Rent of a house | ཁང་གླ་ | *khang-la.* |
| Do. *hon.* | གཟིམ་ཁང་གི་གླ་ | *śim-khang ḱi-la.* |
| Rent, to (house) | ཁང་གླ་བྱས་ནས་བསྡད་ (སྡོད་) པ་ | *khang-la cḱe-ne de-pa.* |
| Do. *hon.* | ཁང་གླ་གནང་ནས་བཞུགས་པ་ | *khang-la nang-ne sḱu-pa.* |
| Repair, to | གསོས་སྐྱོར་བྱེད་པ་ | *sö-kyor cḱe-pa.* |
| Do. *hon.* | གསོས་སྐྱོར་གནང་བ་ | *sö-kyor nang-wa.* |
| Repair, to (a house) | ཞིག་གསོས་བྱེད་པ་ | *sḱik-sö cḱe-pa.* |
| Do. *hon.* | ཞིག་གསོས་གནང་བ་ | *sḱik-sö nang-wa.* |
| Repast | ཁ་ལག། ཏོ་ | *kha-la; to.* |
| Do. *hon.* | ཞལ་ལག་ | *sḱe-la.* |

| | | |
|---|---|---|
| Repay, to | སྐྱིན་ཚབ་སྤྲད་པ་ | *khin-tshap tre-pa.* |
| Do. *hon.* | སྐྱིན་ཚབ་གནང་བ་ | *kyin-tshap nang-wa.* |
| Do. *inf.* to *sup.* | སྐྱིན་ཚབ་ཕུལ་བ་ | *kyin-tshap phü-wa.* |
| Repeat, to (recite) | ཆོས་ཀློག་པ་ | *chhö-lok-pa.* |
| Do. *hon.* | ཆོས་ཀློག་ག་ (པ་) གནང་བ་ | *chhö-lok-ka nang-wa.* |
| Repent, to | འགྱོད་པ་སྐྱེད་པ་ | *gyö-pa kye-pa.* |
| Do. *hon.* | ཐུགས་འགྱོད་གནང་བ་ | *thung-gyö nang-wa.* |
| Repentance | འགྱོད་པ་ | *gyö-pa.* |
| Do. *hon.* | ཐུགས་འགྱོད་ | *thung-gyö.* |
| Reply, *s.* | ལན་ | *len.* |
| Do. *hon.* | བཀའ་ལན་ | *ka-len.* |
| Reply to a letter, *s.* | ཡིག་ལན་ | *yik-len.* |
| Do. *hon.* | ཕྱག་བྲིས་བཀའ་ལན་ | *chha-ri ka-len.* |
| Reply, to | ལན་རྒྱབ་པ་ | *len gyap-pa.* |
| Do. *hon.* | ལྗགས་ལན་སྐྱོན་པ་ | *ja-len kyöm-pa.* |
| Reply, to (letter) | ཡིག་ལན་བཏང་ (གཏོང་) བ་ | *yik-len tang-wa.* |
| Do. *hon.* | ཕྱག་བྲིས་བཀའ་ལན་གནང་བ་ | *chha-ri ka-len nang-wa.* |
| Report (rumour) | སྐད་ཆ། གཏམ་ | *ke-chha; tam.* |
| Report, to | སྙན་ཞུ་བཏང་ (གཏོང་) བ་ | *nyen-sKu tang-wa.* |
| Do. *inf.* to *sup.* | སྙན་ཞུ་ཕུལ་ (འབུལ་) བ་ | *nyen-sKu phü-wa.* |

| | | |
|---|---|---|
| Report, to (after investigation), *inf.* to *sup.* | ཁྲ་མ་ཕུལ་ (འབུལ་) བ་ | *thra-ma phü-wa.* |
| Do. *hon.* | ཁྲ་མ་འབུལ་ར་ (བ་) གནང་བ་ | *thra-ma bü-ra nang-wa.* |
| Repository | བང་མཛོད་ | *ṕang-dzö.* |
| Representative, *s.* | ཚབ། འཐུས་མི་ | *tshaṕ; thü-mi.* |
| Do. *hon.* | སྐུ་ཚབ་ | *ku-tshaṕ.* |
| Reprimand, *s.* | གཤེ་གཤེ་ | *she-she.* |
| Do. *hon.* | བཀའ་བཀྱོན་ | *kaṕ-kyön.* |
| Reprimand, to | གཤེ་གཤེ་བཏང་ (གཏོང་) བ་ | *she-she tang-wa.* |
| Do. *hon.* | བཀའ་བཀྱོན་གནང་བ་ | *kaṕ-kyön nang-wa.* |
| Reproduce, to (copy) | དཔེ་ཤུ་བ་ | *pe-shu-wa.* |
| Do. *hon.* | དཔེ་ཤུ་བ་གནང་བ་ | *pe-shu-wa nang-wa.* |
| Reproduce, to (imitate) | མིག་འདྲེན་བྱེད་པ་ | *miḱ-dren cḱe-pa.* |
| Repulsive | སྐྱུག་བྲོ་པོ་ | *kyuḱ-ťro-po.* |
| Reprove, to | གཤེ་གཤེ་བཏང་ (གཏོང་) བ་ | *she-she tang-wa.* |
| Do. *hon.* | བཀའ་བཀྱོན་གནང་བ་ | *kaṕ-kyön nang-wa.* |
| Reputable | ཡ་རབས་ | *ya-raṕ.* |
| Reputation (fame) | སྐད་གྲགས་ | *ke-ťra.* |
| Do. *hon.* | སྙན་གྲགས་ | *nyen-ťra.* |
| Repute, *s.* | སྐད་གྲགས་ | *ke-ťra.* |

| | | |
|---|---|---|
| Repute, *s. hon.* | སྙན་གྲགས་ | *nyen-ťra.* |
| Request, *s.* | ཞུ་བ་ | *shu-wa.* |
| Request, to | ཞུ་བ་ | *shu-wa.* |
| Do. *hon.* | ཞུ་བ་གནང་བ་ | *shu-wa nang-wa.* |
| Require, to | དགོས་པ་ | *gö-pa.* |
| Do. *hon.* | ཐུགས་དགོས་པ་ | *thu-gö-pa.* |
| Requisite | དགོས་པ་ | *gö-pa.* |
| Do. *hon.* | ཐུགས་ཁོ་ | *thung-kho.* |
| Requite, to (revenge) | དགྲ་ལན་ལོག་པ་ | *dra-len loḱ-pa.* |
| Do. *hon.* | དགྲ་ལན་ལོག་ག་ (པ་) གནང་བ་ | *dra-len loḱ-ka nang-wa.* |
| Rescue, to | བསྐྱབས་པ་ (སྐྱོབ་པ།) སྐྱོང་བ་ | *kyaṗ-pa; kyong-wa.* |
| Do. *hon.* | སྐྱབས་འཇུག་གནང་བ་ | *kyam-juḱ nang-wa.* |
| Resent, to | འཚེར་བ་ | *tsher-wa.* |
| Do. *hon.* | ཐུགས་འཚེར་གནང་བ་ | *thu-tsher nang-wa.* |
| Resentment | ཚིག་པ། ཁོང་ཁྲོ་ | *tshiḱ-pa; khong-thro.* |
| Do. *hon.* | དགོངས་ཚུང་། རྣམ་མཁྱེན་ | *gong-tshung; nam-khyen.* |
| Resentment, to cause | ཁོང་ཁྲོ་སློང་བ་ | *khong-thro lang-wa.* |
| Do. *hon.* | དགོངས་པ་དཀྲུག་པ་ | *gong-pa truḱ-pa.* |

| | | |
|---|---|---|
| Reside, to | བསྡད་པ་ (སྡོད་པ་) | *de-pa.* |
| Do. *hon.* | བཞུགས་པ་ | *sḰu-pa.* |
| Do. *h. hon.* | བཞུགས་གདན་འཇག་པ་ | *sḰu-den jaḱ-pa.* |
| Residence (house) | ཁང་པ། ནང་། སྡོད་ས་ | *khang-pa; nang; dö-sa.* |
| Do. *hon.* | གཟིམ་ཁང་། བཞུགས་ས་ | *śim-khang; sḰuḱ-sa.* |
| Do. *h. hon.* | གཟིམ་ཤག། བཞུགས་གདན་འཇག་ས་ | *śim-sha; sḰu-den ja-sa.* |
| Resident | སྡོད་མཁན་ | *dö-khen.* |
| Do. *hon.* | བཞུགས་མཁན་ | *sḰu-khen.* |
| Do. *h. hon.* | བཞུགས་གདན་འཇག་མཁན་ | *sḰu-den ja-khen.* |
| Residue | ལྷག་མ་ | *hla-ma.* |
| Resistless, to be | བཀག་…མི་ཐུབ་པ་ | *kaḱ...mi-thuṕ-pa.* |
| Resolute | བརྟེན་པོ་ | *tem-po.* |
| Resolve, to (decide) | ཐག་བཅད་ (གཅོད་) པ་ | *tha-che-pa.* |
| Do. *hon.* | ཐག་གཅོད་པ་གནང་བ་ | *tha-chö-pa nang-wa.* |
| Do. *h. hon.* | ཐུགས་ཐག་གཅོད་པ་གནང་བ་ | *thu-tha chö-pa nang-wa.* |
| Respect to, with | དོན་ལ། སྐོར་ལ་ | *tön-la; kor-la.* |
| Respect (reverence) | བསྙེན་བཀུར་ | *nyen-kur.* |
| Respect, to | བསྙེན་བཀུར་བྱེད་པ་ | *nyen-kur cḰe-pa.* |
| Do. *inf.* to *sup.* | བསྙེན་བཀུར་ཞུ་བ་ | *nyen-kur sḰu-wa.* |

| | | |
|---|---|---|
| Respectable (socially) | ཡ་རབས་ | *ya-rap̄.* |
| Respectful language | ཞེ་ས་ | *sk̄e-sa.* |
| Respecting (concerning) | དོན་ལ། སྐོར་ལ་ | *t̄ön-la; kor-la.* |
| Respiration | དབུགས་ | *u.* |
| Do. *hon.* | ལྗགས་དབུགས་ | *ja-u.* |
| Resplendence | གཟི་བརྗིད་ | *śi-ji.* |
| Resplendent | གཟི་བརྗིད་ཆེན་པོ། འོད་ཆེན་པོ་ | *śi-ji chhem-po; ö chhem-po.* |
| Respond, to | ལན་རྒྱབ་པ་ | *len gyap̄-pa.* |
| Do. *hon.* | ལྗགས་ལན་སྐྱོན་པ་ | *ja-len kyöm-pa.* |
| Responsibility | ཁག། འགན་ | *kha; gen.* |
| Do. *hon.* | ཐུགས་ཁག་ | *thu-kha.* |
| Responsible, to become | ཁས་ཁྱག་ (ཁག་ཐེག་) པ་ | *khe-khyak̄-pa.* |
| Do. *hon.* | ཞལ་ཁྱག་ (ཐེག་) གནང་བ་ | *sk̄e-khya nang-wa.* |
| Rest (for Tibetan gun) | མེ་མདའི་རུ་ | *men-de ru.* |
| Do. *hon.* | ཕྱག་མདའི་རུ་ | *chhan-de ru.* |
| Rest, to | ངལ་གསོ་བ་ | *nge-so-wa.* |
| Do. *hon.* | སྐུ་ངལ་གསོ་བ་གནང་བ་ | *ku-nge so-wa nang-wa.* |
| Rest, to (elbows on table, etc.) | སྦོ་སྙེ་རྒྱབ་པ་ | *bo-nye gyap̄-pa.* |
| Do. *hon.* | སྐུ་སྙེ་སྐྱོན་པ་ | *ku-nye kyöm-pa.* |
| Rest, to (lean back) | རྒྱབ་སྙེ་རྒྱབ་པ་ | *gyam-nye gyap̄-pa.* |

| | | |
|---|---|---|
| Rest, to (lean back), *hon.* | སྐུ་སྙེ་སྐྱོན་པ་ | *ku-nye kyöm-pa.* |
| Rest, to (lie down) | ཉལ་བསྡད་ (སྡོད་) པ་ | *nye-de-pa.* |
| Do. *hon.* | གཟིམ་བཞུགས་པ་ | *śim-sḱu-pa.* |
| Restaurant | ཟ་ཁང་ | *śa-khang.* |
| Restrain, to | བཀག་པ་ (འགེགས་པ་) | *kaḱ-pa.* |
| Do. *hon.* | བཀག་ག་ (འགེགས་པ་) གནང་བ་ | *kaḱ-ḱa nang-wa.* |
| Result | སྙིང་པོ་ | *nying-po.* |
| Retain, to | བཞག་པ་ (འཇོག་པ་) | *sḱaḱ-pa.* |
| Do. *hon.* | གཞོག་ག་ (འཇོག་པ་) གནང་བ་ | *sḱoḱ-ḱa nang-wa.* |
| Retaliate, to | དགྲ་ལན་ལོག་པ་ | *dra-len loḱ-pa.* |
| Do. *hon.* | དགྲ་ལན་ལོག་ག་ (པ་) གནང་བ་ | *dra-len loḱ-ḱa nang-wa.* |
| Retaliation | དགྲ་ལན་ | *dra-len.* |
| Retard, to (obstruct) | བཀག་པ་ (འགེགས་པ་) | *kaḱ-pa.* |
| Do. *hon.* | བཀག་ག་ (འགེགས་པ་) གནང་བ་ | *kaḱ-ḱa nang-wa.* |
| Retinue | འཁོར་གཡོག་ | *khor-yo.* |
| Do. *hon.* | ཞབས་ཕྱི་ | *sḱap-chhi.* |

| | | |
|---|---|---|
| Retire, to (retreat) | ཕྱིར་ལོག་རྒྱབ་པ་ | *chhi-lo gyaṕ-pa.* |
| Do. *hon.* | ཕྱིར་ལོག་སྐྱོན་པ་ | *chhi-lo kyöm-pa.* |
| Retreat, *s.* (shelter) | སྐྱབས་གནས་ | *kyam-ne.* |
| Retreat, to | ཕྱིར་ལོག་རྒྱབ་པ་ | *chhi-lo gyaṕ-pa.* |
| Do. *hon.* | ཕྱིར་ལོག་སྐྱོན་པ་ | *chhi-lo kyöm-pa.* |
| Return, to | ལོག་པ་ | *loḱ-pa.* |
| Do. *hon.* | ཚུར་ཕེབ་པ་ | *tshur-phe-pa.* |
| Do. *h. hon.* | ཚུར་འཆིབ་རྒྱུ་གནང་བ་ | *tshur-chhiṕ-gyu nang-wa.* |
| Return, to, *v.t.* (property committed to one's charge) | རྩིས་སྤྲོད་པ་ | *tsi tre-pa.* |
| Do. *hon.* | ཕྱགས་རྩིས་གནང་བ་ | *ja-tsi nang-wa.* |
| Revenge, *s.* | དགྲ་ལན་ | *dra-len.* |
| Revenge, to | དགྲ་ལན་ལོག་པ་ | *dra-len loḱ-pa.* |
| Do. *hon.* | དགྲ་ལན་ལོག་ག་ (པ་) གནང་བ་ | *dra-len loḱ-ka nang-wa.* |
| Revenue | ཁྲལ་དངུལ་ | *thre-ngü.* |
| Revenue, government | ཞུང་གི་འབབ་ | *sḱung-gi baṕ.* |
| Revere, to | བསྙེན་བཀུར་བྱེད་པ་ | *`nyen-kur cḱe-pa.* |
| Do. *inf.* to *sup.* | བསྙེན་བཀུར་ཞུ་བ་ | *nyen-kur sḱu-wa.* |
| Reverence, *s.* | བསྙེན་བཀུར་ | *nyen-kur.* |

| | | |
|---|---|---|
| Reverence, to | བསྙེན་བཀུར་བྱེད་པ་ | *nyen-kur cḱe-pa.* |
| Do. *inf.* to *sup.* | བསྙེན་བཀུར་ཞུ་བ་ | *nyen-kur sḱu-wa.* |
| Reverend (title) | རྗེ་བཙུན་ | *je-tsün.* |
| Reverse, to (turn up-side down) | མགོ་གཞུག་ལོག་པ། ཨ་ལོག་རྒྱབ་པ་ | *go-sḱu loḱ-pa; a-lo gyap̓-pa.* |
| Do. *hon.* | མགོ་གཞུག་ལོག་ག་ (པ་) གནང་བ། ཨ་ལོག་སྐྱོན་པ་ | *go-sḱu loḱ-ḱa nang-wa; a-lo kyöm-pa.* |
| Reverse, to (turn back to front) | ཁ་ཕྱོགས་ལོག་པ་ | *kha-chho loḱ-pa.* |
| Do. *hon.* | ཞལ་ཕྱོགས་ལོག་ག་ (པ་) གནང་བ་ | *sḱe-chho loḱ-ḱa nang-wa.* |
| Revile, to | སྨད་ར་བཏང་ (གཏོང་) བ་ | *me-ra tang-wa.* |
| Do. *hon.* | སྨད་ར་གཏོང་ང་ (བ་) གནང་བ་ | *me-ra tong-nga nang-wa.* |
| Do. *inf.* to *sup* | སྨད་ར་ཞུ་བ་ | *me-ra sḱu-wa.* |
| Revise, to | ཞུ་དག་བཏང་ (གཏོང་) བ་ | *sḱu-t́a tang-wa.* |
| Do. *hon.* | ཞུ་དག་གཏོང་ང་ (བ་) གནང་བ་ | *sḱu-t́a tong-nga nang-wa.* |
| Revision | ཞུ་དག་ | *sḱu-t́a.* |
| Revolt, *s.* | སྡེ་འཁྲུགས་ | *de-thru.* |
| Revolt, to | སྡེ་འཁྲུག་པ་ | *de-thruḱ-pa.* |
| Revolting (disgusting) | སྐྱུག་བྲོ་བོ་ | *kyuḱ-t́ro-po.* |
| Revolve, to | འཁོར་བ་ | *khor-wa.* |

| | | |
|---|---|---|
| Reward | རྔན་པ་ | *ngem-pa.* |
| Do. *hon.* | གསོལ་རས་ | *sö-re.* |
| Reward, to | རྔན་པ་སྟེར་བ་ | *ngem-pa ter-wa.* |
| Do. *hon.* | གསོལ་རས་གནང་བ་ | *sö-re nang-wa.* |
| Rheumatism | འབམ་ | *bam.* |
| Do. *hon.* | ཞབས་འབམ་ | *sKam-bam.* |
| Rhinoceros | བསེ་རུ་ | *se-ru.* |
| Rhododendron | སྟག་མ་ཤིང་ | *ta-ma-shing.* |
| Rhubarb | ཆུ་ཆུ་ | *chhu-chhu.* |
| Rib | རྩིབ་མ་ | *tsi-ma.* |
| Ribbon | ལྷས་མ་ | *hle-ma.* |
| Rice | འབྲས་ | *dre.* |
| Do. *hon.* | བཞེས་འབྲས་ | *sKen-dre.* |
| Rich (wealthy) | ཕྱུག་པོ། ཅ་ (ཆ་) ལག་ཆེན་པོ་ | *chhuk-po; cha-la chhem-po.* |
| Do. *hon.* | སྐུ་ཅས་ (ཆས་) ཆེན་པོ་ | *ku-che chhem-po.* |
| Rich (fertile) | ལུད་ཆུ་འཛོམ་པོ་ | *lü-chhu dzom-po* |
| Ride, to | ཞོན་པ་ | *sKöm-pa.* |
| Do. *hon.* | འཆིབ་པ་ | *chhip-pa.* |
| Ridge | སྒང་ | *gang.* |

| | | |
|---|---|---|
| Ridiculous | དོན་མེད་ | *ťön-me.* |
| Riding horse | ཞོན་རྟ་ | *sḱön-ta.* |
| Do. *hon.* | ཆིབས་པ་ | *chhiḱ-pa.* |
| Riding horse (of very high official or lama) | ཆིབས་ཆེན་ | *chhiṕ-chhen.* |
| Riding mule | ཞོན་དྲེ་ | *sḱön-ťre.* |
| Do. *hon.* | ཆིབས་དྲེ་ | *chhiṕ-ťre.* |
| Riding pony | ཞོན་རྟ་ | *sḱön-ta.* |
| Do. *hon.* | ཆིབས་པ་ | *chhiḱ-pa.* |
| Riding pony (of very high official or lama) | ཆིབས་ཆེན་ | *chhiṕ-chhen.* |
| Rifle | མེ་མདའ་ | *men-da.* |
| Do. *hon.* | ཕྱག་མདའ་ | *chhan-da.* |
| Rift | སེར་ཀ་ | *se-ka.* |
| Right (privilege) | ཐོབ་ཐང་ | *thoṕ-thang.* |
| Right (not left) | གཡས་ | *ye.* |
| Right (not wrong) | དག་པོ་ | *ťaḱ-po.* |
| Right, to be | འགྲིག་པ་ | *driḱ-pa.* |
| Right! (very well) | ལགས་སི། ལགས་ལགས་སི་ | *la-si; la-la-si.* |
| Righteous | དྲང་པོ་ | *ťrang-po.* |
| Rigid | མཁྲགས་པོ་ (མཁྲིགས་པ་) | *thraḱ-po.* |

| | | |
|---|---|---|
| Rind | པགས་པ་ | *pak-pa.* |
| Rinderpest | ཡོར་ | *yor.* |
| Ring (for finger) | ཚིགས་ཁོག་ | *tshi-kho.* |
| Do. *hon.* | ཕྱག་རྒྱུས་ | *chha-gyü.* |
| Ring (for thumb) | སྤྲུས་ཁོག་ | *tre-kho.* |
| Do. *hon.* | ཕྱག་སྤྲུས་ | *chha-tre.* |
| Ring (circle) | ཨ་ལོང་ | *a-long.* |
| Ring, to (bell) | དཀྲོལ་བ་ (འཁྲོལ་བ་) | *tröl-wa.* |
| Ringleader | གདེ་པོ། མི་ཁྲིད་མགོ་ཁྲིད་ཁྲིད་མཁན་ | *te-po; mi-cKe go-cKe cKe-khen.* |
| Rinse, to | བཤལ་བཤལ་བཏང་ (གཏོང་) བ་ | *she-she tang-wa.* |
| Do. *hon.* | བཤལ་བཤལ་གནང་བ་ | *she-she nang-wa.* |
| Ripen, to | སྨིན་པ་ | *mim-pa.* |
| Rise, to (get up) | ལང་བ་ | *lang-wa.* |
| Do. *hon.* | བཞང་བ་ (བཞེང་བ་) | *sKang-wa.* |
| Do. *h. hon.* | སྐུ་བཞང་ (བཞེང་) གནང་བ་ | *ku-sKang nang-wa.* |
| Rise, to (of sun) | ཤར་བ་ | *shar-wa.* |
| Do. (of water) | རྒྱས་པ་ | *gye-pa.* |
| Risk | ཉེན་ཁ་ | *nyen-kha.* |
| Risky | ཉེན་ཁ་ཆེན་པོ་ | *nyen-kha chhem-po.* |

| | | |
|---|---|---|
| Rite, religious | ཆོས་ལུགས་ | *chhö-lu.* |
| Rival | ཁ་ཐེག་ | *khap-the.* |
| River, large | གཙང་པོ་ | *tsang-po.* |
| Do. small | ཆུ་ | *chhu.* |
| Road | ལམ་ཀ་ | *lang-ka.* |
| Do. *hon.* | ཕེབ་ལམ་ | *phep-lam.* |
| Road, main | རྒྱ་ལམ་ | *gya-lam.* |
| Roam, to | ཆམ་ཆམ་ (འཁྱམ་འཁྱམ་) བྱེད་པ་ | *chham-chham cKe-pa.* |
| Do. *hon.* | སྐུ་ཆམ་ (འཁྱམ་) གནང་བ་ | *kün-chham nang-wa.* |
| Roar, to (wild beasts) | ངར་སྐད་རྒྱབ་པ་ | *ngar-ke gyap-pa.* |
| Roast, to | རྔོད་པ་ | *ngö-pa.* |
| Do. *hon.* | རྔོད་པ་གནང་བ་ | *ngö-pa nang-wa.* |
| Rob, to (by stealth) | རྐུ་ (རྐུན་) མ་རྐུ་བ་ | *ku-ma ku-wa.* |
| Do. (openly) | ཇག་པ་རྒྱབ་པ་ | *cKak-pa gyap-pa.* |
| Robber (by stealth) | རྐུ་མ་ (རྐུན་མ་) | *ku-ma.* |
| Do. (openly) | ཇག་པ་ | *cKak-pa.* |
| Robe | དུག་ལོག་ | *tu-lo.* |
| Do. *hon.* | ན་བཟའ་ | *nam-sa.* |
| Robust | ཤེད་ཆེན་པོ་ | *she chhem-po.* |

| | | |
|---|---|---|
| Robust, *hon.* | སྐུ་ཤེད་ཆེན་པོ་ | *ku-she chhem-po.* |
| Rock | བྲག་ | *t́ra.* |
| Rod | འཁར་རྒྱུག་ | *khar-gyu.* |
| Roe (of fish) | ཉའི་སྒོ་ང་ | *nye-go-nga.* |
| Do. *hon.* | བཞེས་ཉའི་བཞེས་སྒོང་ | *sḱe-nye sḱe-gong.* |
| Rogue | བསྟན་བཞིག། འཛབ་ཆེན་ | *ten-sḱi; dzaṕ-chhen.* |
| Roll (of woollen cloth) | བུབས་ | *ṕuṕ.* |
| Do. (of cotton cloth) | ཐ་ན། *Hin.* ཡུག་ | *tha-na; yuḱ.* |
| Do. (of silk) | དབ་རིལ་ | *taṕ-ri.* |
| Roll, to | སྒྲིལ་བ་ | *dril-wa.* |
| Do. *hon.* | སྒྲིལ་ར་ (བ་) གནང་བ་ | *dri-ra nang-wa.* |
| Roof | ཐོག་ཁ་ | *tho-kha.* |
| Rook | ཁྭ་ཏ | *kha-ta.* |
| Room (in house) | ཁང་མིག་ | *khang-mi.* |
| Do. *hon.* | གཟིམས་ཆུང་ | *śim-chhung.* |
| Room (space) | ས་ཆ་ | *sa-chha.* |
| Root | རྩ་བ་ | *tsa-wa.* |
| Rope | ཐག་པ་ | *thaḱ-pa* |
| Rosary | འཕྲང་ང་ (འཕྲེང་བ་) | *thrang-nga.* |
| Do. *hon.* | ཕྱག་འཕྲང་ (ཕྱག་འཕྲེང་) | *chhan-thrang.* |

| | | |
|---|---|---|
| Rose | སེ་བའི་མེ་ཏོག་ | *se-we me-to.* |
| Rosin | ཐང་ཆུ་ | *thang-chhu.* |
| Rot, to | རུལ་བ་ | *rül-wa.* |
| Rotten | རུལ་པ་ | *rü-pa.* |
| Rough | རྩུབ་པོ། རྩིང་པོ་ | *tsup-po; tsing-po.* |
| Round (like a disc) | སྒོར་སྒོར་ | *go-gor.* |
| Do. (like a sphere) | རྡོག་རྡོག་ | *dok-do.* |
| Rouse, to (from sleep) | གཉིད་བསད་ (གསོད་) པ་ | *nyi se-pa.* |
| Do. *hon.* | གཉིད་གསོད་པ་གནང་བ་ | *nyi sö-pa nang-wa.* |
| Do. *inf.* to *sup.* | མཉེན་ (མནལ་) སད་པ་ | *nyen se-pa.* |
| Route | ལམ་ཀ་ | *lang-ka.* |
| Do. *hon.* | ཕེབ་ལམ་ | *phep-lam.* |
| Route (highway) | རྒྱ་ལམ་ | *gya-lam.* |
| Rove, to | ཆམ་ཆམ་ (འཁྱམ་འཁྱམ་) བྱེད་པ་ | *chham-chham cKe-pa.* |
| Do. *hon.* | སྐུ་ཆམ་ (འཁྱམ་) གནང་བ་ | *kün-chham nang-wa.* |
| Row (noise) | ཨུར་སྒྲ་ | *u-dra.* |
| Do. (quarrel) | རྒྱབ་འདྲེ་ | *gyam-dre.* |
| Do. *hon.* | གསུང་འཁྲུག་ | *sung-thru.* |
| Row (line) | གྲལ་ | *ťre.* |

| | | |
|---|---|---|
| Row, to (boat) | སྐྱ་རྒྱབ་པ་ | *kya-gyap-pa.* |
| Royal | རྒྱལ་པོའི་ | *gye-pö.* |
| Rub, to | འཕུར་འཕུར་བྱེད་པ་ | *phu-phu che-pa.* |
| Do. *hon.* | འཕུར་འཕུར་གནང་བ་ | *phu-phu nang-wa.* |
| Rub out, to (erase) | སུབ་པ་ | *sup-pa.* |
| Do. *hon.* | སུབ་པ་གནང་བ་ | *sup-pa nang-wa.* |
| Rubber | སྒྱིགས་ | *gyi.* |
| Rubbish (refuse) | གད་སྙིགས། ཕྱག་སྙིགས་ | *ke-nyi; chha-nyi.* |
| Ruby | པདྨ་རཱ་ག་ | *pe-ma ra-ga.* |
| Rudder | སྐྱ་མཇུག་ | *kyam-ju.* |
| Rude (impolite) | འཛིང་པ་སྦོམ་པོ། གྱོང་པོ་ | *jing-pa bom-po; kyong-po.* |
| Do. (ignorant) | ཡོན་ཏན་མེད་པ་ | *yön-ten me-pa.* |
| Do. (rough) | རྩུབ་པོ་ | *tsup-po.* |
| Do. (robust) | ཤེད་ཆེན་པོ་ | *she chhem-po.* |
| Do. *hon.* | སྐུ་ཤེད་ཆེན་པོ་ | *ku-she chhem-po.* |
| Ruffian | འཛབ་ཆེན་ | *dzap-chhen.* |
| Rug (bedding) | ཉལ་གཟན་ | *nye-śen.* |
| Do. *hon.* | གཟིམ་གཟན་ | *śim-śen.* |
| Rugged | རྩུབ་པོ་ | *tsup-po.* |
| Ruin, to | མེད་པར་བཟོ་བ་ | *me-pa śo-wa.* |

| | | |
|---|---|---|
| Ruin, to, *hon.* | མེད་པར་བཟློ་བ་གནང་བ་ | *me-pa ŝo-wa nang-wa.* |
| Rule (government) | གཞུང་། གཞུང་ཐོག་ | *sKung ; sKung-tho.* |
| Rule (law) | ཁྲིམས་ | *thrim.* |
| Do. *hon.* | བཀའ་ཁྲིམས་ | *ka-thrim.* |
| Do. (religious) | ཆོས་ཁྲིམས་ | *chhö-thrim.* |
| Rule (maxim) | གཏམ་དཔེ་ | *tam-pe.* |
| Rule (power) | དབང་ | *wang.* |
| Do. *hon.* | སྐུ་དབང་ | *ku-wang.* |
| Rule, as a (usually) | ནམ་རྒྱུན་ | *nam-gyün.* |
| Rule, to (govern) | དབང་བྱེད་པ་ | *wang cKe-pa.* |
| Do. *hon.* | སྐུ་དབང་གནང་བ་ | *ku-wang nang-wa.* |
| Rule, to (decide) | ཐག་བཅད་ (གཅོད་) པ་ | *tha-che-pa.* |
| Do. *hon.* | ཐག་གཅོད་པ་གནང་བ་ | *tha-chö-pa nang-wa.* |
| Do. *h. hon.* | ཐུགས་ཐག་གཅོད་པ་གནང་བ་ | *thu-tha chö-pa nang-wa.* |
| Rule a country, to (secular rule) | རྒྱལ་སྲིད་གནང་བ་ | *gye-si nang-wa.* |
| Do. (spiritual rule) | ཆོས་སྲིད་གནང་བ་ | *chhö-si nang-wa.* |
| Ruler (king) | རྒྱལ་པོ་ | *gye-po.* |
| Do. (for drawing lines) | ཐིག་ཤིང་ | *thiK-shing.* |
| Rumour | སྐད་ཆ། གཏམ་ | *ke-chha ; tam.* |

| | | |
|---|---|---|
| Rump (anus) | ཀུབ་ | *kup.* |
| Do. *hon.* | ཞབས་ཕོངས་ | *sham-phong.* |
| Run, to | རྒྱུག་པ་ | *gyuk-pa.* |
| Do. *hon.* | རྒྱུག་ཕེབ་པ་ | *gyuk phe-pa.* |
| Do. *h. hon.* | རྒྱུག་འཆིབ་རྒྱུ་གནང་བ་ | *gyuk chhip-gyu nang-wa.* |
| Run away, to (flee) | བྲོས་ཕྱིན་པ་ | *pö-chhim-pa.* |
| Do. *hon.* | བྲོས་ཕེབ་པ་ | *pö-phep-pa.* |
| Do. *h. hon.* | བྲོས་འཆིབ་རྒྱུ་གནང་བ་ | *pö-chhip-gyu nang-wa.* |
| Rupee | སྒོར་མོ་ | *gor-mo.* |
| Rush, to (run) | རྒྱུག་པ་ | *gyuk-pa.* |
| Do. *hon.* | རྒྱུག་ཕེབ་པ་ | *gyuk phe-pa.* |
| Do. *h. hon.* | རྒྱུག་འཆིབ་རྒྱུ་གནང་བ་ | *gyuk chhip-gyu nang-wa.* |
| Russia | ཨུ་རུ་སུ་ | *u-ru-su.* |
| Russian | ཨུ་རུ་སུ་གི་ | *u-ru-su-ki.* |
| Rust | བཙའ་ | *tsa.* |
| Rut (furrow) | རོལ་ | *röl.* |
| Ruthless, to be | སྙིང་རྗེ་མེད་པ་ | *ṅying-je me-pa* |
| Do. *hon.* | ཐུགས་རྗེ་མེད་པ་ | *thuk-je me-pa.* |

# S

| | | |
|---|---|---|
| Sabbath | ངལ་གསོ་བའི་ཉི་མ་ | *nge-so-we nyi-ma.* |
| Sabre | ཞོག་ལང་ | *sho-lang.* |
| Sack (small) | ཕད་གོག་ | *phe-ḱo.* |
| Do. (large) | སྒྱེ་མོ་ | *gye-mo.* |
| Do. (small, of cotton) | རས་ཁུག་ | *re-khu.* |
| Do. (large, of cotton) | རས་ཕད་ | *re-phe.* |
| Do. leather | ཀྱལ་པ་ | *kye-pa.* |
| Sacred | དམ་པ། ཆོས་ལྡན་ | *t́am-pa; chhön-den.* |
| Sacrifice (religious offering) | མཆོད་པ་ | *chhö-pa.* |
| Sacrifice, to | མཆོད་པ་ཕུལ་ (འབུལ་) བ་ | *chhö-pa phü-wa.* |
| Do. *hon.* | མཆོད་པ་འབུལ་ར་ (བ་) གནང་བ་ | *chhö-pa bü-ra nang-wa.* |
| Sad, to be | སེམས་སྐྱོ་བ། སེམས་སྡུག་པ་ | *sem-kyo-wa; sem-duḱ-pa.* |
| Do. *hon.* | ཐུགས་སེམས་སྐྱོ་བ་གནང་བ། ཐུགས་སེམས་སྡུག་ག་ (པ་) གནང་བ་ | *thu-sem kyo-wa nang-wa; thu-sem duḱ-ḱa nang-wa.* |
| Saddle | སྒ། རྟའི་སྒ་ | *ga; te-ga.* |
| Do. *hon.* | ཆིབས་སྒ་ | *chhiṕ-ga.* |
| Saddle, pack | ཁལ་སྒ་ | *khe-ga.* |

| | | |
|---|---|---|
| Saddle, to | རྟའི་སྒ་རྒྱབ་པ་ | *te-ga gyap-pa.* |
| Do. *hon.* | ཆིབས་སྒ་སྐྱོན་པ་ | *chhip-ga kyöm-pa.* |
| Saddle-bag | རྟ་སྒྲོག་ | *ta-dro.* |
| Do. *hon.* | ཆིབས་སྒྲོག་ | *chhip-dro.* |
| Saddle-cloth | སྨ་སྨྲན་ *Ch.* | *ma-tren.* |
| Do. *hon.* | ཆིབས་སྨ་སྨ་སྨྲན་ | *chhip-ma ma-tren.* |
| Saddle-girth | སྒློ་ | *lo.* |
| Do. *hon.* | ཆིབས་སྒློ་ | *chhip-lo.* |
| Safe (steadfast) | བརྟན་པོ་ | *tem-po.* |
| Safflower (Saffron) | གུར་གུམ་ | *kur-kum.* |
| Saffron | ཁ་ཆེ་ཤ་ཀ་མ་ | *kha-chhe sha-ka-ma.* |
| Sagacious | རིག་པ་ཆེན་པོ་ | *rik-pa chhem-po.* |
| Do. *hon.* | ཐུགས་རིག་ཆེན་པོ་ | *thu-ri chhem-po.* |
| Sagacity | རིག་པ་ | *rik-pa.* |
| Do. *hon.* | ཐུགས་རིག་ | *thu-ri.* |
| Sailor | མཉན་པ་ | *nyem-pa.* |
| Do. *hon.* | མཉན་དཔོན་ལགས་ | *nyem-pön-la.* |
| Saint, Buddhist | བྱང་ཆུབ་སེམས་དཔའ་ | *chang-chhup sem-pa.* |
| Saintly | དམ་པ། ཆོས་ལྡན་ | *tam-pa; chhön-den.* |
| Sake of, for the | དོན་ལ་ | *tön-la.* |

| | | |
|---|---|---|
| Sake of, for the *hon.* | སྐུ་དོན་ལ་ | *ku-tön-la.* |
| Sal ammoniac | རྒྱ་ཚྭ་ | *gya-tsha.* |
| Salary | ཕོགས་ | *pho.* |
| Do. *hon.* | གསོལ་ཕོགས་ | *sö-pho.* |
| Salesman | ཚོང་པ་ | *tshong-pa.* |
| Do. *hon.* | ཚོང་དཔོན་ | *tshong-pön.* |
| Saliva | ཁ་ཆུ་ | *kha-chhu.* |
| Do. *hon.* | ཞལ་ཆུ་ | *sḱe-chhu.* |
| Salt | ཚྭ་ | *tsha* |
| Do. *hon.* | ལྗགས་ཚྭ་ | *ja-tsha.* |
| Saltpetre | ཟེ་ཚྭ་ | *śe-tsha.* |
| Salute, to | ཕྱག་འབུལ་ཞུ་བ་ | *chham-bü sḱu-wa.* |
| Do. *hon.* | ཕྱག་འབུལ་ཞུ་བ་གནང་བ་ | *chham-bü sḱu-wa nang-wa.* |
| Salvation | ཐར་པ་ | *thar-pa.* |
| Same | གཅིག་པ་ | *chiḱ-pa.* |
| Sample | དཔེ། སྤུས་ཚད་ | *pe ; pü-tshe.* |
| Sanctify, to (consecrate) | རབ་གནས་བྱེད་པ་ | *raṗ-ne cḱe-pa.* |
| Do. *hon.* | རབ་གནས་གནང་བ་ | *raṗ-ne nang-wa.* |
| Sanction | དོན་སྨིན་ | *ḱön-min.* |
| Sand | ཕྱེ་མ་ | *chhe-ma.* |

| | | |
|---|---|---|
| Sand-grouse | གང་ག་ལིང་ | *kang-ka-ling.* |
| Sandal | ཀྲད་པ་ | *tre-pa.* |
| Sandal-wood | ཙན་དན་ | *tsen-ten.* |
| Sanskrit | སྔགས་སྐད་ | *nga-ke.* |
| Sap | ཆུ་ | *chhu.* |
| Sapient | ཡོན་ཏན་ཆེན་པོ་ | *yön-ten chhem-po.* |
| Do. *hon.* | སྐུ་ཡོན་ཆེན་པོ་ | *ku-yön chhem-po.* |
| Sapphire | ཨིནྡྲ་ནཱི་ལ་ | *in-tra-ni-la.* |
| Sash | སྐེ་རགས་ | *ke-ra.* |
| Do. *hon.* | སྐུ་རགས་ | *ku-ra.* |
| Satan | བདུད་ | *dü.* |
| Satin (cloth) | ཟུབ་ | *sup.* |
| Satisfied, to be | འདོད་པ་གང་བ་ | *dö-pa kang-wa.* |
| Do. *hon.* | ཐུགས་འདོད་གང་བ་ | *thung-dö kang-wa.* |
| Satisfied, to be (with food) | འགྲང་བ་ | *drang-wa.* |
| Do. (with water) | ཁ་ངོམ་པ་ | *kha ngom-pa.* |
| Do. *hon.* | ཞལ་ངོམ་པ་གནང་བ་ | *ske ngom-pa nang-wa.* |
| Saturday | གཟའ་སྤེན་པ་ | *sa-pem-pa.* |
| Sauce | ཤ་ཁུ་ | *sha-khu.* |
| Do. *hon.* | སྐྱུམ་ཁུ་ | *trung-khu.* |

| | | |
|---|---|---|
| Saucepan | ཚལ་སླང་ | *tshe-lang.* |
| Saucer | ཏྲ་ཀྱ་ | *t́ra-kya.* |
| Do. *hon.* | ཞལ་ཀྱ་ | *sḱe-kya.* |
| Saucy (rude) | འཛིང་པ་སྦོམ་པོ། ཀྱོང་པོ་ | *jing-pa bom-po; ḱyong-po.* |
| Saunter, to (linger) | འགོར་བ་ | *gor-wa.* |
| Do. *hon.* | ཕེབ་འགོར་གནང་བ་ | *phe-gor nang-wa.* |
| Sausage | རྒྱུ་མ་ | *gyu-ma.* |
| Do. *hon.* | བཞེས་རྒྱོང་ (བཞེས་རྒྱུ་) | *sḱe-gyong.* |
| Savage, *s.* (barbarian) | ཀླ་ཀློ་ | *la-lo.* |
| Do. *adj.* (ferocious) | ངན་པ་ | *ngem-pa.* |
| Save, to (rescue) | བསྐྱབས་པ་ (སྐྱོབ་པ་) | *kyaṕ-pa.* |
| Do. *hon.* | སྐྱབས་འཇུག་གནང་བ་ | *kyam-juḱ nang-wa.* |
| Save, to (money) | བསག་པ་ (གསོག་པ་) | *saḱ-pa.* |
| Do. *hon.* | གསོག་ག་ (པ་) གནང་བ་ | *soḱ-ka nang-wa.* |
| Saviour | སྐྱབས་མགོན་ | *kyam-gön.* |
| Savour | བྲོ་ | *t́ro.* |
| Do. *hon.* | ལྗགས་བྲོ་ | *ja-t́ro.* |
| Savoury | ཞིམ་པོ་ | *sḱim-po.* |
| Do. *hon.* | སྨྲོ་པོ་ | *tro-po.* |
| Saw (cutting instrument) | སོག་ལེ་ | *so-le.* |

| | | |
|---|---|---|
| Saw (proverb) | གཏམ་དཔེ་ | *tam-pe.* |
| Saw, to | སོག་ལེ་རྒྱབ་པ་ | *so-le gyaṕ-pa.* |
| Say, to | ལབ་པ། ཟེར་བ་ | *laṕ-pa ; śe-wa.* |
| Do. *hon.* | གསུང་བ་ | *sung-wa.* |
| Saying | སྐད་ཆ་ | *ke-chha.* |
| Scab | རྨ་ཁོག་ | *ma-kho.* |
| Scabbard | ཤུབས་ | *shuṕ.* |
| Scalded, to be | ཆུ་འཁོལ་མས་འཚིག་པ་ | *chhu-khö-me tshiḱ-pa.* |
| Do. *hon.* | ཆབ་ཆུ་འཁོལ་མས་འཚིག་པ་ | *chhaṕ-chhu khö-me tshiḱ-pa.* |
| Scales, a pair of | ཉ་ག་ | *nya-ga.* |
| Scamp | བསྟན་བཞིག། འཛབ་ཆེན་ | *ten-sḱi ; dzaṕ-chhen.* |
| Scan, to (look at) | ལྟ་བ་ | *ta-wa.* |
| Do. *hon.* | གཟིགས་པ་ | *śi-pa.* |
| Scanty | ཉུང་ཉུང་ | *nyung-nyung.* |
| Scar | རྨ་རྗེས་ | *ma-je.* |
| Do. *hon.* | སྐུ་རྨའི་རྗེས་ | *ku-me-je.* |
| Scarce | དཀོན་པོ་ | *köm-po.* |
| Scare, to | ཞེད་སྐྲག་སླང་བ་ | *sḱe-tra lang-wa.* |
| Do. *hon.* | ཞེད་སྐྲག་སློང་ང་(བ་) གནང་བ་ | *sḱe-tra long-nga nang-wa.* |
| Scared, to be | ཞེད་པ་ | *sḱe-pa.* |

| | | |
|---|---|---|
| Scared, to be, *hon.* | ཞེད་པ་གནང་བ་ | *sKe-pa nang-wa.* |
| Scarf, complimentary | ཁ་བཏགས་ | *kha-ta.* |
| Do. *hon.* | མཇལ་དར་ | *je-ťar.* |
| Scarf, complimentary, best | ནང་མཛོད་ | *nang-dzö.* |
| Do. second best | ཨ་ཤེ་ | *a-she.* |
| Do. third best | ཕྱི་ཕྱག་ | *chhi-pa.* |
| Do. fourth best | ཟུར་ཨ་ཤེ་ | *su a-she.* |
| Do. fifth best | ཕྱི་མཛོད་ | *chhi-dzö.* |
| Do. sixth best | ཁ་སྔོན་ | *kha-ngön.* |
| Do. seventh best | གསོལ་བཏགས་ | *sö-ta.* |
| Do. cheapest | རྒྱས་ཕྱག་ | *gye-pa.* |
| Scarlet | དམར་པོ་ | *ma-po.* |
| Scatter, to (strew) | གཏོར་བ་ | *tor-wa.* |
| Do *hon.* | གཏོར་ར་ (བ་) གནང་བ་ | *tor-ra nang-wa.* |
| Schedule | ཟུར་ཐོ་ | *ƀur-tho.* |
| Scent, *s.* | དྲི་མ་ | *ťri-ma.* |
| Sceptre (thunder bolt) | རྡོ་རྗེ་ | *dor-je.* |
| Scholar (pupil) | བསླབ་ཕྲུག་ | *lap-thru.* |
| Scholarly (learned) | ཡོན་ཏན་ཆེན་པོ་ | *yön-ten chhem-po.* |
| Do. *hon.* | སྐུ་ཡོན་ཆེན་པོ་ | *ku-yön chhem-po.* |

| School | བསླབ་གྲྭ་ | *laṕ-t́ra.* |
|---|---|---|
| School-master | དགེ་རྒན་ | *ge-gen.* |
| Science (skill) | རིག་པ་ | *riḱ-pa.* |
| Do. *hon.* | ཐུགས་རིག་ | *thu-ri.* |
| Science (knowledge) | ཤེས་བྱ་ | *she-cḱa.* |
| Scissors | ཛམ་ཙེ་ (ཅམ་ཙེ་) | *cḱem-tse.* |
| Do. *hon.* | ཕྱག་ཛམ་ (ཕྱག་ཅམ་) | *chha-cḱem.* |
| Scoff, to | ཀྱག་ཀྱག་བྱས་ནས་ལབ་པ་ | *kya-kya cḱe-ne laṕ-pa.* |
| Do. *hon.* | ཀྱག་ཀྱག་གནང་ནས་གསུང་བ་ | *kya-kya nang-ne sung-wa.* |
| Scold, to | གཤེ་གཤེ་བཏང་ (གཏོང་) བ་ | *she-she tang-wa.* |
| Do. *hon.* | བཀའ་བཀྱོན་གནང་བ་ | *kaṕ-kyön nang-wa.* |
| Scoop, *s.* | སྐྱོགས་ | *kyo.* |
| Scoop, to | སྐྱོགས་ཀྱིས་བདོན་ (འདོན་) པ་ | *kyo-kyi töm-pa.* |
| Do. *hon.* | སྐྱོགས་ཀྱིས་འདོན་པ་གནང་བ་ | *kyo-kyi döm-pa nang-wa.* |
| Scope (intention) | དོན་དག་ | *t́ön-t́a.* |
| Do. *hon.* | སྐུ་དོན་ | *ku-t́ön.* |
| Scorch, to | འཚིག་པ་ | *tshiḱ-pa.* |
| Score (twenty) | ཉི་ཤུ་ | *nyi-shu.* |
| Scorn, to | ཀྱག་ཀྱག་བྱས་ནས་ལབ་པ་ | *kya-kya cḱe-ne laṕ-pa.* |
| Do. *hon.* | ཀྱག་ཀྱག་གནང་ནས་གསུང་བ་ | *kya-kya nang-ne sung-wa.* |

| | | |
|---|---|---|
| Scorpion | སྡིག་པ་ར་ཛ་ | *diḱ-pa ra-dza.* |
| Scoundrel | བསྟན་བཞིག། འཛབ་ཆེན་ | *ten-sḰi; dzaṕ-chhen.* |
| Scourge, to | ཏའི་ལྕག་གཞུ་བ་ | *te-cha sḰu-wa.* |
| Scraggy (of persons and animals) | ཤ་སྐམ་པོ་ | *sha kam-po.* |
| Do. *hon.* (of persons) | སྐུ་ཤ་སྐམ་པོ་ | *ku-sha kam-po.* |
| Do. *hon.* (of animals) | བཞེས་ཤ་སྐམ་པོ་ | *she-sha kam-po.* |
| Scrap | ཏུམ་བུ་ | *t́um-ṕu.* |
| Scrape, to | བྲད་བྲད་ (འབྲད་འབྲད་) བཏང་ (གཏོང་) བ་ | *t́re-t́re tang-wa.* |
| Do. *hon.* | བྲད་བྲད་ (འབྲད་འབྲད་) གཏོང་ང་ (བ་) གནང་བ་ | *t́re-t́re tong-nga nang-wa* |
| Scrape off, to | ཤུད་ཤུད་བྱེད་པ་ | *shü-shü cḰe-pa.* |
| Do. *hon.* | ཤུད་ཤུད་གནང་བ་ | *shü-shü nang-wa.* |
| Scratch, to | སྦར་ཤད་རྒྱབ་པ་ | *bar-she gyaṕ-pa.* |
| Do. *hon.* | ཕྱག་ཤད་སྐྱོན་པ་ | *chha-she kyöm-pa.* |
| Scream, to | སྐད་རྒྱབ་པ་ | *ke-gyaṕ-pa.* |
| Do. *hon.* | གསུང་སྐད་སྐྱོན་པ་ | *sung-ke kyöm-pa.* |
| Screen | ཡོལ་ལ་ (ཡོལ་བ་) | *yö-la.* |
| Scriptures | གསུང་རབ་ | *sung-raṕ.* |

| | | |
|---|---|---|
| Scroll | ཤུག་གུའི་ཆག་པ་ | *shuk-kü chhak-pa.* |
| Scruple | ཐེ་ཚོམ་ | *the-tshom.* |
| Sea | རྒྱ་མཚོ་ | *gyam-tsho.* |
| Seal | དམ་ཕྲུག། ཐེ་ཙེ་ | *ťam-thru ; the-tse.* |
| Do. *hon.* | ཕྱག་དམ་ | *chha-ťam.* |
| Seal, to | དམ་ཕྲུག་རྒྱབ་པ། ཐེ་ཙེ་རྒྱབ་པ་ | *ťam-thru gyaṕ-pa ; the-tse gyaṕ-pa.* |
| Do. *hon.* | ཕྱག་དམ་སྐྱོན་པ་ | *chha-ťam-kyöm-pa.* |
| Sealing-wax | ལ་ཆ་ | *la-chha.* |
| Seam | ཚེམ་བུ་ | *tshem-ṕu.* |
| Do. *hon.* | ཕྱག་ཚེམ་ | *chha-tshem.* |
| Search, to | འཚལ་བ་ (འཚོལ་བ་) | *tshel-wa.* |
| Do. *hon.* | འཚལ་ར་ (འཚོལ་བ་) གནང་བ་ | *tshe-ra nang-wa.* |
| Season | ནམ་དུས་ | *nam-ťü.* |
| Seat | ཀུབ་ཀྱག། ཁྲིའུ་ཤིང་ | *kuṕ-kya ; thri-u-shing.* |
| Do. *hon.* | ཞབས་ཀྱག་ | *sĥaṕ-kya.* |
| Secluded place | དབེན་གནས་ | *en-ne.* |
| Second | གཉིས་པ་ | *nyi-pa.* |
| Secondly | གཉིས་པར་ | *nyi-pa.* |
| Secret | གསང་བ་ | *sang-wa.* |

| | | |
|---|---|---|
| Secretary | དྲུང་ཡིག་བགྲེས་པ་ | *t́rung-yi dre-pa.* |
| Secretary, Chief | དྲུང་ཡིག་ཆེན་མོ་བ་ | *t́rung-yi chhem-mo-wa.* |
| Secrete, to | སྦེད་པ་ | *be-pa.* |
| Do. *hon.* | སྦེད་པ་གནང་བ་ | *be-pa nang-wa.* |
| Sect (religious) | ཆོས་ལུགས་ | *chhö-lu.* |
| Secular | འཇིག་རྟེན་པ་ | *jiḱ-tem-pa.* |
| Secure (steadfast) | བརྟན་པོ་ | *tem-po.* |
| Security (bail) | ཁས་ཁྱགས་ | *khe-khya.* |
| Do. *hon.* | ཞལ་ཁྱགས་ | *sḱe-khya.* |
| Security, to give | ཁས་ཁྱགས་བྱེད་པ་ | *khe-khya cḱe-pa.* |
| Do. *hon.* | ཞལ་ཁྱགས་གནང་བ་ | *sḱe-khya nang-wa.* |
| Sedan-chair | མགྱོགས་དཔྱང་ (འཁྱོགས་དཔྱང་) | *gyo-chang.* |
| Do. *hon.* | ཕེབ་དཔྱང་ | *phep̍-chang.* |
| Sediment | སྙིགས་ | *nyi.* |
| Seduce, to | སླུ་བ་ | *lu-wa.* |
| Do. *hon.* | སླུ་བ་གནང་བ་ | *lu-wa nang-wa.* |
| See, to | མཐོང་བ་ | *thong-wa.* |
| Do. *hon.* | གཟིགས་པ་ | *śi-pa.* |
| Seed | སོན། ས་བོན་ | *sön ; sa-p̍ön.* |

| | | |
|---|---|---|
| Seek, to | འཚལ་བ་ (འཚོལ་བ་) | *tshel-wa.* |
| Do. *hon.* | འཚལ་ར་ (འཚོལ་བ་) གནང་བ་ | *tshe-ra nang-wa.* |
| Seemingly (probably) | ཡིན་པ་འདྲ་ | *yim-pa-dra.* |
| Seemly (becoming) | འོས་པོ་ | *ö-po.* |
| Seize, to | ཟིན་པ་ (འཛིན་པ་) | *śim-pa.* |
| Do *hon.* | ཟིན་ (འཛིན་) པ་གནང་བ་ | *śim-pa nang-wa.* |
| Select, to | འདམ་པ་ | *dam-pa.* |
| Do. *hon.* | འདམ་པ་གནང་བ་ | *dam-pa nang-wa.* |
| Self | རང་ | *rang.* |
| Selfish | རང་འདོད་ཚ་པོ་ | *rang-dö tsha-po.* |
| Selfishness | རང་འདོད་ | *rang-dö.* |
| Sell, to | འཚོང་བ་ | *tshong-wa.* |
| Do. *hon.* | འཚོང་ང་ (བ་) གནང་བ་ | *tshong-nga nang-wa.* |
| Send, to | བཏང་བ་ (གཏོང་བ་) | *tang-wa.* |
| Do. *hon.* | གཏོང་ང་ (བ་) གནང་བ་ | *tong-nga nang-wa.* |
| Senior | རྒན་པ་ | *gem-pa.* |
| Sense (opinion) | བསམ་པ་ | *sam-pa.* |
| Do. *hon.* | ཐུགས་སེམས་ | *thu-sem.* |
| Sense (purport) | དོན་དག་ | *tön-ťa.* |
| Do. *hon.* | སྐུ་དོན་ | *ku-ťön.* |

| | | |
|---|---|---|
| Sense (understanding) | བློ་གྲོས་ | *lo-trö.* |
| Senseless (nonsensical) | དོན་མེད་ | *tön-me.* |
| Do. (unconscious) | དྲན་མེད་ | *trem-me.* |
| Sensible (intelligent) | རིག་པ་ཡག་པོ་ | *rik-pa yak-po.* |
| Do. *hon.* | ཐུགས་རིག་ཡག་པོ་ | *thu-ri yak-po.* |
| Sentence *s.* (in a book) | ཤོག་ལོ་ | *shok-lo.* |
| Do. a single | ཤོག་ལོ་ཁ་གཅིག་ | *shok-lo kha-chi.* |
| Sentence, to (punish) | ཁྲིམས་བཏང་ (གཏོང་) བ་ | *thrim tang-wa.* |
| Do. *hon.* | ཁྲིམས་གཏོང་ང་ (བ་) གནང་བ་ | *thrim tong-nga nang-wa.* |
| Do. *h. hon.* | བཀའ་ཁྲིམས་གནང་བ་ | *ka-thrim nang-wa.* |
| Sentence, to (fine) | ཉེས་པ་བཏང་ (གཏོང་) བ་ | *nye-pa tang-wa.* |
| Do. *hon.* | ཉེས་པ་གནང་བ་ | *nye-pa nang-wa.* |
| Do. *h. hon.* | བཀའ་ཉེས་གནང་བ་ | *ka-nye nang-wa.* |
| Sentiment (opinion) | བསམ་པ་ | *sam-pa.* |
| Do. *hon.* | ཐུགས་སེམས་ | *thu-sem.* |
| Sentinel | སོ་པ་ | *so-pa.* |
| Separate, to | དབྱེན་ (དབྱེ་བ་) ཕྱེ་བ་ | *yen chhe-wa.* |
| Do. *hon.* | དབྱེན་ (དབྱེ་བ་) ཕྱེ་བ་གནང་བ་ | *yen chhe-wa nang-wa.* |
| Separately | ཁ་ཁ་བྱས་ནས་ | *kha-kha cke-ne.* |
| Sepoy | དམག་མི་ | *ma-mi.* |

| | | |
|---|---|---|
| Sepulchre | རོ་སྦེད་ས་ | *ro be-sa.* |
| Series | རིམ་པ་ | *rim-pa.* |
| Serpent | སྦྲུལ་ | *drü.* |
| Serpent-demon | ཀླུ་ | *lu.* |
| Servant | གཡོག་པོ་ | *yok-po.* |
| Do. *hon.* | ཞབས་ཕྱི་ | *sḰaṕ-chhi.* |
| Servant, female | ཞལ་ཏ་མ་ | *sḰe-ta-ma.* |
| Serve, to | གཡོག་བྱེད་པ་ | *yo cḰe-pa.* |
| Do. *hon.* | ཞབས་ཕྱི་ཞུ་བ་ | *sḰaṕ-chhi sḰu-wa.* |
| Service, religious | ཆོ་ག། སྐུ་རིམ་ | *chho-ga ; ku-rim.* |
| Serviceable, to be | ཕན་ཐོགས་པ་ | *phen-thok-pa.* |
| Do. *hon.* | ཐུགས་ཕན་གསོ་བ་ | *thu-phen so-wa.* |
| Sesamum | ཏིལ་ *Hind* | *til.* |
| Set, to (place) | བཞག་པ་ (འཛོག་པ་) | *sḰak-pa.* |
| Do. *hon.* | གཞོག་ག་ (འཛོག་པ་) གནང་བ་ | *sḰok-ka nang-wa.* |
| Set, to (of the sun) | རྒས་པ་ | *ge-pa.* |
| Set out, to (depart) | འཐོན་པ་ | *thöm-pa.* |
| Do. *hon.* | ཕེབ་པ་ | *phe-pa.* |
| Set right, to (adjust) | སྒྲིག་པ་ | *drik-pa.* |

| | | |
|---|---|---|
| Set right, to (adjust), *hon.* | སྒྲིག་ག་ (པ་) གནང་བ་ | *drik-ḱa nang-wa.* |
| Settle, to (decide) | ཐག་བཅད་ (གཅོད་) པ་ | *tha che-pa.* |
| Do. *hon.* | ཐག་གཅོད་པ་གནང་བ་ | *tha chö-pa nang-wa.* |
| Do. *h. hon.* | ཐུགས་ཐག་གཅོད་པ་གནང་བ་ | *thu-tha chö-pa nang-wa.* |
| Settle, to (a law-suit out of court) | འདུམ་བཏང་ (གཏོང་) བ་ | *dum tang-wa.* |
| Do. *hon.* | བཀའ་འདུམ་གནང་བ་ | *kan-dum nang-wa.* |
| Settle, to (arrange) | སྒྲིག་པ་ | *drik-pa.* |
| Do. *hon.* | སྒྲིག་ག་ (པ་) གནང་བ་ | *drik-ḱa nang-wa.* |
| Seven | བདུན་ | *dün.* |
| Seventh | བདུན་པ་ | *dün-pa.* |
| Seventeen | བཅུ་བདུན་ | *chuṕ-dün.* |
| Seventeenth | བཅུ་བདུན་པ་ | *chuṕ-dün-pa.* |
| Seventieth | བདུན་ཅུ་པ་ | *dün-chu-pa.* |
| Seventy | བདུན་ཅུ་ | *dün-chu.* |
| Sever, to (cut) | བཅད་པ་ (གཅོད་པ་) | *che-pa.* |
| Do. *hon.* | བཅད་ (གཅོད་) པ་གནང་བ་ | *che-pa nang-wa.* |
| Several | འགའ་ཆེན་ | *ga-chhen.* |
| Severally | སོ་སོ་བྱས་ནས་ | *so-so cḱe-ne.* |
| Severe (harsh, of human beings) | གྱོང་པོ་ | *ḱyong-po.* |

| | | |
|---|---|---|
| Severe (of gods) | དྲག་པོ་ | *ťrak-po.* |
| Severe (strict) | དམ་པོ། བཙན་པོ་ | *ťam-po; tsem-po.* |
| Sew, to | འཚེམ་པ། འཚེམ་བུ་རྒྱབ་པ་ | *tshem-pa; tshem-ṕu gyaṕ-pa.* |
| Do. *hon.* | ཕྱག་འཚེམ་གནང་བ། ཕྱག་འཚེམ་སྐྱོན་པ་ | *chha-tshem nang-wa; chha-tshem kyöm-pa.* |
| Sew, to (together) | སྒྲེལ་བ་ | *drel-wa.* |
| Do. *hon.* | སྒྲེལ་ར་ (བ་) གནང་བ་ | *dre-ra nang-wa.* |
| Shackles (for hands) | ལག་ལྕགས་ | *laǩ-cha.* |
| Do. (for feet) | རྐང་ལྕགས་ | *kang-cha.* |
| Shade | བསིལ་གྲིབ་ | *sil-ťriṕ.* |
| Shadow | གྲིབ་མ་ | *ťri-ma.* |
| Shaggy | ཙུབ་པོ་ | *tsuṕ-po.* |
| Shake, to *v.t.* | འགུལ་འགུལ་བཏང་ (གཏོང་) བ། དཀྲུག་དཀྲུག་བྱེད་པ་ | *gü-gü tang-wa; truǩ-truǩ che-pa.* |
| Do. *hon.* | འགུལ་འགུལ་གཏོང་ང་ (བ་) གནང་བ། དཀྲུག་དཀྲུག་གནང་བ་ | *gü-gü tong-nga nang-wa; truǩ-truǩ nang-wa.* |
| Shake, to *v.i.* | འཁྲུག་པ་ | *thruǩ-pa.* |
| Do. (of human being) | འདར་བ་ | *dar-wa.* |

| | | |
|---|---|---|
| Shake, to (of human being), *hon.* | སྐུ་འདར་སྐྱོན་པ་ | *kün-dar kyöm-pa.* |
| Shake, to (of bridge, etc.) | ལྡེམ་ལྡེམ་བྱེད་པ་ | *dem-dem cKe-pa.* |
| Shallow, to be | གཏིང་རིང་པོ་མེད་པ་ | *ting-ring-po me-pa.* |
| Sham (false) | རྫུས་མ་ | *dzü-ma.* |
| Sham, to | གྱོད་བཞད་པ་ | *Kyö she-pa.* |
| Do. *hon.* | གྱོད་གསུང་བ་ | *Kyö sung-wa.* |
| Sham illness, to | ན་རྫུབཏབ་ (འདེབས་) པ་ | *na-dzu taṕ-pa.* |
| Do. *hon.* | སྙུང་རྫུ་བཏབ་ (འདེབས་) པ་ | *nyung-dzu taṕ-pa.* |
| Shame | ངོ་ཚ་ | *ngo-tsha.* |
| Shame, to feel | ངོ་ཚ་བ་ | *ngo-tsha-wa.* |
| Do. *hon.* | ཐུགས་ངོ་ཚ་བ་ | *thu-ngo-tsha-wa.* |
| Shamefaced | ངོ་ཚ་པོ་ | *ngo-tsha-po.* |
| Shameful | ངོ་ཚ་པོ་ | *ngo-tsha-po.* |
| Shameless, to be | ངོ་ཚ་མེད་པ་ | *ngo-tsha me-pa.* |
| Shape, *n.* | བཟོ་བལྟ་ | *śoṕ-ta.* |
| Do. *hon.* | སྐུ་བཟོ་ | *ku-śo.* |
| Share | སྐལ་ལ་ (སྐལ་བ་) | *ke-la.* |
| Do. *hon.* | སྐུ་སྐལ་ | *ku-ke.* |
| Share, to | བགོད་པ། བགོ་བཤའ་རྒྱབ་པ་ | *gö-pa ; goṕ-sha gyaṕ-pa.* |

| | | |
|---|---|---|
| Share, to, *hon.* | བགོད་པ་གནང་བ། བགོ་བ་ཞལ་སྐྱོན་པ་ | *gö-pa nang-wa; gop-sha kyöm-pa.* |
| Sharp (not blunt) | རྣོ་པོ་ | *no-po.* |
| Do. (shrewd) | གཅང་པོ་ | *chang-po.* |
| Do. *hon.* | ཐུགས་གཅང་པོ་ | *thu-chang-po.* |
| Sharpen, to | བདར་བ་ | *dar-wa.* |
| Do. *hon.* | བདར་ར་ (བ་) གནང་བ་ | *dar-ra nang-wa.* |
| Sharpen, to (by blacksmith) | ཁ་འདོན་བྱེད་པ་ | *khan-dön cke-pa.* |
| Shatter, to | ཧྲུག་ཧྲུག་བཏང་ (གཏོང་) བ་ | *hru-hru tang-wa.* |
| Shave, to | སྐྲ་བཞར་བ་ | *tra skar-wa.* |
| Do. *hon.* | དབུ་སྐྲ་བཞར་བ་ | *u-tra skar-wa.* |
| Shaved head, having a (as a monk) | མགོ་རིལ་རིལ་ | *go-ri-ri.* |
| Do. *hon.* | དབུ་རིལ་རིལ་ | *u-ri-ri.* |
| Shawl (of lamas) | གཟན་ | *śen.* |
| Do. *hon.* | སྐུ་གཟན་ | *ku-śen.* |
| She | མོ་ | *mo.* |
| Sheaf | ཆག་པ་ | *chhak-pa.* |
| Shear, to | བལ་བག་ (འབྲེག་) པ་ | *ṕe ṕak-pa.* |

| | | |
|---|---|---|
| Shear, to, *hon.* | བལ་བག་ (འབྲེག་) ག་ (པ་) གནང་བ་ | *ṕe ṕak-ḱa nang-wa.* |
| Sheath | ཤུབས་ | *shuṕ.* |
| Sheep | ལུག་ | *lu.* |
| Sheep, flock of | ལུག་ཁྱུ་ | *luḱ-khyu.* |
| Sheep-skin | ལུག་པགས་ | *luḱ-pa.* |
| Sheet of paper | ཤོག་གུ་ (ཤོག་བུ་) | *shu-ḱu.* |
| Do. *hon.* | ཕྱག་ཤོག་ | *chha-sho.* |
| Shelf | བང་ཁྲི། བང་ག་ | *ṕang-thri; ṕang-ḱa.* |
| Shell | འགྲོན་བུ་ | *dröm-ṕu.* |
| Shell, conch | དུང་ | *t́ung.* |
| Shelter (refuge) | སྐྱབས་གནས་ | *kyam-ne.* |
| Shepherd | ལུག་རྫི་ | *luḱ-dzi.* |
| Shield | ཕུབ་ | *phuṕ.* |
| Shift, to (move) | སྤོ་བ་ | *po-wa.* |
| Do. *hon.* | སྤོ་བ་གནང་བ་ | *po-wa nang-wa.* |
| Shin, shin-bone | ངར་དུང་ | *ngar-t́ung.* |
| Do. *hon.* | ཞབས་པིས་ངར་དུང་ | *sḱaṕ-pi ngar-t́ung.* |
| Shine (brightness) | འོད་ | *ö.* |
| Shine, to | འོད་རྒྱབ་པ་ | *ö gyaṕ-pa.* |

| | | |
|---|---|---|
| Shine, to (of the sun) | ཤར་བ་ | *shar-wa.* |
| Do. (of the moon) | ཟླ་དཀར་ཤར་བ་ | *da-ka shar-wa.* |
| Ship | གྲུ་ | *ťru.* |
| Shirt | འོག་འཇུག་ | *ön-ju.* |
| Do. *hon.* | སྐུ་འཇུག་ | *kün-ju.* |
| Shiver, to (with fear, cold, etc.) | འདར་བ་ | *dar-wa.* |
| Do. *hon.* | སྐུ་འདར་སྐྱོན་པ་ | *kun-dar kyöm-pa.* |
| Shock | ངམས་སྐྲག་ | *ngam-tra.* |
| Shoe | ལྷམ། ལྷམ་ཁོག་ | *hlam; hlam-kho.* |
| Do. *hon.* | ཞབས་ཆགས་ | *sȟap̆-chha.* |
| Shoe (European style) | འཛུ་ད་ *Hin.* | *ju-ta.* |
| Shoe-maker | ལྷམ་བཟོ་ | *hlam-śo.* |
| Shoot, to (with gun, etc.) | རྒྱབ་པ་ | *gyap̆-pa.* |
| Do. *hon.* | སྐྱོན་པ་ | *kyöm-pa.* |
| Shop | ཚོང་ཁང་ | *tshong-khang.* |
| Shore | འགྲམ་ | *dram.* |
| Short | ཐུང་ཐུང་ | *thung-thung.* |
| Short man | དེ་པོ་ | *te-po.* |
| Do. *hon.* | སྐུ་གཟུགས་ཆུང་ཆུང་ | *ku-śu chhung chhung.* |

| | | |
|---|---|---|
| Short-cut (road) | མགྱོགས་ལམ་ | *gyo-lam.* |
| Shorten, to (abbreviate) | སྡུད་པ། དུམ་དུམ་བྱེད་པ་ | *dü-pa ; dum-dum cḱe-pa.* |
| Shortly (soon) | ཧྲིབ་ཙ་ (ཙམ་) གཅིག་ལ་ | *hrip-tsa-chi-la.* |
| Shoulder | དཔུང་པ་ | *pung-pa.* |
| Do. *hon.* | ཕྱག་དཔུང་ | *chha-pung.* |
| Shout, to | སྐད་རྒྱབ་པ་ | *ke-gyaṕ-pa.* |
| Do. *hon.* | གསུང་སྐད་སྐྱོན་པ་ | *sung-ke kyöm-pa.* |
| Shovel | འཇག་མ་ | *ja-ma.* |
| Show | བལྟས་མོ་ | *te-mo.* |
| Do. *hon.* | གཟིགས་མོ་ | *śi-mo.* |
| Show, to | བསྟན་པ་ (སྟོན་པ་) | *tem-pa.* |
| Do. *hon.* | བསྟན་ (སྟོན་) པ་གནང་བ་ | *tem-pa nang-wa.* |
| Do. *inf.* to *sup.* | སྤྱན་ཕེབ་ཞུ་བ། སྤྱན་དར་ཞུ་བ | *chen-phe sḱu-wa; chen-ťar sḱu-wa.* |
| Show off, to (in dress) | དང་འདོད་བྱེད་པ་ | *ťang-dö cḱe-pa.* |
| Do. *hon.* | ཐུགས་དང་འདོད་གནང་བ་ | *thu ťang-dö nang-wa.* |
| Shower of rain, light | སྤྲིན་ཆར་ | *tring-chhar.* |
| Do. mixed with hail | དྲག་ཆར་ | *ťrak-chhar.* |
| Shrewd | གཅང་པོ་ | *chang-po.* |
| Do. *hon.* | ཐུགས་གཅང་པོ་ | *thu-chang-po.* |
| Shrine | ལྷ་ཁང་ | *hla-khang.* |

| | | |
|---|---|---|
| Shrink, to (of cloth, etc.) | འཁུམ་པ་ | *khum-pa.* |
| Shrivel, to | འཁུམ་པ་ | *khum-pa.* |
| Shrub | ཤིང་སྡོང་ཆུང་ཆུང་ | *shing-dong-chung-chung.* |
| Shudder, to | འདར་བ་ | *dar-wa.* |
| Do. *hon.* | སྐུ་འདར་སྐྱོན་པ་ | *kün-dar kyöm-pa.* |
| Shun, to (persons) | དབྱོལ་བ། ཟུར་ནས་འགྲོ་བ་ | *yö-wa ; śur-ne dro-wa.* |
| Do. *hon.* | ཟུར་ནས་ཕེབ་པ་ | *śur-ne phe-pa.* |
| Shun, to (things) | དབྱུག་བཞག་ (འཇོག་) པ། སྤང་བ་ | *yuk-skak-pa ; pang-wa.* |
| Do. *hon.* | དབྱུག་གཞོག་ག་ (འཇོག་པ་) གནང་བ། སྤོང་ང་ (བ་) གནང་བ་ | *yuk-sko-ka nang-wa ; pong-nga nang-wa.* |
| Shut, to (door) | རྒྱབ་པ་ | *gyap-pa.* |
| Do. *hon.* | སྐྱོན་པ་ | *kyöm-pa.* |
| Shut the mouth, to | ཁ་བཙུམ་ (འཛུམ་) པ་ | *kha tsum-pa.* |
| Shut up! (keep quiet) | ཁ་ཁ་སྡོད། ཁ་བཙུམ་ (ཁ་ཚུམ་) | *kha-kha-dö ; kha-tsum.* |
| Do. *hon.* | ཞལ་བཙུམ་ (ཞལ་ཚུམ་) | *ske-tsum.* |
| Shutter | སྒོ་སྤང་ | *go-pang.* |
| Shuttle-cock | ཐེ་བེ་ | *the-be.* |
| Shy, to (of horses) | འདྲོག་པ་ | *drok-pa.* |

| | | |
|---|---|---|
| Shy, to be (bashful) | ངོ་ཚ་བ་ | *ngo-tsha-wa.* |
| Do. *hon.* | ཞལ་རས་ཚ་བ་གནང་བ་ | *sKe-re tsha-wa nang-wa.* |
| Sick, to be | ན་བ་ | *na-wa.* |
| Do. *hon.* | སྙུང་བ་ | *nyung-wa.* |
| Sickle | ཟོར་ར་ ( ཟོར་བ་ ) | *śor-ra.* |
| Sickness | ན་ཚ་ | *na-tsha.* |
| Do. *hon.* | སྙུང་གཞི་ | *nyung-sKi.* |
| Side (of the body) | ཟུར་ | *śur.* |
| Do. (direction) | ཕྱོགས། ངོས་ | *chho; ngö.* |
| Side of, at the | རྩ་ལ་ ( རྩར་ལ་ ) | *tsa-la.* |
| Side of, the far | ཕར་ཕྱོགས་ | *phar-chho.* |
| Side of, the near | ཚུར་ཕྱོགས་ | *tshur-chho.* |
| Sides, on all | ཕན་ཚུན་ | *phen-tshün.* |
| Sift, to | བཙག་པ་ (འཚག་པ་) | *tsak-pa.* |
| Do. *hon.* | བཙག་ག་ (འཚག་པ་) གནང་བ་ | *tsak-ka nang-wa.* |
| Sigh | དབུགས་རིང་ | *u-ring.* |
| Sigh, to | དབུགས་རིང་བཏང་ (གཏོང་) བ་ | *u-ring tang-wa.* |
| Do. *hon.* | དབུགས་རིང་གཏོང་ང་ (བ་) གནང་བ་ | *u-ring tong-nga nang-wa.* |
| Sight (of a gun) | སོ་ཁུང་ | *so-khung.* |

| | | |
|---|---|---|
| Sightless | ལོང་ང་ (ལོང་བ་) | *long-nga.* |
| Do. *hon.* | སྤྱན་ལོང་ང་ (བ་) | *chen-long-nga.* |
| Sign (mark) | རྟགས་ | *ta.* |
| Signal | ལག་བརྡ་ | *laḱ-da.* |
| Signature | ལག་རྟགས་ | *laḱ-ta.* |
| Do. *hon.* | ཕྱག་རྟགས་ | *chha-ta.* |
| Significant (important) | གནད་ཁག་ཆེན་པོ། གལ་ཆེན་པོ་ | *nen-kha chhem-po; ḱe chhem-po.* |
| Signification | དོན་དག་ | *t́ön-t́a.* |
| Do. *hon.* | སྐུ་དོན་ | *ku-t́ön.* |
| Sikkim | འབྲས་ལྗོངས་ | *dren-jong.* |
| Silent, to be | ཁ་ཁ་བསྡད་ (སྡོད་) པ་ | *kha-kha de-pa.* |
| Do. *hon.* | ཞལ་རགས་བཞུགས་པ་ | *sḱe-ra sḱu-pa.* |
| Silk | གོས་ཆེན་ | *ḱö-chhen.* |
| Do. (tussore silk) | འབུ་རས་ | *bu-re.* |
| Silly (weak in intellect) | ལྐུགས་པ། གླེན་པ་ | *kuḱ-pa; lem-pa* |
| Do. (nonsensical) | དོན་མེད་ | *t́ön-me.* |
| Silver, *s.* | དངུལ་ | *ngü.* |
| Do. *adj.* | དངུལ་གྱི་ | *ngü-ḱyi.* |
| Silversmith | དངུལ་བཟོ་བ་ | *ngü śo-wa.* |

| | | |
|---|---|---|
| Similar | ནང་བཞིན། འདྲ་པོ། གཅིག་པ། འདྲ་འདྲ་ | *nang-sḱin ; dra-po ; chiḱ-pa ; dran-dra.* |
| Simple (easy) | ལས་སླ་པོ་ | *le-la-po.* |
| Do. (foolish) | ལྐུགས་པ། གླེན་པ་ | *kuḱ-pa; lem-pa.* |
| Simpleton | ལྐུགས་པ། གླེན་པ་ | *kuḱ-pa ; lem-pa.* |
| Simply (merely) | གཅིག་གོ་ (གཅིག་པོ་) | *chiḱ-ḱo.* |
| Simulate, to | ཀྱོད་བཤད་པ་ | *ḱyö she-pa.* |
| Do. *hon.* | ཀྱོད་གསུང་བ་ | *ḱyö sung-wa.* |
| Sin | སྡིག་པ་ | *diḱ-pa.* |
| Do. *hon.* | སྐུ་སྡིག་ | *ku-di.* |
| Sin, to | སྡིག་པ་བཤགས་ (སོག་) པ་ | *diḱ-pa saḱ-pa.* |
| Do. *hon.* | སྐུ་སྡིག་བཤགས་ག་ (སོག་པ་) གནང་བ་ | *ku-di saḱ-ḱa nang-wa.* |
| Since (afterwards) | གཞུག་ལ། རྗེས་ལ་ | *sḱu-la ; je-la.* |
| Sincere | དྲང་པོ་ | *t́rang-po.* |
| Do. *hon.* | ཐུགས་དྲང་པོ་ | *thuḱ-t́rang-po.* |
| Sincerely | དངོས་ནས་དྲང་ནས་ | *ngö-ne t́rang-ne.* |
| Sinew | རྒྱུས་པ་ | *gyü-pa.* |
| Sinful | ངན་པོ་ | *ngem-po.* |
| Do. *hon.* | ཐུགས་ངན་པོ་ | *thu ngem-po.* |

| | | |
|---|---|---|
| Sing, to | གཞས་བཏང་ (གཏོང་) བ་ | *ske tang-wa.* |
| Do. *hon.* | མགུལ་གླུ་བཞེས་པ་ | *gü-lu ske-pa.* |
| Sing, to (hymns) | མགུར་མ་ལེན་པ་ | *gur-ma lem-pa.* |
| Do. *hon.* | གསུང་མགུར་བཞེས་པ་ | *sung-gur ske-pa.* |
| Single (separate) | གཅིག་པོ་ | *chik-po.* |
| Do. *hon.* | སྐུ་རྐྱང་ | *ku-kyang.* |
| Single (individual) | རེ་རེ་ | *re-re.* |
| Singly | རེ་རེ་བྱས་ནས་ | *re-re che-ne.* |
| Sink, to (of persons) | ཐིམ་པ་ | *thim-pa.* |
| Do. *hon.* | ཐིམ་པ་གནང་བ་ | *thim-pa nang-wa.* |
| Sink, to (of things) | གཟགས་པ་ (འཛོག་པ་) | *śak-pa.* |
| Do. *hon.* | གཟགས་ག་ (འཛོག་པ་) གནང་བ་ | *śak-ka nang-wa.* |
| Sinner | སྡིག་ཅན་ | *dik-chen.* |
| Sinuous | ཀྱོག་ཀྱོག་ | *kyo-kyo.* |
| Sip, to | ཏོག་ཙོ་ཏོག་ཙོ་འཐུང་བ་ | *tok-tso tok-tso thung-wa.* |
| Do. *hon.* | ཏོག་ཙོ་ཏོག་ཙོ་བཞེས་པ་ | *tok-tso tok-tso ske-pa.* |
| Sir | སྐུ་གཞོགས་ (སྐུ་ཞབས་) | *ku-sko.* |
| Sister (general term) | སྤུན་ཀྱག་ | *pün-kya.* |
| Do. *hon.* | སྐུ་མཆེད་ | *kum-chhe.* |

| | | |
|---|---|---|
| Sister, elder | ཨ་ཆེ་ | *a-chhe.* |
| Sister, young | སྤུན་ཀྱག་ཆུང་ང་ (བ་) | *pün-kya chhung-nga.* |
| Do. *hon.* | སྐུ་མཆེད་ཆུང་ང་ (བ་) | *kum-chhe chung-nga.* |
| Sister-in-law (husband's sister) | ཁྱོ་གའི་སྤུན་ཀྱག | *khyo-ge pün-kya.* |
| Do. *hon.* | སྐུ་ཟླའི་སྐུ་མཆེད་ | *kum-de kum-chhe.* |
| Sister-in-law (wife's sister) | སྐྱེ་དམན་གྱི་སྤུན་ཀྱག་ | *kyi-men-k̇yi pün-kya.* |
| Do. *hon.* | སྐུ་ཟླའི་སྐུ་མཆེད་ | *kum-de kum-chhe.* |
| Sister-in-law (brother's wife) | སྤུན་ཀྱག་གི་སྐྱེ་དམན་ | *pün-kya k̇i kyi-men.* |
| Do. *hon.* | སྐུ་མཆེད་ཀྱི་སྐུ་ཟླ་ | *kum-chhe kyi kum-da.* |
| Sit, to | བསྡད་པ་ (སྡོད་པ་) | *de-pa.* |
| Do. *hon.* | བཞུགས་པ་ | *sk̇u-pa.* |
| Do. *h. hon.* | བཞུགས་གདན་འཇག་པ་ | *sk̇u-den jak-pa.* |
| Sit cross-legged, to | སྐྱིལ་ཀྲུང་བྱས་ནས་བསྡད་ (སྡོད་) པ་ | *kyi-trung ck̇e-ne de-pa.* |
| Site | ས་ཆ་ | *sa-chha.* |
| Situation (locality) | ས་ཆ་ | *sa-chha.* |
| Do. (state of affairs, etc.) | གནས་ཚུལ་ | *ne-tshü.* |
| Six | དྲུག་ | *ṫruk̇.* |
| Sixteen | བཅུ་དྲུག་ | *chu-ṫruk̇.* |

| | | |
|---|---|---|
| Sixteenth | བཅུ་དྲུག་པ་ | *chu-ťruk-pa.* |
| Sixth | དྲུག་པ་ | *ťruk-pa.* |
| Sixtieth | དྲུག་ཅུ་པ་ | *ťruk-chu-pa.* |
| Sixty | དྲུག་ཅུ་ | *ťruk-chu.* |
| Size | ཆེ་ཆུང་ | *chhe-chhung.* |
| Skeleton | རུས་ཀྲང་ | *rü-trang.* |
| Sketch | རི་མོ་ | *ri-mo.* |
| Sketch, to | རིས་མོ་བྲིས་པ་ (འབྲི་བ་) | *ri-mo ťri-pa.* |
| Do. *hon.* | རིས་མོ་བྲིས་པ་ (འབྲི་བ་) གནང་བ་ | *ri-mo ťri-pa nang-wa.* |
| Skilful | མཁས་པོ་ | *khe-po.* |
| Skill | རིག་པ་ | *rik-pa.* |
| Do. *hon.* | ཐུགས་རིག་ | *thu-ri.* |
| Skin | པགས་པ་ | *pak-pa.* |
| Skin, to | པགས་པ་ཤུ་བ་ | *pak-pa shu-wa.* |
| Do. *hon* | པགས་པ་ཤུ་བ་གནང་བ་ | *pak-pa shu-wa nang-wa.* |
| Skinny (of persons and animals) | ཤ་སྐམ་པོ་ | *sha kam-po.* |
| Do. *hon.* (of persons) | སྐུ་ཤ་སྐམ་པོ་ | *ku-sha kam-po.* |
| Do. *hon.* (of animals) | བཞེས་ཤ་སྐམ་པོ་ | *sKe-sha kam-po.* |

| | | |
|---|---|---|
| Skull | ཐོད་པ། ཀ་ལི་ *Hind.* | *thö-pa; kap-li.* |
| Skull-drum | ཐོད་རྡམ་ | *thön-tam.* |
| Sky | གནམ། ནམ་མཁའ་ | *nam; nam-kha.* |
| Slack (languid) | ཉ་རེ་ (ར་) ཉོ་རེ་ | *nya-re nyo-re.* |
| Do. (slow) | འགོར་པོ་ | *gor-po.* |
| Slacken, to | ལྷོད་ལྷོད་བཏང་ (གཏོང་) བ་ | *hlö-hlö tang-wa.* |
| Do. *hon.* | ལྷོད་ལྷོད་གཏོང་ང་ (བ་) གནང་བ་ | *hlö-hlö tong-nga nang-wa.* |
| Slander, *s.* | སྨད་ར་ | *me-ra.* |
| Slander, to | སྨད་ར་བཏང་ (གཏོང་) བ་ | *me-ra tang-wa.* |
| Do. *hon.* | སྨད་ར་གཏོང་ང་ (བ་) གནང་བ་ | *me-ra tong-nga nang-wa.* |
| Do. *inf.* to *sup.* | སྨད་ར་ཤུ་བ་ | *me-ra sku-wa.* |
| Slap, to | གཤུ་བ་ | *sku-wa.* |
| Do. *hon.* | གཤུ་བ་གནང་བ་ | *sku-wa nang-wa.* |
| Slate (for writing) | ཡང་བག་ | *yam-pa.* |
| Do. wooden | སྦྱང་ཤིང་ | *jang-shing.* |
| Slaughter, to | བསད་པ་ (གསོད་པ་) | *se-pa.* |
| Do. *hon.* | བསད་ (གསོད་) པ་གནང་བ་ | *se-pa nang-wa.* |
| Slave | ཚེ་གཡོག་ | *tshe-yo.* |
| Slay, to | བསད་པ་ (གསོད་པ་) | *se-pa.* |

| | | |
|---|---|---|
| Slay, to *hon.* | བསད་ (གསོད་) པ་གནང་བ་ | *se-pa nang-wa.* |
| Slay, to (a person of good position) | བཀྲོངས་པ་ (འགྲོང་བ་) | *trong-pa.* |
| Sleep, *s.* | གཉིད་ | *nyi.* |
| Do. *hon.* | མཉལ་ (མནལ་) | *nye.* |
| Sleep, to | ཉལ་བསྡད་ (སྡོད་) པ་ | *nye de-pa.* |
| Do. *hon.* | གཟིམ་བཞུགས་པ་ | *śim sḱu-pa.* |
| Sleep, to go to | གཉིད་ཁུག་པ་ | *nyi khuk-pa.* |
| Do. *hon.* | མཉལ་ (མནལ་) གཟིམ་པ་ | *nye śim-pa.* |
| Sleeping draught | ཞི་སྨན་ | *sḱi-men.* |
| Sleepy, to be | གཉིད་ཚོག་རྒྱབ་པ་ | *nyi-tso gyaṕ-pa.* |
| Do. *hon.* | མཉལ་ (མནལ་) ཚོག་སྐྱོན་པ་ | *nye-tso kyöm-pa.* |
| Sleeve | ཕུ་དུང་ | *phu-ṫung.* |
| Do. *hon.* | ཕྱག་ཕུང་ | *chha-phung.* |
| Slender | ཕྲ་པོ་ | *thra-po.* |
| Slice, to | གདུབ་པ་ | *tuṕ-pa.* |
| Do. *hon.* | གདུབ་པ་གནང་བ་ | *tuṕ-pa nang-wa.* |
| Slice | པྲ་པོ་ | *tra-po.* |
| Slight, *adj.* (thin) | ཤ་སྐམ་པོ་ | *sha kam-po.* |
| Do. *hon.* | སྐུ་ཤ་སྐམ་པོ་ | *ku-sha kam-po.* |

| | | |
|---|---|---|
| Sling (for stone) | སྒུ་རྡོ་ | *gu-do.* |
| Slip, to, *v.i.* | འདྲེད་དག་ཤོར་བ་ | *dre-ťa shor-wa.* |
| Do. *hon.* | ཞབས་འདྲེད་ཤོར་བ་ | *sKam-dre shor-wa.* |
| Slit (fissure) | སེར་ཀ་ | *ser-ka.* |
| Slit, to be (cloth) | རལ་བ་ | *re-wa.* |
| Slope (upward) | གྱེན་ | *kyen.* |
| Do. (downward) | ཐུར་ | *thur.* |
| Slothful | སྙོབས་པོ། ལེ་ལོ་ཆེན་པོ་ | *nyop-po ; le-lo chhem-po.* |
| Slow | འགོར་པོ་ | *gor-po.* |
| Slowly | ག་ལེ་ག་ལེ་ | *ka-le ka-le.* |
| Sluggard | སྙོབས་པོ་ | *nyop-po.* |
| Sluggish (languid) | ཉ་རེ་ (ར་) ཉོ་རེ་ | *nya-re nyo-re.* |
| Slumber, to | གཉིད་ཚོག་རྒྱབ་པ་ | *nyi-tso gyap-pa.* |
| Do. *hon.* | མཉལ་ (མནལ་) ཚོག་སྐྱོན་པ་ | *nye-tso kyöm-pa.* |
| Sly (artful) | གཅང་པོ་ | *chang-po.* |
| Do. *hon.* | ཐུགས་གཅང་པོ་ | *thu-chang-po.* |
| Small | ཆུང་ཆུང་ | *chhung-chhung.* |
| Small-pox | ལྷ་འབྲུམ་ | *hlan-drum.* |
| Smash, to | བཅག་པ་ (གཅོག་པ་) | *chak-pa.* |
| Do. *hon.* | བཅག་ག་ (པ་) གནང་བ་ | *chak-ka nang-wa.* |

| | | |
|---|---|---|
| Smear, to | བྱུག་པ་ (འབྱུག་པ།) སྐུ་བ་ | *chuk-pa ; k̔u-wa.* |
| Do. *hon.* | བྱུགས་ག་ (འབྱུག་པ་) གནང་བ། སྐུ་བ་གནང་བ་ | *chuk-ka nang-wa ; ku-wa nang-wa.* |
| Smell | དྲི་མ་ | *t̔ri-ma.* |
| Smell, to (use the sense of smell) | སྣོམ་པ་ | *nom-pa.* |
| Do. *hon.* | སྣོམ་པ་གནང་བ་ | *nom-pa nang-wa.* |
| Smell, to (have odour) | དྲི་མ་ཁ་བ་ | *t̔ri-ma kha-wa.* |
| Smile, to | ཁ་ཚེ་ཚེ་བྱེད་པ་ | *kha tshe-tshe ck̔e-pa.* |
| Do. *hon.* | ཞལ་ཚེ་ཚེ་གནང་བ་ | *sk̔e tshe-tshe nang-wa.* |
| Smite, to | གཞུ་བ། རྡུང་བ་ | *sk̔u-wa ; dung-wa.* |
| Do. *hon.* | གཞུ་བ་གནང་བ། ཕྱག་འཇུག (འཇུས་) གནང་བ་ | *sk̔u-wa nang-wa ; chhan-ju nang-wa.* |
| Smith | མགར་ར་ (མགར་བ་) | *gar-ra.* |
| Smoke, *s.* | དུ་བ་ (དུད་པ་) | *t̔u-wa.* |
| Smoke, to (tobacco) | འཐུང་བ། འཐེན་པ་ | *thung-wa ; them-pa.* |
| Do. *hon.* | བཞེས་པ་ | *sk̔e-pa.* |
| Smooth | སྙོམ་པོ་ | *nyom-po.* |
| Smother, to | གློ་སུབ་རྒྱབ་པ་ | *lo-sup̔ gyap̔-pa.* |
| Do. *hon.* | གློ་སུབ་སྐྱོན་པ་ | *lo-sup̔ kyöm-pa.* |
| Snake | སྦྲུལ་ | *drü.* |

| | | |
|---|---|---|
| Snap the finger, to | སིར་གོར་ (སེ་གོལ་) རྡབ་པ་ | *sir-k̔or dap̔-pa.* |
| Do. *hon.* | སིར་གོར་ (སེ་གོལ་) རྡབ་པ་ གནང་བ་ | *sir-k̔or dap̔-pa nang-wa.* |
| Snare | རྙི་ | *nyi.* |
| Snatch, to | འཕྲོག་པ་ | *throk-pa.* |
| Do. *hon.* | འཕྲོག་ག་ (པ་) གནང་བ་ | *throk-k̔a nang-wa.* |
| Sneeze, to | ཧབ་བྲིད་ (སྦྲིད་) རྒྱབ་པ་ | *hap̔-t̔ri gyap̔-pa.* |
| Do. *hon.* | ཧབ་བྲིད་ (སྦྲིད་) སྐྱོན་པ་ | *hap̔-t̔ri kyöm-pa.* |
| Sneer, to | ཀྱག་ཀྱག་བྱས་ནས་ལབ་པ་ | *kya-kya cK̔e-ne lap̔-pa.* |
| Do. *hon.* | ཀྱག་ཀྱག་གནང་ནས་གསུང་བ་ | *kya-kya nang-ne sung-wa.* |
| Snore, to | སྔུར་པོ་རྒྱབ་པ་ | *ngur-po gyap̔-pa.* |
| Do. *hon.* | སྔུར་པོ་སྐྱོན་པ་ | *ngur-po kyöm-pa.* |
| Snow | གངས་ | *k̔ang.* |
| Snow, to | གངས་རྒྱབ་པ་ | *k̔ang gyap̔-pa.* |
| Snow, eye-shade for | མིག་ར་ | *mik̔-ra.* |
| Do. *hon.* | སྤྱན་ར་ | *chen-ra.* |
| Snow-avalanche | གངས་རུད་ | *k̔ang-rü.* |
| Snow-blindness | གངས་ཁྲིད་ | *k̔ang-chhi.* |
| Snow-cock, | ལྷ་བྱ་གོང་མོ་ | *lhap̔-cK̔a k̔ong-mo.* |
| Snow-leopard | གསའ་ | *sa.* |

| | | |
|---|---|---|
| Snow-storm | གངས་ཚུབ་ | *kang-tshuṕ.* |
| Snuff | སྣ་ཐག་ | *na-tha.* |
| Do. *hon.* | ཞངས་ཐག་ | *shang-tha.* |
| Snuff-box | སྣ་རུ་ | *na-ru.* |
| Do. *hon.* | ཞངས་རུ་ | *shang-ru.* |
| So and so | དེ་འདྲས་ | *den-dre.* |
| Soak, to | སྦང་བ་ | *bang-wa.* |
| Do. *hon.* | སྦང་ང་ (བ་) གནང་བ་ | *bang-nga nang-wa.* |
| Soap | ཡི་ཙེ་ *Ch.* | *yi-tse.* |
| Do. globular (for washing clothes) | གླང་གླད་ | *lang-le.* |
| Do. powdered (of Tibetan manufacture) | སྦུག་པ་ | *suk-pa.* |
| Do. *hon.* | ཕྱག་སྦུག་ | *chha-su.* |
| Soar, to | ལྡིང་བ་ | *ding-wa.* |
| Sob, to | ངུ་བ་ | *ngu-wa.* |
| Do. *hon.* | ཞུམ་པ་ | *shum-pa.* |
| Sober (not drunk), to be | ར་མ་ཟི་པ་ | *ra ma śi-pa.* |
| Do. *hon.* | སྐུ་ར་མ་བྲད་པ་ | *ku-ra ma be-pa.* |
| Sock | ཨོ་མོ་སུ་ *Mon.* | *o-mo-su.* |
| Do. *hon.* | ཞབས་སུ་ | *shaṕ-su.* |

| | | |
|---|---|---|
| Socket of the eye | མིག་ཁུང་ | *mik-khung.* |
| Do. *hon.* | སྤྱན་ཁུང་ | *chen-khung.* |
| Sod | སྤང་ | *pang.* |
| Soda | བུལ་ཏོག་ | *pü-to.* |
| Soft | འཇམ་པོ་ | *jam-po.* |
| Softly | ག་ལེ་ག་ལེ་ | *ka-le ka-le.* |
| Soil (earth) | ས་ | *sa.* |
| Soil, to | བཙོག་པ་བཟོ་བ་ | *tsok-pa śo-wa.* |
| Do. *hon.* | བཙོག་པ་བཟོ་བ་གནང་བ་ | *tsok-pa śo-wa nang-wa.* |
| Sojourn, to | བསྡད་པ་ (སྡོད་པ་) | *de-pa.* |
| Do. *hon.* | བཞུགས་པ་ | *sku-pa.* |
| Do. *h. hon.* | བཞུགས་གདན་འཇག་པ་ | *sku-den jak-pa.* |
| Solace, to | སེམས་གསོ་བཏང་ (གཏོང་) བ་ | *sem-so tung-wa.* |
| Do. *hon.* | སེམས་གསོ་གཏོང་ང་ (བ་) གནང་བ་ | *sem-so tong-nga nang-wa.* |
| Do. *inf.* to *sup.* | ཐུགས་གསོ་ཕུལ་ (འབུལ་) བ་ | *thu-so phü-wa.* |
| Solder, *s.* | དཀར་ཡ་ | *ka-ya.* |
| Soldier | དམག་མི་ | *ma-mi.* |
| Sole (of foot) | རྐང་མཐིལ་ | *kang-thi.* |
| Do. *hon.* | ཞབས་མཐིལ་ | *skap-thi.* |

| | | |
|---|---|---|
| Sole, *adj*. | གཅིག་པོ་ | *chiḳ-po.* |
| Do. *hon.* | སྐུ་རྐྱང་ | *ku-kyang.* |
| Solely | ཤ་སྟག་ | *sha-ta.* |
| Solicit, to | ཞུ་བ་ | *sḳu-wa.* |
| Do. *hon.* | ཞུ་བ་གནང་བ་ | *sḳu-wa nang-wa.* |
| Solitary | གཅིག་པོ་ | *chiḳ-po.* |
| Do. *hon.* | སྐུ་རྐྱང་ | *ku-kyang.* |
| Solitary place | དབེན་གནས་ | *en-ne.* |
| Solid (firm) | བརྟན་པོ་ | *tem-po.* |
| Sombre, to be, (melancholy) | སེམས་སྐྱོ་སྣང་བྱེད་པ་ | *sem kyo-nang cḳe-pa.* |
| Do. *hon.* | ཐུགས་སེམས་སྐྱོ་སྣང་གནང་བ་ | *thu-sem kyo-nang nang-wa.* |
| Some (a little, *e.g.* salt) | ཏོག་ཙ་ | *toḳ-tsa.* |
| Some (a few, *e.g.* men) | ཁ་ཤས་ | *kha-she.* |
| Something | ག་རེ་ཡིན་ནས་གཅིག་ | *Ḳa-re yin-ne chi.* |
| Sometimes | མཚམས་མཚམས་ | *tsham-tsham.* |
| Do. *hon.* | ཐུགས་སངས་ཐུགས་སངས་ལ་ | *thuḳ-sang thuḳ-sang la.* |
| Somnolent, to be | གཉིད་ཚོག་རྒྱབ་པ་ | *nyi-tso gyaṕ-pa.* |
| Do. *hon.* | མཉལ་ (མནལ་) ཚོག་སྐྱོན་པ་ | *nye-tso kyöm-pa.* |
| Son | བུ་ | *ṕu.* |
| Do. *hon.* | སྲས་ | *se.* |

| | | |
|---|---|---|
| Son-in-law | མག་པ་ | *maḱ-pa.* |
| Do. *hon.* | སྐུ་བག་ | *ku-ṕa.* |
| Song | གཞས་ | *sḱe.* |
| Do. *hon.* | གསུང་གཞས་ | *sung-sḱe.* |
| Song, religious | མགུར་མ་ | *gur-ma.* |
| Do. *hon.* | གསུང་མགུར་ | *sung-gur.* |
| Soon | མགྱོགས་པོར་ | *gyoḱ-po.* |
| Soothsay, to | མངོན་ཤེས་ཤེས་པ་ | *ngön-she she-pa.* |
| Do. *hon.* | མངོན་མཁྱེན་མཁྱེན་པ་ | *ngön-khyen khyem-pa.* |
| Soothsay, to (in a trance) | ལུང་བསྟན་ (སྟོན་) པ་ | *lung tem-pa.* |
| Do. *hon.* | བཀའ་ལུང་བསྟན་ (སྟོན་) པ་གནང་བ་ | *ka-lung tem-pa nang-wa.* |
| Soothsayer | རྩིས་པ་ | *tsi-pa.* |
| Soothsaying | མངོན་ཤེས་ | *ngön-she.* |
| Do. *hon.* | མངོན་མཁྱེན་ | *ngön-khyen.* |
| Soothsaying (in a trance) | ལུང་བསྟན་ | *lung-ten.* |
| Do. *hon.* | བཀའ་ལུང་ | *ka-lung.* |
| Sorcerer | མཐུ་རྒྱབ་མཁན་ | *thu-gyaṕ-khen.* |
| Do. *hon.* | མཐུ་སྐྱོན་མཁན་ | *thu kyön-khen.* |
| Sorcery | མཐུ་ | *thu.* |

| | | |
|---|---|---|
| Sordid (niggardly) | ལག་པ་དམ་པོ་ | *lak-pa ṫam-po.* |
| Do. *hon.* | ཕྱག་དམ་པོ་ | *chha ṫam-po.* |
| Sore, *s.* | རྨ་ | *ma.* |
| Sore throat, to have a | སྐེ་ན་བ་ | *ke-na-wa.* |
| Sorrow | སྡུག་བསྔལ་ | *du-nge.* |
| Do. *hon.* | ཐུགས་འཁྲལ། ཐུགས་བསྔལ་ | *thu-thre; thu-nge.* |
| Sorrowful, to be | སེམས་སྐྱོ་བ། སེམས་སྡུག་པ་ | *sem-kyo-wa; sem-duk-pa.* |
| Do. *hon.* | ཐུགས་སེམས་སྐྱོ་བ་གནང་བ། ཐུགས་སེམས་སྡུག་ག་ (པ་) གནང་བ་ | *thu-sem kyo-wa nang-wa; thu-sem duk-ka nang-wa.* |
| Sorry, to be | སེམས་སྐྱོ་བ་ | *sem-kyo-wa.* |
| Do. *hon.* | ཐུགས་སེམས་སྐྱོ་བ་གནང་བ་ | *thu-sem kyo-wa nang-wa.* |
| Sort, *s.* (class of man) | རྒྱུ། རིགས་ | *gyu; ri.* |
| Do. *hon.* | སྐུ་རྒྱུ། སྐུ་རིགས་ | *ku-gyu; ku-ri.* |
| Sort, *s.* (of things) | རྒྱུ་དག་ | *gyu-ṫa.* |
| Sorts, different | སྣ་ཚོགས་ | *na-tsho.* |
| Soul | སེམས་ | *sem.* |
| Do. *hon.* | ཐུགས་སེམས་ | *thu-sem.* |
| Sound (noise) | སྐད་ | *ke.* |
| Sound (healthy) | གཟུགས་པོ་བདེ་པོ་ | *śuk-po de-po.* |

| | | |
|---|---|---|
| Sound (healthy), *hon.* | སྐུ་གཟུགས་བཟང་པོ་ | *ku-śuk śang-po.* |
| Soup | ཁུ་བ་ | *khu-a.* |
| Do. *hon.* | སྐྱུམ་ཁུ་ | *trung-khu.* |
| Soup (made from meat) | ཤ་ཁུ་ | *sha-khu.* |
| Do. *hon.* | སྐྱུམ་ཁུ་ | *trung-khu.* |
| Sour (acid) | སྐྱུར་པོ་ | *kyur-po.* |
| Source (of river, etc.) | བྱུང་སྟངས་ (འབྱུང་ཁུངས་) | *cKung-tang.* |
| Do. (cause) | རྐྱེན་ | *ḱyen.* |
| South | ལྷོ་ | *hlo.* |
| Sovereign (king) | རྒྱལ་པོ་ | *gye-po.* |
| Sow, *s.* | ཕག་མོ་ | *pha-mo.* |
| Sow, to (seed) | བཏབ་པ་ (འདེབས་པ་) | *tap̍-pa.* |
| Do. (broadcast) | སོན་རྒྱབ་པ་ | *sön gyap̍-pa.* |
| Sower | སོན་རྒྱབ་མཁན་ | *sön gyam-khen.* |
| Space for, sufficient | ཤོང་ས་ | *shong-sa.* |
| Spacious | ཀུ་ཡངས་པོ་ | *ḱu-yang-po.* |
| Spade | འཇག་མ་ | *ja-ma.* |
| Span | མཐོ་ | *tho.* |
| Spare (thin) | ཤ་སྐམ་པོ་ | *sha ḱam-po.* |
| Do. *hon.* | སྐུ་ཤ་སྐམ་པོ་ | *ku-sha ḱam-po.* |

| | | |
|---|---|---|
| Spare time (leisure) | ལོངས་ | *long.* |
| Spark | མེ་ཚག་ | *me-tsha.* |
| Sparkle, to, *v.i.* | འོད་རྒྱབ་པ་ | *ö gyaṕ-pa.* |
| Speak, to | ལབ་པ་ | *laṕ-pa.* |
| Do. *hon.* | གསུང་བ་ | *sung-wa.* |
| Spear | མདུང་ | *dung.* |
| Do. *hon* | ཕྱག་མདུང་ | *chhan-dung.* |
| Specially | ཁྱད་པར་དུ་ | *khye-par-ťu.* |
| Species (of human beings) | རྒྱུ། རིགས་ | *gyu ; ri.* |
| Do. *hon.* | སྐུ་རྒྱུ། སྐུ་རིགས་ | *ku-gyu ; ku-ri.* |
| Species (of things) | རྒྱུ་དག་ | *gyu-ťa.* |
| Do. (different) | སྣ་ཚོགས་ | *na-tsho.* |
| Specimen | དཔེ་ | *pe.* |
| Spectacle | བལྟད་མོ་ | *ťe-mo.* |
| Do. *hon.* | གཟིགས་མོ་ | *śi-mo.* |
| Spectacles | མིག་ཤེར་ (མིག་ཤེལ་) | *mik-sher.* |
| Do. *hon.* | སྤྱན་ཤེར་ (སྤྱན་ཤེལ་) | *chen-sher.* |
| Spectre (ghost) | གདོང་འདྲེ། འདྲེ་ | *dong-dre ; dre.* |
| Speech | སྐད་ | *ke.* |
| Do. *hon.* | གསུང་སྐད་ | *sung-ke.* |

| | | |
|---|---|---|
| Speechless, to be | ཁ་ཁ་བསྡད་ (སྡོད་) པ་ | *kha-kha de-pa.* |
| Do. *hon.* | ཞལ་རགས་བཞུགས་པ་ | *sḱe-ra sḱu-pa.* |
| Speed | ཚ་དྲག་ | *tsha-ťra.* |
| Speed, to | མགྱོགས་པོ་བྱེད་པ་ | *gyoḱ-po cḱe-pa.* |
| Do. *hon.* | རྩོལ་པོ་གནང་བ་ | *tsö-po nang-wa.* |
| Do. *h. hon.* | ཐུགས་རྩོལ་པོ་གནང་བ་ | *thu-tsö-po nang-wa.* |
| Speedy | མགྱོགས་པོ་ | *gyoḱ-po.* |
| Do. *hon.* | རྩོལ་པོ་ | *tsö-po.* |
| Spell, to | སྦྱོར་ཀློག་རྒྱབ་པ་ | *jong-lo gyaṕ-pa.* |
| Spelling | སྦྱོང་ཀློག་ | *jong-lo.* |
| Spend wastefully, to (money) | གཏོར་བ་ | *tor-wa.* |
| Do. *hon.* | གཏོར་ར་ (བ་) གནང་བ་ | *tor-ra nang-wa.* |
| Spice | ཤ་སྨན་ | *sha-men.* |
| Spider | འདོམ་ | *dom.* |
| Spider's web | འདོམ་ཐག་ | *dom-tha.* |
| Spike, iron | ལྕགས་ཕུར་ | *chaḱ-phur.* |
| Do. wooden | ཕུར་པ་ | *phu-pa.* |
| Spill, to | ཕོ་བ་ (འཕོ་བ་) | *pho-wa.* |
| Do. *hon.* | ཕོ་ (འཕོ་) བ་གནང་བ་ | *pho-wa nang-wa.* |

| | | |
|---|---|---|
| Spin, to | འཁལ་བ་ | *khe-wa.* |
| Do. *hon.* | འཁལ་ར་ (བ་) གནང་བ་ | *khe-ra nang-wa.* |
| Spindle | ཡོ་ག་ | *yo-ga.* |
| Do. (another kind) | འཕང་ | *phang.* |
| Spine | རྒལ་ཚིགས་ | *ge-tshi.* |
| Spirit (soul) | སེམས་ | *sem.* |
| Do. (wine) | ཨ་རག་ | *a-ra.* |
| Do. *hon.* | བཞེས་རག་ | *sKe-ra.* |
| Spirit, evil | གདོང་འདྲེ། བདུད་ | *dong-dre ; dü.* |
| Spirited | ཧུར་པོ་ | *hur-po.* |
| Spiritual | དགེ་སེམས་ཆེན་པོ་ | *ge-sem chhem-po.* |
| Spit, to | མཆིལ་མ་གཏོར་བ་ | *chhi-ma tor-wa.* |
| Do. *hon.* | ལྗགས་ཆུ་གཏོར་ར་ (བ་) གནང་བ་ | *ja-chhu tor-ra nang-wa.* |
| Spite | གནོད་སེམས་ | *nö-sem.* |
| Spittle | མཆིལ་མ་ | *chhi-ma.* |
| Do. *hon.* | ལྗགས་ཆུ་ | *ja-chhu.* |
| Splendid | གཟི་བརྗིད་ཆེན་པོ། གཡང་མཛེས་ | *śi-ji chhem-po ; yang-dze.* |
| Splendour | གཟི་བརྗིད་ | *śi-ji.* |

| | | |
|---|---|---|
| Splice, to | འཐུད་རྒྱབ་པ་ | *thü gyap̆-pa.* |
| Do. *hon.* | འཐུད་སྐྱོན་པ་ | *thü kyöm-pa.* |
| Split, to | གཤགས་པ་ | *shak̆-pa.* |
| Do. *hon.* | གཤག་ག་ (པ་) གནང་བ་ | *shak̆-k̆a nang-wa.* |
| Spoil, to | མེད་པར་བཟོ་བ་ | *me-pa śo-wa.* |
| Do. *hon.* | མེད་པར་བཟོ་བ་གནང་བ་ | *me-pa śo-wa nang-wa.* |
| Spoon | ཐུར་མ་ | *thur-ma.* |
| Do. *hon.* | བཞེས་ཐུར་ | *sk̆ip̆-thu.* |
| Sport, *s.* | རྩེད་མོ་ | *tse-mo.* |
| Do. *hon.* | སྐུ་རྩེད་ | *ku-tse.* |
| Sport, to | རྩེད་མོ་རྩེ་བ་ | *tse-mo tse-wa.* |
| Do. *hon.* | སྐུ་རྩེད་གནང་བ་ | *ku-tse nang-wa.* |
| Spot (stain) | ཐིག་པ་ | *thik̆-pa.* |
| Do. (place) | ས་ཆ་ | *sa-chha.* |
| Spouse (wife) | སྐྱེས་དམན་ | *kyi-men.* |
| Do. *hon.* (of well-to-do villager) | སྙི་སྙིང་ལགས་ | *nyi-nying-la.* |
| Do. (of ordinary official) | ལྕམ་སྐུ་གཞོགས་ | *cham ku-sk̆o.* |
| Do. (of third grade and upwards) | ལྷ་ལྕམ་སྐུ་གཞོགས་ | *hla-cham ku-sk̆o.* |
| Sprain, to | ཚིགས་འཁྲོག་ (འབུད་) པ་ | *tshi throk̆-pa.* |

| | | |
|---|---|---|
| Sprain, to, *hon.* | ཞབས་ཆིགས་འཁྲོག་ག་ (འབུད་པ་) གནང་བ་ | *skap-tshi throk-ka nang-wa.* |
| Spread, to (mat, etc.) | བཏིང་བ་ (འདིང་བ་) | *ting-wa.* |
| Do. *hon.* | བཏིང་ང་ (འདིང་བ་) གནང་བ་ | *ting-nga nang-wa.* |
| Spring (season) | དཔྱིད་ཀ་ | *chi-ka.* |
| Spring (of water) | ཆུ་མིག་ | *chhu-mi.* |
| Spring, to (jump) | མཆོངས་པ། མཆོངས་རྒྱག་རྒྱབ་པ་ | *chhong-pa ; chhong-gya gyap-pa.* |
| Do. *hon.* | མཆོངས་རྒྱག་སྐྱོན་པ་ | *chhong-gya kyöm-pa.* |
| Sprinkle, to (*e.g.* water on ground) | གཏོར་བ་ | *tor-wa.* |
| Do. *hon.* | གཏོར་ར་ (བ་) གནང་བ་ | *tor-ra nang-wa.* |
| Sprite | གདོང་འདྲེ། འདྲེ་ | *dong-dre ; dre.* |
| Sprout, to | སྐྱེ་བ་ | *kye-wa.* |
| Spruce (tree) | སད་ཤིང་ | *se-shing.* |
| Spur (of mountain) | སྒང་ | *gang.* |
| Spy, *s.* | སོ་པ་ | *so-pa.* |
| Spy, to | སོ་ལྟ་བ་ | *so ta-wa.* |
| Squabble (row) | རྒྱབ་འདྲེ་ | *gyam-dre.* |
| Do. *hon.* | གསུང་འཁྲུག་ | *sung-thru.* |

| | | |
|---|---|---|
| Squabble, to | རྒྱབ་འདྲེ་རྒྱབ་པ་ | *gyam-dre gyaṕ-pa.* |
| Do. *hon.* | གསུང་འཁྲུག་སྐྱོན་པ་ | *sung-thru kyöm-pa.* |
| Squander, to | གཏོར་བ་ | *tor-wa.* |
| Do. *hon.* | གཏོར་ར་ (བ་) གནང་བ་ | *tor-ra nang-wa.* |
| Square | གྲུ་བཞི་ | *ťruṕ-shi.* |
| Squeeze, to | བཙིར་བ་ (འཚིར་བ) | *tsir-wa.* |
| Do. *hon.* | བཙིར་ར་ (བ་) གནང་བ་ | *tsir-ra nang-wa.* |
| Squirrel | སྲེ་མོང་ | *tre-mong.* |
| Stab, to | བཙུགས་པ་ (འཛུགས་པ་) | *tsuḱ-pa.* |
| Do. *hon.* | བཙུགས་ག་ (འཛུགས་པ་) གནང་བ་ | *tsuḱ-ḱa nang-wa.* |
| Stable, *adj.* (firm) | བརྟན་པོ་ | *tem-po.* |
| Stable, *s.* | རྟ་ར་ | *ta-ra.* |
| Do. *hon.* | ཆིབས་ར་ | *chhiṕ-ra.* |
| Stable gear | རྟ་ཆས་ | *taṕ-chhe.* |
| Stack, to | རྩིག་བཞག་ (འཛོག་) པ་ | *tsiḱ shaḱ-pa.* |
| Do. *hon.* | རྩིག་གཞོག་ག་ (འཛོག་པ་) གནང་བ་ | *tsiḱ shoḱ-ḱa nang-wa.* |
| Staff | འཁར་རྒྱུག། རྒྱུག་པ་ (དབྱུག་པ་) | *khar-gyu ; gyuk-pa.* |

| | | |
|---|---|---|
| Stag | ཤ་ཕོ་ | sha-pho. |
| Do. young | ཤ་ཕྲུག་ | sha-thru. |
| Stage of a journey | ཞག་ས། རྒྱ་ཚུག་ | sKak-sa ; gya-tshu. |
| Do. *hon.* | བཞུགས་ཞག་ | sKu-sKa. |
| Stagger, to, *v.i.* | འཁྱོར་ནས་འགྲོ་བ་ | khyor-ne dro-wa. |
| Do. *hon.* | སྐུ་འཁྱོར་ནས་ཕེབ་པ་ | ku-kyyor-ne phe-pa. |
| Do. *h. hon.* | སྐུ་འཁྱོར་ནས་འཆིབ་རྒྱུ་གནང་བ་ | ku-khyor-ne chhiṗ-gyu nang-wa. |
| Stagger, to (astonish) | ཡ་མཚན་བྱེད་པ་ | yam-tshen cKe-pa. |
| Do. *hon.* | ཡ་མཚན་གནང་བ་ | yam-tshen nang-wa. |
| Stain, *s.* | ཐིག་པ་ | thik-pa. |
| Stain, to | བཙོག་པ་བཟོ་བ་ | tsok-pa ṡo-wa. |
| Do. *hon.* | བཙོག་པ་བཟོ་བ་གནང་བ་ | tsok-pa ṡo-wa nang-wa. |
| Stair-case | ཀན་ཙ་ (སྐས་འཛེག་) | ken-tsa. |
| Do. *hon.* | ཕེབ་སྐས་ | pheṗ-ke. |
| Staircase (of stone) | རྡོ་སྐྱག་ | doṗ-kya. |
| Stake (wager) | རྒྱན་ | gyen. |
| Do. *hon.* | སྐུ་རྒྱན་ | ku-gyen. |
| Stake, to | རྒྱན་བཞག་ (འཛུགས་) པ་ | gyen sKak-pa. |

| | | |
|---|---|---|
| Stake, to, *hon.* | སྐུ་རྒྱན་གཞོག་ག་ (འཛོག་པ་) གནང་བ་ | *ku-gyen sḱok-ka nang-wa.* |
| Stake | སྙིང་པ་ | *nying-pa.* |
| Stalk | ཀང་ | *kang.* |
| Stallion | གསེབ་ | *seṕ.* |
| Do. *hon.* | ཆིབས་གསེབ་ | *chhiṕ-seṕ.* |
| Stalwart | ཤེད་ཆེན་པོ་ | *she chhem-po.* |
| Do. *hon.* | སྐུ་ཤེད་ཆེན་པོ་ | *ku-she chhem-po.* |
| Stammering | ཁ་ལྡིག་ | *kha-di.* |
| Stamp, *s.* (seal) | ཐེ་ཙེ། དམ་ཕྲུག་ | *the-tse ; t́am-thru.* |
| Do. *hon.* | ཕྱག་དམ་ | *chha-t́am.* |
| Stampede, to | འདྲོག་ནས་བོས་ (འབྲོས་) པ་ | *drok-ne ṕö-pa.* |
| Stand, to | ལངས་ནས་བསྡད་ (སྡོད་) པ་ | *lang-ne de-pa.* |
| Do. *hon.* | བཞང་ (བཞེངས་) ནས་བཞུགས་པ་ | *sḱang-ne sḱu-pa.* |
| Standard (flag) | དར་ལྕོག་ | *t́ar-cho.* |
| Star | སྐར་མ་ | *kar-ma.* |
| Stare, to | མིག་འདིར་ (བསྒྲིམས་) ནས་ལྟ་བ་ | *mik-dir-ne ta-wa.* |

| | | |
|---|---|---|
| Stare, to, *hon.* | སྤྱན་འདིར་ (བསྒྲིམས་) ནས་ གཟིགས་པ་ | *chen-dir-ne śi-pa.* |
| Start, to (on a journey) | འགྲོ་བ། ཕྱིན་པ་ | *dro-wa ; chhim-pa.* |
| Do. *hon.* | ཕེབ་པ་ | *phe-pa.* |
| State (condition) | གནས་ཚུལ་ | *ne-tshü.* |
| Do. (kingdom) | རྒྱལ་སྲིད་ | *gye-si.* |
| Station (rank) | གོ་ས་ | *ko-sa.* |
| Statue | སྐུ་འདྲ་ | *kun-dra.* |
| Status quo | ཆབ་སྲིད་སྔོན་ཡོད་ | *chhap-si ngön-yö* |
| Status quo, maintenance of | ཆབ་སྲིད་སྔོན་ཡོད་རང་ འཛགས་བཞག་རྒྱུ་ | *chhap-si ngön-yö rang-ja skak-gyu.* |
| Stay, to | བསྡད་པ་ (སྡོད་པ་) | *de-pa.* |
| Do. *hon.* | བཞུགས་པ་ | *sku-pa.* |
| Do. *h. hon.* | བཞུགས་གདན་འཛག་པ་ | *sku-den jak-pa.* |
| Stay, to (wait) | སྒུག་བསྡད་ (སྡོད་) པ་ | *gu de-pa.* |
| Do. *hon.* | སྒུག་བཞུགས་པ་ | *gu sku-pa.* |
| Steadfast | བརྟན་པོ་ | *tem-po.* |
| Steadily | ཏེན་ཏེན་བྱས་ནས་ | *ten-ten che-ne.* |
| Steady (resolute) | བརྟན་པོ་ | *tem-po.* |
| Steal, to | ཀུན་མ་ཀུ་བ། ཀུ་བ་ | *kü-ma ku-wa ; ku-wa.* |

| | | |
|---|---|---|
| Steam | རླངས་པ་ | *lang-pa.* |
| Steed | རྟ་ | *ta.* |
| Do. *hon.* | ཆིབས་པ་ | *chhi-pa.* |
| Steel | ཁ་ལྕགས་ | *kha-cha.* |
| Steep | གཟར་པོ་ | *śar-po.* |
| Steep, to | སྦང་བ་ | *bang-wa.* |
| Do. *hon.* | སྦང་ང་ (བ་) གནང་བ་ | *bang-nga nang-wa.* |
| Stem | སྡོང་པོ་ | *dong-po.* |
| Stench, to | དྲི་མ་ཁ་བ་ | *ťri-ma kha-wa.* |
| Step (pace) | གོམ་པ་ | *k̄om-pa.* |
| Do. *hon.* | ཞབས་གོམ་ | *sk̄ap̄-k̄om.* |
| Step, to (move by paces) | གོམ་པ་རྒྱབ་པ་ | *k̄om-pa gyap̄-pa.* |
| Do. *hon.* | ཞབས་གོམ་སྐྱོན་པ་ | *sk̄ap̄-k̄om kyöm-pa.* |
| Step-father | ཕ་གཡར་ | *pha-ya.* |
| Step-mother | མ་གཡར་ | *ma-ya.* |
| Steps, flight of wooden | ཀན་ཙ་ (སྐས་འཛེག་) | *ken-tsa.* |
| Do. *hon.* | ཕེབ་སྐས་ | *phep̄-ke.* |
| Steps, stone | རྡོ་ཀྱག་ | *dop̄-kya.* |
| Sterile (of women) | རབས་ཆད་ | *rap̄-chhe.* |
| Do. (of land) | ཙ་ཆུ་འཛོམས་པོ་...མེད་པ་ | *tsa-chhu dzom-po...me-pa.* |

| | | |
|---|---|---|
| Stern, *adj.* | གྱོང་པོ་ | *ḱyong-po.* |
| Steward | ཕྱག་མཛོད་ | *chhang-dzö.* |
| Stick, *s.* | འཁར་རྒྱུག། རྒྱུག་པ་ (དབྱུག་པ་) | *khar-gyu ; gyuk-pa.* |
| Stick, to (paste) *v.t.* | སྦྱར་བ་ | *jar-wa.* |
| Do. *hon.* | སྦྱར་ར་ (བ་) གནང་བ་ | *jar-ra nang-wa.* |
| Stiff | གྱོང་པོ་ | *ḱyong-po.* |
| Stifle to | གློ་སུབ་རྒྱབ་པ་ | *lo-suṕ gyaṕ-pa.* |
| Do. *hon.* | གློ་སུབ་སྐྱོན་པ་ | *lo-suṕ kyöm-pa.* |
| Still, *adv.* | ད་རུང་། ད་འདོ་ | *t́a-rung ; t́an-do.* |
| Still, to sit | ཁ་ཁ་བསྡད་ (སྡོད་) པ་ | *kha-kha de-pa.* |
| Do. *hon.* | ཁ་ཁ་བཞུགས་པ་ | *kha-kha sḱu-pa.* |
| Still-birth | ཤི་རོ་སྐྱེས་པ་ | *shi-ro kye-pa.* |
| Sting, to | སོ་རྒྱབ་པ་ | *so gyaṕ-pa.* |
| Stingy | ལག་པ་དམ་པོ་ | *laḱ-pa t́am-po.* |
| Do. *hon.* | ཕྱག་དམ་པོ་ | *chha-t́am-po.* |
| Stink, to | དྲི་མ་ཁ་བ་ | *t́ri-ma kha-wa.* |
| Stipend | གླ། ཕོགས་ | *la ; pho.* |
| Do. *hon.* | གསོལ་ཕོགས་ | *sö-pho.* |
| Stir, to (move), *v.t.* | དཀྲུག་པ་ | *truḱ-pa.* |

| | | |
|---|---|---|
| Stir, to (move), *v.t., hon.* | དཀྲུག་ག་ (པ་) གནང་བ་ | *truk-ka nang-wa.* |
| Stir, to, *v.i.* | འཁྲུག་པ་ | *thruk-pa.* |
| Do. *hon.* | འཁྲུག་ག་ (པ་) གནང་བ་ | *thruk-ka-nang-wa.* |
| Stirrup | ཡོབ་ | *yop.* |
| Do. *hon.* | ཆིབས་ཡོབ་ | *chhip-yop.* |
| Stirrup-leather | ཡོབ་ཐག་ | *yop-tha.* |
| Do. *hon.* | ཆིབས་ཡོབ་ཀྱི་ཐག་པ་ | *chhip-yop kyi thak-pa.* |
| Stitch, to (clothes) | འཚེམ་པ་ | *tshem-pa.* |
| Do. *hon.* | ཕྱག་འཚེམ་སྐྱོན་པ་ | *chha-tshem kyöm-pa.* |
| Stitch, to (together) | སྦྲེལ་བ་ | *drel-wa.* |
| Do. *hon.* | སྦྲེལ་ར་ (བ་) གནང་བ་ | *dre-ra nang-wa.* |
| Stock (of gun) | སྒྲོམ་ཤིང་ | *gum-shing.* |
| Stocking | ཨོ་མོ་སུ་ *Mon.* | *o-mo-su.* |
| Stocks (for criminals) | ཨན་གདས་ | *an-de.* |
| Stomach | གྲོ་ཁོག་ (གྲོད་ཁོག་) | *tro-kho.* |
| Do. *hon.* | གསོལ་གྲོད་ | *sö-trö.* |
| Stone | རྡོ་ | *do.* |
| Do. *hon.* | ཕྱག་རྡོ་ | *chha-do.* |
| Stool (foot-stool) | རྐང་སྟེགས་ | *kang-tek.* |
| Do. *hon.* | ཞབས་སྟེགས་ | *skap-tek.* |

| | | |
|---|---|---|
| Stoop, to | ཁུག་ཁུག་ (ཁྱུར་ཁྱུར་) བྱེད་པ་ | *kuk-ku che-pa.* |
| Do. *hon.* | ཁུག་ཁུག་ (ཁྱུར་ཁྱུར་) གནང་བ་ | *kuk-ku nang-wa.* |
| Stop, to, *v.t.* | བཀག་པ་ (འགེགས་པ་) | *kak-pa.* |
| Do. *hon.* | བཀག་ག་ (འགེགས་པ་) གནང་བ་ | *kak-ka nang-wa.* |
| Stop, to, *v.i.* | བསྡད་པ་ (སྡོད་པ་) | *de-pa.* |
| Do. *hon.* | བཞུགས་པ་ | *sku-pa.* |
| Do. *h. hon.* | བཞུགས་གདན་འཛག་པ་ | *sku-den jak-pa.* |
| Stop raining, to | ཆར་པ་འཆད་པ་ | *chhar-pa chhe-pa.* |
| Store-house | མཛོད། མཛོད་ཁང་ | *dzö ; dzö-khang.* |
| Stork | ཀྲུང་ཀྲུང་དཀར་མོ་ | *trung-trung ka-mo.* |
| Storm | རླུང་ཚུབ་ | *lung-tshup.* |
| Do. snow | གངས་ཚུབ་ | *kang-tshup.* |
| Story (of house) | ཐོག་ | *tho.* |
| Do. second | བར་ཐོག་ | *par-tho.* |
| Do. third | གསུམ་ཐོག་ | *sum-tho.* |
| Do. top | རྩེ་ཐོག་ | *tse-tho.* |
| Story (legend) | སྒྲུང་། རྣམ་ཐར་ | *drum ; nam-thar.* |
| Do. *hon.* | ཞལ་སྒྲུང་ | *ske-drum.* |

| | | |
|---|---|---|
| Stout (of men and animals) | ཤ་རྒྱགས་པ་ | *sha gyak-pa.* |
| Do. *hon.* | སྐུ་ཤ་འབྱོར་པོ་ | *ku-sha jor-po.* |
| Stout (of things) | སྦོམ་པོ་ | *bom-po.* |
| Stove, iron | ལྕགས་ཐབ་ | *chak-thap.* |
| Straight | འདྲོང་པོ་ (དྲང་པོ་) | *drong-po.* |
| Do. (of road) | ཁ་ཐུག་ | *kha-thu.* |
| Do. (honourable) | དྲང་པོ་ | *ťrang-po.* |
| Straighten, to | འདྲོང་ (དྲང་) པོ་བཟོ་བ་ | *drong-po śo-wa.* |
| Do. *hon.* | འདྲོང་ (དྲང་) པོ་བཟོ་བ་ གནང་བ་ | *drong-po śo-wa nang-wa.* |
| Straightforward (just) | ཁྲིམས་དྲང་པོ་ | *thrim-ťrang-po.* |
| Do. *hon.* | བཀའ་ཁྲིམས་དྲང་པོ་ | *ka-thrim ťrang-po.* |
| Straightway | ལམ་སང་ | *lam-sang.* |
| Strain, to | བཙག་པ་ (འཚག་པ་) | *tsak-pa.* |
| Do. *hon.* | བཙག་ག་ (འཚག་པ་) གནང་བ་ | *tsak-ka nang-wa.* |
| Strainer, tea | ཇ་འཚག་ | *cka-tsha.* |
| Strait (narrow) | དོག་པོ། སྦུགས་སྦུབ་དོག་པོ་ | *ťok-po; bu-su ťok-po.* |
| Strange | ཁྱད་མཚར་པོ་ | *khye-tsha-po.* |
| Stranger | ཕྱི་མི་ | *chhi-mi.* |

| | | |
|---|---|---|
| Strangle, to | སྐེ་བཀག་བཏང་ནས་བསད་ (གསོད་) པ་ | *ke-kak tang-ne se-pa.* |
| Strategy | དམག་ཇུས་ | *mak-chü.* |
| Do. *hon.* | སྐུ་ཇུས་ | *ku-chü.* |
| Straw | ཟན་པ་ | *śem-pa.* |
| Strawberry (Chumbi Valley dialect) | དམར་ལུམ་ | *ma-lum.* |
| Stray, to | ལམ་ཀ་ནོར་པ་ | *lang-ka nor-wa.* |
| Do. *hon.* | ཕེབ་ལམ་ནོར་ར་ (བ་) གནང་བ་ | *pheṕ-lam nor-ra nang-wa.* |
| Stream | རྒྱུག་ཆུ་ | *gyuk-chhu.* |
| Street | ལམ་ཀ་ | *lang-ka.* |
| Do. narrow | སྲང་འགག་ | *hrang-ga.* |
| Strength | ཤེད་ | *she.* |
| Do. *hon.* | སྐུ་ཤེད་ | *ku-she.* |
| Stretch, to | བརྐྱང་བ་ (རྐྱོང་བ་) | *kyang-wa.* |
| Do. *hon.* | རྐྱོང་ང་ (བ་) གནང་བ་ | *kyong-nga nang-wa.* |
| Strew, to (grass, etc.) | གཏོར་བ་ | *tor-wa.* |
| Do. *hon.* | གཏོར་ར་ (བ་) གནང་བ་ | *tor-ra nang-wa.* |
| Strewing oblation | གཏོར་མ་ | *tor-ma.* |

| | | |
|---|---|---|
| Strict | དམ་པོ། བཙན་པོ་ | *ťam-po; tsem-po.* |
| Strife | རྒྱབ་འདྲེ་ | *gyam-dre.* |
| Do. *hon.* | གསུང་འཁྲུག་ | *sung-thru.* |
| Strike, to (hit) | འཕོག་པ་ | *phok-pa.* |
| Strike, to (a blow) | རྡུང་བ་ | *dung-wa.* |
| Do. *hon.* | ཕྱག་འཇུག་ (འཇུས་) གནང་བ་ | *chhan-ju nang-wa.* |
| String | སྐུད་པ་ | *kü-pa.* |
| Do. *hon.* | ཕྱག་སྐུད་ | *chha-kü.* |
| Strive, to | སྙིང་རུས་བྱེད་པ་ | *nying-rü cke-pa.* |
| Do. *hon.* | ཐུགས་རུས་གནང་བ་ | *thuk-rü nang-wa.* |
| Strip, to | ཤུ་བ་ | *shu-wa.* |
| Stroke | ལྕུག་ | *cha.* |
| Stroll, to | ཆམ་ཆམ་ (འཁྱམ་འཁྱམ་) ལ་འགྲོ་བ་ | *chham-chham-la dro-wa.* |
| Do. *hon.* | ཆམ་ཆམ་ (འཁྱམ་འཁྱམ་) ལ་ཕེབ་པ་ | *chham-chham la phe-pa.* |
| Do. *h. hon.* | ཆམ་ཆམ་ (འཁྱམ་འཁྱམ་) ལ་འཆིབ་རྒྱུ་གནང་བ་ | *chham-chham la chhip-gyu nang-wa.* |

| | | |
|---|---|---|
| Strong (of human beings, animals, etc.) | ཤེད་ཆེན་པོ་ | *she chhem-po.* |
| Do. *hon.* | སྐུ་ཤེད་ཆེན་པོ་ | *ku-she chhem-po.* |
| Strong (of forts, houses, etc.) | བཙན་པོ་ | *tsem-po.* |
| Struggle, to (wrestle) | འཛིང་བ། འཛིང་རེ་བཏང་ (གཏོང་) བ་ | *dzing-wa; dzing-re tang-wa.* |
| Do. *hon.* | འཛིང་ང་ (བ་) གནང་བ་ | *dzing-nga nang-wa.* |
| Stubble | སོག་མ་ | *so-ma.* |
| Stubborn | གྱོང་པོ་ | *ḱyong-po.* |
| Student | བསླབ་གྲྭ་ | *laṕ-tra.* |
| Do. religious | གྲྭ་པ་ | *t́ra-pa.* |
| Stumble, to (of persons) | ཁ་རྡབ་པ་ | *kha daṕ-pa.* |
| Do. *hon.* | ཞལ་རྡབ་པ་གནང་བ་ | *sḱe daṕ-pa nang-wa.* |
| Stumble, to (of animals) | ཚིགས་བུར་རྒྱབ་པ་ | *tshik-ṕu gyaṕ-pa.* |
| Stupid (weak in intellect) | ལྐུགས་པ། གླེན་པ་ | *kuḱ-pa; lem-pa.* |
| Do. (senseless, of things) | དོན་མེད་ | *ťön-me.* |
| Sturdy | ཤེད་ཆེན་པོ་ | *she chhem-po.* |
| Do. *hon.* | སྐུ་ཤེད་ཆེན་པོ་ | *ku-she chhem-po.* |
| Stuttering | ཁ་ལྡིག་ | *kha-di.* |
| Sty | ཕག་ཚང་ | *phaḱ-tshang.* |

| | | |
|---|---|---|
| Style (of persons) | རྒྱུ། རིགས་ | *gyu; ri.* |
| Do. *hon.* | སྐུ་རྒྱུ། སྐུ་རིགས་ | *ku-gyu; ku-ri.* |
| Style (of things) | རྒྱུ་དག་ | *gyu-ťa.* |
| Styles, different | སྣ་ཚོགས་ | *na-tsho.* |
| Subdue, to | རྒྱལ་བ། ཀླག་འཁས་པ་ | *gye-wa; la khe-pa.* |
| Do. *hon.* | རྒྱལ་ར་ (བ་) གནང་བ། ཀླག་འཁས་ར་ (པ་) གནང་བ་ | *gye-ra nang-wa; la khe-ra nang-wa.* |
| Subject (of a government), *s.* | མངའ་འབངས་ | *nga-bang.* |
| Do. *hon.* | མངའ་ཞབས་ | *nga-sǩaṕ.* |
| Subjoin, to | འཕུད་རྒྱབ་པ་ | *thü gyaṕ-pa.* |
| Do. *hon.* | འཕུད་སྐྱོན་པ་ | *thü kyöm-pa.* |
| Subjugate, to | རྒྱལ་བ། ཀླག་འཁས་པ་ | *gye-wa; la khe-pa.* |
| Do. *hon.* | རྒྱལ་ར་ (བ་) གནང་བ། ཀླག་འཁས་ར་ (པ་) གནང་བ་ | *gye-ra nang-wa; la khe-ra nang-wa.* |
| Sublime | གཡང་མཛེས་ | *yang-dze.* |
| Submissive (humble) | སེམས་ཆུང་ཆུང་ | *sem-chhung-chhung.* |
| Do. *hon.* | ཐུགས་སེམས་ཆུང་ཆུང་ | *thuǩ-sem chhung-chhung.* |
| Submit, to | མགོ་དགུར་བ་ | *go gur-wa.* |
| Do. *hon.* | དབུ་དགུར་ར་ (བ་) གནང་བ་ | *u gur-ra nang-wa.* |

| | | |
|---|---|---|
| Submit, to (a petition or report) | འབུལ་བ། འབུལ་ལམ་ཞུས་པ་ (ཞུ་བ་) | *bül-wa ; bü-lam sḱü-pa.* |
| Do. *hon.* | འབུལ་ར་ (བ་) གནང་བ། འབུལ་ལམ་ཞུ་བ་གནང་བ་ | *bü-ra nang-wa; bü-lam sḱu-wa nang-wa.* |
| Subside, to (of water, flood, etc.) | ཆག་པ་ | *chhaḱ-pa.* |
| Substance | དངོས་པོ། རྒྱུ་ | *ngö-po ; gyu.* |
| Do. (of document, etc.) | དོན་སྙིང་ | *t́ön-nying.* |
| Substantiate, to (statement) | གཏན་ལྡན་བྱེད་པ་ | *ten-den cḱe-pa.* |
| Do. *hon.* | གཏན་ལྡན་གནང་བ་ | *ten-den nang-wa.* |
| Substitute | ཚབ་ | *tshaṕ.* |
| Do. *hon.* | སྐུ་ཚབ་ | *ku-tshaṕ.* |
| Subtility | གཡོ་སྒྱུ་ | *yo-gyu.* |
| Subtle | གཡོ་ཆེན་པོ་ | *yo chhem-po.* |
| Subtract, to | འཐེན་པ་ | *them-pa.* |
| Do. *hon.* | འཐེན་པ་གནང་བ་ | *them-pa nang-wa.* |
| Succeed, to (be successful) | ཐུབ་པ་ | *thuṕ-pa.* |
| Do. (follow) | གཞུག་ལ་ཕྱིན་པ་ | *sḱu-la chhim-pa.* |
| Do. *hon.* | གཞུག་ལ་ཕེབ་པ་ | *sḱu-la phe-pa.* |
| Do. *h. hon.* | གཞུག་ལ་འཆིབ་རྒྱུ་གནང་བ་ | *sḱu-la chhiṕ-gyu nang-wa* |

| | | |
|---|---|---|
| Successful, to be | མགོ་འཐོན་པ་ | *go thöm-pa.* |
| Succession, (descendants) | རིགས་བརྒྱུད། མི་བརྒྱུད་ | *ri-gyü ; mi-gyü.* |
| Do. *hon.* (of laity) | སྐུ་བརྒྱུད་ | *ku-gyü.* |
| Do. *hon.* (of lamas) | གདུང་བརྒྱུད་ | *dung-gyü.* |
| Succour, *s.* | རོགས་ | *ro.* |
| Do. *hon.* | མགོ་འདྲེན་ | *gön-dren.* |
| Succour, to | རོགས་བྱེད་པ་ | *ro cḱe-pa.* |
| Do. *hon.* | དབུ་འདྲེན་གནང་བ་ | *u-dren nang-wa.* |
| Such | འདི་འདྲ་ | *din-dra.* |
| Suck, to | འཇིབ་པ་ | *jiṕ-pa.* |
| Do. *hon.* | འཇིབ་པ་གནང་བ་ | *jiṕ-pa nang-wa.* |
| Suckle, to | འོ་མ་སྟེར་བ་ | *o-ma ter-wa.* |
| Do. *hon.* | འོ་མ་གནང་བ་ | *o-ma nang-wa.* |
| Suddenly | ལམ་སང་ | *lam-sang.* |
| Suffer, to (endure) | བཟོད་པ་སྒོམ་པ་ | *śö-pa gom-pa.* |
| Do. *hon.* | བཟོད་པ་བཞེས་པ་ | *śö-pa sḱe-pa.* |
| Suffer, to (pain) | གཟུག་རྒྱབ་པ་ | *śu-gyaṕ-pa.* |
| Do. *hon.* | སྙུང་གཟུག་སྐྱོན་པ་ | *nyung-śu kyöm-pa.* |
| Suffer, to (permit) | བཅུག་པ་ (འཇུག་པ་) | *chuḱ-pa.* |
| Do. *hon.* | བཅུག་ག་ (འཇུག་པ་)གནང་བ་ | *chuḱ-ka nang-wa.* |

| | | |
|---|---|---|
| Suffering (mental) | སྡུག་བསྔལ་ | *du-nge.* |
| Do. *hon.* | ཐུགས་འཁྲལ་ | *thu-thre.* |
| Suffering (physical) | གཟུག་ | *śu.* |
| Do. *hon.* | སྙུང་གཟུག་ | *nyung-śu.* |
| Sufficient, to be | ལྡང་བ། འགྲིག་པ་ | *dang-wa; drik-pa.* |
| Suffocate, to | གློ་སྲུབ་རྒྱབ་པ་ | *lo-suṕ gyaṕ-pa.* |
| Do. *hon.* | གློ་སྲུབ་སྐྱོན་པ་ | *lo-suṕ ḱyöm-pa.* |
| Suffocated, to be | དབུགས་འགག་པ་ | *u gaḱ-pa.* |
| Sugar | བྱེ་མ་ཀ་ར་ | *cḱe-ma ḱa-ra.* |
| Sugar-candy | ཤེལ་ཀ་ར་ | *she ḱa-ra.* |
| Suicide, to commit | རང་སྲོག་བཅད་ (གཅོད་) པ་ | *rang-so che-pa.* |
| Do. *hon.* | རང་སྲོག་གཅོད་པ་གནང་བ་ | *rang-so chö-pa nang-wa.* |
| Suit, to (befit) | འོས་པ་ | *ö-pa.* |
| Do. (agree) | འགྲིག་པ། འཆམ་པ་ | *drik-pa; chham-pa.* |
| Suitable | འོས་པོ། འོས་བབས་ | *ö-po; ö-ṕaṕ.* |
| Suite | འཁོར་གཡོག་ | *khor-yo.* |
| Sulk, to | གདོང་ནག་པོ་བསྟན་ (སྟོན་) པ་ | *dong naḱ-po tem-pa.* |
| Do. *hon.* | ཞལ་རས་ནག་པོ་སྟོན་པ་གནང་བ་ | *sḱe-re naḱ-po töm-pa nang-wa.* |
| Sullen | གྱོང་པོ་ | *ḱyong-po.* |

| | | |
|---|---|---|
| Sully, to | བཙོག་པ་བཟོ་བ་ | *sok-pa śo-wa.* |
| Do. *hon.* | བཙོག་པ་བཟོ་བ་གནང་བ་ | *tsok-pa śo-wa nang-wa.* |
| Sulphur | མུ་ཟི་ | *mu-śi.* |
| Sum up, to | སྡོམ་པ་ | *dom-pa.* |
| Do. *hon.* | སྡོམ་པ་གནང་བ་ | *dom-pa nang-wa.* |
| Summer | དབྱར་ཀ་ | *yar-ka.* |
| Summit | རྩེ་ | *tse.* |
| Summon, to | སྐད་བཏང་ (གཏོང་) བ་ | *ke tang-wa.* |
| Do. *hon.* | ཞོག་བཀའ་གནང་བ་ | *sho ka-nang-wa.* |
| Sun | ཉི་མ་ | *nyi-ma.* |
| Do. *hon.* | ཞོ་ཉི་ (ཞུ་ཉི་) | *sko-nyi.* |
| Sunbeam | ཉི་མའི་གཟེར་ | *nyi-me śer.* |
| Sunrise | ཉི་མ་ཤར་ར་ (བ་) | *nyi-ma shar-ra.* |
| Sunset | ཉི་མ་རྒས་པ་ | *nyi-ma ge-pa.* |
| Sunstroke, to get | ཉི་གཟེར་འཕོག་པ་ | *nyi-śer phok-pa.* |
| Sunday | གཟའ་ཉི་མ་ | *śa-nyi-ma.* |
| Sundry (various) | མི་གཅིག་པ་ | *mi-chik-pa.* |
| Superabundant | ཧ་ཅང་མང་པོ། གཡོ་མ་སུ་ | *ha-chang mang-po; yo-ma-su.* |
| Superb | གཡང་མཛེས་ | *yang-dze.* |
| Supercilious (haughty) | ཉམས་ཆེན་པོ། ཛ་ཁོག་ཆེན་པོ་ | *nyam-chhem-po; dza-kho chhem-po.* |

| | | |
|---|---|---|
| Superfluous | ལྷག་པོ་ | *hlak-po.* |
| Superintend | ཏོ་དམ་བྱེད་པ་ | *ťo-ťam cȟe-pa.* |
| Do. *hon.* | ཏོ་དམ་གནང་བ་ | *ťo-ťam nang-wa.* |
| Superintendent | ཏོ་དམ་པ་ | *ťo-ťam-pa.* |
| Superstition | རྣམ་རྟོག་ | *nam-to.* |
| Superior (rank of persons) | མཐོ་པོ་ | *tho-po.* |
| Do. (of things) | ཡག་པོ་ | *yak-po.* |
| Supervise, to | ཏོ་དམ་བྱེད་པ་ | *ťo-ťam cȟe-pa.* |
| Do. *hon.* | ཏོ་དམ་གནང་བ་ | *ťo-ťam nang-wa.* |
| Supper | དགོངས་མོའི་ཁ་ལག་ | *gong-mö kha-la.* |
| Do. *hon.* | དགོངས་མོའི་ཞལ་ལག་ | *gong-mö sȟe-la.* |
| Supple | མཉེན་པོ་ | *nyem-po.* |
| Supplicate, to | ཞུ་བ་ | *sȟu-wa.* |
| Do. *hon.* | ཞུ་བ་གནང་བ་ | *sȟu-wa nang-wa.* |
| Supplication | ཞུ་བ་ | *sȟu-wa.* |
| Supply, to | སྒྲུབ་པ་ | *druṕ-pa.* |
| Do. *hon.* | སྒྲུབ་པ་གནང་བ་ | *druṕ-pa nang-wa.* |
| Support, to (prop up) | སྐྱོར་བ་ | *kyor-wa.* |
| Do. *hon.* | སྐྱོར་ར་ (བ་) གནང་བ་ | *kyor-ra nang-wa.* |
| Support to, (endure) | བཟོད་པ་སྒོམ་པ་ | *śö-pa gom-pa.* |

|  |  |  |
|---|---|---|
| Support, to (endure), *hon.* | བཟོད་པ་སྒོམ་པ་གནང་བ་ | *šö-pa gom-pa nang-wa.* |
| Support, to (nourish) | གསོ་བ་ | *so-wa.* |
| Do. *hon.* | གསོ་བ་གནང་བ་ | *so-wa nang-wa.* |
| Suppose, to | བསམ་པ་ | *sam-pa.* |
| Do. *hon.* | དགོངས་པ་ | *gong-pa.* |
| Supposition (opinion) | བསམ་པ་ | *sam-pa.* |
| Do. *hon.* | ཐུགས་སེམས་ | *thu-sem.* |
| Suppress, to (restrain) | བཀག་པ་ (འགེགས་པ་) | *kak-pa.* |
| Do. *hon.* | བཀག་ག་ (འགེགས་པ་) གནང་བ་ | *kak-ka nang-wa.* |
| Suppression of urine, to suffer from | གཅིན་པ་འགག་པ་ | *chim-pa gak-pa.* |
| Suppurate, to | རྣག་བསག་ (གསོག་) པ་ | *na sak-pa.* |
| Do. *hon.* | རྣག་བསག་ག་ (གསོག་པ་) གནང་བ་ | *na sak-ka nang-wa.* |
| Sure | ཏེན་ཏེན། ཁྲིག་ཁྲིག་ | *ten-ten ; thrik-thri.* |
| Surely | ངེས་པར་ | *nge-par.* |
| Surety | ཁས་ཁྱགས་ | *khe-khya.* |
| Do. *hon.* | ཞལ་ཁྱགས་ | *sKe-khya.* |
| Surety, to stand | ཁས་ཁྱགས་བྱེད་པ་ | *khe-kya cKe-pa.* |

| | | |
|---|---|---|
| Surety, to stand, *hon.* | ཞལ་ཁྲུགས་གནང་བ་ | *sKe-khya nang-wa.* |
| Surgeon | ཨེམ་ཆི་ | *am-chhi.* |
| Surly | གྱོང་པོ་ | *kyong-po.* |
| Surmise, to (suspect) | རྟོགས་པ་ཟ་བ་ | *tok-pa śa-wa.* |
| Do. *hon.* | ཐུགས་རྟོགས་གནང་བ་ | *thu-to nang-wa.* |
| Surmise, to (conjecture) | བསམ་པ་ | *sam-pa.* |
| Do. *hon.* | དགོངས་པ་ | *gong-pa.* |
| Surplus | ལྷག་མ་ | *hla-ma.* |
| Surprise, *s.* | ཡ་མཚན་ | *yam-tshen.* |
| Surprise, to | ཡ་མཚན་བྱེད་པ་ | *yam-tshen cKe-pa.* |
| Do. *hon.* | ཡ་མཚན་གནང་བ་ | *yam-tshen nang-wa.* |
| Surprising | ཡ་མཚན་པོ། ཁྱད་མཚར་པོ་ | *yam-tshem-po; khye-tsha-po.* |
| Surrender, to (abandon) | སྤང་བ་ | *pang-wa.* |
| Do. *hon.* | སྤོང་ང་ (བ་) གནང་བ་ | *pong-nga nang-wa.* |
| Surrender, to (submit) | མགོ་བདགས་ཞུ་བ་ | *goṕ-te sKu-wa.* |
| Surround, to | སྐོར་ར་རྒྱབ་པ་ | *kor-ra gyaṕ-pa.* |
| Do. *hon.* | ཞབས་སྐོར་སྐྱོན་པ་ | *sKaṕ-kor kyöm-pa.* |
| Survey, to (look at) | ལྟ་བ་ | *ta-wa.* |
| Do. *hon.* | གཟིགས་པ་ | *śi-pa.* |
| Suspect, to | རྟོགས་པ་ཟ་བ་ | *tok-pa śa-wa.* |

| | | |
|---|---|---|
| Suspect, to, *hon.* | ཐུགས་དོགས་གནང་བ་ | *thu-t́o nang-wa.* |
| Suspense (doubt) | ཐེ་ཚོམ་ | *the-tshom.* |
| Suspense, to be in (doubt) | ཐེ་ཚོམ་ཟ་བ་ | *the-tshom śa-wa.* |
| Do. *hon.* | ཐེ་ཚོམ་གནང་བ་ | *the-tshom nang-wa.* |
| Suspend, to | བཀལ་བ་ (འགེལ་བ་) | *kel-wa.* |
| Do. *hon.* | བཀལ་ར་ (འགེལ་བ་) གནང་བ་ | *ke-ra nang-wa.* |
| Suspend, to (from office) | བཏོན་པ་ (འདོན་པ་) | *tӧm-pa.* |
| Do. *hon.* | བཏོན་ (འདོན་) པ་གནང་བ་ | *tӧm-pa nang-wa.* |
| Suspicion | དོགས་པ་ | *t́oḱ-pa.* |
| Do. *hon.* | ཐུགས་དོགས་ | *thu-t́o.* |
| Suspicious and angry, to be | བལྟ་ཕྱོགས་བྱེད་པ་ | *ta-chhoḱ cḱe-pa.* |
| Do. *hon.* | གཟིགས་ཕྱོགས་གནང་བ་ | *śi-chhoḱ nang-wa.* |
| Sustain, to (endure) | བཟོད་པ་སྒོམ་པ་ | *śö-pa gom-pa.* |
| Do. *hon.* | བཟོད་པ་སྒོམ་པ་གནང་བ་ | *śö-pa gom-pa nang-wa.* |
| Sustain, to (nourish) | གསོ་བ་ | *so-wa.* |
| Do. *hon.* | གསོ་བ་གནང་བ་ | *so-wa nang-wa.* |
| Sustain, to (prop) | སྐྱོར་བ་ | *kyor-wa.* |
| Do. *hon.* | སྐྱོར་ར་ (བ་) གནང་བ་ | *kyor-ra nang-wa.* |
| Swallow, to | མིད་པ་ | *mi-pa.* |

| | | |
|---|---|---|
| Swarm (crowd) | ཚོགས་ | *tsho.* |
| Sway | དབང་ | *wang.* |
| Do. *hon.* | སྐུ་དབང་ | *ku-wang.* |
| Sway, to (govern) | དབང་བྱེད་པ་ | *wang-cḱe-pa.* |
| Do. *hon.* | སྐུ་དབང་གནང་བ་ | *ku-wang nang-wa.* |
| Swear, to | མནའ་སྐྱེལ་བ་ | *na kyel-wa.* |
| Do. *hon.* | དབུ་མནའ་བཞེས་པ་ | *u-na sḱe-pa.* |
| Sweat, *s.* | རྔུལ་ནག་ | *ngü-na.* |
| Sweat, to | རྔུལ་ནག་འཐོན་པ་ | *ngü-na thöm-pa.* |
| Do. *hon.* | རྔུལ་ནག་འཐོན་པ་གནང་བ་ | *ngü-na thöm-pa nang-wa.* |
| Sweep, to | གེ་རྒྱབ་པ་ | *ḱe gyaṕ-pa.* |
| Do. *hon.* | གེ་སྐྱོན་པ་ | *ḱe-kyöm-pa.* |
| Sweeper | གེ་པ། ར་རྒྱ་པ་ | *ḱe-pa; ra-gya-pa.* |
| Do. chief | ར་རྒྱ་དཔོན་པོ་ | *ra-gya pöm-po.* |
| Sweet, *adj.* | མངར་མོ། ཞིམ་པོ་ | *ngar-mo; sḱim-po.* |
| Sweetheart | སྙིང་སྡུག་ | *nying-du.* |
| Sweetmeat | བྱི་རིལ་ | *cḱi-ri.* |
| Sweet-scented | དྲི་མ་ཞིམ་པོ་ | *ṫri-ma sḱim-po.* |
| Swell, to | སྐྲང་བ་ | *trang-wa.* |
| Do. *hon.* | སྐྲང་ང་ (བ་) གནང་བ་ | *trang-nga nang-wa.* |

| | | |
|---|---|---|
| Swift | མགྱོགས་པོ་ | *gyoḱ-po.* |
| Do. *hon.* | རྩོལ་པོ་ | *tsö-po.* |
| Swim, to | རྐྱལ་རྒྱབ་པ་ | *kye gyaṕ-pa.* |
| Do. *hon.* | རྐྱལ་སྐྱོན་པ་ | *kye kyöm-pa.* |
| Swine | ཕག་པ་ | *phaḱ-pa.* |
| Swineherd | ཕག་རྫི་ | *phaḱ-dzi.* |
| Swing, (*e.g.* branch in wind) | ལིང་ལིང་བྱེད་པ་ | *ling-ling cḱe-pa.* |
| Do. (brandish) | དབྱུག་དབྱུག་བྱེད་པ་ | *yuk-yuḱ cḱe-pa.* |
| Do. *hon.* | དབྱུག་དབྱུག་གནང་བ་ | *yuk-yuḱ nang-wa.* |
| Switch | ཏེའི་ལྕག ། ལྕང་སྨྱུག་ | *te-cha ; chang-nyu.* |
| Do. *hon.* | ཆིབས་ལྕག་ | *chhiṕ-cha.* |
| Swoon, to | དྲན་མེད་བརྒྱལ་བ་ | *t́ren-me gyel-wa.* |
| Do. *hon.* | ཐུགས་དྲན་མེད་བརྒྱལ་ར་ (བ་) གནང་བ་ | *thu-t́ren-me gye-ra nang-wa.* |
| Sword | དཔའ་དམ ། ཞོག་ལང་ | *pa-dam ; sho-lang.* |
| Do. (two-edged) | རལ་གྲི་ | *re-t́ri.* |
| Do. short | རྩེབ་སག་ | *tseṕ-sa.* |
| Symbol | རྟགས་ | *ta.* |
| Symmetry (proportion) | ཚོད་ | *tshö.* |

| | | |
|---|---|---|
| Sympathy | སྙིང་རྗེ། བྱམས་སྙིང་རྗེ་ | *nying-je; cham-nying-je.* |
| Do. *hon.* | ཐུགས་རྗེ་ | *thuk-je.* |
| Symptom (of disease) | ན་སྟངས་ | *na-tang.* |
| Do. *hon.* | སྙུང་སྟངས་ | *nyung-tang.* |
| Syphilis | སྲི་མོག་ | *se-mo.* |
| System (method) | ཐབས་ | *thap.* |

# T

| | | |
|---|---|---|
| Table, small | ལྕོག་ཙེ་ | *choḱ-tse.* |
| Do. *hon.* | གསོལ་ལྕོག་ | *sö-cho.* |
| Table, European | རྒྱ་ལྕོག་ | *gya-cho.* |
| Table-cloth | ལྕོག་ཁེབས་ | *cho-kheṕ.* |
| Taciturn, to be | ཁ་ཁ་བསྡད་ (སྡོད་) པ་ | *kha-kha de-pa.* |
| Do. *hon.* | ཞལ་ཁ་བཞུགས་པ་ | *sḱe-kha sḱu-pa.* |
| Tact | ཐབས་མཁས་ | *thaṕ-khe.* |
| Tail | གཞུག་གུ་ | *sḱu-gu.* |
| Tailor | ཚེམ་བུ་ | *tshem-ṕu.* |
| Do. *hon.* | དབུ་མཛད་ | *um-dze.* |
| Taint (contamination) | གྲིབ་ | *t́riṕ.* |
| Do. *hon.* | སྐུ་གྲིབ་ | *ku-t́riṕ.* |
| Take, to | ལེན་པ་ | *lem-pa.* |
| Do. *hon.* | བཞེས་པ་ | *sḱe-pa.* |
| Take, to (carry) | འཁྱེར་འགྲོ་བ་ | *khe dro-wa.* |
| Do. *hon.* | སྣོམ་ཕེབ་པ་ | *nom phe-pa.* |
| Do. *h. hon.* | སྣོམ་འཚིབ་རྒྱུ་གནང་བ་ | *nom chhiṕ-gyu nang-wa.* |
| Take, to (conduct) | འཁྲིད་འགྲོ་བ་ | *thri dro-wa.* |
| Do. *hon.* | འཁྲིད་ཕེབ་པ་ | *thri phe-pa.* |

| | | |
|---|---|---|
| Take, to (conduct), *h. hon.* | འཁྲིད་འཆིབ་རྒྱུ་གནང་བ་ | *thri chhiṕ-gyu nang-wa.* |
| Take, to (forcibly | འཕྲོག་པ་ | *phoḱ-pa.* |
| Do. *hon.* | འཕྲོག་ག་ (པ་) གནང་བ་ | *phoḱ-ka nang-wa.* |
| Take hold of, to | ཟིན་པ་ | *śim-pa.* |
| Do. *hon.* | ཟིན་པ་གནང་བ་ | *śim-pa nang-wa.* |
| Take off, to (clothes, etc.) | ཕིས་པ་ (འབུད་པ་) | *pi-pa.* |
| Do. *hon.* | བསིལ་ར་ (བ་) གནང་བ་ | *si-ra nang-wa.* |
| Take out, to | བཏོན་པ་ (འདོན་པ་) | *töm-pa.* |
| Do. *hon.* | འདོན་པ་གནང་བ་ | *döm-pa nang-wa.* |
| Tale | སྒྲུང་། རྣམ་ཐར་ | *drum; nam-thar.* |
| Do. *hon.* | ཞལ་སྒྲུང་ | *sḱe-drum.* |
| Talent (natural gift) | ཡོན་ཏན་ | *yön-ten.* |
| Talented (person) | རིག་པ་ཆེན་པོ་ | *riḱ-pa chhem-po.* |
| Do. *hon.* | ཐུགས་རིག་ཆེན་པོ་ | *thu-ri chhem-po.* |
| Talisman | སྲུང་བ་ | *hrung-nga.* |
| Do. (used by high lamas) | སྲིད་པ་ཧོ་ | *si-pa-ho.* |
| Talk, *s.* (conversation) | སྐད་ཆ་ | *ḱe-chha.* |
| Do. *hon.* | གསུང་གྲོས་ | *sung-ṫrö.* |
| Talk (rumour) | སྐད་ཆ། གཏམ་ | *ḱe-chha; tam.* |
| Talk, to | ལབ་པ་ | *laṕ-pa.* |

| | | |
|---|---|---|
| Talk, to, *hon.* | གསུང་བ་ | *sung-wa.* |
| Do. *h. hon.* | བཀའ་གནང་བ་ | *ka nang-wa.* |
| Tall | གཟུགས་པོ་རིང་པོ་ | *śuk-po ring-po.* |
| Do. *hon.* | སྐུ་གཟུགས་རིང་པོ་ | *ku-śu ring-po.* |
| Tallow | ཚིལ་ལུ་ ( ཚིལ་བུ་ ) | *tshi-lu.* |
| Talon | སྡེར་མོ་ | *der-mo.* |
| Tame, to | ཧླིང་པོ་བཟོ་བ་ | *hling-po śo-wa.* |
| Do. *hon.* | ཧླིང་པོ་བཟོ་བ་གནང་བ་ | *hling-po śo-wa nang-wa.* |
| Tan, to | མཉེད་པ་ | *nye-pa.* |
| Tanner | ཀོ་བ་མཉེད་མཁན་ | *ko-wa nye-khen.* |
| Tap, to | དག་དག་བཏང་ (གཏོང་) བ་ | *taḱ-ta tang-wa.* |
| Do. *hon.* | དག་དག་གཏོང་ང་ (བ་) གནང་བ་ | *taḱ-ta tong-nga nang-wa.* |
| Tape, measuring | ཐག་ཚད་ | *thaḱ-tshe.* |
| Tape-worm | ཀུབ་འབུ་ | *kup-bu.* |
| Tardy | ཕྱི་པོ་ | *chhi-po.* |
| Target | རྒྱབ་འབེན་ | *gyam-be.* |
| Tarnish, to | བཙོག་པ་བཟོ་བ་ | *tsoḱ-pa śo-wa.* |
| Do. *hon.* | བཙོག་པ་བཟོ་བ་གནང་བ་ | *tsoḱ-pa śo-wa nang-wa.* |
| Tarry, to | འགོར་པོ་བྱེད་པ་ | *gor-po cḱe-pa.* |

| | | |
|---|---|---|
| Tarry, to, *hon.* | འགོར་པོ་གནང་བ་ | *gor-po nang-wa.* |
| Tartar (on the teeth) | སོ་དྲེག་ | *so-ťre.* |
| Do. *hon.* | ཚེམས་དྲེག་ | *tshem-ťre.* |
| Task | ལས་ཀ་ | *le-ka.* |
| Do. *hon.* | ཕྱག་ལས་ | *chha-le.* |
| Task, school | ཡིག་ཚད་ | *yiḱ-tshe.* |
| Tassel (for hat) | དོང་སྐྱུད་ | *tong-kü.* |
| Taste, *s.* | བྲོ་བ་ | *ťro-a.* |
| Do. *hon.* | ཞལ་བྲོ་ | *ja-ťro.* |
| Taste, to | བྲོ་བ་ལྟ་བ་ | *ťro-a ta-wa.* |
| Do. *hon.* | ཞལ་བྲོ་གཟིགས་པ་ | *ja-ťro ś́i-pa.* |
| Taunt, to | ཀྱག་ཀྱག་བྱས་ནས་ལབ་པ་ | *kya-kya ćhe-ne lap̌-pa.* |
| Do. *hon.* | ཀྱག་ཀྱག་གནང་ནས་གསུང་བ་ | *kya-kya nang-ne sung-wa.* |
| Tavern | ཆང་ཁང་ | *chhang-khang.* |
| Tax (general) | ཁྲལ། འབབ་ | *thre ; bap̌.* |
| Do. (customs-duty) | ཤོ་ཁྲལ་ | *sho-thre.* |
| Do. on land | ས་ཁྲལ་ | *sa-thre.* |
| Tax, to pay | ཁྲལ་འཇལ་བ་ | *thre-je-wa.* |
| Tea | ཇ་ | *ćha.* |
| Do. *hon.* | གསོལ་ཇ་ | *sö-ćha.* |

| | | |
|---|---|---|
| Tea, best quality | འབྲུ་ཐང་ | *dru-thang.* |
| Do. 2nd quality | འབྲུ་གཉིས་ | *dru-nyi.* |
| Do. 3rd quality | བཅུ་པ་ | *chu-pa.* |
| Do. 4th quality | བརྒྱད་པ་ | *gye-pa.* |
| Tea, brick of | ཇ་བག་ | *cḱa-ṕa-ka.* |
| Do. *hon.* | གསོལ་ཇ་བག་ | *sö-cḱa ṕa-ka.* |
| Tea-pot | ཁོག་ཏི་ | *kho-ti.* |
| Do. *hon.* | གསོལ་ཏི་ | *sö-ti.* |
| Tea-strainer | ཇ་ཚགས་ | *cḱa-tsha.* |
| Teach, to | བསླབ་པ་ (སློབ་པ་) | *laṕ-pa.* |
| Do. *hon.* | བསླབས་ (སློབ་) པ་གནང་བ་ | *laṕ-pa nang-wa.* |
| Teacher | དགེ་རྒན། སློབ་དཔོན་ | *ge-gen; lo-pön.* |
| Tear, *s.* | མིག་ཆུ་ | *miḱ-chhu.* |
| Do. *hon.* | སྤྱན་ཆབ་ | *chen-chhaṕ.* |
| Tear, to (cloth, etc.) | རལ་བ་ | *re-wa.* |
| Do. *hon.* | རལ་ར་ (བ་) གནང་བ་ | *re-ra nang-wa.* |
| Tear, to (flesh) | བཀོག་པ་ (འགོག་པ་) | *koḱ-pa.* |
| Do. *hon.* | བཀོག་ག་ (འགོག་པ་) གནང་བ་ | *koḱ-ka nang-pa.* |
| Tears, to shed | མིག་ཆུ་ཤོར་བ་ | *miḱ-chhu shor-wa.* |

| | | |
|---|---|---|
| Tears, to shed, *hon.* | སྤྱན་ཆབ་ཤོར་བ་ | *chen-chhaṕ shor-wa.* |
| Tedious | དཀའ་ལས་ཁག་པོ་ | *ka-le khaḱ-po.* |
| Do. *hon.* | སྐུ་མཉེལ་པོ་ | *ku-nye-po.* |
| Telegram | གློག་སྐུད་ཡི་གེ་ | *lo-kü yi-ge.* |
| Telegraph | ལྕགས་སྐུད། གློག་སྐུད་ | *cha-kü; lo-kü.* |
| Telephone | ཁ་པར་ | *kha-ṕar.* |
| Do. *hon.* | ཞལ་པར་ | *sḱe-ṕar.* |
| Telescope | རྒྱང་ཤེལ་ | *gyang-she.* |
| Tell, to | ལབ་པ་ | *laṕ-pa.* |
| Do. *hon.* | གསུང་བ་ | *sung-wa.* |
| Do. *h. hon.* | བཀའ་གནང་བ་ | *ka nang-wa.* |
| Temper (passion) | ཚིག་པ། ཁོང་ཁྲོ | *tshik-pa ; khong-thro.* |
| Tempered, good | བློ་རྒྱུ་རིང་པོ་ | *lo-gyu ring-po.* |
| Do. *hon.* | ཐུགས་རྒྱུ་རིང་པོ་ | *thu-gyu ring-po.* |
| Tempered, bad | རུ་ངར་པོ་ | *ru ngar-po.* |
| Do. *hon.* | ཐུགས་རུ་ངར་པོ་ | *thu-ru ngar-po.* |
| Temperate (climate) | བསིལ་དྲོས་སྙོམ་པོ་ | *si-t́rö nyom-po.* |
| Temperate, to be (moderate) | ཚོད་ཟིན་པ་ | *tshö-śim-pa.* |
| Temperature | གྲང་ལོས་ | *t́rang-lö.* |
| Tempest | རླུང་ཚུབ་ | *lung-tshuṕ.* |

| | | |
|---|---|---|
| Temple | མཆོད་ཁང་ | *chhö-khang.* |
| Tempt, to (cheat) | མགོ་སྐོར་བཏང་ (གཏོང་) བ་ | *go-kor tang-wa.* |
| Do. *hon.* | མགོ་སྐོར་གཏོང་ང་ (བ་) གནང་བ་ | *go-kor tong-nga nang-wa.* |
| Tempt, to (entice) | སེམས་བསླུས་པ་ | *sem lü-pa.* |
| Do. *hon.* | སེམས་བསླུས་པ་གནང་བ་ | *sem lü-pa nang-wa.* |
| Do. *inf.* to *sup.* | ཐུགས་སེམས་བསླུས་པ་ | *thuk-sem lü-pa.* |
| Tenacious (obstinate) | གྱོང་པོ་ | *kyong-po.* |
| Tenant | མི་སེར། འབངས་ | *mi-ser; bang.* |
| Do. poorer class of | མོ་ཡན་ | *mo-yen.* |
| Tender | འཇམ་པོ་ | *jam-po.* |
| Tendon | རྒྱུས་པ་ | *gyü-pa.* |
| Tenet | ཆོས་ལུགས་ | *chhö-lu.* |
| Ten | བཅུ་ | *chu.* |
| Tenth | བཅུ་པ་ | *chu-pa.* |
| Ten thousand | ཁྲི་ | *thri.* |
| Tent | གུར་ | *kur.* |
| Do. *hon.* | དབུ་གུར་ | *u-kur.* |
| Tent-pole | གུར་རྒྱུག་ | *kur-gyu.* |
| Tepid | དྲོས་འཇམ་ | *trön-jam.* |

| | | |
|---|---|---|
| Term (limit) | མཐའ་ | *tha.* |
| Do. (period) | དུས། བསྐལ་པ་ | *tü; kel-pa.* |
| Do. (word) | ཚིག་ | *tshi.* |
| Terminate, to | འཚར་བ་ | *tshar-wa.* |
| Do. *hon.* | གྲུབ་པ་ | *ťrup-pa.* |
| Terrible | ཞེད་སྐྲག་ཚ་པོ་ | *sḱe-tra tsha-po.* |
| Terribly | ཞེད་སྐྲག་ | *sḱe-tra.* |
| Terrified, to be | ཞེད་པ་ | *sḱe-pa.* |
| Do. *hon.* | ཞེད་པ་གནང་བ་ | *sḱe-pa nang-wa.* |
| Terrify, to | ཞེད་སྐྲག་སླང་བ་ | *sḱe-tra lang-wa.* |
| Do. *hon.* | ཞེད་སྐྲག་སློང་ང་ (བ་) གནང་བ་ | *sḱe-tra long-nga nang-wa.* |
| Terrifying | ཞེད་སྐྲག་ཚ་པོ་ | *sḱe-tra tsha-po.* |
| Territory | ས་ཆ་ | *sa-chha.* |
| Terror | ཞེད་སྐྲག་ | *sḱe-tra.* |
| Test, to | ཚོད་ལྟ་བ་ | *tshö ta-wa.* |
| Do. *hon.* | ཚོད་གཟིགས་པ་ | *tshö śi-pa.* |
| Testament (will) | ཁ་ཆེམས་ | *kha-chhem.* |
| Do. *hon.* | ཞལ་ཆེམས་ | *sḱe-chhem.* |
| Testicle | རླིག་པ་ | *lik-pa.* |

| | | |
|---|---|---|
| Testify, to | དཔང་པོ་བྱེད་པ་ | *pang-po cḱe-pa.* |
| Do. *hon.* | དཔང་པོ་གནང་བ་ | *pang-po nang-wa.* |
| Than | ལས་ | *le.* |
| Thankful, to be | དྲིན་དྲན་པ་ | *ťrin ťrem-pa.* |
| Do. *hon.* | དྲིན་དྲན་པ་གནང་བ་ | *ťrin ťrem-pa nang-wa.* |
| Do. *inf.* to *sup.* | བཀའ་དྲིན་དྲན་པ་ | *ka-ťrin ťrem-pa.* |
| Thank you! | འོ་ཡག་བྱུང་ | *o ya-cḱung.* |
| Do. *hon.* | ཐུགས་ཆེ་ | *thu-chhe.* |
| Do. *h. hon.* | ཐུགས་རྗེ་ཆེ་གནང་ | *thu-je chhe-nang.* |
| That | དེ་ | *ťe.* |
| That down there | མ་གི་ | *ma-ḱi.* |
| That, just like | ད་ག་རང་། དེ་འདྲ་ | *ťa-ḱa-rang; ťen-dra.* |
| That over there | ཕ་གི་ | *pha-ḱi.* |
| That up there | ཡ་གི་ | *ya-ḱi.* |
| That very | ཕ་གེ་རང་ | *pha-ḱe-rang.* |
| Thaw, to | ཞུ་བ་ | *sḱu-wa.* |
| The, *def. art.* | འདི། དེ་ | *di; ťe.* |
| Theft | རྐུན་མ་ | *ku-ma.* |
| Their | ཁོ་ཚོའི་ | *ḱhon-tshö.* |
| Them | ཁོ་ཚོ་ | *ḱhon-tsho.* |

| | | |
|---|---|---|
| Then (after that) | དེ་ནས་ | *t́e-ne.* |
| Do. (at that time) | དེའི་སྐང་ལ་ | *t́e-i gang-la.* |
| There | དད་ (དེ་ཙ།) ཕ་གི་ | *t́e ; pha-gi.* |
| Therefore | བྱས་ཚང་། དེའི་རྐྱེན་བྱས་ནས། དེའི་རྐྱེན་གྱིས་ | *cḱe-tsang ; t́e-i kyen cḱe-ne ; t́e-i kyen-kyi* |
| Thermometer | ཚ་གྲང་ལྟ་ཡ་ | *tsha-t́rang ta-ya.* |
| These | འདི་ཚོ་ | *di-tsho.* |
| They | ཁོ་ཚོ་ | *khon-tsho.* |
| Thibet | བོད་ | *ṕo.* |
| Thibetan | བོད་པ་ | *ṕö-pa.* |
| Do. language | བོད་སྐད་ | *ṕö-ke.* |
| Do. manuscript characters | དབུ་མེད་ | *u-me.* |
| Do. printed characters | དབུ་ཅན་ | *u-chen.* |
| Thick (of flat objects) | འཐུག་པོ་ | *thuk-po.* |
| Do. (of round objects) | སྦོམ་པོ་ | *bom-po.* |
| Do. (turbid) | རྙོག་པོ་ | *nyok-po.* |
| Thief | རྐུན་མ་ | *ku-ma.* |
| Thieve, to | རྐུན་མ་རྐུ་བ་ | *ku-ma ku-wa.* |
| Thigh | བརླ་ཤ་ | *le-sha.* |

| | | |
|---|---|---|
| Thigh-bone trumpet | རྐང་གླིང་ | *kang-ling.* |
| Thimble | ཅོ་མོ་ | *cho-mo.* |
| Thin (of flat objects) | སྲབ་པོ་ | *trap̄-po.* |
| Do. (of round objects) | ཕྲ་པོ་ | *thra-po.* |
| Do. (of persons and animals) | ཤ་སྐམ་པོ་ | *sha kam-po.* |
| Do. *hon.* (of persons) | སྐུ་ཤ་སྐམ་པོ་ | *ku-sha kam-po.* |
| Do. *hon.* (of animals) | བཞེས་ཤ་སྐམ་པོ་ | *sḱe-sha kam-po.* |
| Thine | ཁྱོད་རེའི་ (ཁྱོད་ཀྱི་) | *khyö-re.* |
| Do. *hon.* | ཁྱེད་ཀྱི་ | *khye-kyi.* |
| Do. *h. hon.* | སྐུ་གཞོགས་ཀྱི་ | *ku-sḱo kyi.* |
| Thing | ཅ་ལག་ (ཆ་ལག་) | *cha-la.* |
| Do. *hon.* | སྐུ་ཅས་ (སྐུ་ཆས་) | *ku-che.* |
| Think, to (suppose) | བསམ་པ་ | *sam-pa.* |
| Do. *hon.* | དགོངས་པ་ | *gong-pa.* |
| Think, to (reflect) | བསམ་བློ་བཏང་ (གཏོང་) བ་ | *sam-lo tang-wa.* |
| Do. *hon.* | ཐུགས་བསམ་བཞེས་པ་ | *thu-sam sḱe-pa.* |
| Third | གསུམ་པ་ | *sum-pa.* |
| Thirdly | གསུམ་པར་ | *sum-pa.* |
| Thirsty, to be | ཁ་སྐོམ་པ་ | *kha kom-pa.* |
| Do. *hon.* | ཞལ་སྐྱེམས་པ་ | *sḱe kyem-pa.* |

| | | |
|---|---|---|
| Thirteen | བཅུ་གསུམ་ | *chuk-sum.* |
| Thirteenth | བཅུ་གསུམ་པ་ | *chuk-sum-pa.* |
| Thirty | སུམ་ཅུ་ | *sum-chu.* |
| Thirtieth | སུམ་ཅུ་པ་ | *sum-chu-pa.* |
| This | འདི་ | *di.* |
| This very | ད་ག་རང་ | *ťa-ka-rang.* |
| Thither | དད་ (དེ་རུ་) | *ťe.* |
| Thorn | ཚེར་མ་ | *tsher-ma.* |
| Thorough, to be (complete) | ཕུགས་འཁྱོལ་བ་ | *phu khyö-wa.* |
| Thoroughly | བད་དེ་ | *be-ťe.* |
| Those | དེ་ཚོ་ | *ťe-tsho.* |
| Thou | ཁྱོད། ཁྱོད་རང་ | *khyö ; khyö-rang.* |
| Do. *hon.* | ཁྱེད་ | *khye.* |
| Do. *h. hon.* | སྐུ་གཞོགས་ | *ku-sko.* |
| Though | ནས། ཀྱང་། རུང་། ན་ཡང་ | *ne ; kyang ; rung ; nu-yang.* |
| Thought (intention) | དོན་དག་ | *ťön-ťa.* |
| Do. *hon.* | སྐུ་དོན་ | *ku-ťön.* |
| Thought (opinion) | བསམ་པ་ | *sam-pa.* |
| Do. *hon.* | ཐུགས་སེམས་ | *thu-sem.* |

| | | |
|---|---|---|
| Thousand | སྟོང་ཕྲག་ | *tong-thra.* |
| Thousand, hundred | འབུམ་ | *bum.* |
| Thousand, ten | ཁྲི་ | *thri.* |
| Thrash, to | གཡོ་མ་སྲུ་རྡུང་བ་ | *yo-ma-su dung-wa.* |
| Thread | སྐུད་པ་ | *kü-pa.* |
| Threaten, to | འཛོག་འཛོག་ (འཛིག་འཛིག་) བཏང་ (གཏོང་) བ་ | *dzik-dzik tang-wa.* |
| Three | གསུམ་ | *sum.* |
| Thresh, to (corn) | རྡུང་བ་ | *dung-wa.* |
| Threshhold | ཐེམ་པ་ | *them-pa.* |
| Thrice | ཚར་གསུམ་ | *tshar-sum.* |
| Thriving | གཡང་ཆེན་པོ་ | *yang-chhem-po.* |
| Throat | མིག་པ་ | *mik-pa.* |
| Do. *hon.* | མགུལ་མིག་ | *gü-mi.* |
| Throne | བཞུགས་ཁྲི་ | *sḱuk-thri.* |
| Throng (of men) | མི་ཚོགས་ | *mi-tsho.* |
| Through (by the agency of) | བརྒྱུད་ནས་ | *gyü-ne.* |
| Throw, to | རྒྱབ་པ། དབྱུག་པ་ | *gyaṕ-pa ; yuk-pa.* |
| Do. *hon.* | དབྱུག་ག་ (པ་) གནང་བ་ | *yuk-ka nang-wa.* |
| Throw at, to | གཞུ་བ་ | *sḱu-wa.* |

| | | |
|---|---|---|
| Throw at, to, *hon.* | སྐྱོན་པ་གནང་བ་ | *kyöm-pa nang-wa.* |
| Thumb | མཐེ་བོ་ | *the-ṕo.* |
| Do. *hon.* | ཕྱག་མཐེ་ | *chha-the.* |
| Thunder | འབྲུག་སྐད་ | *druḱ-ke.* |
| Thunder, to | འབྲུག་སྐད་སྐྱོན་པ་ | *druḱ-ke kyöm-pa.* |
| Thunderbolt | ཐོག་ | *tho.* |
| Do. sacred | རྡོ་རྗེ་ | *dor-je.* |
| Thursday | གཟའ་ཕུར་བུ་ | *śa-phur-ṕu.* |
| Thus | འདི་འདྲས། དག་ག་ཟེ་ | *din-dre ; ťa-ka-śe.* |
| Thwart, to | བཀག་པ་ (འགེགས་པ་) | *kaḱ-pa.* |
| Do. *hon.* | བཀག་ག་ (འགེགས་པ་) གནང་བ་ | *kaḱ-ḱa nang-wa.* |
| Tibet | བོད་ | *ṕö.* |
| Tibetan | བོད་པ་ | *ṕö-pa.* |
| Do. language | བོད་སྐད་ | *ṕö-ke.* |
| Do. printed characters | དབུ་ཅན་ | *u-chen.* |
| Do. manuscript characters | དབུ་མེད་ | *u-me.* |
| Tickle, to | ཨི་ཀུ་ལུ་ཀུ་སག་པ་ | *i-ḱu lu-ḱu saḱ-pa.* |
| Tidings | གནས་ཚུལ། གསར་འགྱུར་ | *ne-tshü ; sang-gyu.* |

| | | |
|---|---|---|
| Tiffin | ཉིན་གུང་ཁ་ལག་ | *nyin-kung kha-la.* |
| Do. *hon.* | ཉིན་གུང་ཞལ་ལག་ | *nyin-kung she-la.* |
| Tie, to | བསྡམས་པ་ (སྡོམ་པ་) | *dam-pa.* |
| Do. *hon.* | བསྡམས་ (སྡོམ་) པ་གནང་བ་ | *dam-pa nang-wa.* |
| Tiger | སྟག་ | *ta.* |
| Tight | དམ་པོ་ | *tam-po.* |
| Till | ཐུག་ལ། བར་དུ་ | *thuk-la; par-tu.* |
| Till, to | རྨོན་པ་རྒྱབ་པ་ | *möm-pa gyap-pa.* |
| Tillage | སོ་ནམས་ | *so-nam.* |
| Tiller, *s.* (one who tills) | རྨོན་པ་རྒྱབ་མཁན། ཐོན་ཁས་ (ཐོང་པ་) | *möm-pa gyang-khen; thön-khe.* |
| Timber | ཤིང་ཆ་ | *shing-chha.* |
| Time | དུས། དུས་ཚོད་ | *tü; tü-tshö.* |
| Do. (o'clock) | ཆུ་ཚོད་ | *chhu-tshö.* |
| Do. (proper time for doing something) | རན་ | *ren.* |
| Do. (three times, etc.) | ཚར། ཐེངས་ | *tshar; theng.* |
| Do. (life) | ཚེ་ | *tshe.* |
| Time, at the present (now-a-days) | དེ་རིང་སང་། དེང་སང་ | *te-ring sang; teng-sang.* |
| Time, to pass the | དགོ་འཁོར་བ་ | *go-khor-wa.* |

| | | |
|---|---|---|
| Time, to pass the, *hon.* | དབུ་འཁོར་བ་ | *u-khor-wa.* |
| Tin | ཤ་དཀར་ | *sha-ka.* |
| Tinder | སྤྲ་བ་ | *pa-a.* |
| Tip (point) | རྩེ་ | *tse.* |
| Tip (gratuity) | ཆང་རིན་ | *chhang-ring.* |
| Do. *hon.* | གསོལ་རས་ | *sö-re.* |
| Tipsy | ར་བཟི་ | *rap-śi.* |
| Do. to be | ར་བཟི་བ་ | *ra-śi-wa.* |
| Do. *hon.* | སྐུ་ར་བྱེད་པ་ | *ku-ra be-pa.* |
| Tired | བཀའ་ལས་ཁག་པོ་ | *ka-le khak-po.* |
| Do. *hon.* | སྐུ་མཉེལ་པོ་ | *ku-nye-po.* |
| Tired, to be | ཐང་ཆད་པ་ | *thang-chhe-pa.* |
| Do. *hon.* | སྐུ་ཐང་ཆད་པ་གནང་བ་ | *ku-thang chhe-pa nang-wa.* |
| Tiresome (tedious) | དཀའ་ལས་ཁག་པོ་ | *ka-le khak-po.* |
| Do. *hon.* | སྐུ་མཉེལ་པོ་ | *ku-nye-po.* |
| Titan (demi-god) | ལྷ་མ་ཡིན་ | *hla-ma-yin.* |
| Title | གོ་ས། གོ་གནས་ | *ko-sa; ko-ne.* |
| To (in presence of a person) | རྩ་ལ་ | *tsa-la.* |
| Do. *inf.* to *sup.* | སྐུ་མདུན་ལ་ | *kun-dün-la.* |
| To (as far as) | བར་ལ་ | *par-la.* |

| | | |
|---|---|---|
| Tobacco | ཐ་མག་ | *tha-ma.* |
| Do. *hon.* | བཞེས་ཐ་ | *sḱe-tha.* |
| Tobacco pipe | གང་ཟག་ | *kang-śa.* |
| Do. *hon.* | བཞེས་ཟག་ | *sḱe-śa.* |
| Tobacco pouch | ཐ་ཁུག་ | *tha-khu.* |
| Do. *hon.* | བཞེས་ཁུག་ | *sḱe-khu.* |
| To-day | དེ་རིང་ | *ťe-ring.* |
| Toe | རྐང་པའི་མཛུག་གུ་ | *kang-pe dzuḱ-ḱu.* |
| Do. *hon.* | ཞབས་ཀྱི་ཕྱག་མཛུག་ | *sḱaṕ-kyi chhan-dzu.* |
| Toe, the big | རྐང་པའི་མཐེ་བོ་ | *kang-pe the-ṕo.* |
| Do. *hon.* | ཞབས་ཀྱི་མཐེ་བོ་ | *sḱaṕ-kyi the-ṕo.* |
| Together with, *prep.* | དང་མཉམ་དུ་ | *ťang-nyam-ťu.* |
| Together, *adv.* (jointly) | མཉམ་སྦྲེལ་ | *nyam-drel.* |
| Do. *hon.* | ཕྱག་སྦྲེལ་ | *chha-drel.* |
| Toilsome | དཀའ་ལས་ཁག་པོ་ | *ka-le khaḱ-po.* |
| Do. *hon.* | སྐུ་མཉེལ་པོ་ | *ku-nye-po.* |
| Token | རྟགས་ | *ta.* |
| Tolerate, to (endure) | བཟོད་པ་སྒོམ་པ་ | *śö-pa gom-pa.* |
| Do. *hon.* | བཟོད་པ་སྒོམ་པ་གནང་བ་ | *śö-pa gom-pa nang-wa.* |
| Tolerate to (permit) | བཅུག་པ་ (འཇུག་པ་) | *chuḱ-pa.* |

| | | |
|---|---|---|
| Tolerate, to (permit), *hon.* | བཅུག་ག་ (འཇུག་པ་) གནང་བ་ | *chuk-ka nang-wa.* |
| Tomb | དུར་ཁུང་ | *ťur-khung.* |
| Tom-cat | ཕོ་ཞིམ་ | *pho-sǩim.* |
| To-morrow | སང་ཉིན་ | *sang-nyi.* |
| To-morrow morning | སང་ཞོགས་སྔ་པོ་ | *sang-sǩo nya-po.* |
| Tone | གདངས་ | *dang.* |
| Tongue | ལྕེ་ | *che.* |
| Do. *hon.* | ལྗགས་ | *ja.* |
| Tongue (dialect) | སྐད་ལུགས་ | *ǩe-lu.* |
| To-night | དོ་དགོངས་དགོངས་མོ་ | *ťo-gong gong-mo.* |
| Too, *conj.* | ཡང་ | *yang.* |
| Too (very) | ཧ་ཅང་ | *ha-chang.* |
| Too few, to be | ཉུང་དྲག་པ་ | *nyung ťrak-pa.* |
| Too little, to be | ཆུང་དྲག་པ་ | *chhung ťrak-pa.* |
| Too many, to be | མང་དྲག་པ་ | *mang ťrak-pa.* |
| Too much, to be | ལྷག་པ་ | *hlak-pa.* |
| Tool | ལག་ཆ་ | *lak-chha.* |
| Tooth | སོ་ | *so.* |
| Do. *hon.* | ཚེམས་ | *tshem.* |

| | | |
|---|---|---|
| Toothless | སོ་མེད་ | *so-me.* |
| Do. *hon.* | ཚེམས་མེད་ | *tshem-me.* |
| Tooth, front | མདུན་སོ་ | *dün-so.* |
| Do. *hon.* | མདུན་གྱི་ཚེམས་ | *dün-kyi tshem.* |
| Tooth, lower | སྨད་སོ་ | *me-so.* |
| Do. *hon.* | སྨད་ཀྱི་ཚེམས་ | *me-kyi tshem.* |
| Tooth, molar | འགྲམ་སོ་ | *dram-so.* |
| Do. *hon.* | ཞལ་འགྲམ་གྱི་ཚེམས་ | *sKe-dram kyi-tshem* |
| Tooth, upper | ཡ་སོ་ | *ya-so.* |
| Do. *hon.* | ཡས་ཀྱི་ཚེམས་ | *ye-kyi tshem.* |
| Top (summit) | རྩེ་ | *tse.* |
| Do. (lid) | ཁ་གཅོད་ | *khap-chö.* |
| Do. *hon.* | ཞལ་གཅོད་ | *sKe-chö.* |
| Torch | སྤྱད་འབར་ ( སྤྱ་འབར་ ) | *pem-bar.* |
| Torment, to (annoy) | ཁོང་ཁྲོ་སློང་བ་ | *khong-thro lang-wa.* |
| Do. *hon.* | དགོངས་པ་དཀྲུག་པ་ | *gong-pa truk-pa.* |
| Torn, to be | རལ་བ་ | *re-wa.* |
| Tortoise | རུས་སྦལ་ | *rü-be.* |
| Tortuous (crooked) | ཀྱོག་ཀྱོག་ | *kyo-kyo.* |
| Do. (deceitful) | གཡོ་ཅན། བློ་སྐྱོགས་སྐྱོགས་ | *yo-chen ; lo kyok-kyok.* |

| | | |
|---|---|---|
| Tortuous (deceitful), *hon.* | ཐུགས་གཡོ་ཅན། ཐུགས་སྐྱོགས་སྐྱོགས་ | *thu yo-chen; thu kyok-kyok.* |
| Torture (agony of mind) | སྡུག་བསྔལ་ | *du-nge.* |
| Do. *hon.* | ཐུགས་འཁྲམ་ | *thu-thre.* |
| Total, in the | བསྡོམས་ནས་ | *dom-ne.* |
| Totter, to | འཁྱོར་ནས་འགྲོ་བ་ | *khyor-ne dro-wa.* |
| Do. *hon.* | སྐུ་འཁྱོར་ནས་ཕེབ་པ་ | *ku-khyor-ne phe-pa.* |
| Do. *h. hon.* | སྐུ་འཁྱོར་ནས་འཆིབ་རྒྱུ་གནང་བ་ | *ku-khyor-ne chhip-gyu nang-wa.* |
| Touch, to | ཐུག་པ། འཆང་བ་ | *thuk-pa; chhang-wa.* |
| Do. *hon.* | ཐུག་ག་ (པ་) གནང་བ་ | *thuk-ka nang-wa.* |
| Touch, to (by stretching out hand, etc.) | སྙོབ་པ་ | *nyop-pa.* |
| Do. *hon.* | སྙོབ་པ་གནང་བ་ | *nyop-pa nang-wa.* |
| Towards | ཕྱོགས་ལ། ངོས་ལ་ | *chhok-la; ngö-la.* |
| Towel | ཨ་ཅོར་ | *a-chor.* |
| Do. *hon.* | ཞལ་ཅོར་ | *sKe-chor.* |
| Town | གྲོང་ཁྱེར་ | *trong-khyer.* |
| Toy | རྩེད་མོ་རྩེ་ཡ་ | *tse-mo tse-ya.* |
| Do. *hon.* | སྐུ་རྩེ་གནང་ཡ་ | *ku-tse nang-ya.* |

| | | |
|---|---|---|
| Track (path) | ལམ་ཀ་ | *lang-ka.* |
| Do. *hon.* | ཕེབ་ལམ་ | *pheṕ-lam.* |
| Track (on face of cliff) | ཕྲང་ | *thrang.* |
| Track (foot-print) | རྐང་རྗེས་ | *kang-je.* |
| Do. *hon.* | ཞབས་རྗེས་ | *sḱaṕ-je.* |
| Tract (of country) | ལུང་པ་ | *lung-pa.* |
| Trade, *s.* | ཚོང་ | *tshong.* |
| Do. *hon.* | རྒྱ་ཚོང་ | *gya-tshong.* |
| Trade, to | ཚོང་རྒྱབ་པ་ | *tshong-gyaṕ-pa.* |
| Do. *hon.* | རྒྱ་ཚོང་སྐྱོན་པ་ | *gya-tshong kyöm-pa.* |
| Trader, tradesman | ཚོང་པ་ | *tshong-pa.* |
| Do. *hon.* | ཚོང་དཔོན་ | *tshong-pön.* |
| Traduce, to | སྨད་ར་བཏང་ (གཏོང་) བ་ | *me-ra tang-wa.* |
| Do. *hon.* | སྨད་ར་གཏོང་ང་ (བ་) གནང་བ་ | *me-ra tong-nga nang-wa.* |
| Do. *inf.* to *sup.* | སྨད་ར་ཞུ་བ་ | *me-ra sḱu-wa.* |
| Traffic | ཚོང་ | *tshong.* |
| Do. *hon.* | རྒྱ་ཚོང་ | *gya-tshong.* |
| Train, to (teach) | བསླབས་པ་ (སློབ་པ་) | *laṕ-pa.* |
| Do. *hon.* | བསླབས་ (སློབ་) པ་གནང་བ་ | *laṕ-pa nang-wa.* |
| Trammel *s.* (hindrance) | བཀག་ཆ་ | *kaḱ-chha.* |

| | | |
|---|---|---|
| Trammel, to | བཀག་པ་ (འགེགས་པ་) | *kak-pa.* |
| Do. *hon.* | བཀག་ག་ (འགེགས་པ་) གནང་བ་ | *kak-ka nang-wa.* |
| Tramp, *s* (loafer) | རྒྱལ་ཁམས་སྐོར་མཁན་ | *gyeng-kham kor-khen.* |
| Trample, to | རྐང་པས་རྫི་བ་ | *kang-pe dzi-wa.* |
| Do. *hon.* | ཞབས་ཀྱིས་རྫི་བ་གནང་བ་ | *sk̄ap-kyi dzi-wa nang-wa.* |
| Tranquil (of places) | ཁ་གུ་སིམ་བུ་ | *kha-ku sim-p̄u.* |
| Do. *hon.* | ཞལ་གུ་སིམ་བུ་ | *sk̄e-ku sim-p̄u.* |
| Transfer, to | རྗེ་བ་ | *je-wa.* |
| Do. (soldiers, etc.) | རྗེ་པོ་རྒྱབ་པ་ | *je-po gyap̄-pa.* |
| Do. *hon.* | རྗེ་པོ་སྐྱོན་པ་ | *je-po kyöm-pa.* |
| Transgress, to | སྡིག་པ་བསགས་ (སོག་) པ་ | *dik-pa sak-pa.* |
| Do. *hon.* | སྐུ་སྡིག་བསགས་ག་ (སོག་པ་) གནང་བ་ | *ku-di sak-ka nang-wa.* |
| Transgression | སྡིག་པ་ | *dik-pa.* |
| Do. *hon.* | སྐུ་སྡིག་ | *ku-di.* |
| Translate, to | སྒྱུར་བ་ | *gyur-wa.* |
| Do. *hon.* | སྒྱུར་ར་ (བ་) གནང་བ་ | *gyur-ra nang-wa.* |
| Transmigrate, to | སྐྱེ་བ་འཕོས་པ་ | *kye-wa phö-pa.* |
| Do. *hon.* | སྐུ་སྐྱེ་འཕོས་པ་ | *ku-kye phö-pa.* |

| | | |
|---|---|---|
| Transmigration, cycle of | སྲིད་པ་འཁོར་ལོ་ | *si-pa khor-lo.* |
| Transport | ཁལ་མ་ | *khe-ma.* |
| Do. *hon.* | ཆིབས་ཁལ་ | *chhip-khe.* |
| Transport (compulsory service) | རྟའུ་ | *ta-u.* |
| Do. *hon.* | ཆིབས་རྟའུ་ | *chhip-ta-u.* |
| Transport, to | རྟའུ་སྐྱེལ་བ་ | *ta-u kyel-wa.* |
| Do. *hon.* | ཆིའུ་སྐྱེལ་ར་ (བ་) གནང་བ་ | *chhi-u kye-ra nang-wa.* |
| Trap | རྙི་ | *nyi.* |
| Travail (child-birth) | སྐྱེ་གཟུག་ | *kye-śu.* |
| Traveller | འགྲུལ་པ་ | *drü-pa.* |
| Tray | ཤིང་ཁྲོལ་ | *shing-thrö.* |
| Do. *hon.* | གསོལ་ཁྲོལ་ | *sö-thrö.* |
| Tread, to | རྐང་ལེབ་འཐེབ་པ་ | *kang-le thep-pa.* |
| Do. *hon.* | ཞབས་ལེབ་འཐེབ་པ་ | *sKap-le thep-pa.* |
| Treasure, *s.* | བཀང་འཇུག་ | *kang-juk.* |
| Treasurer | ཕྱག་མཛོད་ | *chhan-dzö.* |
| Treasury | དངུལ་ཁང་ | *ngü-khang.* |
| Treat, *s.* (feast) | མགྲོན་པོ་ | *dröm-po.* |
| Do. *hon.* | ཐུགས་སྤྲོ་ | *thu-tro.* |

| | | |
|---|---|---|
| Treat, to (entertain) | མགྲོན་པོ་བཏང་ (གཏོང་) བ་ | *dröm-po tang-wa.* |
| Do. *hon.* | ཐུགས་སྤྲོ་གཏོང་ང་ (བ་) གནང་བ་ | *thu-tro tong-nga nang-wa.* |
| Treaty | འཆིང་ཡིག་ | *chhing-yi.* |
| Tree | ཤིང་སྡོང་ | *shing-dong.* |
| Tremble, to (of animate beings) | འདར་བ་ | *dar-wa.* |
| Do. *hon* | སྐུ་འདར་སྐྱོན་པ་ | *kun-dar kyöm-pa.* |
| Tremble, to (of inanimate things) | འཁྲུག་པ་ | *thruk-pa.* |
| Trench | དོང་ | *ťong.* |
| Trial (experiment) | ཞིབ་ཆ་ | *sKip̌-chha.* |
| Do. (by judge) | ཞིབ་དཔྱོད་ | *sKip̌-chö.* |
| Do. *hon.* | བཀའ་ཞིབ་ | *ka-sKip̌.* |
| Trial, to make a | ཞིབ་ཆ་ལྟ་བ་ | *sKip̌-chha ta-wa.* |
| Do. *hon.* | ཞིབ་ཆ་གཟིགས་པ་ | *sKip̌-chha śi-pa.* |
| Triangle | ཟུར་གསུམ་ | *śur-sum.* |
| Tribe | མི་བརྒྱུད། རིགས་བརྒྱུད་ | *mi-gyü ; ri-gyü.* |
| Tribunal | ཁྲིམས་ཁང་ | *thrim-khang.* |
| Tribute | ཁྲལ། འབབ་ | *thre ; bap̌.* |
| Trick (deceit) | མགོ་སྐོར་ | *go-kor.* |

| | | |
|---|---|---|
| Trick (deceit), *hon.* | དབུ་སྐོར་ | *u-kor.* |
| Trickle, to | ཐིགས་པ་རྒྱབ་པ་ | *thiḱ-pa gyaṕ-pa.* |
| Tricky (artful) | གཙང་པོ་ | *chang-po.* |
| Do. *hon.* | ཐུགས་གཙང་པོ་ | *thu-chang-po.* |
| Trident | ཁ་ཊཾ་ | *kha-tam.* |
| Trifling, (matter), *adj.* | དོན་གནད་ཆུང་ཆུང་ | *t́ön-ne chhung-chhung.* |
| Do. *hon.* | ཐུགས་དོན་ཆུང་ཆུང་ | *thuḱ-t́ön chhung-chhung.* |
| Trigger | སྐམ་པ་ | *kam-pa.* |
| Tripod | ཀང་གསུམ་ | *kang-sum.* |
| Do. iron (for fire) | ལྕགས་སྒྱིད་ | *cha-gyi.* |
| Trivial | དོན་གནད་ཆུང་ཆུང་ | *t́ön-ne chhung-chhung.* |
| Do. *hon.* | ཐུགས་དོན་ཆུང་ཆུང་ | *thuḱ-t́ön chhung-chhung.* |
| Tromowa (inhabitant of Chumbi Valley) | གྲོ་མོ་བ་ | *t́ro-mo-wa.* |
| Troop | དམག་དཔུང་ | *maḱ-pung.* |
| Trot, to | གོམ་ས་རྒྱབ་པ་ | *ḱom-sa gyaṕ-pa.* |
| Do. *hon.* | གོམ་ས་སྐྱོན་པ་ | *ḱom-sa kyöm-pa.* |
| Trouble | དཀའ་ལས་ | *ka-le.* |
| Do. to be in | དཀའ་ལས་བྱུང་བ་ | *ka-le cḱung-wa.* |

| | | |
|---|---|---|
| Troublesome (of persons) | ཅ་སྙིང་པོ་ | *cha-sing-po.* |
| Do. *hon.* | ཐུགས་ཅ་སྙིང་པོ་ | *thuk-cha sing-po.* |
| Troublesome (of things) | དཀའ་ལས་ཁག་པོ་ | *ka-le khak-po.* |
| Do. *hon.* | སྐུ་མཉེལ་པོ་ | *ku-nye-po.* |
| Trousers | གོ་ཐུང་ (གོས་ཐུང་།) དོར་མ་ | *ko-thung; tor-ma.* |
| Do. *hon.* | ཞབས་དོར་ | *skap-to.* |
| True | ངོ་ཐོག། དངོས་ནས་ | *ngo-tho; ngö-ne.* |
| Truly | དངོས་ནས་ | *ngö-ne.* |
| Trumpet | དུང་ | *tung.* |
| Trumpet, thigh bone | རྐང་གླིང་ | *kang-ling.* |
| Trunk (box) | སྒམ་ | *gam.* |
| Do. *hon.* | ཕྱག་སྒམ་ | *chha-gam.* |
| Trunk (of elephant) | མཆུ་དོ་ | *chhu-do.* |
| Trunk, iron (box) | ལྕགས་སྒམ་ | *cha-gam.* |
| Do. leather (box) | ཀོ་སྒམ་ | *ko-gam.* |
| Trunk (of tree) | སྡོང་པོ་ | *dong-po.* |
| Trust (confidence) | བློ་གཏད་ | *lo-te.* |
| Trust, to | བློས་བཀལ་བ་ | *lö ke-wa.* |
| Do. *hon* | ཐུགས་བློ་བཀལ་ར་ (བ་) གནང་བ་ | *thu-lo ke-ra nang-wa.* |

| | | |
|---|---|---|
| Trustworthy | བློས་ (བློ་) ཁེལ་ར་ (བ་) | *lö khe-ra.* |
| Do. *hon.* | ཐུགས་བློ་ཁེལ་ར་ (བ་) | *thu-lo khe-ra.* |
| Truth | ངོ་ཐོག། དངོས་ནས་ | *ngo-tho; ngö-ne.* |
| Try, to (make effort) | སྙིང་རུས་བྱེད་པ་ | *nying-rü cḱe-pa.* |
| Do. *hon.* | ཐུགས་རུས་གནང་བ་ | *thuk-rü nang-wa.* |
| Try, to (test) | ཚོད་ལྟ་བ། ཁོག་པ་ལེན་པ་ | *tshö ta-wa; khok-pa lem-pa.* |
| Do. *hon.* | ཚོད་གཟིགས་པ་ | *tshö śi-pa.* |
| Tuesday | གཟའ་མིག་དམར་ | *śa mik-mar.* |
| Tumble, to (on ground which one is already touching) | འགྱེལ་བ་ | *gye-wa.* |
| Do. *hon.* | འགྱེལ་ར་ (བ་) གནང་བ་ | *gye-ra nang-wa.* |
| Tumble, to (from a height) | གཟགས་པ་ (འཛོག་པ་) | *śak-pa.* |
| Do. *hon.* | གཟགས་ག་ (འཛོག་པ་) གནང་བ་ | *śak-ka nang-wa.* |
| Tumour | གཉེན་འབུར་ | *nyem-bur.* |
| Tumult | རྒྱབ་འདྲེ། འཁྲུག་པ་ | *gyam-dre; thruk-pa.* |
| Tune | གདངས་ | *dang.* |
| Turban | ལེ་དོས་ | *le-tö.* |
| Turbid | རྙོག་པོ་ | *nyok-po.* |

| | | |
|---|---|---|
| Turf | སྤང་ | *pang.* |
| Turkistan | ཧོར་ལུང་པ། ཧོར་ཡུལ་ | *hor lung-pa; hor-yü.* |
| Do. man of | ཧོར་པ་ | *hor-pa.* |
| Turn round, to, *v.i.* | འཁོར་བ་ | *khor-wa.* |
| Do. *hon.* | ཞབས་འཁོར་གནང་བ་ | *sḱaṕ-khor nang-wa.* |
| Turn round, to, *v.t.* | སྐོར་ར་ (བ་) རྒྱབ་པ་ | *kor-ra gyaṕ-pa.* |
| Do. *hon.* | སྐོར་ར་ (བ་) སྐྱོན་པ་ | *kor-ra kyöm-pa.* |
| Turn back to front, to | ཁ་ཕྱོགས་ལོག་པ་ | *kha-chho loḱ-pa.* |
| Do. *hon.* | ཁ་ཕྱོགས་ལོག་ག་ (པ་) གནང་བ་ | *kha-chho loḱ-ḱa nang-wa.* |
| Turn upside down, to | མགོ་གཤུག་ལོག་པ། ཨ་ལོག་རྒྱབ་པ་ | *go-sḱu loḱ-pa; a-lo gyaṕ-pa.* |
| Do. *hon.* | མགོ་གཤུག་ལོག་ག་ (པ་) གནང་བ། ཨ་ལོག་སྐྱོན་པ་ | *go-sḱu loḱ-ḱa nang-wa; a-lo kyöm-pa.* |
| Turnip | ཉུང་མ་ | *nyung-ma.* |
| Do. *hon.* | བཞེས་ཉུང་ | *sḱe-nyung.* |
| Turquoise | གཡུ་ | *yu.* |
| Do. *hon.* | ཕྱག་གཡུ་ | *chha-yu.* |
| Turquoise ear-ring | ཟི་གཡུ་ | *śi-yu.* |
| Turquoise (worn in head-dress) | གཡུ་ | *yu.* |

| | | |
|---|---|---|
| Turquoise (worn in head-dress) *hon.* | དབུ་གཡུ་ | *u-yu.* |
| Tusk | མཆེ་བ་ | *chhe-wa.* |
| Tutelary deity | ཡི་དམ་ | *yi-dam.* |
| Tutor | དགེ་རྒན་ | *ge-gen.* |
| Do. *hon.* | དགེ་རྒན་ལགས་ | *ge-gen-la.* |
| Twelfth | བཅུ་གཉིས་པ་ | *chu-nyi-pa.* |
| Twelve | བཅུ་གཉིས་ | *chu-nyi.* |
| Twentieth | ཉི་ཤུ་པ་ | *nyi-shu-pa.* |
| Twenty | ཉི་ཤུ་ | *nyi-shu.* |
| Twice | ཚར་གཉིས་ | *tshar-nyi.* |
| Twilight, at | ས་རིབ་ (སྲིབ་) ནས་ | *sa rip-ne.* |
| Twin | མཚེ་མ་ | *tshe-ma.* |
| Do. *hon.* | ཨ་ཝ་མཚེ་མ་ | *a-wa tshe-ma.* |
| Twine | སྐུད་པ་ | *kü-pa.* |
| Do. *hon.* | ཕྱག་སྐུད་ | *chha-kü.* |
| Twist, to | སྒྲིམ་པ་ | *drim-pa.* |
| Do. *hon.* | སྒྲིམ་པ་གནང་བ་ | *drim-pa nang-wa.* |
| Two | གཉིས་ | *nyi.* |
| Do. (in weighing, measuring, etc.) | དོ་ | *t̕o.* |

# U

| | | |
|---|---|---|
| Udder | གཞོས་ | *sḱö.* |
| Ugly | ཁ་མདོག་ཉེས་པོ་ | *kha-do nye-po.* |
| Do. *hon.* | ཞལ་མདོག་ཉེས་པོ་ | *sḱe-do nye-po.* |
| Ulcer | ཤུ་བ་ | *shu-wa.* |
| Do. *hon.* | སྐུ་ཤུ་ | *ku-shu.* |
| Ultimate | གཞུག་ཤོས་ | *sḱuk-shö.* |
| Umbrage, to take | འཚེར་བ་ | *tsher-wa.* |
| Do. *hon.* | ཐུགས་འཚེར་གནང་བ་ | *thu-tsher nang-wa.* |
| Umbrella | ཉི་གདུགས་ | *nyi-du.* |
| Do *hon.* | དབུ་གདུགས་ | *u-du.* |
| Unable, to be | མི་ཐུབ་པ་ | *mi thuṕ-pa.* |
| Unavailing, to be (useless) | ཕན་མི་ཐོགས་པ་ | *phen mi thoḱ-pa.* |
| Do. *hon.* | ཐུགས་ཕན་མི་གསོ་བ་ | *thu-phen mi so-wa.* |
| Unbearable (pain) | སྒོང་མི་ཐུབ་པ་ | *gong mi thuṕ-pa.* |
| Do. *hon.* | སྒོང་ང་ (སྒོམ་པ་) གནང་མི་ ཐུབ་པ་ | *gong-nga nang mi thuṕ-pa.* |
| Unbiassed | ཁྲིམས་དྲང་པོ་ | *thrim ťrang-po.* |
| Do. *hon.* | བཀའ་ཁྲིམས་དྲང་པོ་ | *ka-thrim ťrang-po.* |
| Unbreakable, to be | ཆག་རྒྱུ་མེད་པ་ | *chhaḱ-gyu me-pa.* |

| | | |
|---|---|---|
| Unbridled (licentious) | འདོད་ཆགས་ཆེན་པོ་ | *dö-chha chhem-po.* |
| Unceasing | རྒྱུན་ཆད་རྒྱུ་མེད་པ་ | *gyün-chhe-gyu me-pa.* |
| Unceasingly | རྣམ་རྒྱུན། དུས་རྒྱུན་ | *nam-gyün; tü-gyün.* |
| Uncertain, to be | ཐེ་ཚོམ་ཟ་བ་ | *the-tshom śa-wa.* |
| Do. *hon.* | ཐེ་ཚོམ་གནང་བ་ | *the-tshom nang-wa.* |
| Uncertainty | ཐེ་ཚོམ་ | *the-tshom.* |
| Unchaste | འདོད་ཆགས་ཆེན་པོ་ | *dö-chha chhem-po.* |
| Uncivil | སྒྲིག་མེད་ | *drik-me.* |
| Uncle, maternal | ཞང་ཞང་ (ཨ་ཞང་) | *shang·shang.* |
| Do. paternal | ཨ་ཀུ་ | *a-ku.* |
| Unclean | བཙོག་པ་ | *tsok-pa.* |
| Unclothed | དམར་ཧྲང་ང་ | *mar-hrang-nga.* |
| Uncommon (rare) | དཀོན་པོ་ | *köm-po.* |
| Unconquerable | གླགས་···མི་ཁ་བ་ | *la...mi kha-wa.* |
| Undaunted | བློ་ཁོག་ཆེན་པོ་ | *lo-kho chhem-po.* |
| Do. *hon.* | ཐུགས་ཁོག་ཆེན་པོ་ | *thu-kho chhem-po.* |
| Undefined | བརྟན་པོ་མེད་པ་ | *tem-po me-pa.* |
| Under | འོག་ལ་ | *o-la.* |
| Understand, to | ཤེས་པ། ཧ་གོ་བ་ | *she-pa; ha-ko-wa.* |
| Do. *hon.* | མཁྱེན་པ་ | *khyem-pa.* |

| | | |
|---|---|---|
| Understand, to, *h. hon.* | དགོངས་པ་རྟོགས་པ་ | *gong-pa tok-pa.* |
| Understanding | རིག་པ་ | *rik-pa.* |
| Do. *hon.* | ཐུགས་རིག་ | *thu-ri.* |
| Undo, to (nullify) | མེད་པར་བཟོ་བ་ | *me-pa śo-wa.* |
| Do. *hon.* | མེད་པར་བཟོ་བ་གནང་བ་ | *me-pa śo-wa nang-wa.* |
| Undo, to (untie) | བཀྲོལ་བ་ (འགྲོལ་བ།) བཤིག་པ་ | *tröl-wa; sKik-pa.* |
| Do. *hon.* | བཀྲོལ་ར་ (འགྲོལ་བ་) གནང་བ། བཤིག་ག་ (པ་) གནང་བ་ | *trö-ra nang-wa; sKik-ka nang-wa.* |
| Undress, to | ཕིས་པ་ (འབུད་པ་) | *pi-pa.* |
| Do. *hon.* | ཕིས་ (འབུད་) པ་གནང་བ་ | *pi-pa nang-wa.* |
| Unendurable (pain) | སྒྲོང་ (སྒྲོམ་) མི་ཐུབ་པ་ | *gong mi thup-pa.* |
| Do. *hon.* | སྒྲོང་ང་ (སྒྲོམ་པ་) གནང་མི་ཐུབ་པ་ | *gong-nga nang mi thup-pa.* |
| Uneven, to be | སྙོམས་པོ་མེད་པ་ | *nyom-po me-pa.* |
| Unfasten, to (button, etc.) | སྦྱིད་པ་ | *pi-pa.* |
| Do. *hon.* | སྦྱིད་པ་གནང་བ་ | *pi-pa nang-wa.* |
| Unfasten, to (knot, etc.) | བཤིག་པ་ | *sKik-pa.* |
| Do. *hon.* | བཤིག་ག་ (པ་) གནང་བ་ | *sKik-ka nang-wa.* |

| | | |
|---|---|---|
| Unfit | འོས་པོ་མེད་པ་ | *ö-po me-pa.* |
| Do. *hon.* | ཐུགས་འོས་པོ་མེད་པ་ | *thu-ö-po me-pa.* |
| Unfortunate | བསོད་བདེ་མེད་པ། བསོད་བདེ་ཆུང་ཆུང་ | *so-de me-pa; so-de chhung-chhung.* |
| Do. *hon.* | སྐུ་བསོད་མེད་པ། སྐུ་བསོད་ཆུང་ཆུང་ | *ku-sö me-pa; ku-sö chhung-chhung.* |
| Unfortunate, to be | བསོད་བདེ་མེད་པ་ | *so-de me-pa.* |
| Do. *hon.* | སྐུ་བསོད་མེད་པ་ | *ku-sö me-pa.* |
| Unintelligible | མི་གོ་བ་ | *mi ko-wa.* |
| Do. *hon.* | མི་གསན་པ་ | *mi sem-pa.* |
| Unhappy, to be | སྐྱིད་པོ་མེད་པ་ | *kyi-po me-pa.* |
| Do. *hon.* | ཐུགས་སྤྲོ་པོ་མེད་པ་ | *thu-tro-po me-pa.* |
| Uniform (dress) | དམག་ཆས་ | *mak-chhe.* |
| Uniform (alike) | གཅིག་པ། འདྲ་འདྲ་ | *chik-pa; dran-dra.* |
| Unimportant | དོན་དག་ཆུང་ཆུང་ | *tön-ta chhung-chhung.* |
| Do. *hon.* | ཐུགས་དོན་ཆུང་ཆུང་ | *thuk-tön chhung-chhung* |
| Uninterrupted | རྒྱུན་ཆད་རྒྱུ་མེད་བ་ | *gyün-chhe-gyu me-pa.* |
| Uninterruptedly | རྣམ་རྒྱུན། དུས་རྒྱུན་ | *nam-gyün; tü-gyün.* |
| Unite, to | འཐུད་རྒྱབ་པ་ | *thü-gyap-pa.* |
| Do. *hon.* | འཐུད་སྐྱོན་པ་ | *thü-kyöm-pa.* |

| | | |
|---|---|---|
| Unitedly (jointly) | མཉམ་སྦྲེལ་ | *nyam-drel.* |
| Do. *hon.* | ཕྱག་སྦྲེལ་ | *chha-drel.* |
| Universal (all) | ཚང་མ། ཐམས་ཅད། སྒང་ཁ། རུ་ | *tshang-ma; tham-che; gang-kha; ru.* |
| Unlawful | ཁྲིམས་མེད་ | *thrim-me.* |
| Unlearned | ཡོན་ཏན་མེད་པ་ | *yön-ten me-pa.* |
| Do. *hon.* | སྐུ་ཡོན་མེད་པ་ | *ku-yön me-pa.* |
| Unless, with *verb* "to do" | མ་བྱེད་ན་ | *ma che-na.* |
| Unlimited | ཚོད་མེད་པ་ | *tshö me-pa.* |
| Unloose, to (dress, etc.) | སྤྱིད་པ་ | *pi-pa.* |
| Do. *hon.* | སྤྱིད་པ་གནང་བ་ | *pi-pa nang-wa.* |
| Unlucky | བསོད་བདེ་མེད་པ། བསོ་ (བསོད་) བདེ་ཆུང་ཆུང་ | *so-de me-pa; so-de chhung-chhung* |
| Do. *hon.* | སྐུ་བསོད་མེད་པ། སྐུ་བསོད་ཆུང་ཆུང་ | *ku-sö me-pa; ku-sö chhung-chhung.* |
| Unlucky, to be | བསོད་བདེ་མེད་པ་ | *so-de me-pa.* |
| Do. *hon.* | སྐུ་བསོད་མེད་པ་ | *ku-sö me-pa.* |
| Unmarried man | ཕོ་ཧྲང་ང་ | *pho-hrang-nga.* |
| Do. woman | མོ་ཧྲང་ང་ | *mo-hrang-nga.* |
| Unmerciful, to be | སྙིང་རྗེ་མེད་པ་ | *nying-je me-pa.* |

| | | |
|---|---|---|
| Unmerciful, to be, *hon.* | ཐུགས་རྗེ་མེད་པ་ | *thuk-je me-pa.* |
| Unprejudiced (of judge) | ཁྲིམས་དྲང་པོ་ | *thrim t̔rang-po.* |
| Do. *hon.* | བཀའ་ཁྲིམས་དྲང་པོ་ | *ka-thrim t̔rang-po.* |
| Unprofitable, to be | ཕན་མི་ཐོགས་པ་ | *phen mi thok-pa.* |
| Do. *hon.* | ཐུགས་ཕན་མི་གསོ་བ་ | *thu-phen mi so-wa.* |
| Unreasonable | དོན་མེད་ | *t̔ön-me.* |
| Unrelenting, to be | སྙིང་རྗེ་མེད་པ་ | *nying-je me-pa.* |
| Do. *hon.* | ཐུགས་རྗེ་མེད་པ་ | *thuk-je me-pa.* |
| Unserviceable, to be | ཕན་མི་ཐོགས་པ་ | *phen mi thok-pa.* |
| Do. *hon.* | ཐུགས་ཕན་མི་གསོ་བ་ | *thu-phen mi so-wa.* |
| Unsettled (indefinite) | བརྟན་པོ་མེད་པ་ | *tem-po me-pa.* |
| Untie, to | བཀྲོལ་བ་ (འགྲོལ་བ།) བཤིག་པ་ | *tröl-wa ; sk̔ik-pa.* |
| Do. *hon.* | བཀྲོལ་ར་ (འགྲོལ་བ་) གནང་བ། བཤིག་ག་ (པ་) གནང་བ་ | *trö-ra nang-wa ; sk̔ik-ka nang-wa.* |
| Until | ཐུག་ལ་ | *thuk-la.* |
| Untruth | ཧམ་པ། ཀྱག་རྫུན | *ham-pa ; kyak-dzün.* |
| Do. *hon.* | ཞལ་རྫུན | *sk̔e-dzün.* |
| Unusual (rare) | དཀོན་པོ་ | *köm-po.* |

| | | |
|---|---|---|
| Unusual (extraordinary) | ཡ་མཚན་པོ། ཁྱད་མཚར་པོ་ | *yam-tshem-po ; khye-tsha-po.* |
| Unwell, to be | བདེ་པོ་མེད་པ། གཟུགས་པོ་ཐང་པོ་མེད་པ་ | *de-po me-pa ; śuḱ-po thang-po me-pa.* |
| Do. *hon.* | སྐུ་གཟུགས་བདེ་པོ་མེད་པ། སྐུ་གཟུགས་ཐང་པོ་མེད་པ་ | *ku-śu de-po me-pa ; ku-śu thang-po me-pa.* |
| Up | ཡར་ | *ya.* |
| Up to | ཐུག་ལ་ | *thuḱ-la.* |
| Up-hill | གྱེན་ | *kyen.* |
| Do. steep | གྱེན་དམ་པོ་ | *kyen-ťam-po.* |
| Upon | སྟེང་ལ། སྒང་ལ་ | *teng-la ; gang-la.* |
| Upper | ཡ་གི་ | *ya-ki.* |
| Upper arm | ལག་ཉ་ | *laḱ-nya.* |
| Do. *hon.* | ཕྱག་ཉ་ | *chha-nya.* |
| Upper tooth | ཡ་སོ་ | *ya-so.* |
| Do. *hon.* | ཡས་ཀྱི་ཚེམས་ | *ye-kyi tshem.* |
| Upraid, to | གཤེ་གཤེ་བཏང་ (གཏོང་) བ་ | *she-she tang-wa.* |
| Do. *hon.* | བཀའ་བཀྱོན་གནང་བ་ | *kaṕ-kyön nang-wa.* |
| Upright (erect) | ཀྱེ་རེ་ | *kye-re.* |
| Do. (just) | ཁྲིམས་དྲང་པོ་ | *thrim ťrang-po.* |
| Do. *hon.* | བཀའ་ཁྲིམས་དྲང་པོ་ | *ka-thrim ťrang-po.* |

| | | |
|---|---|---|
| Upright (moral, virtuous) | ཚུལ་ལྡན་ | *tshün-den.* |
| Upshot | སྙིང་པོ་ | *nying-po.* |
| Upstairs | ཡ་ཐོག་ | *yap-tho.* |
| Urge, to (insist) | ཨུ་ཚུགས་བྱེད་པ་ | *u-tshu cKe-pa.* |
| Do. *hon.* | ཨུ་ཚུགས་གནང་བ་ | *u-tshu nang-wa.* |
| Urgent (work) | འཕྲལ་འཕྲལ་བྱེད་དགོས་ཡ་ | *thre-thre cKe gö-ya.* |
| Urine | གཅིན་པ་ | *chim-pa.* |
| Do. *hon.* | ཆབ་གསང་ | *chhap-sang.* |
| Do. *h. hon.* | སྐུ་གསང་ | *ku-sang.* |
| Urine, to discharge | གཅིན་པ་བཏང་ (གཏོང་) བ་ | *chim-pa tang-wa.* |
| Do. *hon.* | ཆབ་གསང་བཏང་ (གཏོང་) བ་ | *chhap-sang tang-wa.* |
| Do. *h. hon.* | སྐུ་གསང་གནང་བ་ | *ku-sang nang-wa.* |
| Urn (containing ashes of dead lama) | སྐུ་གདུང་ | *ku-dung.* |
| Us | ང་ཚོ་ | *nga-tsho.* |
| Usage | ལུགས་སྲོལ་ | *luk-sö.* |
| Use (custom) | ལུགས་སྲོལ་ | *luk-sö.* |
| Use, to (employ) | སྐོ་བ་ | *ko-wa.* |
| Do. *hon.* | སྐོ་བ་གནང་བ་ | *ko-wa nang-wa.* |
| Use, to be of | ཕན་ཐོགས་པ་ | *phen thok-pa.* |

| | | |
|---|---|---|
| Use, to be of *hon.* | ཐུགས་ཕན་གསོ་བ་ | *thu-phen so-wa.* |
| Used to, to be | གོམས་པ་ | *ḱom-pa.* |
| Used to, to become | གོམས་སོང་བ་ | *ḱom-song-wa.* |
| Used up, to be | རྫོགས་པ་ | *dzoḱ-pa.* |
| Do. *hon.* | རྫོགས་ཀ་ (པ་) གནང་བ་ | *dzoḱ-ḱa nang-wa.* |
| Useful, to be | ཕན་ཐོགས་པ་ | *phen thoḱ-pa.* |
| Do. *hon.* | ཐུགས་ཕན་གསོ་བ་ | *thu-phen so-wa.* |
| Useless, to be | ཕན་མི་ཐོགས་པ་ | *phen mi thoḱ-pa.* |
| Do. *hon.* | ཐུགས་ཕན་མི་གསོ་བ་ | *thu-phen mi so-wa.* |
| Usually | ཕལ་ཆེར་ | *phe-chhe.* |
| Usurp, to | འཕྲོག་པ་ | *throḱ-pa.* |
| Do. *hon.* | འཕྲོག་ཀ་ (པ་) གནང་བ་ | *throḱ-ḱa nang-wa.* |
| Utensils | ལག་ཆ་ | *laḱ-chha.* |
| Do. cooking | ཐབ་ཆས་ | *thaṕ-chhe.* |
| Utter (entire) | ཚང་མ། ཐམས་ཅད། སྒང་ཁ་ | *tshang-ma; thum-che; gang-kha.* |
| Utter, to (speak) | ལབ་པ་ | *laṕ-pa.* |
| Do. *hon.* | གསུང་བ་ | *sung-wa.* |
| Utterance | སྐད་ | *ke.* |
| Do. *hon.* | གསུང་སྐད་ | *sung-ke.* |
| Utterly (used negatively) | བྲད་དེ། ཁྱོན་ནས་ | *be-ṭe; khyön-ne.* |

# V

| | | |
|---|---|---|
| Vacant | སྟོང་པ་ | *tong-pa.* |
| Vagrant | རྒྱལ་ཁམས་སྐོར་མཁན་ | *gyeng-kham kor-khen.* |
| Vaccine lymph | ཐོར་པའི་སྨན་ | *thor-pe-men.* |
| Vacillate, to | ཐེ་ཚོམ་ཟ་བ་ | *the-tshom śa-wa.* |
| Do. *hon.* | ཐེ་ཚོམ་གནང་བ་ | *the-tshom nang-wa.* |
| Vacillation | ཐེ་ཚོམ་ | *the-tshom.* |
| Vague | ཏན་པོ་མེད་པ་ | *tem-po me-pa.* |
| Vain | རང་སྟོད་ཚ་པོ་ | *rang-tö tsha-po.* |
| Do. in personal appearance | དང་འདོད་ཚ་པོ་ | *ťang-dö tsha-po.* |
| Valiant | སྙིང་ཆེན་པོ་ | *nying-chhem-po.* |
| Do. *hon.* | ཐུགས་སྙིང་ཆེན་པོ་ | *thu-nying chhem-po.* |
| Valley | རོང་། ལུང་པ་ | *rong; lung-pa.* |
| Do. upper part of | ལུང་པའི་ཕུ་ | *lung-pe phu.* |
| Do. lower part of | ལུང་པའི་མདོ་ | *lung-pe do.* |
| Valorous | སྙིང་ཆེན་པོ་ | *nying-chhem-po.* |
| Do. *hon.* | ཐུགས་སྙིང་ཆེན་པོ་ | *thu-nying chhem-po.* |
| Valuable | རྩ་ཆེན་པོ་ | *tsa chhem-po.* |
| Value, *s.* | གོང་ | *kong.* |

| | | |
|---|---|---|
| Value, *hon.* | ལྗགས་གོང་ | *ja-kong.* |
| Valueless | གོང་མེད་ | *kong-me.* |
| Vanish, to | ཡལ་བ་ | *ye-wa.* |
| Vanity | རང་སྟོད་ | *rang-tö.* |
| Do. in personal appearance | ཐང་འདོད་ | *ťang-dö.* |
| Vanquish, to | རྒྱལ་བ། ཀླག་འཁས་པ་ | *gye-wa; la khe-pa.* |
| Do. *hon.* | རྒྱལ་ར་ (བ་) གནང་བ། ཀླག་འཁས་ར་ (པ་) གནང་བ་ | *gye-ra nang-wa; la khe-ra nang-wa.* |
| Vanquished, to be | འཕམ་པ་ | *pham-pa.* |
| Do. *hon.* | འཕམ་པ་གནང་བ་ | *pham-pa nang-wa.* |
| Vapour | རླངས་པ་ | *lang-pa.* |
| Variable, to be | བརྟན་པོ་……མེད་པ་ | *tem-po...me-pa.* |
| Variation (difference) | ཁྱད། ཧེ་བག་ | *khye; he-ṕa.* |
| Do. *hon.* | ཐུགས་ཁྱད་ | *thu-khye.* |
| Variety | ཁྱད། ཧེ་བག་ | *khye; he-ṕa.* |
| Do. *hon.* | ཐུགས་ཁྱད་ | *thu-khye.* |
| Various | མི་གཅིག་པ། མི་འདྲ་བ་ | *mi chik-pa; min dra-wa.* |
| Various kinds of | སྣ་ཚོགས་ | *na-tsho.* |
| Vase | བུམ་པ་ | *ṕum-pa.* |

| | | |
|---|---|---|
| Vase, *hon.* | ཕྱག་བུམ་ | *chha-pum.* |
| Vast | རྒྱ་ཆེན་པོ་ | *gya-chhem-po.* |
| Vaunt, to | རང་སྟོད་བྱེད་པ་ | *rang-tö ch́e-pa.* |
| Veal | བེ་བའི་ཤ་ | *ṕe-ṕe sha.* |
| Vegetable | ཚལ་ *Ch.* | *tshe.* |
| Vegetable drug | སྔོ་སྨན་ | *ngo-men.* |
| Vegetable garden | ཚལ་གཡང་ཚེ་ *Ch.* | *tshe yang-tse.* |
| Vein | རྩ་ | *tsa.* |
| Do. *hon.* | སྐུ་རྩ་ | *ku-tsa.* |
| Velveteen | སྤུ་མ་ | *pu-ma.* |
| Venerable (title) | རྗེ་བཙུན་ | *je-tsün.* |
| Venerate, to | བསྙེན་བཀུར་བྱེད་པ་ | *nyen-kur ch́e-pa.* |
| Do. *inf.* to *sup.* | བསྙེན་བཀུར་ཞུ་བ་ | *nyen-kur sḱu-wa.* |
| Veneration | བསྙེན་བཀུར་ | *nyen-kur.* |
| Vengeance | དགྲ་ལན་ | *dra-len.* |
| Vengeance, to take | དགྲ་ལན་ལེན་པ་ | *dra-len lem-pa.* |
| Do. *hon.* | དགྲ་ལན་བཞེས་པ་ | *dra-len sḱe-pa.* |
| Venial (trivial) | དོན་གནད་ཆུང་ཆུང་ | *t́ön-ne chhung-chhung.* |
| Do. *hon.* | ཐུགས་དོན་ཆུང་ཆུང་ | *thuḱ-t́ön chhung-chhung.* |
| Venison | ཤྭ་གི་ཤ་ (ཤྭ་བའི་ཤ་) | *sha-ḱi sha.* |

| | | |
|---|---|---|
| Venom (poison) | དུག་ | *ṫu.* |
| Do. *hon.* | གསོལ་དུག་ | *sö-ṫu.* |
| Venom (spite) | གནོད་སེམས་ | *nö-sem.* |
| Venture, to | ནུས་པ་ | *nü-pa.* |
| Do. *hon.* | ནུས་པ་གནང་བ་ | *nü-pa nang-wa.* |
| Venturesome | ཁ་མེད་མིག་མེད་ | *kha-me mik̇-me.* |
| Verandah (roofed in) | ཐོག་གཡང་ | *tho-yang.* |
| Do. (in upper story) | གཡབ་སྟེང་ | *yaṗ-teng.* |
| Do. (upper, running round a house) | གཡབ་འཁོར་ | *yaṗ-khor.* |
| Verbal | ཁའི་ | *khe.* |
| Verbally | ཁ་ནས་ | *kha-ne.* |
| Verdict (judgment) | བཅད་མཚམས་། ཁྲ་མ་ | *che-tsham; thra-ma.* |
| Vermilion | མཚལ། རྒྱ་མཚལ་ | *tshe; gyam-tshe.* |
| Vermin | འབུ་ | *bu.* |
| Verse | ཚིགས་བཅད་ | *tshik̇-che.* |
| Vertebræ | སྒལ་ཚིགས་ | *ge-tshi.* |
| Do. *hon.* | སྐུ་སྟོད་ཚིགས་ | *ku-tö tshi.* |
| Vertigo | བད་རླུང་མགོ་འཁོར་ | *ṗe-lung go-khor.* |
| Very | ཧ་ཅང་ | *ha-chang.* |

| | | |
|---|---|---|
| Vessel (for water) | ཆུ་སྣོད་ | *chhu-nö.* |
| Do. *hon.* | ཆབ་སྣོད་ | *chhaṕ-nö.* |
| Vessel (ship) | གྲུ་ | *t́ru.* |
| Do. *hon.* | ཕེབ་གྲུ་ | *pheṕ-t́ru.* |
| Vex, to | ཁོང་ཁྲོ་སློང་བ་ | *ḱhong-thro lang-wa.* |
| Do. *hon.* | དགོངས་པ་དཀྲུག་པ་ | *gong-pa truḱ-pa.* |
| Vexed, to be | ཚིག་པ་ཟ་བ་ | *tshiḱ-pa śa-wa.* |
| Do. *hon.* | དགོངས་པ་ཚུང་པ་ | *gong-pa tshung-pa.* |
| Viands | ཁ་ལག། ལྟོ་ | *ḱha-la ; to.* |
| Do. *hon.* | ཞལ་ལག་ | *sḱe-la.* |
| Vibrate, to | འཁྲུག་པ་ | *thruḱ-pa.* |
| Vice | སྡིག་པ་ | *diḱ-pa.* |
| Do. *hon.* | སྐུ་སྡིག་ | *ḱu-di.* |
| Vicinity | ཉེ་འཁོར་ | *nye-khor.* |
| Vicious | ངན་པོ་ | *ngem-po.* |
| Do. *hon.* | ཐུགས་ངན་པོ་ | *thu ngem-po.* |
| Victorious, to be | རྒྱལ་བ་ | *gye-wa.* |
| Do. *hon.* | རྒྱལ་ར་ (བ་) གནང་བ་ | *gye-ra nang-wa.* |
| Victuals | ཁ་ལག། ལྟོ་ | *kha-la ; to.* |
| Do. *hon.* | ཞལ་ལག་ | *sḱe-la.* |

| | | |
|---|---|---|
| View (opinion) | བསམ་པ་ | *sam-pa.* |
| Do. *hon.* | ཐུགས་སེམས་ | *thu-sem.* |
| View (purpose) | དོན་དག་ | *tön-t́a.* |
| Do. *hon.* | སྐུ་དོན་ | *ku-t́ön.* |
| View, to | མཐོང་བ། ལྟ་བ་ | *thong-wa ; ta-wa.* |
| Do. *hon.* | གཟིགས་པ་ | *śi-pa.* |
| Vigorous | ཤེད་ཆེན་པོ་ | *she chhem-po.* |
| Do. *hon.* | སྐུ་ཤེད་ཆེན་པོ་ | *ku-she chhem-po.* |
| Vigour | ཤེད་ | *she.* |
| Do. *hon.* | སྐུ་ཤེད་ | *ku-she.* |
| Vile (dirty) | བཙོག་པ་ | *tsoḱ-pa.* |
| Do. (odious) | སྐྱུག་བྲོ་པོ་ | *kyuḱ-t́ro-po.* |
| Vilification | སྨད་ར་ | *me-ra.* |
| Vilify, to | སྨད་ར་བཏང་ (གཏོང་) བ་ | *me-ra tang-wa.* |
| Do. *hon.* | སྨད་ར་གཏོང་ང་ (བ་) གནང་བ་ | *me-ra tong-nga nang-wa.* |
| Do. *inf.* to *sup.* | སྨད་ར་ཞུ་བ་ | *me-ra sḱu-wa.* |
| Village | གྲོང་པ་ | *t́rong-pa.* |
| Villager | གྲོང་པ་ | *t́rong-pa.* |
| Villain | འཛབ་ཆེན་ | *dzaṕ-chhen.* |
| Vine | རྒུན་འབྲུམ་ཤིང་ | *gün-drum-shing.* |

| | | |
|---|---|---|
| Vinegar | ཚུའུ་ *Ch.* | *tshu-u.* |
| Violence (force) | དབང་ཡོད་ | *wang-yö.* |
| Violence, to show | དབང་ཡོད་བྱེད་པ་ | *wang-yö cKe-pa.* |
| Violet (colour) | གུན་འབྲུམ་མདོག་ | *gün-drum do.* |
| Virgin | བུ་མོ་ | *ṕu-mo.* |
| Virtue | དགེ་བ་ | *ge-wa.* |
| Virtuous | ཚུལ་ལྡན་ | *tshün-den.* |
| Virus (poison) | དུག་ | *ťu.* |
| Do. *hon.* | གསོལ་དུག་ | *sö-tu.* |
| Visible, to be | མཐོང་བ་ | *thong-wa.* |
| Do. *hon.* | གཟིགས་པ་ | *śi-pa.* |
| Vision (spectre) | གདོང་འདྲེ། འདྲེ་ | *dong-dre ; dre.* |
| Visit, to (a person) | བཅར་བ་ | *char-wa.* |
| Do. *inf.* to *sup.* | སྐུ་མདུན་ལ་བཅར་བ་ | *kun-dün-la char-wa.* |
| Vituperate, to | སྨོད་ར་བཏང་ (གཏོང་) བ་ | *me-ra tang-wa.* |
| Do. *hon.* | སྨོད་ར་གཏོང་ང་ (བ་) གནང་བ་ | *me-ra tong-nga nang-wa.* |
| Do. *inf.* to *sup.* | སྨོད་ར་ཞུ་བ་ | *me-ra sKu-wa.* |
| Vituperation | སྨོད་ར་ | *me-ra.* |
| Vocabulary | མིང་མཛོད་ | *ming-dzö.* |
| Vocation | ལས་ཀ་ | *le-ka.* |

| | | |
|---|---|---|
| Vocation, *hon.* | ཕྱག་ལས་ | *chha-le.* |
| Voice | སྐད། སྒྲ | *ke ; dra.* |
| Do. *hon.* | གསུང་ | *sung.* |
| Void (empty) | སྟོང་པ་ | *tong-pa.* |
| Volume (of book) | པོ་ཏི | *po-ti.* |
| Vomit, to | སྐྱུག་པ་ | *kyuk-pa.* |
| Do. *hon.* | ཞལ་སྐྱུག་གནང་བ་ | *sǩe-kyu nang-wa.* |
| Voracious (gluttonous) | གྲོད་ཆེན་པོ་ | *ťrö-chhem-po.* |
| Vouch, to | ཁས་ཁྲུགས་བྱེད་པ་ | *khe-khya cǩe-pa.* |
| Do. *hon.* | ཞལ་ཁྲུགས་གནང་བ་ | *sǩe-khya nang-wa.* |
| Voucher (guarantor) | ཁས་ཁྲུགས་བྱེད་མཁན་ | *khe-khya cǩe-khen.* |
| Do. *hon.* | ཞལ་ཁྲུགས་གནང་མཁན་ | *sǩe-khya nang-khen.* |
| Vow (religious) | དམ་བཅའ་ | *ťam-cha.* |
| Do. to make) | དམ་བཅའ་ཕུལ་ (འབུལ་) བ་ | *ťam-cha phü-wa.* |
| Do. *hon.* | དམ་བཅའ་འབུལ་ར་ (བ་) གནང་བ་ | *ťam-cha bü-ra nang-wa.* |
| Vowels | དབྱངས་ | *yang.* |
| Vulgar (of language, *opp.* to *hon.*) | ཞེ་ས་མེད་པ་ | *sǩe-sa me-pa.* |
| Do. (of persons, *opp.* to high-born) | དཀྱུས་མ་ | *kyü-ma.* |

# W

| | | |
|---|---|---|
| Wag (jester) | དབུ་འཁོར་ཞུ་མཁན་ | *u-khor sKu-khen.* |
| Wag, to (shake) | དབྱུག་དབྱུག་བྱེད་པ་ | *yuk-yu cKe-pa.* |
| Do. *hon.* | དབྱུག་དབྱུག་གནང་བ་ | *yuk-yu nang-wa.* |
| Wag, to (dog's tail) | རིལ་རིལ་བྱེད་པ་ | *ri-ri cKe-pa.* |
| Wager | རྒྱན་ | *gyen.* |
| Do. *hon.* | སྐུ་རྒྱན་ | *ku-gyen.* |
| Wager, to | རྒྱན་བཞག་ (འཛོག་) པ་ | *gyen sKak-pa.* |
| Do. *hon.* | སྐུ་རྒྱན་གཞོག་ག་ (འཛོག་པ་) གནང་བ་ | *ku-gyen sKok-ka nang-wa.* |
| Wages | གླ། ཕོགས་ | *la ; pho.* |
| Waggish | བགད་མོ་བྲོ་པོ་ | *ge-mo t́ro-po.* |
| Do. *hon.* | ཞལ་མོ་བྲོ་པོ་ | *sKe-mo t́ro-po.* |
| Waggon | ཤིང་རྟ་འཁོར་ལོ་ | *shing-ta khor-lo.* |
| Wail, to | ངུ་བ་ | *ngu-wa.* |
| Do. *hon.* | ཤུམ་པ་ | *shum-pa.* |
| Waist | ཀེད་པ་ | *ke-pa.* |
| Do. *hon.* | སྐུ་ཀེད་ | *ku-ke.* |
| Waist band | སྐེད་རགས་ | *ke-ra.* |
| Do. *hon.* | སྐུ་རགས་ | *ku-ra.* |

| | | |
|---|---|---|
| Waistcoat | ཁན་སྦྱར་ | *khen-jar.* |
| Wait, to, *v.t.* | སྒུག་བསྡད་ (སྡོད་) པ་ | *gu de-pa.* |
| Do. *hon.* | སྒུག་བཞུགས་པ་ | *gu-sku-pa.* |
| Wait on, to | སྐུ་མདུན་ལ་བཅར་བ་ | *kun-dün-la char-wa.* |
| Wake, to | གཉིད་སད་པ་ | *nyi se-pa.* |
| Do. *hon.* | མཉན་ (མནལ་) སད་པ་ | *nyen se-pa.* |
| Walk, to | རྐང་ཐང་ལ་འགྲོ་བ་ | *kang-thang la dro-wa.* |
| Do. *hon.* | ཞབས་ཐང་ལ་ཕེབ་པ་ | *skap-thang la phe-pa.* |
| Do. *h. hon.* | ཞབས་ཐང་ལ་འཆིབ་རྒྱུ་གནང་བ་ | *skap-thang la chhip-gyu nang-wa.* |
| Walk, to (of horses) | གོམ་པ་འགྲོ་བ་ | *kom-pa dro-wa.* |
| Walk, to take a | ཆམ་ཆམ་ (འཁྲམ་འཁྲམ་) ལ་འགྲོ་བ་ | *chham-chham la dro-wa.* |
| Do. *hon.* | སྐུ་ཆམ་ (འཁྲམ་) ལ་ཕེབ་པ་ | *kün-chham la phe-pa.* |
| Do. *h. hon.* | སྐུ་ཆམ་ (འཁྲམ་) ལ་འཆིབ་རྒྱུ་གནང་བ་ | *kün-chham la chhip-gyu nang-wa.* |
| Wall | རྩིག་པ་ | *tsik-pa.* |
| Do. city | ལྕགས་རི་ | *cha-ri.* |
| Do. fortified | འཛིང་ར་ | *dzing-ra.* |
| Walnut | སྟར་ཀ་ | *tar-ka.* |

| | | |
|---|---|---|
| Wan | དཀར་པོ་དཀར་ཀྱང་ | *kar-po kar-kyang.* |
| Wander, to (stroll) | ཆམ་ཆམ་ (འཁྱམ་འཁྱམ་) ལ་འགྲོ་བ་ | *chham-chham la dro-wa.* |
| Do. *hon.* | སྐུ་ཆམ་ (འཁྱམ་) ལ་ཕེབ་པ་ | *kün-chham la phe-pa.* |
| Do. *h. hon.* | སྐུ་ཆམ་ (འཁྱམ) ལ་འཆིབ་རྒྱུ་གནང་བ་ | *kün-chham la chhip-gyu nang-wa.* |
| Wander, to (go astray) | ལམ་ཀ་ནོར་བ་ | *lam-ka nor-wa.* |
| Do. *hon.* | ཕེབ་ལམ་ནོར་ར་ (བ་) གནང་བ་ | *phep-lam nor-ra nang-wa.* |
| Want, to (need) | དགོ་བ་ (དགོས་པ་) | *go-wa.* |
| Do. *hon.* | དགོ་བ་གནང་བ་ | *go-wa nang-wa.* |
| Want, to (wish) | འདོད་པ་བྱེད་པ་ | *dö-pa c‘he-pa.* |
| Do. *hon.* | ཐུགས་འདོད་གནང་བ་ | *thung-dö nang-wa.* |
| Wanton | འདོད་ཆགས་ཆེན་པོ་ | *dö-chha chhem-po.* |
| War | དམག་ | *ma.* |
| Wardrobe | དུག་ལོག་བླུག་སའི་སྒམ་ | *t‘u-lo luk-se gam.* |
| Do. *hon.* | ན་བཟའ་བླུག་སའི་ཕྱག་སྒམ་ | *nam-śa luk-se chha-gam.* |
| Wares | ཚོང་ཡ་ | *tshong-ya.* |
| Do. *hon.* | རྒྱ་ཚོང་གནང་ཡ་ | *gya-tshong nang-ya.* |
| Warm | དྲོ་པོ་ | *t‘ro-po.* |
| Warn, to | བསླབ་བྱ་བྱེད་པ་ | *lap-c‘ha c‘he-pa.* |

| | | |
|---|---|---|
| Warn, to, *hon.* | བསླབ་བྱ་གནང་བ་ | *lap-cha nang-wa.* |
| Warp, *s.* (of loom) | རྒྱུ་ | *gyu.* |
| Do. *hon.* | ཕྱག་རྒྱུ་ | *chha-gyu.* |
| Warrant, to (authorize) | དབང་སྤྲད་པ་ | *wang tre-pa.* |
| Do. *hon.* | དབང་གནང་བ་ | *wang nang-wa.* |
| Warrant, to (guarantee) | ཁས་ཁྱགས་བྱེད་པ་ | *khe-khya che-pa.* |
| Do. *hon.* | ཞལ་ཁྱགས་གནང་བ་ | *she-khya nang-wa.* |
| Warranty | ཁས་ཁྱགས་ | *khe-khya.* |
| Do. *hon.* | ཞལ་ཁྱགས་ | *she-khya.* |
| Warrior | དམག་མི་ | *ma-mi.* |
| Wart, *s.* | སྨེན་ (སྨེ་བ་) | *men.* |
| Do. *hon.* | སྐུ་སྨེན་ (སྐུ་སྨེ་) | *ku-men.* |
| Wash, to | འཁྲུད་པ་ | *thrü-pa.* |
| Do. *hon.* | བསིལ་ར་ (བ་) གནང་བ་ | *si-ra nang-wa.* |
| Wasp | དུག་སྦྲང་ | *t́uk-drang.* |
| Waste, to | གཏོར་བ་ | *tor-wa.* |
| Do. *hon.* | གཏོར་ར་ (བ་) གནང་བ་ | *tor-ra nang-wa.* |
| Watch, *s.* | ཆུ་ཚོད་འཁོར་ལོ་ | *chhu-tshö khor-lo.* |
| Watch, to | མིག་ལྟ་བ་ | *mik ta-wa.* |
| Do. *hon.* | སྤྱན་གཟིགས་པ་ | *chen śi-pa.* |

| | | |
|---|---|---|
| Watch, to (guard) | སྲུང་བ་ | *sung-wa.* |
| Do. *hon.* | སྲུང་ང་ (བ་) གནང་བ་ | *sung-nga nang-wa.* |
| Watchman | མིག་ལྟ་མཁན། སྲུང་མཁན་ | *mik-ta-khen ; sung-khen.* |
| Water | ཆུ་ | *chhu.* |
| Do. *hon.* | ཆབ་ | *chhaṕ.* |
| Water (for drinking) | འཐུང་ཡ་གི་ཆུ་ | *thung-ya-ki chhu.* |
| Do. *hon.* | བཞེས་ཡ་གི་ཆབ་ | *sḱe-ya-ḱi chhaṕ.* |
| Waterfall | བབ་ཆུ་ (འབབ་ཆུ་) | *ṕaṕ-chhu.* |
| Do. over rocks | བྲག་ཆུ་ | *ťraḱ-chhu.* |
| Water-mill | ཆུ་འཁོར་ | *chhu-kho.* |
| Water-vessel | ཆུ་སྣོད་ | *chhu-nö.* |
| Do. *hon.* | ཆབ་སྣོད་ | *chhaṕ-nö.* |
| Wave, *s.* | དབའ་རླབས་ | *ba-laṕ.* |
| Wave, to | དབྱུག་དབྱུག་བྱེད་པ་ | *yuḱ-yu cḱe-pa.* |
| Waver, to | ཐེ་ཚོམ་ཟ་བ་ | *the-tshom śa-wa.* |
| Do. *hon.* | ཐེ་ཚོམ་གནང་བ་ | *the-tshom nang-wa.* |
| Wavering | ཐེ་ཚོམ་ | *the-tshom.* |
| Wax, sealing | ལ་ཆ་ | *la-chha.* |
| Way (road) | ལམ་ཀ་ | *lang-ḱa.* |
| Do. *hon.* | ཕེབ་ལམ་ | *pheṕ-lam.* |

| | | |
|---|---|---|
| Way (highway) | རྒྱ་ལམ་ | *gya-lam.* |
| Way (manner) | ཐབས་ | *thap.* |
| We | ང་ཚོ། ང་རང་ཚོ་ | *nga-tsho ; nga-rang-tsho.* |
| Weak (in muscle) | ཤེད་ཆུང་ཆུང་ | *she chhung-chhung.* |
| Do. *hon.* | སྐུ་ཤེད་ཆུང་ཆུང་ | *ku-she chhung-chhung.* |
| Weak (prone to illness) | གཟུགས་པོ་གཙོང་པོ་ | *śuk-po chong-po.* |
| Do. *hon.* | སྐུ་གཟུགས་གཙོང་པོ་ | *ku-śuk chong-po.* |
| Weakminded | ལྐུགས་པ། གླེན་པ་ | *kuk-pa ; lem-pa.* |
| Wealthy | ཕྱུག་པོ། ཅ་ (ཆ་) ལག་ཆེན་པོ་ | *chhuk-po ; cha-la chhem-po.* |
| Do. *hon.* | སྐུ་ཅས་ (ཆས་) ཆེན་པོ་ | *ku-che chhem-po.* |
| Weapon | མཚོན་ཆ་ | *tshön-chha.* |
| Wear, to | གོན་པ་ | *köm-pa.* |
| Do. *hon.* | བཞེས་པ་ | *ske-pa.* |
| Wearisome | དཀའ་ལས་ཁག་པོ་ | *ka-le khak-po.* |
| Do. *hon.* | སྐུ་མཉེལ་པོ་ | *ku-nye-po.* |
| Weariness | ངལ་ | *ngel.* |
| Do. *hon.* | སྐུ་ངལ་ | *ku-ngel.* |
| Weary, to be | ཐང་ཆད་པ་ | *thang chhe-pa.* |
| Do. *hon.* | སྐུ་ཐང་ཆད་པ་གནང་བ་ | *ku-thang chhe-pa nang-wa.* |

| Weasel | སྲེ་མོང་ | *tre-mong.* |
|---|---|---|
| Weather | གནམ་ | *nam.* |
| Do. clear | གནམ་དྭངས་པོ་ | *nam ťang-po.* |
| Weave, to | འཐག་འཐག་པ་ | *tha thaḱ-pa.* |
| Do. *hon.* | འཐག་འཐག་ག་ (པ་) གནང་བ་ | *tha thaḱ-ḱa nang-wa.* |
| Weaver | འཐག་མཁན་ | *thang-khen.* |
| Web | ཐགས་ | *tha.* |
| Do. *hon.* | ཕྱག་ཐགས་ | *chha-tha.* |
| Wed, to (take husband) | མག་པ་བསླང་ (སློང་) བ་ | *maḱ-pa lang-wa* |
| Do. *hon.* | སྐུ་བག་བཞེས་པ་ | *ku-ṕa sḱe-pa.* |
| Wed, to (take wife) | མནའ་མ་ལེན་པ་ | *na-ma lem-pa.* |
| Do. *hon.* | མནའ་མ་བཞེས་པ་ | *na-ma sḱe-pa.* |
| Wedding | ཆང་ས་ | *chhang-sa.* |
| Do. *hon.* | འཁྲུང་ས་ | *thrung-sa.* |
| Wedge | གེའུ་ | *ke-u.* |
| Wednesday | གཟའ་ལྷག་པ་ | *śa-hlaḱ-pa.* |
| Weed | རྩ་ངན་ | *tsa-ngen.* |
| Weed, to | ཡུར་མ་རྒྱབ་པ་ | *yur-ma gyaṕ-pa.* |
| Do. *hon.* | ཡུར་མ་སྐྱོན་པ་ | *yur-ma kyöm-pa* |
| Week | བདུན་ཕྲག་ | *dün-thra.* |

| | | |
|---|---|---|
| Weep, to | ངུ་བ་ | *ngu-wa.* |
| Do. *hon.* | ཤུམ་པ་ | *shum-pa.* |
| Weft | སྤུན་ | *pün.* |
| Do. *hon.* | ཕྱག་སྤུན་ | *chha-pün.* |
| Weigh, to | ཀྱག་ (འགྱོགས་) པ་ | *kyak-pa.* |
| Do. *hon.* | ཀྱག་ག་ (འགྱོགས་པ་) གནང་བ་ | *kyak-ka nang-wa.* |
| Weigh, to (consider) | བསམ་བློ་བཏང་ (གཏོང་) བ་ | *sam-lo tang-wa.* |
| Do. *hon.* | ཐུགས་བསམ་བཞེས་པ་ | *thu-sam ske-pa.* |
| Weight | ཡང་ལྗི་ | *yang-chi.* |
| Weighty (heavy) | ལྗི་པོ་ | *ji-po.* |
| Do. (important) | གནད་ཁག་ཆེན་པོ། གལ་ཆེན་པོ་ | *nen-kha chhem-po ; ke chhem-po.* |
| Welcome! | ཕྱག་ཕེབ་གནང་བྱུང་ | *chha-phe nang-chung.* |
| Well, *s.* | ཁྲོམ་པ་ (ཁྲོན་པ་) | *throm-pa.* |
| Do. *adj.* | ཡག་པོ་ | *yak-po.* |
| Well, to be (in health) | གཟུགས་པོ་བདེ་པོ་ཡོད་པ་ | *śuk-po de-po yö-pa.* |
| Do. *hon.* | སྐུ་གཟུགས་བཟང་པོ་ཡོད་པ་ | *ku-śuk śang-po yö-pa.* |
| Well! *interj.* | འོ་ན་ | *o-na.* |
| Well-behaved | ཡ་རབས་ | *ya-rap.* |
| Well-known (celebrated) | སྐད་གྲགས་ཆེན་པོ་ | *ke-tra chhem-po.* |

| | | |
|---|---|---|
| Well-known (celebrated), *hon.* | མཚན་སྙན་གྲགས་ཆེན་པོ་ | *tshen-nyen-t́ra chhem-po.* |
| Well-modelled (of metal-work, wood-work, etc.) | བཀོད་པ་ཏོད་པོ་ | *kö-pa t́ö-po.* |
| West | ནུབ་ | *nuṕ.* |
| Westward | ནུབ་ངོས། ནུབ་ཕྱོགས་ | *nuṕ-ngö ; nuṕ-chho.* |
| Wet | རློན་པ་ | *löm-pa.* |
| Wet, to | སྦང་བ་ | *bang-wa.* |
| Do. *hon.* | སྦང་ང་ (བ་) གནང་བ་ | *bang-nga nang-wa.* |
| Wether | ལུག་ཕོ་ | *luḱ-pho.* |
| What, *interr.* and *rel.* | ག་རེ་ | *ḱa-re.* |
| Whatever it is | ག་རེ་ཡིན་ནས་ | *ḱa-re yin-ne.* |
| Wheat | གྲོ་ | *t́ro.* |
| Wheat-flour | གྲོ་ཞིབ་ | *t́ro-sḱiṕ.* |
| Wheedle, to (for good object) | བསླབ་བྱ་རྒྱབ་པ་ | *laṕ-cḱa gyaṕ-pa.* |
| Do. *hon.* | བཀའ་སློབ་གནང་བ་ | *ka-loṕ nang-wa.* |
| Wheedle, to (for bad object) | སླུ་བ་ | *lu-wa.* |
| Do. *hon.* | སླུ་བ་གནང་བ་ | *lu-wa nang-wa.* |
| Wheel | འཁོར་ལོ་ | *khor-lo.* |
| When, *rel.* | དུས་ (w. root of verb) | *t́ü.* |

| | | |
|---|---|---|
| When, *interr.* | ག་དུས་ | *ḱa-ťü.* |
| Whenever | ག་དུས་……ཡང་ | *ḱa-ťü...yang.* |
| Whence | ག་ནས་ | *ḱa-ne.* |
| Where, *interr.* and *rel.* | ག་པ་ | *ḱa-pa.* |
| Wherever | ག་པ་……ཡང་ | *ḱa-pa...yang* |
| Whet, to | རྡར་བ་ | *dar-wa.* |
| Do. *hon.* | རྡར་ར་ (བ་) གནང་བ་ | *dar-ra nang-wa.* |
| Whether | ནས་ (ན་) | *ne.* |
| Whetstone | བདར་རྡོ་ | *dar-do.* |
| Which, *interr.* and *rel.* | ག་རེ་ | *ḱa-re.* |
| Which of them | ག་གི་ | *ḱa-ḱi.* |
| While, *adv.* | དུས་ (w. root of verb) | *ťü.* |
| Whip | རྟའི་ལྕག་ | *te-cha.* |
| Do. *hon.* | ཆིབས་ལྕག་ | *chhiṕ-cha.* |
| Whirlwind | རླུང་ཚུབ་ | *lung-tshuṕ.* |
| Whiskers | རྒྱའུ་ | *gya-u.* |
| Whisper, *s.* | ཤབ་ཤོབ་ (ཤབ་ཤུབ་) | *shaṕ-shoṕ.* |
| Whisper, to | ཤབ་ཤོབ་ (ཤབ་ཤུབ་) ལབ་པ་ | *shaṕ-shoṕ laṕ-pa.* |
| Do. *hon.* | ཤབ་ཤོབ་ (ཤབ་ཤུབ་) གསུང་བ་ | *shaṕ-shoṕ sung-wa.* |

| | | |
|---|---|---|
| Whistle, to | སི་རྒྱབ་པ་ | *si gyap̄-pa.* |
| Do. *hon.* | སི་སྐྱོན་པ་ | *si kyöm-pa.* |
| Whistle a tune, to | སི་གླུ་བཏང་ (གཏོང་) བ་ | *si-lu tang-wa.* |
| Do. *hon.* | སི་གླུ་བཞེས་པ་ | *si-lu sk̄e-pa.* |
| White | དཀར་པོ་ | *kar-po.* |
| Whitewash | ས་དཀར། དཀར་རྩི་ | *sa-kar ; kar-tsi.* |
| Whither | ག་པ་ | *k̄a-pa.* |
| Who | སུ་ | *su.* |
| Whoever (you, he, etc.) be | སུ་ཡིན་ནས་ | *su yin-ne.* |
| Whole | ཚང་མ། ཐམས་ཅད། སྒང་ཁ | *tshang-ma ; tham-che ; gang-kha.* |
| Do. (healthy) | གཟུགས་པོ་བདེ་པོ་ | *śuk-po de-po.* |
| Do. *hon.* | སྐུ་གཟུགས་བཟང་པོ་ | *ku-śuk̄ śang-po.* |
| Wholly (used negatively) | ཐད་དེ། ཁྱོན་ནས་ | *be-t̄e ; khyön-ne.* |
| Whore | གཞང་ཚོང་མ་ | *sk̄ang-tshong-ma.* |
| Why, *interr.* | ག་རེ་དོན་ལ་ | *k̄a-re tön-la.* |
| Do. *interj.* | འོ་ན་ | *o-na.* |
| Wick | སྡོང་རས་ | *dong-re.* |
| Wicked | ངན་པོ་ | *ngem-po.* |
| Do. *hon.* | ཐུགས་ངན་པོ་ | *thu ngem-po.* |

| | | |
|---|---|---|
| Wickedness | སྡིག་པ་ | *diḱ-pa.* |
| Do. *hon.* | སྐུ་སྡིག་ | *ku-di.* |
| Wide | ཞང་ (ཞེང་) ཆེན་པོ་ | *sḱang-chhem-po.* |
| Do. (of valley, etc.) | རྒྱ་ཆེན་པོ་ | *gya chhem-po.* |
| Widow (term of reproach) | ཡུགས་ཟ་མ་ | *yuḱ-śa-ma.* |
| Width | ཞང་ (ཞེང་) | *sḱang.* |
| Wife | སྐྱེ་དམན་ | *kyi-men.* |
| Do. (of well-to-do villager) | སྙི་སྙིང་ལགས་ | *nyi-nying-la.* |
| Do. (of ordinary official) | ལྕམ་སྐུ་གཞོགས་ | *cham ku-sḱo.* |
| Do. (of third grade and upwards) | ལྷ་ལྕམ་སྐུ་གཞོགས་ | *hla-cham ku-sḱo.* |
| Wild (fierce, of human beings) | ངན་པ་ | *ngem-pa.* |
| Do. (of animals) | ཚུབ་པོ་ | *tshuṕ-po.* |
| Wild animal | རི་དྭགས་ | *ri-t́a.* |
| Wilderness | བྱེ་ཐང་ | *cḱe-thang.* |
| Wile, *s.* | མགོ་སྐོར་ | *go-kor.* |
| Do. *hon.* | དབུ་སྐོར་ | *u-kor.* |
| Will, *s.* (wish) | འདོད་པ་ | *dö-pa.* |
| Do. *hon.* | ཐུགས་འདོད་ | *thung-dö.* |
| Will, *s.* (testament) | ཁ་ཆེམས་ | *kha-chhem.* |

| | | |
|---|---|---|
| Will, *s* (testament), *hon.* | ཞལ་ཆེམས་ | *sk̄e-chhem.* |
| Willing, to be | འདོད་པ་ཡོད་པ་ | *dö-pa yö-pa.* |
| Do. *hon.* | ཐུགས་འདོད་ཡོད་པ་ | *thung-dö yö-pa.* |
| Willow | ལྕང་མ་ | *chang-ma.* |
| Wily | གཅང་པོ་ | *chang-po.* |
| Do. *hon.* | ཐུགས་གཅང་པོ་ | *thu chang-po.* |
| Win, to (conquer) | རྒྱལ་བ་ | *gyel-wa.* |
| Do. *hon.* | རྒྱལ་ར་ (བ་) གནང་བ་ | *gye-ra nang-wa.* |
| Win, to (obtain) | འབྱོར་བ། ཐོབ་པ་ | *jor-wa ; thop̄-pa.* |
| Do. *hon.* | ཕྱག་འབྱོར་ཡོང་བ་ | *chhan-jor yong-wa.* |
| Wind | ལྷགས་པ། རླུང་ | *hlak̄-pa ; lung.* |
| Wind, to | སྒྲིལ་བ་ | *dril-wa.* |
| Do. *hon.* | སྒྲིལ་ར་ (བ་) གནང་བ་ | *dri-ra nang-wa.* |
| Winding | ཀྱོག་ཀྱོག་ | *kyo-kyo.* |
| Window | སྒེ་ཁུང་ (རྒྱལ་ཁུང་) | *gi-khung.* |
| Window-grating | ཁྲ་མ་ (དྲ་མ་) | *thra-ma.* |
| Do. *hon.* | ཞལ་ཁྲ་ | *sk̄e-thra.* |
| Wine (beer) | ཆང་ | *chhang.* |
| Do. *hon.* | མཆོད་ཆང་ | *chhö-chhang.* |
| Wing | ཤོག་པ་ | *shok̄-pa.* |

| | | |
|---|---|---|
| Wink, to | མིག་ཁྲབ་ཁྲབ་བྱེད་པ་ | *mik thrap-thrap cke-pa.* |
| Do. *hon.* | སྤྱན་ཁྲབ་ཁྲབ་གནང་བ་ | *chen thrap-thrap nang-wa.* |
| Winter | དགུན་ཀ་ | *gün-ka.* |
| Wintry (cold) | གྲང་མོ། བསིལ་པོ་ | *ťrang-mo ; si-po.* |
| Do. *hon.* | སྐུ་བསིལ་པོ་ | *ku-si-po.* |
| Wipe, to | འཕྱིད་པ་ | *chhi-pa.* |
| Do. *hon.* | འཕྱིད་པ་གནང་བ་ | *chhi-pa nang-wa.* |
| Wipe out, to (efface) | སྲུབ་པ་ | *sup-pa.* |
| Do. *hon.* | སྲུབ་པ་གནང་བ་ | *sup-pa nang-wa.* |
| Wire | ལྕགས་སྐུད་ | *cha-kü.* |
| Wireless telegraphy | ལྕགས་སྐུད་མེད་པའི་དར་ | *cha-kü me-pe tar.* |
| Wisdom | བློ་གྲོས་ | *lo-ťrö.* |
| Wise (skilful) | མཁས་པོ་ | *khe-po.* |
| Do. (learned) | ཡོན་དན་ཆེན་པོ་ | *yön-ten chhem-po.* |
| Do. *hon.* | སྐུ་ཡོན་ཆེན་པོ་ | *ku-yön chhem-po.* |
| Wish | འདོད་པ་ | *dö-pa.* |
| Do. *hon.* | ཐུགས་འདོད་ | *thung-dö.* |
| Wish, to | འདོད་པ་བྱེད་པ་ | *dö-pa cke-pa.* |
| Do. *hon.* | ཐུགས་འདོད་གནང་བ་ | *thung-dö nang-wa.* |
| Wit (intellect) | བློ་གྲོས་ | *lo-ťrö.* |

| | | |
|---|---|---|
| Witchcraft | མཐུ་ | *thu.* |
| With (together with) | དང་མཉམ་དུ་ | *t́ang-nyam-tu.* |
| Do. *hon.* | ལྷན་རྒྱས་ | *hlen-gye.* |
| With regard to | དོན་ལ། སྐོར་ལ་ | *t́ön-la; kor-la.* |
| Withdraw, to, *v.i.* (retreat) | ཕྱིར་ལོག་རྒྱབ་པ་ | *chhi-lo gyap̒-pa.* |
| Do. *hon.* | ཕྱིར་ལོག་སྐྱོན་པ་ | *chhi-lo kyöm-pa.* |
| Wither, to | རྙིད་པ་ | *nyi-pa.* |
| Within | ནང་ལ་ | *nang-la.* |
| Withhold, to (restrain) | བཀག་པ་ (འགེགས་པ་) | *kak̒-pa.* |
| Do. *hon.* | བཀག་ག་ (འགེགས་པ་) གནང་བ་ | *kak̒-k̒a nang-wa.* |
| Without (*opp.* to "with") | མེད་པར་ | *me-pa.* |
| Without (*opp.* to "within") | ཕྱི་ལོགས་ལ་ | *chhi-lo-la.* |
| Withstand, to (restrain) | བཀག་པ་ (འགེགས་པ་) | *kak̒-pa.* |
| Do. *hon.* | བཀག་ག་ (འགེགས་པ་) གནང་བ་ | *kak̒-k̒a nang-wa.* |
| Witless | ལྐུགས་པ། གླེན་པ་ | *kuk̒-pa; lem-pa.* |
| Witness | དཔང་པོ་ | *pang-po.* |
| Witness, to | དཔང་པོ་བྱེད་པ་ | *pang-po cK̒e-pa.* |
| Do. *hon.* | དཔང་པོ་གནང་བ་ | *pang-po nang-wa.* |

| | | |
|---|---|---|
| Woe | སྡུག་བསྔལ། སེམས་འཁྲལ་ | *du-nge; sem-thre.* |
| Do. *hon.* | ཐུགས་འཁྲལ་ | *thuk-thre.* |
| Wolf | སྤྱང་ཀུ་ | *chang-ku.* |
| Woman | སྐྱེས་དམན་ | *kyi-men.* |
| Do. (wife of well-to-do villager) | སྙི་སྙིང་ལགས་ | *nyi-nying-la.* |
| Do. (wife of ordinary official) | ལྕམ་སྐུ་གཞོགས་ | *cham ku-sKo.* |
| Do. (third grade and upwards) | ལྷ་ལྕམ་སྐུ་གཞོགས་ | *hla-cham ku-sKo.* |
| Womb | བུ་སྣོད་ | *pu-nö.* |
| Wonder | ཡ་མཚན་ | *yam-tshen.* |
| Wonder, to | ཁྱད་མཚར་བ་ | *khye tshar-wa.* |
| Do. *hon.* | ཐུགས་ཁྱད་མཚར་ར་ (བ་) གནང་བ་ | *thu-khye tshar-ra nang-wa.* |
| Wonderful | ཡ་མཚན་པོ། ཁྱད་མཚར་པོ་ | *yam-tshem-po; khye-tsha-po.* |
| Wondrous | ཡ་མཚན་པོ། ཁྱད་མཚར་པོ་ | *yam-tshem-po; khye-tsha-po.* |
| Wood | ཤིང་ | *shing.* |
| Do. (forest) | ཤིང་ནགས། ནགས་གསེབ་ | *shing-na; nak-sep.* |
| Wooden | ཤིང་གི་ | *shing-ki.* |
| Woof, *s.* (of loom) | སྤུན་ | *pün.* |

| | | |
|---|---|---|
| Woof, *s.* (of loom), *hon.* | ཕྱག་སྤུན་ | *chha-pün.* |
| Wool | བལ་ | *ṕe.* |
| Woollen | བལ་གྱི་ | *ṕe-ḱyi.* |
| Woollen cloth | སྣམ་བུ་ | *nam-ṕu.* |
| Do. *hon.* | ཕྱག་སྣམ་ | *chha-nam.* |
| Word | ཚིག | *tshi.* |
| Do. (tidings) | གནས་ཚུལ། གསར་འགྱུར་ | *ne-tshü ; sang-gyu.* |
| Do. (command) | བཀའ་ | *ka.* |
| Word, to give one's (promise) | ཁས་བླང་བ་ | *khe-lang-wa.* |
| Do. *hon.* | ཞལ་བཞེས་པ་ | *sḱe-sḱe-pa.* |
| Work | ལས་ཀ་ | *le-ka.* |
| Do. *hon.* | ཕྱག་ལས་ | *chha-le.* |
| Work, to | ལས་ཀ་བྱེད་པ་ | *le-ka cḱe-pa.* |
| Do. *hon.* | ཕྱག་ལས་གནང་བ་ | *chha-le nang-wa.* |
| Work, to be, occupied with | བྲེལ་བ་ཡོད་པ་ | *t́re-wa yö-pa.* |
| Do. *hon.* | ཐུགས་བྲེལ་ཡོད་པ་ | *thu-t́re yö-pa.* |
| World | འཛམ་བུ་གླིང་། འཇིག་རྟེན་ | *dzam-ṕu-ling ; jik-ten.* |
| Worm | འབུ་ | *bu.* |
| Worry, to, *v.t.* (vex) | ཁོང་ཁྲོ་སློང་བ་ | *khong-thro lang-wa.* |
| Do. *hon.* | དགོངས་པ་དཀྲུག་པ་ | *gong-pa truk-pa.* |

| | | |
|---|---|---|
| Worry, to, *v.i.* | སེམས་འཁྲུལ་བྱེད་པ་ | *sem-thre cḱe-pa.* |
| Do. *hon.* | ཐུགས་འཁྲུལ་གནང་བ་ | *thuḱ-thre nang-wa.* |
| Worship, to (extempore prayers) | སྨོན་ལམ་བཏབ་ (འདེབས་) པ་ | *mö-lam taṕ-pa.* |
| Do. *hon.* | ཐུགས་སྨོན་གནང་བ་ | *thu-mön nang-wa.* |
| Worship, to (written prayers) | ཁ་འདོན་བྱེད་པ་ | *khan-dön cḱe-pa.* |
| Do. *hon.* | ཞལ་འདོན་གནང་བ་ | *sḱen-dön nang-wa.* |
| Worst | སྡུག་ཤོས་ | *duḱ-shö.* |
| Worst of, to get the | འཕམ་པ་ | *pham-pa.* |
| Do. *hon.* | འཕམ་པ་གནང་བ་ | *pham-pa nang-wa.* |
| Worth | གོང་ | *ḱong.* |
| Do. *hon.* | ལྗགས་གོང་ | *ja-ḱong.* |
| Worth, to be | གོང་བྱེད་པ་ | *ḱong-cḱe-pa.* |
| Worthless (valueless) | གོང་མེད་ | *ḱong-me.* |
| Do. (useless) | དོན་མེད་ | *t́ön-me.* |
| Do. (wicked) | ངན་པོ་ | *ngem-po.* |
| Do. *hon.* | ཐུགས་ངན་པོ་ | *thu ngem-po.* |
| Worthy | འོས་པོ་ | *ö-po.* |
| Wound, *s.* | རྨ་ | *ma.* |
| Wound, to | རྨ་བཟོ་བ་ | *ma śo-wa.* |

| | | |
|---|---|---|
| Wound, to, *hon.* | སྨ་བཟློ་བ་གནང་བ་ | *ma śo-wa nang-wa.* |
| Wrangle, to | རྒྱབ་འདྲེ་རྒྱབ་པ་ | *gyam-dre gyap-pa.* |
| Do. *hon.* | གསུང་འཁྲུག་སྐྱོན་པ་ | *sung-thru kyöm-pa.* |
| Wrap, to | སྒྲིལ་བ་ | *dril-wa.* |
| Do. *hon.* | སྒྲིལ་ར་ (བ་) གནང་བ་ | *dri-ra nang-wa.* |
| Wrath | ཚིག་པ། ཁོང་ཁྲོ་ | *tshik-pa ; khong-thro.* |
| Do. *hon.* | དགོངས་ཚུང་། རྣམ་མཁྱེན་ | *gong-tshung ; nam-khyen.* |
| Wrathful, to be | ཚིག་པ་ཟ་བ། ཁོང་ཁྲོ་ཟ་བ་ | *tshik-pa śa-wa ; khong-thro śa-wa.* |
| Do. *hon.* | དགོངས་པ་ཚུང་པ། རྣམ་མཁྱེན་འགལ་བ་ | *gong-pa tshung-pa ; nam-khyen gel-wa.* |
| Wrest, to | འཕྲོག་པ་ | *throk-pa.* |
| Do. *hon.* | འཕྲོག་ག་ (པ་) གནང་བ་ | *throk-ka nang-wa.* |
| Wrestle, to | འཛིང་རེ་བཏང་ (གཏོང་) བ་ | *dzing-re tang-wa.* |
| Wretched (bad) | སྡུག་རུལ་ | *duk-rü.* |
| Do. (unhappy) | སྡུག་བསྔལ་ཆེན་པོ་ | *dung-nge chhem-po.* |
| Do. *hon.* | ཐུགས་བསྔལ་ཆེན་པོ་ | *thuk-nge chhem-po.* |
| Wretchedness | སྡུག་བསྔལ། སེམས་འཁྲལ་ | *dung-nge ; sem-thre.* |
| Do. *hon.* | ཐུགས་འཁྲལ་ | *thuk-thre.* |
| Wring, to (twist) | སྒྲིམ་པ་ | *drim-pa.* |

| | | |
|---|---|---|
| Wring, to. (twist), *hon.* | སྒྲིམ་པ་གནང་བ་ | *drim-pa nang-wa* |
| Wrinkle (on face) | གཉེར་མ་ | *nye-ma.* |
| Wrist | ལག་ཚིགས་ | *lak-tshi.* |
| Do. *hon.* | ཕྱག་ཚིགས་ | *chhak-tshi.* |
| Write, to | བྲིས་པ་ (འབྲི་བ་) | *t́ri-pa.* |
| Do. *hon.* | ཕྱག་བྲིས་གནང་བ་ | *chha-t́ri nang-wa.* |
| Writer (author) | རྩོམ་མཁན་ | *tsom-khen.* |
| Do. *hon.* | རྩོམ་པ་གནང་མཁན་ | *tsom-pa nang-khen.* |
| Writer (clerk) | དྲུང་ཡིག་ | *t́rung-yi.* |
| Do. *hon.* | དྲུང་ཡིག་ལགས་ | *t́rung-yi-la.* |
| Wrong, *adj.* (incorrect) | མ་དག་པ་ | *ma…t́ak-pa.* |
| Do. (unjust) | ཁྲིམས་མེད་ | *thrim-me.* |
| Do. (wicked) | ངན་པ་ | *ngem-pa.* |
| Wrong, *s.* (error) | ནོར་ | *nor.* |
| Do. (guilt) | སྐྱོན། ཉེས་པ་ | *kyön; nye-pa.* |
| Do. (sin) | སྡིག་པ་ | *dik-pa.* |
| Do. *hon.* | སྐུ་སྡིག་ | *ku-di.* |
| Wrong (crime), to commit | ཁྲིམས་འགལ་བ་ | *thrim gel-wa.* |
| Do. *hon.* | བཀའ་ཁྲིམས་འགལ་ར་ (བ་) གནང་བ་ | *ka-thrim ge-ra nang-wa.* |

# X

| | | |
|---|---|---|
| Xylograph, to make a | ཤིང་བརྐོས་རྒྱབ་པ་ | *shing-kö gyap-pa.* |
| Do. *hon.* | ཤིང་བརྐོས་སྐྱོན་པ་ | *shing-kö kyöm-pa.* |

# Y

| | | |
|---|---|---|
| Yak, *m.* | གཡག་ | *ya.* |
| Do. *f.* | འབྲི་ | *dri.* |
| Yak, wild | འབྲོང་ | *drong.* |
| Yak, half-breed with ordinary cattle | མཛོ་ | *dzo.* |
| Yak-dung | ལྕོ་ (ལྕི་བ་) | *cho.* |
| Yak's meat | ཚག་ཤ་ | *tshak̄-sha.* |
| Yama | གཤིན་རྗེ་ཆོས་རྒྱལ་ | *shin-je chhö-gye.* |
| Yap, to | འཆང་བ་ | *chhang-wa.* |
| Yard, court | སྒོ་ར་ | *go-ra.* |
| Yarn | སྲིང་སྐུད་ | *hring-kü.* |
| Do. black | སྲིང་ནག་ | *hring-na.* |
| Do. blue | སྲིང་སྔོན་ | *hring-ngön.* |
| Do. green | སྲིང་ལྗང་ | *hring-jang.* |
| Do. red | སྲིང་དམར་ | *hring-mar.* |
| Do. white | སྲིང་དཀར་ | *hring-kar.* |
| Do. yellow | སྲིང་སེར་ | *hring-ser.* |
| Yawn, to | ཨ་སྟོང་རྒྱབ་པ་ | *a-tong gyap̄-pa.* |
| Do. *hon.* | ཨ་སྟོང་སྐྱོན་པ་ | *a-tong kyöm-pa.* |

| | | |
|---|---|---|
| Year | ལོ་ | *lo.* |
| Year, this | ད་ལོ་ | *t́a-lo.* |
| Year, last | ཟླ་ཉིང་ (ན་ནིང་) | *da-nyi.* |
| Year before last | ཞི་ཉིང་ (ཞི་ནིང་) | *sḱi-nyi.* |
| Year, next | ཕྱི་ལོ། སང་ཕོད་ | *chhi-lo; sang-pö.* |
| Year, first four months of a | ཟླ་སྟོད་ | *da-tö.* |
| Year, middle four months of a | ཟླ་དཀྱིལ་ | *da-kyi.* |
| Year, last four months of a | ཟླ་སྨད་ | *da-me.* |
| Yearn for, to | དྲན་པ་ | *t́rem-pa.* |
| Do. *hon.* | ཐུགས་དྲན་པ་གནང་བ་ | *thu-t́rem-pa nang-wa.* |
| Yeast (for bread) | ཕྱི་སྨན་ | *chhi-men.* |
| Do. (for fermenting liquor) | ཕབ་ | *phap̆.* |
| Yell, to (of children crying) | ངུ་བ་ | *ngu-wa.* |
| Do. *hon.* | ཤུམ་པ་ | *shum-pa.* |
| Yell, to (of dogs) | ཀྲུག་སྐད་རྒྱབ་པ་ | *duḱ-ḱe gyap̆-pa.* |
| Yellow | སེར་པོ་ | *se-po.* |
| Yellow, dark | སྙུག་སེ་ | *nyuk-se.* |
| Yelp, to (of dogs) | འཆང་བ་ | *chhang-wa.* |
| Yes | ལགས་སི། ལགས་ w. auxiliary verb | *la-si; la.* |

| | | |
|---|---|---|
| Yes, *hon.* | ལགས་ལགས་སི། ལ་འོང་ | *la-la-si; la-ong.* |
| Do. *h. hon.* | ལགས་བཀའ་གནང་རང་ | *la ka-nang-rang.* |
| Yesterday | ཁས་ས (ཁ་སང་) ཁ་སང་ | *khe-sa.* |
| Yesterday evening | མདང་དགོང་ | *dang-gong.* |
| Yet, *adv.* (in addition) | ད་འདོ། ད་རུང་ | *ťan-do; ťa-rung.* |
| Yet, *conj.* (nevertheless) | ཡིན་ནས། ཡིན་ཀྱང་། ཡིན་ན་ཡང་ | *yin-ne; yin-kyang; yin-na-yang.* |
| Yield, to (admit) | ཁས་ལེན་པ་ | *khe-lem-pa.* |
| Do. *hon.* | ཞལ་བཞེས་གནང་བ། ཞལ་གྱིས་བཞེས་པ་ | *sḱe-sḱe nang-wa; sḱe-kyi sḱe-pa.* |
| Yield, to (forego) | སྤང་བ་ | *pang-wa.* |
| Do. *hon.* | སྤོང་ང་ (བ་) གནང་བ་ | *pong-nga nang-wa.* |
| Yield, to (give) | སྟེར་བ་ | *ter-wa.* |
| Do. *hon.* | གནང་བ་ | *nang-wa.* |
| Yield, to (surrender) | མགོ་དགུར་བ་ | *go gur-wa.* |
| Do. *hon.* | དབུ་དགུར་ར་ (བ་) གནང་བ་ | *u gur-ra nang-wa.* |
| Yielding (flexible) | མཉེན་པོ་ | *nyem-po.* |
| Yoke (for oxen) | གཉའ་ཤིང་ | *nya-shing.* |
| Yolk | སེར་སྒོང་། སེར་སྤྲིན་ | *ser-gong; ser-trin.* |
| Yonder | ཕ་གི་ | *pha-gi.* |

| | | |
|---|---|---|
| You | ཁྱོད། ཁྱོད་རང་ | *khyö ; khyö-rang.* |
| Do. *hon.* | ཁྱེན་ (ཁྱེད་) | *khyen.* |
| Do. *h. hon.* | སྐུ་གཞོགས་ | *ku-sK̄o.* |
| Young | གཞོན་པ། ལོ་གཞོན་གཞོན་ | *sK̄öm-pa ; lo sK̄ön-sK̄ön.* |
| Your | ཁྱོད་རེའི་ (ཁྱོད་ཀྱི་) | *khyö-re.* |
| Do. *hon.* | ཁྱེན་གྱི་ (ཁྱེད་ཀྱི་) | *khyen-K̄yi.* |
| Do. *h. hon.* | སྐུ་གཞོགས་ཀྱི་ | *ku-sK̄o kyi.* |
| Youthful | གཞོན་པ། ལོ་གཞོན་གཞོན་ | *sK̄öm-pa ; lo sK̄ön-sK̄ön.* |

## Z

| | | |
|---|---|---|
| Zeal | སྙིང་རུས་ | *nying-rü.* |
| Do. *hon.* | ཐུགས་རུས་ | *thu-rü.* |
| Zealous | སྙིང་རུས་ཆེན་པོ་ | *nying-rü chhem-po.* |
| Do. *hon.* | ཐུགས་རུས་ཆེར་པོ་ | *thu-rü.* |
| Zealous, to be | སྙིང་རུས་བྱེད་པ་ | *nying-rü cKe-pa.* |
| Do. *hon.* | ཐུགས་རུས་གནང་བ་ | *thu-rü nang-wa.* |
| Zealously | སྙིང་རུས་བྱས་ནས་ | *nying-rü cKe-ne.* |
| Do. *hon.* | ཐུགས་རུས་གནང་ནས་ | *thu-rü nang-ne.* |
| Zero | ཀླད་སྐོར་ | *le-kor.* |
| Zigzag | ལམ་སྐྱོགས་ | *lam-kyo.* |

THE END.